TAKING SIDES

Clashing Views in

United States History, Volume II, Reconstruction to the Present

TWELFTH EDITION

McGraw-Hill **Contemporary Learning Series**

A Division of The McGraw-Hill Companies

TAKING SIDES

Clashing Views in

United States History, Volume II, Reconstruction to the Present

TWELFTH EDITION

Selected, Edited, and with Introductions by

Larry Madaras
Howard Community College

and

James M. SoRelle
Baylor University

Contemporary Learning Series

A Division of The McGraw-Hill Companies

To Maggie and Cindy

Photo Acknowledgment
Cover Image: Library of Congress

Cover Acknowledgment
Maggie Lytle

Manufactured in the United States of America

Twelfth Edition

123456789DOCDOC9876

Library of Congress Cataloging-in-Publication Data
Main entry under title:

Taking sides: clashing views on controversial issues in American history, volume ii,
reconstruction to the present/selected, edited, and with introductions by
Larry Madaras and James M. SoRelle—12th ed.

Includes bibliographical references and index.
1. United States—History—1865– I. Madaras, Larry, *comp.* II. SoRelle, James M., *comp.*
973

0-07-352722-X
978-0-07352722-2
ISSN: 1091-8833

Printed on Recycled Paper

Preface

The success of the past eleven editions of *Taking Sides: Clashing Views in United States History* has encouraged us to remain faithful to its original objectives, methods, and format. Our aim has been to create an effective instrument to enhance classroom learning and to foster critical thinking. Historical facts presented in a vacuum are of little value to the educational process. For students, whose search for historical truth often concentrates on *when* something happened rather than on *why*, and on specific events rather than on the *significance* of those events, *Taking Sides* is designed to offer an interesting and valuable departure. The understanding that the reader arrives at based on the evidence that emerges from the clash of views encourages the reader to view history as an *interpretive* discipline, not one of rote memorization.

As in previous editions, the issues are arranged in chronological order and can be easily incorporated into any American history survey course. Each issue has an issue *introduction*, which sets the stage for the debate that follows in the pro and con selections and provides historical and methodological background to the problem that the issue examines. Each issue concludes with a *postscript*, which ties the readings together, briefly mentions alternative interpretations, and supplies detailed *suggestions for further reading* for the student who wishes to pursue the topics raised in the issue. Also, Internet site addresses (URLs), which should prove useful as starting points for further research, have been provided on the *On the Internet* page that accompanies each part opener. At the back of the book is a listing of all the *contributors to this volume* with a brief biographical sketch of each of the prominent figures whose views are debated here.

Changes to this Edition

In this edition, we have continued our efforts to maintain a balance between the traditional political, diplomatic, and cultural issues and the new social history, which depicts a society that benefited from the presence of African Americans, women, and workers of various racial and ethnic backgrounds. With this in mind, we present nine new issues, some at the request of teachers who want some of the earlier issues revisited. These are: "Did William M. Tweed Corrupt Post–Civil War New York?" (Issue 3); "Did Booker T. Washington's Philosophy and Actions Betray the Interests of African Americans?" (Issue 6); "Was It Necessary to Drop the Atomic Bomb on Japan to End World War II?" (Issue 11); "Was Richard Nixon America's Last Liberal President?" (Issue 15); and "Is George W. Bush the Worst President in American History?" (Issue 18).

A word to the instructor *An Instructor's Manual With Test Questions* (multiple-choice and essay) is available through the publisher for the instructor using *Taking*

Sides in the classroom. A general guidebook, *Using Taking Sides in the Classroom*, which discusses methods and techniques for integrating the procon approach into any classroom setting, is also available. An online version of *Using Taking Sides in the Classroom* and a correspondence service for *Taking Sides* adopters can be found at http://www.mhcls.com/usingts/.

Taking Sides: Clashing Views in United States History is only one title in the *Taking Sides* series. If you are interested in seeing the table of contents for any other titles, please visit the *Taking Sides* Web site at http://www.mhcls.com/takingsides/.

Acknowledgments Many individuals have contributed to the successful completion of past editions. We appreciate the evaluations submitted to McGraw-Hill/CLS by those who have used *Taking Sides* in the classroom. Special thanks to those who responded with specific suggestions for the previous editions:

Gary Best
University of Hawaii–Hilo

James D. Bolton
Coastline Community College

Mary Borg
University of Northern Colorado

John Whitney Evans
College of St. Scholastica

Mark Hickerson
Chaffey College

Maryann Irwin
Diablo Valley College

Tim Koerner
Oakland Community College

Gordon Lam
Sierra College

Jon Nielson
Columbia College

Andrew O'Shaugnessy
University of Wisconsin–Oshkosh

Manian Padma
DeAnza College

Elliot Pasternack
Middlesex County College (N.J.)

Robert M. Paterson
Armstrong State College

Charles Piehl
Mankato State University

Ethan S. Rafuse
University of Missouri–Kansas City

John Reid
Ohio State University–Lima

Murray Rubinstein
CUNY Baruch College

Neil Sapper
Amarillo College

Preston She
Plymouth State College

Jack Traylor
William Jennings Bryan College

We are particularly indebted to Maggie Cullen, Cindy SoRelle, the late Barry A. Crouch, Virginia Kirk, Joseph and Helen Mitchell, and Jean Soto, who shared their ideas for changes, pointed us toward potentially useful historical works, and provided significant editorial assistance. Lynn Wilder performed indispensable typing duties connected with this project. Susan E. Myers, Ela Ciborowski, and Karen Higgins in the library at Howard Community College provided essential help in acquiring books and articles on interlibrary loan. Finally, we are sincerely grateful for the commitment, encouragement, and patience provided over the years by David Dean, former list manager for the *Taking Sides* series; David Brackley, former senior developmental editor; and the entire staff of McGraw-Hill/CLS. Indispensable to this project are Ted Knight, the former list manager, and Jill Peter, the current editor-in-charge of the *Taking Sides* series.

Larry Madaras
Howard Community College

James M. SoRelle
Baylor University

Contents In Brief

Contents

Oscar Handlin insists that historical truth is absolute and knowable by historians who adopt the scientific method of research to discover factual evidence that provides both a chronology and context for their findings. William McNeill argues that historical truth is general and evolutionary and is discerned by different groups at different times and in different places in a subjective manner that has little to do with a scientifically absolute methodology.

Matthew Josephson depicts John D. Rockefeller as an unconscionable manipulator who employed a policy of deception, bribery, and outright conspiracy to restrain free trade in order to eliminate his competitors for control of the oil industry in the United States. Ron Chernow recognizes that Rockefeller was guilty of misdeeds that were endemic among both small and large corporate leaders of the industrial age, but he concludes that some of the most egregious claims attributed to Rockefeller were without merit and often represented actions taken by Standard Oil associates without Rockefeller's knowledge.

Professor emeritus of history Alexander B. Callow, Jr., asserts that by exercising a corrupting influence over the city and state governments as well as over key elements within the business community, William M.

"Boss" Tweed and his infamous "ring" extracted enormous sums of ill-gotten money for their own benefit in post–Civil War New York. Professor of history Leo Hershkowitz portrays Tweed as a devoted public servant who championed New York City's interests during his 20-year career and whose reputation as the symbol for urban political corruption is grossly undeserved.

Elaine Tyler May, a professor of American studies and history, argues that the Industrial Revolution in the United States, with its improved technology, increasing income, and emerging consumerism, led to higher rates of divorce because family wage earners failed to meet rising expectations for material accumulation. History professors Jacquelyn Dowd Hall, Robert Korstad, and James Leloudis contend that the cotton mill villages of the New South, rather than destroying family work patterns, fostered a labor system that permitted parents and children to work together as a traditional family unit.

Professor of history Christine Stansell contends that women on the Great Plains were torn from their eastern roots, isolated in their home environment, and separated from friends and relatives. She concludes that they consequently endured lonely lives and loveless marriages. Professor of history Glenda Riley argues that in spite of enduring harsh environmental, political, and personal conditions on the Great Plains, women created rich and varied social lives through the development of strong support networks.

W. E. B. Du Bois, a founding member of the National Organization for the Advancement of Colored People, argues that Booker T. Washington failed to articulate the legitimate demands of African Americans for full civil and political rights. Professor of history Louis R. Harlan portrays Washington as a political realist whose policies and actions were designed to benefit black society as a whole.

Issue 7.   Was Early Twentieth-Century American Foreign Policy in the Caribbean Basin Dominated by Economic Concerns?   141

Professor of history Walter LaFeber argues that the United States developed a foreign policy that deliberately made the Caribbean nations its economic dependents from the early nineteenth century on. Professor of history David Healy maintains that the two basic goals of American foreign policy in the Caribbean were to provide security against the German threat and to develop the economies of the Latin American nations, whose peoples were considered to be racially inferior.

Issue 8.   Did the Progressives Fail?   165

Professor of history Richard M. Abrams maintains that progressivism was a failure because it tried to impose a uniform set of values upon a culturally diverse people who never seriously confronted the inequalities that still exist in American society. Professors of history Arthur S. Link and Richard L. McCormick argues that the Progressives were a diverse group of reformers who confronted and ameliorated the worst abuses that emerged in urban industrial America during the early 1900s.

Issue 9.   Was Prohibition a Failure?   189

David E. Kyvig admits that alcohol consumption declined sharply in the prohibition era but that federal actions failed to impose abstinence among an increasingly urban and heterogeneous populace that resented

and resisted restraints on their individual behavior. John C. Burnham states that the prohibition experiment was more a success than a failure and contributed to a substantial decrease in liquor consumption, reduced arrests for alcoholism, fewer alcohol-related diseases and hospitalizations, and destroyed the old-fashioned saloon that was a major target of the law's proponents.

Professor of history Gary Dean Best argues that Roosevelt established an antibusiness environment with the creation of the New Deal regulatory programs, which retarded the nation's economic recovery from the Great Depression until World War II. Professor of history Roger Biles contends that, in spite of its minimal reforms and non-revolutionary programs, the New Deal created a limited welfare state that implemented economic stabilizers to avert another depression.

Professor of American history Robert James Maddox contends that the atomic bomb became the catalyst that forced the hard-liners in the Japanese army to accept the emperor's plea to surrender, thus avoiding a costly, bloody invasion of the Japanese mainland. Professor of American history Tsuyoshi Hasegawa argues that the Soviet entrance into the war played a greater role in causing Japan to surrender than did the dropping of the atomic bombs.

History professors John Earl Haynes and Harvey Klehr argue that army code-breakers during World War II's "Venona Project" uncovered a disturbing number of high-ranking U.S. government officials who seriously damaged American interests by passing sensitive information to the Soviet Union. Professor of history Richard M. Fried argues that the early 1950s were a "nightmare in red" during which American citizens had their First

and Fifth Amendment rights suspended when a host of national and state investigating committees searched for Communists in government agencies, Hollywood, labor unions, foundations, universities, public schools, and even public libraries.

Peter Irons argues that, despite evidence that integration improves the status of African Americans, the school integration prescribed by the *Brown* decision was never seriously tried, with the consequence that major gaps between white and black achievement persist and contribute to many of the social problems confronting African Americans today. Richard Kluger concludes that fifty years after the *Brown* decision, African Americans are better educated, better housed, and better employed than they were before 1954 in large part because the Supreme Court's ruling spawned the modern civil rights movement that culminated in the Civil Rights Act of 1964, the 1965 Voting Rights Act, and many programs of Lyndon Johnson's Great Society that were designed to improve the status of African Americans.

Professor of history Brian VanDeMark argues that President Lyndon Johnson failed to question the viability of increasing U.S. involvement in the Vietnam War because he was a prisoner of America's global containment policy and because he did not want his opponents to accuse him of being soft on communism or endanger support for his Great Society reforms. H.R. McMaster, an active-duty army tanker, maintains that the Vietnam disaster was not inevitable but a uniquely human failure whose responsibility was shared by President Johnson and his principal military and civilian advisers.

According to professor of history Joan Hoff-Wilson, the Nixon presidency reorganized the executive branch and portions of the federal bureaucracy and implemented domestic reforms in civil rights, welfare, and economic planning, despite its limited foreign policy successes and the Watergate scandal. According to Professor Bruce J. Schulman, Richard Nixon was the first conservative president of the post-World War II era who undermined the Great Society legislative program of President Lyndon Baines Johnson and built a new Republican majority coalition of white, northern blue-collar workers, and southern and sunbelt conservatives.

Professor of history John Lewis Gaddis argues that President Ronald Reagan combined a policy of militancy and operational pragmatism that perplexed his hard-line advisers when he made the necessary compromises to bring about the most significant improvement in Soviet-American relations since the end of World War II. Professors of political science Daniel Deudney and G. John Ikenberry contend that the cold war ended only when Soviet president Mikhail Gorbachev accepted Western liberal values and the need for global cooperation.

Social scientist Tamar Jacoby maintains that the newest immigrants keep America's economy strong because they work harder and take jobs that native-born Americans reject. Syndicated columnist Patrick J. Buchanan argues that America is no longer a nation because immigrants from Mexico and other Third World Latin American and Asian countries have turned America into a series of fragmented multicultural ethnic enclaves that lack a common culture.

Bancroft prize-winning historian Sean Wilentz argues that the current president ranks with Presidents James Buchanan, Andrew Johnson, and Herbert Hoover in having divided the nation, governed erratically, and left the nation worse off than when he came into office. FDR biographer

Conrad Black believes that President Bush is, with the exception of FDR, the most important president since Lincoln in accomplishing a highly successful domestic and foreign policy.

Introduction

The Study of History

Larry Madaras

James M. SoRelle

In a pluralistic society such as ours, the study of history is bound to be a complex process. How an event is interpreted depends not only on existing evidence but also on the perspective of the interpreter. Consequently, understanding history presupposes the evaluation of information, a task that often leads to conflicting conclusions. An understanding of history, then, requires the acceptance of the idea of historical relativism. Relativism means the redefinition of our past is always possible and desirable. History shifts, changes, and grows with new and different evidence and interpretations. As is the case with the law and even with medicine, beliefs that were unquestioned 100 or 200 years ago have been discredited or discarded since.

Relativism then encourages revisionism. There is a maxim that says, "The past must remain useful to the present." Historian Carl Becker argued that every generation should examine history for itself, thus ensuring constant scrutiny of our collective experience through new perspectives. History, consequently, does not remain static, in part because historians cannot avoid being influenced by the times in which they live. Almost all historians commit themselves to revising the views of other historians by either disagreeing with earlier interpretations or creating new frameworks that pose different questions.

Schools of Thought

Three predominant schools of thought have emerged in American history since the first graduate seminars in history were given at the Johns Hopkins University in Baltimore, Maryland, in the 1870s. The *progressive* school dominated the professional field in the first half of the twentieth century. Influenced by the reform currents of populism, progressivism, and the New Deal, these historians explored the social and economic forces that energized America. The progressive scholars tended to view the past in terms of conflicts between groups, and they sympathized with the underdog.

The post–World War II period witnessed the emergence of a new group of historians who viewed the conflict thesis as overly simplistic. Writing against the backdrop of the Cold War, these *neoconservative* and *consensus* historians argued that Americans possess a shared set of values and that the areas of agreement within the nation's basic democratic and capitalistic framework are more important than the areas of disagreement.

In the 1960s, however, the civil rights movement, women's liberation, and the student rebellion (with its condemnation of the war in Vietnam) fragmented the consensus of values upon which historians of the 1950s centered their interpretations. This turmoil set the stage for the emergence of another group of scholars. *New Left* historians began to reinterpret the past once again. They emphasized the significance of conflict in American history, and they resurrected interest in those groups ignored by the consensus school. In addition, New Left history is still being written. The most recent generation of scholars, however, focuses upon social history. Their primary concern is to discover what the lives of "ordinary Americans" were really like. These new social historians employ previously overlooked court and church documents, house deeds and tax records, letters and diaries, photographs, and census data to reconstruct the everyday lives of average Americans. Some employ new methodologies, such as quantifications (enhanced by advanced computer technology) and oral history, while others borrow from the disciplines of political science, economics, sociology, anthropology, and psychology for their historical investigations.

The proliferation of historical approaches, which are reflected in the issues debated in this book, has had mixed results. On the one hand, historians have become so specialized in their respective time periods and methodological styles that it is difficult to synthesize the recent scholarship into a comprehensive text for the general reader. On the other hand, historians now know more about new questions or ones that previously were considered to be germane only to scholars in other social sciences. Although there is little agreement about the answers to these questions, the methods employed and the issues explored make the "new history" a very exciting field to study.

The topics that follow represent a variety of perspectives and approaches. Each of these controversial issues can be studied for its individual importance to American history. Taken as a group, they interact with one another to illustrate larger historical themes. When grouped thematically, the issues reveal continuing motifs in the development of American history.

Intellectual and Economic Questions

Issue 1 explores the big question that historians face. Is history true? Two prize-winning historians who write from a macro-perspective disagree. Oscar Handlin argues that "truth is absolute; it is as absolute as the world is real . . . truth is knowable and will out if earnestly pursued and science is the procedure or set of procedures for approximating it." But William H. McNeill disagrees. "[W]hat seems true to one historian will seem false to another, so one historian's truth becomes another's myth, even at the moment of utterance."

Issue 2 explores the dynamics of the modern American economy through investigations of the nineteenth-century entrepreneurs. Were these industrial leaders robber barons, as portrayed by contemporary critics and many history texts? Or were they industrial statesmen and organizational geniuses? Matthew Josephson argues that John D. Rockefeller is a key example of a monopoly capitalist who utilized ruthless and violent methods in organizing the oil industry. More favorable and representative of the business historian approach is the interpretation of prize-winning author Ron Chernow. He concludes that Rockefeller was among the earliest organizational innovators and that he standardized production and procedures and created a large integrated industrial corporation.

The Outsiders: Laborers, Farmers, Blacks, Women, Family, and Immigrants

In recent years, historians have shifted their focus to social issues. New questions have been asked and new frameworks have been developed. Issue 4 ponders whether the Industrial Revolution disrupted the American family. In her study of changing patterns of divorce between 1880 and 1920, Elaine Tyler May find that higher consumer expectations, which resulted from the Industrial Revolution, disproportionately strained marital relations among the lower-middle and working classes because the husbands were unable to fulfill the economic demands of their wives. But in their study of cotton mill people in the Piedmont region of North and South Carolina, Jacquelyn Dowd Hall, Robert Korstad, and James Leloudis argue that rural families were able to use the mills to make a living and to keep their families and farms intact.

The Piedmont mills were composed of white workers only. By the 1890s rigid segregation laws and customs separated the white and black races in the South. Did segregation hurt or harm the black community? Issue 6 asks whether Booker T. Washington's philosophy and actions betrayed the interests of African Americans. The most famous black intellectual, W. E. B. Du Bois, a founding member of the National Organization of the Advancement of Colored People, argues that Booker T. Washington failed to articulate the legitimate demands of African Americans for full civil and political rights. Professor of history Louis R. Harlan portrays Washington as a political realist whose policies and actions were designed to benefit black society as a whole.

One of the less well-known areas of American history is the impact of the frontier on the women who migrated West. In Issue 5, Christine Stansell maintains that women who migrated West in the late nineteenth century lost their networks of family and friends back East and that they were isolated and lonely on the Great Plains. Glenda Riley agrees that women faced many hardships on the frontier. However, she argues that women rebuilt friendships through church gatherings and quilting bee sessions.

One of the major controversies of the present time is whether or not the United States should remain a nation of immigrants. Tamar Jacoby, who supports allowing immigration to continue, maintains in Issue 17 that the newest immigrants keep America's economy strong because they work harder and take jobs that native-born Americans reject. Patrick J. Buchanan, however, argues that America is no longer a nation because immigrants from Mexico and other Third World Latin American and Asian countries have turned it into a series of fragmented multicultural ethnic enclaves that lack a common culture. Therefore, he contends, immigration should be drastically curbed.

Political and Social Successes and Failure, 1880–1920

Issue 9 discusses one of the major progressive "social control" reforms—Prohibition. The "noble experiment" to prohibit the manufacture, sale, and transportation of alcoholic beverages had a rather short life. Originally passed in 1919, the Prohibition amendment was repealed fourteen years later. To this day, it remains the only amendment ever to have been removed from the Constitution. John C. Burnham revises the traditional image of the decade of the 1920s as the "lawless years." He points out that when the "Prohibition experiment" was passed, two-thirds of the states, which encompassed over half of the population, were already dry. The purpose of the legislation, he argues, was to control the political and social practices of the immigrant working classes who lived in the cities. He denies that crime increased dramatically in the decade, attributing the so-called crime waves to the overblown accounts in the newspapers and newsreels. Gambling, rather than the sale of illegal liquor, remained the major source of revenue for organized crime. Burnham also marshals statistical evidence to document a decline in per capita drinking in the early 1920s as well as in the diseases and deaths related to alcohol. David Kyvig concedes that Prohibition "sharply reduced the consumption of alcohol in the United States." But images of lawbreaking through Hollywood films and newsreels and the inability of law enforcement officials in all levels of government to enforce the law, especially unpopular in American cities, "disenchanted many Americans and moved some to an active effort to bring an end to the dry law."

In Issue 3, post–Civil War political corruption is discussed with a focus on William M. "Boss" Tweed and his activities at Tammany Hall, the Democratic machine's headquarters in New York City. Alexander B. Callow, Jr., asserts that Tweed exercised a corrupting influence over the city and state governments and the business community. Leo Hershkowitz emphasizes the services that Tweed provided to benefit New York City.

The Progressive movement is examined in Issue 8. Richard M. Abrams attributes the failure of the movement to its limited scope. He maintains that it imposed a uniform set of values on a diverse people and did not address the inequalities that prevailed in American society. Arthur S. Link and Richard L. McCormick, however, emphasize the reforms introduced by the Progressives that checked the abuses of industrialization and urbanization during the early 1900s.

A second reform movement took place in the 1930s. The Great Depression of the 1930s remains one of the most traumatic events in U.S. history. The characteristics of that decade are deeply etched in American folk memory, but the remedies that were applied to these social and economic ills—known collectively as the New Deal—are not easy to evaluate. In Issue 10, Roger Biles contends that the economic stabilizers created by the New Deal programs prevented the recurrence of the Great Depression. Gary Dean Best, on the other hand, criticizes the New Deal from a 1990s conservative perspective. In his view, because New Deal agencies were antibusiness, they overregulated the economy and did not allow the free enterprise system to work out the depression that FDR's programs prolonged.

The 1960s brought about a third era of domestic reforms. In the early 1960s, President Lyndon Johnson initiated the Great Society anti-poverty programs and civil rights laws. Did his successor Richard Nixon continue or attempt to kill the Great Society? In Issue 15, Professor Joan Hoff-Wilson believes the Nixon presidency reorganized the executive branch and portions of the federal bureaucracy and implemented domestic reforms in civil rights, welfare, and economic planning, despite its limited foreign policy successes and the Watergate scandal. But Professor Bruce Schulman argues that Nixon was not the last liberal twentieth-century president, but America's first modern conservative executive. By 1971, Nixon had recognized that the center of the American political spectrum had shifted rightward, and he shifted his policies accordingly in the areas of civil rights, environmentalism, and welfare reform.

In the 30-plus years since Nixon's departure, the American political spectrum has continued to shift to the right. Even Democratic presidents Carter and Clinton could by no stretch of the imagination be considered liberals. Our present executive, George W. Bush, traces his economic legacy of tax cuts as a fiscal stimulus back to the Regan presidency. Issue 18 presents two diametrically opposed views of the current president. Princeton historian Sean Wilentz thinks that George Bush will be considered one of the worst presidents in American history because he is oblivious to the major economic and social problems facing the nation, has waged a partisan war in Iraq under false pretenses, and has turned an inherited surplus into the largest deficit ever with his proposed tax cuts for the wealthiest Americans. But publishing mogul Conrad Black disagrees; George Bush, he argues, will rank with Lincoln and FDR among our most important presidents because he is waging a successful war against terrorism, while his nation-building agenda will bring peace, stability, freedom, and democracy to the Arab world.

The United States and the World

As the United States developed a preeminent position in world affairs, the nation's politicians were forced to consider the proper relationship between their country and the rest of the world. To what extent, many asked, should the United States seek to expand its political, economic, and moral influence around the world? This was a particularly intriguing question for early twentieth-century American presidents Roosevelt, Taft, and Wilson, who actively intervened in the internal affairs in the Caribbean basin of Cuba, Haiti, and the Dominican Republic as well as in the Central American countries of Mexico, Nicaragua, and Panama. Were these forays spurred by a need for security or by economic concerns? In Issue 7, the well-known diplomatic historian Walter LaFeber argues that the United States developed a foreign policy that deliberately made the Caribbean nations its economic dependents from the early nineteenth century on. Professor of history David Healy maintains that the two basic goals of American foreign policy in the Caribbean were to provide security against the German threat and to develop the economies of the Latin American nations, whose peoples were considered to be racially inferior.

The United States became a major participant in two world wars in the twentieth century. At the end of the First World War, President Wilson tried to enlarge the United States' role in the world by brokering the peace and establishing a League of Nations to prevent the outbreak of another war. Whether the Second World War could have been prevented if the United States had joined the League of Nations and abandoned its isolationist traditional foreign policy is a subject of debate for historians. Certainly, President FDR hoped that the United Nations would resolve future world conflicts.

But the Second World War produced a major unintended consequence. The Manhattan Project was a secret enclave of thousands of scientists who lived in the desert in Los Alamos, New Mexico, in order to develop an atomic bomb. The first successful test in the desert of New Mexico occurred two months after the war in Germany had ended. Two atomic bombs—Fat Man and Little Boy— were ready to be used against the Japanese. Were there alternatives to dropping the atomic bombs on Japan to end the war? Were the alternatives rejected for political reasons: (1) keep Russia out of the Asian war; (2) make the Russians "more manageable" in Eastern European peace negotiations? In the first selection in Issue 11, Professor Robert James Maddox rejects these contentions and argues that military considerations were dominant. President Truman, he says, dropped both atomic bombs in order to shorten the war, save American and Japanese lives, and convince the military hard-liners to surrender because there were no acceptable alternatives. Professor Tsuyoshi Hasegawa plays down the role of the A-bombs in bringing about Japan's surrender. After a careful examination of Japanese, Russian, and American archives, he concludes that it was the Russian declaration of war and not the two atomic bombs at Hiroshima and Nagasaki that caused the Japanese to surrender out of fear of having part of northern Japan occupied by the Russians after the war ended.

After World War II, many Americans believed that the Russians not only threatened world peace but could also subvert America's own democratic form of government. How legitimate was the great Red scare? Did communist subversion threaten America's internal security? In the first reading in Issue 12, John Earl Haynes and Harvey Klehr contend that recently released World War II intelligence intercepts prove that a sizable number of high-level government officials passed sensitive information to Russian intelligence. But Richard M. Fried argues that the 1950s became a "Red nightmare" when state and national government agencies overreacted in their search for communists in government agencies, schools, labor unions, and even Hollywood, violating citizens' rights of free speech and defense against self-incrimination under the First and Fifth Amendments.

No discussion of American foreign policy is complete without some consideration of the Vietnam War. Was America's escalation of the war inevitable in 1965? In Issue 14, Brian VanDeMark argues that President Lyndon Johnson was a prisoner of America's global "containment" policy and was afraid to pull out of Vietnam because he feared that his opponents would accuse him of being soft on communism and that they would also destroy his Great Society reforms. H. R. McMaster blames Johnson and his civilian and military advisers for failing to develop a coherent policy in Vietnam.

Now that the Cold War is over, historians must assess why it ended so suddenly and unexpectedly. Did President Ronald Reagan's military buildup in the 1980s force the Soviet Union into economic bankruptcy? In Issue 16, John Lewis Gaddis gives Reagan high marks for ending the Cold War. By combining a policy of militancy and operational pragmatism, he argues, Reagan brought about the most significant improvement in Soviet-American relations since the end of World War II. According to Daniel Deudney and G. John Ikenberry, however, the Cold War ended only when the Soviets saw the need for international cooperation to end the arms race, prevent a nuclear holocaust, and liberalize their economy. They contend that Western global ideas, not the hard-line containment policy of the early Regan administration, caused Soviet president Mikhail Gorbechev to abandon traditional Russian communism.

Conclusion

The process of historical study should rely more on thinking than on memorizing data. Once the basics of who, what, when, and where are determined, historical thinking shifts to a higher gear. Explanation, analysis, evaluation, comparison, and contrast take command. These skills not only increase our knowledge of the past, but they also provide general tools for the comprehension of all the topics about which human beings think.

The diversity of a pluralistic society, however, creates some obstacles to comprehending the past. The spectrum of differing opinions on any particular subject eliminates the possibility of quick and easy answers. In the final analysis, conclusions are often built through a synthesis of several different interpretations, but even then they may be partial and tentative.

The study of history in a pluralistic society allows each citizen the opportunity to teach independent conclusions about the past. Since most, if not all, historical issues affect the present and future, understanding the past becomes necessary if society is to progress. Many of today's problems have a direct connection with the past. Additionally, other contemporary issues may lack obvious direct antecedents, but historical investigation can provide illuminating analogies. At first, it may appear confusing to read and to think about opposing historical views, but the survival of our democratic society depends on such critical thinking by acute and discerning minds.

On the Internet . . .

Internet Web sites containing historical material relevant to the subjects discussed in all the issues can be reached through the McGraw-Hill history site.

http://www.Mhhe.comsocscience/history/usa/link/linktop.html

Important journal articles and book reviews that reflect the most recent scholarship on all the issues can be found on the following site:

http://H-NE.msu.edu

John D. Rockefeller and the Standard Oil Company

This site, created by Swiss entrepreneur Francois Micheloud, provides a highly detailed history of the American oil industry, with John D. Rockefeller as a main focus. It includes the discovery of oil, the main players in the oil industry, the rise of the Standard Oil Company, the passing of the Sherman Antitrust Act, and the dismantling of Standard Oil, as well as both short and detailed chronologies of the company.

http://www.micheloud.com./FXM/SO/rock.htm

Industrial Revolution

This site provides an extensive list of links to pages on the Industrial Revolution grouped into categories, including Child Labor, Disparity of Wealth, Unions, and Urban Planning.

http://members.aol.com/TeacherNet/Industrial.html

Documenting the American South

This Web site is a collection of sources on southern history, literature, and culture from the colonial period through the first decades of the twentieth century. It is organized into several projects according to subject, such as "First-Person Narratives of the American South," "North American Slave Narratives," and "The Church in the Southern Black Community."

http://docsouth.unc.edu

PART 1

Reconstruction and the Industrial Revolution

*E*conomic expansion and the seemingly unlimited resources available in postbellum America offered great opportunity and created new political, social, and economic challenges. Political freedom and economic opportunity provided incentives for immigration to America. The need for cheap labor to run the machinery of the Industrial Revolution created an atmosphere for potential exploitation that was intensified by the concentration of wealth in the hands of a few capitalists. The labor movement took root, with some elements calling for an overthrow of the capitalist system, while others sought to establish political power within the existing system. Strains began to develop between immigrant and native-born workers as well as between workers and owners, husbands and wives, and parents and their children.

With the growth of industry, urban problems became more acute. Improvements in water and sewage, street cleaning, housing, mass transit, and fire and crime prevention developed slowly because incredible population growth strained municipal services. Urban governments had limited powers, which often fell under the control of political bosses. Historians disagree as to whether or not attempts to remedy these problems through a brokered political system were successful. Meanwhile, the last frontier had been reached with the end of the Indian wars. Were the western communities more violent than the large industrial cities of the 1890s? Or have radio, television, and the movies portrayed a mythical West?

- Is History True?

- Was John D. Rockefeller a "Robber Baron"?

- Did William M. Tweed Corrupt Post–Civil War New York?

- Did the Industrial Revolution Disrupt the American Family?

- Did Nineteenth-Century Women of the West Fail to Overcome the Hardships of Living on the Great Plains?

1

ISSUE 1

Is History True?

YES: Oscar Handlin, from *Truth in History* (The Belknap Press of Harvard University Press, 1979)

NO: William H. McNeill, from "Mythistory, or Truth, Myth, History, and Historians," *American Historical Review* (February 1986)

ISSUE SUMMARY

YES: Oscar Handlin insists that historical truth is absolute and knowable by historians who adopt the scientific method of research to discover factual evidence that provides both a chronology and context for their findings.

NO: William McNeill argues that historical truth is general and evolutionary and is discerned by different groups at different times and in different places in a subjective manner that has little to do with a scientifically absolute methodology.

The basic premise of this volume of readings is that the study of history is a complex process that combines historical facts and the historian's interpretation of those facts. Underlying this premise is the assumption that the historian is committed to employing evidence that advances an accurate, truthful picture of the past. Unfortunately, the historical profession in the last several years has been held up to close public scrutiny as a result of charges that a few scholars, some quite prominent, have been careless in their research methods, have cited sources that do not exist, and have reached conclusions that were not borne out by the facts. The result has been soiled or ruined reputations and the revocation of degrees, book awards, and tenure. Certainly, this is not the end to which most historians aspire, and the failures of a few should not cast a net of suspicion on the manner in which the vast majority of historians practice their craft.

In reflecting upon her role as a historian, the late Barbara Tuchman commented, "To write history so as to enthrall the reader and make the subject as captivating and exciting to him as it is to me has been my goal. . . . A prerequisite . . . is to be enthralled one's self and to feel a compulsion to communicate the magic." For Tuchman, it was the historian's responsibility to the reader to conduct thorough research on a particular topic, sort through the mass of facts to determine what was essential and what was not, and to formulate what remained into a dramatic narrative. Tuchman and most practicing historians also agree with the nineteenth-century German historian Leopold von Ranke that the task of the historian is to discover what really happened. In most instances, however, historians write about events at which they were not present. According to Tuchman, "We can never be certain that we have recaptured [the past] as it really was. But the least we can do is to stay within the evidence."

David Hackett Fischer has written about the difficulties confronting historians as they attempt to report a truthful past, and he is particularly critical of what he terms the "absurd and pernicious doctrine" of historical relativism as it developed in the United States in the 1930s under the direction of Charles Beard and Carl Becker. Becker's suggestion that each historian will write a history based upon his or her own values or the climate of opinion in a particular generation strikes Fischer as a slippery slope leading to the loss of historical accuracy. In conclusion, Fischer writes, "The factual errors which academic historians make today are rarely deliberate. The real danger is not that a scholar will delude his readers, but that he will delude himself."

The selections that follow explore the topic of historical truth. In the late 1970s, Oscar Handlin, like Fischer, became extremely concerned about the impact of the historical and cultural relativism of postmodern and deconstructionist approaches to the study of history. For Handlin, historical truth is absolute and knowable if pursued by the historian adopting the scientific method of research. The value of history, he believes, lies in the capacity to advance toward the truth by locating discrete events, phenomena, and expressions in the historical record.

In contrast, William McNeill recognizes a very thin line between fact and fiction. He claims that historians distinguish between the truth of their conclusions and the myth of those conclusions they reject. The result is what he terms "mythistory." Moreover, the arrangement of historical facts involves subjective judgments and intellectual choices that have little to do with the scientific method. Historical truth, McNeill proposes, is evolutionary, not absolute.

YES

Oscar Handlin

The Uses of History

Why resist the temptation to be relevant? The question nags historians in 1978 as it does other scholars. The world is turning; it needs knowledge; and possession of learning carries an obligation to attempt to shape events. Every crisis lends weight to the plea: transform the library from an ivory tower into a fortress armed to make peace (or war), to end (or extend) social inequality, to alter (or preserve) the existing economic system. The thought boosts the ego, as it has ever since Francis Bacon's suggestion that knowledge is power. Perhaps authority really does lie in command of the contents of books!

In the 1960s the plea became an order, sometimes earnest, sometimes surly, always insistent. Tell us what we need to know—straight answers. Thus, students to teachers, readers to authors. The penalties for refusal ranged from mere unpopularity to organized boycotts and angry confrontations—in a few cases even to burning manuscripts and research notes. Fear added to the inducements for pleasing the audience, whether in the classroom or on the printed page.

To aim to please is a blunder, however. Sincere as the supplicants generally are, it is not knowledge they wish. Having already reached their conclusions, they seek only reassuring confirmation as they prepare to act. They already know that a unilateral act of will could stop wars, that the United States is racist, and that capitalism condemns the masses to poverty. The history of American foreign policy, of the failure of post-Civil War Reconstruction, and of industrial development would only clutter the mind with disturbing ambiguities and complexities.

At best, the usable past demanded of history consists of the data to flesh out a formula. We must do something about the war, the cities, pollution, poverty, and population. Our moral sense, group interest, and political affiliation define the goals; let the historian join the other social scientists in telling us how to reach them. At worst, the demand made of the past is for a credible myth that will identify the forces of good and evil and inspire those who fight with slogans or fire on one side of the barricades or the other.

The effort to meet either demand will frustrate the historian true to his or her craft. Those nimble enough to catch the swings of the market in the classroom or in print necessarily leave behind interior standards of what is important and drop by the wayside the burden of scrupulous investigation and rigorous judgment. Demands for relevance distort the story of ethnicity as they corrupt the historical novel.

Whoever yields, forgoes the opportunity to do what scholars are best qualified to do. Those who chase from one disaster to another lose sight of the long-term trend; busy with the bandaids, they have no time to treat the patient's illness. The family did not originate yesterday, or the city, or addiction to narcotics; a student might well pick up some thoughts on those subjects by shifting his sights from the 1970s to Hellenistic society.

Above all, obsession with the events of the moment prevents the historian from exercising the faculty of empathy, the faculty of describing how people, like us, but different, felt and behaved as they did in times and places similar to, but different, from our own. The writer or teacher interested only in passing judgment on the good guys and the bad will never know what it meant to be an Irish peasant during a famine, or the landlord; an Alabama slave in the 1850s, or the master; a soldier at Antietam, or a general.

❧

The uses of history arise neither from its relevance nor from its help in preparing for careers—nor from its availability as a subject which teachers pass on to students who become teachers and in turn teach others to teach.

Nevertheless, again and again former pupils who come back for reunions after twenty-five years or more spontaneously testify to the utility of what they had learned at college in the various pursuits to which life's journey had taken them. Probing usually reveals not bits of information, not a general interpretation, but a vague sense that those old transactions of classroom and library had somehow expanded their knowledge of self. The discipline of history had located them in time and space and had thereby helped them know themselves, not as physicians or attorneys or bureaucrats or executives, but as persons.

These reassuring comments leave in suspense the question of why study of the past should thus help the individuals understand himself or herself. How do those who learn this subject catch a glimpse of the process of which they are part, discover places in it?

Not by relevance, in the competition for which the other, more pliable, social sciences can always outbid history. Nor by the power of myth, in the peddling of which the advantage lies with novelists. To turn accurate knowledge to those ends is, as C. S. Peirce noted, "like running a steam engine by burning diamonds."

The use of history lies in its capacity for advancing the approach to truth.

The historian's vocation depends on this minimal operational article of faith: Truth is absolute; it is as absolute as the world is real. It does not exist because individuals wish it to anymore than the world exists for their convenience. Although observers have more or less partial views of the truth, its actuality is unrelated to the desires or the particular angles of vision of the viewers. Truth is knowable and will out if earnestly pursued; and science is the procedure or set of procedures for approximating it.

❧

What is truth? Mighty above all things, it resides in the small pieces which together form the record.

History is not the past, any more than biology is life, or physics, matter. History is the distillation of evidence surviving from the past. Where there is no evidence, there is no history. Much of the past is not knowable in this way, and about those areas the historian must learn to confess ignorance.

No one can relive the past; but everyone can seek truth in the record. Simple, durable discoveries await the explorer. So chronology—the sequential order of events reaching back beyond time's horizon—informs the viewer of the long distance traversed and of the immutable course of occurrences: no reversal of a step taken; no after ever before. The historian cannot soar with the anthropologists, who swoop across all time and space. Give or take a thousand years, it is all one to them in pronouncements about whether irrigation systems succeeded or followed despotisms, or in linking technology, population, food, and climatic changes. In the end they pick what they need to prop up theory. The discipline of dates rails off the historian and guards against such perilous plunges. No abstraction, no general interpretation, no wish or preference can challenge chronology's dominion, unless among those peoples who, lacking a sense of time, lack also a sense of history. And whoever learns to know the tyranny of the passing hours, the irrecoverable nature of days passed, learns also the vanity of all aspirations to halt the clock or slow its speed, of all irridentisms, all efforts to recapture, turn back, redeem the moments gone by.

Another use of history is in teaching about vocabulary, the basic component of human communication. Words, singularly elusive, sometimes flutter out of reach, hide in mists of ambiguity, or lodge themselves among inaccessible logical structures, yet form the very stuff of evidence. The historian captures the little syllabic clusters only by knowing who inscribed or spoke them—a feat made possible by understanding the minds and hearts and hands of the men and women for whom they once had meaning. Words released by comprehension wing their messages across the centuries. A use of history is to instruct in the reading of a word, in the comprehension of speakers, writers different from the listener, viewer.

And context. Every survival bespeaks a context. Who graved or wrote or built did so for the eyes of others. Each line or shape denotes a relation to people, things, or concepts—knowable. The identities of sender and recipient explain the content of the letter; the mode of transmission explains the developing idea, the passions of employers and laborers, the organization of the factory. A use of history is its aid in locating discrete events, phenomena, and expressions in their universes.

The limits of those universes were often subjects of dispute. Early in the nineteenth century Henry Thomas Buckle complained, in terms still applicable decades thereafter, of "the singular spectacle of one historian being ignorant of political economy; another knowing nothing of law; another nothing of ecclesiastical affairs and changes of opinion; another neglecting the philosophy of statistics, another physical science," so that those important pursuits, being cultivated, "some by one man, and some by another, have been isolated rather than united," with no disposition to concentrate them upon history. He thus echoed Gibbon's earlier injunction to value all facts. A Montesquieu, "from the meanest of them, will draw conclusions unknown to ordinary men" and arrive at "philosophical history."

On the other hand, a distinguished scholar fifty years later pooh-poohed the very idea that there might be a relation among the Gothic style, feudalism, and scholasticism, or a link between the Baroque and Jesuitism. Nevertheless, the dominant thrust of twentieth-century historians has been toward recognition of the broader contexts; in a variety of fashions they have searched for a totality denominated civilization, culture, or spirit of an epoch, and which they have hoped would permit examination of enlightening linkages and reciprocal relations. Even those who deny that history is a single discipline and assert that it is only "congeries of related disciplines" would, no doubt, expect each branch to look beyond its own borders.

In the final analysis, all the uses of history depend upon the integrity of the record, without which there could be no counting of time, no reading of words, no perception of the context, no utility of the subject. No concern could be deeper than assaults upon the record, upon the very idea of a record.

◦◀❀▶◦

Although history is an ancient discipline, it rests upon foundations laid in the seventeenth century, when a century of blood shed in religious and dynastic warfare persuaded those who wrote and read history to accept a vital difference in tolerance between facts and interpretation. The text of a charter or statute was subject to proof of authenticity and validity, whatever the meanings lawyers or theologians imparted to its terms. The correct date, the precise phrasing, the seal were facts which might present difficulties of verification, but which, nevertheless, admitted of answers that were right or wrong. On the other hand, discussion of opinions and meanings often called for tolerance among diverse points of view, tolerance possible so long as disputants distinguished interpretation from the fact, from the thing in itself. Scholars could disagree on large matters of interpretation; they had a common interest in agreeing on the small ones of fact which provided them grounds of peaceful discourse.

From that seminal insight developed the scientific mechanisms that enabled historians to separate fact from opinion. From that basis came the Enlightenment achievements which recognized the worth of objectivity and asserted the possibility of reconstructing the whole record of the human past.

True, historians as well as philosophers often thereafter worried about the problems of bias and perspective; and some despaired of attaining the ideal of ultimate objectivity. None were ever totally free of bias, not even those like Ranke who most specifically insisted on the integrity of the fact which he struggled to make the foundation of a truly universal body of knowledge. But, however fallible the individual scholar, the historian's, task, Wilhelm von Humboldt explained, was "to present what actually happened."

It may have been a dream to imagine that history would become a science meaningful to all people, everywhere. If so, it was a noble dream.

By contrast, historians in the 1970s and increasingly other scientists regarded the fact itself as malleable. As the distinction between fact and interpretation faded, all became faction—a combination of fact and fiction. The passive acceptance of that illegitimate genre—whatever mixes with fiction ceases to be fact—revealed the erosion of scholarly commitment. More and more often, the factual elements in an account were instrumental to the purpose the author-manipulator wished them to serve. It followed that different writers addressing different readers for different purposes could arrange matters as convenient. In the end, the primacy of the fact vanished and only the authority of the author, the receptivity of the audience, and the purpose intended remained.

Whence came this desertion, this rejection of allegiance to the fact?

Chroniclers of the past always suffered from external pressure to make their findings relevant, that is, to demonstrate or deny the wisdom, correctness, or appropriateness of current policies. They resisted out of dedication to maintaining the integrity of the record; and long succeeded in doing so. In the 1970s, however, the pressures toward falsification became more compelling than ever before.

Although the full fruits of the change appeared only in that decade, its origins reached back a half-century. It was one of Stalin's most impressive achievements to have converted Marxism from its nineteenth-century scientific base to an instrument of state purpose, and it was not by coincidence that history was the first discipline to suffer in the process. The Soviet Union did more than impose an official party line on interpretations of Trotsky's role in the revolution of 1917; it actually expunged the name Trotsky from the record, so that the fact of the commissar's existence disappeared. What started in the domain of history led in time to Lysenko's invasion of the natural sciences. The Nazis, once in power, burned the nonconforming books; and after 1945 the assault spread to all countries subject to totalitarian control. Those developments were neither surprising nor difficult to comprehend; they followed from the nature of the regimes which fostered them.

More surprising, more difficult to comprehend, was the acquiescence by the scholars of free societies in the attack on history, first, insofar as it affected colleagues less fortunately situated, then as it insinuated itself in their own ranks. External and internal circumstances were responsible.

In a sensate society the commercial standards of the media governed the dissemination of information. Since whatever sold was news, the salient consideration was one of attracting attention; factual accuracy receded to the remote background. An affluent and indulgent society also mistook flaccid permissiveness for tolerance. Everything went because nothing was worth defending, and the legitimate right to err became the disastrous obliteration of the difference between error and truth.

Difficult critical issues tempted the weak-minded to tailor fact to convenience. In the United States, but also in other parts of the world, the spread of a kind of tribalism demanded a history unique to and written for the specifications of particular groups. Since knowledge was relative to the knowers, it was subject to manipulation to suit their convenience. The process by which blacks, white ethnics, and women alone were conceded the capability of understanding and writing their own histories wiped out the line between truth and myth.

That much was comprehensible; these forces operated outside the academy walls and were not subject to very much control. More important, more susceptible to control, and less explicable was the betrayal by the intellectuals of their own group interests and the subsequent loss of the will to resist. A variety of elements contributed to this most recent *trahison des clercs*. Exaggerated concern with the problems of bias and objectivity drove some earnest scholars to despair. Perhaps they reacted against the excessive claims of the nineteenth century, perhaps against the inability of historians, any more than other scholars, to withstand the pressures of nationalism in the early decades of the twentieth century. In any case, not a few followed the deceptive path from acknowledgment that no person was entirely free of prejudice or capable of attaining a totally objective view of the past to the conclusion that all efforts to do so were vain and that, in the end, the past was entirely a recreation emanating from the mind of the historian. Support from this point of view came from the philosophers Benedetto Croce in Italy and, later, R. G. Collingwood in England. Support also came from a misreading of anthropological relativism, which drew from the undeniable circumstances that different cultures evolved differently, the erroneous conclusion that judgments among them were impossible.

Perhaps playfully, perhaps seriously, Carl L. Becker suggested that the historical fact was in someone's mind or it was nowhere, because it was "not the past event," only a symbol which enabled later writers to recreate it imaginatively. His charmingly put illustrations deceived many a reader unaware that serious thinkers since Bayle and Hume had wrestled with the problem. "No one could ever object to the factual truth that Caesar defeated Pompey; and whatever the principles one wishes to use in dispute, one will find nothing less questionable than this proposition—Caesar and Pompey existed and were not just simple modification of the minds of those who wrote their lives"—thus Bayle.

The starting point in Becker's wandering toward relativism, as for others among his contemporaries, was the desire to be useful in solving "the everlasting riddle of human experience." Less subtle successors attacked neutrality "toward the main issues of life" and demanded that society organize all its forces in support of its ideals. "Total war, whether it be hot or cold, enlists everyone and calls upon everyone to assume his part. The historian is no freer from this obligation than the physicists." Those too timid to go the whole way suggested that there might be two kinds of history, variously defined: one, for instance, to treat the positive side of slavery to nurture black pride; another, the negative, to support claims for compensation."

Historians who caved in to pressure and ordered the past to please the present neglected the future, the needs of which would certainly change and in unpredictable ways. Scholarship could no more provide the future than the present with faith, justification, self-confidence, or sense of purpose unless it first preserved the record, intact and inviolable.

History does not recreate the past. The historian does not recapture the bygone event. No amount of imagination will enable the scholar to describe exactly what happened to Caesar in the Senate or to decide whether

Mrs. Williams actually lost two hundred pounds by an act of faith. History deals only with evidence from the past, with the residues of bygone events. But it can pass judgment upon documentation and upon observers' reports of what they thought they saw.

Disregarding these constraints, Becker concluded that, since objectivity was a dream, everyman could be his own historian and contrive his own view of the past, valid for himself, if for no one else. He thus breached the line between interpretation, which was subjective and pliable, and fact, which was not.

Internal specialization allowed historians to slip farther in the same direction. The knowledge explosion after 1900 made specialization an essential, unavoidable circumstance of every form of scholarly endeavor. No individual could presume to competence in more than a sector of the whole field; and the scope of the manageable sector steadily shrank. One result was the dissolution of common standards; each area created its own criteria and claimed immunity from the criticism of outsiders. The occupants of each little island fortress sustained the illusion that the dangers to one would not apply to others. Lines of communication, even within a single faculty or department, broke down so that, increasingly, specialists in one area depended upon the common mass media for knowledge about what transpired in another.

The dangers inherent in these trends became critical as scholarship lost its autonomy. Increasingly reliance on support from external sources—whether governments or foundations—circumscribed the freedom of researchers and writers to choose their own subjects and to arrive at their own conclusions. More generally, the loss of autonomy involved a state of mind which regarded the fruits of scholarship as dependent and instrumental—that is, not as worthy of pursuit for their own sake, not for the extent to which they brought the inquirer closer to the truth, but for other, extrinsic reasons. Ever more often, scholars justified their activity by its external results—peace, training for citizenship, economic development, cure of illness, and the like—in other words, by its usefulness. The choice of topics revealed the extent to which emphasis had shifted from the subject and its relation to the truth to its instrumental utility measured by reference to some external standard.

The plea from utility was dangerous. In the 1930s it blinded well-intentioned social scientists and historians to the excesses of totalitarianism. It was inevitable in creating the omelette of a great social experiment that the shells of a few eggs of truth would be broken, so the argument ran. So, too, in the avid desire for peace, in the praiseworthy wish to avoid a second world war, Charles A. Beard abandoned all effort at factual accuracy. Yet the errors to which the plea for utility led in the past have not prevented others from proceeding along the same treacherous path in pursuit of no less worthy, but equally deceptive utilitarian goals.

Finally, the reluctance to insist upon the worth of truth for its own sake stemmed from a decline of faith by intellectuals in their own role as intellectuals. Not many have, in any conscious or deliberate sense, foresworn their allegiance to the pursuit of truth and the life of the spirit. But power tempted them as it tempts other men and women. The twentieth-century intellectual had unparalleled access to those who actually wielded political or military influence. And few could resist the temptation of being listened to by presidents and ministers, of seeing ideas translated into action. Moreover, a more subtle, more insidious temptation nested in the possibility that possession of knowledge may itself become a significant source of power. The idea that a name on the letterhead of an activist organization or in the endorsement of a political advertisement might advance some worthy cause gives a heady feeling of sudden consequence to the no-longer-humble professor. Most important of all is the consciousness that knowledge can indeed do good, that it is a usable commodity, not only capable of bringing fame to its possessor but actually capable of causing beneficent changes in the external world.

All too few scholars are conscious that in reducing truth to an instrument, even an instrument for doing good, they necessarily blunt its edge and expose themselves to the danger of its misuse. For, when truth ceases to be an end in itself and becomes but a means toward an end, it also becomes malleable and manageable and is in danger of losing its character—not necessarily, not inevitably, but seriously. There may be ways of avoiding the extreme choices of the ivory tower and the marketplace, but they are far from easy and call for extreme caution.

❦

In 1679 Jacques Bossuet wrote for his pupil the Dauphin, heir apparent to the throne of France, a discourse on universal history. Here certainly was an opportunity to influence the mind of the future monarch of Europe's most powerful kingdom. Bossuet understood that the greatest service he could render was to tell, not what would be pleasant to hear, but the truth about the past, detached and whole, so that in later years his pupil could make what use he wished of it.

Therein Bossuet reverted to an ancient tradition. The first law for the historian, Cicero had written, "is never to dare utter an untruth and the second, never to suppress anything true." And, earlier still, Polybius had noted that no one was exempt from mistakes made out of ignorance. But "deliberate misstatements in the interest of country or of friends or for favour" reduced the scholar to the level of those who gained "their living by their pens" and weighed "everything by the standard of profit."

In sum, the use of history is to learn from the study of it and not to carry preconceived notions or external objectives into it.

❦

The times, it may be, will remain hostile to the enterprise of truth. There have been such periods in the past. Historians would do well to regard the example of those clerks in the Dark Ages who knew the worth of the task. By retiring from an alien world to a hidden monastic refuge, now and again one of them at least was able to maintain a true record, a chronicle that survived the destructive passage of armies and the erosion of doctrinal disputes and informed the future of what had transpired in their day. That task is ever worthy. Scholars should ponder its significance.

William H. McNeill  **NO**

Mythistory, or Truth, Myth, History, and Historians

Myth and history are close kin inasmuch as both explain how things got to be the way they are by telling some sort of story. But our common parlance reckons myth to be false while history is, or aspires to be, true. Accordingly, a historian who rejects someone else's conclusions calls them mythical, while claiming that his own views are true. But what seems true to one historian will seem false to another, so one historian's truth becomes another's myth, even at the moment of utterance.

A century and more ago, when history was first established as an academic discipline, our predecessors recognized this dilemma and believed they had a remedy. Scientific source criticism would get the facts straight, whereupon a conscientious and careful historian needed only to arrange the facts into a readable narrative to produce genuinely scientific history. And science, of course, like the stars above, was true and eternal, as Newton and Laplace had demonstrated to the satisfaction of all reasonable persons everywhere.

Yet, in practice, revisionism continued to prevail within the newly constituted historical profession, as it had since the time of Herodotus. For a generation or two, this continued volatility could be attributed to scholarly success in discovering new facts by diligent work in the archives; but early in this century thoughtful historians began to realize that the arrangement of facts to make a history involved subjective judgments and intellectual choices that had little or nothing to do with source criticism, scientific or otherwise.

In reacting against an almost mechanical vision of scientific method, it is easy to underestimate actual achievements. For the ideal of scientific history did allow our predecessors to put some forms of bias behind them. In particular, academic historians of the nineteenth century came close to transcending older religious controversies. Protestant and Catholic histories of post-Reformation Europe ceased to be separate and distinct traditions of learning—a transformation nicely illustrated in the Anglo-American world by the career of Lord Acton, a Roman Catholic who became Regius Professor of History at Cambridge and editor of the first *Cambridge Modern History*. This was a great accomplishment. So was the accumulation of an enormous fund of exact and reliable data through painstaking source criticism that allowed the writing of history in the western world to assume a new depth, scope, range, and precision as compared to anything possible in earlier times. No heir of that scholarly tradition should scoff at the faith of our predecessors, which inspired so much toiling in archives.

Yet the limits of scientific history were far more constricting than its devotees believed. Facts that could be established beyond all reasonable doubt remained trivial in the sense that they did not, in and of themselves, give meaning or intelligibility to the record of the past. A catalogue of undoubted and indubitable information, even if arranged chronologically, remains a catalogue. To become a history, facts have to be put together into a pattern that is understandable and credible; and when that has been achieved, the resulting portrait of the past may become useful as well—a font of practical wisdom upon which people may draw when making decisions and taking action.

Pattern recognition of the sort historians engage in is the chef d'oeuvre of human intelligence. It is achieved by paying selective attention to the total input of stimuli that perpetually swarm in upon our consciousness. Only by leaving things out, that is, relegating them to the status of background noise deserving only to be disregarded, can what matters most in a given situation become recognizable. Suitable action follows. Here is the great secret of human power over nature and over ourselves as well. Pattern recognition is what natural scientists are up to; it is what historians have always done, whether they knew it or not.

Only some facts matter for any given pattern. Otherwise, useless clutter will obscure what we are after: perceptible relationships among important facts. That and that alone constitutes an intelligible pattern, giving meaning to the world, whether it be the world of physics and chemistry or the world of interacting human groups through time, which historians take as their special domain. Natural scientists are ruthless in selecting aspects of available sensory inputs to pay attention to, disregarding all else. They call their patterns theories and inherit most of them from predecessors. But, as we now know, even Newton's truths needed adjustment. Natural science is neither eternal nor universal; it is instead historical and evolutionary, because scientists accept a new theory only when the new embraces a wider range of phenomena or achieves a more elegant explanation of (selectively observed) facts than its predecessor was able to do.

No comparably firm consensus prevails among historians. Yet we need not despair. The great and obvious difference between natural scientists and historians is the greater complexity of the behavior historians seek to understand. The principal source of historical complexity lies in the fact that human beings react both to the natural world and to one another chiefly through the mediation of symbols. This means, among other things, that any theory about human life, if widely believed, will alter actual behavior, usually by inducing people to act as if the theory were true. Ideas and ideals thus become self-validating within remarkably elastic limits. An extraordinary behavioral motility results. Resort to symbols, in effect, loosened up the connection between external reality and human responses, freeing us from instinct by setting us adrift on a sea of uncertainty. Human beings thereby acquired a new capacity to err, but also to change, adapt, and learn new ways of doing things. Innumerable errors, corrected by experience, eventually made us lords of creation as no other species on earth has ever been before.

The price of this achievement is the elastic, inexact character of truth, and especially of truths about human conduct. What a particular group of persons understands, believes, and acts upon, even if quite absurd to outsiders, may nonetheless cement social relations and allow the members of the group to act together and accomplish feats otherwise impossible. Moreover, membership in such a group and participation in its sufferings and triumphs give meaning and value to individual human lives. Any other sort of life is not worth living, for we are social creatures. As such we need to share truths with one another, and not just truths about atoms, stars, and molecules but about human relations and the people around us.

Shared truths that provide a sanction for common effort have obvious survival value. Without such social cement no group can long preserve itself. Yet to outsiders, truths of this kind are likely to seem myths, save in those (relatively rare) cases when the outsider is susceptible to conversion and finds a welcome within the particular group in question.

The historic record available to us consists of an unending appearance and dissolution of human groups, each united by its own beliefs, ideals, and traditions. Sects, religions, tribes, and states, from ancient Sumer and Pharaonic Egypt to modern times, have based their cohesion upon shared truths—truths that differed from time to time and place to place with a rich and reckless variety. Today the human community remains divided among an enormous number of different groups, each espousing its own version of truth about itself and about those excluded from its fellowship. Everything suggests that this sort of social and ideological fragmentation will continue indefinitely.

Where, in such a maelstrom of conflicting opinions, can we hope to locate historical truth? Where indeed?

Before modern communications thrust familiarity with the variety of human idea-systems upon our consciousness, this question was not particularly acute. Individuals nearly always grew up in relatively isolated communities to a more or less homogeneous world view. Important questions had been settled long ago by prophets and sages, so there was little reason to challenge or modify traditional wisdom. Indeed there were strong positive restraints upon any would-be innovator who threatened to upset the inherited consensus.

To be sure, climates of opinion fluctuated, but changes came surreptitiously, usually disguised as commentary upon old texts and purporting merely to explicate the original meanings. Flexibility was considerable, as the modern practice of the U.S. Supreme Court should convince us; but in this traditional ordering of intellect, all the same, outsiders who did not share the prevailing orthodoxy were shunned and disregarded when they could not be converted. Our predecessors' faith in a scientific method that would make written history absolutely and universally true was no more than a recent example of such a belief system. Those who embraced it felt no need to pay attention to ignoramuses who had not accepted the truths of "modern science." Like other true believers, they were therefore spared the task of taking others' viewpoints seriously or wondering about the limits of their own vision of historical truth.

But we are denied the luxury of such parochialism. We must reckon with multiplex, competing faiths—secular as well as transcendental, revolutionary as well as traditional—that resound amongst us. In addition, partially autonomous professional idea-systems have proliferated in the past century or so. Those most important to historians are the so-called social sciences—anthropology, sociology, political science, psychology, and economics—together with the newer disciplines of ecology and semeiology. But law, theology, and philosophy also pervade the field of knowledge with which historians may be expected to deal. On top of all this, innumerable individual authors, each with his own assortment of ideas and assumptions, compete for attention. Choice is everywhere; dissent turns into cacaphonous confusion; my truth dissolves into your myth even before I can put words on paper.

The liberal faith, of course, holds that in a free marketplace of ideas, Truth will eventually prevail. I am not ready to abandon that faith, however dismaying our present confusion may be. The liberal experiment, after all, is only about two hundred and fifty years old, and on the appropriate world-historical time scale that is too soon to be sure. Still, confusion is undoubted. Whether the resulting uncertainty will be bearable for large numbers of people in difficult times ahead is a question worth asking. Iranian Muslims, Russian communists, and American sectarians (religious and otherwise) all exhibit symptoms of acute distress in face of moral uncertainties, generated by exposure to competing truths. Clearly, the will to believe is as strong today as at any time in the past; and true believers nearly always wish to create a community of the faithful, so as to be able to live more comfortably, insulated from troublesome dissent.

The prevailing response to an increasingly cosmopolitan confusion has been intensified personal attachment, first to national and then to subnational groups, each with its own distinct ideals and practices. As one would expect, the historical profession faithfully reflected and helped to forward these shifts of sentiment. Thus, the founding fathers of the American Historical Association and their immediate successors were intent on facilitating the consolidation of a new American nation by writing national history in a WASPish mold, while also claiming affiliation with a tradition of Western civilization that ran back through modern and medieval Europe to the ancient Greeks and Hebrews. This version of our past was very widely repudiated in the 1960s, but iconoclastic revisionists felt no need to replace what they attacked with any architectonic vision of their own. Instead, scholarly energy concentrated on discovering the history of various segments of the population that had been left out or ill-treated by older historians: most notably women, blacks, and other ethnic minorities within the United States and the ex-colonial peoples of the world beyond the national borders.

Such activity conformed to our traditional professional role of helping to define collective identities in ambiguous situations. Consciousness of a common past, after all, is a powerful supplement to other ways of defining who "we" are. An oral tradition, sometimes almost undifferentiated from the practical wisdom embodied in language itself, is all people need in a stable social universe where in-group boundaries are self-evident. But with civilization, ambiguities multi pled, and formal written history became useful in defining "us" versus "them." At first, the central ambiguity ran between rulers and ruled. Alien conquerors who lived on taxes collected from their subjects were at best a necessary evil when looked at from the bottom of civilized society. Yet in some situations, especially when confronting natural disaster or external attack, a case could be made for commonality, even between taxpayers and tax consumers. At any rate, histories began as king lists, royal genealogies, and boasts of divine favor—obvious ways of consolidating rulers' morale and asserting their legitimacy vis-à-vis their subjects.

Jewish history emphasized God's power over human affairs, narrowing the gap between rulers and ruled by subjecting everybody to divine Providence. The Greeks declared all free men equal, subject to no one, but bound by a common obedience to law. The survival value of both these visions of the human condition is fairly obvious. A people united by their fear and love of God have an ever-present help in time of trouble, as Jewish history surely proves. Morale can survive disaster, time and again; internal disputes and differences diminish beneath the weight of a shared subjection to God. The Greek ideal of freedom under law is no less practical in the sense that willing cooperation is likely to elicit maximal collective effort, whether in war or peace.

Interplay between these two ideals runs throughout the history of Western civilization, but this is not the place to enter into a detailed historiographical analysis. Let me merely remark that our professional heritage from the liberal and nationalist historiography of the nineteenth century drew mainly on the Greek, Herodotean model, emphasizing the supreme value of political freedom within a territorially defined state.

World War I constituted a catastrophe for that liberal and nationalist vision of human affairs, since freedom that permitted such costly and lethal combat no longer seemed a plausible culmination of all historic experience. Boom, bust, and World War II did nothing to clarify the issue, and the multiplication of subnational historiographies since the 1950s merely increased our professional confusion.

What about truth amidst all this weakening of old certainties, florescence of new themes, and widening of sensibilities? What really and truly matters? What should we pay attention to? What must we neglect?

All human groups like to be flattered. Historians are therefore under perpetual temptation to conform to expectation by portraying the people they write about as they wish to be. A mingling of truth and falsehood, blending history with ideology, results. Historians are likely to select facts to show that we—whoever "we" may be—conform to our cherished principles: that we are free with Herodotus, or saved with Augustine, or oppressed with Marx, as the case may be. Grubby details indicating that the group fell short of its ideals can be skated over or omitted entirely. The result is mythical: the past as we want it to be, safely simplified into a contest between good guys and bad guys, "us" and "them." Most national history and most group history is of this kind, though the intensity of chiaroscuro varies greatly, and sometimes an historian turns traitor to the group he studies by setting out to unmask its pretensions. Groups struggling toward self-consciousness and groups whose accustomed status seems threatened are likely to demand (and get) vivid, simplified portraits of their admirable virtues and undeserved sufferings. Groups accustomed to power and surer of their internal cohesion can afford to accept more subtly modulated portraits of their successes and failures in bringing practice into conformity with principles.

Historians respond to this sort of market by expressing varying degrees of commitment to, and detachment from, the causes they chronicle and by infusing varying degrees of emotional intensity into their pages through particular choices of words. Truth, persuasiveness, intelligibility rest far more on this level of the historians' art than on source criticism. But, as I said at the beginning, one person's truth is another's myth, and the fact that a group of people accepts a given version of the past does not make that version any truer for outsiders.

Yet we cannot afford to reject collective self-flattery as silly, contemptible error. Myths are, after all, often self-validating. A nation or any other human group that knows how to behave in crisis situations because it has inherited a heroic historiographical tradition that tells how ancestors resisted their enemies successfully is more likely to act together effectively than a group lacking such a tradition. Great Britain's conduct in 1940 shows how world politics can be redirected by such a heritage. Flattering historiography does more than assist a given group to survive by affecting the balance of power among warring peoples, for an appropriately idealized version of the past may also allow a group of human beings to come closer to living up to its noblest ideals. What is can move toward what ought to be, given collective commitment to a flattering self-image. The American civil rights movement of the fifties and sixties illustrates this phenomenon amongst us.

These collective manifestations are of very great importance. Belief in the virtue and righteousness of one's cause is a necessary sort of self-delusion for human beings, singly and collectively. A corrosive version of history that emphasizes all the recurrent discrepancies between ideal and reality in a given group's behavior makes it harder for members of the group in question to act cohesively and in good conscience. That sort of history is very costly indeed. No group can afford it for long.

On the other hand, myths may mislead disastrously. A portrait of the past that denigrates others and praises the ideals and practice of a given group naively and without restraint can distort a people's image of outsiders so that foreign relations begin to consist of nothing but nasty surprises. Confidence in one's own high principles and good intentions may simply provoke others to resist duly accredited missionaries of the true faith, whatever that faith may be. Both the United States and the Soviet Union have encountered their share of this sort of surprise and disappointment ever since 1917, when Wilson and Lenin proclaimed their respective recipes for curing the world's ills. In more extreme cases, mythical, self-flattering versions of the past may push a people toward suicidal behavior, as Hitler's last days may remind us.

More generally, it is obvious that mythical, self-flattering versions of rival groups' pasts simply serve to intensify their capacity for conflict. With the recent quantum jump in the destructive power of weaponry, hardening of group cohesion at the sovereign state level clearly threatens the survival of humanity; while, within national borders, the civic order experiences new strains when subnational groups acquire a historiography replete with oppressors living next door and, perchance, still enjoying the fruits of past injustices.

The great historians have always responded to these difficulties by expanding their sympathies beyond narrow in-group boundaries. Herodotus set out to award a due meed of glory both to Hellenes and to the barbarians; Ranke inquired into what really happened to Protestant and Catholic, Latin and German nations alike. And other pioneers of our profession have likewise expanded the range of their sympathies and sensibilities beyond previously recognized limits without ever entirely escaping, or even wishing to escape, from the sort of partisanship involved in accepting the general assumptions and beliefs of a particular time and place.

Where to fix one's loyalties is the supreme question of human life and is especially acute in a cosmopolitan age like ours when choices abound. Belonging to a tightly knit group makes life worth living by giving individuals something beyond the self to serve and to rely on for personal guidance, companionship, and aid. But the stronger such bonds, the sharper the break with the rest of humanity. Group solidarity is always maintained, at least partly, by exporting psychic frictions across the frontiers, projecting animosities onto an outside foe in order to enhance collective cohesion within the group itself. Indeed, something to fear, hate, and attack is probably necessary for the full expression of human emotions; and ever since animal predators ceased to threaten, human beings have feared, hated, and fought one another.

Historians, by helping to define "us" and "them," play a considerable part in focusing love and hate, the two principal cements of collective behavior known to humanity. But myth making for rival groups has become a dangerous game in the atomic age, and we may well ask whether there is any alternative open to us.

In principle the answer is obvious. Humanity entire possesses a commonality which historians may hope to understand just as firmly as they can comprehend what unites any lesser group. Instead of enhancing conflicts, as parochial historiography inevitably does, an intelligible world history might be expected to diminish the lethality of group encounters by cultivating a sense of individual identification with the triumphs and tribulations of humanity as a whole. This, indeed, strikes me as the moral duty of the historical profession in our time. We need to develop an ecumenical history, with plenty of room for human diversity in all its complexity.

Yet a wise historian will not denigrate intense attachment to small groups. That is essential to personal happiness. In all civilized societies, a tangle of overlapping social groupings lays claim to human loyalties. Anyone person may therefore be expected to have multiple commitments and plural public identities, up to and including membership in the human race and the wider DNA community of life on planet Earth. What we need to do as historians and as human beings is to recognize this complexity and balance our loyalties so that no one group will be able to command total commitment. Only so can we hope to make the world safer for all the different human groups that now exist and may come into existence.

The historical profession has, however, shied away from an ecumenical view of the human adventure. Professional career patterns reward specialization; and in all the well-trodden fields, where pervasive consensus on important matters has already been achieved, research and innovation necessarily concentrate upon minutiae. Residual faith that truth somehow resides in original documents confirms this direction of our energies. An easy and commonly unexamined corollary is the assumption that world history is too vague and too general to be true, that is, accurate to the sources. Truth, according to this view, is only attainable on a tiny scale when the diligent historian succeeds in exhausting the relevant documents before they exhaust the historian. But as my previous remarks have made clear, this does not strike me as a valid view of historical method. On the contrary, I call it naive and erroneous.

All truths are general. All truths abstract from the available assortment of data simply by using words, which in their very nature generalize so as to bring order to the incessantly fluctuating flow of messages in and messages out that constitutes human consciousness. Total reproduction of experience is impossible and undesirable. It would merely perpetuate the confusion we seek to escape. Historiography that aspires to get closer and closer to the documents—all the documents: and nothing but the documents—is merely moving closer and closer to incoherence, chaos, and meaninglessness. That is a dead end for sure. No society will long support a profession that produces arcane trivia and calls it truth.

Fortunately for the profession, historians' practice has been better than their epistemology. Instead of replicating confusion by paraphrasing the totality of relevant and available documents, we have used our sources to discern, support, and reinforce group identities at national, transnational, and subnational levels and, once in a while, to attack or pick apart a group identity to which a school of revisionists has taken a scunner.

If we can now realize that our practice already shows how truths may be discerned at different levels of generality with equal precision simply because different patterns emerge on different time-space scales, then, perhaps, repugnance for world history might diminish and a juster proportion between parochial and ecumenical historiography might begin to emerge. It is our professional duty to move toward ecumenicity, however real the risks may seem to timid and unenterprising minds.

With a more rigorous and reflective epistemology, we might also attain a better historiographical balance between Truth, truths, and myth. Eternal and universal Truth about human behavior is an unattainable goal, however delectable as an ideal. Truths are what historians achieve when they bend their minds as critically and carefully as they can to the task of making their account of public affairs credible as well as intelligible to an audience that shares enough of their particular outlook and assumptions to accept what they say. The result might best be called mythistory perhaps (though I do not expect the term to catch on in professional circles), for the same words that constitute truth for some are, and always will be, myth for others, who inherit or embrace different assumptions and organizing concepts about the world.

This does not mean that there is no difference between one mythistory and another. Some clearly are more adequate to the facts than others. Some embrace more time and space and make sense of a wider variety of human behavior than others. And some, undoubtedly, offer a less treacherous basis for collective action than others. I actually believe that historians' truths, like those of scientists, evolve across the generations, so that versions of the past acceptable today are superior in scope, range, and accuracy to versions available in earlier times. But such evolution is slow, and observable only on an extended time scale, owing to the self-validating character of myth. Effective common action can rest on quite fantastic beliefs. *Credo quia absurdum* may even become a criterion for group membership, requiring initiates to surrender their critical faculties as a sign of full commitment to the common cause. Many sects have prospered on this principle and have served their members well for many generations while doing so.

But faiths, absurd or not, also face a long-run test of survival in a world where not everyone accepts anyone set of beliefs and where human beings must interact with external objects and nonhuman forms of life, as well as with one another. Such "foreign relations" impose limits on what any group of people can safely believe and act on, since actions that fail to secure expected and desired results are always costly and often disastrous. Beliefs that mislead action are likely to be amended; too stubborn an adherence to a faith that encourages or demands hurtful behavior is likely to lead to the disintegration and disappearance of any group that refuses to learn from experience.

Thus one may, as an act of faith, believe that our historiographical myth making and myth breaking is bound to cumulate across time, propagating mythistories that fit experience better and allow human survival more often, sustaining in-groups in ways that are less destructive to themselves and to their neighbors than was once the case or is the case today. If so, ever-evolving mythistories will indeed become truer and more adequate to public life, emphasizing the really important aspects of human encounters and omitting irrelevant background noise more efficiently so that men and women will know how to act more wisely than is possible for us today.

This is not a groundless hope. Future historians are unlikely to leave out blacks and women from any future mythistory of the United States, and we are unlikely to exclude Asians, Africans, and Amerindians from any future mythistory of the world. One hundred years ago this was not so. The scope and range of historiography has widened, and that change looks as irreversible to me as the widening of physics that occurred when Einstein's equations proved capable of explaining phenomena that Newton's could not.

It is far less clear whether in widening the range of our sensibilities and taking a broader range of phenomena into account we also see deeper into the reality we seek to understand. But we may. Anyone who reads historians of the sixteenth and seventeenth centuries and those of our own time will notice a new awareness of social process that we have attained. As one who shares that awareness, I find it impossible not to believe that it represents an advance on older notions that focused attention exclusively, or almost exclusively, on human intentions and individual actions, subject only to God or to a no less inscrutable Fortune, while leaving out the social and material context within which individual actions took place simply because that context was assumed to be uniform and unchanging.

Still, what seems wise and true to me seems irrelevant obfuscation to others. Only time can settle the issue, presumably by outmoding my ideas and my critics' as well. Unalterable and eternal Truth remains like the Kingdom of

Heaven, an eschatological hope. Mythistory is what we actually have—a useful instrument for piloting human groups in their encounters with one another and with the natural environment.

To be a truth-seeking mythographer is therefore a high and serious calling, for what a group of people knows and believes about the past channels expectations and affects the decisions on which their lives, their fortunes, and their sacred honor all depend. Formal written histories are not the only shapers of a people's notions about the past; but they are sporadically powerful, since even the most abstract and academic historiographical ideas do trickle down to the level of the commonplace, if they fit both what a people want to hear and what a people need to know well enough to be useful.

As members of society and sharers in the historical process, historians can only expect to be heard if they say what the people around them want to hear—in some degree. They can only be useful if they also tell the people some things they are reluctant to hear—in some degree. Piloting between this Scylla and Charybdis is the art of the serious historian, helping the group he or she addresses and celebrates to survive and prosper in a treacherous and changing world by knowing more about itself and others.

Academic historians have pursued that art with extraordinary energy and considerable success during the past century. May our heirs and successors persevere and do even better!

POSTSCRIPT

Is History True?

Closely associated to the question of historical truth is the matter of historical objectivity. Frequently, we hear people begin statements with the phrase "History tells us . . ." or "History shows that . . . ," followed by a conclusion that reflects the speaker or writer's point of view. In fact, history does not directly tell or show us anything. That is the job of historians, and as William McNeill argues, much of what historians tell us, despite their best intentions, often represents a blending of historical evidence and myth.

Is there such a thing as a truly objective history? Historian Paul Conkin agrees with McNeill that objectivity is possible only if the meaning of that term is sharply restricted and is not used as a synonym for certain truth. History, Conkin writes, "is a story about the past; it is not the past itself. . . . Whether one draws a history from the guidance of memory or of monuments, it cannot exactly mirror some directly experienced past nor the feelings and perceptions of people in the past." He concludes, "In this sense, much of history is a stab into partial darkness, a matter of informed but inconclusive conjecture. . . . Obviously, in such areas of interpretation, there is no one demonstrably correct 'explanation,' but very often competing, equally unfalsifiable, theories. Here, on issues that endlessly fascinate the historian, the controversies rage, and no one expects, short of a great wealth of unexpected evidence, to find a conclusive answer. An undesired, abstractive precision of the subject might so narrow it as to permit more conclusive evidence. But this would spoil all the fun." For more discussion on this and other topics related to the study of history, see Paul K. Conkin and Roland N. Stromberg, *The Heritage and Challenge of History* (Dodd, Mead & Company, 1971).

The most thorough discussion of historical objectivity in the United States is Peter Novick, *That Noble Dream: The 'Objectivity Question' and the American Historical Profession* (Cambridge University Press, 1988), which draws its title from Charles A. Beard's article in the *American Historical Review* (October 1935) in which Beard reinforced the views expressed in his 1933 presidential address to the American Historical Association. [See "Written History as an Act of Faith," *American Historical Review* (January 1934).] Novick's thorough analysis generated a great deal of attention, the results of which can be followed in James T. Kloppenberg, "Objectivity and Historicism: A Century of American Historical Writing," *American Historical Review* (October 1989), Thomas L. Haskell, "Objectivity Is Not Neutrality: Rhetoric vs. Practice in Peter Novick's *That Noble Dream*," *History & Theory* (1990), and the scholarly forum "Peter Novick's *That Noble Dream*: The Objectivity Question and the Future of the Historical Profession," *American Historical Review* (June 1991). A critique of recent historical writing that closely follows the concerns expressed by Handlin can be found in Keith Windschuttle, *The Killing of History: How Literary Critics and Social Theorists Are Murdering Our Past* (The Free Press, 1996).

Readers interested in this subject will also find the analyses in Barbara W. Tuchman, *Practicing History: Selected Essays* (Alfred A. Knopf, 1981) and David Hackett Fischer, *Historians' Fallacies: Toward a Logic of Historical Thought* (Harper & Row, 1970) to be quite stimulating. Earlier, though equally rewarding, volumes include Harvey Wish, *The American Historian: A Social-Intellectual History of the Writing of the American Past* (Oxford University Press, 1960); John Higham, with Leonard Krieger and Felix Gilbert, *History: The Development of Historical Studies in the United States* (Prentice-Hall, 1965); and Marcus Cunliffe and Robin Winks, eds., *Pastmasters: Some Essays on American Historians* (Harper & Row, 1969).

ISSUE 2

Was John D. Rockefeller a "Robber Baron"?

YES: Matthew Josephson, from *The Robber Barons: The Great American Capitalists, 1861–1901* (Harcourt, Brace & World, 1962)

NO: Ron Chernow, from *Titan: The Life of John D. Rockefeller, Sr.* (Random House, 1998)

ISSUE SUMMARY

YES: Matthew Josephson depicts John D. Rockefeller as an unconscionable manipulator who employed a policy of deception, bribery, and outright conspiracy to restrain free trade in order to eliminate his competitors for control of the oil industry in the United States.

NO: Ron Chernow recognizes that Rockefeller was guilty of misdeeds that were endemic among both small and large corporate leaders of the industrial age, but he concludes that some of the most egregious claims attributed to Rockefeller were without merit and often represented actions taken by Standard Oil associates without Rockefeller's knowledge.

Between 1860 and 1914, the United States was transformed from a country of farms, small towns, and modest manufacturing concerns to a modern nation dominated by large cities and factories. During those years, the population tripled, and the nation experienced astounding urban growth. A new proletariat emerged to provide the necessary labor for the country's developing factory system. Between the Civil War and World War I, the value of manufactured goods in the United States increased twelvefold, and the capital invested in industrial pursuits multiplied twenty-two times. In addition, the application of new machinery and scientific methods to agriculture produced abundant yields of wheat, corn, and other foodstuffs, despite the decline in the number of farmers.

Why did this industrial revolution occur in the United States during the last quarter of the nineteenth century? What factors contributed to the rapid pace of American industrialization? In answering these questions, historians often point to the first half of the 1800s and the significance of the "transportation revolution," which produced better roads, canals, and railroads to move people and goods more efficiently and cheaply from one point to another. Technological improvements such as the Bessemer process, refrigeration, electricity, and the telephone also made their mark in the nation's "machine age." Government cooperation with business, large-scale immigration from Europe and Asia, and the availability of foreign capital for industrial investments provided still other underpinnings for this industrial growth. Finally, American industrialization depended upon a number of individuals in the United States who were willing to organize and finance the nation's industrial base for the sake of anticipated profits. These, of course, were the entrepreneurs.

American public attitudes have reflected a schizophrenic quality with regard to the activities of the industrial leaders of the late nineteenth century. Were these entrepreneurs "robber barons," who employed any means necessary to enrich themselves at the expense of their competitors? Or were they "captains of industry" whose shrewd and innovative leadership brought order out of industrial chaos and generated great fortunes that enriched the public welfare through the workings of various philanthropic agencies that these leaders established? Although the "robber baron" stereotype emerged as early as the 1870s, it probably gained its widest acceptance in the 1930s when, in the midst of the Great Depression, many critics were proclaiming the apparent failure of American capitalism. Since the depression, however, some historians, including Allan Nevins, Alfred D. Chandler, and Maury Klein, have sought to revise the negative assessments offered by earlier generations of scholars. In the hands of these business historians, the late-nineteenth-century businessmen have become "industrial statesmen" who skillfully oversaw the process of raising the United States to a preeminent position among the nations of the world. The following selections reveal the divergence of scholarly opinion as it applies to one of the most notable of these American entrepreneurs—John D. Rockefeller Sr., the founder of the Standard Oil Company, who came to epitomize both the success and excess of corporate capitalism in the United States.

Matthew Josephson, whose 1934 attack on monopolistic capitalism became the model for the "robber baron" thesis for post-depression era historians, characterizes Rockefeller as a parsimonious, deceptive, and conspiratorial businessman. Rockefeller's fortune, Josephson argues, was built upon a series of secret agreements that wrung concessions from America's leading railroad magnates and allowed Rockefeller to decimate his competitors through the establishment of the South Improvement Company and, subsequently, Standard Oil.

In a chapter from his recent biography of Rockefeller, Ron Chernow analyzes the indictment against the nation's leading oil magnate crafted by muckraking journalist Ida Tarbell at the turn of the last century. Chernow points out that Tarbell, motivated in part by the belief that her father and brother had suffered financial setbacks as a result of Rockefeller's business dealings, painted a portrait of scandalous misdeeds on the part of Rockefeller, some of which was undeserved.

The Robber Barons

John Rockefeller who grew up in Western New York and later near Cleveland, as one of a struggling family of five children, recalls with satisfaction the excellent practical training he had received and how quickly he put it to use. His childhood seemed to have been darkened by the misdeeds of his father, a wandering vendor of quack medicine who rarely supported his family, and was sometimes a fugitive from the law; yet the son invariably spoke of his parent's instructions with gratitude. He said:

> . . . He himself trained me in practical ways. He was engaged in different enterprises; he used to tell me about these things . . . and he taught me the principles and methods of business. . . . I knew what a cord of good solid beech and maple wood was. My father told me to select only solid wood . . . and not to put any limbs in it or any punky wood. That was a good training for me.

But the elder Rockefeller went further than this in his sage instructions, according to John T. Flynn, who attributes to him the statement:

> I cheat my boys every chance I get, I want to make 'em sharp. I trade with the boys and skin 'em and I just beat 'em every time I can. I want to make 'em sharp.

If at times the young Rockefeller absorbed a certain shiftiness and trading sharpness from his restless father, it was also true that his father was absent so often and so long as to cast shame and poverty upon his home. Thus he must have been subject far more often to the stern supervision of his mother, whom he has recalled in several stories. His mother would punish him, as he related, with a birch switch to "uphold the standard of the family when it showed a tendency to deteriorate." Once when she found out that she was punishing him for a misdeed at school of which he was innocent, she said, "Never mind, we have started in on this whipping and it will do for the next time." The normal outcome of such disciplinary cruelty would be deception and stealthiness in the boy, as a defense.

But his mother, who reared her children with the rigid piety of an Evangelist, also started him in his first business enterprise. When he was seven years old she encouraged him to raise turkeys, and gave him for this purpose the family's surplus milk curds. There are legends of Rockefeller as a boy stalking a turkey with the most patient stealth in order to seize her eggs.

This harshly disciplined boy, quiet, shy, reserved, serious, received but a few years' poor schooling, and worked for neighboring farmers in all his spare time. His whole youth suggests only abstinence, prudence and the growth of parsimony in his soul. The pennies he earned he would save steadily in a blue bowl that stood on a chest in his room, and accumulated until there was a small heap of gold coins. He would work, by his own account, hoeing potatoes for a neighboring farmer from morning to night for 37 cents a day. At a time when he was still very young he had fifty dollars saved, which upon invitation he one day loaned to the farmer who employed him.

"And as I was saving those little sums," he relates, "I soon learned that I could get as much interest for $50 loaned at seven per cent—then the legal rate of interest—as I could earn by digging potatoes for ten days." Thereafter, he tells us, he resolved that it was better "to let the money be my slave than to be the slave of money."

In Cleveland whither the family removed in 1854, Rockefeller went to the Central High School and studied bookkeeping for a year. This delighted him. Most of the conquering types in the coming order were to be men trained early in life in the calculations of the bookkeeper, Cooke, Huntington, Gould, Henry Frick and especially Rockefeller of whom it was said afterward: "He had the soul of a bookkeeper."

In his first position as bookkeeper to a produce merchant at the Cleveland docks, when he was sixteen, he distinguished himself by his composed orderly habits. Very carefully he examined each item on each bill before he approved it for payment. Out of a salary which began at $15 a month and advanced ultimately to $50 a month, he saved $800 in three years, the lion's share of his total earnings! This was fantastic parsimony.

He spent little money for clothing, though he was always neat; he never went to the theater, had no amusements, and few friends. But he attended his Baptist Church in Cleveland as devoutly as he attended to his accounts. And to the cause of the church alone, to its parish fund and mission funds, he demonstrated his only generosity by gifts that were large for him then—first of ten cents, then later of twenty-five cents at a time.

In the young Rockefeller the traits which his mother had bred in him, of piety and the economic virtue—worship of the "lean goddess of Abstinence"— were of one cloth. The pale, bony, small-eyed young Baptist served the Lord and pursued his own business unremittingly. His composed manner, which had a certain languor, hid a feverish calculation, a sleepy strength, cruel, intense, terribly alert.

As a schoolboy John Rockefeller had once announced to a companion, as they walked by a rich man's ample house along their way: "When I grow up I want to be worth $100,000. And I'm going to be too." In almost the same words, Rockefeller in Cleveland, Cooke in Philadelphia, Carnegie in Pittsburgh, or a James Hill in the Northwestern frontier could be found voicing the same hope. And Rockefeller, the bookkeeper, "not slothful in business . . . serving the Lord," as John T. Flynn describes him, watched his chances closely, learned every detail of the produce business which engaged him, until finally in 1858 he made bold to open a business of his own in partnership with a young

Englishman named Clark (who was destined to be left far behind). Rockefeller's grimly accumulated savings of $800, in addition to a loan from his father at the usurious rate of 10 per cent, yielded the capital which launched him, and he was soon "gathering gear" quietly. He knew the art of using loan credit to expand his operations. His first bank loan against warehouse receipts gave him a thrill of pleasure. He now bought grain and produce of all kinds in carload lots rather than in small consignments. Prosperous, he said nothing, but began to dress his part, wearing a high silk hat, frock coat and striped trousers like other merchants of the time. His head was handsome, his eyes small, birdlike; on his pale bony cheeks were the proverbial side-whiskers, reddish in color.

At night, in his room, he read the Bible, and retiring had the queer habit of talking to his pillow about his business adventures. In his autobiography he says that "these intimate conversations with myself had a great influence upon my life." He told himself "not to get puffed up with any foolish notions" and never to be deceived about actual conditions. "Look out or you will lose your head—go steady."

He was given to secrecy; he loathed all display. When he married, a few years afterward, he lost not a day from his business. His wife, Laura Spelman, proved an excellent mate. She encouraged his furtiveness, he relates, advising him always to be silent, to say as little as possible. His composure, his self-possession was excessive. Those Clevelanders to whom Miss Ida Tarbell addressed herself in her investigations of Rockefeller, told her that he was a hard man to best in a trade, that he rarely smiled, and almost never laughed, save when he struck a good bargain. Then he might clap his hands with delight, or he might even, if the occasion warranted, throw up his hat, kick his heels and hug his informer. One time he was so overjoyed at a favorable piece of news that he burst out: "I'm bound to be rich! *Bound to be rich!*" . . .

The discovery of oil in the northwestern corner of Pennsylvania by [Edwin L.] Drake in 1859 was no isolated event, but part of the long overdue movement to exploit the subsoil of the country. When thousands rushed to scoop the silver and gold of Nevada, Colorado and Montana, the copper of Michigan, the iron ore of Pennsylvania and New York, technical knowledge at last interpreted the meaning of the greasy mineral substance which lay above ground near Titusville, Pennsylvania, and which had been used as a patent medicine ("Kier's Medicine") for twenty years. The rush and boom, out of which numerous speculators such as Andrew Carnegie had drawn quick profits and sold out—while so many others lost all they possessed—did not escape the attention of Rockefeller. The merchants of Cleveland, interested either in handling the new illuminating oil or investing in the industry itself, had sent the young Rockefeller to spy out the ground.

He had come probably in the spring of 1860 to the strange, blackened valleys of the Oil Regions where a forest of crude derricks, flimsy shacks and storehouses had been raised overnight. Here he had looked at the anarchy of the pioneer drillers or diggers of oil, the first frenzy of exploitation, with a deep disfavor that all conservative merchants of the time shared. There were continual fires, disasters and miracles; an oil well brought a fortune in a week, with the market price at twenty dollars a barrel; then as more wells came in the price fell to three and even two dollars a barrel before the next season! No one could tell at what price it was safe to buy oil, or oil acreage, and none knew how long the supply would last.

Returning to Cleveland, Rockefeller had counseled his merchant friends against investments in oil. At best the refining trade might be barely profitable if one could survive the mad dance of the market and if the supply of oil held out. Repugnance was strong in the infinitely cautious young merchant against the pioneering of the Oil Creek rabble. Two years were to pass before he approached the field again, while his accumulations increased with the fruitful wartime trade in provisions.

In 1862, when small refineries were rising everywhere, when more and more oil fields were being opened, the prospects of the new trade were immensely more favorable. A Clevelander named Samuel Andrews, owner of a small still, now came to the firm of Rockefeller & Clark with a proposal that they back him in setting up a sizable oil-refinery. The man Andrews was something of a technologist: he knew how to extract a high percentage of kerosene oil from the crude; he was one of the first to use the by-products developed in the refining process. Rockefeller and his partner, who appreciated the man's worth, invested $5,000 at the start with him. The affair flourished quickly, as demand widened for the new illuminant. Soon Rockefeller missed not a day from the refinery, where Andrews manufactured a kerosene better, purer than his competitors', and Rockefeller kept the books, conducted the purchasing of crude oil in his sharp fashion, and saved old iron, waste oils, made his own barrels, watched, spared, squirmed, for the smallest bargains.

In 1865, with uncanny judgment, Rockefeller chose between his produce business and the oil-refining trade. He sold his share in the house of Rockefeller & Clark, and purchased Clark's share in the oil-refinery, now called Rockefeller & Andrews. At this moment the values of all provisions were falling, while the oil trade was widening, spreading over all the world. Several great new wells had come in; supply was certain—10,000 barrels a day. Concentrating all his effort upon the new trade, he labored unremittingly to entrench himself in it, to be ready for all the hazards, which were great. He inaugurated ruthless economies; giving all his attention "to little details," he acquired a numerous clientele in the Western and Southern states; and opened an export selling agency in New York, headed by his brother William Rockefeller. "Low-voiced, soft-footed, humble, knowing every point in every man's business," Miss Tarbell relates, "he never tired until he got his wares at the lowest possible figures." "John always got the best of the bargain," the old men of Cleveland recall: "savy fellow he was!" For all his fierce passion for money, he was utterly impassive in his bearing, save when some surprisingly good purchase of oil had been made at the creek. Then he could no longer restrain his shouts of joy. In the oil trade, John Rockefeller grew up in a hard school of struggle; he endured the merciless and unprincipled competition of rivals; and his own unpitying logic and coldly resolute methods were doubtless the consequence of the brutal free-for-all from which he emerged with certain crushing advantages.

While the producers of crude oil contended with each other in lawless fashion to drill the largest quantities, the refiners at different industrial centers who processed and reshipped the crude oil were also engaged in unresting trade conflicts, in which all measures were fair. And behind the rivalry of the producers and the refiners in different cities lay the secret struggles of the large railroad interests moving obscurely in the background. Drew's Erie, Vanderbilt's New York Central, Thomson and Scott's Pennsylvania, extending their lines to the Oil Regions, all hunted their fortune in the huge new traffic, pressing the interests of favored shipping and refining centers such as Cleveland or Pittsburgh or Buffalo to suit themselves. It would have been simplest possibly to have oilrefineries at the source of the crude material itself; but the purpose of the railroads forbade this; and there was no way of determining the outcome in this matter, as in any other phase of the organization of the country's new resources, whose manner of exploitation was determined only through pitched battles between the various gladiators, wherein the will of Providence was seen.

Rockefeller, who had no friends and no diversions, who was "all business," as John T. Flynn describes him, now gave himself to incessant planning, planning that would defeat chance itself. His company was but one of thirty oil-refiners located in Cleveland; in the Oil Regions, at Oil City and Titusville, there were numerous others, including the largest refineries of all, more favorably placed for shipping. But in 1867 Rockefeller invited into his firm as a partner, a business acquaintance of his, Henry M. Flagler, son-in-law of the rich whiskey distiller and salt-maker S. V. Harkness. Flagler, a bold and dashing fellow, was deeply attracted by the possibilities of the oil business. Thanks to Harkness, he brought $70,000 into the business, which at once opened a second refinery in Cleveland. Within a year or two the firm of Rockefeller, Flagler & Andrews was the biggest refinery in Cleveland, producing 1,500 barrels a day, having its own warehouses, its export agency in New York, its own wooden tank cars, its own staff of chemists or experts who labored to improve or economize the manufacturing processes. The company moved steadily to the front of the field, surpassing its rivals in quality, and outselling them by a small, though not certain or decisive, margin. How was this done?

In the struggle for business, Rockefeller's instinct for conspiracy is already marked. The partnership with Flagler brought an access of fresh capital and even more credit. Then in a further step of collusion, this of profound importance, Rockefeller and Flagler approached the railroad which carried so many carloads of their oil toward the seaboard, and whose tariff figured heavily in the ultimate cost. They demanded from it concessions in freight rates that would enable them to meet the advantages of other refining centers such as Pittsburgh, Philadelphia and New York. Their company was now large enough to force the hand of the railroad, in this case, a branch of Vanderbilt's New York Central system; and they were granted their demands: a secret reduction or "rebate" on all their shipments of oil. "Such was the railroad's method," Rockefeller himself afterward admitted. He relates:

> A public rate was made and collected by the railroad companies, but so far as my knowledge extends, was seldom retained in full; a portion of it was repaid to the shipper as a rebate. By this method the real rate of freight

which any shipper paid was not known by his competitors, nor by other railroads, the amount being a matter of bargain with the carrying companies.

Once having gained an advantage Rockefeller pressed forward relentlessly. The volume of his business increased rapidly. Thanks to the collaboration of the railroad, he had placed his rivals in other cities and in Cleveland itself under a handicap, whose weight he endeavored to increase.

The railroads, as we see, possessed the strategic power, almost of life and death, to encourage one industrial group or cause another to languish. Their policy was based on the relative costs of handling small or large volume shipments. Thus as the Rockefeller company became the largest shipper of oil, its production rising in 1870 to 3,000 barrels a day, and offered to guarantee regular daily shipments of as much as sixty carloads, the railroads were impelled to accept further proposals for rebates. It was to their interest to do so in view of savings of several hundred thousand dollars a month in handling. On crude oil brought from the Oil Regions, Rockefeller paid perhaps 15 cents a barrel less than the open rate of 40 cents; on refined oil moving from Cleveland toward New York, he paid approximately 90 cents against the open rate of $1.30. These momentous agreements were maintained in utter secrecy, perhaps because of the persisting memory of their illegality, according to the common law ever since Queen Elizabeth's time, as a form of "conspiracy" in trade.

In January, 1870, Rockefeller, Flagler & Andrews were incorporated as a joint-stock company, a form increasingly popular, under the name of the Standard Oil Company of Ohio. At this time their worth was estimated at one million dollars; they employed over a thousand workers and were the largest refiners in the world. Despite deeply disturbed conditions in their trade during 1870, profits came to them in a mounting flood, while in the same year, it is noteworthy, four of their twenty-nine competitors in Cleveland gave up the ghost. The pious young man of thirty who feared only God, and thought of nothing but his business, gave not a sign of his greatly augmented wealth, which made him one of the leading personages of his city. His income was actually a fabulous one for the time. The Standard Oil Company from the beginning earned something like 100 per cent on its capital; and Rockefeller and his brother owned a full half-interest in it in 1870. But with an evangelistic fervor John Rockefeller was bent only upon further conquests, upon greater extensions of the power over industry which had come into the hands of the group he headed.

In the life of every conquering soul there is a "turning point," a moment when a deep understanding of the self coincides with an equally deep sense of one's immediate mission in the tangible world. For Rockefeller, brooding, secretive, uneasily scenting his fortune, this moment came but a few years after his entrance into the oil trade, and at the age of thirty. He had looked upon the disorganized conditions of the Pennsylvania oil fields, the only source then known, and found them not good: the guerilla fighting of drillers, or refining firms, of rival railroad lines, the mercurial changes in supply and market value—very alarming in 1870—offended his orderly and methodical spirit. But one could see that petroleum was to be the light of the world. From the source, from the chaotic oil fields where thousands of drillers toiled, the grimy stream of the precious commodity, petroleum, flowed along many diverse channels to narrow into the hands of several hundred refineries, then to issue once more in a continuous stream to consumers throughout the world. Owner with Flagler and Harkness of the largest refining company in the country, Rockefeller had a strongly entrenched position at the narrows of this stream. Now what if the Standard Oil Company should by further steps of organization possess itself wholly of the narrows? In this period of anarchic individual competition, the idea of such a movement of rationalization must have come to Rockefeller forcibly, as it had recently come to others.

Even as early as 1868 the first plan of industrial combination in the shape of the pool had been originated in the Michigan Salt Association. Desiring to correct chaotic market conditions, declaring that "in union there is strength," the saltproducers of Saginaw Bay had banded together to control the output and sale of nearly all the salt in their region, a large part of the vital national supply. Secret agreements had been executed for each year, allotting the sales and fixing the price at almost twice what it had been immediately prior to the appearance of the pool. And though the inevitable greed and self-seeking of the individual salt-producers had tended to weaken the pool, the new economic invention was launched in its infantile form. Rockefeller's partners, Flagler and Harkness, had themselves participated in the historic Michigan Salt Association.

This grand idea of industrial rationalization owed its swift, ruthless, methodical execution no doubt to the firmness of character we sense in Rockefeller, who had the temper of a great, unconscionable military captain, combining audacity with thoroughness and shrewd judgment. His plan seemed to take account of no one's feelings in the matter. Indeed there was something revolutionary in it; it seemed to fly in the fact of human liberties and deep-rooted custom and common law. The notorious "South Improvement Company," with its strange charter, ingeniously instrumenting the scheme of combination, was to be unraveled amid profound secrecy. By conspiring with the railroads (which also hungered for economic order), it would be terribly armed with the power of the freight rebate which garrotted all opposition systematically. This plan of combination, this unifying conception Rockefeller took as his ruling idea; he breathed life into it, clung to it grimly in the face of the most menacing attacks of legislatures, courts, rival captains, and, at moments, even of rebellious mobs. His view of men and events justified him, and despite many official and innocent denials, he is believed to have said once in confidence, as Flynn relates:

> I had our plan clearly in mind. It was right. I knew it as a matter of conscience. It was right between me and my God. If I had to do it tomorrow I would do it again in the same way—do it a hundred times.

The broad purpose was to control and direct the flow of crude petroleum into the hands of a narrowed group of refiners. The refiners would be supported by the combined railroad trunk lines which shipped the oil; while the producers' phase of the stream would be left unorganized— *but with power over their outlet to market* henceforth to be concentrated into the few hands of the refiners.

Saying nothing to others, bending over their maps of the industry, Rockefeller and Flagler first drew up a short list of the principal refining companies who were to be asked to combine with them. Then having banded together a sufficient number, they would persuade the railroads to give them special freight rates—on the ground of "evening" the traffic—guaranteeing equitable distribution of freight business; and this in turn would be a club to force other elements needed into union with them. They could control output, drive out competitors, and force all foreign countries throughout the world to buy their product from them at their own terms. They could finally dictate market prices on crude oil, stabilize the margin of profit at their own process, and do away at last with the dangerously speculative character of their business.

Their plans moved forward rapidly all through 1871. For a small sum of money the "conspirators" obtained the Pennsylvania charter of a defunct corporation, which had been authorized to engage in almost any kind of business under the sun. Those who were approached by the promoters, those whom they determined to use in their grand scheme, were compelled in a manner typical of all Rockefeller's projects to sign a written pledge of secrecy:

> I, —— ——, do solemnly promise upon my honor and faith as a gentleman that I will keep secret all transactions which I may have with the corporation known as the South Improvement Company; that should I fail to complete any bargains with the said company, all the preliminary conversations shall be kept strictly private; and finally that I will not disclose the price for which I dispose of any products or any other facts which may in any way bring to light the internal workings or organization of the company. All this I do freely promise.

At the same time, in confidential pourparlers with the officials of the Erie, the Pennsylvania and the New York Central Railroads, the men of the Standard Oil represented themselves as possessing secret control of the bulk of the refining interest. Thus they obtained conditions more advantageous than anything which had gone before; and this weapon in turn of course ensured the triumph of their pool.

The refiners to be combined under the aegis of the South Improvement Company were to have a rebate of from 40 to 50 per cent on the crude oil they ordered shipped to them and from 25 to 50 per cent on the refined oil they shipped out. The refiners in the Oil Regions were to pay *twice as much* by the new code (though nearer to New York) as the Standard Oil Company at Cleveland. But besides the rebate the members of the pool were to be given also a "drawback" consisting of part of the increased tariff rate which "outsiders" were forced to pay. Half of the freight payments of a rival refiner would in many cases be paid over to the Rockefeller group. Their competitors were simply to be decimated; and to make certain of this the railroads agreed—all being set down in writing, in minutest detail—"to make manifests or way-bills of all petroleum or its product transported over any portion of its lines . . . which manifests shall state the name of the consignee, the place of shipment and the place of destination," this information to be furnished faithfully to the officers of the South Improvement Company.

The railroad systems, supposedly public-spirited and impartial, were to open all their knowledge of rival private business to the pool, thus helping to concentrate all the oil trade into the few hands chosen. In return for so much assistance, they were to have their freight "evened," and were enabled at last to enter into a momentous peace pact with each other by which the oil traffic (over which they had quarreled bitterly) was to be fairly allotted among themselves.

By January, 1872, after the first decade of the oil business, John Rockefeller, with the aid of the railroad captains, was busily carrying out a most "elaborate national plan" of his own for the control of his industry—such planned control as the spokesman of the business system asserted ever afterward was impossible. The first pooling of 1872, beautiful as was its economic architecture and laudable its motive, had defects which were soon plainly noticeable. All the political institutions, the whole spirit of American law still favored the amiable, wasteful individualism of business, which in Rockefeller's mind had already become obsolete and must be supplanted by a centralized, one might say almost *collectivist* —certainly cöoperative rather than competitive—form of operation. Moreover, these "revolutionists" took little account of the social dislocations their juggernaut would bring. Like the railroad baron, Vanderbilt, working better than they knew, their eyes fixed solely upon the immediate task rather than upon some millennium of the future, they desired simply, as they often said, to be "the biggest refiners in the world. . . ."

To the principal oil firms in Cleveland Rockefeller went one by one, explaining the plan of the South Improvement Company patiently, pointing out how important it was to oppose the creek refiners and save the Cleveland oil trade. He would say:

"You see, this scheme is bound to work. There is no chance for anyone outside. But we are going to give everybody a chance to come in. You are to turn over your refinery to my appraisers, and I will give you Standard Oil Company stock or cash, as you prefer, for the value we put upon it. I advise you to take the stock. It will be for your good."

Then if the men demurred, according to much of the testimony at the Senate Investigation of 1876, he would point out suavely that it was useless to resist; opposition would certainly be crushed. The offers of purchase usually made were for from a third to a half the actual cost of the property.

Now a sort of terror swept silently over the oil trade. In a vague panic, competitors saw the Standard Oil officers come to them and say (as Rockefeller's own brother and rival, Frank, testified in 1876): "If you don't sell your property to us it will be valueless, because we have got the advantage with the railroads."

The railroad rates indeed were suddenly doubled to the outsiders, and those refiners who resisted the pool came and expostulated; then they became frightened and disposed of their property. One of the largest competitors in Cleveland, the firm of Alexander, Scofield & Co., held out for a time, protesting before the railroad officials at the monstrous unfairness of the deal. But these officials when consulted said mysteriously: " *Better sell—better get clear—better sell out—no help for it.*" Another powerful refiner, Robert Hanna, uncle of the famous Mark Alonzo, found that the railroads would give him no relief, and also was glad to sell out at 40 or 50 cents on the dollar for his property value. To one of these refiners, Isaac L. Hewitt, who had been his employer in boyhood, Rockefeller himself spoke with intense emotion. He urged Hewitt to take stock. Hewitt related: "He told me that it would be sufficient to take care of my family for all time. . . and asking for reasons, he made this expression, I remember: '*I have ways of making money that you know nothing of.*'"

All this transpired in secret. For "silence is golden," the rising king of oil believed. Though many were embittered by their loss, others joined gladly. The strongest capitalists in Cleveland, such as the wealthy Colonel Oliver H. Payne, were amazed at the swift progress Rockefeller had made, at the enormous profits he showed them in confidence to invite their cöoperation. Payne, among others, as a man of wealth and influence, was taken into the board of directors and made treasurer of the Standard Oil Company. (The officers of the South Improvement Company itself were "dummies.") Within three months by an economic *coup d'état* the youthful Rockefeller had captured all of Cleveland's oil-refining trade, all twenty-five competitors surrendered to him and yielded him command of one-fifth of America's output of refined oil.

Tomorrow all the population of the Oil Regions, its dismayed refiners, drillers, and workers of oil, might rise against the South Improvement Company ring in a grotesque uproar. The secret, outwardly peaceful campaigns would assume here as elsewhere the character of violence and lawlessness which accompanied the whole program of the industrial revolution. But Rockefeller and his comrades had stolen a long march on their opponents; their tactics shaped themselves already as those of the giant industrialists of the future conquering the pigmies. Entrenched at the "narrows" of the mighty river of petroleum they could no more be dislodged than those other barons who had formerly planted their strong castles along the banks of the Rhine could be dislodged by unarmed peasants and burghers.

Avenging Angel

. . . In stalking Standard Oil, Teddy Roosevelt had no more potent ally than the press. In the spring of 1900, Rockefeller could still reassure a correspondent that favorable publicity about him overshadowed adverse coverage. "No man can succeed in any calling without provoking the jealousy and envy of some," he observed. "The strong level-headed man will go straight forward and do his work, and history will rightly record."

Several trends gave birth to a newly assertive press. The gigantic trusts swelled the ranks of national advertisers, fattening the pages of many periodicals. Aided by new technologies, including linotype and photoengraving, glossy illustrated magazines streamed forth in such numbers that the era would be memorialized as the golden age of the American magazine. Paralleling this was the rise of mass-circulation newspapers, which catered to an expanding reading public. Competing in fierce circulation wars, Joseph Pulitzer, William Randolph Hearst, and other press barons plied readers with scandals and crusades. Nonetheless, the turn of the century marked more than the heyday of strident tabloids and yellow journalism, as sophisticated publications began to tackle complex stories, illustrating them lavishly and promoting them aggressively. For the first time in history, college graduates went to work on newspapers and magazines, bringing a new literary flair to a world once considered beneath the dignity of the educated elite.

Studded with star writers and editors, the most impressive periodical was *McClure's Magazine*, which was started by Samuel S. McClure in 1893. In September 1901, the same month that Roosevelt ascended to the presidency, the magazine's managing editor, Ida Minerva Tarbell, sailed to Europe to confer with McClure, then taking a rest from his strenuous life in Vevey, Switzerland. In her suitcase she carried an outline for a three-part series on the Standard Oil Company, though she wondered whether anyone would ever wade through a long, factual account of a business empire—a journalistic enterprise never assayed before.

The Standard Oil story was intertwined with Tarbell's early life. Born in 1857 in a log cabin thirty miles from where Drake struck oil two years later, she was a true daughter of the Oil Regions. "I had grown up with oil derricks, oil tanks, pipe lines, refineries, oil exchanges," she wrote in her memoirs. Her father, Franklin Tarbell, crafted vats from hemlock bark, a trade easily converted into barrel making after Drake's discovery. The Tarbells lived beside his

Rouseville barrel shop, and Ida as a child rolled luxuriously in the heaps of pine shavings. Down the hill from her house, across a ravine, lived an amiable young refiner named Henry H. Rogers, who later recalled seeing the young girl picking wildflowers on the slope.

Ida watched men with queer gleams in their eyes swarming through Rouseville en route to the miracle-turned-mirage of Pithole Creek. Franklin Tarbell set up a barrel shop there and cashed in on the boom before Pithole's oil gave out. But Franklin's prosperity was tenuous, based on an antiquated technology. Wooden barrels were soon replaced by iron tanks—the first of several times that Ida's father was hurt by progress. He then sought his fortune as an independent oil producer and refiner, just as Rockefeller was consolidating the industry and snuffing out small operators.

In 1872, as an impressionable fifteen-year-old, Ida saw her paradise torn asunder by the South Improvement Company. As her father joined vigilantes who sabotaged the conspirators' tanks, she thrilled to the talk of revolution. "On the instant the word became holy to me," she later wrote. The SIC darkened her sunlit world. The father who once sang, played the Jew's harp, and told funny stories became a "silent and stern" man, breeding in his sensitive daughter a lifelong hatred of Standard Oil. For her, Standard Oil symbolized the triumph of grasping men over decent folk, like her father, who played fair and square.

She remembered the Titusville of her teenage years as divided between the valiant majority who resisted the octopus and the small band of opportunists who defected to it. On the street, Franklin pointed out turncoats to his daughter. "In those days I looked with more contempt on the man who had gone over to the Standard than on the one who had been in jail," she said. After a time, Franklin's family would not speak to blackguards who had sold out to Rockefeller. It revolted Ida that the trust could turn proud; independent entrepreneurs into beaten men taking orders from distant bosses.

Although Tarbell had a more genteel upbringing than Rockefeller, with more books, magazines, and small luxuries, one is struck by the similarity of the Rockefellers' Baptist and the Tarbells' Methodist households. The straitlaced Franklin Tarbell forbade cards and dancing and supported many causes, including the temperance movement. Ida attended prayer meetings on Thursday nights and taught an infant class of the Sunday school. Shy and bookish, she tended, like Rockefeller, to arrive at brilliant solutions by slow persistence.

What set Tarbell apart from Rockefeller was her intellectual daring and fearless curiosity. As a teenager, despite her family's fundamentalism, she tried to prove the truth of evolution. By the time she enrolled at Allegheny College in Meadville, Pennsylvania, in 1876—she was the sole girl in the freshman class of this Methodist school—she loved to peer through microscopes and planned to become a biologist. What distinguished her as a journalist was how she united a scientific attention to detail, with homegrown moral fervor. After graduation, Tarbell taught for two years at the Poland Union Seminary in Poland, Ohio, then got a job on the editorial staff of *The Chautauquan*, an offshoot of the summer adulteducation movement, which originated as a Methodist camp meeting. The fiery, militant Christian spirit of the movement made Ida even more high-minded in her expectations.

Tall and attractive, with dark hair, large gray eyes, and high cheekbones, Tarbell had an erect carriage and innate dignity and never lacked suitors. Yet she decided never to marry and to remain self-sufficient. She steeled herself against any feelings that might compromise her ambitions or integrity, and she walked through life, perhaps a little self-consciously, in a shining moral armor.

In 1891, the thirty-four-year-old Tarbell moved to Paris with friends and set up Bohemian quarters on the Left Bank—an unusually courageous decision for a young American woman at the time. She was determined to write a biography of the Girondist Madame Roland while selling freelance articles to Pennsylvania and Ohio newspapers and attending classes at the Sorbonne. Hardworking and levelheaded, she mailed off two articles during her first week in Paris alone. Even though the prim Tarbell was taken aback when lascivious Frenchmen flirted with her, she adored her time in Paris. She interviewed eminent Parisians, ranging from Louis Pasteur to Emile Zola, for American newspapers and won many admirers for her clean, accurate reportage; she claimed that her writing had absorbed some of the beauty and clarity of the French language. Still, she struggled on the "ragged edge of bankruptcy" and was susceptible when McClure wooed her as an editor of his new magazine.

While she was still in Paris, two events occurred that would lend an emotional tinge to her Standard Oil series. One Sunday afternoon in June 1892, she found herself roaming the Paris streets, unable to shake off a sense of doom. Later that afternoon, she read in the Paris newspapers that Titusville and Oil City had been ravaged by flood and fire, with 150 people either drowned or burned to death. The next day, her brother, Will, sent a single-word cable—"Safe"—relieving her anxieties, but the event reinforced a guilty feeling that she had neglected her family. In 1893, one of her father's oil partners shot himself in despair because of poor business, forcing Franklin Tarbell to mortgage his house to settle the debts he inherited. Ida's sister was in the hospital at the time, and "here was I across the ocean writing picayune pieces at a fourth of a cent a word while they struggled there," she later recalled. "I felt guilty, and the only way I had kept myself up to what I had undertaken was the hope that I could eventually make a substantial return." While in Paris, Ida Tarbell laid hands on a copy of *Wealth Against Commonwealth*, where she rediscovered the author of her father's woes: John D. Rockefeller.

Once in New York in 1894, Tarbell published two biographies in serial form that might have predisposed her to focus on a single figure at Standard Oil. Anticipating her portrait of Rockefeller, she presented Napoleon as a gifted megalomaniac, a great but flawed man lacking "that fine sense of proportion which holds the rights of others in the same solemn reverence which it demands for its own." Lifted by this series, *McClure's* circulation leaped from 24,500 in late 1894 to more than 100,000 in early 1895. Then followed Tarbell's celebrated twenty-part series on Lincoln, which absorbed four years of her life (1895–1899) and boosted the magazine's circulation to 300,000. She honed her investigative skills as she excavated dusty documents and forgotten courthouse records. In 1899, after being named managing editor of *McClure's*, Tarbell took an apartment in Greenwich Village and befriended many literary notables, including Mark Twain, who would soon provide her with entrée to

Henry H. "Hell Hound" Rogers. By this time, having sharpened her skills, she was set to publish one of the most influential pieces of journalism in American business history. The idea of writing about Standard Oil had fermented in her mind for many years before she worked for *McClure's*. "Years ago, when I dreamed of some day writing fiction. . . . I had planned to write the great American novel, having the Standard Oil Company as a backbone!"

After receiving McClure's blessing, Ida Tarbell launched the series in November 1902, feeding the American public rich monthly servings of Rockefeller's past misdeeds. She went back to the early Cleveland days and laid out his whole career for careful inspection. All the depredations of a long career, everything Rockefeller had thought safely buried and forgotten, rose up before him in haunting and memorable detail. Before she was done, Ida Tarbell turned America's most private man into its most public and hated figure. . . .

❧

Although Tarbell pretended to apply her scalpel to Standard Oil with surgical objectivity, she was never neutral and not only because of her father. Her brother, William Walter Tarbell, had been a leading figure in forming the Pure Oil company, the most serious domestic challenger to Standard Oil, and his letters to her were laced with anti-Standard venom. Complaining of the trust's price manipulations in one letter, Will warned her, "Some of those fellows will get killed one of those days." As Pure Oil's treasurer in 1902, Will steered legions of Rockefeller enemies to his sister and even vetted her manuscripts. Far from cherishing her neutrality, Tarbell in the end adhered to the advice she had once received from Henry James: "Cherish your contempts." Amazingly enough, nobody made an issue of Tarbell's veritable partnership with her brother in exposing his chief competitor. . . .

❧

From the perspective of nearly a century later, Ida Tarbell's series remains the most impressive thing ever written about Standard Oil—a tour de force of reportage that dissects the trust's machinations with withering clarity. She laid down a clear chronology, provided a trenchant account of how the combine had evolved, and made the convoluted history of the oil industry comprehensible. In the dispassionate manner associated with *McClure's*, she sliced open America's most secretive business and showed all the hidden gears and wheels turning inside it. Yet however chaste and clearly reasoned her prose, it was always informed by indignation that throbbed just below the surface. It remains one of the great case studies of what a single journalist, armed with the facts, can do against seemingly invincible powers.

Tarbell is perhaps best appreciated in comparison with her predecessor, Henry Demarest Lloyd, who was sloppy with his facts, florid in his prose, and too quick to pontificate. A meticulous researcher, Tarbell wrote in a taut, spare language that conveyed a sense of precision and restraint—though she had more than her quota of strident moments. By writing in such a relatively cool style, she made her readers boil with anger. Instead of invoking political panaceas or sweeping ideological prescriptions, she appealed to the reader's sense of common decency and fair play and was most effective where she showed something small and mean-spirited about the Standard Oil style of business.

Like Teddy Roosevelt, Tarbell did not condemn Standard Oil for its size but only for its abuses and did not argue for the automatic dismantling of all trusts; she pleaded only for the preservation of free competition in the marketplace. While she was by no means evenhanded, she was quick to acknowledge the genuine achievements of Rockefeller and his cohorts and even devoted one chapter to "The Legitimate Greatness of the Standard Oil Company." "There was not a lazy bone in the organization, not an incompetent hand, nor a stupid head," she wrote. It was the very fact that they could have succeeded without resorting to unethical acts that so exasperated her. As she said, "They had never played fair, and that ruined their greatness for me."

If Tarbell gave an oversimplified account of Standard Oil's rise, her indictment was perhaps the more forceful for it. In the trust's collusion with the railroads, the intricate system of rebates and drawbacks, she found her smoking gun, the irrefutable proof that Rockefeller's empire was built by devious means. She was at pains to refute Rockefeller's defense that everybody did it. "Everybody did not do it," she protested indignantly. "In the nature of the offense everybody could not do it. The strong wrested from the railroads the privilege of preying upon the weak, and the railroads never dared give the privilege save under the promise of secrecy." To the contention that rebates were still legal, Tarbell countered with the questionable theory that they violated the common law. She argued that Rockefeller had succeeded by imbuing subordinates with a ferocious desire to win at all costs, even if that meant trampling upon others. "Mr. Rockefeller has systematically played with loaded dice, and it is doubtful if there has ever been a time since 1872 when he has run a race with a competitor and started fair." Tarbell rightly surmised that Standard Oil received secret kickbacks from the railroads on a more elaborate scale than its rivals did. This is abundantly borne out by Rockefeller's private papers, which show that the practice was even more pervasive than Tarbell realized.

Beginning with the Cleveland Massacre of 1872, Tarbell showed that Rockefeller had taken over rival refineries in an orchestrated atmosphere of intimidation. She exposed the deceit of an organization that operated through a maze of secret subsidiaries in which the Standard Oil connection was kept secret from all but the highest-ranking employees. She sketched out many abuses of power by the Standard Oil pipelines, which used their monopoly position to keep refractory producers in line while favoring Standard's own refineries. And she chronicled the terror tactics by which the trust's marketing subsidiaries got retailers to stock their product exclusively. Like Lloyd, she also decried the trust's threat to democracy and the subornation of state legislators, although she never guessed the depths of corruption revealed by Rockefeller's papers.

Nevertheless, as Allan Nevins and other defenders of Rockefeller pointed out, Tarbell committed numerous errors, and her work must be cited with caution. To begin with, the SIC was initiated by the railroads, not Rockefeller, who doubted the plan's efficacy. And for all its notoriety, the SIC did not cause the oil crisis of the early 1870s but was itself a response to the glut that forced almost everybody to operate at a loss. It is also true that, swayed by childhood memories, Tarbell ennobled the Oil Creek drillers, portraying them as exemplars of a superior morality. As she wrote: "They believed in independent effort—every man for himself and fair play for all. They wanted competition, loved open fight." To support this statement, she had to overlook the baldly anticompetitive agreements proposed by the producers themselves. Far from being free-marketeers, they repeatedly tried to form their own cartel to restrict output and boost prices. And, as Rockefeller pointed out, they happily took rebates whenever they could. The world of the early oil industry was not, as Tarbell implied, a morality play of the evil Standard Oil versus the brave, noble independents of western Pennsylvania, but a harsh dog-eat-dog world.

Though billed as a history of Standard Oil, the Tarbell series presented Rockefeller as the protagonist and center of attention. Tarbell made Standard Oil and Rockefeller interchangeable, even when covering the period after Rockefeller retired. Sometimes it is hard to tell whether Rockefeller is a real person or a personification of the trust. Significantly, Tarbell chose for her epigraph the famous line from Emerson's essay on self-reliance, "An Institution is the lengthened shadow of one man." When Henry Rogers questioned this approach, Tarbell noted the dramatic effect of focusing on one individual, writing in her notes after the meeting, "Illustrate it by Napoleon work and the effort to keep the attention centered on Napoleon, never mentioning anybody if I could help it." This great-man approach to history gave a human face to the gigantic, amorphous entity known as Standard Oil but also turned the full force of public fury on Rockefeller. It did not acknowledge the bureaucratic reality of Standard Oil, with its labyrinthine committee system, and stigmatized Rockefeller to the exclusion of his associates. So Flagler came off relatively unscathed, even though he had negotiated the secret freight contracts that bulk so large in the *McClure's* exposé.

However pathbreaking in its time and richly deserving of its accolades, the Tarbell series does not, finally, stand up as an enduring piece of history. The more closely one examines it, the more it seems a superior screed masquerading as sober history. In the end, Tarbell could not conquer her nostalgia for the Titusville of her girlhood, that lost paradise of heroic friends and neighbors who went forth doughtily to do battle with the all-devouring Standard Oil dragon.

☙❦❧

The most celebrated and widely quoted charge that Tarbell made against Rockefeller was the least deserved: that he had robbed Mrs. Fred M. Backus—forever known to history as "the Widow Backus"—blind when buying her Cleveland lubricating plant in 1878. If every melodrama needs a poor, lorn widow, cheated by a scheming cad, then Mrs. Backus perfectly fitted Tarbell's portrait of Rockefeller. "If it were true," Rockefeller later conceded, it "would represent a shocking instance of cruelty in crushing a defenceless woman. It is probable that its wide circulation and its acceptance as true by those who know nothing of the facts has awakened more hostility against the Standard Oil Company and against me personally than any charge which has been made."

The background of the story is simple. In his early Cleveland days, Rockefeller had befriended Fred M. Backus, who worked as a bookkeeper in his office and taught in the Sunday school of their church. In time, Backus married, had three children, and started a small lubricating company. In 1874, the forty-year-old Backus died, likely from consumption, and his widow inherited an obsolete plant that consisted of little more than a primitive cluster of sheds, stills, and tanks. Its hilltop site meant that raw materials had to be hauled up the slope at great expense, and then the lubricating oils had to be carted down the same steep path—not the most efficient of venues. Before it entered the lubricating business, Standard Oil had tolerated this marginal operation. When it branched out into lubricating oils and greases in the late 1870s, it absorbed three small lubricating companies, of which Backus Oil was probably the most backward. In fact, the Backus operation was so outmoded that Standard Oil eventually shut it down. This did not prevent the Widow Backus from stirring up a rabid national controversy about Rockefeller's supposed theft of her priceless plant.

When Standard Oil first approached her about the purchase, she insisted upon dealing with Rockefeller who, for old time's sake, agreed to meet her in her house. Appealing to her status as a widow and trusting to his gentlemanly honor, she pleaded for a fair price for her property. As she recalled, "he promised, with tears in his eyes, that he would stand by me in this transaction, and that I should not be wronged. . . . I thought that his feelings were such on the subject that I could trust him and that he would deal honourably by me." Backus told a friend that Rockefeller suggested that they kneel together in prayer. Up until this point, her story tallied closely with Rockefeller's, who said that he had been "moved by kindly consideration to an old employee."

While Backus wanted Rockefeller to conduct the negotiations for her plant, he knew nothing about lubricants and sent his associates instead. According to Backus, Rockefeller's hirelings bilked her unmercifully. She valued her operation between $150,000 and $200,000, whereas the Standard Oil people refused to pay more than $79,000—$19,000 for the oil on hand, plus $60,000 for the factory and goodwill. (Out of regard for Backus, Rockefeller had had his appraisers bump up this last figure by $10,000.) Backus's negotiator, Charles H. Marr, later swore that his client, in an estimated inventory of her assets, had written down $71,000 for plant and goodwill—not much more than Rockefeller finally paid. Yet she grew incensed over the purchase price and drafted a savage letter to Rockefeller, accusing him of double-dealing, to which he made the following reply:

> In regard to the reference that you make as to my permitting the business of the Backus Oil Company to *be taken* from you, I say that in this, as in all else that you have written . . . you do me most grievous wrong. It was of but little moment to the interests represented by me whether the business

of the Backus Oil Company was purchased or not. I believe that it was for your interest to make the sale, and am entirely candid in this statement, and beg to call your attention to the time, some two years ago, when you consulted Mr. Flagler and myself as to selling out your interests to Mr. Rose, at which time you were desirous of selling at *considerably less price*, and upon time, than you have now received in cash, and which sale you would have been glad to have closed if you could have obtained satisfactory security for the deferred payments.

He then pointed out that the $60,000 paid for the property was two or three times the cost of constructing equal or better facilities—a statement corroborated by a Mr. Maloney, superintendent of the Backus plant. "I believe that if you would reconsider what you have written in your letter . . . you must admit having done me great injustice, and I am satisfied to await upon [your] innate sense of right for such admission." In closing, Rockefeller offered to restore her business in return for the money or give her stock in the company at the same price paid by Standard Oil. It was an eminently fair offer, and yet the histrionic Backus flung the letter in the fire.

Because Ida Tarbell insisted upon reviving this hoary story—Henry Demarest Lloyd had already wrung tears from readers with it—in 1905 Rockefeller's attorneys leaked to the press a letter written by H. M. Backus, the widow's brother-in-law. Having lived with his sister-in-law during the period in question, he was present the day Rockefeller paid his visit. As he told Rockefeller, "I know of the ten thousand dollars that was added to the purchase price of the property at your request, and I know that you paid 3 times the value of the property, and I know that all that ever saved our company from ruin was the sale of its property to you, and I simply want to easy my mind by doing justice to you by saying so." It was exceedingly lucky for Backus that she bowed out of business, for Standard Oil built more modern lubricating plants, marketed 150 different lubricants, and drove prices far below the price at which she could have operated profitably. Had she stayed in business, she would have been bankrupt within a few years.

By investing her proceeds in Cleveland real estate instead, Backus, far from being reduced to filth and misery, became an extremely rich woman. According to Allan Nevins, she was worth approximately $300,000 at her death. Nevertheless, the supposed theft of Backus Oil became an idée fixe, and she dredged up the story for anyone who cared to listen. The notion of Rockefeller gleefully ruining a poor widow was such a good story, with so fine a Dickensian ring, that gullible reporters gave it fresh circulation for many years.

If Tarbell perpetuated one myth about Rockefeller, she also had the honesty to debunk another: that Rockefeller had blown up a competing refinery in Buffalo. It was this allegation that so upset Henry Rogers that he cooperated with Tarbell to clear his name. Swallowed whole by Lloyd and constantly brandished by the *World*, the tale was a hardy perennial of the anti-Standard Oil literature.

Like the Backus case, the incident dated back to the period when Standard Oil entered the lubricating business in the late 1870s. The trust had coveted the Vacuum Oil Works in Rochester, New York, owned by a father-and-son team,

Hiram and Charles Everest. One day, John Archbold shepherded Hiram Everest into Rockefeller's office and asked him point-blank to name a price for his firm. When Everest obliged, Archbold threw back his head and roared with laughter, dismissing the figure as absurd. Taking a suaver approach, Rockefeller leaned forward, touched Everest on the knee, and said, "Mr. Everest, don't you think you would be making a mistake to go into a fight with young, active men, who mean to develop the entire petroleum industry?" When Everest shot back that he was a fighter, Rockefeller just smiled.

Everest eventually realized he was dealing with an immovable force and sold a three-fourths interest in his firm to Henry Rogers, John Archbold, and Ambrose McGregor, acting as agents for Standard Oil. Because the Everests remained the managers, the Standard executives were involved only tangentially. In 1881, a trio of Vacuum employees—J. Scott Wilson, Charles B. Matthews, and Albert Miller—defected to start a rival refinery, the Buffalo Lubricating Oil Company. They brazenly planned to re-create their old firm by transferring technology, poaching clients, and copying processes patented by Vacuum. When the Everests learned of this, they threatened legal action. Albert Miller repented and sought help from Hiram Everest. Together, they consulted a Rochester lawyer, and at this meeting Everest allegedly floated the idea of Miller sabotaging the new plant: "Suppose he should arrange the machinery so it would bust up, or smash up, what would the consequences be?" A tall edifice of speculation would be erected on this query.

According to a later conspiracy charge, on June 15, 1881, Miller ordered the fireman at the Buffalo plant to heat the still to such explosive temperatures that the heavy crude oil began to stir and boil. Pretty soon, the brickwork cracked, the safety valve blew off, and a large volume of gas hissed out— without kindling a fire. A week later, Miller met in New York with Hiram Everest and Henry Rogers, who packed him off to work at a California cannery. When the Everests filed patent-infringement suits against the Buffalo refinery, Charles Matthews, ringleader of the renegades, retaliated with his own civil suit, charging a conspiracy to blow up his Buffalo works and seeking $250,000 in damages. The three Standard Oil worthies on the Vacuum board— Rogers, Archbold, and McGregor—despite the distant nature of their involvement in Rochester, were indicted along with the Everests. Only vaguely aware of the brouhaha, never having met Miller, Rockefeller was roped into the case for publicity purposes and subpoenaed as a prosecution witness. The case always struck him as a petty irritant, distracting him from more pressing matters. Nothing in Rockefeller's papers suggests that he regarded the suit as anything other than outright extortion.

In May 1887, Rockefeller sat captive in a packed Buffalo courtroom for eight days. Resentful of being turned into a public spectacle, he felt he was being served up as a sideshow freak to "this curious class of wonder-worshippers, the class whom P. T. Barnum capitalized [on] and made his fortune out of." When Rockefeller testified, he displayed, as always, total forgetfulness, but in this instance he really knew little about the case. At the end of eight days, the judge dropped charges against Rogers, Archbold, and McGregor. While Rogers hugged a bunch of pansies given by a well-wisher, Rockefeller, in a rare display of public fury, rose from his seat, jaw clenched, and said, "I have no congratulations to offer you, Rogers. What should be done with people who bring an action against men in this way—what?" Wheeling about, he shook his fist at Charles Matthews. Then, muttering "what an unheard-of-thing," he strode briskly from the courtroom, his retinue in tow. In later years, he fulminated against Matthews as a "scheming, trouble-making blackmailer" who offered to sell his refinery to Standard Oil for $100,000 and only initiated his nuisance suit after being rebuffed.

The Buffalo suit, in truth, had scant merit. The prosecution never established that an explosion had taken place or even that a high flame was necessarily hazardous when starting up the still. Though the Everests were convicted and fined $250 apiece, this small figure mirrored the jurors' belief that the Everests did not conspire to blow up the refinery and were guilty only of luring away Albert Miller. If Henry Rogers cooperated with Ida Tarbell for the sake of vindication in the Buffalo case, he was amply rewarded. She stated categorically: "As a matter of fact, no refinery was burned in Buffalo, nor was it ever proved that Mr. Rogers knew anything of the attempts the Everests made to destroy Matthews' business." Yet the notion that Rockefeller enjoyed blowing up rival plants so tickled the popular fancy that it remained enshrined as a story much too good to retire, and it was duly revived, along with the musty canard about the Widow Backus, by Matthew Josephson in his 1934 book *The Robber Barons*. . . .

POSTSCRIPT

Was John D. Rockefeller a "Robber Baron"?

Regardless of how American entrepreneurs are perceived, there is no doubt that they constituted a powerful elite and were responsible for defining the character of society in the Gilded Age. For many Americans, these business-men represented the logical culmination of the country's attachment to laissez-faire economics and rugged individualism. In fact, it was not unusual at all for the nation's leading industrialists to be depicted as the reallife mod-els for the "rags-to-riches" theme epitomized in the self-help novels of Horatio Alger. Closer examination of the lives of most of these entrepreneurs, how-ever, reveals the mythical dimensions of this American ideal. Simply put, the typical business executive of the late nineteenth century did not rise up from humble circumstances, a product of the American rural tradition or the immi-grant experience, as frequently claimed. Rather, most of these big business-men were of Anglo-Saxon origin and reared in a city by middle-class parents. According to one survey, over half the leaders had attended college at a time when even the pursuit of a high school education was considered unusual. In other words, instead of having to pull themselves up by their own bootstraps from the bottom of the social heap, these individuals usually started their climb to success at the middle of the ladder or higher.

The reader may be surprised to learn that in spite of the massive influx of immigrants from Asia and southern and eastern Europe in the years 1880 to 1924, today's leaders are remarkably similar in their social and economic back-grounds to their nineteenth-century counterparts. A 1972 study by Thomas Dye listing the top 4,000 decision-makers in corporate, governmental, and public-interest sectors of American life revealed that 90 percent were affluent, white, Anglo-Saxon males. There were only two African Americans in the whole group; there were no Native Americans, Hispanics, or Japanese-Americans, and very few recognizable Irish, Italians, or Jews.

A useful contextual framework for examining the role of the American entrepreneur can be found in Thomas C. Cochran and William Miller, *The Age of Enterprise: A Social History of Industrial America* (rev. ed.; Harper & Row, 1961) and Glenn Porter, *The Rise of Big Business, 1860–1910* (Harlan Davidson, 1973). Earl Latham and Peter D.A. Jones have assembled an excellent collection of the major viewpoints on the "robber baron" thesis in their respective edited anthologies *John D. Rockefeller: Robber Baron or Industrial Statesman* (D.C. Heath, 1949) and *The Robber Barons Revisited* (D.C. Heath, 1968). For a critique of Josephson's work, see Maury Klein, "A Robber Historian," *Forbes* (October 26, 1987). Studies focusing specifically upon Rockefeller include Allan Nevins, *John D. Rockefeller: The Heroic Age of American Enterprise*, 2 vols. (Scribner's,

1940), *Study in Power: John D. Rockefeller, Industrialist and Philanthropist*, 2 vols. (Scribner's, 1953), and David Freeman Hawke, *John D.: The Founding Father of the Rockefellers* (1980). Biographical studies of other late-nineteenth-century businessmen include Harold Livesay, *Andrew Carnegie and the Rise of Big Business* (Little, Brown, 1975) and Maury Klein, *The Life and Legend of Jay Gould* (Johns Hopkins Press, 1986). Robert Sobel's *The Entrepreneurs: Explorations Within the American Business Tradition* (Weybright and Talley, 1974) presents sympathetic sketches of the builders of often-neglected industries of the nineteenth and twentieth centuries.

The works of Alfred D. Chandler, Jr., are vital to the understanding of American industrialization. Chandler almost single-handedly reshaped the way in which historians write about American corporations. Instead of arguing about the morality of nineteenth-century businessmen, he employed organizational theories of decision making borrowed from the sociologists and applied them to case studies of corporate America. For example, see *Strategy and Structure: Chapters in the History of American Industrial Enterprise* (MIT Press, 1962); *The Visible Hand: The Managerial Revolution in American Business* (Harvard University Press, 1977); and *Scale and Scope: The Dynamics of Industrial Capitalism* (Harvard University Press, 1990). Chandler's most important essays are collected in Thomas K. McCraw, ed., *The Essential Alfred Chandler: Essays Toward a Historical Theory of Big Business* (Harvard Business School Press, 1988). For an assessment of Chandler's approach and contributions, see Louis Galambos, "The Emerging Organizational Synthesis in Modern American History," *Business History Review* (Autumn 1970) and Thomas K. McCraw, "The Challenge of Alfred D. Chandler, Jr.: Retrospect and Prospect," *Reviews in American History* (March 1987).

ISSUE 3

Did William M. Tweed Corrupt Post–Civil War New York?

YES: Alexander B. Callow, Jr., from *The Tweed Ring* (Oxford University Press, 1966)

NO: Leo Hershkowitz, from *Tweed's New York: Another Look* (Anchor Press, 1977)

ISSUE SUMMARY

YES: Professor emeritus of history Alexander B. Callow, Jr., asserts that by exercising a corrupting influence over the city and state governments as well as over key elements within the business community, William M. "Boss" Tweed and his infamous "ring" extracted enormous sums of ill-gotten money for their own benefit in post–Civil War New York.

NO: Professor of history Leo Hershkowitz portrays Tweed as a devoted public servant who championed New York City's interests during his 20-year career and whose reputation as the symbol for urban political corruption is grossly undeserved.

On the eve of the Civil War, the United States remained primarily a rural, agrarian nation. Of the country's 31 million inhabitants, 80 percent were characterized as "rural" dwellers by the United States Bureau of the Census; only 392 "urban" places (incorporated towns with 2,500 or more residents, or unincorporated areas with at least 2,500 people per square mile) dotted the national landscape; a mere nine U.S. cities contained populations in excess of 100,000.

After 1865 the growth of urban America was directly linked to the economic and technological changes that produced the country's Industrial Revolution, as well as to rapid immigration, which filled the nation's cities with what seemed to native-born Americans to be a multitude of foreigners from around the globe. Reflecting many of the characteristics of modern America, these industrial cities produced a number of problems for the people who lived in them—problems associated with fire and police protection, sanitation, utilities, and a wide range of social services. These coincided with increased concerns over employment opportunities and demands for transportation and housing improvements. Typically, municipal governments became the clearinghouses for such demands. They also became the targets for charges of corruption.

Political corruption is virtually synonymous with the post–Civil War era. From the scandals of the Grant administration at the beginning of the so-called Gilded Age to the almost universal condemnation of the activities of alleged political opportunists (carpetbaggers and scalawags) involved in reconstructing the former states of the Confederacy, these years have traditionally been portrayed as being saturated by intrigue, malfeasance, and betrayal of the public trust. Whether at the local, state, or national levels of government, and regardless of party affiliation, charges of corruption seemed commonplace. Nowhere did this appear to be more the case than in the realm of New York politics dominated by the Tammany Hall Democratic "machine" and its notorious "boss," William M. Tweed.

Born in New York City in 1823 to Irish immigrant parents, Tweed rose to political prominence by serving as alderman, congressman, and state senator. He developed a power base in local and state politics both during and immediately after the Civil War, and he controlled that base until reform initiatives by the *New York Times* and Samuel J. Tilden brought him down. He died in jail, serving a sentence for failing to audit claims against the city, in 1878.

Undoubtedly, James Lord Bryce had Tweed and the infamous "Tweed Ring" in mind when he depicted city government in the United States as a "conspicuous failure." But does Tweed deserve the charges of wrongdoing that have been heaped upon him? Did his activities run counter to the best interests of his constituents? Is it conceivable that this long-standing symbol of corruption in urban America has been unduly maligned? These questions are addressed in the selections that follow.

According to Alexander B. Callow, Jr., William Tweed's malefic reputation is well deserved. "Boss" Tweed, he says, perfected the art of political corruption by controlling three vital sources of graft: the city, the state, and the business community. Under Tweed's direction, the Tweed Ring extracted wealth from New York's city and state governments by controlling the key legislative and financial agencies that awarded charters and franchises and were responsible for city improvements. The record of bribery and excessive charges for construction, says Callow, are incontrovertible, and Tweed used his political power to benefit personally from the graft collected.

Leo Hershkowitz, on the other hand, defends Tweed's reputation and insists that the "Boss's" image was fabricated by journalists, such as cartoonist Thomas Nast, to sell newspapers in New York. New York's diversity of peoples and interests, says Hershkowitz, made it impossible for one person to control the political realm to the extent that is attributed to Tweed. Hershkowitz points out that Tweed was never convicted on charges of graft or theft and concludes that, in fact, the Tammany leader effectively represented the interests of New York residents by opening schools, building hospitals, paving streets, and providing a wide variety of other necessary services.

YES

Alexander B. Callow, Jr.

"Honest" Graft

Post-Civil-War New York has been described as being encircled by a host of political rings, rings within rings, each depending on the other. There was the Gravel Ring, the Detective Ring, the Supervisors' Ring, the Courthouse Ring, the Albany Ring, the Street Commissioners' Ring, the Manure Ring, the Market Ring, and, consolidating and hovering above all, the Tweed Ring. And what was a political ring? It was the source of "magic wisdom" that made Tammany Hall a political power, said a big chief of the Tammany braves. Samuel Tilden, who almost became President of the United States on the claim he had smashed a "ring," said:

> The very definition of a "Ring" is that it encircles enough influential men in the organization of each party to control the action of both party machines; men who in public push to extremes the abstract ideas of their respective parties, while they secretly join their hands in schemes for personal power and profit.

Scholars and public alike have generally accepted Tilden's definition of the Tweed Ring. Why was it that later city bosses like [Richard] Croker had a "machine," while Tweed had a "Ring"—a word, as it were, with a more ominous ring, a political synonym for conspiracy, venality, and corruption? If the Tweed Ring's skills at organization have never been rightfully emphasized, its achievements in corruption certainly have, although large-scale graft existed before the emergence of the Tweed Ring, and continued after its downfall.

We shall probably never know exactly how much the Ring stole. Calculations have run as high as $300 million, which was probably too high, even for the Tweed Ring. The *New York Evening Post* estimated it at $59 million; the *Times* thought it was more like $75 million to $80 million. . . .

Years after the fall of the Ring, Matthew J. O'Rourke, who had made a study of the Ring's plunders, estimated that if fraudulent bonds were included, the Ring probably stole about $200 million. Henry J. Taintor made the closest study. For six years he had been employed by the City to determine the amount of the Ring's graft. It cost the City over $73,000 to maintain Taintor's investigation, and for a moment during the Tweed Ring investigation in 1877 there was the suspicion, later dispelled, that a dreadful irony had occurred: that Taintor, in investigating graft, had been tempted himself, and had padded his bills. At any rate, he testified his research showed that the Ring had stolen at least $60 million, but even this was not an accurate figure, he said, because he did not possess all the records. Whatever the figure, in order to maintain a political machine as well as to increase their personal fortune, the Tweed Ring's operation was on a gigantic scale.

There [were] three primary sources of graft: the city, the state, and the business community. In the city, the Ring's control of the key legislative and financial agencies, from the Supervisors and Aldermen to the Comptroller and Mayor, gave it command of New York's financial machinery and bountiful opportunity for graft. Every warrant, then, charged against the city treasury passed the Ring's scrutiny and was subject to its manipulation. Every scheme for city improvement, be they new streets, new buildings, new city parks, had to be financed from the city treasury, controlled by the Ring. The results were often graft, reflected in excessive charges and needless waste. Every charter and franchise for new businesses had to meet the approval of the city legislature and the Mayor, and many companies, therefore, had to pay the tribute of the bribe to get them passed. All the city's financial affairs, such as bond issues, tax-collecting, rentals on city properties, were vulnerable as sources of graft. In effect, there was a direct relationship between power and graft. The Ring's political influence was so extensive that one roadblock to graft, the check and balance system—pitting the upper house of the City legislature against the lower house, and the Mayor as a check to the combined houses of the legislature—was simply nullified. When this happened, the city's financial operations became an open target.

This was largely true for the State legislature as well. Any check and balance between state and city, governor and legislature, was nullified. The Ring controlled the governor, John Hoffman; it controlled the powerful block of city Democrats in the State legislature. When he was elected State Senator in 1867 (and assumed office in 1868, when the Senate convened), Boss Tweed, as Chairman of the influential State Finance Committee, and as a member of the important Internal Affairs of Towns and Counties, Charitable and Religious, and Municipal Affairs committees, was in a commanding position to influence tax-levies, bond issues, and special projects for the city—all sources of graft. As the leader of the Black Horse Cavalry, a corrupt band of State legislators, he could control legislation leading to graft.

Not all the money came from the City and State treasury. The business community was an important source of profit, both as allies and victims. The Tweed Ring operated as lobby brokers for businessmen seeking to pass or kill legislation vital to their interests. Services rendered for the Erie Railroad, for example, brought in thousands of dollars. Businessmen provided large "kickbacks" in payment for receiving profitable contracts. The "cinch" bill, legislative extortion threatening business firms and individuals, was used extensively by the Ring through both the City and State legislatures.

Unlike the sly, sophisticated tactics of modern-day graft—the highly complicated dummy corporation, the undercover payoff via the "respectable" attorney—the Ring operated in a remarkably open and straightforward fashion. In effect, the shortest distance to the city treasury was a straight line. While the Ring used several methods for plunder, the largest share of the booty was gained by a method simple, direct, brazen, daring—and often sloppy. Every person who received a contract from the city, whether for supplies or for work on the city buildings and public works was instructed to alter his bills before submitting them for payment. At first the tribute was levied somewhat irregularly at 10 percent, then it was raised to

55 percent; in July 1869 it jumped to 60 percent; and from November 1869 on, the tradesmen received 35 percent and the Ring 65 percent on all bills and warrants. When bills from contractors and tradesmen did not come in fast enough, Tweed ordered vouchers to be made out to imaginary firms and individuals. On large contracts, Tweed acted directly and got immediately to the point. When he was told that electric fire alarms would cost the city $60,000, he asked the contractor, "If we get you a contract for $450,000 will you give us $225,000?" No time was wasted. The contractor answered with a simple yes and got the contract. Nor did the Boss quibble over small sums. Once a merchant told Tweed that Comptroller [Richard B.] Connolly had refused to pay his bill. Only by "kicking-back" 20 percent of the bill, would the merchant ever get paid. Tweed wrote Connolly: "For God's sake pay—'s bill. He tells me you people ask 20 percent. The whole d—d thing isn't but $1100. If you don't pay it, I will. Thine."

The division of the spoils varied: Tweed received from 10 to 25 percent; Connolly from 10 to 20 percent; [Peter B.] Sweeny 10 percent; [A. Oakey] Hall 5 to 10 percent. There was a percentage for the "sinking fund," and James Watson and W. E. Woodward shared 5 percent. These last two, clerks of the gang, did the paper work and forging. "You must do just as Jimmy tells you, and you will get your money," was a well-known saying among Tweed Ring contractors.

James Watson, the Ring's bookkeeper, was City Auditor in Connolly's office. He first demonstrated his talents while a convict. In 1850 Watson was an agent for a prosperous firm which suddenly began to experience severe losses that Watson found inconvenient to explain. He fled to California. He was brought back to New York in irons and clapped in Ludlow Street jail. An active fellow with pleasant manners, he soon won the friendship of the warden. He took charge of the prison records and performed with such admirable efficiency, especially in calculations, that he was released, with the warden's help, and was appointed a collector in the Sheriff's office. He held that position under three Sheriffs. When the Tweed Ring was formed in 1866, he was made City Auditor, a position that paid a small salary. Four years later, he was worth anywhere from two to three million dollars. It was said that he was a simple man and lived in a curious state of "ostentatious modesty." He had only one luxury—fast trotting horses, a passion that later helped to ruin the Tweed Ring.

W. E. Woodward occupied a key post as clerk to the Supervisors; he helped to rig the percentages of the business that came through that office. At the time of the Aldermen's investigation of the Ring in 1877, the Aldermen were curious how a mere clerk could own a $150,000 home, the best home, in fact, in Norwalk, Connecticut. Asked how he could do this on a salary that never exceeded $5000, Woodward gave a straightforward answer. "I used to take all I could get, and the Board of Supervisors were very liberal to me."

In the Comptroller's Office, Slippery Dick Connolly performed feats that justified his name, as his successor in 1871, the reformer, Andrew Green, confirmed when he found the treasury thoroughly sacked. As Comptroller, Connolly served the Ring three ways. He spent the money collected through the city's regular channels of revenue—taxes, rents from such city properties as markets, docks armories, etc. While some of the money was spent legitimately, a good deal of it was either embezzled or found its way into fraudulent contracts, excessive rents, or padded payrolls, a percentage of which was "kicked-back" into the Ring's coffers. However, only about a third of the city's money came from taxes or rents; the rest came from securities. Thus when a tax-levy of some $30 or more million was spent, usually at a brisk pace, Connolly's next job was to realize $30 to $50 millions more by issuing stocks and bonds.

Connolly performed this task like a financial conjuror. He created a litter of stocks and bonds raised for every conceivable project, ingenious in wording and intent. There were Accumulated Debt Bonds, Assessment Fund bonds, Croton Aqueduct Bonds, Croton Reservoir Bonds, Central Park Improvement Fund Stocks, City Improvement Stocks, Street Improvement Bonds, Fire Department Stocks, Tax Relief Bonds, Bridge Revenue Bonds, New Court House Stock. Repairs to the County Offices and Building Stocks, Dock Bonds, and bonds for the Soldiers' Relief Fund. The war chest to provide funds for padded payrolls, for example, was raised by the sale of appropriately named Riot Damages Indemnity Bonds. As a result of Connolly's various enterprises, the city groaned under a debt which increased by nearly $70 million from 1869 to 1871.

Finally, it was Connolly's responsibility to mask the Ring's fraudulent expenditures by slippery accounting techniques. In this, he was helped by the extensive power of the Ring which nullified an elaborate series of regulations established to prevent fraud. By state law, every warrant and claim drawn against the City must be itemized and accompanied by a signed affidavit certifying its authenticity. Before it could be cashed it must be thoroughly examined and signed by the Comptroller, City Auditor, the Board of Supervisors, and the Mayor. But since the Ring "owned" all these offices, it was relatively simple to rig a phony warrant and get the required signatures. Indeed, the Ring became so powerful that it owned its own bank, the Tenth National, to ensure the safe deposit of its booty. (Tweed, Connolly, Hall, James Ingersoll, and James Fisk, Jr., were the Tenth National's distinguished directors.) . . .

Added to all this was another lush source for graft. Connolly and his lieutenant James Watson were in a position to audit and pay off fictitious claims against the city. With logic, the New York City Council of Political Reform said: "In a sound fiscal system one officer *adjusts* claims and another *pays* them. From the weakness of human nature it is not deemed wise or prudent for the government of any great city or county to allow the *same* officer to adjust a claim *who* is to *pay* it; lest he may be tempted by a share of the money to conspire with the claimant and allow an unjust claim. But in our city, in 1868 and 1870, a *single* officer, the Comptroller, *adjusted* and *paid*, by adding so much to the permanent debt, $12,500,000 of claims!"

The Comptroller's office was also a point of frustration for those with legitimate claims against the city. They were kept waiting sometimes for years, before they could get their money. Subsequently, they often sold their claim to one of the Ring's agents for 50 or 60 cents on the dollar. Immediately after the transaction took place, the new owner was promptly paid. A clerk in Connolly's office, named Mike Moloney, was in charge of this branch of business.

> Moloney sits opposite the door by which his victims enter and watches for them with all the avidity that a spider might watch the approach of a fly. The moment an unlucky claimant makes his appearance Moloney jumps on his

feet and steps forward to the counter to meet him. Bending forward he listens to the application of the victim, and then by a series of ominous shakes of his head, and "the oft-told tale" repeated in half-smothered whispers, he tries to convince the applicant that there is no prospect of him receiving his money for some time to come, and that, if he really needs it, he had better go over to City Hall and see Mr. Thomas Colligan. (The victim sees Mr. Colligan) . . . and comes out feeling much the same as if he had lost his pocketbook, while the genial Mr. Colligan pockets the "little difference," invites Moloney to dinner, and quietly divides the spoils while sipping Champagne or smoking a Havana.

It is difficult to know where to begin in dealing with the many specific schemes of the Tweed Ring. Perhaps it is best to begin with what E. L. Godkin once called "one of those neat and profitable little curiosities of fraud which the memory holds after graver things are forgotten."

In 1841, a man named Valentine, a clerk in the Common Council, persuaded the city to finance the publication of a city almanac which he would edit. Initially, it was a small volume of not quite 200 pages, which had a map of the city and a list of all persons associated with the government of New York City and their business and home addresses. Although the City Directory contained the same information, for some obscure reason the almanac seemed valuable. Down through the years, the almanac increased in bulkiness, and, more important, in cost to the taxpayers, until it became "a manual of folly, extravagance, and dishonesty." By 1865, *Valentine's Manual*, as it was called, had become a 879-page monument of costliness and superficiality. Among 141 pictures was a large, folding four-page lithograph, illustrating— "O precious gift to posterity!"—a facsimile of each Alderman's autograph. Expensive lithographs covered a number of vital subjects: a fur store built in 1820; a house that Valentine had once lived in; a grocery and tea store of ancient vintage; Tammany Hall as it looked in 1830; a Fifth Avenue billiard saloon; and a host of "portraits of undistinguished persons." Well over 400 pages were cluttered with extracts from old government documents, newspapers, and "memories." The cost of printing was $57,172.30; the number of copies printed, 10,000. A few copies found their way into secondhand bookstores, which paid two dollars apiece for them, $3.36 less than a copy cost the city. An outraged public opinion forced Mayor Hoffman to veto the resolution authorizing a similar expenditure for 1866. He found that Appleton's or Harper's would have published the same number of copies for $30,000 instead of $53,672. The Aldermen, however, overrode his veto. . . .

The Tweed Ring created several companies which moved in to monopolize every phase of city printing as well as city advertising. One such firm was the New York Printing Company. Its expansion reflected all the gusto of American business enterprises. It began in a shabby little office on Centre Street, but almost at once business became so good that it absorbed three of the largest printing establishments in the city. The New York Printing Company was growing, said a newspaper, "but like other mushrooms it grows in the dark. It is spreading under the cover of night, and running its roots into the Treasury by deep underground passages." On a capital stock of $10,000 it paid a dividend of $50,000 to $75,000 to each of its stockholders. The city apparently liked its work, for during 1870–71 the firm obtained $260,283.81 of its business. All these amounts incorporated a 25 percent tribute to the Ring. The company became so versatile in printing all kinds of material that the city paid it another

$300,000 for printing in book form the records of New York City from 1675 to 1776. Nor did the firm confine its customers to the City and County. Insurance companies and steamboat and ferry companies were extremely vulnerable to a legislative bill which, in the public interest, could hurt them by regulating their activities and profits. Hence, they all received a notice that the New York Printing Company would be happy to do their printing.

The Tweed Ring composed the major stockholders of the Manufacturing Stationers' Company, which sold stationery supplies to city offices and schools. In 1870 the City and County paid it over $3 million. Among its many bills, there was this interesting one: for six reams of note paper, two dozen penholders, four ink bottles, one dozen sponges, and three dozen boxes of rubber bands, the city paid $10,000. James Parton singled out the Manufacturing Stationers' Company for its treachery.

> We have before us a successful bid for supplying the city offices with stationery, in which we find the bidder offering to supply "blue folio post" at one cent per ream; "magnum bonum pens," at one cent per gross; "lead pencils," at one cent per dozen; "English sealing-wax," at one cent per pound; and eighty-three other articles of stationery, at the uniform price of one cent for the usual parcel. This was the "lowest bid," and it was, of course, the one accepted. It appeared, however, when the bill was presented for payment, that the particular kind of paper styled "blue folio post" had never been called for, nor any considerable quantity of the other articles proposed to be supplied for one cent. No one, strange to say, had ever wanted "magnum bonum" pens at one cent a gross, but in all the offices the cry had been for "Perry's extra fine," at three dollars. Scarcely any one had used "envelopes letter-size" at one cent per hundred but there had been countless calls for "envelopes note-size" at one cent each. Between the paper called "blue folio post," at one cent per ream, and paper called "foolscap extra ruled," at *five dollars and a half*, the difference was too slight to be perceived; but every one had used the foolscap. Of what avail are contracts, when the officials who award them, and the other officials who pay the bill, are in league with the contractor to steal the public money?

As the fictional Boss Blossom Brick said, "Official advertising is the Pain Killer of Politics." During the Civil War three men started an insignificant newspaper titled *The Transcript*. They were George Stout, "a journalist unknown to fame," Charles E. Wilbour, a court stenographer and "literary man, somewhat less unknown," and Cornelius Corson, "an employee in the City Hall, and not devoid of influence in that quarter." When Tweed, Connolly, and Sweeny became their partners, business, but not circulation, picked up. The Common Council (the Aldermen and Assistant Aldermen) ordered that a full list of all persons liable to serve in the army, amounting to some 50,000 names, should be printed in the *Transcript*. Later, thirty-five copies of the list were published in book-form, "though the bill was rendered for a large edition." From then on the *Transcript* enjoyed days of high prosperity. It published the major share of all "city advertising," which meant official records of the courts, and official statements and declarations, statistical reports, new ordinances, in effect, the facts and figures of city business. The rates were exorbitant enough to ensure a heady profit; for example, messages from the Mayor cost a dollar a line. A great deal of the advertisements came from Tweed's

Department of Public Works, and from the Bureau of Assessments, where Richard Tweed was in control. Although the newspaper never sold more than a hundred copies, the city paid it $801,874 from 1869 to 1871 for publishing its official business and advertisements. The December 3, 1870, issue, for example, consisted of 504 pages. Advertisements were charged at a rate of 25 cents a line, higher than prevailing newspaper rates. It was estimated that the Ring received $68,000 in profits for that issue alone. The Christmas number for that year was a special: a double extra of 1000 pages, all advertisements, for which double rates were charged. It appeared to one newspaper that the Ring paid for its Christmas presents out of the public till. The profits, then, made by the three companies of the Ring which corralled city printing reached a grand total over a three-year period of $2,641,828.30, of which nine-tenths was pure profit.

As Boss Blossom Brick said, "Give the people plenty of taffy and the newspapers plenty of advertising—then help yourself to anything that's lying around loose." Funneling the taxpayers' dollars through the *Transcript* was a way to finance Tweed's mansion on Fifth Avenue and his palatial estate in Greenwich, Connecticut; but there was another method of using city advertising which ensured, for a few years at least, that gracious living could be enjoyed. The Tweed Ring found that the best way to protect itself against newspaper criticism was to distribute city advertising as a token of peace. It became a kind of hush money which bound the press to silence. Until the storm broke, in 1871, probably no New York political regime ever enjoyed less newspaper criticism than the Tweed Ring, and only when the evidence became painfully obvious and practically overwhelming did the press join the crusade against evil begun by the *New York Times* and *Harper's Weekly*. Before the storm, there had been some criticism, but it was spotty and half-hearted. The *Tribune* might thunder for a while, the *Sun* became nasty—as was its style—but a general grant of advertising had the same effect as placing alum on the tongue.

By law, the city corporation was limited to nine daily and eight weekly papers in which to advertise. But the Tweed Ring, with its usual disregard for procedure, extended delicious morsels of city advertising to twenty-six daily and forty-four weekly newspapers in the city alone, and seventeen weekly journals outside the city, making a total of eighty-seven organs. Probably no political regime in the history of New York City had exerted so much influence on the press. . . .

Not content with the method of using advertising, the Ring also won the hearts of City Hall reporters by giving them $200 gifts at Christmas. This practice had started as early as 1862, under the administration of Mayor George Opdyke (who disapproved), but the Ring elaborated on the scheme. It also subsidized six to eight reporters on nearly all the city papers with fees of $2000 to $2500 to exercise the proper discretion when it came to writing about politics. There was the reward of patronage for the especially deserving: Stephen Hayes, on the *Herald* staff during the high days of the Ring, was rewarded with a sinecure in the Marine Court ($2500 a year), and Michael Kelly, also of the *Herald*, received positions in both the Fire Department and the Department of Public Works. Moreover, reporters from various newspapers of the country, from a Cleveland newspaper to the *Mobile Register*, were hired to write favorable notices of the Democratic administration in New York. And if a firm went too far and tried to print a pamphlet exposing the

Ring, it might find its offices broken into by the Ring's men and the type altered to present a glowing account of the Ring's activities—as did the printing company of Stone, Jordan and Thomson.

At the time the Ring was breaking up, the City found itself confronted with claims amounting to over a million and a half dollars negotiated between newspapers and the Ring, some fraudulent and some not, for not all journals which received city advertising did so on the basis of a conspiracy with the Ring. But enough of them did to ensure the complacency and the apathy which seemed to grip many during the Ring's rule.

The Ring needed complacency and apathy when it came to operations behind the opening, widening, and improving of the city streets. With the city's enormous growth came a legitimate demand for new streets and the improvement of old ones. It became one of the Ring's most lucrative forms of graft. It was, indeed, a democratic form of graft—laborers got work; City Hall clerks were able to supplement their incomes; political debts were paid off in commissionerships, judges no longer had to rely entirely on their salaries; Ring members and friends prospered from the assessments involved and the excitement of "gambling" in real estate. As in the case of Recorder and Street Commissioner [John] Hackett, the key factor was the appointment of reliable Commissioners by the Ring judges, upon the suggestion of Corporation Counsel [John] O'Gorman. From then on a pattern emerged: Tammany favorites and members of the Ring's families constantly appeared as Commissioners; awards for damages were exorbitantly high; Commissioners charged "from ten to one hundred times as much as the law allowed" for their services and expenses, despite the fact that the Commissioners as employees of the city were disqualified by law from receiving any pay.

To "open" a new street did not mean to begin construction work. It was a legal term signifying that the land had been bought and was now officially "opened." Announcements of the transaction were published, and those property owners involved were invited to declare any objections to the Commissioners. The clerk drew up a report and the thing was done. Actually it usually amounted to a mere formality.

The cost for this activity under the Tweed Ring, however, would seem to indicate that an enormous amount of work went into it. What usually happened was that the surveyor reproduced a map of the street from maps made in 1811, when Manhattan island, except for a small area at its northern end, was surveyed so well that the maps were still adequate in post-Civil War New York. On the borders of the copy made by the surveyor, the clerk wrote the names of the owners of the lots on both sides of the street, copying his information from the tax books. Then the fun began. "The surveyor charges as though he had made original surveys and drawn original maps. The clerk charges as though his reports were the result of original searchers and researchers. The commissioners charge as though the opening had been the tardy fruit of actual negotiations." For the year ending in June 1866, it was estimated that the cost for "opening" twenty-five streets was $257,192.12. Of this cost, $4433 was charged for rent of an office, which ordinarily rented for $300 a year; "disbursements and postagestamps" cost $950; and one surveyor's bill alone accounted for an astounding $54,000.

The Broadway widening "job" was a good example of the Ring in action. On May 17, 1869, the State legislature passed an act providing for the widening of Broadway between Thirty-fourth and Fifty-ninth streets, whereupon the Ring seized control of the legal machinery that decided assessments and damages to the property involved. With the friendly judge Albert Cardozo presiding, and two of the three Commissioners good Ring men, the Ring and a selected few began to buy property. Two of them paid $24,500 for a lot for which the Commissioners generously awarded them damages of $25,100. The new front was worth $10,000 more. Another lot sold for $27,500, but this payment was absorbed by a $30,355 award in damages. It was the resale value of the property, however, where the profit was made, and lots on Broadway were worth thousands. With tactics of this sort, the Ring managed to purchase some of the most valuable property in New York City.

With minor variations, the Broadway widening scheme was repeated in the Madison Avenue extension, the Church Street extension, the opening of Lexington Avenue through Stuyvesant Park, the Park Place widening, and the so-called "Fifth Avenue raid," where the Ring profited from the widening, extending, and "improvement" of that street. To one writer, who greatly exaggerated, it seemed that streets were opened "which no mortal had seen, no foot had trod; and they appeared only on the city map as spaces between imaginary lines leading from No-where to No-place." To a New York citizen in 1871 who examined the New York State *Senate Journal* of 1869, it might have seemed that the State legislature had gone No-where. On page 61 was an act entitled, "An act to afford relief against frauds and irregularities in assessments for local improvements in the city of New York."

Whether the source of graft was street openings, real estate speculation, city advertising, padded contractor's bills, juggled city records and bond issues fat with graft, a simple but imaginative profit on the City Directory, or a straightforward attack on the city treasury by supplying printing and stationery goods, the Tweed Ring explored the various paths to civic dishonesty. The roads to graft, however, were paved by the very interests the Ring exploited. The financial community, consumed in its own self-interests, stood to gain from the massive pump-priming in city improvements. The "open door" policy of state and city welfare deadened the voice of religious and philanthropic organizations; the newspapers, split by political partisanship and competitive self-interest, were softened by the morsels of political handouts; and the "people" were indifferent. The Tweed Ring thrived on the lack of civic conscience, and the result was graft.

Tweed's New York: Another Look

Myth

William M. Tweed, the notorious "Boss" Tweed, is one of the great myths of American history. His ugly features, small beady eyes, huge banana-like nose, vulturish expression and bloated body are the personification of big-city corruption. Thomas Nast, political propagandist and executioner of *Harper's Weekly*, has made them a triumph of the caricaturist art. Tweed's deeds, or rather misdeeds, as fashioned by historians and the like, are perhaps even better known. They have been told and retold in countless textbooks, monographs, biographies, articles, reminiscences, and have become an American epic whose proportions with each recounting become more fantastic, more shocking. Here are fables of monumental robberies of the New York City treasury, of fraud, deceit, treachery, of monstrous villainies, of carpets, furniture and of courthouses. Like fables, they are largely untrue, but like most legends, they perpetuate themselves and are renewed and enlarged with each telling.

The myth has become so much a part of history and Tweed such a convenient reference for the after-dinner speaker, pulp writer, or simply something to frighten little children with, that if there wasn't a Tweed, he would have to be invented, and he was.

Tweed is a fat, urban Jesse James without any saving graces. James is a western Robin Hood, a sort of criminal St. Francis. Tweed's patron saint is an eastern St. Tammany, refuge for the greedy, vulgar, corrupt—in short, consummate—politician. Tweed is the essence of urban rot, malodorous, the embodiment of all that is evil and cancerous in American municipal and political life. The monster lives. In a recent tax-evasion case, the prosecution charged a defendant with failure to report income allegedly obtained illegally. During the course of the trial, an enlarged Nast cartoon of "Boss Tweed" was produced to illustrate the similarity of crimes. The jury voted for conviction. Interestingly, the United States Court of Appeals reversed the verdict partly because the court felt use of the cartoon had prejudiced the jury. Eternally threatened plans to destroy the "Tweed Courthouse" (the name itself is an example of the myth) still standing behind New York's City Hall caused many New Yorkers to ask that the building be spared as a monument to graft and a reminder of the necessity of rooting out piggish politicians who take their slops at the public trough. Almost miraculously, the building, though supposedly built by corrupt politicians and contractors, is one of the finest examples of Italian Renaissance design in the country. It has not collapsed into a pile of plaster and sawdust, as critics predicted it would.

A popular cast-iron bank depicts an oily-faced tuxedoed figure, supposedly a banker, greedily swallowing the pennies of innocent children. What really "sells" the bank is calling it "Boss Tweed," even if one has nothing to do with the other. The myth is so salable and so deeply rooted that it is as American as "apple pie" or "Mother." A noted TV station produced a "documentary" on Tweed. When told that a mass of evidence exists that questions the "facts," representatives of the station offered an opinion, without pausing even to look at the material, that they wished all such records were destroyed. What price integrity as long as the legend lives, and it does so with abandon.

When political leaders think of New York, the vile image of Tweed taught them with their earliest history lessons returns to mind and appeals on behalf of the city fall on deaf ears. When Congress or the state legislature meet to debate New York's future, Tweed like some ghoulish specter rises up and beckons an end to discussion.

The myth is outrageously simple. Tweed was born in New York. Big, strong, ambitious and ruthless, he climbed out of the streets, and leaped like a snarling "Tammany Tiger" on unsuspecting citizens. Through fraud, deceit and intimidation, he was elected to various city and state offices, and even served a term in Congress. Tweed yearned for bigger and better things. He met kindred souls whom he placed in strategic places as members of "The Ring" to pillage the city treasury, conquer the state and finally the nation. By using the simple device of padded or fictitious bills for items not delivered or not needed, millions were stolen. The county courthouse, the "Tweed Courthouse," became the symbol and center of the operation. Subservient members of "The Ring" were Peter B. ("Brains") Sweeny, city chamberlain; Richard B. ("Slippery Dick") Connolly, city comptroller; A. Oakey Hall ("The Elegant One"), mayor; and John T. ("Toots") Hoffman, mayor and governor. Hoffman would hopefully become President to serve Tweed better. An army of poor, unwashed and ignorant were also recruited. These were recent Irish and German immigrants, whose largely illegal votes were cheaply bought in return for jobs given away at City Hall or a turkey at Christmas. Judges were necessary to stay the hands of the law, so added to the conspiracy were George G. Barnard, John H. McCunn and Albert Cardozo. Misguided though willing contractors like Andrew Garvey, "Prince of Plasterers"; James H. Ingersoll, the "Chairmaker"; John Keyser, the "Plumber"; and numerous others were awarded contracts, but kicked back up to 75 per cent to Tweed and "The Ring." Tweed received the lion's or rather "Tiger's" share of perhaps 50 to 200 million dollars at a time when an average workman received two to three dollars a day.

The fable continues that this monumental looting was halted by courageous, honest men. There were Democrats like Samuel J. Tilden, who on the strength of his attacks against "The Ring" became governor and presidential candidate. Honest Republicans like George Jones, editor of the *Times*, combined to disgrace "The Ring" with the help of Nast and *Harper's Weekly*. Indictments were handed down against Tweed, who was found guilty and sentenced to the penitentiary. Finally, like most of the others of "The Ring," he fled the country.

Recognized in Spain by a sailor, or someone or other who just happened to be an avid reader of *Harper's Weekly*—the myth is never clear on details—and was quite familiar with the Boss's features, he was returned to prison to die a lonely but deserved death, a lesson to evildoers.

With great delight, happy historians, political activists, popularizers, drooled over juicy tidbits like carpets and plumbing and people named Dummy and Cash, never bothering to look at dust-gathering records, or even those quite dust-free. It would seem that research would interfere with exorcising the devil or prevent the development of some interesting theories. One theory concerned the failure of adequate communication in an evolving, increasingly complicated metropolis. It was a lack of such communication as seen in a decentralized and chaotic government which explains the emergence of Tweed and the "Big Pay-off." Others see Tweed emerging from the schismatic web of Tammany politics to seize and consolidate power by "pulling wires," hiring professional toughs and modernizing control within Tammany.

Lord James Bryce, a hostile critic of American urban government, in his classic *American Commonwealth* found Tweed the end product of "rancid dangerous Democracy." The scornful Englishman felt that "The time was ripe, for the lowest class of voters, foreign and native, had now been thoroughly organized and knew themselves able to control the city."

This voting mob was ready to follow Tammany Hall, which he concluded "had become the Acropolis of the city; and he who could capture it might rule as tyrant." Bryce found Tweed's unscrupulousness matched by the crafty talents of others, creating a perfect blend of flagrant corruption. But the essential ingredient was democracy and failure to follow traditional leadership. It was such democracy which allowed a Falstaff-like Tweed to emerge as a hero; a "Portuguese Jew" like Albert Cardozo who was born in New York to "prostitute" his legal talents for party purposes; or a Fernando Wood, Tweed's predecessor in Tammany, to become a major figure from such small beginnings that he was "reported to have entered New York as the leg of an artificial elephant in a travelling show." Bryce thus denounced Tweed and a form of government that had little if any respect for birth or breeding, but rewarded the mean, the base-born for their audacity and treachery.

It all sounds so plausible, but does it help Tweed emerge from behind Thomas Nast's leering cartoons? The problem with Tweed and the myth is that it is all so much vapor and so little substance, and what has been written has not dispelled shadows; only deepened them. So little has been done to obtain even basic information about the man, and what is known is generally wrong. Perhaps never has so much nonsense been written about an individual.

A few questions to start. Was it possible for one man or even a group of men to plan such a vast swindle involving hundreds if not thousands of officials, clerks, laborers, contractors, and hope to succeed? If Tweed plotted such an operation which supposedly involved bribing the state legislature, coercing judges, muzzling the press, aborting the gossip of bank officers and city auditors, he must have been a genius, a Houdini, Machiavelli, Napoleon rolled into one. Such a mind surely would have withstood the trivial intrusion of a hundred brash reformers. Yet he was shaken from his lofty perch, tumbled into prison and hounded to death. All this was done without organized resistance and in literally the twin-kling of an eye. Tweed had such "power" that he was thrown out of his party without a word spoken in his behalf, even before he was found guilty of any-thing. There was, except for counsel, no one to defend him, no congressman, senator, assemblyman, no one in authority. "The Ring" was so strongly forged that it shattered at the slightest pressure, its component parts flying about with no other thought than every man for himself. If "The Ring" was supposed to be a strong political or financial alliance well led and directed, then it like "Boss" Tweed was simply a figment of historical imagination, a pretty bit of caricature.

At no time did such a "Ring" dominate New York City politics, let alone the state or national scene. Supposed "Ring" members rarely had much to do with one another, socially or otherwise. Sweeny was a friend of Victor Hugo's, Hall aspired to make a mark in the theater, Tweed aspired to office, Connolly had Connolly. There was little to bind the so-called "Ring." Except by an accident of history that they served in various city posts at the same time, there is little to relate one with the other.

Even the dreaded "Tammany Tiger" was a paper one. Certainly in Tweed's day Tammany did not dominate New York politics. Perhaps it never did. The city was and is a complex, competitive system of diverse interest. It was then and is now too heterogeneous, too much made up of various groups, classes, outlooks, beliefs for any part or let alone one person to control. New Yorkers' cosmopolitanism and tolerance have a tragic price.

The city cannot send representatives to Washington or to Albany who can express the single-minded view of smaller, simpler communities. Its large im-migrant population creates suspicion: is New York an American city? A rural backwater has more political clout than all of the city when it comes to power on national or state levels.

Partly this is in consequence of an age-old struggle between the city and the farm, and eternal tug of war between the city in its search for greater self-government and rural conservative interests who find New York a threat to themselves and their entrenched power. There were some deeply rooted animosities. Cities are not natural. God made the earth, trees, animals and man. Cities are man-made. Natural things are pure, innocent and obedient to order, while man is sinful, evil, disobedient, whose works like cities are suspect. There may be a Garden of Eden, but there is no City of Eden, only Sodom and Gomorrah. This kind of morality underlines economic and political selection. It is served by the Tweed myth, since the horrors of municipal corruption and Tammany bossism plainly demonstrate the impossibility of the city even governing itself. It is in a deeper sense an implied failure of man governing himself apart from some external power. As New York cannot be given greater home rule, it must even be more closely regulated and watched by the state; so too man must observe a higher authority.

To make matters worse, New York also destroys its political talent, its best lost in the heat of murderous combat. It was a rare aspirant indeed who could emerge from his trials to become a national figure of any permanence. Alexander Hamilton and Aaron Burr were testimony to this. De Witt Clinton and Edward Livingston were further examples of early casualties. By mid-nineteenth century, no New York City politician had any voice in national or state affairs. Fernando Wood, potentially a great politician and a champion of the city's interest against the state rural lobby, was destroyed by bitter intra-party fighting. William Tweed might have provided the city with a voice and he too was destroyed, but in such a way that the city too suffered in countless ways—not the least of which forever identified the metropolis as a spawning ground for corruption and filth. Why then pay it any attention? Why spend money on the sewers? Tweed was and is a convenient stick with which to beat the city over the head, preferably at regular intervals. In many ways, the tragedy of New York is that Tweed did not succeed, that a strong unified political force was not created, that the paper tiger was not real.

As for Tweed, there remain the stories. There is no evidence that he created the "Tammany Tiger" or ordered it to be used as his personal symbol. The clawing, snarling, toothed tiger was Nast's idea, part of the image he wished to create. It was plastered on Tweed and Tammany and sold. What politician would use such a symbol to win votes or influence people, except a madman or a cartoonist like Nast?

One of the universally accepted myths is that of Tweed's reactions to the July 1871 disclosures exposing "The Ring." He is supposed to have snarled like his tiger to a group of cowering reporters, reformers and the public at large, "What are you going to do about it?" Again, what politician, especially in this country, would make such an asinine statement, no matter how sure he was of his position? It was certainly not Tweed's style, and if he made "The Ring," he was not that stupid. In truth, the phrase was never used by Tweed, but invented by Nast as a caption for a June 10, 1871, cartoon a month before Tweed and "The Ring" made headlines. Reporters asked Tweed that question after the deluge and his troubles with the law. It was never Tweed's question. It was all "Boss," all Nast and all nonsense.

Tweed was no saint, but he was not the Nast creature. He was more a victim than a scoundrel or thief. Characteristically, Tweed was intensely loyal, warmhearted, outgoing, given to aiding the underdog and the underprivileged. But he was also gullible, naïve and easily fooled. If he were a real "boss," he should have been able, like Sweeny and others, to avoid inundating calamity. He was a good family man, and there simply is no scandal to report so far as his personal habits are concerned. Even his bitterest enemies could find nothing. He was not an intellectual, he was not at home with a Sweeny or an Oakey Hall, but found a close friendship with Jubilee Jim Fisk, the brilliant short-lived Roman candle and bon vivant.

Why then Tweed? First, he was what he was. In his prime, he reportedly weighed close to three hundred pounds. A "slim" Tweed would not be as inviting a target. Point one, for dieters. His features could be easily exaggerated by someone like Nast, and he was enough in the public eye for the *Times* and *Harper's*. He was ambitious, but not ruthless. He had money, but not enough to throw a scare into or buy off his opponents. He had power, but not enough to withstand attacks by newspapers, law, rivals and supposed friends.

Further, and much more importantly, he represented the interests of New York. He had established legislative programs which opened schools, hospitals, museums, programs tailored to meet the needs of a rapidly expanding constituency. His identification with the interests of the city was enough for the traditional rural-suburban leadership to seek his destruction. He provided a means for Republicans from President U.S. Grant on down to those in the local level to make people forget the corruptions in Republican circles, like the Whisky Ring, Indian Ring or Crédit Mobilier—all schemes to defraud millions from the government—but see instead the balloon-like figure of Tweed, Tammany and the defeat of Democratic opposition. National Democrats like Horatio Seymour and the inept "Sammy" Tilden could point to Tweed and gain cheers and votes for their efforts to "delouse" the party. If there ever was a scapegoat, its name was Tweed.

The Tweed story does not need exaggeration, lies, half-truths, rumors to make it interesting. It is in itself an incredible story. Debunking the myth is part of it, but there is much more. There are bigots like Nast, George T. Strong and others who saw in Tweed an outsider threatening their position by his supposedly championing the "drunken-ignorant Irish," the overly ambitious German-Jewish immigrants and those seeking to change the status quo. That he sought to provide answers to the increasing complications of urban life did not help. Tweed never traveled in upper-class society. With all his apparent success, he was never able to wash away the tarnish of the Lower East Side. Moreover, there are some of the most incredible trials and abuses of the judicial process on record. There are hand-picked judges and juries, not as might be expected by Tweed, but by the prosecution. The misuse of grand jury indictments should become legendary.

Tweed was never tried for or found guilty of graft or theft, the crime Tweed stands accused of by history. He was convicted after some strange, improper, even illegal judicial proceedings, which were in many ways worse than anything Tweed supposedly committed, of a misdemeanor—failing to audit claims against the city. Hall was tried three times on the same charge and was not convicted. Connolly and Sweeny were never tried.

Tweed died in prison after having spent some four years there, and he would have remained longer but for his death—only one of these years was he in a penitentiary, on the misdemeanor conviction. The remaining years he spent in the county jail because he could not raise an exorbitant bail in a civil suit. The manipulation of the law by those sworn to uphold the law was a real crime. Then add the threatening, tampering with, and intimidation of witnesses, as well as the use of informers and agent provocateurs. Under these conditions, Snow White would have been hanged for loitering to commit prostitution.

The threat to individual liberty by an unbridled omnipresent legal system is rarely as clear as in the Tweed case. The innocent and guilty are too often given the same even-handed justice.

Couple this with yellow journalism and abuse of power by the press and Nast. Horace Greeley in his bid for the presidency in 1871 complained that he did not know whether he was running for that office or the penitentiary. Tweed was as much a victim of irresponsible journalism. Tweed, too, was "hot copy." He was also tried and convicted by newspapers in a too often repeated process in which rabid reporters and editors became judge and jury and headlines substitute for trial and district attorneys, while editors scratch each other's backs for the sake of publicity—where an indictment is often all that is necessary to make a point, sell papers and win votes. . . .

Epilogue

And so Tweed passed into history to become the fabled legend. It was an undeserved fate. Except for Tweed's own very questionable "confession," there was really no evidence of a "Tweed Ring," no direct evidence of Tweed's thievery, no evidence, excepting the testimony of the informer contractors, of "wholesale" plunder by Tweed. What preceded is a story of political profiteering at the expense of Tweed, of vaulting personal ambitions fed on Tweed's carcass, of a conspiracy of self-justification of the corruption of law by the upholders of that law, of a venal irresponsible press and a citizenry delighting in the exorcism of witchery. If Tweed was involved then all those about him were equally guilty. He was never tried for theft. The only criminal trial that was held was for a misdemeanor of failing to audit, and this trial was held before a hand-picked judge and jury at a time when Tweed-hunting was at its height.

Probably the "truth" about Tweed, "The Ring" and the "stolen" millions will never be known. It is possible to measure the difference between graft and profit? If Keyser charged so much for plastering, perhaps another could do the work for less, but would it be the same work, could it be done on time? How do you compare the cost of one carpet with that of another? Price is only one consideration. At one point, a decision has to be reached on any contract, no matter who is selected; there will always be someone who could have done it cheaper. Surely there were overcharges, but by how much? The throwing about of figures, 10, 30, 50, 200 million, is of no help. Is it possible to decide at what point profit becomes graft? It is difficult to answer these questions or work out an almost insoluble puzzle. In the end, the easiest solution is of course to blame Tweed, rather than examine financial records, vouchers, warrants. These were allowed to lie dormant silently collecting the dust of a century, in the end hopefully to disappear. How much easier to nail the "Elephant" to a wall or listen to the romanticism of history and the excesses of rhetoric created by Godkin, Bryce, Wingate, Lynch and so many others.

Tweed emerges as anything but a master thief. It was the contractors who willingly padded bills, never calling attention to any undue pressure upon them to do so; it was those lower-echelon agents in the city, especially Woodward and Watson, who were in direct liaison with the contractors, not Tweed. And lastly blame should be placed on the city and state. The former because it did not regulate expenditures properly and failed to pay its bills on time, a point brought up time and again by the contractors, and the latter because it interfered in city business; the city's welfare was subverted by state political interests. The Tweed story, or better the contractors' story, is about as good a reason for New York City home rule as can be offered.

Where did the legendary millions go? None of the contractors, with the possible exception of Garvey, had sizable sums of money, and even he wasn't to be compared to the "robber barons" like Morgan or Whitney or Rockefeller. These could sneeze out in a moment what purported to be the total Tweed plunder.

What of Hall, Connolly, Sweeny, Hoffman? There is nothing to show they received any princely sums. No one connected with the so-called "Ring" set up a dynasty or retired to luxurious seclusion. Certainly not Tweed. If money was stolen, it held a Pharaoh's curse. Those who touched it did not enjoy it. So many died suddenly, so many died in dishonor and loneliness. None suffered as much as did William Magear Tweed and the City of New York.

Tweed spent some twenty years in public service. In the Fire Department, as alderman, member of the Board of Supervisors and Board of Education, member of Congress, state senator, commissioner of public works—it was a long list and resulted in a great deal of public good. He was instrumental in modernizing governmental and educational institutions, in developing needed reforms in public welfare programs, in incorporating schools, hospitals, establishing public baths, in preserving a site in Central Park for the Metropolitan Museum of Art, in widening Broadway, extending Prospect Park and removing fences from around public parks, establishing Riverside Park and Drive, annexing the Bronx as a forerunner of the incorporation of Greater New York, in building the Brooklyn Bridge, in founding the Lenox Library. He was of considerable service during the Civil War. Tweed moved the city forward in so many ways and could have been, if he had not been destroyed, a progressive force in shaping the interests and destiny of a great city and its people.

Tweed's concepts about urbanization and accommodation while not philosophically formalized were years beyond their time. Twenty or thirty years later such programs were adopted by reformers and urban planners. Tweed was a pioneer spokesman for an emerging New York, one of the few that spoke for its interests, one of the very few that could have had his voice heard in Albany. Tweed grew with the city, his death was a tragedy for the future metropolis.

His life in the end was wasted, not so much by what he did, but by what was done to him, his work and the city being relegated to the garbage heap, both branded by the same indelible iron. He became a club with which to beat New York, really the ultimate goal of the blessed reformers.

It is time to seek a re-evaluation of Tweed and his time. If Tweed was not so bad, neither was the city. Old legends die hard, old ideas have deep roots, but hopefully some of the old legends will die and the deep roots wither away.

What was learned from the episode? Practically nothing. Politics, politicians, jurists and venal journalists certainly continued to ply their trade, spurred by their success, as in the past, with hardly a glance or hesitation, comforted in the downfall of the "Boss." The devil had been killed; would anyone bother to look at the judges or ask anyone else to do the Lord's work? Every once in a while, a bill is introduced in the Massachusetts legislature to have the Salem witches exonerated and declared non-witches. Some are. It might be time to have the New York state legislature and history provide a similar service for Tweed. Surely, there are other devils around to take his place. And a statue for Tweed? Yes, it would be his city alive and well.

POSTSCRIPT

Did William M. Tweed Corrupt Post–Civil War New York?

The opposing viewpoints of Callow and Hershkowitz regarding "Boss" Tweed's place in history is representative of a long-standing scholarly debate about the consequences of machine politics in the United States. James Bryce, *The American Commonwealth*, 2 vols. (Macmillan, 1888); Moisei Ostrogorski, *Democracy and the Organization of Political Parties* (1902; reprint, Anchor Books, 1964); Lincoln Steffens, *The Shame of the Cities* (McClure, Phillips, 1904); and Ernest S. Griffith, *A History of American City Government: The Conspicuous Failure, 1870–1900* (National Civic League Press, 1974) present a litany of misdeeds associated with those who controlled municipal government.

Efforts to rehabilitate the sullied reputations of the machine politicians can be dated to the comments of Tammany Hall ward healer George Washington Plunkitt, whose turn-of-the-century observations included a subtle distinction between "honest" and "dishonest" graft. A more scholarly explanation was presented by Robert K. Merton, a political scientist, who identified numerous "latent functions" of the political machine. A generally positive description of the operations of urban government can also be found in Jon C. Teaford, *The Unheralded Triumph: City Government in America, 1860–1900* (Johns Hopkins University Press, 1984).

There are several excellent urban history texts that devote space to the development of municipal government, including discussions of political machines, in the nineteenth century. Among these are Howard P. Chudacoff and Judith E. Smith, *The Evolution of American Urban Society*, 3d ed. (Prentice Hall, 1981) and Charles N. Glaab and A. Theodore Brown, *A History of Urban America*, 3d ed. (Macmillan, 1983). Various developments in the post–Civil War period are discussed in Raymond A. Mohl, *The New City: Urban America in the Industrial Age, 1860–1920* (Harlan Davidson, 1985). Boss politics is analyzed in Robert K. Merton, *Social Theory and Social Structure* (Free Press, 1957) and John M. Allswang, *Bosses, Machines, and Urban Voters: An American Symbiosis* (Kennikat Press, 1977). In addition to the studies by Callow and Hershkowitz excerpted here, the most famous of the nineteenth-century urban bosses is evaluated in Seymour Mandelbaum, *Boss Tweed's New York* (John Wiley, 1965). For a study of New York City in the early years of Tweed's career, see Edward K. Spann, *The New Metropolis: New York City, 1840–1857* (Columbia University Press, 1981).

ISSUE 4

Did the Industrial Revolution Disrupt the American Family?

YES: Elaine Tyler May, from "The Pressure to Provide: Class, Consumerism, and Divorce in Urban America, 1880–1920," *Journal of Social History* (Winter 1978)

NO: Jacquelyn Dowd Hall, Robert Korstad, and James Leloudis, from "Cotton Mill People: Work, Community, and Protest in the Textile South, 1880–1940," *The American Historical Review* (April 1986)

ISSUE SUMMARY

YES: Elaine Tyler May, a professor of American studies and history, argues that the Industrial Revolution in the United States, with its improved technology, increasing income, and emerging consumerism, led to higher rates of divorce because family wage earners failed to meet rising expectations for material accumulation.

NO: History professors Jacquelyn Dowd Hall, Robert Korstad, and James Leloudis contend that the cotton mill villages of the New South, rather than destroying family work patterns, fostered a labor system that permitted parents and children to work together as a traditional family unit.

The Industrial Revolution fueled the rise of the United States to a preeminent position among the nations of the world by 1914. It affected virtually every institution—political, economic, and social—in the country. Politically, municipal, state, and federal governments recognized the benefits of cooperating in a variety of ways with corporate America, so much so that the doctrine of laissez-faire existed more in theory than in actual practice. Economically, industrialization laid the foundation for monopolization; fueled occupational opportunities for residents, both native and foreignborn; placed in jeopardy the value of skilled artisans; and transformed the workplace for millions of Americans. Socially, the economic forces dominating the United States in the last quarter of the nineteenth century played a significant role in encouraging geographical mobility, subordinating rural values to those associated with large industrial cities, and generating tensions and conflicts along racial, ethnic, class, and gender lines.

As the factory came to replace the farm as the workplace for more and more Americans, the United States developed an identifiable proletariat—a mass of unskilled, often propertyless workers whose labor was controlled by someone other than themselves. Moreover, despite the optimistic promises of "rags-to-riches" advancement associated with the American Dream, these workers could anticipate that they would remain unskilled and propertyless for their entire lives. Within the factories, mills, and mines of industrial America, corporate managers dictated company policy regarding wages, hours, and other conditions of employment and tended to view themselves, not the laborers, as the producers. Wages may have been relatively higher but so, too, were prices, and a dollar a day was not enough for a man to feed, clothe, and house his family, to say nothing of providing medical attention. Consequently, many working-class, married women entered the labor force to help make ends meet, not because they found the prospect of wage earning to be liberating. In doing so, they were accused of stepping outside their proper sphere of domesticity and of violating the Victorian "cult of true womanhood." Their children also moved into the industrial workforce since little physical strength was required to carry out many of the tasks of the factory. Also, the owners could justify paying youngsters lower wages, which reduced production costs.

This scenario suggests that the processes of industrialization had the potential to alter the traditional structure of the American family wherein the husband and father was expected to provide the necessities of life. What happened to the family during the Industrial Revolution? How similar or different was it from the preindustrial family? Did industrialization have a sustaining or transformative impact on family life in the United States? These questions are addressed from different perspectives by the selections that follow.

Elaine Tyler May compares divorce records in California and New Jersey for the 1880s and 1920 and finds that the increased prosperity of the industrial era created money problems that affected marriages among the wealthy and the poor alike. In particular, assumptions of vastly improved material circumstances did not always match the realities of household income. As a result, arguments over money created a "pressure to provide" that led to the breakup of many families.

In contrast, Jacquelyn Dowd Hall, Robert Korstad, and James Leloudis emphasize factors that maintained family stability during the Industrial Revolution. Their study of the culture of cotton mill villages in the South after Reconstruction presents a portrait of a much smoother transition from farm to factory than is often associated with the Industrial Revolution. Specifically, they describe a work environment in the cotton mills that preserved rather than destroyed the traditional family labor system.

YES

Elaine Tyler May

The Pressure to Provide

In an era of massive production of consumer goods, what determines the normative standard of living, and what constitutes the necessities of life? These questions became increasingly difficult to answer during the decades surrounding the turn of the century, when profound economic changes ushered in corporate America. Scholars have documented a number of crucial developments, including standardized industrial technology, a mushrooming national bureaucracy, a shorter work week, and increased wages. Some observers hail these changes for providing security and material abundance to enhance the home and enrich private life. Others lament the loss of the craft tradition, and the intrinsic satisfactions that went with it. Still others claim that consumerism was a ploy to buy off workers and women, making them complacent while discouraging effective unionization and political action. But, as yet, no study has used empirical data to probe the impact of these developments on American families, or determined how they affected individuals on different levels of the class order. This article examines and compares the effects of heightened material aspirations upon wealthy, white-collar, and blue-collar Americans. While the rising standard of living may well have enhanced family life for some among the comfortable classes, it often wreaked havoc in the homes of those who could not afford the fruits of abundance. It is no accident that the emergence of the affluent society paralleled the skyrocketing of the American divorce rate.

One way to explore the way in which prosperity took its toll is to examine the casualties themselves. I have used hundreds of divorce cases filed during these years to uncover some of the economic problems that plagued American marriages. The samples include 500 litigations from Los Angeles in the 1880s, and another 500 from 1920. A comparative sample includes 250 divorces filed throughout New Jersey in 1920. The proceedings cover a developing west-coast city with little manufacturing, and an eastern industrial state with a large rural population. Within the samples are individuals from virtually every ethnic group and occupational category. By comparing the accusations mentioned in the 1880s and in 1920, we can determine the effects of economic change over time, during these crucial transitional years. The testimonies of the litigants in these cases reveal the limits of abundance, and suggest that no class or locale was immune to the ill effects of rising material aspirations.

From Elaine Tyler May, "The Pressure to Provide: Class, Consumerism, and Divorce in Urban America, 1880–1920," *Journal of Social History*, vol. 12, no. 2 (Winter 1978). Copyright © 1978 by *Journal of Social History*. *Reprinted by permission of Journal of Social History*; permission conveyed via Copyright Clearance Center. Notes omitted.

Obviously, financial problems did not erupt in American homes with the onset of the corporate economy. In fact, money conflicts appeared in divorce cases well before the 20th century. Yet the turn-of-the-century decades did witness a profound change. In the first place, the number of divorces increased dramatically. Secondly, issues surrounding money—who should make it, how much is adequate, and how it should be spent—became increasingly prevalent. The divorce samples from Los Angeles and New Jersey reflect this trend. Although the percentage of cases filed on the grounds of "neglect to provide" did not rise significantly between the two samples taken, these problems did become more complicated in the later decades. The Lynds found a similar development in Muncie, Indiana. In spite of the fairly constant rate of neglect complaints in divorce litigations from 1890 to the 1920s, "economic considerations figure possibly more drastically than formerly as factors in divorce."

At first glance, this appears rather perplexing. The nation was more prosperous in the later period than the earlier, and the standard of living was rising steadily for all classes. Moreover, women found greater opportunities to work, and both males and females experienced increasing wages and more free time off the job. During the same years, an unprecedented abundance of consumer goods became available on a mass level. Presumably, these developments would contribute to easing tensions between husbands and wives rather than creating them, while fostering a more pleasant, epressive, and comfortable existence. However, with the standard of living rising, and affluence filtering down to a greater proportion of the population, the "provider" was often expected to fulfill the increased demands sparked by widespread prosperity.

The evidence in the divorce proceedings suggests that this was not a major problem in the 1880s. Although financial conflicts appeared often, there was no controversy over what constituted the necessities of life. Either a husband supported his family, or he did not. Virtually all of the cases in the early sample that dealt with issues of neglect were clear-cut. If a man did not provide enough food, clothing, and shelter for his wife to live comfortably, she was entitled to a divorce. No husband questioned that; and no quarrels ensued over what his obligation entailed.

. . . Women who placed heavy demands upon their husbands were not merely selfish or lazy. Although these were the years of women's presumed "emancipation," females still faced limited options outside the home. Middle-class wives in particular may have felt restless as well as powerless. While their numbers in the work force increased, it was still considered undesirable for a married woman to work. If a wife did seek employment, she did not have access to the most lucrative, prestigious, and rewarding occupations. Most jobs available to women were routine and monotonous, with low pay and few chances for advancement.

What was left, then, to give these married females personal satisfaction? Even at home they may have felt a sense of uselessness. Childbearing and household responsibilities utilized less of a woman's creative energies as the birth rate declined and labor-saving devices proliferated. New avenues for self-expression had to be explored. The economy offered little in the way of jobs;

yet it provided seemingly unlimited possibilities for consumerism. Indeed, female emancipation found its most immediate expression not in the work force, but in the realms of styles and leisure pursuits. These were purchasable, provided one had the means. If wives began spending to adorn their homes and themselves, it may have reflected their constraints elsewhere. It is no wonder that, for some women, this gave rise to an obsession with material goods and private indulgence. Thus, they turned the full force of their pent-up energies to these endeavors.

With limited financial resources of their own, women often looked to men to provide the means for their consumption desires. This pressure was one of many new challenges facing 20th-century males. While public notice focused on new female activities, parallel shifts that affected men went virtually unnoticed. Males continued to work, their clothing styles remained practically unaltered, and their public behavior did not change dramatically. Yet they were experiencing a subtle transformation in sex-role expectations that, while not as obvious as the new status of women, was no less profound.

For white-collar men, the most far-reaching changes came with the maturation of the corporate system. The engulfing bureaucracies stabilized many uncertainties of the earlier era, and offered at least a modicum of security. The 20th-century businessman was less likely to enter business on his own, with the full burden of success or failure resting on his shoulders. If one followed the rules, he would advance up the hierarchy in a steady, predictable manner, and reach a moderate level of success and prosperity. There may have been [a] few examples of men making a fortune overnight within the modern system; but, in fact, the Carnegies of the previous era served as little more than encouragement to fantasies. The top of the ladder was virtually closed then as well as later. However, successful men had been models of 19th-century striving. In spite of new rewards, the corporations took away some of the unique triumphs of individual enterprise.

With the mechanization of industry, increasing production, the declining work week, and a rising standard of living, the benefits were obvious. In terms of purely material considerations, the corporate economy offered abundance and leisure. The tragedy, however, was that the aspiration for affluence was more widespread than the luxurious life itself. Even if an individual entered the white-collar ranks, he still faced enormous pressures to advance and succeed. Supplying increased demands necessitated continual striving. This was difficult enough for relatively successful businessmen, but infinitely more so for employees with modest salaries, or for petty proprietors without the cushion of corporate security.

We know from national statistics that the white-collar level of society shifted away from self-employed businessmen to corporate bureaucrats and clerical workers. Our Los Angeles samples reflect a similar trend. These white-collar groups, possibly more than any other level in society, were striving for upward mobility, afraid of slipping down the socioeconomic ladder, and concerned with deriving the fruits of their labor in tangible material goods. Arno Mayer has suggested that, historically, the petite bourgeoisie was possibly the most insecure and status-conscious level in western nations. This group had its own unique aspirations and cultural forms geared toward emulating the more affluent groups above them. If this premise holds for 20th-century America, and I believe it does, then petty proprietors facing competition from large corporations, as well as rank and file white-collar workers, would be feeling these pressures most intensely.

Looking at the divorce samples from Los Angeles, we find that, by 1920, the low-white-collar level is overrepresented, compared to its proportion of the general population. In the later sample, the proportion of divorces granted to the wealthy classes declined dramatically as the more bureaucratic clerical and sales categories mushroomed. At the same time, the percentage of petty proprietors in the work force shrank; but these small businessmen remained heavily overrepresented in the divorce samples. Those who remained among the entrepreneurial ranks may well have felt new pressures. As large chains and department stores began drawing local patrons and customers away from independent enterprises, owners of small shops and businesses may have faced increasing insecurity. To add to these burdens, many of them had to purchase goods from larger firms, making them dependent upon a national marketing system. Undersold by large competitors who often controlled production and supply as well as distribution, and bound by wholesale merchandise prices, they may have tried to cut costs by turning to family labor. This was not always a satisfactory solution, especially if proprietors of small concerns had to cope with diminishing returns as well as increasing consumer demands. It is perhaps no wonder that this group had more than its share of divorce.

Unfortunately, relatively few of the divorce litigants articulated how financial and status considerations affected their marriages and their lives. As with virtually every complex issue that eroded these relationships, we must glean insights from a handful of cases where evidence is rich and detailed. In terms of material considerations, we are able to discern a pattern of discontent for each of the major socioeconomic levels represented. . . . [A]ffluence did not preclude the possibility of money squabbles. The leisured wife of a man with means might make a quasi-career out of purchasing goods and adorning herself and her abode. Even wealthy husbands may have reacted against frivolous or wasteful expenditures. But if a man's income was consistently a measure below his wife's aspirations for comfortable living, the tension could become chronic and destroy a marriage that otherwise might have survived.

In the divorce proceedings, conflicts over status and mobility stand out in bold relief, particularly among white-collar families on the west coast. It is here that we can best perceive the intensified pressures placed upon men to supply heightened material desires. Norman Shinner, for example, admitted that he deserted his wife after five years of marriage because of his "inability to support her in the manner she desired on my salary, and on this account we could not live together in an amiable manner." Rather than struggling to meet up to his wife's aspirations, Norman Shinner simply left.

Oscar Lishnog faced similar difficulties. He married Martha in Chicago in 1908, and had four children prior to their Los Angeles divorce. While the Lishnogs appeared to be a fairly comfortable suburban family, financial strain ultimately caused their union to collapse. Oscar was in the insurance and real estate business, working as an employee or salesman rather than executive or proprietor. His income was steady but modest. He spent some time living apart from his family while working in San Pedro; nevertheless, Oscar and Martha exchanged frequent loving, chatty, but slightly distant letters to each other. He sent her money, she tried to save, and they expressed affection for one another. Now and then Martha would tell Oscar to "mind the store and not waste time or money." Revealing her material aspirations, she wrote that many of her neighbors owned automobiles, for there was no street car line nearby. This suggests that their Los Angeles home was in a fairly new suburban development, removed from the downtown district and transportation network. Martha also reminded her husband that she was paying mortgage on the house, and the "kids want a hammock." She usually closed with affection, saying she was "waiting for him."

But in 1920, Martha filed for divorce on the grounds of willful neglect, saying that Oscar spent his $35 per week salary in "riotous living away from his family," squandering his money while depriving his wife and children. Claiming that she was not skilled in any vocation, Martha said she had to rely on the charity of friends. She asked for custody of the children. Oscar denied the charges, insisting that he earned only $21 per week and gave it all to his wife except a small amount for living expenses. He asked that the divorce be denied, and, assuming that they would remain living apart, requested joint custody of the children. Nevertheless, the court granted Martha the divorce, plus custody, $9 per week for the children, and $3 per month for her "personal recreation." This final item, though minimal in amount, suggests that courts were willing to designate some money for amusements and consumption within the category of necessities—which men were required to provide. Whatever other problems may be hidden from our view that contributed to this couple's woes, it is clear that money was a sore spot for a long time. Oscar's salary was hardly abundant, and he was finally unable to supply the demands of his wife and children to maintain their suburban lifestyle.

Perhaps one of the most telling of these cases was the Los Angeles divorce of Margaret and Donald Wilton. She was a devout midwestern Protestant whose marriage to her clerk husband lasted two years. At one point, she wrote to her estranged spouse, hoping to be reconciled. She recommended that he read some bible passages relating to the duties of husbands and wives, and promised to be a "good Christian wife." In a revealing passage at the end, she wrote, "I heard something about you that made my heart sing with joy; you have climbed another rung on the ladder of success. I am proud to know it, dear. . . ." In spite of Donald's improved status, their marriage was beyond repair. After a rather bitter case, Margaret Wilton was granted a divorce.

Families such as the ones mentioned above may not have suffered severe deprivation. But, like other 20th-century couples, they faced a greater potential for disappointment when a modicum of luxury became the anticipated norm. As the standard of living continued to climb, the golden age of affluence seemed imminent, and it was anticipated with almost religious fervor. For much of the American population, increasing prosperity appeared as a signal from the Divine that the culmination of progress was at hand. One observer perceived, "To most people a millennium implies spiritual overtones.

So does the standard of living." For a male provider, then, inability to keep up with this sanctified progress meant failure and damnation.

Although these pressures were particularly acute for the lower middle class, they were also severe for workers. Financial difficulties among working-class couples, however, were qualitatively different from those facing white-collar families. Laborers faced a double-edged problem. They may not have felt the same status anxieties as petty proprietors or rank and file bureaucrats, but it was often difficult for them to make ends meet. Blue-collar families lived with the uncertainties of a fluid labor market and usually lacked the cushion of corporate security. Weak or non-existent labor unions left them virtually unprotected. This is not to deny the fact that some of the abundance filtered down among the working classes. By 1900, their improved circumstances prompted Samuel Gompers, when asked if he thought the conditions of workers were worsening, to reply, "Oh, that is perfectly absurd." In our samples, we find that financial conflicts among blue-collar families actually decreased somewhat between 1880 and 1920. However, their percentage of the total number of litigants increased markedly. This may reflect a number of factors. It is possible that in the 1880s, the very price of a divorce precluded legal action for many blue-collar couples. When they did come to court, nearly one-third of them included money conflicts among their complaints. By 1920, more workers may have been able to afford a divorce, and the wives might have been less likely to complain of financial desperation. Yet status and spending concerns might well have helped erode these unions as well. To add to the problem of meeting basic needs, working-class families also shared new consumer desires with their more affluent peers. But for those with meager incomes, luxuries were out of the question, and the affluence they saw everywhere around them only served to heighten frustrations.

Working-class couples, then, faced compounded difficulties. Often the breadwinner's earnings were inadequate and his job insecure. Moreover, he was subject to the same sorts of demands for mass-produced goods as his white-collar contemporaries. One of the crucial features of the consumer-oriented economy was the way it transcended class boundaries. On one level, this contributed to a certain superficial "classless" quality. But, on another level, it served to homogenize tastes in a society where wealth remained unequally distributed. Once self-esteem and validation came to rest upon supplying material goods, those on the bottom rungs would be considered less worthy. . . .

Alberta Raschke was a blue-collar wife in Los Angeles with a five-year-old daughter. She filed for a divorce on the grounds of desertion and neglect, claiming that her husband forced her to rely on her parents' charity. The couple married in Indiana in 1913, and separated four years later. At some point, Alberta came to California and William remained in Chicago. In a letter, she accused him of refusing to support her, and claimed that she was in a " weakened condition." "You have had ample time to *make a man of yourself* in all these six years, if you cared for your wife and baby, instead of driving a wagon for $12 a week. You would not take work offered you at $21 a week, so it is not because you could not find better. I stood for all the terrible abuse you gave me, and went without the very necessities of life to see if you would not come to your senses, but now I am tired of waiting and have decided to file suit for divorce . . . I am as ever Alberta."

Although Alberta Raschke probably had a valid complaint, the pressure put upon William to "make a man" of himself may have been unfair. It is not clear why he did not take the job allegedly offered to him for more pay, but perhaps he simply enjoyed what he was doing. The conflict between working at a job one liked and working for money may have ultimately led to this divorce. Although William Raschke apparently found the lower paying job more satisfying, as far as his wife was concerned the primary purpose of his work was to make money. Undoubtedly, it was not easy for this woman to live on $12 a week with a five-year-old child. However, the equation of manhood with the ability to provide placed a particularly heavy burden on a working-class husband.

In general, working-class wives were less obsessed with status considerations and more concerned with bread and butter issues. Most blue-collar divorces that included money difficulties revolved around basic needs, similar to the conflicts that surfaced in the 1880s proceedings. These problems erupted frequently in New Jersey, where the majority of divorces were among blue-collar couples. It is important to keep in mind that New Jersey only permitted divorces on the grounds of adultery and desertion—not financial neglect. Nevertheless, money was at the heart of many New Jersey litigations. In fact, a number of these couples struggled, quite literally, just to keep a roof over their heads.

A severe housing shortage in urban areas placed serious strains on several marriages. Providers with meager earnings often found themselves unable to provide a home. Numerous couples lived with parents or other relatives, or moved from one form of lodging to another. For these couples, the inability to acquire adequate housing was the fundamental issue that destroyed their marriages. The Shafers were one such family. "I want one thing," pleaded Anna Shafer to her husband. "Won't you please come back and make a home for me, I don't care if it is only two rooms, if you can afford to pay for two rooms." They had been married since 1910, when they ran away together to Hoboken, New Jersey. Anna claimed that William deserted her three years later. She said that her husband was "a drinking man who never made a home or provided for her and their child," although he worked for an insurance company. Anna was granted a divorce and restored to her maiden name. The same problems ended the marriage of Harris and Catherine Martin, two blue-collar workers in Newark. "I told him I would go anyplace with him as long as he could furnish me with a home," explained Catherine. "I didn't care where it was, even if it was only one room and I was alone." But after three months they separated, and Catherine was granted a divorce plus the return of her maiden name.

Lack of housing and insecure work also disrupted the marriage of a Jewish couple in New Jersey, Sarah and Morris Dubin, who married in 1910, and had one child that died. Morris was a tailor by trade, but was unable to practice his craft. Instead, he worked for the railroad, and as a cook in a sanitarium. It appears that this duo had a rather stormy marriage, with Morris deserting now and then and Sarah continually begging him to make a home for her. Whenever she asked, "Why won't you make me a home and support me?" he replied, "I won't and can't live in Newark with you." Newark was particularly plagued by the housing shortage at this time, which aggravated the situation for Morris, who was unable to find work that utilized his tailoring skills. But the court had little mercy. The interviewer concluded that Morris was "apparently one of those people who find it difficult to settle down and perform his obligations for any length of time." Sarah won her suit and the return of her maiden name.

Although a chronic shortage of basic needs eroded most of these blue-collar marriages, a number of working-class couples quarreled over consumer spending and status concerns as well. A few cases illustrate how squabbles might ensue over how money should be spent. Emma Totsworth was 19 when she married David Totsworth, a 22-year-old machinist, in Jersey City. Five years later she deserted. When asked about their difficulties, David said they argued "over different things, like going out and clothes, no clean clothes and all around jealousy. Simple meanness. She spent money on clothes that should have gone for eating." It appears that David Totsworth preferred to see his hard-earned income used for less frivolous items.

Charles and Ada Davis were plagued by similar problems. They were married in New Jersey in 1902 and had one child. After nine years, Ada deserted and went to New York. Apparently Charles, a railroad brakeman, never managed to provide for her in the style that she wanted. According to the interviewer, Ada became "dissatisfied with her surroundings and complained of the style of life her husband afforded her. She wouldn't speak or recognize her husband sometimes for days at a time. Finally she left, saying she wanted to live where she wanted to, and also wanted him to support her." Charles' brother stood up for the aggrieved husband, saying that he "always worked steadily and was a good provider for his home and did everything he could for his wife and family that a man could do under his circumstances." But apparently it was not enough. Charles testified that Ada "insisted upon telling me how much more the neighbors had than she had, and what the neighbor's husband did, and what they didn't do. I told her that if she would stop listening to outsiders and live for me and our little girl as she had done up to that time, everything could be very nice and we could get along." But Ada's dissatisfaction increased until she finally left, and Charles was granted a New Jersey divorce on the grounds of desertion.

These blue-collar couples were plagued by status anxieties. Both Emma Totsworth and Ada Davis had aspirations for material goods beyond the reach of their husbands' pay checks. Some wives not only held their spouses' incomes in disdain, they also looked down upon the work itself. Olivia Garside was a New Jersey housekeeper bent on feverish social climbing. After 26 years of marriage and three children, she finally left her husband Frederick, a machinist, who could not supply the lifestyle she craved. According to Frederick,

> My wife never considered me her equal. She told me this shortly after her marriage, and she was never satisfied with anything I might undertake to do and that I was not as neat appearing as a professional man. She would say my conversation wasn't as it should be and she felt I was socially beneath her. I have always turned over every cent I made to my wife

outside of my travelling expenses. I have never been intoxicated in my life. I would very often work overtime and on Sundays around the neighborhood to earn a few dollars more. My wife always complained I wasn't making enough money.

This husband took pride in his hard work, his efforts to support his wife, his sobriety and discipline. But to his wife, he lacked polish and grace—and the ample income to go with it. The court granted Frederick a divorce on the grounds of desertion.

The evidence in these cases suggests that mass consumption was not necessarily a positive outgrowth of the society's industrial development, even though it held the potential for increased financial security and a more comfortable lifestyle. Rather, these marital conflicts represent a failure or inability to come to terms with the changing economic order. For affluent couples, tensions emerged over how the family's resources should be spent. For those among the lower-white-collar ranks, status considerations clashed with limited incomes, creating enormous pressures upon the family breadwinner. For many working-class couples, mass consumption remained virtually out of reach, contributing to a greater sense of economic insecurity and heightened frustrations.

The testimonies of divorce litigants reflect the discrepancy between material desires and reality, for it was difficult to meet the soaring demands put before every consumer's eyes. Perhaps many Americans did indeed benefit from new opportunities created by the mature industrial system. But among those whose marriages fell apart during these years, and undoubtedly among thousands more whose thoughts and feelings are beyond the reach of scholars, there was a great deal of disappointment, disillusion, and despair that the good life they had hoped for could not be grasped.

Jacquelyn Dowd Hall, Robert Korstad, and James Leloudis

Cotton Mill People

Textile mills built the New South. Beginning in the 1880s, business and professional men tied their hopes for prosperity to the whirring of spindles and the beating of looms. Small-town boosterism supplied the rhetoric of the mill-building campaign, but the impoverishment of farmers was industrialization's driving force. The post–Civil War rise of sharecropping, tenantry, and the crop lien ensnared freedmen, then eroded yeoman society. Farmers of both races fought for survival by clinging to subsistence strategies and habits of sharing even as they planted cash crops and succumbed to tenantry. Meanwhile, merchants who had accumulated capital through the crop lien invested in cotton mills. As the industry took off in an era of intensifying segregation, blacks were relegated to the land, and white farmers turned to yet another strategy for coping with economic change. They had sold their cotton to the merchant; now they supplied him with the human commodity needed to run his mills. This home-grown industry was soon attracting outside capital and underselling northern competitors. By the end of the Great Depression, the Southeast replaced New England as the world's leading producer of cotton cloth, and the industrializing Piedmont replaced the rural Coastal Plain as pacesetter for the region.

Despite the lasting imprint of textile manufacturing on regional development and labor relations, we have no modern survey of the industry's evolution. Nor has the outpouring of research on working-class history been much concerned with factory workers in the New South. To be sure, recent studies have uncovered sporadic, and sometimes violent, contention over the shape of the industrial South. But those findings have done little to shake the prevailing wisdom: The South's mill villages supposedly bred a "social type" compounded of irrationality, individualism, and fatalism. Unable to unite in their own interests, textile workers remained "silent, incoherent, with no agency to express their needs."

We have reached different conclusions. Our research began with a collaborative oral history project aimed at discovering how working people made sense of their own experience. We did not view memory as a direct window on the past. But we did presume the moral and intellectual value of listening to those who lacked access to power and, thus, the means of affecting historical debate. Our effort was repaid in two major ways. Oral autobiographies dissolved static images, replacing them with portrayals of mill village culture drawn by the men and women who helped create it. Workers' narratives also steered us away from psychological interpretations and toward patterns of resistance, cultural creativity, and structural evolution. Later we turned to the trade press, particularly the *Southern Textile Bulletin*. Published by David Clark in Charlotte, North Carolina, the *Bulletin* spoke for factory owners at the cutting edge of industrial innovation. Finally, from the eloquent letters textile workers wrote to Franklin D. Roosevelt and the National Recovery Administration, we gained a view of the New Deal from below. Together, retrospective and contemporary evidence revealed the social logic that underlay daily practices and suggested an analysis that distinguished one epoch from another in a broad process of technological, managerial, and cultural change.

⁓◈⁓

Nothing better symbolized the new industrial order than the mill villages that dotted the Piedmont landscape. Individual families and small groups of local investors built and owned most of the early mills. Run by water wheels, factories flanked the streams that fell rapidly from the mountains toward the Coastal Plain. Of necessity, owners provided housing where none had been before. But the setting, scale, and structure of the mill village reflected rural expectations as well as practical considerations. Typically, a three-story brick mill, a company store, and a superintendent's house were clustered at one end of the village. Three- and four-room frame houses, owned by the company but built in a vernacular style familiar in the countryside, stood on lots that offered individual garden space, often supplemented by communal pastures and hog pens. A church, a company store, and a modest schoolhouse completed the scene. By 1910 steam power and electricity had freed the mills from their dependence on water power, and factories sprang up on the outskirts of towns along the route of the Southern Railway. Nevertheless, the urban mill village retained its original rural design. Company-owned villages survived in part because they fostered management control. Unincorporated "mill hills" that surrounded towns such as Charlotte and Burlington, North Carolina, and Greenville, South Carolina, enabled owners to avoid taxes and excluded workers from municipal government. But the mill village also reflected the workers' heritage and served their needs.

Like the design of the mill village, the family labor system helped smooth the path from field to factory. On farms women and children had always provided essential labor, and mill owners took advantage of these traditional roles. They promoted factory work as a refuge for impoverished women and children from the countryside, hired family units rather than individuals, and required the labor of at least one worker per room as a condition for residence in a mill-owned house. But this labor system also dovetailed with family strategies. The first to arrive in the mills were those least essential to farming and most vulnerable to the hazards of commercial agriculture: widows, female heads of households, single women, and itinerant laborers. By the turn of the century, families headed by men also lost their hold on the land. Turning to the mills, they sought not a "family wage" that would enable a man to support his dependents but an arena in which parents and children could work together as they had always done.

The deployment of family labor also helped maintain permeable boundaries between farm and mill. The people we interviewed moved with remarkable ease from farming to mill work and back again or split their family's time between the two. James Pharis's father raised tobacco in the Leaksville-Spray area of North Carolina until most of his six children were old enough to obtain mill jobs. The family moved to a mill village in the 1890s because the elder Pharis "felt that all we had to do when we come to town was to reach up and pull the money off of the trees." From the farm Pharis saved his most valuable possession: his team of horses. While the children worked in the mill, he raised vegetables on a plot of rented ground and used his team to do "hauling around for people." Betty Davidson's landowning parents came up with the novel solution of sharing a pair of looms. "My father would run the looms in the wintertime," Davidson remembered, "and go to and from work by horseback. And in the summertime, when he was farming, my mother run the looms, and she stayed in town because she couldn't ride the horse. Then, on the weekends, she would come home."

This ability to move from farming to factory work—or combine the two—postponed a sharp break with rural life. It also gave mill workers a firm sense of alternative identity and leverage against a boss's demands. Lee Workman recalled his father's steadfast independence. In 1918 the superintendent of a nearby cotton mill came to the Workmans' farm in search of workers to help him meet the demand for cloth during World War I. The elder Workman sold his mules and cow but, contrary to the superintendent's advice, held on to his land. Each spring he returned to shoe his neighbors' horses, repair their wagons and plows, and fashion the cradles they used to harvest grain. "He'd tell the superintendent, 'You can just get somebody else, because I'm going back to make cradles for my friends.' Then he'd come back in the wintertime and work in the mill." This type of freedom did not sit well with the mill superintendent, but the elder Workman had the upper hand. "'Well,' he told them, 'if you don't want to do that, I'll move back to the country and take the family.'"

Although Lee Workman's father periodically retreated to the farm, his sons and daughters, along with thousands of others, eventually came to the mills to stay. There they confronted an authority more intrusive than anything country folk had experienced before. In Bynum, North Carolina, the mill owner supervised the Sunday School and kept tabs on residents' private lives. "If you stubbed your toe they'd fire you. They'd fire them here for not putting out the lights late at night. Old Mr. Bynum used to go around over the hill at nine o'clock and see who was up. And, if you were up, he'd knock on the door and tell you to cut the lights out and get into bed." Along with surveillance came entanglement with the company story. Mill hands all too familiar with the crop lien once again found themselves in endless debt. Don Faucette's father often talked about it. "Said if you worked at the mill they'd just take your wages and put it in the company store and you didn't get nothing. For years and years they didn't get no money, just working for the house they lived in and what they got at the company store. They just kept them in the hole all the time."

The mill village undeniably served management's interests, but it also nurtured a unique workers' culture. When Piedmont farmers left the land and took a cotton mill job, they did not abandon old habits and customs. Instead, they fashioned familiar ways of thinking and acting into a distinctively new way of life. This adaptation occurred at no single moment in time; rather, it evolved, shaped and reshaped by successive waves of migration off the farm as well as the movement of workers from mill to mill. Village life was based on family ties. Kinship networks facilitated migration to the mill and continued to play a powerful integrative role. Children of the first generation off the land married newcomers of the second and third, linking households into broad networks of obligation, responsibility, and concern. For many couples, marriage evolved out of friendships formed while growing up in the village. One married worker recalled, "We knowed each other from childhood. Just raised up together, you might say. All lived here on the hill, you see, that's how we met." As single workers arrived, they, too, were incorporated into the community. Mary Thompson explained that the boarding houses run by widowed women and older couples "were kind of family like. There ain't no place like home, but I guess that's the nearest place like home there is, a boarding house." Mill folk commonly used a family metaphor to describe village life. Hoyle McCorkle remembered the Highland Park mill village in Charlotte as a single household knit together by real and fictive kin: "It was kind of one big family; it was a 200–house family."

Mill hands also brought subsistence strategies from the countryside, modifying them to meet mill village conditions. Just as farmers had tried to bypass the furnishing merchant, mill workers struggled to avoid "living out of a tin can." Edna Hargett's father planted a large garden every spring but could not afford a mule to help till the land. He made do by putting a harness around himself and having his children "stand behind and guide the plow." Louise Jones's family also gardened and raised "homemade meat." Her parents "had a big garden and a corn patch and a few chickens around the yard. We'd have maybe six or eight hens, and we'd let the hens set on the eggs and hatch chickens and have frying-size chickens, raise our own fryers." Self-sufficiency, however, was difficult to achieve, especially when every family member was working a ten- to twelve-hour day for combined wages that barely made ends meet. Even with their gardens, few families could sustain a varied diet through the winter months. As a result, pellagra was a scourge in the mill villages. Life was lived close to the bone.

Under these conditions, necessity and habit fostered rural traditions of mutual aid. Although each family claimed a small plot of land, villagers shared what they grew and "live[d] in common." In late summer and early fall, they gathered for the familiar rituals of harvest and hog killing. Paul and Don Faucette remembered how it was done in Glencoe, North Carolina. "We'd kill our hogs this time, and a month later we'd kill yours. Well, you can give us some, and we can give you some. They'd have women get together down in the church basement. They'd have a quilting bee, and they'd go down and they'd all quilt. They'd have a good crop of cabbage, [and] they'd get together and all make kraut." Villagers helped one another, not with an expectation of immediate return but with the assurance of community support in meeting their individual needs. "They'd just visit around and work voluntarily. They all done it, and nobody owed nobody nothing."

Cooperation provided a buffer against misery and want at a time when state welfare services were limited and industrialists often refused to assume responsibility for job-related sickness and injury. It bound people together and reduced their dependence on the mill owners' charity. When someone fell ill, neighbors were quick to give the stricken family a "pounding." "They'd all get together and help. They'd cook food and carry it to them—all kinds of food—fruits, vegetables, canned goods." Villagers also aided sick neighbors by taking up a "love offering" in the mill. Edna Hargett organized such collections in the weave room at the Chadwick-Hoskins Mill in Charlotte. "When the neighbors got paid they'd come and pay us, and we'd take their money and give it to [the family of the weaver who was ill], and they'd be so proud of it, because they didn't have any wage coming in." To the people we interviewed, the village was "just one big community and one big family" whose members "all kind of hung together and survived."

Community solidarity did not come without a price. Neighborliness could shade into policing; it could repress as well as sustain. Divorced women and children born out of wedlock might be ostracized, and kinship ties could give mill supervisors an intelligence network that reached into every corner of the village. Alice Evitt of Charlotte remarked that "people then couldn't do like they do now. They was talked about. My daddy would never allow us to be with people that was talked about. This was the nicest mill hill I ever lived on. If anybody done anything wrong and you reported them, they had to move." A Bynum proverb summed up the double-edged quality of village life. "If you went along, they'd tend to their business and yours, too, if you let them, your neighbors would. Tend to your business and theirs, too. And the old saying here, you know, 'Bynum's red mud. If you stick to Bynum, it'll stick to you when it rains.'"

Given such tensions, we were struck by how little ambivalence surfaced in descriptions of mill village life. Recollections of factory work were something else again, but the village—red mud and all—was remembered with affection. The reasons are not hard to find. A commitment to family and friends represented a realistic appraisal of working people's prospects in the late nineteenth and early twentieth-century South. Only after World War II, with the expansion of service industries, did the Piedmont offer alternatives to lowwage factory work to more than a lucky few. Until then, casting one's lot with others offered more promise and certainly more security than the slim hope of individual gain. To be sure, mill people understood the power of money; they struggled against dependency and claimed an economic competence as their due. Nevertheless, they had "their own ideas . . . about what constitute[d] the 'good life.'" Communal values, embodied in everyday behavior, distance mill folk from the acquisitiveness that characterized middle-class life in New South towns. . . .

The physical and social geography of the mill village . . . was less a product of owners' designs than a compromise between capitalist organization and workers' needs. For a more clear-cut embodiment of the manufacturers' will, we must look to the factory. The ornate facades of nineteenth-century textile mills reflected their builders' ambitions and the orderly world they hoped to create. The mill that still stands at Glencoe is an excellent example. Situated only a few hundred yards from the clapboard houses that make up the village, the mill is a three-story structure complete with "stair tower, corbelled cornice, quoined stucco corners, and heavily stuccoed window labels." In contrast to the vernacular form of the village, the architecture of the factory, modeled on that of New England's urban mills, was highly self-conscious, formal, and refined.

At Glencoe, and in mills throughout the Piedmont, manufacturers endeavored to shape the southern yeomanry into a tractable industrial workforce. Workers' attitudes toward factory labor, like those toward village life, owed much to the cycles and traditions of the countryside. Owners, on the other hand, sought to substitute for cooperation and task orientation a labor system controlled from the top down and paced by the regular rhythms of the machine. Barring adverse market conditions, work in the mills varied little from day to day and season to season. Workers rose early in the morning, still tired from the day before, and readied themselves for more of the same. For ten, eleven, and twelve hours they walked, stretched, leaned, and pulled at their machines. Noise, heat, and humidity engulfed them. The lint that settled on their hair and skin marked them as mill workers to the outside world. The cotton dust that silently entered their lungs could also kill them.

Owners enforced this new pattern of labor with the assistance of a small coterie of supervisors. As a rule, manufacturers delegated responsibility for organizing work and disciplining the help to a superintendent and his overseers and second hands. A second hand in a pre-World War I mill recalled, "You had the cotton, the machinery, and the people, and you were supposed to get out the production. How you did it was pretty much up to you; it was production management was interested in and not how you got it." Under these circumstances, supervision was a highly personal affair; there were as many different approaches to its problems as there were second hands and overseers. As one observer explained, "There was nothing that could be identified as a general pattern of supervisory practice."

At times, discipline could be harsh, erratic, and arbitrary. This was particularly true before 1905, when most workers in southern mills were women and children. Even supervisors writing in the *Southern Textile Bulletin* admitted that "some overseers, second hands, and section men have a disposition to abuse the help. Whoop, holler, curse, and jerk the children around." James Pharis remembered that "you used to work for the supervisor because you were scared. I seen a time when I'd walk across the road to keep from meeting my supervisor. They was the hat-stomping kind. If you done anything, they'd throw their hat on the floor and stomp it and raise hell."

In the absence of either state regulation or trade unions, management's power seemed limitless, but there were, in fact, social and structural constraints. Although manufacturers relinquished day-to-day authority to underlings, they were ever-present figures, touring the mill, making decisions on wages and production quotas, and checking up on the help. These visits were, in part, attempts to maintain the appearance of paternalism and inspire hard work and company loyalty. At the same time, they divided power in the mill. Workers had direct access to the owner and sometimes saw him as a buffer between themselves and supervisors, a "force that could bring an arbitrary and unreasonable [overseer] back into line." Mack Duncan recalled that in the early years "most all the mill owners seemed like they had a little milk of human kindness about them, but some of the people they hired didn't. Some of the managers didn't have that. They were bad to exploit people." Under these circumstances, the commands of an overseer were always subject to review. Workers felt free to complain about unjust treatment, and owners, eager to keep up production, sometimes reversed their lieutenants' orders. Federal labor investigators reported in 1910 that "when an employee is dissatisfied about mill conditions he may obtain a hearing from the chief officer of the mill . . . and present his side of the case. Not infrequently when complaints are thus made, the overseer is overruled and the operative upheld." . . .

⋅◈⋅

[The] tradeoff between a relatively relaxed work pace on the one hand and long hours and low wages on the other was tenuous at best. Despite manufacturers' efforts to create a secure world in the mill and village, there were recurrent symptoms of unrest. During the 1880s and 1890s, southern mill hands turned first to the Knights of Labor and then to the National Union of Textile Workers (NUTW) to defend their "freedom and liberty." In 1900 an intense conflict led by the NUTW flared in Alamance County, center of textile manufacturing in North Carolina, when an overseer at the Haw River Mill fired a female weaver for leaving her loom unattended. The next day, September 28, union members "threw up" their machines, defending the woman's right to "go when she pleased and where she pleased." By mid-October, workers at other mills throughout the county had joined in a sympathy strike.

The mill owners, conveniently overstocked with surplus goods, posted armed guards around their factories, declared they would employ only nonunion labor, and threatened to evict union members from company-owned houses. Undeterred, the workers resolved to stand together as "free men and free women"; five thousand strong, they brought production in Alamance mills virtually to a halt. But by the end of November evictions had overwhelmed the NUTW's relief fund, and the Alamance mill hands were forced to accept a settlement on management's terms.

The Haw River strike capped more than two decades of unrest. During those years, Populists and factory laborers challenged the power of planters, merchants, and industrialists. Between 1895 and 1902, southern Democrats turned to race baiting, fraud, and intimidation to destroy this interracial movement. The passage of state constitutional amendments disfranchising blacks and many poor whites, accompanied by a flurry of Jim Crow laws, restructured the political system, narrowing the terms of public discourse, discouraging lower-class political participation, and making it impossible for opposition movements to survive.

As prospects for collective protest diminished, Piedmont mill hands opted for a personal strategy as old as the industry itself—relocation. In Alamance County alone, more than three hundred workers left to find new jobs in south Carolina and Georgia. "Among them," reported the *Alamance Gleaner*, "are a great many excellent people who prefer to go elsewhere rather than surrender rights and privileges which they as citizens deem they should own and enjoy." In choosing to leave in search of better conditions, the Haw River workers set a pattern for decades to come. Until the end of World War I, quitting was textile workers' most effective alternative to public protest or acquiescence. One student of the southern textile industry declared that a mill hand's "ability to move at a moment's notice was his Magna Carta, Declaration of Independence, and Communist Manifesto."

This movement from job to job could be touched off by any number of factors—curtailed production, a promise of higher wages, or a simple desire to move on—but it could also be a response to a perceived abuse of authority. Josephine Glenn of Burlington explained. "A lot of people in textile mills come and go. They're more or less on a cycle. They're not like that as a whole, but a lot of them are. They're dissatisfied, you might say, restless. They just go somewhere and work awhile, and, if everything don't go just like they think it should, why, they walk out. Sometimes they'd be mad, and sometimes they'd just get on a bender and just not come back. Maybe something personal, or maybe something about the work, or just whatever they got mad about. They'd just [say], 'I've had it,' and that was it." Workers expected to be treated with respect; when it was lacking, they left. George Dyer of Charlotte offered this advice: "Sometimes some boss don't like you, gets it in for you. It's best then just to quit. Don't work under conditions like that. I didn't want to work under a man that don't respect me."

The decision to move was usually made by men, and it could be hard on women and children. Family ties could fray under the wear and tear of factory life. Although Edna Hargett also worked in the mills, she was evicted from her house every time her husband quit his job. "He was bad about getting mad and quitting. He was just hot-tempered and didn't like it when they wanted to take him off his job and put him on another job. When you work in the card room, you have to know how to run about every piece of machinery in there. He liked to be a slubber, and they wanted to put him on drawing or something else. Well, he didn't like to do that." Edna understood her husband's motives but finally left to settle down and rear their children on her own.

Divorce, however, was uncommon. Most families stayed together, and their moves from mill to mill were facilitated by kinship and cushioned by community. A study completed in the late 1920s revealed that 41 percent of mill families had moved less than three times in ten years. Most settled families were headed by middle-aged men and women who had "just kept the road hot" before and immediately after marriage and had then stayed in a village they liked. This relatively stable core of residents made movement possible by providing the contacts through which other workers learned of job opportunities.

Established residents also mitigated the ill effects of transiency and preserved ways of life that made it easy for newcomers to feel at home. Women played central roles in this process, keeping up with the events in the village, coordinating informal acts of relief, and keeping the web of social relations intact.

In these ways, the Piedmont became what journalist Arthur W. Page described in 1907 as "one long mill village." Individual communities were woven together—through kinship, shared occupational experiences, and popular culture—into an elaborate regional fabric. According to Lacy Wright, who worked at Greensboro's White Oak Mill, "We had a pretty fair picture, generally speaking, of what you might say was a 200-mile radius of Greensboro. News traveled by word of mouth faster than any other way in those days, because that's the only way we had. In other words, if something would happen at White Oak this week, you could go over to Danville, Virginia, by the weekend and they'd done heard about it. It looked like it always worked out that there would be somebody or another that would carry that information all around." Rooted in a regional mill village culture, workers like Wright took the entire Piedmont as their frame of reference.

POSTSCRIPT

Did the Industrial Revolution Disrupt the American Family?

In his study of family life in Plymouth Colony, John Demos identifies six important functions performed by the family in preindustrial America. As the central social unit, says Demos, the family served as business, school, vocational institute, church, house of correction, and welfare institution. This pattern prevailed for the most part until the Industrial Revolution, when these traditional functions began to be delegated to institutions outside the household. For example, children received their formal education in public schools and private academies established for that purpose, rather than from their parents. Similarly, religious instruction occurred more often than not in a church building on Sunday morning, not in a home where family members gathered around a table for Bible readings. The explanation for this change is that work opportunities existed outside the home, and various family members were spending less and less time in the physical presence of one another because of the exigencies of the industrial workplace. See John Demos, *A Little Commonwealth: Family Life in Plymouth Colony* (Oxford University Press, 1970) and *Past, Present, and Personal: The Family and the Life Course in American History* (Oxford University Press, 1986).

May's work offers a variation of Demos's interpretation by focusing upon the destructive influence of industrialization on the family, but May is less concerned with the altered functions of the family than with the powerful influence of heightened expectations of the acquisition of material wealth. Hall, Korstad, and Leloudis, on the other hand, suggest that the changes produced in American families were not as drastic as some scholars believe. Their portrait of cotton mill workers reveals significant levels of continuity with the rural past and the family labor patterns that were not all that different from those described by Demos for seventeenth-century Plymouth.

The study of the history of families is an outgrowth of the "new social history" that began to emerge in the 1960s. Since that time, scholars have devoted considerable attention to such topics as changing household structure and the influence of economic forces on family units and individual family members. For a general summary of the scholarly attention given to the American family, see Estelle B. Freedman's essay "The History of the Family and the History of Sexuality," in Eric Foner, ed., *The New American History*, rev. and exp. ed. (Temple University Press, 1997). Carl Degler, *At Odds: Women and the Family in America* (Oxford University Press, 1980); Steven Mintz and Susan Kellogg, *Domestic Revolutions: A Social History of American Family Life* (Free Press, 1988); and Stephanie Coontz, *The Social Origins of Private Life: A History of American Families, 1600–1900* (Verso, 1988) present introductory surveys of American family history. May expands the coverage of some of the issues explored in her essay in *Great Expectations: Marriage and Divorce in Post-Victorian America* (University of Chicago Press, 1980). Additional works addressing southern families in the industrial era include Carol Bleser, ed., *In Joy and in Sorrow: Women, Family, and Marriage in the Victorian South* (Oxford University Press, 1991) and Peter Bardaglio, *Reconstructing the Household: Families, Sex and the Law in the Nineteenth-Century South* (University of North Carolina Press, 1995). Tamara Hareven, *Family Time and Industrial Time: The Relationship Between the Family and Work in a New England Industrial Community* (Cambridge University Press, 1982) and Michael Grossberg, *Governing the Hearth: Law and the Family in Nineteenth-Century America* (University of North Carolina Press, 1985) are important monographs of the industrial era. For studies of family life among African Americans and immigrants, see E. Franklin Frazier, *The Negro Family in the United States* (University of Chicago Press, 1939); Herbert G. Gutman, *The Black Family in Slavery and Freedom, 1750-1925* (Pantheon, 1976); Virginia Yans McLaughlin, *Family and Community: Italian Immigrants in Buffalo, 1880-1930* (Cornell University Press, 1977); and Judith Smith, *Family Connections: A History of Italian and Jewish Immigrant Lives in Providence, Rhode Island, 1900-1940* (State University of New York Press, 1985). Finally, for the past quarter century, cutting-edge scholarship on the American family has appeared in the issues of the *Journal of Family History.*

ISSUE 5

Did Nineteenth-Century Women of the West Fail to Overcome the Hardships of Living on the Great Plains?

YES: Christine Stansell, from "Women on the Great Plains 1865–1890," *Women's Studies* (vol. 4, 1976)

NO: Glenda Riley, from *A Place to Grow: Women in the American West* (Harlan Davidson, 1992)

ISSUE SUMMARY

YES: Professor of history Christine Stansell contends that women on the Great Plains were torn from their eastern roots, isolated in their home environment, and separated from friends and relatives. She concludes that they consequently endured lonely lives and loveless marriages.

NO: Professor of history Glenda Riley argues that in spite of enduring harsh environmental, political, and personal conditions on the Great Plains, women created rich and varied social lives through the development of strong support networks.

In 1893 young historian Frederick Jackson Turner (1861–1932) delivered an address before the American Historical Association entitled "The Significance of the Frontier in American History." Turner's essay not only sent him from Wisconsin to Harvard University, it became one of the most important essays ever written in American history. According to Turner's thesis, American civilization was different from European civilization because the continent contained an abundance of land that was settled in four waves of migration from 1607 through 1890. During this process the European heritage was shed and the American characteristics of individualism, mobility, nationalism, and democracy developed.

This frontier theory of American history did not go unchallenged. Some historians argued that Turner's definition of the frontier was too vague and imprecise; he underestimated the cultural forces that came to the West from

Europe and the eastern states; he neglected the forces of urbanization and industrialization in opening the West; he placed an undue emphasis on sectional developments and neglected class struggles for power; and, finally, his provincial view of American history prolonged the isolationist views of a nation that had become involved in world affairs in the twentieth century. By the time Turner died, his thesis had been widely discredited. Historians continued to write about the West, but new fields and new theories were competing for attention.

Younger historians have begun to question the traditional interpretation of western expansion. For example, the older historians believed that growth was good and automatically brought forth progress. New historians William Cronin, Patricia Limerick, and others, however, have questioned this assumption in examining the disastrous ecological effects of American expansionism, such as the elimination of the American buffalo and the depletion of forests.

Until recently, most historians did not consider women part of western history. One scholar who searched 2,000 pages of Turner's work could find only one paragraph devoted to women. Men built the railroads, drove the cattle, led the military expeditions, and governed the territories. "Women," said one writer, "were invisible, few in number, and not important to the taming of the West."

When scholars did acknowledge the presence of women on the frontier, perceptions were usually based on stereotypes that were created by male observers and had become prevalent in American literature. According to professor of history Sandra L. Myres (1933–1991), there were three main images. The first image was that of a frightened, tearful woman who lived in a hostile environment and who was overworked and overbirthed, depressed and lonely, and resigned to a hard life and an early death. The second image, in contrast, was of a helpmate and a civilizer of the frontier who could fight Indians as well as take care of the cooking, cleaning, and rearing of the children. A third image of the westering woman was that of the "bad woman," who was more masculine than feminine in her behavior and who was "hefty, grotesque and mean with a pistol."

The proliferation of primary source materials since the early 1970s—letters, diaries, and memoirs written by frontierswomen—led to a reassessment of the role of westering women. They are no longer what professor of history Joan Hoff-Wilson once referred to as the "orphans of women's history." There are disagreements in interpretation, but they are based upon sound scholarship. One area where scholars disagree is how women were changed by their participation in the westward movements of the nineteenth century.

In the following selection, Christine Stansell, arguing from a feminist perspective, asserts that women on the Great Plains were torn from their eastern roots, isolated in their home environments, and forced to endure lonely lives and loveless marriages because they could not create networks of female friendships. In the second selection, Glenda Riley argues that in spite of harsh environmental, political, and personal conditions on the Great Plains, women were able to create rich and varied social lives through the development of strong support networks.

Women on the Great
Plains 1865–1890

In 1841, Catharine Beecher proudly attested to the power of her sex by quoting some of Tocqueville's observations on the position of American women. On his tour of 1831, Tocqueville had found Americans to be remarkably egalitarian in dividing social power between the sexes. In his opinion, their ability to institute democratic equality stemmed from a clearcut division of work and responsibilities: "in no country has such constant care been taken . . . to trace two clearly distinct lines of action for the two sexes, and to make them keep pace with the other, but in two pathways which are always different." In theory, men and women controlled separate "spheres" of life: women held sway in the home, while men attended to economic and political matters. Women were not unaware of the inequities in a trade-off between ascendancy in the domestic sphere and participation in society as a whole. Attached to the metaphorical bargain struck between the sexes was a clause ensuring that women, through "home influence," could also affect the course of nation-building. For Miss Beecher, domesticity was also imperial power "to American women, more than to any others on earth, is committed the exalted privilege of extending over the world those blessed influences, which are to renovate degraded man, and 'clothe all climes with beauty.'"

Yet despite Beecher's assertions to the contrary, by 1841 one masculine "line of action" was diverging dangerously from female influences. Increasing numbers of men were following a pathway which led them across the Mississippi to a land devoid of American women and American homes. In the twenty-odd years since the Santa Fe trade opened the Far West to American businessmen, only men, seeking profits in furs or trading, had gone beyond the western farmlands of the Mississippi Valley; no women participated in the first stages of American expansion. Consequently, by 1841 the West was in one sense a geographical incarnation of the masculine sphere, altogether untouched by "home influence." Although in theory American development preserved a heterosexually balanced democracy, in actuality, the West, new arena of political and economic growth, had become a man's world.

In 1841, the first Americans intending to settle in the trans-Mississippi region rather than only trap or trade began to migrate over the great overland road to the coast. For the first time, women were present in the caravans, and in the next decades, thousands of women in families followed. Their wagon trains generally carried about one-half men, one-half women and children: a population with the capacity to reinstate a heterosexual culture. Only during the Gold Rush years, 1849–1852, were most of the emigrants once again male. Many of the forty-niners, however, chose to return East rather than to settle. In the aftermath of the Rush, the numerical balance of men and women was restored. By 1860, the sex ratio in frontier counties, including those settled on the Great Plains, was no different from the average sex ratio in the East.

Despite the heterosexual demography, however, the West in the years after 1840 still appeared to be masculine terrain. Everywhere, emigrants and travellers saw "such lots of men, but very few ladies and children." In mining camps, "representatives of the gentler sex were so conspicuous by their absence that in one camp a lady's bonnet and boots were exhibited for one dollar a look." Similarly, "the Great Plains in the early period was strictly a man's country." Even later, historians agree that "the Far West had a great preponderance of men over women," and that the absence of "mothers and wives to provide moral anchorage to the large male population" was a primary cause of its social ills. What accounts for the disparity between these observations and the bare facts of demography? In many frontier regions, women failed to reinstitute their own sphere. Without a cultural base of their own, they disappeared behind the masculine preoccupations and social structure which dominated the West. Despite their numbers, women were often invisible, not only in the first two decades of family settlement but in successive phases as well.

In this [selection], I try to sketch out some ways of understanding how the fact of this masculine imperium affected women's experiences in the great trans-Mississippi migrations. The following pages are in no way a monograph but rather a collection of suggestions which I have developed through reading and teaching about the West, and which I hope will encourage others to begin investigating this neglected area. Western migration constituted a critical rite of passage in nineteenth century culture; its impact still reverberates a century later in our own "Western" novels, movies, and television serials. Women's relationship to this key area of the "American experience" has remained submerged and unquestioned. There are only a few secondary books on women in the West, and the two best-known works are simplistic and sentimental. Few writers or scholars have attempted to look at frontier women in the light of the newer interpretations of women's history which have evolved over the last four years. There are a wealth of questions to investigate and a wealth of sources to use. To demonstrate how new analyses can illuminate conventional teaching and lecture material, I have chosen one clearly defined area of "pioneer experience," settlers on the Great Plains from 1865–1890. . . .

Until after the Civil War, emigrants usually travelled over the Great Plains without a thought of stopping. Explorers, farmers, and travellers agreed that the dry grasslands of the "Great American Desert"—the Dakotas, western Kansas, and western Nebraska—were not suitable for lucrative cultivation. In the late 60's, however, western land-grant railroads attempting to boost profits from passenger fares and land sales by promoting settlement in the region launched an advertising campaign in America and Europe which portrayed the Plains as a new Eden of verdant grasslands, rich soil, and plenteous streams. The railroad propaganda influenced a shift in public opinion, but technological advances in wheat-growing and steadily expanding urban markets for crops were far mare significant in attracting settlers from Europe and the Mississippi Valley to the region. Emigrants came to take advantage of opportunities for more land, more crops, and more profits.

Who decided to move to the new lands? In the prevailing American notions of family relations, decisions about breadwinning and family finances were more or less in the hands of the male. Of course, removal to the Plains was a significant matter, and it is doubtful that many husbands and fathers made a unilateral decision to pull up stakes. Unfortunately, no large body of evidence about the choice to migrate to the Plains has been found or, at least, utilized in scholarly studies. I have sampled, however, some of the more than seven hundred diaries of men and women travelling to California and Oregon twenty years earlier. These indicate that the man usually initiated a plan to emigrate, made the final decision, and to a greater or lesser degree imposed it on his family. Men's involvement with self-advancement in the working world provided them with a logical and obvious rationale for going West.

The everyday concerns of "woman's sphere," however, did not provide women with many reasons to move. In the system that Tocqueville praised and Beecher vaunted, women's work, social responsibilities, and very identities were based almost entirely in the home. Domesticity involved professionalized housekeeping, solicitous child-rearing, and an assiduous maintenance of a proper moral and religious character in the family. Clearly, women could keep house better, literally and metaphorically, in "civilized" parts, where churches, kinfolk, and women friends supported them. The West held no promise of a happier family life or a more salutary moral atmosphere. On the contrary, it was notoriously destructive to those institutions and values which women held dear.

The Plains region was an especially arid prospect for the transplantation of womanly values. Lonely and crude frontier conditions prevailed into the 90's; in some areas, the sparse population actually declined with time: "following the great boom of the 80's, when the tide of migration began to recede, central Dakota and western Nebraska and Kansas presented anything but a land of occupied farms." The loneliness which women endured "must have been such as to crush the soul," according to one historian of the region. Another asserts that "without a doubt" the burden of the adverse conditions of Plains life—the aridity, treelessness, heat, perpetual wind, and deadening cold—fell upon the women. Almost without exception, others concur: "although the life of the frontier farmer was difficult special sympathy should go to his wife" . . . "it is certain that many stayed until the prairie broke them in spirit or body while others fled from the monotonous terror of it." An observer who visited the Plains in the 50's found life there to be "peculiarly severe upon women and oxen." The duration as well as the severity of cultural disruption which Plains women experienced was perhaps without parallel in the history of nineteenth-century frontiers.

First of all, emigrant women did not move into homes like the ones they had left behind, but into sod huts, tarpaper shacks, and dugouts. Seldom as temporary as they planned to be, these crude structures still existed as late as the nineties. Most settlers lived in one room "soddies" for six or seven years: if luck left a little cash, they might move into a wooden shack. Thus a farmer's wife often spent years trying to keep clean a house made of dirt. The effort became especially disheartening in rainstorms, when leaking walls splattered mud over bedclothes and dishes: "in those trying times the mud floors were too swampy to walk upon and wives could cook only with an umbrella held over the stove; after they were over every stitch of clothing must be hung out to dry." Dry weather gave no respite from dirt, since dust and straw incessantly sifted down from the walls. Housekeeping as a profession in the sense that Catharine Beecher promulgated it was impossible under such circumstances. Soddies were so badly insulated that during the winter, water froze away from the stove. In summer, the paucity of light and air could be stifling.

Often there was simply no money available to build a decent house. Drought, grasshoppers, or unseasonable rains destroyed many of the harvests of the 80's and 90's. Even good crops did not necessarily change a family's living conditions, since debts and mortgages which had accrued during hard times could swallow up any profits. But in any case, home improvements were a low priority, and families often remained in soddies or shacks even when there was cash or credit to finance a frame house. The farmer usually earmarked his profits for reinvestment into the money-making outlay of better seeds, new stock, machinery, and tools. Farm machinery came first, labor-saving devices for women last: "there was a tendency for the new homesteader to buy new machinery to till broad acres and build new barns to house more stock and grain, while his wife went about the drudgery of household life in the old way in a little drab dwelling overshadowed by the splendour of machine farming." Washers and sewing machines graced some farms in the 80's, but "for the most part . . . the machine age did not greatly help woman. She continued to operate the churn, carry water, and run the washing machine—if she were fortunate enough to have one—and do her other work without the aid of horse power which her more fortunate husband began to apply in his harvesting, threshing, and planting."

Against such odds, women were unable to recreate the kinds of houses they had left. Nor could they reinstate the home as a venerated institution. A sod house was only a makeshift shelter; no effort of the will or imagination could fashion it into what one of its greatest defenders eulogized as "the fairest garden in the wide field of endeavour and achievement." There were other losses as well. Many feminine social activities in more settled farm communities revolved around the church, but with the exception of the European immigrant enclaves, churches were scarce on the Plains. At best, religious observance was makeshift; at worst, it was non-existent. Although "it is not to be supposed that only the ungodly came west," one historian noted, "there seemed to exist in some parts of the new settlements a spirit of apathy if not actual hostility toward religion." Circuit-riders and evangelical freelancers drew crowds during droughts and depressions, but during normal times, everyday piety was rare. Few families read the Bible, sang hymns, or prayed together: "when people heard that a family was religious, it was thought that the head of the household must be a minister."

Women were also unable to reconstitute the network of female friendships which had been an accustomed and sustaining part of daily life "back home." Long prairie winters kept everyone housebound for much of the year. During summers and warmer weather, however, men travelled to town to buy supplies and negotiate loans, and rode to nearby claims to deliver mail, borrow tools, or share news. "As soon as the storms let up, the men could get away from the isolation," wrote Mari Sandoz, Nebraska writer and daughter of a homesteader: "But not their women. They had only the wind and the cold and the problems of clothing, shelter, food, and fuel." On ordinary days men could escape, at least temporarily, "into the fields, the woods, or perhaps to the nearest saloon where there was warmth and companionship, but women had almost no excuses to leave. Neighbors lived too far apart to make casual visiting practicable; besides, a farmer could seldom spare a wagon team from field work to take a woman calling. Hamlin Garland, who moved to the Plains as a young boy, remembered that women visited less than in Wisconsin, his former home, since "the work on the new farms was never-ending": "I doubt if the women—any of them—got out into the fields or meadows long enough to enjoy the birds and the breezes."

In most respects, the patterns of life rarely accommodated women's needs. Plains society paid little mind to women, yet women were essential, not incidental, to its functioning. Without female labor, cash-crop agriculture could never have developed. A man could not farm alone, and hired help was almost impossible to come by. Ordinarily, a farmer could count only on his wife and children as extra hands. On the homestead, women's responsibilities as a farmhand, not as a home-maker or a mother, were of first priority. Women still cooked, sewed, and washed, but they also herded livestock and toted water for irrigation.

The ambitious farmer's need for the labor power of women and children often lent a utilitarian quality to relations between men and women. For the single settler, marriage was, at least in part, a matter of efficiency. Courtships were typically brief and frank. Molly Dorsey Sanford, a young unmarried homesteader in Nebraska territory, recorded in her diary over half a dozen proposals in a few years. Most of her suitors were strangers. One transient liked her cooking, another heard about a "hull lot of girls" at the Dorsey farm and came to try his luck, and an old man on the steamboat going to Nebraska proposed after an hour's acquaintance. Jules Sandoz, father of Mari Sandoz, married four times. Three wives fled before he found a woman who resigned herself to the emotionless regimen of his farm. Stolid and resilient, the fourth, Mari's mother, lived to a taciturn old age, but her daughter could not forget others of her mother's generation who had not survived their hasty marriages: "after her arrival the wife found that her husband seldom mentioned her in his letters or manuscripts save in connection with calamity. She sickened and left her work undone . . . so the pioneer could not plow or build or hunt. If his luck was exceedingly bad, she died and left him his home without a housekeeper until she could be replaced." With characteristic ambivalence, Sandoz added, "at first this seems a calloused, even a brutal attitude, but it was not so intended."

Instrumentality could also characterize other family relations. Jules Sandoz "never spoke well of anyone who might make his words an excuse for less prompt jumping when he commanded. This included his wife and children." Garland described himself and his fellows as "a Spartan lot. We did not believe in letting our wives and children know they were an important part of our contentment." Jules' wife "considered praise of her children as suspect as self praise would be." Preoccupied by her chores, she maintained only minimal relationships with her family and assigned the care of the younger children to Mari, the oldest daughter.

In the domestic ideology of the family, careful and attentive child-rearing was especially important. Unlike the stoic Mrs. Sandoz, the American women who emigrated were often openly disturbed and troubled by a situation in which mothering was only peripheral to a day's work, and keenly felt the absence of cultural support for correct child-rearing. Mrs. Dorsey, the mother of diarist Molly Sanford, continually worried that her children, exiled from civilization, would turn into barbarians. In towns like Indianapolis, the family's home, schools, churches, and mothers worked in concert. In Nebraska, a mother could count on few aids. The day the Dorseys reached their claim, Molly wrote, "Mother hardly enters into ecstasies . . . she no doubt realizes what it is to bring a young rising family away from the world . . . if the country would only fill up, if there were only schools or churches or even some society. We do not see women at all. All men, single, or bachelors, and one gets tired of them." Molly occasionally responded to her mother's anxiety by searching herself and her siblings for signs of mental degeneration, but Mrs. Dorsey's fears were never warranted. The children grew up healthy and dutiful: in Molly's words, "the wild outdoor life strengthens our physical faculties, and the privations, our powers of endurance." To her confident appraisal, however, she appended a cautionary note in her mother's mode: "so that we do not degenerate mentally, it is all right; Heaven help us." Mrs. Dorsey, however, could seldom be reassured. When a snake bit one of the children, "Poor Mother was perfectly prostrated . . . she sometimes feels wicked to think she is so far away from all help with her family." On her mother's fortieth birthday, Molly wrote, "I fear she is a little blue today. I do try so hard to keep cheerful. I don't know as it is hard work to keep myself so, but it is hard with her. She knows now that the children ought to be in school. We will have to do the teaching ourselves." . . .

As Mrs. Dorsey saw her ideas of child-rearing atrophy, she also witnessed a general attenuation of the womanliness which had been central to her own identity and sense of importance in the world. Her daughters particularly taxed her investment in an outmoded conception of womanhood. Molly, for instance, was pleased with her facility in learning traditionally male skills. "So it seems I can put my hand to almost anything," she wrote with pride after helping her father roof the house. Mrs. Dorsey regarded her daughter's expanding capacities in a different light. When Molly disguised herself as a man to do some chores, "it was very funny to all but Mother, who fears I am losing all the dignity I ever possessed." Molly was repentant but defensive: "I know I am getting demoralized, but I should be more so, to mope around and have no fun."

Mrs. Dorsey's partial failure to transmit her own values of womanhood to her daughter is emblematic of many difficulties of the first generation of woman settlers. Women could not keep their daughters out of men's clothes, their children in shoes, their family Bibles in use, or their houses clean; at every step, they failed to make manifest their traditions, values, and collective sensibility. It was perhaps the resistance of the Plains to the slightest feminine modification rather than the land itself which contributed to the legend of woman's fear of the empty prairies: "literature is filled with women's fear and distrust of the Plains . . . if one may judge by fiction, one must conclude that the Plains exerted a peculiarly appalling effect on women." The heroine of [O. E.] Rolvaag's *Giants in the Earth* echoed the experience of real women in her question to herself: "how will human beings be able to endure this place? . . . Why, there isn't even a thing that one can *hide behind*!" The desolation even affected women who passed through on their way to the coast. Sarah Royce remembered shrinking from the "chilling prospect" of her first night on the Plains on the Overland Trail: "surely there would be a few trees or a sheltering hillside. . . . No, only the level prairie. . . . Nothing indicated a place for us—a cozy nook, in which for the night we might be guarded."

Fright was not a rarity on the Plains. Both men and women knew the fear of droughts, blizzards, and accidental death. Yet the reported frequency of madness and suicide among women is one indication that [Everett] Dick may have been right in his contention that "the real burden . . . fell upon the wife and mother." Men's responsibilities required them to act upon their fears. If a blizzard hung in the air, they brought the cattle in; if crops failed, they renegotiated the mortgages and planned for the next season. In contrast, women could often do nothing in the face of calamity. "If hardships came," Sandoz wrote, "the women faced it at home. The results were tersely told by the items in the newspapers of the day. Only sheriff sales seem to have been more numerous than the items telling of trips to the insane asylum."

Men made themselves known in the acres of furrows they ploughed up from the grassland. Women, lacking the opportunities of a home, had few ways to make either the land or their neighbors aware of their presence. The inability of women to leave a mark on their surroundings is a persistent theme in Sandoz's memoirs. When Mari was a child, a woman killed herself and her three children with gopher poison and a filed down case knife. The neighbors agreed that "she had been plodding and silent for a long time," and a woman friend added sorrowfully, "If she could a had even a geranium, but in that cold shell of a shack. . . ." In Sandoz's memory, the women of her mother's generation are shadows, "silent . . . always there, in the dark corner near the stove."

I have emphasized only one side of woman's experience on the Plains. For many, the years brought better times, better houses, and even neighbors. A second generation came to maturity: some were daughters like the strong farm women of Willa Cather's novels who managed to reclaim the land that had crushed their mothers. Yet the dark side of the lives of the first women on the Plains cannot be denied. Workers in an enterprise often not of their own making, their labor was essential to the farm, their womanhood irrelevant. Hamlin Garland's *Main Travelled Roads*, written in part as a condemnation of "the futility of woman's life on a farm," elicited this response from his mother: "you might have said more but I'm glad you didn't. Farmer's wives have enough to bear as it is."

Glenda Riley

NO

Women, Adaptation, and Change

Gender norms and expectations affected all types of western women—African American, Native American, Asian American, Anglo, and Spanish-speaking—in some way. Yet many women pushed at customary boundaries and tested limits. Sometimes they had feminist intentions, but other times they sought to fulfill their own needs, talents, and desires. As a result, women turned up everywhere, and often in unexpected places: holding jobs, fighting for the right of suffrage, forming labor organizations, and divorcing their spouses at a higher rate than women in any other region of the country.

Other women, who are less obvious in the historical record, fought against other forms of injustice—prejudicial attitudes and discriminatory practices. Although historical accounts often present women of color only as victims of oppression and exploitation, in reality they frequently resisted and developed their own ways to live in an often hostile world. A wide variety of resources gave women of diverse races and ethnic backgrounds the strength to live in a West composed of groups of people who persistently belittled and shunned other groups who differed from them.

Women's Responses to the Challenges of Plains Living

The Great Plains region is an especially revealing case study of women's adaptation and survival in the West. Here, women, as in other western regions, carried the primary responsibility for home and family. Not only wives and mothers, but all women, young or old, single or married, white or black, Asian or Hispanic, whether employed outside the home or not, were expected to attend to, or assist with, domestic duties. In addition, women helped with the family enterprise and often held paid employment outside the home. They were also socially, and sometimes even politically, active. In all these realms, women had to deal on a daily basis with the particular limitations imposed upon them by the harsh and demanding Plains environment. This essay examines how the Plains affected women's duties and concerns, and how the majority of women triumphed over these exigencies.

Between the early 1860s and the early 1910s the Great Plains attracted much controversy. It had vehement boosters and equally determined detractors. Land promoters and other supporters were quick to claim that a salubrious climate, rich farming and grazing lands, and unlimited business opportunities awaited newcomers. This "boomer" literature presented an attractive image that did not always seem completely truthful to those men and women who actually tried to profit from the area's purported resources.

Particularly during the early years of settlement, many migrants widely bemoaned the lack of water and relatively arid soil as well as their own inability to grapple effectively with these natural features of the Plains. At times their hardships were so severe that special relief committees and such groups as the Red Cross and the United States Army had to supply food, clothing, and other goods to help them survive.[1] Consequently, twentieth-century historical accounts have often focused on the ongoing struggles of existence. Until recently, only a few of these studies documented or analyzed the special problems that the Plains posed to women. Fortunately, a growing sensitivity to women's roles in history has led to an examination of women's own writings. This analysis of diaries, letters, and memoirs has clearly and touchingly revealed the details of their lives.[2]

The challenges that confronted women on the Plains can be grouped into three categories: the natural environment; political upheavals over such crucial issues as slavery, racism, and economic policy; and personal conflict with other people, including spouses. Obviously, all these factors also affected men, but they had a particular impact upon women.

The Natural Environment

The physical environment of the Plains created numerous difficulties for women. They showed, for instance, tremendous creativity and energy in obtaining the water that constantly was in such short supply. They carried water in pails attached to neck yokes or in barrels on "water sleds." They melted snow to obtain cooking and wash water. They used sal soda to 'break' the alkali content of water. Women also helped build windmills and dig wells. And in their desperation they even resorted to hiring a 'water-witch' or diviner to help them locate a vein of water.[3]

The aridity of the Plains created another problem for women—horribly destructive prairie fires. Men feared these fires because they endangered the animals, crops, and buildings that were largely their responsibilities, but women thought first of their children and homes as well as their cows, pigs, and chickens. In 1889 a fire in North Dakota destroyed one man's horses and barn and also claimed his wife's precious cows and chickens. Four years later, another fire in Fargo, North Dakota, burned to the ground both the shops where primarily men labored and the homes where primarily women worked. Recalling her childhood, a Kansas woman explained that because most buildings were made of wood, the "greatest danger" they faced was fire. She added that her father immediately turned all stock loose in the face of an oncoming fire because the animals instinctively headed for the safety of the river valley, while her mother placed her in the middle of the garden on the presumption that fire would not "pass into the ploughed land." Other women described the deafening noise and blinding smoke of the fires that threatened their families and homes.[4]

In addition, many women claimed that the Plains climate plagued them and interfered with their work. Destructive storms and blizzards were a constant threat, while summer heat and winter cold were regular annoyances. A Norwegian woman confronted her cold kitchen each winter morning dressed in overshoes, heavy clothing, and a warm head-scarf. Another woman simply wrote in her journal, "the snow falls upon my book while I write by the stove."[5]

Ever-present insects and animals also challenged women at every turn. Grasshoppers not only demolished crops, but could destroy homes and household goods as well. The "hoppers" gnawed their way through clothing, bedding, woodwork, furniture, mosquito netting, and stocks of food. Bliss Isely of Kansas claimed that she could remember the grasshopper "catastrophe" of 1874 in vivid detail for many years after its occurrence. As she raced down the road trying to outrun the "glistening white cloud" of grasshoppers thundering down from the sky, she worried about the baby in her arms. When the grasshoppers struck, they ate her garden to the ground, devoured fly netting, and chewed a hole in her black silk shawl. "We set ourselves to live through a hungry winter," she remembered. In the months that followed, she "learned to cook wheat and potatoes in every way possible." She made coffee from roasted wheat and boiled wheat kernels like rice for her children. Another Kansas woman who survived the grasshopper attack bitterly declared that Kansas had been "the state of cyclones, the state of cranks, the state of mortgages—and now grasshopper fame had come!"[6]

Political Upheaval

As if the physical environment wasn't enough to discourage even the hardiest and most determined women, another problem, political conflict, beset them as well. The ongoing argument over slavery especially affected the Kansas Territory when in 1856 an outbreak of violence between free-staters and proslavery factions erupted. "Border ruffians" added to the chaos by crossing frequently into "Bleeding Kansas" from Missouri in an attempt to impose slavery on the territory by force. Sara Robinson of Lawrence felt terrorized by frequent "street broils" and saw her husband imprisoned during what she termed the "reign of terror" in Kansas. Another Kansas woman lamented that there was no respite between this convulsive episode and the Civil War, which plucked men out of homes for military service. Women not only lost the labor and income of their men, but they feared the theft of food and children and the threat of rape for themselves and their daughters at the hands of raiders, thieves, and other outlaws made bold by the absence of men. In addition, the departure of men caused the burden of families, farms, and businesses to fall on the shoulders of already beleaguered women.[7]

The disputes that followed in the wake of the Civil War continued to disrupt women's lives. The period of Reconstruction between 1865 and 1877 included, for example, the chaotic entry of Exodusters (former slaves) into Kansas and other Plains states. In turn, prejudice against Exodusters created difficulties for African American women who had hoped they were migrating to a more hospitable region than the American South. Also during this period, economic unrest and dissatisfaction with federal and state government policies resulted in Populist agitation through the Plains during the 1880s and 1890s. By 1900, it seemed to many women that their lives had been entangled in a long series of political upheavals.

Personal Conflict

Women experienced personal conflict as well. Prejudice against Catholics, Jews, and people of other faiths led to intolerance at best and violence at worst. Ethnic and racial groups also received their share of distressing treatment. African American, Asian, and Mexican women were expected to work in the most menial, low-paid jobs, were barred from shops and other businesses, and were personally treated with disdain by many other migrants. This situation was especially difficult for women because they were frequently told that they were to be the arbitrators of society, yet they felt helpless to right this situation. Women also wanted desperately to shield their children from such treatment.

Some women also faced trouble within their own homes. Anecdotal evidence demonstrates that some husbands were domineering, demanding, and physically or verbally abusive. A young Jewish woman whose father had insisted that his family migrate to North Dakota remembered continual strife between her mother and father. "How can one bring the close, intimate life of the Russian *shtetl* to the vast open wilderness of the prairie?" she asked. But her mother tried. According to her daughter, "she rose early and cooked and baked and washed and scrubbed and sewed. She prayed and observed the fast days and holidays by making special dishes." Yet she also regretted and complained. Unable to understand her sorrow or offer her some much-needed sympathy, her husband argued and remonstrated. One day, much to his daughter's relief, he ran from the house storming and raging. Jumping into a buggy and seizing the reins, he shouted, "Goodbye, goodbye—I am leaving. This is more than human flesh can bear. . . . This is the end. I can take no more. It is beyond enduring. Goodbye, goodbye." When he soon returned, her joy dissipated: "My father had not kept his promise to go away and leave us in peace. He had returned. We were all trapped."[8]

On the Plains, and throughout the West, thousands of women deserted such husbands or sought relief in divorce courts. Census figures indicate that western women sought and received a higher proportion of divorces than women in other regions of the country. Whether economic opportunities encouraged this proclivity to divorce or whether western women had a spirit that sought independence is as yet unclear.[9]

Given the many difficulties that beset women, a reasonable person might ask why they stayed on the Plains. In fact, many did not stay. They and their families returned to former homes or moved onward to try life in another western region or town. After spending two years in Kansas, Helen Carpenter was delighted to become a new bride about to migrate to California. In 1857, Carpenter began her trail journal by going "back in fancy" over the two years she had spent in Kansas. She recalled the initial "weary journey of three weeks on a river boat" when all the children fell ill. Then, she wrote, it was "the struggle to get a roof over our heads . . . then followed days of longing for youthful companions . . . and before the summer waned, the entire community was stricken with fever and ague." Just as she finally made some friends and established something of a social life, "such pleasures were cut short by border troubles and an army of 'Border Ruffians' . . . who invaded the neighborhood, with no regard for life or property." She admitted that Kansas was "beautiful country" with its tall grass and lush wildflowers, but added that "the violent thunderstorms are enough to wreck the nerves of Hercules and the rattlesnakes are as thick as the leaves on the trees, and lastly 'but not leastly,' the fever and ague are corded up ever ready for use." Given the nature of her memories, it is not surprising that Carpenter concluded, "in consideration of what we have undergone physically and mentally, I can bid Kansas Good Bye without a regret." Another Kansas woman whose family left the region said that her father had taken sick and that her "Auntie wanted to get away from a place always hideous in her eyes."[10]

Fortunately, not all women felt so strongly about the drawbacks of their environment. Many women had already experienced a demanding life and, as Laura Ingalls Wilder put it, they saw the rigors of the Plains as "a natural part of life." They hung on because they had hope for the future, or according to one migrant, because they didn't expect the hard times to last. Often, their optimism was rewarded, and conditions did improve. Innovative technology gradually conquered the arid Plains, and economic booms occasionally appeared. A Nebraska woman of the early 1900s summed up her triumph in a pithy way when she wrote, "we built our frame house and was thru with our old leaky sod house. . . . We now had churches, schools, Telephones, Rural Mail."[11]

Still we must ask: did the women who remained on the Plains suffer disillusionment and despair, growing old and ill before their time? Did they blame their menfolk who had seen economic opportunity in the Plains for their misfortunes? The answer is "yes": many women who stayed on the Plains did so with resentment and hostility. Their writings tell of crushing work loads, frequent births, illnesses and deaths, recurring depression, loneliness, homesickness, and fear. A common complaint was the absence of other women; Plains women also longed for family members who had stayed at home. A Wyoming woman even claimed that the wind literally drove her crazy and that she could no longer bear to spend long winters on a remote ranch with no other women.[12]

Some women's lamentations were unrelenting, but others gradually included more pleasant observations. They noted that other people, including women, soon moved in and that often members of their own families joined them. Gradually, the depression of many hostile women ebbed and was replaced by a sense of affection for their new homes. Even the Wyoming woman who feared for her own mental stability later maintained that "those years on the Plains were hard years but I grew to like the West and now I would not like to live any other place."[13]

Numerous women did blame men for their circumstances. But it is often difficult to determine which women had fair cause to lay blame.

Because women were hesitant to record personal troubles in journals or letters sent back home, it is not always clear how responsible men were for women's difficulties. Certainly, sad stories do exist of men who verbally or physically abused women or who were alcoholic, lazy, financially inept, or generally irresponsible. In the patriarchal family structure of the time, men were often slow to recognize the importance of women's labor, allow women a voice in family decisions, and extend understanding for women's concerns. As early as 1862, the U.S. Commissioner of Agriculture's annual report suggested that the supposedly prevalent insanity of plainswomen resulted more from the harsh treatment doled out by their own men than from the Plains climate, family finances, or infant mortality. In following years, newspaper reports of wife-beating or journal accounts of alcoholic husbands gave credence to his assertion.[14]

Here again, the negative testimony is balanced by other accounts. Countless women wrote about the energy, responsibility, support, community participation, and kindness of fathers, brothers, husbands, and sons. Women spoke of men's "cheerful spirits," patience, thoughtfulness, sympathy, and companionship. Army wives Ada Vogdes and Elizabeth Custer both felt that the hardships of their lives as women in western forts were greatly offset by the courtesy and consideration of their husbands, other officers, and enlisted men. More important, a considerable number of plucky women faced challenges with creativity, energy, optimism, and motivation. They battled the circumstances of their environment by confronting the necessities of each day while maintaining hope for a better future. They met political upheaval and violence with religious faith and a commitment to help establish order. And they endured conflict with family members, neighbors, and members of other cultural groups by persevering and seeking the companionship of others, especially other women.

A Kansan of the 1880s, Flora Moorman Heston, is one example of a woman who confronted poverty, hard work, loneliness, and other problems with buoyant spirits. In a letter home, she maintained that "we have the best prospect of prosperity we ever had and believe it was right for us to come here." She added that "I have a great deal more leasure [sic] time than I used to have it dont take near the work to keep one room that it does a big house."[15] Like women in the Midwest, Southwest, and Far West, plainswomen relied on their inner strength and kept a positive outlook. Although these qualities are often forgotten in conventional descriptions of the darker side of Plains living, they did indeed exist.

How Women Adapted

Most women who ventured to the Plains states were highly motivated. They sought wealth, health, a more promising future for their children, lower taxes, and end to slavery, less prejudice or more freedom from governmental control. During the hard times and disasters, their hopes sustained them. When their fathers, brothers, or husbands talked of moving elsewhere, they often reminded the men of the particular dream that had brought them to the Plains in the first place. Others relied upon religious faith, or clung to their belief that they were civilizing a raw region, or some other commitment to keep them strong in the face of adversity.

Many women migrants created rich and varied social lives out of limited opportunities. They relieved their own isolation by writing in cherished journals or penning letters to friends and family. A young Nebraska woman who lamented the lack of women in the neighborhood wrote daily in her journal. "What should I do without my journal!" she exclaimed on one of its pages. Yet, as time passed, her entries became less frequent while her apologies to her neglected journal increased.[16]

Women also turned to the books and newspapers they had brought with them, borrowed from others, or had purchased with hoarded butter-and-egg money. Bliss Isely explained that even when she and her husband could "not afford a shotgun and ammunition to kill rabbits" they subscribed to newspapers and bought books. She made it a personal rule that "no matter how late at night it was or how tired [she] was, never to go to bed without reading a few minutes from the Bible and some other book." Other women wrote of their longing for more books, of feeling settled when their books were unpacked, and of borrowing books from others. Faye Cashatt Lewis poignantly wrote: "Finishing the last book we borrowed from the Smiths, and having it too stormy for several days to walk the mile and a half to return it and get more, was a frequent and painful experience. Seeing the end of my book approaching was like eating the last bite of food on my plate, still hungry, and no more food in sight."[17]

Music also provided solace and sociability. Frequently women insisted upon bringing guitars, pianos, and miniature parlor organs to the Plains. Despite the fact that Ada Vogdes and her husband were transported from fort to fort in army ambulances with limited space, she clung to her guitar. In her journal, she frequently mentioned the pleasure that playing guitar and singing along brought to her and others.[18] Vogdes, like many others, also depended upon mail to keep her amused and sane. When a snowstorm stopped the mail for two long weeks, Vogdes proclaimed that she could not wait much longer. To many women, the arrival of the mail provided a lifeline to home and family and brought news of the larger world through magazines, journals, ethnic and other newspapers, and books.[19]

The coming of the railroad had great social implications. Not only did railroad companies bring additional people, but they sponsored fairs and celebrations and provided ties with other regions of the country. An Indian agent's wife in Montana wrote that "the coming of the Northern Pacific Railroad in 1883 brought us in closer touch with civilization, with kin and friends, with medical and military aid, but put an end to the old idyllic days." In 1907, a Wyoming woman was delighted to see the railroad come into her area and claimed that its very existence alleviated her depression. She explained that with "no trees and few buildings" to hamper her view of passing trains, she felt that she kept "in touch with the outside pretty well."[20]

Women also became effective instigators and organizers of a huge variety of social events including taffy pulls, oyster suppers, quilting bees, dinners, picnics, box suppers, church "socials," weddings and chivarees, spelling bees, dances, theatricals, song fests, puppet shows, and readings. Perhaps most important were the celebration of such special holidays as Thanksgiving, Hanukkah, Christmas, and the Fourth of July. The menus concocted by women on special occasions often confounded other women. After a particularly splendid dinner, one woman wrote, "however she got up such a variety puzzled me, as she cooks by the fireplace and does her baking in a small covered skillet."[21]

A third way in which women adapted was in their belief that they were family and cultural conservators. Women often derived great satisfaction and a sense of significance by establishing "real" homes for their families, preserving traditional values, folkways, and mores, passing on family and ethnic traditions, contributing to local schools and churches, and establishing women's organizations. Many would have probably agreed with the poetic woman who said of them, "Without their gentle touch, the land/Would still be wilderness." Certainly, women spent a good deal of time and energy recording and relating their cultural activities.[22]

In this role, women placed a great deal of emphasis on material goods. They preserved, but also used, family treasures. Some insisted on fabric rather than oilcloth table coverings, served holiday eggnog to cowhands in silver goblets, and used their best silver and chinaware whenever the occasion arose. Years after coming to the Plains, Faye Lewis still proudly displayed her mother's Haviland china. She explained that "Father had urged strongly that this china be sold, but the thought was so heartbreaking to mother that he relented and helped her pack it." Lewis perceptively saw that her mother's china was "more than a set of dishes to her, more than usefulness, or even beauty. They were a tangible link, a reminder, that there are refinements of living difficult to perpetuate . . . perhaps in danger of being forgotten." Certainly Mary Ronan felt this way. On an isolated Indian reservation in Montana, she still regularly set her dinner table with tablecloths and ivory napkin rings. She explained that "heavy, satiny damask" cloths gave her "exquisite satisfaction" although her children did not like them. She added that she had "one beautiful set of dishes" but used them only on "gala occasions."[23]

Rituals such as the celebration of Christmas were also important. In the early years, the Christmas trees in many Plains homes were scraggly, ornaments few and homemade, and Christmas dinner far from lavish. But as their situations improved financially, women provided more festive trees, elaborate presents, and special foods. They placed trees decorated with nuts, candy, popcorn balls, strings of cranberries, wax candles, and homemade decorations in schools and churches. They then surrounded the trees with gifts for family and friends as well as presents for poor children who might otherwise be deprived of a Christmas celebration. Often music, singing, speeches, and prayers preceded the arrival of a local man dressed as Santa Claus.[24]

It is important to note that women contributed to a diversity of cultural patterns because of their own mixed ethnic and racial stock. European, Native American, African American, Mexican, and Asian women who desired to preserve their own rich heritages subscribed to a variety of newspapers and magazines in their own languages, continued to wear traditional clothing, practiced their customary holiday rituals, and added their own words, foods, and perspectives to the evolving society. A Norwegian woman in Nebraska continued to speak Norwegian in her home, sent her children to parochial school, and cooked Norwegian food. African American women were another group who added their folkways to the cultural blend, especially after the Civil War when significant numbers of them migrated to Plains states as Exodusters.[25]

Jewish women were yet another group who brought their own culture to the Plains. Although many Jewish settlers first came to the Plains as members of agricultural communities, particularly under the auspices of the Jewish Colonization Association and the Hebrew Emigrant Aid Society, they soon relocated in such cities as Omaha, Nebraska, and Grand Forks, North Dakota. Here they established businesses and communities that could support rabbis and supply other religious needs. This relocation was important to many Jewish women who despaired of their inability to provide their children with religious education and keep a kosher home when separated from a sizable Jewish community.[26]

A fourth, and crucial, factor that aided many women in their adaptation to life on the Plains was their ability to bond with other women and to create what we would today call supportive networks. On the Plains, as elsewhere, women turned to each other for company, encouragement, information, and help in times of need. Women's longing for female companionship is clearly revealed by their laments about the lack of other women. One of only three known women migrants in a remote region of North Dakota stated simply, "Naturally I was very lonely for women friends."

Consequently, women frequently overcame barriers of age, ethnicity, social class, and race in forming friendships. Arriving in Oklahoma Territory in the early 1900s, Leola Lehman formed an extremely close friendship with a Native American woman whom she described as "one of the best women" she had known in her lifetime. A Kansas woman similarly characterized an African American woman who was first a domestic, then a confidante and friend, as "devoted, kind-hearted, hard-working." Still other women told how they found a way around language barriers in order to gain companionship from women of other races and cultures.[27]

Typically, women began a friendship with a call or chat. Lehman was hanging out her wash when the Indian woman who became her friend quietly appeared and softly explained, "I came to see you. . . . I thought you might be lonesome." The company of other women was especially important in male-dominated military forts, where a woman began receiving calls upon arrival. Ada Vogdes recorded her gratitude for being whisked off by another officer's wife the moment she first arrived at Fort Laramie. Her journal overflowed with mention of calls, rides, and other outings with women friends. When her closest friends left the fort, Vogdes described herself as feeling "forsaken and forlorn" and overwhelmed by an aching heart. Some years later, Fanny McGillycuddy at Fort Robinson in South Dakota also logged calls and visits with other women and noted their great importance to her.[28]

Women also established friendships, gave each other information and support and passed on technical information, often through quilting bees and sewing circles. Bliss Isely remembered that as a young woman she was always invited to the "sewings and quiltings" held by the married women in her neighborhood. On one occasion, she invited them in return and was pleased that "they remained throughout the day." Isely felt that these events gave her invaluable training in much-needed domestic skills and that the women had "a good time helping each other" with their work.[29]

Older women lavished new brides with maternal attention and were often very generous in sharing their time, energy, and skills with the novice. In 1869 the *Bozeman Chronicle* quoted a recent bride as saying, "In all there were just fourteen women in the town in 1869, but they all vied with each other to help us and make us welcome." This hospitality even included much-needed cooking lessons for the seventeen-year-old wife. A decade later, another bride arriving in Miles City, Montana, recalled that she met with a similar welcome: "Ladies called. . . . I wasn't at all lonely."[30]

Women were also quick to offer their services to other women in times of childbirth, illness, and death. Such aid in time of need created strong bonds between women that often stretched beyond racial, ethnic, and class lines. In 1871, the *Nebraska Farmer* quoted a settler who claimed that such women acted "without a thought of reward" and that their mutual aid transformed women into "unbreakable friends." During the early 1880s, a Jewish woman in North Dakota explained that when a woman was about to give birth she would send her children "to the neighbors to stay for the time" so that she "could have rest and quiet the first few days, the only rest many of these women ever knew." She added that "the rest of us would take home the washing, bake the bread, make the butter, etc." Other women said that in time of illness or death they would take turns watching the patient, prepare medicines, bring food, prepare a body with herbs, sew burial clothes, organize a funeral, and supply food.[31] The crucial nature of another woman's assistance in time of physical need was perhaps best expressed by Nannie Alderson, a Montana ranch wife during the 1880s. When she was ill, male family members and ranch hands strongly urged her to call a doctor from Miles City. Her reply: "I don't want a doctor. I want a woman!" When the men surrounding her failed to understand her need, they again pressed her to call a doctor. She sent for a neighbor woman instead. After her recovery, she justified her action by saying, "I simply kept quiet and let her wait on men, and I recovered without any complications whatever."[32]

As the number of women increased in an area, women began to join together in the public arena as well as in private. They formed a myriad of social, education, and reform associations. Women's literary clubs studied books and started libraries. Temperance societies—the most famous of which was the national Women's Christian Temperance Union—attempted to help control the evil of alcoholism that was so damaging to women and children who were economically dependent upon men. And woman suffrage groups fought for the right to vote. Nebraskan Clara Bewick Colby, suffragist and editor of *The Woman's Tribune*, noted again and again that the Plains states were particularly fertile ground for suffrage reform.[33]

Plainswomen split, however, on the issue of suffrage. Nebraskan Luna Kellie explained that she "had been taught that it was unwomanly to concern oneself with politics and that only the worst class of women would ever vote if they had a chance." But when a tax reform proposed to cut the length of the school term, Kellie, a mother of several small children, "saw for the first time that a woman might be interested in politics and want a vote." With her father's and husband's help, she promoted a campaign that resulted in woman suffrage in local school elections. Kellie's husband urged her to continue her efforts to obtain women's right to vote in general elections.[34] In 1888, one Kansas women placed a cap bearing presidential candidate Belva Lockwood's name on her daughter's head. Still, many women opposed the suffrage cause, maintaining that the vote should belong to men only. These women believed that women should focus on their homes and families rather than on making political decisions. Some of these women even organized anti-suffrage associations.[35]

But advocates of woman suffrage were not so easily deterred. After the National Woman Suffrage Association was organized in 1869 (the same year that Wyoming Territory granted women the right to vote), Elizabeth Cady Stanton and Susan B. Anthony traveled through the West promoting suffrage. Stanton thought that Wyoming was a "blessed land . . . where woman is the political equal of man." Although Esther Morris is usually given credit for bringing woman suffrage to Wyoming Territory and was later called the Mother of Woman Suffrage, some people dispute the centrality of her role. Evidently, many women worked to convince the Democratic legislature to adopt a Women's Rights Bill in December 1869 and persuaded Republican governor John A. Campbell to sign the bill on December 10, 1869.[36]

In addition to suffrage organizations, thousands of other women's clubs and associations existed, including hospital auxiliaries, housekeepers' societies, current events clubs, musical groups, tourist clubs, world peace groups, Red Cross units, and Women's Relief Corps chapters. By the 1880s, so many organizations existed that one Wyoming woman termed the era "the golden age of women's clubs." One leading Oklahoma clubwoman established or led over forty associations during her life.[37]

Unfortunately, much of the sharing that had existed during the early days of a region now began to dissipate. Many women's clubs were segregated; women of color formed their own groups and fought for suffrage or reforms in their own way. For instance, African American women worked energetically within their own communities to provide medical care, playgrounds, and better educational facilities.

Some men's organizations also invited women (usually only white women, however) to join their membership and support their causes. A few even expanded their platforms to include women's issues. As a result, women joined the Patrons of Husbandry (the Grange), the Farmers' Alliance, and the Populist party. Annie La Porte Diggs of Kansas, for example, was an active Populist speaker and writer known for her religious liberalism. Of course, the most famous Populist woman orator was Mary Elizabeth Lease, a woman who was admitted to the Kansas bar in 1885 and who gave in 1890 over 160 speeches in support of the Populist cause. She became famous for her admonition to farmers to "raise less corn and more hell" and was dubbed by the media "Mary Yellin'." So many other women spoke from wagons and platforms, carried banners, and marched in parades that political humorist Joseph Billings wrote, "Wimmin is everywhere."[38]

Women also began to run for office on the Populist ticket. They had long held elected positions on local, county, and state school boards so the idea was not totally unacceptable to many women and men. In 1892, Ella Knowles, a Montana lawyer who in 1889 successfully lobbied for a statute allowing women to practice law in the state, ran unsuccessfully for attorney general. She was, however, appointed to a four-year term as assistant attorney general, and during the mid 1890s was a delegate to Populist conventions and a member of the Populist National Committee. During this period, Olive Pickering Rankin served as the only woman on the school board in Missoula, Montana. She was also the mother of Jeanette Rankin, the first woman to serve in the U.S. Congress and the person who introduced the "Anthony Amendment" for woman suffrage into the U.S. House of Representatives.[39]

Many men also supported women in other areas of life. Cases of supportive, helpful, sympathetic men who offered a helping hand and a listening ear when needed abounded in all communities. Faye Cashatt Lewis, whose mother so plaintively complained that the great trouble with North Dakota was that "there is nothing to make a shadow," claimed that her father was her mother's "saving support" throughout her various travails. Lewis said that her mother "could never have felt lost while he was by her side."[40] Children too offered assistance, company, and comfort to the older women of a family. While the men were gone in the fields, working in a shop, practicing a profession, or making trips, children were often women's solace, friends, and helpers. According to Lewis, she and her siblings were not only her mother's assistants, but her friends and confidantes as well.[41]

The ability of many women to concentrate on their hopes and dreams, create and enjoy socializing, serve as cultural conservators, and form strong bonds with others—both female and male—helped them triumph over the innumerable demands of the West. Although the Plains was an especially difficult environment for women, they were not generally disoriented, depressed, or in disarray. Rather, the majority of them managed to maintain homes and families, carry out domestic functions, and perpetuate the many values associated with the home. While depression, insanity, or bitterness characterized some women's lives, many more were able to respond to the challenges and hardships involved in Plains living in ways that insured survival and often brought contentment and satisfaction as well.

Notes

1. Gilbert C. Fite, "The United States Army and Relief to Pioneer Settlers, 1874–1875," *Journal of the West* 6 (January 1967), 99–107.

2. Louise Pound, *Pioneer Days in the Middle West: Settlement and Racial Stocks* (Lincoln: Nebraska State Historical Society, n.d.); Mary W. M. Hargreaves, "Homesteading and Homemaking on the Plains: A Review," *Agricultural History* 47 (April 1973), 156–63; Lillian Schlissel, "Women's Diaries on the Western Frontier," *American Studies* 18 (Spring 1977), 87–100, and Lillian

Schlissel, "Mothers and Daughters on the Western Frontier," *Frontiers* 3 (1979), 29–33; Christine Stansell, "Women on the Great Plains, 1865–1900," *Women's Studies* 4 (1976), 87–98; John Mack Faragher and Christine Stansell, "Women and Their Families on the Overland Trail to California and Oregon, 1842–1867," *Feminist Studies* 2 (1975), 150–66; Glenda Riley, *The Female Frontier: A Comparative View of Women on the Prairie and the Plains* (Lawrence: University Press of Kansas, 1988).

3. See Myra Waterman Bickel, Lydia Burrows Foote, Eleanor Schubert, and Anna Warren Peart, Pioneer Daughters Collection, SDHRC; Abbie Bright, Diary, 1870–1871, KHS; Barbara Levorsen, "Early Years in Dakota," *Norwegian-American Studies* 21 (1961), 167–69; Kathrine Newman Webster, "Memories of a Pioneer," in *Old Times Tales*, Vol. 1, Part 1 (Lincoln: Nebraska State Historical Society, 1971); Bertha Scott Hawley Johns, "Pioneer Memories 1975," WSAMHD; Emma Crinklaw (interview by Mary A. Thon), "One Brave Homesteader of '89," 1989, WSAMHD. Regarding 'witching' for water in Kansas see Bliss Isely, *Sunbonnet Days* (Caldwell, Idaho: Caxton Printers, 1935), 176–79.

4. Ellen Stebbins Emery, letter to "Dear Sister Lizzie," December 31, 1889, from Emerado, SHSND (used by permission); "Prairie Pioneer: Some North Dakota Homesteaders," *North Dakota History* 43 (Spring 1976), 22; Adela E. Orpen, *Memories of the Old Emigrant Days in Kansas, 1862–1865* (New York: Harper & Brothers, 1928), 65–69; Florence Marshall Stote, "Of Such is the Middle West," n.d., KHS; Meri Reha, Pioneer Daughters Collection, SDHRC.

5. Amanda Sayle Walradth, Pioneer Daughters Collection, SDHRC, and Ada Vogdes, Journal, 1868–1872, HL.

6. Isely, *Sunbonnet Days*, 196–201, and Anne E. Bingham, "Sixteen Years on a Kansas Farm,] 1870–1886," Kansas State Historical Society *Collections* 15 (1919/ 20), 516.

7. Sara Tappan Doolittle Robinson, *Kansas, Its Interior and Exterior Life* (Freeport, New York: Books for Libraries Press, 1856), 85, 249–69, 347; Georgiana Packard, "Leaves from the Life of a Kansas Pioneer," 1914, KHS; Marian Lawton Clayton, "Reminiscences—The Little Family," 1961, KHS.

8. From Sophie Trupin, *Dakota Diaspora: Memoirs of a Jewish Homesteader* (Lincoln: University of Nebraska Press, 1984), 35, 39, 41–42.

9. For a fuller discussion of western divorce see Glenda Riley, *Divorce: An American Tradition* (New York: Oxford University Press, 1991), ch. 4.

10. Helen M. Carpenter, "A Trip Across the Plains in an Ox Wagon," 1857, HL, and Orpen, *Memories of the Old Immigrant Days*, 8.

11. Laura Ingalls Wilder, *The First Four Years* (New York: Harper & Row, 1971); Mollie Dorsey Sanford, *Mollie: The Journal of Mollie Dorsey Sanford in Nebraska and Colorado Territories, 1857–1886* (Lincoln: University of Nebraska Press, 1976), 54; Eva Klepper, "Memories of Pioneer Days," n.d., in May Avery Papers, NHS.

12. Sarah Ettie Armstrong, "Pioneer Days," n.d., WSAMHD.

13. Ibid.

14. U.S. Commissioner of Agriculture, *Annual Report*, 1862, 462–70; *Laramie Sentinel*, October 10, 1885; Martha Farnsworth, Diary, 1882–1922, KHS. See also John Mack Faragher, "History from the Inside-Out: Writing the History of Women in Rural America," *American Quarterly* 33 (Winter 1981), 537–57, and Melody Graulich, "Violence Against Women in Literature of the Western Family," *Frontiers* 7 (1984), 14–20.

15. Flora Moorman Heston, "'I think I will Like Kansas': The Letters of Flora Moorman Heston, 1885–1886," *Kansas History* 6 (Summer 1983), 92.

16. Sanford, *Mollie*, 38.

17. Isely, *Sunbonnet Days*, 180, and Lewis, *Nothing to Make a Shadow*, 76.

18. Vogdes, Journal.

19. Ibid.

20. Margaret Ronan, *Frontier Woman: The Story of Mary Ronan* (Helena: University of Montana, 1973), 123, and Mrs. Charles Robinson, "Pioneer Memories," 1975, WSAMHD.

21. Sanford, *Mollie*, 63. Descriptions of social events can be found in Nannie T. Alderson and Helen H. Smith, *A Bride Goes West* (Lincoln: University of Nebraska Press, 1969), 169; Mary and George Baillie, "Recollections in the Form of a Duet," 1939, WSAMHD; Enid Bennets, "Rural Pioneer Life," 1939, WSAMHD; Minnie Doehring, "Kansas One-Room Public School," 1981, KHS; W. H. Elznic, Pioneer Daughters Collection, SDSHRC; Lottie Holmberg (recorder), Laura Ingraham Bragg, Recollections, n.d., WSAMHD; Lena Carlile Hurdsman, "Mrs. Lena Hurdsman of Mountain View," 1939, WSAMHD; Levorson, "Early Years in Dakota," 161; Alice Richards McCreery, "Various Happenings in the Life of Alice Richards McCreery," n.d., WSAMHD; Minnie Dubbs Millbrook, ed., "Rebecca Visits Kansas and the Custers: The Diary of Rebecca Richmond," *Kansas Historical Quarterly* 42 (Winter 1976), 366–402; Graphia Mewhirter Wilson, "Pioneer Life," 1939, WAHC.

22. Catherine E. Berry, "Pioneer Memories," 1975, WSAMHD. For discussions of women reconstructing their known lifestyle patterns on the Plains see James I. Fenton, "Critters, Sourdough, and Dugouts: Women and Imitation Theory on the Staked Plains, 1875–1910," in John R. Wunder, ed., *At Home on the Range: Essays on the History of Western Social and Domestic Life* (Westport, Conn.: Greenwood Press, 1985), 19–38; Jacqueline S. Reinier, "Concepts of Domesticity on the Southern Plains Agricultural Frontier," in Wunder, ed., *At Home on the Range*, 55–70.

23. Mrs. G. W. Wales, Reminiscences, 1866–1877, SHSND; Florence McKean Knight, "Anecdotes of Early Days in Box Butte County," *Nebraska History* 14 (April–June 1933), 142; Alderson and Smith, *A Bride Goes West*, 89; Lewis, *Nothing to Make a Shadow*, 71–72; Ronan, *Frontier Woman*, 115.

24. Lorshbough, "Prairie Pioneers," 78–79; Walter F. Peterson, "Christmas on the Plains," *American West* 1 (Fall 1964), 53–57; Anna Warren Peart, Pioneer Daughters Collection, SDHRC; Mabel Cheney Moudy, "Through My Life," n.d., WAHC.

25. Hannah, Birkley, "Mrs. Iver O. Birkley," 1957, NHS. For descriptions of Exodusters see Roy Garvin, "Benjamin, or 'Pap' Singleton and His Followers," *Journal of Negro History* 33 (January 1948), 7–8; Glen Schwendemann, "Wyandotte and the First 'Exodusters' of 1879," *Kansas Historical Quarterly* 26 (Autumn 1960), 233–49, and "The 'Exodusters' on the Missouri," *Kansas Historical Quarterly* 29 (Spring 1963), 25–40; Arvarh E. Strickland, "Toward the Promised Land: The Exodus to Kansas and Afterward," *Missouri Historical Review* 69 (July 1975), 405–12; Nell Irvin Painter, *Exodusters: Black Migration to Kansas after Reconstruction* (New York: Alfred A. Knopf, 1977; reprint, Lawrence: University Press of Kansas, 1986), 108–17; George H. Wayne, "Negro Migration and Colonization in Colorado, 1870–1930," *Journal of the West* 15 (January 1976), 102–20; "Washwomen, Maumas, Exodusters, Jubileers," in *We Are Your Sisters: Black Women in the Nineteenth Century*, ed. Dorothy Sterling (New York: Norton, 1984), 355–94.

26. For descriptions of Jewish women and men on the Plains see Lipman Goldman Feld, "New Light on the Lost Jewish Colony of Beersheba, Kansas, 1881–1886," *American Jewish Historical Quarterly* 60 (December 1970), 159, 165–67; Susan Leaphart, ed., "Frieda and Belle Fligelman: A Frontier-City Girlhood in the 1890s," *Montana: The Magazine of Western History* 32 (Summer 1982), 85–92; James A. Rudin, "Beersheba, Kansas: 'God's Pure Air on Government Lands,'"

Kansas Historical Quarterly 34 (Autumn 1968), 282–98; Elbert L. Sapinsley, "Jewish Agricultural Colonies in the West: The Kansas Example," *Western States Jewish Historical Quarterly* 3 (April 1971), 157–69; Lois Fields Schwartz, "Early Jewish Agricultural Colonies in North Dakota," *North Dakota History* 32 (October 1965), 217, 222–32; William C. Sherman, *Prairie Mosaic: An Ethnic Atlas of Rural North Dakota* (Fargo: North Dakota Institute for Regional Studies, 1983), 19–20, 53–54, 70, 112.

27.   Mrs. W. M. Lindsay, "My Pioneer Years in North Dakota," 1933, SHSND; Leola Lehman, "Life in the Territories," *Chronicles of Oklahoma* 41 (Fall 1963), 373; Orpen, *Memories of the Old Emigrant Days*, 219; Lucy Horton Tabor, "An Old Lady's Memories of the Wyoming Territory," n.d., WSAMHD; Emma Vignal Borglum, "The Experience at Crow Creek: A Sioux Indian Reservation at South Dakota," 1899, SDHRC.

28.   Lehman, "Life in the Territories," 373; Vogdes, Journal; Fanny McGillycuddy, Diary, 1877–78, SDHRC.

29.   Isely, *Sunbonnet Days*, 78–79. For other descriptions of the importance of quilting see Mrs. Henry (Anna) Crouse, Reminiscence, January 12, 1939, MSU; Ellen Calder Delong, "Memories of Pioneer Days in Cavalier County," n.d., SHSND; Agnes Henberg, Interview, September 6, 1979, WAHC; Olivia Holmes, Diary, 1872, KHS; Sarah Bessey Tracy, Diary, 1869, MSU.

30.   *Bozeman Chronicle*, August 10, 1954; unidentified newspaper clipping, "Journey from Missouri to Montana in 1880 Great Adventure According to Mrs. Mary Myer," n.d., MSU.

31.   *Nebraska Farmer*, December 8, 1934; Martha Thal, "Early Days: The Story of Sarah Thal, Wife of a Pioneer Farmer of Nelson County, N.D.," *American Jewish Archives* 23 (April 1971), 59; Mary Raymond, "My Experiences as a Pioneer," 1929, 1933, NHS; Allen, Diary; Lindsay, "My Pioneer Years"; Eleanor Schubert and Mary Louise Thomson, Pioneer Daughters Collection, SDHRC.

32.   Alderson and Smith, *A Bride Goes West*, 205–06.

33.   Clara Bewick Colby, Scrapbook of Clippings from *The Woman's Tribune*, 1883–1891, Clara Colby Collection, HL. See in particular pp. 24, 25, 257.

34.   Luna Kellie, "Memoirs," n.d., NHS.

35.   Catherine Wiggins Porter, "Sunday School Houses and Normal Institutes: Pupil and Teacher in Northern Kansas, 1886–1895," KHS, and Bingham, "Sixteen Years on a Kansas Farm," 502.

36.   Stanton is quoted in Beverly Beeton and G. Thomas Edwards, "Susan B. Anthony's Woman Suffrage Crusade in the American West," *Journal of the West* 21 (April 1982), 5. See also Virginia Scharff, "The Case for Domestic Feminism: Woman Suffrage in Wyoming," *Annals of Wyoming* 56 (Fall 1984), 29–37; Dr. Grace Raymond Hebard, "How Woman Suffrage Came to Wyoming," n.d., WSAMHD; Katharine A. Morton, "How Woman Suffrage Came to Wyoming," n.d., Woman Suffrage Collection, WSAMHD; Staff of the Library of the University of Wyoming, "Esther Hobart Morris and Suffrage," n.d., Woman Suffrage File, WAHC; and Mary Lee Stark, "One of the First Wyoming Women Voters Tells How Franchise Was Granted," n.d., WAHC.

37.   Mathilda C. Engstad, "The White Kid Glove Era," n.d., SHSND, and Marilyn HoderSalmon, "Myrtyle Archer McDougal: Leader of Oklahoma's 'Timid Sisters,'" *Chronicles of Oklahoma* 60 (Fall 1982), 332–43.

38.   Marilyn Dell Brady, "Populism and Feminism in a Newspaper by and for Women of the Kansas Farmers' Alliance, 1891–1894," *Kansas History* 7 (Winter 1984/85), 280–90; O. Gene Clanton, "Intolerant Populist? The Disaffection of Mary Elizabeth Lease," *Kansas Historical Quarterly* 34 (Summer 1968), 189–200; Katherine B. Clinton, "What Did You Say, Mrs. Lease?" *Kansas Quarterly* 1

(Fall 1969), 52–59; and Richard Stiller, *Queen of the Populists: The Story of Mary Elizabeth Lease* (New York: Crowell, 1970). See also Elizabeth Cochran, "Hatchets and Hoopskirts: Women in Kansas History," *Midwest Quarterly* 2 (April 1961), 229–49.

39. Richard B. Knowles, "Cross the Gender Line: Ella L. Knowles, Montana's First Woman Lawyer," *Montana: The Magazine of Western History* 32 (Summer 1982), 6475, and Olive Pickering Rankin, Montana American Mothers Bicentennial Project, MHSA.

40. Stote, "Of Such is the Middle West," KHS; Bingham, "Sixteen Years on a Kansas Farm," 517; Alderson and Smith, *A Bride Goes West*, 206, 233–34, Elizabeth B. Custer, *"Boots and Saddles" Or Life in Dakota With General Custer* (New York: Harper & Brothers, 1885), 126, 145; Vogdes, Journal; Faye Cashatt Lewis, *Nothing to Make a Shadow* (Ames: Iowa State University Press, 1971), 33–34.

41. Lewis, *Nothing to Make a Shadow*, 33–34.

POSTSCRIPT

Did Nineteenth-Century Women of the West Fail to Overcome the Hardships of Living on the Great Plains?

In her study of 700 letters, journals, and diaries, Stansell concludes that nineteenth-century women were forced by their husbands to move to a primitive, isolated environment and to live in sod houses far removed from their families and friends in the more civilized states east of the Mississippi River. In Stansell's view, women regressed from the traditional cult of motherhood adhered to by middle-class eastern women who attended to the moral and physical needs of their homes and their children. Out on the frontier, says Stansell, women were isolated from their support systems of other women, and their marriages were often dominated by males who showed their wives neither love and affection nor respect. In short, Stansell paints a very grim picture of frontier life for women.

Riley grants that women on the Great Plains faced physical hardships, political disputes, and personal family tragedies. But she also shows how women adapted to the new environment and developed close friendships through church services, holiday parties, and quilting bees. In addition, it was in the West that women began to move out of the home through the Prohibition and Populist reform movements and eventually achieved voting rights.

Riley's research indicates the new directions in which western women's history has been moving. First, she has established the multicultural links that women felt toward one another on the frontier, exemplified by the friendships that developed between white and Indian women. Second, Riley has studied the West as a continuum that transcends several generations down to the present time. See *Building and Breaking Families in the American West* (University of New Mexico Press, 1996).

Two major anthologies that sample new western history are William Cronon, George Miles, and Jay Gitlin, eds., *Under an Open Sky: Rethinking America's Western Past* (W. W. Norton, 1992) and Patricia N. Limerick, Charles Rankin, and Clyde A. Milner, Jr., eds., *Trails: Toward a New Western History* (University of Kansas Press, 1991). These readers deal with the environment, industrialization, painting, film, minorities, and women—areas of the West neglected by Frederick Jackson Turner and his followers.

The two best overviews of the new western history are Patricia N. Limerick's *The Legacy of Conquest: The Unbroken Past of the American West* (W. W. Norton, 1988) and Richard White's *"It's Your Misfortune and None of My Own": A New History of the American West* (University of Oklahoma Press, 1992).

On the Internet . . .

Anacostia Museum/Smithsonian Institution

This is the home page of the Center for African American History and Culture of the Smithsonian Institution.

http://www.si.edu/archives/historic/anacost.htm

The Age of Imperialism

During the late nineteenth and early twentieth centuries, the United States pursued an aggressive policy of expansionism, extending its political and economic influence around the globe. That pivotal era in the nation's history is the subject of this interactive site. Maps and photographs are provided.

http://www.smplanet.com/imperialism/toc.html

Gilded Age and Progressive Era Resources

General Resources on the Gilded Age and Progressive Era including numerous links for research and further reading.

http://www.tintech.edu/history/gilprog.html

Prohibition

The National Archives offers visitors the chance to view "The Volstead Act and Related Prohibition Documents." Documents reproduced on the site include the amendments establishing and repealing Prohibition, photographs, and more.

http://www.archives.gov/

New Deal Network

Launched by the Frank and Eleanor Roosevelt Institute (FERI) in October 1996, the New Deal Network (NDN) is a research and teaching resource on the World Wide Web devoted to the public works and arts project of the New Deal.

http://www.newdeal.feri.org

Hiroshima Archive

The Hiroshima Archive is intended to serve as a research and educational guide to those who want to gain and expand their knowledge of the atomic bombing.

http://www.lclark.edu/~history/HIROSHIMA/

The Enola Gay

The official Web site of Brigadier General Paul W. Tibbets, Jr. (Ret.) offers a wealth of historical analysis and photographs of the events surrounding the use of atomic weapons on Japan in 1945.

http://www.theenolagay.com/index.html

PART 2

The Response to Industrialism: Reform and War

*T*he maturing of the industrial system, a major economic depression, agrarian unrest, and labor violence all came to a head in 1898 with the Spanish-American War. The victory gave overseas territorial possessions to the United States and served notice to the world that the United States was a "great power." At the end of the nineteenth century, the African American population began fighting for civil rights, political power, and integration into society. Spokespersons for the blacks began to emerge, but their often unclear agendas frequently touched off controversy among both black and white people. At the turn of the century, reformers known as the Progressives attempted to ameliorate the worst abuses brought about in the factories and slums of America's cities. However, it is argued that the most serious problems of inequality were never addressed by the Progressives.

In the 1920s, tensions arose between the values of the nation's rural past and the new social and moral values of modem America. There is controversy over whether the prohibition movement curbed drinking or whether it created a climate of lawlessness in the 1920s. The onset of a more activist federal government accelerated with the Great Depression. With more than one-quarter of the workforce unemployed, Franklin D. Roosevelt was elected on a promise to give Americans a "New Deal." World War II short-circuited these plans and led to the development of a Cold War between the United States and the Soviet Union.

But the New Deal and the use of the atomic bombs against the Japanese transformed the American presidency into the most powerful political institution in both the United States and the entire world.

- Did Booker T. Washington's Philosophy and Actions Betray the Interests of African Americans?

- Was Early Twentieth-Century American Foreign Policy in the Caribbean Basin Dominated by Economic Concerns?

- Did the Progressives Fail?

- Was Prohibition a Failure?

- Did the New Deal Prolong the Great Depression?

- Was It Necessary to Drop the Atomic Bomb on Japan to End World War II?

ISSUE 6

Did Booker T. Washington's Philosophy and Actions Betray the Interests of African Americans?

YES: W. E. B. Du Bois, from *The Souls of Black Folk* (1903, Reprint, Fawcett Publications, 1961)

NO: Louis R. Harlan, from "Booker T. Washington and the Politics of Accommodation," in John Hope Franklin and August Meier, eds., *Black Leaders of the Twentieth Century* (University of Illinois Press, 1982)

ISSUE SUMMARY

YES: W. E. B. Du Bois, a founding member of the National Organization for the Advancement of Colored People, argues that Booker T. Washington failed to articulate the legitimate demands of African Americans for full civil and political rights.

NO: Professor of history Louis R. Harlan portrays Washington as a political realist whose policies and actions were designed to benefit black society as a whole.

In the late nineteenth and early twentieth centuries, most black Americans' lives were characterized by increased inequality and powerlessness. Although the Thirteenth Amendment had fueled a partial social revolution by emancipating approximately four million Southern slaves, the efforts of the Fourteenth and Fifteenth Amendments to provide all African Americans with the protections and privileges of full citizenship had been undermined by the United States Supreme Court.

By 1910, seventy-five percent of all African Americans resided in rural areas. Ninety percent lived in the South, where they suffered from abuses associated with the sharecropping and crop-lien systems, political disfranchisement, and antagonistic race relations, which often boiled over into acts of violence, including race riots and lynchings. Black Southerners who moved north in the decades preceding World War I to escape the ravages of racism instead discovered a society in which the color line was drawn more rigidly to limit black opportunities. Residential segregation led to the emergence of racial ghettos. Jim Crow also affected Northern education, and competition for jobs produced frequent clashes between black and white workers. By the early twentieth century, then, most African Americans endured a second-class citizenship reinforced by segregation laws (both customary and legal) in the "age of Jim Crow."

Prior to 1895, the foremost spokesman for the nation's African American population was former slave and abolitionist Frederick Douglass, whose crusade for blacks emphasized the importance of civil rights, political power, and immediate integration. August Meier has called Douglass "the greatest living symbol of the protest tradition during the 1880s and 1890s." At the time of Douglass's death in 1895, however, this tradition was largely replaced by the emergence of Booker T. Washington. Born into slavery in Virginia in 1856, Washington became the most prominent black spokesman in the United States as a result of a speech delivered at the Cotton States Exposition in Atlanta, Georgia. Known as the "Atlanta Compromise," this address, with its conciliatory tone, found favor among whites and gave Washington, who was president of Tuskegee Institute in Alabama, a reputation as a "responsible" spokesman for black America.

What did Booker T. Washington really want for African Americans? Did his programs realistically address the difficulties confronted by blacks in a society where the doctrine of white supremacy was prominent? Is it fair to describe Washington simply as a conservative whose accommodationist philosophy betrayed his own people? Did the "Sage of Tuskegee" consistently adhere to his publicly stated philosophy of patience, self-help, and economic advancement?

One of the earliest and most outspoken critics of Washington's program was his contemporary, W. E. B. Du Bois. In a famous essay in *The Souls of Black Folk*, Du Bois levels an assault upon Washington's narrow educational philosophy for blacks and his apparent acceptance of segregation. By submitting to disfranchisement and segregation, Du Bois charges, Washington had become an apologist for racial injustice in the United States. He also claims that Washington's national prominence was bought at the expense of black interests throughout the nation.

Louis R. Harlan's appraisal of Washington, while not totally uncritical, illuminates the complexity of Washington's personality and philosophy. Washington, according to Harlan, understood the reality of Southern race relations and knew what he was capable of accomplishing without endangering his leadership position, which was largely controlled by whites. He was, then, a consummate politician—master of the art of the possible in turn-of-the-century race relations.

Of Mr. Booker T. Washington and Others

Easily the most striking thing in the history of the American Negro since 1876 is the ascendancy of Mr. Booker T. Washington. It began at the time when war memories and ideals were rapidly passing; a day of astonishing commercial development was dawning; a sense of doubt and hesitation overtook the freedmen's sons,—then it was that his leading began. Mr. Washington came, with a single definite programme, at the psychological moment when the nation was a little ashamed of having bestowed so much sentiment on Negroes, and was concentrating its energies on Dollars. His programme of industrial education, conciliation of the South, and submission and silence as to civil and political rights, was not wholly original; . . . But Mr. Washington first indisolubly linked these things; he put enthusiasm, unlimited energy, and perfect faith into this programme, and changed it from a by-path into a veritable Way of Life. And the tale of the methods by which he did this is a fascinating study of human life.

It startled the nation to hear a Negro advocating such a programme after many decades of bitter complaint; it startled and won the applause of the South, it interested and won the admiration of the North; and after a confused murmur of protest, it silenced if it did not convert the Negroes themselves.

To gain the sympathy and coöperation of the various elements comprising the white South was Mr. Washington's first task; and this, at the time Tuskegee was founded, seemed, for a black man, well-nigh impossible. And yet ten years later it was done in the word spoken at Atlanta: "In all things purely social we can be as separate as the five fingers, and yet one as the hand in all things essential to mutual progress." This "Atlanta Compromise" is by all odds the most notable thing in Mr. Washington's career. The South interpreted it in different ways: the radicals received it as a complete surrender of the demand for civil and political equality; the conservatives, as a generously conceived working basis for mutual understanding. So both approved it, and to-day its author is certainly the most distinguished Southerner since Jefferson Davis, and the one with the largest personal following.

Next to this achievement comes Mr. Washington's work in gaining place and consideration in the North. Others less shrewd and tactful had formerly essayed to sit on these two stools and had fallen between them; but as

Mr. Washington knew the heart of the South from birth and training, so by singular insight he intuitively grasped the spirit of the age which was dominating the North. And so thoroughly did he learn the speech and thought of triumphant commercialism, and the ideals of material prosperity, that the picture of a lone black boy poring over a French grammar amid the weeds and dirt of a neglected home soon seemed to him the acme of absurdities. One wonders what Socrates and St. Francis of Assisi would say to this.

And yet this very singleness of vision and thorough oneness with his age is a mark of the successful man. It is as though Nature must needs make men narrow in order to give them force. So Mr. Washington's cult has gained unquestioning followers, his work has wonderfully prospered, his friends are legion, and his enemies are confounded. To-day he stands as the one recognized spokesman of his ten million fellows, and one of the most notable figures in a nation of seventy millions. One hesitates, therefore, to criticise a life which, beginning with so little, has done so much. And yet the time is come when one may speak in all sincerity and utter courtesy of the mistakes and shortcomings of Mr. Washington's career, as well as of his triumphs, without being thought captious or envious, and without forgetting that it is easier to do ill than well in the world.

The criticism that has hitherto met Mr. Washington has not always been of this broad character. In the South especially has he had to walk warily to avoid the harshest judgments,—and naturally so, for he is dealing with the one subject of deepest sensitiveness to that section. Twice—once when at the Chicago celebration of the Spanish-American War he alluded to the color-prejudice that is "eating away the vitals of the South," and once when he dined with President Roosevelt—has the resulting Southern criticism been violent enough to threaten seriously his popularity. In the North the feeling has several times forced itself into words, that Mr. Washington's counsels of submission overlooked certain elements of true manhood, and that his educational programme was unnecessarily narrow. Usually, however, such criticism has not found open expression, although, too, the spiritual sons of the Abolitionists have not been prepared to acknowledge that the schools founded before Tuskegee, by men of broad ideals and self-sacrificing spirit, were wholly failures or worthy of ridicule. While, then, criticism has not failed to follow Mr. Washington, yet the prevailing public opinion of the land has been but too willing to deliver the solution of a wearisome problem into his hands, and say, "If that is all you and your race ask, take it."

Among his own people, however, Mr. Washington has encountered the strongest and most lasting opposition, amounting at times to bitterness, and even to-day continuing strong and insistent even though largely silenced in outward expression by the public opinion of the nation. Some of this opposition is, of course, mere envy; the disappointment of displaced demagogues and the spite of narrow minds. But aside from this, there is among educated and thoughtful colored men in all parts of the land a feeling of deep regret, sorrow, and apprehension at the wide currency and ascendancy which some of Mr. Washington's theories have gained. These same men admire his sincerity of purpose, and are willing to forgive much to honest endeavor which is doing something worth the doing. They coöperate with Mr. Washington as far as they conscientiously can; and, indeed, it is no ordinary tribute to this man's tact and power that, steering as he must between so many diverse interests and opinions, he so largely retains the respect of all.

But the hushing of the criticism of honest opponents is a dangerous thing. It leads some of the best of the critics to unfortunate silence and paralysis of effort, and others to burst into speech so passionately and intemperately as to lose listeners. Honest and earnest criticism from those whose interests are most nearly touched,—criticism of writers by readers, of government by those governed, of leaders by those led,—this is the soul of democracy and the safeguard of modern society. If the best of the American Negroes receive by outer pressure a leader whom they had not recognized before, manifestly there is here a certain palpable gain. Yet there is also irreparable loss,—a loss of that peculiarly valuable education which a group receives when by search and criticism it finds and commissions its own leaders. The way in which this is done is at once the most elementary and the nicest problem of social growth. History is but the record of such group-leadership; and yet how infinitely changeful is its type and character! And of all types and kinds, what can be more instructive than the leadership of a group within a group?—that curious double movement where real progress may be negative and actual advance be relative retrogression. All this is the social student's inspiration and despair.

Now in the past the American Negro has had instructive experience in the choosing of group leaders, founding thus a peculiar dynasty which in the light of present conditions is worth while studying. When sticks and stones and beasts form the sole environment of a people, their attitude is largely one of determined opposition to and conquest of natural forces. But when to earth and brute is added an environment of men and ideas, then the attitude of the imprisoned group may take three main forms,—a feeling of revolt and revenge; an attempt to adjust all thought and action to the will of the greater group; or, finally, a determined effort at self-realization and self-development despite environing opinion. The influence of all of these attitudes at various times can be traced in the history of the American Negro, and in the evolution of his successive leaders. . . .

Booker T. Washington arose as essentially the leader not of one race but of two,—a compromiser between the South, the North, and the Negro. Naturally the Negroes resented, at first bitterly, signs of compromise which surrendered their civil and political rights, even though this was to be exchanged for larger chances of economic development. The rich and dominating North, however, was not only weary of the race problem, but was investing largely in Southern enterprises, and welcomed any method of peaceful coöperation. Thus, by national opinion, the Negroes began to recognize Mr. Washington's leadership; and the voice of criticism was hushed.

Mr. Washington represents in Negro thought the old attitude of adjustment and submission; but adjustment at such a peculiar time as to make his programme unique. This is an age of unusual economic development, and Mr. Washington's programme naturally takes an economic cast, becoming a gospel of Work and Money to such an extent as apparently almost completely to overshadow the higher aims of life. Moreover, this is an age when the more advanced races are coming in closer contact with the less developed races, and the race-feeling is therefore intensified; and Mr. Washington's programme practically accepts the alleged inferiority of the Negro races. Again, in our own land, the reaction from the sentiment of war time has given impetus to race-prejudice against Negroes, and Mr. Washington withdraws many of the high demands of Negroes as men and American citizens. In other periods of intensified prejudice all the Negro's tendency to self-assertion has been called forth; at this period a policy of submission is advocated. In the history of nearly all other races and peoples the doctrine preached at such crises has been that manly self-respect is worth more than lands and houses, and that a people who voluntarily surrender such respect, or cease striving for it, are not worth civilizing.

In answer to this, it has been claimed that the Negro can survive only through submission. Mr. Washington distinctly asks that black people give up, at least for the present three things,—

First, political power,
Second, insistence on civil rights,
Third, higher education of Negro youth,—

and concentrate all their energies on industrial education, the accumulation of wealth, and the conciliation of the South. This policy has been courageously and insistently advocated for over fifteen years, and has been triumphant for perhaps ten years. As a result of this tender of the palm-branch, what has been the return? In these years there have occurred:

1. The disfranchisement of the Negro.
2. The legal creation of a distinct status of civil inferiority for the Negro.
3. The steady withdrawal of aid from institutions for the higher training of the Negro.

These movements are not, to be sure, direct results of Mr. Washington's teachings; but his propaganda has, without a shadow of doubt, helped their speedier accomplishment. The question then comes: Is it possible, and probable, that nine millions of men can make effective progress in economic lines if they are deprived of political rights, made a servile caste, and allowed only the most meagre chance for developing their exceptional men? If history and reason give any distinct answer to these questions, it is an emphatic *No*. And Mr. Washington thus faces the triple paradox of his career:

1. He is striving nobly to make Negro artisans business men and property-owners; but it is utterly impossible, under modern competitive methods, for workingmen and property-owners to defend their rights and exist without the right of suffrage.
2. He insists on thrift and self-respect, but at the same time counsels a silent submission to civic inferiority such as is bound to sap the manhood of any race in the long run.

3. He advocates common-school and industrial training, and depreciates institutions of higher learning; but neither the Negro common-schools, nor Tuskegee itself, could remain open a day were it not for teachers trained in Negro colleges, or trained by their graduates.

This triple paradox in Mr. Washington's position is the object of criticism by two classes of colored Americans. One class is spiritually descended from Toussaint the Savior, through Gabriel, Vesey, and Turner, and they represent the attitude of revolt and revenge; they hate the white South blindly and distrust the white race generally, and so far as they agree on definite action, think that the Negro's only hope lies in emigration beyond the borders of the United States. And yet, by the irony of fate, nothing has more effectually made this programme seem hopeless than the recent course of the United States toward weaker and darker peoples in the West Indies, Hawaii, and the Philippines,—for where in the world may we go and be safe from lying and brute force?

The other class of Negroes who cannot agree with Mr. Washington has hitherto said little aloud. They deprecate the sight of scattered counsels, of internal disagreement; and especially they dislike making their just criticism of a useful and earnest man an excuse for a general discharge of venom from small-minded opponents. Nevertheless, the questions involved are so fundamental and serious that it is difficult to see how men like the Grimkes, Kelly Miller, J. W. E. Bowen, and other representatives of this group, can much longer be silent. Such men feel in conscience bound to ask of this nation three things:

1. The right to vote.
2. Civic equality.
3. The education of youth according to ability.

They acknowledge Mr. Washington's invaluable service in counselling patience an courtesy in such demands; they do not ask that ignorant black men vote when ignorant whites are debarred, or that any reasonable restrictions in the suffrage should not be applied; they know that the low social level of the mass of the race is responsible for much discrimination against it, but they also know, and the nation knows, that relentless color-prejudice is more often a cause than a result of the Negro's degradation; they seek the abatement of this relic of barbarism, and not its systematic encouragement and pampering by all agencies of social power from the Associated Press to the Church of Christ. They advocate, with Mr. Washington, a broad system of Negro common schools supplemented by thorough industrial training; but they are surprised that a man of Mr. Washington's insight cannot see that no such educational system ever has rested or can rest on any other basis than that of the well-equipped college and university, and they insist that there is a demand for a few such institutions throughout the South to train the best of the Negro youth as teachers, professional men, and leaders.

This group of men honor Mr. Washington for his attitude of conciliation toward the white South; they accept the "Atlanta Compromise" in its broadest interpretation; they recognize, with him, many signs of promise, many men of high purpose and fair judgment, in this section; they know that no easy task has been laid upon a region already tottering under heavy burdens. But, nevertheless, they insist that the way to truth and right lies in straightforward honesty, not in indiscriminate flattery; in praising those of the South who do well and criticising uncompromisingly those who do ill; in taking advantage of the opportunities at hand and urging their fellows to do the same, but at the same time remembering that only a firm adherence to their higher ideals and aspirations will ever keep those ideals within the realm of possibility. They do not expect that the free right vote, to enjoy civic rights, and to be educated, will come in a moment; they do not expect to see the bias and prejudices of years disappear at the blast of a trumpet; but they are absolutely certain that the way for a people to gain their reasonable rights is not by voluntarily throwing them away and insisting that they do not want them; that the way for a people to gain respect is not by continually belittling and ridiculing themselves; that, on the contrary, Negroes must insist continually, in season and out of season, that voting is necessary to modern manhood, that color discrimination is barbarism, and that black boys need education as well as white boys.

In failing thus to state plainly and unequivocally the legitimate demands of their people, even at the cost of opposing an honored leader, the thinking classes of American Negroes would shirk a heavy responsibility,—a responsibility to themselves, a responsibility to the struggling masses, a responsibility to the darker races of men whose future depends so largely on this American experiment, but especially a responsibility to this nation,—this common Fatherland. It is wrong to encourage a man or a people in evil-doing; it is wrong to aid and abet a national crime simply because it is unpopular not to do so. The growing spirit of kindliness and reconciliation between the North and South after the frightful difference of a generation ago ought to be a source of deep congratulation to all, and especially to those whose mistreatment caused the war; but if that reconciliation is to be marked by the industrial slavery and civic death of those same black men, with permanent legislation into a position of inferiority, then those black men, if they are really men, are called upon by every consideration of patriotism and loyalty to oppose such a course by all civilized methods, even though such opposition involves disagreement with Mr. Booker T. Washington. We have no right to sit silently by while the inevitable seeds are sown for a harvest of disaster to our children, black and white.

First, it is the duty of black men to judge the South discriminatingly. The present generation of Southerners are not responsible for the past, and they should not be blindly hated or blamed for it. Furthermore, to no class is the indiscriminate endorsement of the recent course of the South toward Negroes more nauseating than to the best thought of the South. The South is not "solid"; it is a land in the ferment of social change, wherein forces of all kinds are fighting for supremacy; and to praise the ill the South is to-day perpetrating is just as wrong as to condemn the good. Discriminating and broad-minded criticism is what the South needs,—needs it for the sake of her own white sons and daughters, and for the insurance of robust, healthy mental and moral development.

To-day even the attitude of the Southern whites toward the blacks is not, as so many assume, in all cases the same; the ignorant Southerner hates the Negro, the workingmen fear his competition, the money-makers wish to use him as a laborer, some of the educated see a menace in his upward development, while others—usually the sons of masters—wish to help him to rise. National opinion has enabled this last class to maintain the Negro common schools, and to protect the Negro partially in property, life, and limb. Through the pressure of the money-makers, the Negro is in danger of being reduced to semi-slavery, especially in the country districts; the workingmen, and those of the educated who fear the Negro, have united to disfranchise him, and some have urged his deportation; while the passions of the ignorant are easily aroused to lynch and abuse any black man. To praise this intricate whirl of thought and prejudice is nonsense; to inveigh indiscriminately against "the South" is unjust; but to use the same breath in praising Governor [Charles B.] Aycock, exposing Senator [John T.] Morgan, arguing with Mr. Thomas Nelson Page, and denouncing Senator Ben Tillman, is not only sane, but the imperative duty of thinking black men.

It would be unjust to Mr. Washington not to acknowledge that in several instances he has opposed movements in the South which were unjust to the Negro; he sent memorials to the Louisiana and Alabama constitutional conventions, he has spoken against lynching, and in other ways has openly or silently set his influence against sinister schemes and unfortunate happenings. Notwithstanding this, it is equally true to assert that on the whole the distinct impression left by Mr. Washington's propaganda is, first, that the South is justified in its present attitude toward the Negro because of the Negro's degradation; secondly, that the prime cause of the Negro's failure to rise more quickly is his wrong education in the past; and, thirdly, that his future rise depends primarily on his own efforts. Each of these propositions is a dangerous half-truth. The supplementary truths must never be lost sight of: first, slavery and race-prejudice are potent if not sufficient causes of the Negro's position; second, industrial and common-school training were necessarily slow in planting because they had to await the black teachers trained by higher institutions,—it being extremely doubtful if any essentially different development was possible, and certainly a Tuskegee was unthinkable before 1880; and, third, while it is a great truth to say that the Negro must strive and strive mightily to help himself, it is equally true that unless his striving be not simply seconded, but rather aroused and encouraged, by the initiative of the richer and wiser environing group, he cannot hope for great success.

In his failure to realize and impress this last point, Mr. Washington is especially to be criticised. His doctrine has tended to make the whites, North and South, shift the burden of the Negro problem to the Negro's shoulders and stand aside as critical and rather pessimistic spectators; when in fact the burden belongs to the nation, and the hands of none of us are clean if we bend not our energies to righting these great wrongs.

The South ought to be led, by candid and honest criticism, to assert her better self and do her full duty to the race she has cruelly wronged and is still wronging. The North—her co-partner in guilt—cannot salve her conscience by plastering it with gold. We cannot settle this problem by diplomacy and suaveness, by "policy" alone. If worse come to worst, can the moral fibre of this country survive the slow throttling and murder of nine millions of men?

The black men of America have a duty to perform, a duty stern and delicate,—a forward movement to oppose a part of the work of their greatest leader. So far as Mr. Washington preaches Thrift, Patience, and Industrial Training for the masses, we must hold up his hands and strive with him, rejoicing in his honors and glorying in the strength of this Joshua called of God and of man to lead the headless host. But so far as Mr. Washington apologizes for injustice, North or South, does not rightly value the privilege and duty of voting, belittles the emasculating effects of caste distinctions, and opposes the higher training and ambition of our brighter minds,—so far as he, the South, or the Nation, does this,—we must unceasingly and firmly oppose them. By every civilized and peaceful method we must strive for the rights which the world accords to men, clinging unwaveringly to those great words which the sons of the Fathers would fain forget: "We hold these truths to be self-evident: That all men are created equal; that they are endowed by their Creator with certain unalienable rights; that among these are life, liberty, and the pursuit of happiness."

Booker T. Washington and the Politics of Accommodation

It is ironic that Booker T. Washington, the most powerful black American of his time and perhaps of all time, should be the black leader whose claim to the litle is most often dismissed by the lay public. Blacks often question his legitimacy because of the role that favor by whites played in Washington's assumption of power, and whites often remember him only as an educator or, confusing him with George Washington Carver, as "that great Negro scientist." This irony is something that Washington will have to live with in history, for he himself deliberately created the ambiguity about his role and purposes that has haunted his image. And yet, Washington was a genuine black leader, with a substantial black following and with virtually the same long-range goals for Afro-Americans as his rivals. This presentation is concerned with Washington's social philosophy, such as it was, but it also addresses his methods of leadership, both his Delphic public utterances that meant one thing to whites and another to blacks and his adroit private movements through the brier patch of American race relations. It does not try to solve the ultimate riddle of his character.

Washington's own view of himself was that he was the Negro of the hour, whose career and racial program epitomized what blacks needed to maintain themselves against white encroachments and to make progress toward equality in America. The facts of his life certainly fitted his self-image. He was the last of the major black leaders to be born in slavery, on a small farm in western Virginia in 1856. Growing up during the Reconstruction era in West Virginia, he believed that one of the lessons he learned was that the Reconstruction experiment in racial democracy failed because it began at the wrong end, emphasizing political means and civil rights acts rather than economic means and self-determination. Washington learned this lesson not so much through experiences as a child worker in the salt works and coal mines as by what he was taught as a houseboy for the leading family of Malden, West Virginia, and later as a student at Hampton Institute in Virginia. Hampton applied the missionary method to black education and made its peace with the white South.

After teaching school in his home town, Washington briefly studied in a Baptist seminary and in a lawyer's office. But he soon abandoned these alternative careers, perhaps sensing that disfranchisement and the secularization of society would weaken these occupations as bases for racial leadership. He returned to Hampton Institute as a teacher for two years and then founded Tuskegee Normal and Industrial Institute in Alabama in 1881. Over the next quarter of a century, using Hampton's methods but with greater emphasis on the skilled trades, Washington built up Tuskegee Institute to be an equal of Hampton.

Washington's bid for leadership went beyond education and institution-building, however. Symbolic of his fresh approach to black-white relations was a speech he gave in 1895 before a commercial exposition, known as the Atlanta Compromise Address, and his autobiography, *Up from Slavery* (1901). As Washington saw it, blacks were toiling upward from slavery by their own efforts into the American middle class and needed chiefly social peace to continue in this steady social evolution. Thus, in the Atlanta Compromise he sought to disarm the white South by declaring agitation of the social equality question "the merest folly" and proclaiming that in "purely social" matters "we can be as separate as the fingers, yet one as the hand in all things essential to mutual progress." These concessions came to haunt Washington as southerners used segregation as a means of systematizing discrimination, and northerners followed suit. And they did not stop at the "purely social."

Washington's concessions to the white South, however, were only half of a bargain. In return for downgrading civil and political rights in the black list of priorities, Washington asked whites to place no barriers to black economic advancement and even to become partners of their black neighbors "in all things essential to mutual progress." Washington saw his own role as the axis between the races, the only leader who could negotiate and keep the peace by holding extremists on both sides in check. He was always conscious that his unique influence could be destroyed in an instant of self-indulgent flamboyance.

Washington sought to influence whites, but he never forgot that it was the blacks that he undertook to lead. He offered blacks not the empty promises of the demagogue but a solid program of economic and educational progress through struggle. It was less important "just now," he said, for a black person to seek admission to an opera house than to have the money for the ticket. Mediating diplomacy with whites was only half of Washington's strategy; the other half was black solidarity, mutual aid, and institution-building. He thought outspoken complaint against injustice was necessary but insufficient, and he thought factional dissent among black leaders was self-defeating and should be suppressed.

Washington brought to his role as a black leader the talents and outlook of a machine boss. He made Tuskegee Institute the largest and best-supported black educational institution of his day, and it spawned a large network of other industrial schools. Tuskegee's educational function is an important and debatable subject, of course, but the central concern here is Washington's use of the school as the base of operations of what came to be known as the Tuskegee Machine. It was an all-black school with an all-black faculty at a time when most black colleges were still run by white missionaries. Tuskegee taught self-determination. It also taught trades designed for economic independence in a region dominated by sharecrop agriculture. At the same time, by verbal juggling tricks, Washington convinced the southern whites that Tuskegee was not educating black youth away from the farms. Tuskegee also functioned as a model black community, not only by acquainting its students with a middle-class way of life, but by buying up the surrounding farmland and selling it at low rates of interest to create a community of small landowners and homeowners. The Institute became larger than the town.

Washington built a regional constituency of farmers, artisans, country teachers, and small businessmen; he expanded the Tuskegee Machine nation-wide after the Atlanta Compromise seemed acceptable to blacks all over the country, even by many who later denounced it. His first northern black ally was T. Thomas Fortune, editor of the militant and influential New York *Age* and founder of the Afro-American Council, the leading forum of black thought at the time. Washington was not a member, but he usually spoke at the annual meetings, and his lieutenants so tightly controlled the council that it never passed an action or resolution not in Washington's interest. Seeking more direct allies, Washington founded in 1900 the National Negro Business League, of which he was president for life. The league was important not so much for what it did for black business, which was little, but because the local branch of the league was a stronghold of Washington men in every substantial black population center.

Other classes of influential blacks did not agree with Washington's stated philosophy but were beholden to him for the favors he did them or offered to do for them. He was not called the Wizard for nothing. White philanthropists who approved of him for their own reasons gave him the money to help black colleges by providing for a Carnegie library here, a dor-mitory there. Through Washington Andrew Carnegie alone gave buildings to twenty-nine black schools. Not only college administrators owed him for favors, but so did church leaders, YMCA directors and many others. Though never much of a joiner, he became a power in the Baptist church, and he schemed through lieutenants to control the secret black fraternal orders and make his friends the high potentates of the Pythians, Odd Fellows, and so on. Like any boss, he turned every favor into a bond of obligation.

It was in politics, however, that Washington built the most elaborate ten-tacle of the octopus-like Tuskegee Machine. In politics as in everything else, Washington cultivated ambiguity. He downgraded politics as a solution of black problems, did not recommend politics to the ambitious young black man, and never held office. But when Theodore Roosevelt became president in 1901 and asked for Washington's advice on black and southern appoint-ments, Washington consented with alacrity. He became the chief black advisor of both Presidents Roosevelt and William Howard Taft. He failed in his efforts to liberalize Republican policy on voting rights, lynching, and racial discrimina-tion, however, and relations between the Republican party and black voters reached a low ebb.

In patronage politics, however, Washington found his opportunity. For a man who minimized the importance of politics, Washington devoted an inordi-nate amount of his time and tremendous energy to securing federal jobs for his machine lieutenants. These men played a certain role in the politics of the period, but their first obligation was to the Tuskegean. Washington advised the presidents to replace the old venal officeholding class of blacks with men who had proven themselves in the independent world of business, but in practice it took only loyalty to Washington to cleanse miraculously an old-time political hack. . . .

Washington's outright critics and enemies were called "radicals" because they challenged Washington's conservatism and bossism, though their tactics of verbal protest would seem moderate indeed to a later generation of activists. They were the college-educated blacks, engaged in professional pursuits, and proud of their membership in an elite class—what one of them called the Talented Tenth. The strongholds of the radicals were the northern cities and southern black colleges. They stood for full political and civil rights, liberal education, free expression, and aspiration. They dreamed of a better world and believed Booker T. Washington was a menace to its achievement. . . .

Washington dismissed his black critics by questioning their motives, their claim to superior wisdom, and—the politician's ultimate argument—their numbers. Washington understood, if his critics did not, that his leadership of the black community largely depended on his recognition by whites as the black leader. If he did not meet some minimal standards of satisfactoriness to whites, another Washington would be created. He obviously could not lead the whites; he could not even divide the whites. He could only, in a limited way, exploit the class divisions that whites created among themselves. He could work in the cracks of their social structure, move like Brer Rabbit through the brier patch, and thus outwit the more numerous and powerful whites.

While Washington recognized the centrality of black-white relations in his efforts to lead blacks, he was severely restricted by the historical context of his leadership. It was an age of polarization of black and white. The overheated atmosphere of the South at the turn of the century resembled that of a crisis center on the eve of war. Lynching became a more than weekly occurrence; discrimination and humiliation of blacks were constant and pervasive and bred a whole literature and behavioral science of self-justification. Race riots terrorized blacks in many cities, and not only in the South. It would have required not courage but foolhardiness for Washington, standing with both feet in Alabama, to have challenged this raging white aggression openly and directly. Even unqualified verbal protest would have brought him little support from either southern blacks or white well-wishers. Du Bois took higher ground and perhaps a better vision of the future when he urged forthright protest against every white injustice, on the assumption that whites were rational beings and would respond dialectically to black protest. But few white racists of the early twentieth century cared anything for the facts. And when Du Bois in his Atlanta years undertook to implement his protest with action, he was driven to the negative means of refusing to pay his poll tax or refusing to ride segregated streetcars and elevators.

Instead of either confronting all of white America or admitting that his Faustian bargain for leadership had created a systemic weakness in his program, Washington simply met each day as it came, pragmatically, seeking what white allies he could against avowed white enemies. A serious fault of this policy was that Washington usually appealed for white support on a basis of a vaguely conceived mutual interest rather than on ideological agreement. For example, in both the South and the North Washington allied himself with the white upper class against the masses. In the South he joined with the planter class and when possible with the coal barons and railroad officials against the populists and other small white farmer groups who seemed to him to harbor the most virulent anti-black attitudes born of labor competition. Similarly, in the North, Washington admired and bargained with the big business class. The bigger the businessman, the more Washington admired him, as the avatar and arbiter of American society. At the pinnacle in his measure of men were the industrialists Carnegie, John D. Rockefeller, and Henry H. Rogers and the merchant princes Robert C. Ogden and Julius Rosenwald. To be fair to Washington, he appreciated their philanthropic generosity at least as much as he admired their worldly success, but his lips were sealed against criticism of even the more rapacious and ungenerous members of the business elite.

Washington made constructive use of his philanthropic allies to aid not only Tuskegee but black education and black society as a whole. He guided the generous impulse of a Quaker millionairess into the Anna T. Jeanes Foundation to improve the teaching in black public schools. He persuaded the Jewish philanthropist Julius Rosenwald to begin a program that lasted for decades for building more adequate black schoolhouses all over the South. Washington's influence on Carnegie, Rockefeller, Jacob Schiff, and other rich men also transcended immediate Tuskegee interests to endow other black institutions. In short, Washington did play a role in educational statesmanship. There were limits, however, to his power to advance black interests through philanthropy. When his northern benefactors became involved in the Southern Education Board to improve the southern public school systems, for example, he worked repeatedly but without success to get this board to redress the imbalance of public expenditures or even to halt the rapid increase of discrimination against black schools and black children. He had to shrug off his failure and get from these so-called philanthropists whatever they were willing to give.

Having committed himself to the business elite, Washington took a dim view of the leaders of the working class. Immigrants represented to him, as to many blacks, labor competitors; Jews were the exception here, as he held them up to ambitious blacks as models of the work-ethic and group solidarity. He claimed in his autobiography that his disillusionment with labor unions went back to his youthful membership in the Knights of Labor and stemmed from observation of their disruption of the natural laws of economics. In his heyday, however, which was also the age of Samuel Gompers, Washington's anti-union attitudes were explained by the widespread exclusion of blacks from membership in many unions and hence from employment in many trades. There is no evidence that Washington ever actively supported black strikebreaking, but his refusal to intervene in behalf of all-white unions is understandable. It was more often white employees rather than employers who excluded blacks, or so Washington believed. He worked hard to introduce black labor into the non-union, white-only cotton mills in the South, even to the extent of interesting northern capitalists in investing in black cotton mills and similar enterprises.

Washington was a conservative by just about any measure. Though he flourished in the Progressive era it was not he, but his opponents who were the men of good hope, full of reform proposals and faith in the common man. Washington's vision of the common man included the southern poor white full of rancor against blacks, the foreign-born anarchist ready to pull down the temple of American business, and the black sharecropper unqualified by education or economic freedom for the ballot. Though Washington opposed the grandfather clause and every other southern device to exclude the black man from voting solely on account of his color, Washington did not favor universal suffrage. He believed in literacy and property tests, fairly enforced. He was no democrat. And he did not believe in woman suffrage, either.

In his eagerness to establish common ground with whites, that is, with some whites, Washington overstepped his purpose in public speeches by telling chicken-thief, mule, and other dialect stories intended to appeal to white stereotypes of blacks, and he occasionally spoke of the Afro-American as "a child race." No doubt his intent was to disarm his listeners, and before mixed audiences he often alternately addressed the two groups, reassuring whites that blacks should cooperate with their white neighbors in all constructive efforts, but saying to blacks that in their cooperation there should be "no unmanly cowering or stooping." At the cost of some forcefulness of presentation, Washington did have a remarkable capacity to convince whites as well as blacks that he not only understood them but agreed with them. It is one of Washington's intangible qualities as a black leader that he could influence, if not lead, so many whites. The agreement that whites sensed in him was more in his manner than in his program or goals, which always included human rights as well as material advancement for blacks.

In his constant effort to influence public opinion, Washington relied on the uncertain instruments of the press and the public platform. A flood of books and articles appeared over his name, largely written by his private secretary and a stable of ghostwriters, because he was too busy to do much writing. His ghostwriters were able and faithful, but they could not put new words or new ideas out over his signature, so for the crucial twenty years after 1895, Washington's writings showed no fresh creativity or real response to events, only a steady flood of platitudes. Washington's speeches generally suffered from an opposite handicap, that he was the only one who could deliver them. But he was too busy making two or three speeches a day to write a new one for each occasion, so the audiences rather than the speeches changed. But everywhere he went, North, South, or West, he drew large crowds ready to hear or rehear his platitudes.

Washington did try to change his world by other means. Some forms of racial injustice, such as lynching, disfranchisement, and unequal facilities in education and transportation, Washington dealt with publicly and directly. Early in his career as a leader he tried to sidestep the lynching question by saying that, deplorable though it was, he was too busy working for the education of black youth to divide his energies by dealing with other public questions. Friends and critics alike sharply told him that if he proposed to be a leader of blacks, he was going to have to deal with this subject. So he began an annual letter on lynching that he sent to all the southern white dailies, and he made Tuskegee Institute the center of statistical and news information on lynching.

He always took a moderate tone, deplored rape and crime by blacks, but always denied that the crime blacks committed was either the cause of or justification for the crime of lynching. He tried to make up for his moderation by persistence, factual accuracy, and persuasive logic. Disfranchisement of black voters swept through the South from Texas to Virginia during Washington's day. He publicly protested in letters to the constitutional conventions and legislatures in Alabama, Georgia, and Louisiana and aided similar efforts in several other states. He failed to stop lynching, to prevent the loss of voting rights, and to clean up the Jim Crow cars or bring about even minimal standards of fairness in the public schools. But he did try.

As for social segregation, Washington abided by southern customs while in the South but forthrightly declared it unreasonable for white southerners to dictate his behavior outside of the South. His celebrated dinner at the White House in 1901, therefore, though it caused consternation and protest among white southerners, was consistent with his lifetime practice. Tuskegee Institute underwent an elaborate ritual of segregation with every white visitor, but the man who came to dinner at the White House, had tea with the queen of England, and attended hundreds of banquets and private meals with whites outside the South certainly never internalized the attitudes of the segregators.

What Washington could not do publicly to achieve equal rights, he sought to accomplish secretly. He spent four years in cooperation with the Afro-American Council on a court case to test the constitutionality of the Louisiana grandfather clause, providing funds from his own pocket and from northern white liberal friends. In his own state of Alabama, Washington secretly directed the efforts of his personal lawyer to carry two grandfather-clause cases all the way to the U.S. Supreme Court, where they were lost on technicalities. He took the extra precaution of using code names in all the correspondence on the Atlabama cases. Through private pressure on railroad officials and congressmen, Washington tried to bring about improvement in the Jim Crow cars and railroad waiting rooms. He had more success in the Dan Rogers case, which overturned a criminal verdict against a black man because blacks were excluded from the jury. He also secretly collaborated with two southern white attorneys to defend Alonzo Bailey, a farm laborer held in peonage for debt; the outcome here was also successful, for the Alabama peonage law was declared unconstitutional. These and other secret actions were certainly not enough to tear down the legal structure of white supremacy, but they show that Washington's role in Afro-American history was not always that of the accommodationist "heavy." He was working, at several levels and in imaginative ways, and always with vigor, toward goals similar to those of his critics. If his methods did not work, the same could be said of theirs. And he did not take these civil rights actions as a means of answering criticism, because he kept his part in the court cases a secret except to a handful of confidants, a secret not revealed until his papers were opened to historians in recent decades.

There was another, uglier side of Washington's secret behavior, however—his ruthless spying and sabotage against his leading black critics. Washington never articulated a justification for these actions, perhaps because, being secret, they did not require defense. And yet Washington and Emmett Scott left the evidence of his secret machinations undestroyed in his papers, apparently in the faith that history would vindicate him when all the facts were known. Then, too, Washington was not given to explaining himself. . . .

The Booker T. Washington who emerges into the light of history from his private papers is a complex, Faustian character quite different from the paragon of self-uplift and Christian forbearance that Washington projected in his autobiography. On the other hand, there is little evidence for and much evidence against the charge of some of his contemporaries that he was simply an accommodationist who bargained away his race's birthright for a mess of pottage. Nor does he fit some historians' single-factor explanations of his career: that he offered "education for the new slavery," that he was a proto-black-nationalist, that he was or must have been psychologically crippled by the constraints and guilt feelings of his social role.

Washington's complexity should not be overstressed, however, for the more we know about anybody the more complex that person seems. And through the complexity of Washington's life, its busyness and its multiple levels, two main themes stand out, his true belief in his program for black progress and his great skill in and appetite for politics, broadly defined, serving both his goals and his personal power.

First, let us look closely at Washington's industrial education and small business program. It may have been anachronistic preparation for the age of mass production and corporate gigantism then coming into being, but it had considerable social realism for a black population which was, until long after Washington's death, predominantly rural and southern. Furthermore, it was well attuned to the growth and changing character of black business in his day. Increasingly, the nineteenth-century black businesses catering to white clients surrendered predominance to ghetto businesses such as banks, insurance companies, undertakers, and barbers catering to black customers. These new businessmen, with a vested interest in black solidarity, were the backbone of Washington's National Negro Business League. Washington clearly found congenial the prospect of an elite class of self-made businessmen as leaders and models for the struggling masses. There was also room for the Talented Tenth of professional men in the Tuskegee Machine, however. Washington welcomed every college-educated recruit he could secure. Directly or through agents, he was the largest employer in the country of black college graduates.

Second, let us consider Washington as a powerful politician. Though he warned young men away from politics as a dead-end career, what distinguished Washington's career was not his rather conventional goals, which in public or private he shared with almost every other black spokesman, but his consummate political skill, his wheeling and dealing. . . .

Washington's program was not consensus politics, for he always sought change, and there was always vocal opposition to him on both sides that he never tried to mollify. Denounced on the one hand by the Niagara Movement and the NAACP for not protesting enough, he was also distrusted and denounced by white supremacists for bringing the wooden horse within the walls of Troy. All of the racist demagogues of his time—Benjamin Tillman, James Vardaman, Theodore Bilbo, Thomas Dixon, and J. Thomas Heflin, to name a few—called

Washington their insidious enemy. One descriptive label for Washington might be centrist coalition politics. The Tuskegee Machine had the middle and undecided majority of white and black people behind it. Washington was a rallying point for the southern moderates, the northern publicists and makers of opinion, and the thousands who read his autobiography or crowded into halls to hear him. Among blacks he had the businessmen solidly behind him, and even, as August Meier has shown, a majority of the Talented Tenth of professional men, so great was his power to reward and punish, to make or break careers. He had access to the wellsprings of philanthropy, political preferment, and other white sources of black opportunity. For blacks at the bottom of the ladder, Washington's program offered education, a self-help formula, and, importantly for a group demoralized by the white aggression of that period, a social philosophy that gave dignity and purpose to lives of daily toil.

It could be said with some justification that the Tuskegee Machine was a stationary machine, that it went nowhere. Because the machine was held together by the glue of self-interest, Washington was frequently disappointed by the inadequate response of his allies. The southern upper class did not effectively resist disfranchisement as he had hoped and never gave blacks the equal economic chance that he considered an integral part of the Atlanta Compromise. Washington's philanthropist-friends never stood up for equal opportunity in public education. Black businessmen frequently found their own vested interest in a captive market rather than a more open society. And Washington himself often took the view that whatever was good for Tuskegee and himself was good for the Negro.

To the charge that he accomplished nothing, it can only be imagined what Washington would have answered, since he did not have the years of hindsight and self-justification that some of his critics enjoyed. He would probably have stressed how much worse the southern racial reaction would have been without his coalition of moderates, his soothing syrup, and his practical message to blacks of self-improvement and progress along the lines of least resistance. Washington's power over his following, and hence his power to bring about change, have probably been exaggerated. It was the breadth rather than the depth of his coalition that was unique. Perhaps one Booker T. Washington was enough. But even today, in a very different society, Washington's autobiography is still in print. It still has some impalpable power to bridge the racial gap, to move new readers to take the first steps across the color line. Many of his ideas of self-help and racial solidarity still have currency in the black community. But he was an important leader because, like Frederick Douglass before him and Martin Luther King after him, he had the program and strategy and skill to influence the behavior of not only the Afro-American one-tenth, but the white nine-tenths of the American people. He was a political realist.

POSTSCRIPT

Did Booker T. Washington's Philosophy and Actions Betray the Interests of African Americans?

Discussions of race relations in the late nineteenth- and early twentieth-century United States invariably focus upon the ascendancy of Booker T. Washington, his apparent accommodation to existing patterns of racial segregation, and the conflicting traditions within black thought, epitomized by the clash between Washington and Du Bois. Seldom, however, is attention given to black nationalist thought in the "age of Booker T. Washington."

Black nationalism, centered on the concept of racial solidarity, has been a persistent theme in African American history and reached one of its most important stages of development between 1880 and 1920. In the late 1800s, Henry McNeal Turner and Edward Wilmot Blyden encouraged greater interest in the repatriation of black Americans to Africa, especially Liberia. This goal continued into the twentieth century and culminated in the "Back-to-Africa" program of Marcus Garvey and his Universal Negro Improvement Association. Interestingly, Booker T. Washington also exhibited nationalist sentiment by encouraging blacks to withdraw from white society, develop their own institutions and businesses, and engage in economic and moral uplift. Washington's nationalism concentrated on economic self-help and manifested itself in 1900 with the establishment of the National Negro Business League.

A thorough assessment of the protest and accommodationist views of black Americans is presented in August Meier, *Negro Thought in America, 1880–1915* (University of Michigan Press, 1963). See Rayford Logan, *The Betrayal of the Negro: From Rutherford B. Hayes to Woodrow Wilson* (Macmillan, 1965). By far the best studies of Booker T. Washington are two volumes by Louis R. Harlan: *Booker T. Washington: The Making of a Black Leader, 1856–1901* (Oxford University Press, 1972) and *Booker T. Washington: The Wizard of Tuskegee, 1901–1915* (Oxford University Press, 1983). In addition, Harlan has edited the 13-volume *Booker T. Washington Papers* (University of Illinois Press, 1972–1984). For assessments of two of Booker T. Washington's harshest critics, see David Levering Lewis, *W. E. B. Du Bois: Biography of a Race, 1868–1919* (Henry Holt, 1993) and *W. E. B Du Bois: The Fight for Equality and the American Century, 1919–1963* (Henry Holt, 2000), and Stephen R. Fox, *The Guardian of Boston: William Monroe Trotter* (Atheneum, 1970). John H. Bracey, Jr., August Meier, and Elliott Rudwick, *Black Nationalism in America* (Bobbs-Merrill, 1970), provide an invaluable collection of documents pertaining to black nationalism. See also Edwin S. Redkey, *Black Exodus: Black Nationalist and Back-to-Africa Movements, 1890–1910* (Yale University Press, 1969), and Hollis R. Lynch, *Edward Wilmot Blyden: Pan-Negro*

Patriot, 1832–1912 (Oxford University Press, 1967). Diverse views of Marcus Garvey, who credited Booker T. Washington with inspiring him to seek a leadership role on behalf of African Americans, are found in Edmund David Cronon, *Black Moses: The Story of Marcus Garvey and the Universal Negro Improvement Association* (University of Wisconsin Press, 1955); Tony Martin, *Race First: The Ideological and Organizational Struggles of Marcus Garvey and the UNIA* (Greenwood Press, 1976); and Judith Stein, *The World of Marcus Garvey: Race and Class in Modern Society* (Louisiana State University Press, 1986). Some of Garvey's own writings are collected in Amy Jacques-Garvey, ed., Philosophy and Opinions of Marcus Garvey (1925; Atheneum, 1969).

ISSUE 7

Was Early Twentieth-Century American Foreign Policy in the Caribbean Basin Dominated by Economic Concerns?

YES: Walter LaFeber, from *Inevitable Revolutions: The United States in Central America* (W. W. Norton, 1983)

NO: David Healy, from *Drive to Hegemony: The United States in the Caribbean, 1898–1917* (University of Wisconsin Press, 1988)

ISSUE SUMMARY

YES: Professor of history Walter LaFeber argues that the United States developed a foreign policy that deliberately made the Caribbean nations its economic dependents from the early nineteenth century on.

NO: Professor of history David Healy maintains that the two basic goals of American foreign policy in the Caribbean were to provide security against the German threat and to develop the economies of the Latin American nations, whose peoples were considered to be racially inferior.

$\mathbf{G}$eographically, the Caribbean area runs from the tip of the Gulf of Mexico into the Caribbean Sea and includes two major sets of countries. First, the six Central American nations of Guatemala, Honduras, El Salvador, Nicaragua, Costa Rica, and Panama stretch along a narrow 300-mile strip between Mexico and Colombia, which separates the Pacific and Atlantic oceans. Second are a number of islands—Cuba, Haiti, the Dominican Republic, and Puerto Rico—which extend below Florida eastward into the Atlantic Ocean. Ironically, parts of Cuba, which has been a major enemy of the United States for the past 30 years, lie only 90 miles from Key West, Florida.

U.S. involvement in Central America was minimal until the mid-nineteenth century, when the acquisition of California and the subsequent discovery of gold there spurred interest in the building of a canal in Panama or Nicaragua to connect the two oceans. Worried about England's desire to build a similar canal, the United States had Great Britain sign the Clayton-Bulwer Treaty in 1850, which provided that neither country would seek exclusive control over an Isthmian route.

Ironically, America's first excursions into Nicaragua were by invitation. In 1855 the Liberals in Nicaragua grew tired of trying to unseat the Conservative president who had Guatemalan aid. They hired William Walker, a Tennessee-born soldier of fortune to fight the Conservatives. In a bizarre turn of events, Walker not only assembled an army and captured the capital, he also became Nicaragua's president in 1856. During his 10 months in office, Walker tried to impose Anglo-Saxon values on the unwilling Nicaraguans. An invasion financed by Peru, Britain, Cornelius Vanderbilt, and the rest of the Central American countries succeeded in overthrowing Walker. U.S. Marines escorted him out of the country in 1857. He attempted a comeback but was caught and executed in Honduras in 1860.

During the next four decades the United States became preoccupied with its own internal affairs. But by the turn of the twentieth century, three events brought the United States back to the Caribbean area—the Spanish-American War, the Panama Canal controversy, and the Roosevelt Corollary to the Monroe Doctrine. In 1898 U.S. soldiers liberated Cuba in a "splendid little war" with Spain and acquired Puerto Rico as an American territory. Five years later President Theodore Roosevelt supported a revolution in Panama to overthrow Colombian rule and proceeded to negotiate a treaty to build a canal 15 days after the new government of Panama had been created. Finally, in 1904 Roosevelt redefined the Monroe Doctrine. Worried that European countries might intervene in the Dominican Republic because of the money owed to European banks, Roosevelt declared that America should help "backward" states pay their bills. The United States took over the customs office of the Dominican Republic and used the revenues to pay off European bill collectors. The Roosevelt Corollary stated that the United States would actively intervene on behalf of the Central American nations. The "insurrectionary habit" brought U.S. Marines to the Dominican Republic in 1916. American troops were also sent to Haiti, Honduras, and Nicaragua.

Why did the United States constantly intervene in the affairs of the Caribbean nations during the first two decades of the twentieth century? In the following essays, Walter LaFeber argues that, given the nineteenth-century racial attitudes which considered all races other than white to be inferior, the United States easily justified its expansion across the continent. Therefore, says LaFeber, the United States adopted a foreign policy which deliberately made the Caribbean nations its *economic* dependents from the early nineteenth century on. David Healy disagrees with the theory of economic neodependency, stating that U.S. interventions were motivated by two factors: to stabilize the area by having American businesses help these radically backward Caribbean nations develop their resources and to provide security against a military threat from Germany.

YES

Walter LaFeber

Inevitable Revolutions

An Overview of the System

Central America is the most important place in the world for the United States today.

U.S. Ambassador to the United Nations,
Jeane Kirkpatrick, 1981

What we see in Central America today would not be much different if Fidel Castro and the Soviet Union did not exist.

U.S. Ambassador to Panama,
Ambler Moss, 1980

No area in the world is more tightly integrated into the United States political-economic system, and none—as President Ronald Reagan warned a joint session of Congress in April 1983—more vital for North American security, than Central America. Washington, D.C. is closer to El Salvador than to San Francisco. Nearly two-thirds of all U.S. trade and the nation's oil imports, as well as many strategic minerals, depend on the Caribbean sea lanes bordered by the five Central American nations.

North Americans have always treated the region differently from the remainder of Latin America. The five nations cover only a little more than one-hundredth of the Western Hemisphere's land area, contain a mere one-fortieth of its population, stretch only nine hundred miles north to south and (at the widest points) less than three hundred miles from ocean to ocean. But this compact region has been the target of a highly disproportionate amount of North American investment and—especially—military intervention. Every twentieth-century intervention by U.S. troops in the hemisphere has occurred in the Central American-Caribbean region. The unusual history of the area was captured by former Chilean President Eduardo Frei, who observed that the Central American states "to a man from the deep South [of the Americas] seem at times more remote than Europe." Frei's remark also implied that the largest South American nations (Argentina, Chile, Brazil) historically looked east to Europe, while the Central Americans have turned north to the United States.

From INEVITABLE REVOLUTIONS: THE UNITED STATES IN CENTRAL AMERICA, 1983, pp. 7–8, 15–18, 30–38. Copyright © 1983 by W. W. Norton. Reprinted by permission.

No region in the world is in greater political and economic turmoil than Central America. And there are few areas about which North Americans are more ignorant. The following is a capsule view of the five nations which, over the past century, have become dependent on the U.S. system. Each is quite different from the other four, but all five share a dependence on the United States that is deeply rooted in history. They also share poverty and inequality that have spawned revolutions in the seventies and eighties. . . .

These five countries are changing before our eyes. Such instability, importance to U.S. security, and North American ignorance about them form a combustible mixture. One explosion has already rocked the hemisphere: the Nicaraguan revolution became the most significant political event in the Caribbean region since 1959 when Fidel Castro seized power in Cuba. Revolutionary movements have since appeared in every other Central American nation except Costa Rica, and even that democracy has not been safe from terrorism.

The United States has countered those revolutions with its military power. Washington's recent policy, this book argues, is historically consistent for two reasons: first, for more than a century (if not since 1790), North Americans have been staunchly antirevolutionary; and second, U.S. power has been the dominant outside (and often inside) force shaping the societies against which Central Americans have rebelled. The reasons for this struggle between the Goliaths and Davids of world power (or what former Guatemalan President Juan José Arévalo called "the Shark and the Sardines") lie deeply embedded in the history of U.S.-Central American relations. As U.S. Ambassador to Panama Ambler Moss phrased the problem in 1980, "What we see in Central America today would not be much different if Fidel Castro and the Soviet Union did not exist."

These two themes—the U.S. fear of revolution and the way the U.S. system ironically helped cause revolutions in Central America—form the basis of this book. Before that story is told in detail, however, a short overview introduces the two themes.

The Revolutions of the 1970s and 1770s

Washington officials have opposed radical change not because of pressure from public opinion. Throughout the twentieth century, the overwhelming number of North Americans could not have identified each of the five Central American nations on a map, let alone ticked off the region's sins that called for an application of U.S. force.

The United States consistently feared and fought such change because it was a status quo power. It wanted stability, benefited from the on-going system, and was therefore content to work with the military-oligarchy complex that ruled most of Central America from the 1820s to the 1980s. The world's leading revolutionary nation in the eighteenth century became the leading protector of the status quo in the twentieth century. Such protection was defensible when it meant defending the more equitable societies of Western Europe and Japan, but became questionable when it meant bolstering poverty and inequality in Central America.

How North Americans turned away from revolution toward defense of oligarchs is one of the central questions in U.S. diplomatic history. The process, outlined in Chapter 1, no doubt began with the peculiar nature of the revolution in 1776. It was radical in that it proclaimed the ideal of personal freedom. The power of the British mercantilist state, Thomas Jefferson and some of his colleagues declared, had to be more subordinate to individual interest. North Americans, especially if they were white and male, could moreover realize such an ideal in a society that was roughly equitable at its birth, and possessed a tremendous landed frontier containing rich soil and many minerals that could provide food and a steadily growing economy for its people.

Central Americans have expressed similar ideals of freedom, but the historical sources of those ideals—not to mention the geographical circumstances in which they could be realized—have been quite different from the North American. Fidel Castro quoted the Declaration of Independence and compared burning Cuban cane fields in 1958 to the Boston Tea Party of 1773. But his political program for achieving the Declaration's principles flowed from such native Cuban revolutionaries as José Martí, not from Thomas Jefferson.

The need of Cubans and Central Americans to find different means for achieving their version of a just society arose in large part from their long experience with North American capitalism. This capitalism has had a Jekyll and Hyde personality. U.S. citizens see it as having given them the highest standard of living and most open society in the world. Many Central Americans have increasingly associated capitalism with a brutal oligarchy-military complex that has been supported by U.S. policies—and armies. Capitalism, as they see it, has too often threatened the survival of many for the sake of freedom for a few. For example, Latin Americans bitterly observed that when the state moved its people for the sake of national policy (as in Cuba or Nicaragua), the United States condemned it as smacking of Communist tyranny. If, however, an oligarch forced hundreds of peasants off their land for the sake of his own profit, the United States accepted it as simply the way of the real world. . . .

For the United States, capitalism and military security went hand-in-hand. They have, since the nineteenth-century, formed two sides of the same policy in Central America. Early on, the enemy was Great Britain. After 1900 it became Germany. Only after World War I were those dangers replaced by a Soviet menace. Fencing out Communists (or British, or Germans) preserved the area for North American strategic interests and profits. That goal was not argued. The problem arose when Washington officials repeatedly had to choose which tactic best preserved power and profits: siding with the status quo for at least the short term, or taking a chance on radical change that might (or might not) lead to long-term stability. Given the political and economic pressures, that choice was predetermined. As former Secretary of State Dean Acheson observed, there is nothing wrong with short-term stability. "When you step on a banana peel you have to keep from falling on your tail, you don't want to be lurching all over the place all the time. Short-term stability is all right, isn't it? Under the circumstances." The "circumstances" Acheson alluded to were the revolutions that began to appear in the newly emerging countries during the 1950s.

When applied to Central America, Acheson's view missed a central tenet of the region's history: revolutions have served the functions of elections in the United States; that is, they became virtually the only method of transferring power and bringing about needed change. Acheson's short-term stability too often turned out to be Washington's method for ensuring that Central American oligarchs did not have to answer to their fellow citizens.

The revolutionaries of the 1770s thus had less and less to say to the revolutionaries of the 1970s and 1980s. The latter were more anticapitalist, pro-statist, and concerned much less with social stability than were the former. These differences appeared as the upheavals increased in number and intensity. . . . Revolutions in such areas as Central America were inevitable. The only choice was whether North Americans would work with those revolutionaries to achieve a more orderly and equitable society, or whether—as occurred in Guatemala and Nicaragua—Washington officials would try to cap the upheavals until the pressure built again to blow the societies apart with even greater force.

Neodependency: The U.S. System

Central American revolutions have thus not only been different from, but opposed to, most of the U.S. revolutionary tradition. This opposition can be explained historically. For in rebelling against their own governments, Central Americans have necessarily rebelled against the U.S. officials and entrepreneurs who over many decades made Central America a part of their own nation's system. Not that day-to-day control, in Washington's view, was necessary or desirable. Actually governing such racially different and politically turbulent nations as Guatemala or Honduras was one headache that U.S. officials tried to avoid at every turn. They instead sought informal control, and they finally obtained it through a system that can be described as "neodependency."

First outlined in the 1960s, the theory of "dependency" has been elaborated until it stands as the most important and provocative method of interpreting U.S.-Latin American relations. Dependency may be generally defined as a way of looking at Latin American development, not in isolation, but as part of an international system in which the leading powers (and since 1945, the United States in particular), have used their economic strength to make Latin American development dependent on—and subordinate to—the interests of those leading powers. This dependence, the theory runs, has stunted the Latins' economic growth by forcing their economies to rely on one or two main export crops or on minerals that are shipped off to the industrial nations. These few export crops, such as bananas or coffee, make a healthy domestic economy impossible, according to the theory, because their price depends on an international marketplace which the industrial powers, not Central America can control. Such export crops also blot up land that should be used to grow foodstuffs for local diets. Thus malnutrition, even starvation, grow with the profits of the relatively few producers of the export crops.

Dependency also skews Central American politics. The key export crops are controlled by foreign investors or local elites who depend on foreigners for capital, markets, and often for personal protection. In the words of a Chilean scholar, these foreign influences become a "kind of 'fifth column'" that distorts economic and political development without taking direct political control of the country. Thus dependency theory denies outright a cherished belief of many North Americans: that if they are allowed to invest and trade freely, the result will be a more prosperous and stable Central America. To the contrary, dependency theorists argue, such investment and trade has been pivotal in misshaping those nations' history until revolution appears to be the only instrument that can break the hammerlock held by the local oligarchy and foreign capitalists. Latin American development, in other words, has not been compatible with United States economic and strategic interests.

[The next section] outlines how Central America became dependent on the United States. But as the story unfolds, it becomes clear that the economic aspects of dependency theory are not sufficient to explain how the United States gained such control over the region. Other forms of power, including political and military, accompanied the economic. In Nicaragua from 1909 to 1912, for example, or in Guatemala during the 1954 crisis, or in El Salvador during the eighties, economic leverage proved incapable of reversing trends that North American officials despised and feared. Those officials then used military force to destroy the threats. The United States thus has intervened frequently with troops or covert operations to ensure that ties of dependency remained.

In this respect, U.S. foreign policy has sharply distinguished Central America and the Caribbean nations from the countries in South America. In the latter region, U.S. political threats have been rarer. Direct, overt military intervention has been virtually nonexistent. Central American nations, however, have received special attention. Washington officials relied primarily on their nation's immense economic power to dominate Central America since 1900 . . . but they also used military force to ensure that control. Hence the term neodependency to define that special relationship.

To return to the original theme of [this discussion], no region in the world is more tightly integrated into the United States economic and security system than Central America. That region, however, is being ripped apart by revolutions that have already begun in Nicaragua, El Salvador, and Guatemala, and threaten Honduras. Even Costa Rica, with the most equitable and democratic system in Central America, is unsettled. As the dominant power in the area for a century, the United States bears considerable responsibility for the conditions that burst into revolution. The U.S. system was not designed accidentally or without well-considered policies. It developed slowly between the 1820s and 1880s, then rapidly, reaching maturity in the 1940s and 1950s. It was based on principles that had worked, indeed on principles that made the United States the globe's greatest power: a confidence in capitalism, a willingness to use military force, a fear of foreign influence, and a dread of revolutionary instability.

The application of those principles to Central America has led to a massive revolutionary outbreak. This history of U.S.-Central American relations during the past 150 years attempts to explain why this occurred. . . .

T.R. and TAFT: Justifying Intervention

In 1898 an awesome North American force needed fewer than three months to crush the remnants of Spain's New World empire and then establish bases in territory as close as the Caribbean and as distant as the Philippines. In 1901 the United States forced the British to terminate the Clayton-Bulwer treaty so Washington could fully control the building and defense of an isthmian canal. That same year William McKinley was assassinated and Theodore Roosevelt became president of the United States.

The famed Rough Rider, who fought publicly if not brilliantly in Cuba during the 1898 war, believed as much as Blaine that the United States was the "natural protector"—and should be the main beneficiary—of Central American affairs. But Roosevelt's methods were characteristically more direct than Blaine's. Nor was he reluctant to use them on Latin Americas whom he derisively called "Dagoes" because, in his view, they were incapable of either governing themselves or—most important in T. R.'s hierarchy of values—maintaining order. The U.S. emergence as a world power and Roosevelt's ascendency to the White House were accompanied by a third historic event during the years from 1898 to 1901: the largest export of North American capital to that time. The country remained an international debtor until World War I, but the force of the new U.S. industrial and agricultural complexes was felt many years before. A large-scale capital market centered in New York City allowed further expansion and concentration of those complexes.

England's investments in Central America meanwhile peaked in 1913 at about $115 million. More than two-thirds of the money, however, was in Costa Rica and Guatemala. And of the total amount, about $75 million—almost wholly in Costa Rica and Guatemala—represented British railroad holdings. Another $40 million was invested in government bonds, most of which were worthless. U.S. investments in Central America, on the other hand, climbed rapidly from $21 million in 1897 to $41 million in 1908, and then to $93 million by the eve of World War I. These differed from the British not only in the rapidity of growth, but in the overwhelming amount (over 90 percent) that went into such direct investments as banana plantations and mining, rather than into government securities, and in the power—perhaps even a monopoly power—these monies were buying in Honduran and Nicaraguan politics. Not that the two British bastions were invulnerable. In Guatemala, U.S. railroad holdings amounted to $30 million between 1897 and 1914 until they rapidly closed ground on England's investment of slightly over $40 million. U.S. fruit companies alone nearly equalled Great Britain's entire investment in Costa Rica's economic enterprises.

No one understood these movements and their implications as well as Elihu Root, T. R.'s secretary of state between 1905 and 1909, the nation's premier corporate lawyer, and perhaps his generation's shrewdest analyst of the new corporate America. Returning from a trip through Latin America in 1906, Root told a convention of businessmen that during the past few years three centuries of that nation's history had suddenly closed. The country's indebtedness had given way to a "surplus of capital" that was "increasing with extraordinary rapidity." As this surplus searched throughout the world for markets to conquer and vast projects to build, the mantle of world empire was being passed: "As in their several ways England and France and Germany have stood, so we in our own way are beginning to stand and must continue to stand toward the industrial enterprise of the world."

The northern and southern hemispheres perfectly suited each other, Root observed. People to the south needed North American manufacturers and the latter needed the former's raw materials. Even the personalities complemented each other: "Where we accumulate, they spend. While we have less of the cheerful philosophy" which finds "happiness in the existing conditions of life," as the Latins do, "they have less of the inventive faculty which strives continually to increase the productive power of men." Root closed by putting it all in historical perspective: "Mr. Blaine was in advance of his time. . . . Now, however, the time has come; both North and South America have grown up to Blaine's policy."

In important respects Root's speech of 20 November 1906 resembled Frederick Jackson Turner's famous essay of 1893 on the closing of the North American frontier. Both men understood that three centuries of U.S. development had terminated during their lifetime and that a new phase of the nation's history had begun. Both revealed social and racial views which shaped the new era's policies. Both were highly nationalistic if not chauvinistic. Most important, both used history as a tool to rationalize the present and future: the dynamic new United States necessarily prepared itself to find fresh frontiers abroad to replace the closed frontier at home.

Unfortunately for Root's plans, internal revolts and external wars tormented Central America at the time. The upheavals and the consequent danger of European intervention posed special problems after 1903. For in that year Roosevelt helped Panama break away from Colombia and he then began to build the isthmian canal. In a private letter of 1905 Root drew the lesson: "The inevitable effect of our building the Canal must be to require us to police the surrounding premises. In the nature of things, trade and control, and the obligation to keep order which go with them, must come our way." The conclusion was unarguable.

It must be noted, however, that one of Root's assumptions was faulty. The Panama Canal was only an additional, if major, reason for injecting U.S. power into Central America. That power had actually begun moving into the region a half-century before. It could claim de facto political and military predominance years before canal construction began. And as Root himself argued in his 1906 speech, United States development, especially in the economic realm, foretold a new relationship with Latin America even if the canal were never built. The Panamanian passageway accelerated the growth of U.S. power in Central America. It also magnificently symbolized that power. But it did not create the power or the new relationship.

For many reasons, therefore—to ensure investments, secure the canal, act as a "natural protector," and, happily, replace the declining presence of the British—Roosevelt announced in 1905 that henceforth the United States would act as the policeman to maintain order in the hemisphere. He focused this

Roosevelt Corollary to the Monroe Doctrine on the Caribbean area, where Santo Domingo was beset by revolutions and foreign creditors, but his declaration had wider meaning: "All that this country desires is that the other republics on this continent shall be happy and prosperous; and they cannot be happy and prosperous unless they maintain order within their boundaries and behave with a just regard for their obligations toward outsiders."

Perhaps Roosevelt's major gift to U.S. statecraft was his formulation of why revolutions were dangerous to his nation's interest, and the justification he then provided to use force, if necessary, to end them. But his Corollary meant more than merely making war for peace. It exemplified North American disdain for people who apparently wanted to wage revolts instead of working solid ten-hour days on the farm. Roosevelt saw such people as "small bandit nests of a wicked and inefficient type," and to U.S. Progressives such as T.R., the only sin greater than inefficiency was instability. A top U.S. naval official called the outbreaks "so-called revolutions" that "are nothing less than struggles between different crews of bandits for the possession of the customs houses—and the loot." A fellow officer agreed that only the civilized Monroe Doctrine held "a large part of this hemisphere in check against cosmic tendencies."

Of course that view completely reversed the meaning of the original Doctrine. Monroe and Adams had originally intended it to protect Latin American revolutions from outside (that is, European) interference. Eighty years later the power balance had shifted to the United States, and the Doctrine itself shifted to mean that Latin Americans should now be controlled by outside (that is, North American) intervention if necessary. Roosevelt justified such intervention as only an exercise of "police" power, but that term actually allowed U.S. presidents to intervene according to any criteria they were imaginative enough to devise. In the end they could talk about "civilization," and "self-determination," but their military and economic power was its own justification.

Roosevelt's successor, William Howard Taft, and Secretary of State Philander C. Knox hoped that T.R.'s military "Big Stick" could be replaced by the more subtle and constructive dollar. They held to the traditional North American belief in the power of capital for political healing. To bestow such blessings Knox thought it only proper that the United States seize other nations' customs revenues so they could not become the target of "devastating and unprincipled revolutions." To stabilize Central America—and to have U.S. investors do well while doing good—Taft and Knox searched for an all-encompassing legal right for intervention. The president bluntly told a Mexican diplomat that North Americans could "not be content until we have secured some formal right to compel the peace between those Central American Governments," and "have the right to knock their heads together until they should maintain peace between them." Such a general right was never discovered because legal experts in the State Department warned Knox that such a thing did not exist. Taft and Knox fell back on straight dollar diplomacy; that instrument, given their views of Central Americans, then led them to use force in the T.R. manner. As noted below, Knox soon relied upon what he termed "the moral value" of naval power.

To argue, therefore, that the United States intervened in Central America simply to stop revolutions and bestow the blessings of stability tells too little too simply. The Roosevelt Corollary and Taft's dollar diplomacy rested on views on history, the character of foreign peoples, and politics that anticipated attitudes held by North Americans throughout much of the twentieth century. These policies were applied by presidents who acted unilaterally and set historic precedents for the global application of U.S. power in later years.

North Americans seldom doubted that they could teach people to the south to act more civilized. The potential of U.S. power seemed unlimited, and as that power grew so did the confidence with which it was wielded. Brooks Adams, the grandson and great-grandson of presidents, and a brilliant eccentric who was a friend and adviser of Roosevelt, studied history deeply, then emerged to declare that the 1898 war was "the turning point in our history. . . . I do believe that we may dominate the world, as no nation has dominated it in recent time." In a personal letter, Adams spoke for his generation when he asserted that the years from 1900 to 1914 would "be looked back upon as the grand time. We shall, likely enough, be greater later, but it is the dawn which is always golden. The first taste of power is always the sweetest."

Drive to Hegemony

After experiencing a heady victory in the Spanish-American War, the United States acquired a small but far-flung empire and embarked upon a more energetic course in foreign affairs. For the next generation its diplomatic efforts were focused principally on two regions, northern Latin America and the Far East. In both regions Washington sought to become a leading shaper of events and fount of influence, but with very different results. In spite of its pretentious Open Door policy, the United States repeatedly met with frustration and failure in its Far Eastern efforts; by 1917 it had little to show for them but an enduring rivalry with Japan and a Philippine colony already coming to be seen as a white elephant. In the Caribbean area, by contrast, it had established an effective regional hegemony.

The reasons for the nation's differing success rate in these areas are not hard to find, for they emerge clearly in even a superficial comparison of the two. First of all, in the Far East the United States was a latecomer to a long-standing rivalry involving a number of competitors: Great Britain, Russia, Germany, France, and the rising local power, Japan. Located halfway around the globe from the United States, the region was never regarded in Washington as vital, however intense the occasional burst of diplomatic involvement might become, and certainly no one at the time ever suggested that it had any bearing upon the security of the United States.

The Caribbean region, by contrast, was close to the United States and far from the other great powers. No other major power challenged United States hegemony there. Great Britain, with a large economic presence, the world's mightiest navy, and secure bases in Jamaica, Trinidad, the Lesser Antilles, British Guiana, and British Honduras, was best positioned to mount such a challenge but consciously refrained. Although Americans [The use of *American* to mean *from the United States* is widely accepted in much of the world. In Latin America, *North American* is the term most used to denote United States origin. Since there is no generally satisfactory term available, I have used both interchangeably.] long feared that Germany would pick up the gauntlet, no significant opposition to Washington's growing power came from Berlin. The region was of secondary or marginal importance to the other nations of real weight, and of primary importance only to the United States. If necessary, the Americans were ready to fight for their aims in the Caribbean, and the other powers knew it. Locked into their own European tensions, they found nothing in the area worth a war with a rising naval and industrial power. As continental tensions rose steadily, then exploded into general war in 1914, Europe was increasingly debarred from any meaningful power commitments in the New World.

In addition to being the only major power with a free hand in the Caribbean, the United States possessed other regional advantages. Again, these emerge plainly from a regional comparison. American ambitions in the Far East initially included hopes of economic penetration, particularly into the markets of China. While these were at that time not large, Europeans and Americans alike shared a mistaken conviction that China was on the brink of rapid westernization and economic development which would make it a large consumer of western manufactures. In practice, China's trade with the developed world was not only rather static but overwhelmingly dominated by the British, while Japan emerged as a formidable regional business rival. As a result, the American economic stake in the Far East never became very large.

Once more the Caribbean was different. The British were also well entrenched in Caribbean trade, investment, and shipping in 1898, but not so strongly as in the Far East, while North American enterprise made steady inroads from the late nineteenth century on. By 1917 United States economic influence in the Caribbean had passed that of Great Britain, particularly in the countries in which Washington was most interested. The First World War clinched the American advantage by closing off the supply of European goods and money. Yankee businessmen quickly moved in to fill the void, making gains which substantially survived the end of the war.

A final contrast is even more striking: that between the vastness of China and the relative smallness of the Caribbean states. Both were vulnerable and disorganized at the turn of the century, but the teeming population of China had for centuries passively absorbed a succession of conquerors. To use force effectively in China might require considerable and expensive efforts extended over years, and the problem was compounded by the number of great-power rivals to be considered. The Russo-Japanese War of 1904–1905 was a grim warning of the price which the unwary could be obliged to pay; the winners as well as the losers suffered scores of thousands of casualties and paid dearly in gold as well as blood.

The scale of the effort required in the Caribbean was drastically smaller. Unchallenged by major rivals, Washington could overawe each small state one to one, in most cases not even needing to use its forces to make its point. When the United States did commit troops to action, seldom as many as two thousand were involved, and never more than three. There were normally enough marines stationed in the region or available nearby on the mainland to handle even small local wars without much extra expenditure, and never were they very bloody—for the North Americans, at any rate. Divided into many small, weak states, the Caribbean region posed little resistance to a determined great-power drive for hegemony.

Given these strategic and economic advantages, the United States quickly became dominant in the Caribbean. This . . . is an account of that rise to dominance, which began in 1898 and was substantially completed by 1917. The pages that follow do not, however, deal with the entire Gulf-Caribbean region. Mexico, important as it was, and however intimately entangled with the United States, constitutes another story. Like Colombia and Venezuela, it was not a part of the central system of Caribbean control erected in this period by the United States, but rather an indicator of the limits of that system. These larger countries also felt the weight of Washington's power and, in Mexico's case especially, played host to a myriad of North American enterprises, but never passed wholly within the circle of North American hegemony. Thus while Mexico's story has much in common with those of its neighbors, it is different in kind and will not be told here. Also omitted are the Caribbean colonies of Great Britain, France, and the Netherlands, with which Washington made no effort to interfere. This . . . is about United States relations, official and unofficial, with the independent states of Central America and the Greater Antilles, and the former Spanish colonies which passed under United States control in 1898. It is about the techniques developed to exercise hegemony over the small sovereign states of the Caribbean, the reasons why North Americans desired such hegemony, and some of the effects which resulted from its establishment. . . .

Assumptions, Biases, and Preconceptions

As the twentieth century got under way, the United States stood poised to extend its interests far beyond the initial Caribbean stepping-stones of Cuba and Puerto Rico. Even as this process began, many of the nation's people and policy makers already harbored a set of shared assumptions which would condition their future actions in the area. These assumptions touched upon the relations between the powerful industrialized states and the weaker and less developed ones, the economic potential of the Caribbean region and the capabilities of its peoples, and the probability of a European threat to the region's security.

Such preconceptions did not necessarily originate in the United States; some were borrowed from European views and experience, while many were jointly held on both sides of the Atlantic. By 1900, the European powers had a long history of interaction with other societies in every part of the world, and had established an extensive set of behavioral norms, many of which were accepted in the United States as a matter of course. The Old World was still a world of empires, and the thirty years before 1900 had witnessed a massive advance of European colonialism across Africa and Southeast Asia. Europeans of the Victorian age tended to divide the peoples of the world into the civilized and the barbarous, and their nations into the progressive and the stagnant. They saw non-European peoples lacking modern industrial societies as not merely different, but inferior, and worse yet, obstructive. These peoples, they felt, had no right to stand in the way of the world's development; "civilization" needed their raw materials, their agricultural production, and the economic opportunities which they represented. . . .

This assumed need raised problems in dealing with preindustrial nations. This was especially true of those with exotic legal and commercial codes, those prone to political violence, and those whose magnates or governments failed to honor contracts with the outside world. Once European men and money had committed themselves to enterprises in such places, their home governments must be ready to protect their lives and property against local misbehavior. The Palmerston Circular, issued by the government of Great Britain in 1849, formally claimed the right to intervene for its citizens abroad either in their individual capacity or as members of corporate organizations. Other governments claimed the same right, and the diplomatic protection of citizens' economic activities abroad became an increasingly important function of foreign offices and their legations and consulates.

It was not always clear when a citizen or corporation had been wronged, of course; frequently the disputes were murky, with much to blame on both sides. Furthermore, the issue may have been formally decided after due process by the legal system of the host country, but the imperial powers refused to accept this as decisive. . . .

The borrowers soon learned the tactics of evasion. Some Latin American governments regularly defaulted on their loans, and most did so at least once. Almost all of them contracted new loans to repay the old, usually enlarging the total in order to have fresh funds in hand for current needs. Governments regularly pledged specific sources of revenue—most often customs collections or export taxes—to the service of existing debts, then used them for other purposes in violation of their promises. It was not long before the whole process of contracting such debts became a vicious game without rules, in which each side tried to take advantage of the other. By the turn of the century some semblance of order began to emerge, as the complex and sordid controversies of the past were increasingly settled by compromise. In such settlements the debtor government paid only an agreed fraction of the sometimes fantastic totals charged against them by the bondholders. Even in 1900, however, the whole field of Caribbean government loans was still dangerous to the uninitiated, and too often tarred with scandal. . . .

If belief in special enterprisers' rights under international law commanded a consensus in the United States, so did confidence that the Caribbean countries contained a rich field for enterprise. American travelers of the period almost invariably saw vast economic promise in the region. The genuinely fertile island of Cuba set the standard, while the lush foliage of the tropics suggested a similar productivity for most of the other areas. Thus Nicaragua, for example, was widely regarded as having equal possibilities. Speaking of that country, a traveler of the 1880s concluded: "Nature has blessed it with wonderful resources, and a few years of peace and industry would make the country prosperous without comparison. . . ." Some years later the navy's Admiral James G. Walker echoed the sentiment: "The country's natural resources are immense. Millions of acres of rich land . . . need but little development to yield enormous harvests." In 1906 the United States minister drew a dismal picture of the present state of the country, then went on to contrast this with its latent potential: "This lamentable picture is one of the most fertile, beautiful countries in tropical America, which would rapidly advance in wealth and population were there security of life or property." A half dozen years later, another transient Yankee saw the future prosperity of the land in the cultivation of sugar and rubber by foreign investors, once political stability should be restored. "For these people and for this country as much can be done as we did for Cuba," he wrote, "and without firing a shot." . . .

Almost invariably, each glowing forecast of future prosperity was accompanied by harsh criticisms of the current society of the country under discussion. Thus Nicaragua had heretofore failed to flourish because "so much attention has been paid to politics that little is left for anything else," and frequently recurring civil wars disrupted labor and production. Bad government was reputed to be almost universal. The same British diplomat who saw such material promise in all of the Central American states found in their rulers a major obstacle to development. "Their dishonest methods, total lack of justice, and their shiftiness make it almost useless to endeavor to deal with these Governments as with civilized nations," he declared. "Presidents, Ministers, Judges, police and all other Government or local officials appear to have but one object, namely, to extort and steal as much as possible during their term of office." Elihu Root dismissed the public life of Santo Domingo in a sentence: "Her politics are purely personal, and have been a continual struggle of this and that and the other man to secure ascendancy and power."

To these outside observers, the failure of government was closely associated with the defects of the population. Witness after witness testified that the Caribbean peoples were ignorant, lazy, backward, perhaps vicious. The London *Times* correspondent who gave such a favorable report of Santo Domingo's land and resources described the people as "easy-going and improvident," devoid of initiative or enterprise. When he asked a rural cultivator why he did not dig a ditch and irrigate his field, the man replied that if such a thing were necessary, God would have made it. Admiral Walker saw the Nicaraguans as "dreaming the years away" without past traditions or future ambitions to inspirit them. The American author of a 1910 travel book on Central America did not attempt to conceal his contempt for the people of that region: "Barbarism, enervated by certain civilized forms, without barbarism's vigor, tells all in a word. Scenes of disgust I might repeat to the point of nausea; utter lack of sanitation, of care of body as well as mind, expose a scrofulous people to all the tropical diseases. . . ." To this writer, Central America was not properly a part of the larger Latin American whole, for the South Americans were civilized and progressive, the Central Americans not so. They would be better called "Indo-Americans," he thought, to indicate their inferiority. . . .

The truth was that the American public of the early twentieth century expected to find inferior qualities in nonwhite peoples from tropical societies. Racism in the United States was older than the nation itself; Indians and blacks had suffered from the stigma of inequality since early colonial times. The legacies of the frontier and slavery had long since hardened into fixed attitudes, only superficially changed by the passing of Indian resistance or the episodes of the Civil War and Reconstruction. By the late nineteenth century the South was resubmerging its black population under grandfather clauses, Jim Crow legislation, and lynch law, while Indians were consigned to segregated "reservations" and forgotten. Even the newer European immigrants, flocking in from Southern and Eastern Europe and bringing different cultural backgrounds into the mainstream, were received with deep suspicion and scarcely concealed intimations of inferiority. The inequality of peoples was a pervasive idea in turn-of-the-century America; the Indians, mestizos, and blacks of the Caribbean could hope for little from United States public opinion.

The period entertained not only racial, but geographical biases. A widely read book entitled *The Control of the Tropics* appeared in 1898 with a large impact in both England and America. Written by an Englishman named Benjamin Kidd, its thesis centered on the allegation that the tropical peoples were always and everywhere incapable of self-government and economic development, and their societies were typically characterized by anarchy and bankruptcy. The roots of this alleged condition were not merely racial; white men of "high efficiency," living too long amid slack standards in an enervating climate, were themselves in danger of degeneration. Such men must return regularly to their homelands to renew their mental, moral, and physical vigor, or succumb in time to the universal tropical decay. If tropical areas were to be developed, therefore, they must be governed and managed by career executives and civil servants sent out from the vigorous societies of the north, and regularly replaced by new blood. Since the last great field for the world's economic growth lay in the tropics, Kidd declared, the matter was of more than theoretical importance, and scores of reviewers and readers in the United States agreed with him. . . .

Potentially rich, but peopled by inferior stocks and retarded by inimical tropical conditions, the future of the region lay primarily with outsiders: that was the message, implicit or explicit, received by public opinion in the United States. Yet a plethora of witnesses asserted their confidence in the area's future. Given even a modest degree of order and stability, they chorused, foreign business enterprise would soon be able to tap the varied riches awaiting its fulfilling hand. With economic development under way, a generalized prosperity would soon transform the lives, the institutions, perhaps even the nature of the local populations. For the benefits of economic growth would assuredly be mutual; the native peoples of the Caribbean would gain at least as much as the entrepreneurs who came from abroad to invest their money and talents. A rising level of wealth would bring peace, education, and progress to currently benighted areas, provided of course that the developers enjoyed a relatively free hand. Furthermore, the glowing prospects so often described were typically placed, not in the remote future, but in the next decade or sooner. The driving engine of this economic miracle was to lie primarily in tropical agriculture: the sugar, coffee, bananas, or tobacco in which foreign investors were already so interested. In addition some infrastructure would be needed, particularly in the form of railroads and public utilities, while mining and lumbering represented further fields of action. . . .

In the unsparing light of hindsight, it is easy to indict these prophets of progress and prosperity for their hypocrisy. After a century of partial and selective foreign development, the Caribbean region is not rich, but poor. While the enterprisers often made money, and local elites received a more modest share, their activities produced nothing like a generalized prosperity. On the contrary, a vast inequality of incomes left many in penury and most barely above the subsistence level. And in the long run, even the investors' profits were limited; most of the twentieth century has seen agricultural products exchange at a disadvantage with industrial goods, the terms of trade being largely controlled by the industrial and financial centers. World market surpluses of sugar, coffee, and other tropical staples have further driven prices down, so that only during major wars does a true agricultural prosperity bloom in the tropical world.

In the light of these facts, it is tempting to conclude that the claims and promises by which foreign enterprisers justified themselves in the early twentieth century were insincere and self-serving. Self-serving they certainly were, but not necessarily insincere. It is, after all, easiest to believe what is welcome; belief and self-interest typically run hand in hand. More seriously, the enterpriser of 1900 or 1915 had persuasive reasons to believe in the viability of an agriculturally based economic development. At that very time, Argentina was rapidly emerging as the most prosperous and "modern" of Latin American states, making a major success of selling wheat and beef to a hungry Europe. Since the bulk of Argentina's population sprang from recent European immigrants, the lesson seemed to be that the more efficient "races" could indeed wring wealth out of the soil, and that the process was inhibited elsewhere mainly by the deficiencies of the natives. Furthermore, Argentine economic development had been managed and financed to a notable extent from England, demonstrating the efficacy of foreign enterprise. With a fast-growing productive base, a solid infrastructure, and a relatively stable political system, Argentina was widely seen as a role model for all of the Latin America.

Closer to home, the enterprising Yankee had an even more compelling example of the possibilities of market agriculture. The United States itself had long flourished through the export of huge agricultural surpluses, which had played an essential role in financing nineteenth-century industrialization. Nor was this a phenomenon of the past; American food and fibers still dominated the world market, and their profitability had continued to spur the development of large sections of the nation. The Great Plains constituted the last great agricultural frontier, and in 1900 that region was just approaching full development. Within the memory of millions of living Americans, vast areas west of the Mississippi had been settled and broken to the plow. With startling speed, railroads were built, cities founded, churches, opera houses, universities created—an entire new society, comprising numerous states of the union, had appeared as if by magic in a few decades, quickly achieving American standards of wealth, productivity, and material consumption.

The undeniable fact was that united States economic development had historically been tightly linked to a varied and prosperous agriculture. Its modern industrial economy was built on a foundation of soil-based wealth; its citizens took it as a given that the one was a natural precondition for the other. What they had done at home, right up to the early twentieth century, they assumed they could do anywhere else where a reasonable resource base existed. They had little reason to doubt that a healthy economic development could spring from the export of agricultural surpluses to a world market, and every reason to have faith in the process.

In retrospect, of course, there are obvious flaws in this assumption. The relatively favorable terms of trade enjoyed by agricultural products at the beginning of the century were to disappear almost permanently after the First World War. A crop like sugar, considered as an enterprise, differed significantly from grain or meat, given sugar's special demand for cheap seasonal labor and its wildly fluctuating world price. Large-scale corporate farming by foreign businesses was hardly the same as the family farming which prevailed for so long in the United States. And nowhere in the Caribbean, except perhaps in Cuba, were there large tracts of land possessing anything like the incomparable richness of soil and climate which characterized the more prosperous farming areas of the United States. At the time, however, it appeared otherwise. The Great Plains, with their harsh climate, insect plagues, lack of trees, and inadequate rivers seemed the ultimate in nature's resistance to exploitation. Surely the nation which had brought such a region to productivity could repeat its success in the lush, warm valleys of the Caribbean, where the limitations of tropical soils were still imperfectly understood. Flush with surplus capital, confident of their new technology, and glorying in past success, it never occurred to Yankee enterprisers to doubt their ability to pluck riches from the neighboring lands to the south. Neither did they doubt that their success in this would bring the region progress and prosperity. What had happened so often at home was now to be duplicated abroad, they believed, and so did their contemporaries.

What American businessmen and policy makers feared in the Caribbean was not economic failure, but the challenge of their transatlantic rivals to United States control of the region. If they saw the principal barrier to Caribbean development in the supposed deficiencies of the native peoples, they were only slightly less concerned with the threat of European intervention in the area. France's invasion of Mexico in the 1860s, the French Panamá canal project of the 1880s, and the events leading to the Venezuelan crisis with England in the mid-1890s all mobilized long-standing fears in the United States that Europe's imperial rivalries might spill over into the Americas. As Richard Olney's "twenty-inch gun" note of 1895 had so dramatically stated, most Americans would regard such outside intervention in the hemisphere as disastrous, threatening United States security, prestige, and future economic growth. The Monroe Doctrine's dictum against the possibility had long expressed a central tenet of United States foreign policy, and commanded the most widespread popular support. . . .

In general, however, contemporary Americans were united in their opposition to European expansion in the New World, and after 1900 they came quickly to focus their strongest fears and suspicions, no longer on France or Great Britain, but on the rising power of imperial Germany. From the beginning of the twentieth century, this perceived "German threat" constituted one of the ongoing assumptions behind United States policies in the Caribbean.

Belief in a German threat to the Americas was growing rapidly even before Theodore Roosevelt became president in 1901, and it became pervasive in the policy-making circles of the Roosevelt administration. As early as 1898, Roosevelt himself believed that "of all the nations of Europe it seems to me that Germany is by far the most hostile to us." By 1901, he was certain that only a major naval building program could deter the kaiser's ambitions. "I find that the Germans regard our failure to go forward in building up the navy this year as a sign that our spasm of preparation, as they think it, has come to an end," he wrote, that we shall sink back, so that in a few years they will be in a position to take some step in the West Indies or South America which will make us either put up or shut up on the Monroe Doctrine; they counting upon their ability to trounce us if we try the former horn of the dilemma.

To an English correspondent, Roosevelt confided that "as things are now the Monroe Doctrine does not touch England . . . the only power that needs to be reminded of its existence is Germany." In particular, he feared the Germans would find ways to acquire the Dutch and Danish possessions in the Americas to use as bases for the insertion of their power. By 1905, however, the president felt that his firm stance, accompanied by a continuing program of naval expansion, had become an effective deterrent: "I think I succeeded in impressing on the Kaiser, quietly and unofficially . . . that the violation of the Monroe Doctrine by territorial aggrandizement on his part around the Caribbean meant war, not ultimately, but immediately, and without any delay." It was, however, a deterrent which required continual alertness and preparation, he thought. . . .

These fears of hostile German intentions were not confined to administration insiders, but were matters of common knowledge and objects of frequent discussion in the press. They outlived the end of the Roosevelt administration, to be reinvigorated by the events of the First World War. Why were Americans so sure that Germany's power was dangerous to them, and how accurate was their assumption?

Germany, like the United States, was a fast-rising industrial power and a relative newcomer to the imperial scramble for colonies. Also like the United States, it had recently entered the international competition to become a leading naval power. Its flamboyant kaiser, fond of military show and symbolism, talked altogether too freely at times of his grandiose ambitions. The Prussian military tradition dominated the new German Empire, and if its navy aimed to become one of the strongest in due time, the position of its army was already fixed at or near the top. This was, in short, a formidable, energetic state, which appeared both ambitious and menacing to powers with established claims. . . .

There were also reasons to tie a prospective German threat to the Caribbean. Admiral Alfred von Tirpitz, the powerful German naval chief, wished to acquire bases in the western hemisphere to match those already held by Great Britain and France. He thought of finding such bases on the coast of Brazil, where three hundred thousand German immigrants had settled in the recent past, or in the Galapagos Islands on the Pacific side of South America. He also talked, however, of gaining possession for Germany of the Dutch or Danish colonies in the Caribbean area and thereby gaining a base at Curaçao, Surinam, or the Virgin Islands, a possibility that worried American naval strategists.

Between 1897 and 1905, German naval staff officers elaborated a series of war plans involving an attack upon the east coast of the United States. Their original concept of a direct descent upon New York, Norfolk, Boston, or elsewhere was eventually modified to include the prior seizure of an advanced base in Puerto Rico or Cuba. Such a staging point would make an invasion less risky, and had the added advantage that its seizure would force the American fleet to come out and fight at a time and place chosen by the Germans. By 1901 the Army General Staff had joined the Admiralty Staff in joint planning, General Alfred von Schlieffen originally estimating that fifty thousand men would be required to take and hold Cuba. A later version of the plan substituted Puerto Rico for Cuba, and reduced the troop strength for its seizure to something over twelve thousand men. Finally, in 1906, the war operations plan was reduced to a mere theoretical exercise, as rising tensions in Europe made it too dangerous to consider committing Germany's entire naval strength to operations in another part of the world. The continued increase in United States naval strength also acted to discourage German planners, and in 1909 the German navy's Caribbean–South Atlantic squadron was discontinued.

While Germany's war plans were kept secret, some idea of their nature leaked through to the United States, where American naval leaders added a real fear of invasion to their earlier anti-German bias. Repeated rumors of the German General Staff's hostile activity confirmed Theodore Roosevelt in his belief in a Teutonic threat and his determination to keep the navy strong. Interestingly, his conviction in 1905 that he had succeeded in deterring the kaiser's ambitions through a policy of firmness and strength came reasonably close to the moment when Berlin itself ceased to consider an American adventure. By 1909 President William Howard Taft would call talk of German aggression in the hemisphere "absurd," and even the navy became less convinced that a clash was imminent.

By that time, however, Americans perceived another kind of threat, as Germany's economic penetration of Latin America and success in selling its exports there identified her as a leading trade rival. The large German immigration to South America and the prominent role of resident German businessmen in many Latin American cities reinforced the picture of a drive for economic domination. Such domination was achieved in fact only in tiny, poverty-stricken Haiti, where German merchants did control the great bulk of international trade. Elsewhere, however, the growth of United States trade outpaced that of its rivals, including Germany; rapid Latin American economic growth in the early twentieth century had in fact increased the exports of all the leading suppliers to the area, but none more than the United States.

Whether there really was a "German threat" to the United States or its Caribbean interests is still a matter of debate. H. H. Herwig and David Trask have argued that the intensive German war planning at the beginning of the century indicated a serious interest in naval and military circles in an aggressive war against the United States. Admiral von Tirpitz made no secret of his ambitions in the western hemisphere, and he had considerable influence over the impressionable kaiser. True, such a war now appears adventurist and dangerous, risking German power far from home for distinctly marginal purposes, and the Germans themselves eventually thought better of it. However, they long discounted American naval, and more especially military, strength on the assumption that the United States armed forces were weakened by indiscipline and inefficiency. Thus, according to this view, it was only the growing crisis in Europe itself that finally acted to cancel out Berlin's aspirations in the New World.

Melvin Small agrees that Americans long feared a German attack, but concludes that the decision makers in Berlin never seriously considered Latin

American conquest or North American aggression. Whatever intellectual gymnastics the service leaders undertook, they did not reflect actual government policy, his argument implies. Certainly after 1903, he says, the kaiser's government hoped for good relations with the United States, not confrontation. All in all, Small believes, the "German threat" had been more apparent than real. Yet Small omits a close scrutiny of the period from 1898 to 1903, where lay the strongest indications of a hostile German purpose. On the other hand, no one has made much of a case for a German threat after 1906, even if one existed earlier. One is forced to conclude that the *continuation* of the fear of German designs in the hemisphere was ill founded, even as one concedes the sincerity of most of its prophets.

Justified or not, fear of Germany played a significant part in American thinking about the area as a vital security zone. Concern for the national security blended in turn with economic objectives, status ambition, and even reforming zeal to motivate a quest for United States hegemony. As they looked southward, Americans saw a potentially rich area awaiting development. They believed its resident peoples backward and inferior, incapable by themselves of achieving progress or material development. They feared that European rivals might challenge American power and policies in the region, and in particular that Germany would do so, perhaps go even further and unleash armed aggression against the United States. And they accepted a European-made concept of international law which upheld the rights and interests of foreign enterprisers in undeveloped countries. All of these assumptions, singly and together, encouraged Americans to feel that they should play a leading role in the Caribbean, in order to benefit themselves, develop the region, and forestall foreign threats. Most Americans soon came to see United States hegemony as practical, right, legally justified, and even necessary.

POSTSCRIPT

Was Early Twentieth-Century American Foreign Policy in the Caribbean Basin Dominated by Economic Concerns?

In *Drive to Hegemony,* Healy provides us with a sophisticated summary of the most recent scholarship. Yet, in a number of ways Healy supports the views of Samuel F. Bemis, which are developed in *Latin American Policy of the United States* (Harcourt, Brace & World, 1943). Both argue that U.S. foreign policy was primarily concerned with the German threat to the security in the Caribbean. Both recognize the importance of economic factors, yet maintain that American businesses would invest or trade in the Caribbean only when encouraged by the U.S. government.

Healy gives the economic argument a new twist when he says that it was understandable why so many Yankees believed that the Caribbean was ripe for economic development. Since the United States built its industrial revolution upon its agricultural export surpluses, the assumption was that the Latin American nations could do likewise. But Healy is not willing to call the North Americans "benevolent imperialists" as Bemis does. Instead, he recognizes that American policy makers considered their neighbors to be of "racially inferior" stock and used this to partially explain the lack of economic progress in the Caribbean.

LaFeber has a different perspective than Healy in his view of U.S. relations with Central America. "From the beginning," argues LaFeber, "North American leaders believed their new republic was fated to be dominant in Spanish-held Mexico, Central America, and, indeed, the regions beyond. . . . Capitalism and military security went hand in hand . . . and since the nineteenth century, formed two sides of the same policy in Central America." LaFeber's emphasis on economic forces determining our relationship in the Caribbean is hardly new. In 1934 Charles Beard and George H. E. Smith anticipated many of Bemis's arguments and presented a detailed account of the penetration of Latin America by big business in *The Idea of National Interest* (Macmillan, 1934). LaFeber's broadened definition of imperialism is also not a new concept. Over 30 years ago, William Appleman Williams, LaFeber's graduate school mentor, in *The Tragedy of American Diplomacy,* 2d rev., enlarged ed. (Delta, 1972), argued that the United States created an informal empire in Latin America, Asia, and later Europe via the penetration of American business interests.

What distinguishes LaFeber's analysis is his application of the economic theory of "neodependency" to describe U.S. relations in the Caribbean. First outlined in the 1960s by a number of radical economists, the theory of dependency argues that the United States has used its economic strength to make the development of Latin American countries economically dependent upon the United States. Highly controversial, this theory has been criticized by David Ray in "The Dependency Model of Latin America Underdevelopment: Three Basic Fallacies," *Journal of Interamerican Studies and World Affairs* (February 1973). Ray's critique is very general, but it very easily applies to LaFeber's use of the dependency theory in his discussion of U.S. policy in the Caribbean area. He argues that "the model claims that dependency is caused by the economics of capitalism." If this is true, how can Soviet economic imperialism in Eastern Europe be explained? These countries are economically dominated by Russia, a country that lacks a capitalist economic system. The dependency model also assumes "that private foreign investment is invariably exploitative and invariably detrimental to Latin American development." But not all foreign investments are bad. Although investments in extractive industries can distort a country's economy, investments in industries that seek to expand the domestic market may be beneficial to the Central American nation. Finally, the model assumes that these countries face only two choices: dependent capitalism or nondependent "popular revolutionary governments which open the way to socialism." Consider the examples of Cuba and Nicaragua today. To what extent are they less dependent upon the Soviet bloc trade than they previously had been on trade with the West? How vulnerable are they to Soviet pressures on political and economic issues? In short, "the dependency theorists," says Ray, "conceptualize dependency/nondependency as a dichotomous variable, rather than a continuous one."

Many fine monographic studies have appeared on this subject in the last 20 years. Good overviews of this research can be found in David M. Pletcher's "United States Relations with Latin America: Neighborliness and Exploitation," *American Historical Review* (February 1977) and Richard V. Salisbury's "Good Neighbors? The United States and Latin America in the Twentieth Century," in Gerald K. Haines and J. Samuel Walker, eds., *American Foreign Relations: A Historiographical Overview* (Greenwood Press, 1981).

In a review essay of David Healy's *Drive to Hegemony* in *Diplomatic History* (Summer 1990), David M. Pletcher provides an annotated bibliographical review of all the major works on this subject for the past 75 years. An accessible and acerbic critique of the Williams-LaFeber economic analysis of United States–Caribbean relations can be found in Arthur M. Schlesinger, Jr., *The Cycles of American History* (Houghton Mifflin, 1986).

ISSUE 8

Did the Progressives Fail?

YES: Richard M. Abrams, from "The Failure of Progressivism," in Richard Abrams and Lawrence Levine, eds., *The Shaping of the Twentieth Century,* 2d ed. (Little, Brown, 1971)

NO: Arthur S. Link and Richard L. McCormick, from *Progressivism* (Harlan Davidson, 1983)

ISSUE SUMMARY

YES: Professor of history Richard M. Abrams maintains that progressivism was a failure because it tried to impose a uniform set of values upon a culturally diverse people and never seriously confronted the inequalities that still exist in American society.

NO: Professors of history Arthur S. Link and Richard L. McCormick argue that the Progressives were a diverse group of reformers who confronted and ameliorated the worst abuses that emerged in urban industrial America during the early 1900s.

*P**rogressivism* is a word used by historians to define the reform currents in the years between the end of the Spanish-American War and America's entrance into the Great War in Europe in 1917. The so-called Progressive movement had been in operation for over a decade before the label was first used in the 1919 electoral campaigns. Former president Theodore Roosevelt ran as a third-party candidate in the 1912 election on the Progressive party ticket, but in truth the party had no real organization outside of the imposing figure of Theodore Roosevelt. Therefore, as a label, "progressivism" was rarely used as a term of self-identification for its supporters. Even after 1912, it was more frequently used by journalists and historians to distinguish the reformers of the period from socialists and old-fashioned conservatives.

The 1890s was a crucial decade for many Americans. From 1893 until almost the turn of the century, the nation went through a terrible economic depression. With the forces of industrialization, urbanization, and immigration wreaking havoc upon the traditional political, social, and economic structures of American life, changes were demanded. The reformers responded in a variety of ways. The proponents of good government believed that democracy was threatened because the cities were ruled by corrupt political machines while the state legislatures were dominated by corporate interests. The cure was to purify democracy and place government directly in the hands of the people through such devices as the initiative, referendum, recall, and the direct election of local school board officials, judges, and U.S. senators.

Social justice proponents saw the problem from a different perspective. Settlement workers moved into cities and tried to change the urban environment. They pushed for sanitation improvements, tenement house reforms, factory inspection laws, regulation of the hours and wages of women, and the abolition of child labor.

A third group of reformers considered the major problem to be the trusts. They argued for controls over the power of big business and for the preservation of the free enterprise system. Progressives disagreed on whether the issue was size or conduct and on whether the remedy was trust-busting or the regulation of big business. But none could deny the basic question: How was the relationship between big business and the U.S. government to be defined?

How successful was the Progressive movement? What triggered the reform impulse? Who were its leaders? How much support did it attract? More important, did the laws that resulted from the various movements fulfill the intentions of its leaders and supporters?

In the following selections, Richard M. Abrams distinguishes the Progressives from other reformers of the era, such as the Populists, the Socialists, the mainstream labor unions, and the corporate reorganization movement. He then argues that the Progressive movement failed because it tried to impose a uniform set of middle-class Protestant moral values upon a nation that was growing more culturally diverse, and because the reformers supported movements that brought about no actual changes or only superficial ones at best. The real inequalities in American society, says Abrams, were never addressed.

In contrast, Arthur S. Link and Richard L. McCormick view progressivism from the point of view of the reformers and rank it as a qualified success. They survey the criticisms of the movement made by historians since the 1950s and generally find them unconvincing. They maintain that the Progressives made the first real attempts to change the destructive direction in which modern urban-industrial society was moving.

YES

Richard M. Abrams

The Failure of Progressivism

Our first task is definitional, because clearly it would be possible to beg the whole question of "failure" by means of semantical niceties. I have no intention of being caught in that kind of critics' trap. I hope to establish that there was a distinctive major reform movement that took place during most of the first two decades of this century, that it had a mostly coherent set of characteristics and long-term objectives, and that, measured by its own criteria—not criteria I should wish, through hindsight and preference, to impose on it—it fell drastically short of its chief goals.

One can, of course, define a reform movement so broadly that merely to acknowledge that we are where we are and that we enjoy some advantages over where we were would be to prove the "success" of the movement. In many respects, Arthur Link does this sort of thing, both in his and William B. Catton's popular textbook, *American Epoch*, and in his article, "What Happened to the Progressive Movement in the 1920's?" In the latter, Link defines "progressivism" as a movement that "began convulsively in the 1890's and waxed and waned afterward to our own time, to insure the survival of democracy in the United States by the enlargement of governmental power to control and offset the power of private economic groups over the nation's institutions and life." Such a definition may be useful to classify data gathered to show the liberal sources of the enlargement of governmental power since the 1890's; but such data would not be finely classified enough to tell us much about the *non*liberal sources of governmental power (which were numerous and important), about the distinctive styles of different generations of reformers concerned with a liberal society, or even about vital distinctions among divergent reform groups in the era that contemporaries and the conventional historical wisdom have designed as progressive. . . .

Now, without going any further into the problem of historians' definitions which are too broad or too narrow—there is no space here for such an effort—I shall attempt a definition of my own, beginning with the problem that contemporaries set themselves to solve and that gave the era its cognomen, "progressive." That problem was *progress*—or more specifically, how American society was to continue to enjoy the fruits of material progress without the accompanying assault upon human dignity and the erosion of the conventional values and moral assumptions on which the social order appeared to rest. . . .

To put it briefly and yet more specifically, a very large body of men and women entered into reform activities at the end of the nineteenth century to translate "the national credo" (as Henry May calls it) into a general program for social action. Their actions, according to Richard Hofstadter, were "founded upon the indigenous Yankee-Protestant political tradition [that] assumed and demanded the constant disinterested activity of the citizen in public affairs, argued that political life ought to be run, to a greater degree than it was, in accordance with general principles and abstract laws apart from and superior to personal needs, and expressed a common feeling that government should be in good part an effort to moralize the lives of individuals while economic life should be intimately related to the stimulation and development of individual character."

The most consistently important reform impulse, among *many* reform impulses, during the progressive era grew directly from these considerations. It is this reform thrust that we should properly call "the progressive movement." We should distinguish it carefully from reform movements in the era committed primarily to other considerations.

The progressive movement drew its strength from the old mugwump reform impulse, civil service reform, female emancipationists, prohibitionists, the social gospel, the settlement-house movement, some national expansionists, some world peace advocates, conservation advocates, technical efficiency experts, and a wide variety of intellectuals who helped cut through the stifling, obstructionist smokescreen of systematized ignorance. It gained powerful allies from many disadvantaged business interests that appealed to politics to redress unfavorable trade positions; from some ascendant business interests seeking institutional protection; from publishers who discovered the promotional value of exposes; and from politicians-on-the-make who sought issues with which to dislodge long-lived incumbents from their place. Objectively it focused on or expressed (1) a concern for responsive, honest, and efficient government, on the local and state levels especially; (2) recognition of the obligations of society— particularly of an affluent society—to its underprivileged; (3) a desire for more rational use of the nation's resources and economic energies; (4) a rejection, on at least intellectual grounds, of certain social principles that had long obstructed social remedies for what had traditionally been regarded as irremediable evils, such as poverty; and, above all, (5) a concern for the maintenance or restoration of a consensus on what conventionally had been regarded as *fixed moral* principles. "The first and central faith in the national credo," writes Professor May, "was, as it always had been, the reality, certainty, and eternity of moral values. . . . A few thought and said that ultimate values and goals were unnecessary, but in most cases this meant that they believed so deeply in a consensus on these matters that they could not imagine a serious challenge." Progressives shared this faith with most of the rest of the country, but they also conceived of themselves, with a grand sense of stewardship, as its heralds, and its agents.

The progressive movement was (and is) distinguishable from other Contemporary reform movements not only by its devotion to social conditions regarded, by those within it as well as by much of the generality, as *normative*, but also by its definition of what forces threatened that order. More specifically, progressivism directed its shafts at five principal enemies, each in its own way representing reform:

1. The *socialist reform movement*—because, despite socialism's usually praiseworthy concern for human dignity, it represented the subordination of the rights of private property and of individualistic options to objectives that often explicitly threatened common religious beliefs and conventional standards of justice and excellence.
2. The corporate reorganization of American business, which I should call *the corporate reform movement* (its consequence has, after all, been called "the corporate revolution")—because it challenged the traditional relationship of ownership and control of private property, because it represented a shift from production to profits in the entrepreneurial definition of efficiency, because it threatened the proprietary small-business character of the American social structure, because it had already demonstrated a capacity for highly concentrated and socially irresponsible power, and because it sanctioned practices that strained the limits of conventionality and even legality.
3. *The labor union movement*—because despite the virtues of unionized labor as a source of countervailing force against the corporations and as a basis for a more orderly labor force, unionism (like corporate capitalism and socialism) suggested a reduction of individualistic options (at least for wage-earners and especially for small employers), and a demand for a partnership with business management in the decision-making process by a class that convention excluded from such a role.
4. *Agrarian radicalism*, and populism in particular—because it, too, represented (at least in appearance) the insurgency of a class conventionally believed to be properly excluded from a policy-making role in the society, a class graphically represented by the "Pitchfork" Bens and "Sockless" Jerrys, the "Cyclone" Davises and "Alfalfa" Bills, the wool hat brigade and the rednecks.
5. *The ethnic movement*—the demand for specific political and social recognition of ethnic or ex-national affiliations—because accession to the demand meant acknowledgment of the fragmentation of American society as well as a retreat from official standards of integrity, honesty, and efficiency in government in favor of standards based on personal loyalty, partisanship, and sectarian provincialism.

Probably no two progressives opposed all of these forces with equal animus, and most had a noteworthy sympathy for one or more of them. . . .

So much for what progressivism was not. Let me sum it up by noting that what it rejected and sought to oppose necessarily says much about what it was—perhaps even more than can be ascertained by the more direct approach.

My thesis is that progressivism failed. It failed in what it—or what those who shaped it—conceived to be its principal objective. And that was, over and above everything else, to restore or maintain the conventional consensus on a particular view of the universe, a particular set of values, and a particular constellation of behavioral modes in the country's commerce, its industry, its social relations, and its politics. Such a view, such values, such modes were challenged by the influx of diverse religious and ethnic elements into the nation's social and intellectual stream, by the overwhelming economic success and power of the corporate form of business organization, by the subordination of the work-ethic bound up within the old proprietary and craft enterprise system, and by the increasing centrality of a growing proportion of low-income, unskilled, wage-earning classes in the nation's economy and social structure. Ironically, the *coup de grâce* would be struck by the emergence of a philosophical and scientific rationale for the existence of cultural diversity within a single social system, a rationale that largely grew out of the very intellectual ferment to which progressivism so substantially contributed.

Progressivism sought to save the old view, and the old values and modes, by educating the immigrants and the poor so as to facilitate their acceptance of and absorption into the Anglo-American mode of life, or by excluding the "unassimilable" altogether; by instituting antitrust legislation or, at the least, by imposing regulations upon corporate practices in order to preserve a minimal base for small proprietary business enterprise; by making legislative accommodations to the newly important wage-earning classes—accommodations that might provide some measure of wealth and income redistribution, on-the-job safety, occupational security, and the like—so as to forestall a forcible transfer of policy-making power away from the groups that had conventionally exercised that power; and by broadening the political selection process, through direct elections, direct nominations, and direct legislation, in order to reduce tensions caused unnecessarily by excessively narrow and provincial cliques of policymakers. When the economic and political reforms failed to restore the consensus by giving the previously unprivileged an ostensible stake in it, progressive energies turned increasingly toward using the force of the state to proscribe or restrict specifically opprobrious modes of social behavior, such as gaming habits, drinking habits, sexual habits, and Sabbatarian habits. In the ultimate resort, with the proliferation of sedition and criminal syndicalist laws, it sought to constrict political discourse itself. And (except perhaps for the disintegration of the socialist movement) *that* failed, too.

One measure of progressivism's failure lies in the xenophobic racism that reappeared on a large scale even by 1910. In many parts of the country, for example, in the far west and the south, racism and nativism had been fully blended with reform movements even at the height of progressive activities there. The alleged threats of "coolie labor" to American living standards, and of "venal" immigrant and Negro voting to republican institutions generally, underlay the alliance of racism and reform in this period. By and large, however, for the early progressive era the alliance was conspicuous only in the south and on the west coast. By 1910, signs of heightening ethnic animosities, most notably anti-Catholicism, began appearing in other areas of the country as well. As John Higham has written, "It is hard to explain the rebirth of anti-Catholic ferment [at this time] except as an outlet for expectations which progressivism raised and then failed to fulfill." The failure here was in part the inability of reform to deliver a meaningful share of the social surplus to the groups left out of the general national progress, and in part the inability of reform to achieve its objective of assimilation and consensus.

The growing ethnic animus, moreover, operated to compound the difficulty of achieving assimilation. By the second decade of the century, the objects of the antagonism were beginning to adopt a frankly assertive posture. The World War, and the ethnic cleavages it accentuated and aggravated, represented only the final blow to the assimilationist idea; "hyphenate" tendencies had already been growing during the years before 1914. It had only been in 1905 that the Louisvilleborn and secular-minded Louis Brandeis had branded as "disloyal" all who "keep alive" their differences of origin or religion. By 1912, by now a victim of anti-Semitism and aware of a rising hostility toward Jews in the country, Brandeis had become an active Zionist; before a Jewish audience in 1913, he remarked how "practical experience" had convinced him that "to be good Americans, we must be better Jews, and to be better Jews, we must become Zionists."

Similarly, American Negroes also began to adopt a more aggressive public stance after having been subdued for more than a decade by antiblack violence and the accommodationist tactics suggested in 1895 by Booker T. Washington. As early as 1905, many black leaders had broken with Washington in founding the Niagara Movement for a more vigorous assertion of Negro demands for equality. But most historians seem to agree that it was probably the Springfield race riot of 1908 that ended illusions that black people could gain an equitable share in the rewards of American culture by accommodationist or assimilationist methods. The organization of the NAACP in 1909 gave substantive force for the first time to the three-year-old Niagara Movement. The year 1915 symbolically concluded the demise of accommodationism. That year, the Negro-baiting movie, "The Birth of a Nation," played to massive, enthusiastic audiences that included notably the president of the United States and the chief justice of the Supreme Court; the KKK was revived; and Booker T. Washington died. The next year, black nationalist Marcus Garvey arrived in New York from Jamaica.

Meanwhile, scientific knowledge about race and culture was undergoing a crucial revision. At least in small part stimulated by a keen self-consciousness of his own "outsider" status in American culture, the German-Jewish immigrant Franz Boas was pioneering in the new anthropological concept of "cultures," based on the idea that human behavioral traits are conditioned by historical traditions. The new view of culture was in time to undermine completely the prevailing evolutionary view that ethnic differences must mean racial inequality. The significance of Boas's work after 1910, and that of his students A. L. Kroeber and Clyde Kluckhohn in particular, rests on the fact that the racist thought of the progressive era had founded its intellectual rationale on the monistic, evolutionary view of culture; and indeed much of the progressives' anxiety over the threatened demise of "the American culture" had been founded on that view.

Other intellectual developments as well had for a long time been whittling away at the notion that American society had to stand or fall on the unimpaired coherence of its cultural consensus. Yet the new work in anthropology, law, philosophy, physics, psychology, and literature only unwittingly undermined that assumption. Rather, it was only as the ethnic hostilities grew, and especially as the power of the state came increasingly to be invoked against dissenting groups whose ethnic "peculiarities" provided an excuse for repression, that the new intelligence came to be developed. "The world has thought that it must have its culture and its political unity coincide," wrote Randolph Bourne in 1916 while chauvinism, nativism, and antiradicalism were mounting; now it was seeing that cultural diversity might yet be the salvation of the liberal society—that it might even serve to provide the necessary countervailing force to the power of the state that private property had once served (in the schema of Locke, Harrington, and Smith) before the interests of private property became so highly concentrated and so well blended with the state itself.

The telltale sign of progressivism's failure was the violent crusade against dissent that took place in the closing years of the Wilson administration. It is too easy to ascribe the literal hysteria of the postwar years to the dislocations of the War alone. Incidents of violent repression of labor and radical activities had been growing remarkably, often in step with xenophobic outbreaks, for several years before America's intervention in the War. To quote Professor Higham once more. "The seemingly unpropitious circumstances under which antiradicalism and anti-Catholicism came to life [after 1910] make their renewal a subject of moment." It seems clear that they both arose out of the sources of the reform ferment itself. When reform failed to enlarge the consensus, or to make it more relevant to the needs of the still disadvantaged and disaffected, and when in fact reform seemed to be encouraging more radical challenges to the social order, the old anxieties of the 1890's returned.

The postwar hysteria represented a reaction to a confluence of anxiety-laden developments, including the high cost of living, the physical and social dislocations of war mobilization and the recruitment of women and Negroes into war production jobs in the big northern cities, the Bolshevik Revolution, a series of labor strikes, and a flood of radical literature that exaggerated the capabilities of radical action. "One Hundred Per Cent Americanism" seemed the only effective way of meeting all these challenges at once. As Stanley Coben has written, making use of recent psychological studies and anthropological work on cultural "revitalization movements"; "Citizens who joined the crusade for one hundred per cent Americanism sought, primarily, a unifying forte which would halt the apparent disintegration of their culture. . . . The slight evidence of danger from radical organizations aroused such wild fear only because Americans had already encountered other threats to cultural stability."

Now, certainly during the progressive era a lot of reform legislation was passed, much that contributed genuinely to a more liberal society, though more that contributed to the more absolutistic moral objectives of progressivism. Progressivism indeed had real, lasting effects for the blunting of the sharper edges of self-interest in American life, and for the reduction of the harsher cruelties suffered by the society's underprivileged. These achievements deserve emphasis, not least because they derived directly from the progressive habit of looking to standards of conventional morality and human decency for the solution of diverse social conflicts. But the deeper nature of the problem Confronting American society required more than the invocation of conventional standards; the conventions themselves were at stake, especially as they bore upon the allocation of privileges and rewards. Because most of the progressives never confronted that problem, in a way their efforts were doomed to failure.

In sum, the overall effect of the period's legislation is not so impressive. For example, all the popular government measures put together have not Conspicuously raised the quality of American political life. Direct nominations and elections have tended to make political campaigns so expensive as to reduce the number of eligible candidates for public office to (1) the independently wealthy; (2) the ideologues, especially on the right, who can raise the needed campaign money from independently wealthy ideologues like themselves, or from the organizations set up to promote a particular ideology; and (3) party hacks who payoff their debt to the party treasury by whistle-stopping and chicken dinner speeches. Direct legislation through the Initiative and Referendum device has made cities and states prey to the best-financed and organized special-interest group pressures, as have so-called nonpartisan elections. Which is not to say that things are worse than before, but only that they are not conspicuously better. The popular government measures did have the effect of shaking up the established political organizations of the day, and that may well have been their only real purpose.

But as Arthur Link has said, in his text, *The American Epoch*, the popular government measures "were merely instruments to facilitate the capture of political machinery. . . . They must be judged for what they accomplished or failed to accomplish on the higher level of substantive reform." Without disparaging the long list of reform measures that passed during the progressive era, the question remains whether all the "substantive reforms" together accomplished what the progressives wanted them to accomplish.

Certain social and economic advantages were indeed shuffled about, but this must be regarded as a short-term achievement for special groups at best. Certain commercial interests, for example, achieved greater political leverage in railroad policy-making than they had had in 1900 through measures such as the Hepburn and Mann-Elkins Acts—though it was not until the 1940's that any real change occurred in the general rate structure, as some broad regional interests had been demanding at the beginning of the century. Warehouse, farm credits, and land-bank acts gave the diminishing numbers of farm owners enhanced opportunities to mortgage their property, and some business groups had persuaded the federal government to use national revenues to educate farmers on how to increase their productivity (Smith-Lever Act, 1914); but most farmers remained as dependent as ever upon forces beyond their control—the bankers, the middlemen, the international market. The FTC, and the Tariff Commission established in 1916, extended the principle of using government agencies to adjudicate intra-industrial conflicts ostensibly in the national interest, but these agencies would develop a lamentable tendency of deferring to and even confirming rather than moderating the power of each industry's dominant interests. The Federal Reserve Act made the currency more flexible, and that certainly made more sense than the old system, as even the bankers agreed. But depositers would be as prey to defaulting banks as they had been in the days of the Pharaoh—bank deposit insurance somehow was "socialism" to even the best of men in this generation. And despite Woodrow Wilson's brave promise to end the banker's stifling hold on innovative small business, one searches in vain for some provision in the FRA designed specifically to encourage small or new businesses. In fact, the only constraints on the bankers' power that emerged from the era came primarily from the ability of the larger corporations to finance their own expansion out of capital surpluses they had accumulated from extortionate profits during the War.

A major change almost occurred during the war years when organized labor and the principle of collective bargaining received official recognition and a handful of labor leaders was taken, temporarily, into policy-making councils (e.g., in the War Labor Board). But actually, as already indicated, such a development, if it had been made permanent, would have represented a defeat, not a triumph, for progressivism. The progressives may have fought for improved labor conditions, but they jealously fought against the enlargement of union power. It was no aberration that once the need for wartime productive efficiency evaporated, leading progressives such as A. Mitchell Palmer, Miles Poindexter, and Woodrow Wilson himself helped civic and employer organizations to bludgeon the labor movement into disunity and docility. (It is possible, I suppose, to argue that such progressives were simply inconsistent, but if we understand progressivism in the terms I have outlined above I think the consistency is more evident.) Nevertheless, a double irony is worth noting with respect to progressivism's objectives and the wartime labor developments. On the one hand, the progressives' hostility to labor unions defeated their own objectives of (1) counterbalancing the power of collectivized capital (i.e., corporations), and (2) enhancing workers' share of the nation's wealth. On the other hand, under wartime duress, the progressives did grant concessions to organized labor (e.g., the Adamson Eight-Hour Railway Labor Act, as well as the WLB) that would later serve as precedents for the very "collectivization" of the economic situation that they were dedicated to oppose.

Meanwhile, the distribution of advantages in the society did not change much at all. In some cases, from the progressive reformers' viewpoint at least, it may even have changed for the worse. According to the figures of the National Industrial Conference Board, even income was as badly distributed at the end of the era as before. In 1921, the highest 10 percent of income recipients received 38 percent of total personal income, and that figure was only 34 percent in 1910. (Since the share of the top S percent of income recipients probably declined in the 1910–20 period, the figures for the top 10 percent group suggest a certain improvement in income distribution at the top. But the fact that the share of the lowest 60 percent also declined in that period, from 35 percent to 30 percent, confirms the view that no meaningful improvement can be shown.) Maldistribution was to grow worse until after 1929.

American farmers on the whole and in particular seemed to suffer increasing disadvantages. Farm life was one of the institutional bulwarks of the mode of life the progressives ostensibly cherished. "The farmer who owns his land" averred Gifford Pinchot, "is still the backbone of the Nation; and one of the things we want most is more of him, . . . [for] he is the first of home-makers." If only in the sense that there were relatively fewer farmers in the total population at the end of the progressive era, one would have to say farm life in the United States had suffered. But, moreover, fewer owned their own farms. The number of farm tenants increased by 21 percent from 1900 to 1920; 38.1 percent of all farm operators in 1921 were tenants; and the figures look even worse when one notices that tenancy *declined* in the most *impoverished* areas during this period, suggesting that the family farm was surviving mostly in the more marginal agricultural areas. Finally, although agriculture had enjoyed some of its most prosperous years in history in the 1910–20 period, the 21 percent of the nation's gainfully employed who were in agriculture in 1919 (a peak year) earned only 16 percent of the national income.

While progressivism failed to restore vitality to American farming, it failed also to stop the vigorous ascendancy of corporate capitalism, the most conspicuous challenge to conventional values and modes that the society faced at the beginning of the era. The corporation had drastically undermined the very basis of the traditional rationale that had supported the nation's free-wheeling system of resource allocation and had underwritten the permissive-ness of the laws governing economic activities in the nineteenth century. The new capitalism by-passed the privately-owned proprietary firm, it featured a separation of ownership and control, it subordinated the profit motive to var-ied and variable other objectives such as empire-building, and, in many of the techniques developed by financial brokers and investment bankers, it appeared to create a great gulf between the making of money and the produc-ing of useful goods and services. Through a remarkable series of judicial soph-istries, this nonconventional form of business enterprise had become, in law, a *person*, and had won privileges and liberties once entrusted only to men, who were presumed to be conditioned and restrained by the moral qualities that inhere in human nature. Although gaining legal dispensations from an oblig-ing Supreme Court, the corporation could claim no theoretical legitimacy beyond the fact of its power and its apparent inextricable entanglement in the business order that had produced America's seemingly unbounded material success.

Although much has been written about the supposed continuing vitality of small proprietary business enterprise in the United States, there is no gainsaying the continued ascendancy of the big corporation nor the fact that it still lacks legitimation. The fact that in the last sixty years the number of small proprietary businesses has grown at a rate that slightly exceeds the rate of population growth says little about the character of small business enter-prise today as compared with that of the era of the American industrial revolution; it does nothing to disparage the apprehensions expressed in the antitrust campaigns of the progressives. To focus on the vast numbers of automobile dealers and gasoline service station owners, for example, is to miss completely their truly humble dependence upon the very few giant auto-mobile and oil companies, a foretold dependence that was the very point of

progressives' anticorporation, antitrust sentiments. The progressive movement must indeed be credited with placing real restraints upon monopolistic
tendencies in the United States, for most statistics indicate that at least until
the 1950's business concentration showed no substantial increase from the
turn of the century (though it may be pertinent to note that concentration
ratios did increase significantly in the decade immediately following the progressive era). But the statistics of concentration remain impressive—just as
they were when John Moody wrote *The Truth About the Trusts* in 1904 and Louis
Brandeis followed it with *Other People's Money* in 1914. That two hundred corporations (many of them interrelated) held almost one-quarter of all business
assets, and more than 40 percent of all corporate assets in the country in 1948;
that the fifty largest manufacturing corporations held 35 percent of all industrial assets in 1948, and 38 percent by 1962; and that a mere twenty-eight
corporations or one one-thousandth of a percentage of all nonfinancial firms
in 1956 employed 10 percent of all those employed in the nonfinancial industries, should be sufficient statistical support for the apprehensions of the
progressive era—*just as it is testimony to the failure of the progressive movement
to achieve anything substantial to alter the situation.*

Perhaps the crowning failure of progressivism was the American role in
World War I. It is true that many progressives opposed America's intervention, but it is also true that a great many more supported it. The failure in
progressivism lies not in the decision to intervene but in the futility of intervention measured by progressive expectations.

Arthur S. Link and
Richard L. McCormick

 **NO**

Progressivism in History

Convulsive reform movements swept across the American landscape from the 1890s to 1917. Angry farmers demanded better prices for their products, regulation of the railroads, and the destruction of what they thought was the evil power of bankers, middlemen, and corrupt politicians. Urban residents crusaded for better city services and more efficient municipal government. Members of various professions, such as social workers and doctors, tried to improve the dangerous and unhealthy conditions in which many people lived and worked. Businessmen, too, lobbied incessantly for goals which they defined as reform. Never before had the people of the United States engaged in so many diverse movements for the improvement of their political system, economy, were calling themselves progressives. Ever since, historians have used the term *progessivism* to describe the many reform movements of the early twentieth century.

Yet in the goals they sought and the remedies they tried, the reformers were a varied and contradictory lot. Some progressives wanted to increase the political influence and control of ordinary people, while other progressives wanted to concentrate authority in experts. Many reformers tried to curtail the growth of large corporations; others accepted bigness in industry on account of its supposed economic benefits. Some progressives were genuinely concerned about the welfare of the "new" immigrants from southern and eastern Europe; other progressives sought, sometimes frantically, to "Americanize" the newcomers or to keep them out altogether. In general, progressives sought to improve the conditions of life and labor and to create as much social stability as possible. But each group of progressives had its own definitions of improvement and stability. In the face of such diversity, one historian, Peter G. Filene, has even argued that what has been called the progressive movement never existed as a historical phenomenon ("An Obituary for 'The Progressive Movement,'" *American Quarterly*, 1970).

Certainly there was no *unified* movement, but, like most students of the period, we consider progessivism to have been a real, vital, and significant phenomenon, one which contemporaries recognized and talked and fought about. Properly conceptualized, progessivism provides a useful framework for the history of the United States in the late nineteenth and early twentieth centuries.

One source of confusion and controversy about progressives and progressivism is the words themselves. They are often used judgmentally to describe people and changes which historians have deemed to be "good," "enlightened," and "farsighted." The progressives themselves naturally intended the words to convey such positive qualities, but we should not accept their usage uncritically. It might be better to avoid the terms progressive and progressivism altogether, but they are too deeply embedded in the language of contemporaries and historians to be ignored. Besides, we think that the terms have real meaning. In this [selection] the words will be used neutrally, without any implicit judgment about the value of reform.

In the broadest sense, progressivism was the way in which a whole generation of Americans defined themselves politically and responded to the nation's problems at the turn of the century. The progressives made the first comprehensive efforts to grapple with the ills of a modern urban-industrial society. Hence the record of their achievements and failures has considerable relevance for our own time.

Who Were the Progressives?

Ever since the early twentieth century, people have argued about who the progressives were and what they stood for. This may seem to be a strange topic of debate, but it really is not. Progressivism engaged many different groups of Americans, and each group of progressives naturally considered themselves to be the key reformers and thought that their own programs were the most important ones. Not surprisingly, historians ever since have had trouble agreeing on who really shaped progressivism and its goals. Scholars who have written about the period have variously identified farmers, the old middle classes, professionals, businessmen, and urban immigrants and ethnic groups as the core group of progressives. But these historians have succeeded in identifying *their* reformers only by defining progressivism narrowly, by excluding other reformers and reforms when they do not fall within some specific definition, and by resorting to such vague, catch-all adjectives as "middle class." . . .

The advocates of the middle-class view might reply that they intended to study the leaders of reform, not its supporters, to identify and describe the men and women who imparted the dominant character to progressivism, not its mass base. The study of leadership is surely a valid subject in its own right and is particularly useful for an understanding of progressivism. But too much focus on leadership conceals more than it discloses about early twentieth-century reform. The dynamics of progressivism were crucially generated by ordinary people—by the sometimes frenzied mass supporters of progressive leaders, by rank-and-file voters willing to trust a reform candidate. The chronology of progressivism can be traced by events which aroused large numbers of people—a sensational muckraking article, an outrageous political scandal, an eye-opening legislative investigation, or a tragic social calamity. Events such as these gave reform its rhythm and its power.

Progressivism cannot be understood without seeing how the masses of Americans perceived and responded to such events. Widely circulated magazines gave people everywhere the sordid facts of corruption and carried the clamor for reform into every city, village, and county. State and national election campaigns enabled progressive candidates to trumpet their programs. Almost no literate person in the United States in, say, 1906 could have been unaware that ten-year-old children worked through the night in dangerous factories, or that many United States senators served big business. Progressivism was the only reform movement ever experienced by the whole American nation. Its national appeal and mass base vastly exceeded that of Jacksonian reform. And progressivism's dependence on the people for its objectives and timing has no comparison in the executive-dominated New Deal of Franklin D. Roosevelt or the Great Society of Lyndon B. Johnson. Wars and depressions had previously engaged the whole nation, but never reform. And so we are back to the problem of how to explain and define the outpouring of progressive reform which excited and involved so many different kinds of people.

A little more than a decade ago, Buenker and Thelen recognized the immense diversity of progressivism and suggested ways in which to reorient the study of early twentieth-century reform. Buenker observed that divergent groups often came together on one issue and then changed alliances on the next ("The Progressive Era: A Search for a Synthesis," *Mid-America*, 1969). Indeed, different reformers sometimes favored the same measure for distinctive, even opposite, reasons. Progressivism could be understood only in the light of these shifting coalitions. Thelen, in his study of Wisconsin's legislature, also emphasized the importance of cooperation between different reform groups. "The basic riddle in Progressivism," he concluded, "is not what drove groups apart but what made them seek common cause."

There is a great deal of wisdom in these articles, particularly in their recognition of the diversity of progressivism and in the concept of shifting coalitions of reformers. A two-pronged approach is necessary to carry forward this way of looking at early twentieth-century reform. First, we should study, not an imaginary unified progressive movement, but individual reforms and give particular attention to the goals of their diverse supporters, the public rationales given for them, and the results which they achieved. Second, we should try to identify the features which were more or less common to different progressive reforms.

The first task—distinguishing the goals of a reform from its rhetoric and its results—is more difficult than it might appear to be. Older interpretations of progressivism implicitly assumed that the rhetoric explained the goals and that, if a proposed reform became law, the results fulfilled the intentions behind it. Neither assumption is a sound one: purposes, rationale, and results are three different things. Samuel P. Hays' influential article, "The Politics of Reform in Municipal Government in the Progressive Era" (*Pacific Northwest Quarterly*, 1964), exposed the fallacy of automatically equating the democratic rhetoric of the reformers with their true purposes. The two may have coincided, but the historian has to demonstrate that fact, not take it for granted. The unexamined identification of either intentions or rhetoric with results is also invalid, although it is still a common feature of the scholarship on progressivism. Only within the last decade have historians begun to examine the actual achievements of the reformers. To carry out this first task, in the following . . . we will distinguish between the goals and rhetoric of individual reforms and will discuss the results of reform whenever the current literature permits. To do so is to observe the ironies, complexities, and disappointments of progressivism.

The second task—that of identifying the common characteristics of progressivism—is even more difficult than the first but is an essential base on which to build an understanding of progressivism. The rest of this [selection] focuses on identifying such characteristics. The place to begin that effort is the origins of progressivism. . . .

The Character and Spirit of Progressivism

Progressivism was characterized, in the first place, by a distinctive set of attitudes toward industrialism. By the turn of the century, the overwhelming majority of Americans had accepted the permanence of large-scale industrial, commercial, and financial enterprises and of the wage and factory systems. The progressives shared this attitude. Most were not socialists, and they undertook reform, not to dismantle modern economic institutions, but rather to ameliorate and improve the conditions of industrial life. Yet progressivism was infused with a deep outrage against the worst consequences of industrialism. Outpourings of anger at corporate wrongdoing and of hatred for industry's callous pursuit of profit frequently punctuated the course of reform in the early twentieth century. Indeed, antibusiness emotion was a prime mover of progressivism. That the acceptance of industrialism *and* the outrage against it were intrinsic to early twentieth-century reform does not mean that progressivism was mindless or that it has to be considered indefinable. But it does suggest that there was a powerful irony in progressivism: reforms which gained support from a people angry with the oppressive aspects of industrialism also assisted the same persons to accommodate to it, albeit to an industrialism which was to some degree socially responsible.

The progressives' ameliorative reforms also reflected their faith in progress—in mankind's ability, through purposeful action, to improve the environment and the conditions of life. The late nineteenth-century dissidents had not lacked this faith, but their espousal of panaceas bespoke a deep pessimism: "Unless this one great change is made, things will get worse." Progressive reforms were grounded on a broader assumption. In particular, reforms could protect the people hurt by industrialization, and make the environment more humane. For intellectuals of the era, the achievement of such goals meant that they had to meet Herbert Spencer head on and confute his absolute "truths." Progressive thinkers, led by Lester Frank Ward, Richard T. Ely, and, most important, John Dewey, demolished social Darwinism with what Goldman has called "reform Darwinism." They asserted that human adaptation to the environment did not interfere with the evolutionary process, but was, rather, part and parcel of the law of natural change. Progressive intellectuals and their popularizers produced a vast literature to condemn laissez faire and to promote the concept of the active state.

To improve the environment meant, above all, to intervene in economic and social affairs in order to control natural forces and impose a measure of order upon them. This belief in interventionism was a third component of progressivism. It was visible in almost every reform of the era, from the supervision of business to the prohibition of alcohol John W. Chambers II, *The Tyranny of Change: America in the Progressive Era, 1900–1917,* 1980). Interventionism could be both private and public. Given their choice, most progressives preferred to work noncoercively through voluntary organizations for economic and social changes. However, as time passed, it became evident that most progressive reforms could be achieved only by legislation and public control. Such an extension of public authority made many progressives uneasy, and few of them went so far as Herbert Croly in glorifying the state in his *The Promise of American Life* (1909) and *Progressive Democracy* (1914). Even so, the intervention necessary for their reforms inevitably propelled progressives toward an advocacy of the use of governmental power. A familiar scenario during the period was one in which progressives called upon public authorities to assume responsibility for interventions which voluntary organizations had begun.

The foregoing describes the basic characteristics of progressivism but says little about its ideals. Progressivism was inspired by two bodies of belief and knowledge—evangelical Protestantism and the natural and social sciences. These sources of reform may appear at first glance antagonistic to one another. Actually, they were complementary, and each imparted distinctive qualities to progressivism.

Ever since the religious revivals from about 1820 to 1840, evangelical Protestantism had spurred reform in the United States. Basic to the reform mentality was an all-consuming urge to purge the world of sin, such as the sins of slavery and intemperance, against which nineteenth-century reformers had crusaded. Now the progressives carried the struggle into the modern citadels of sin—the teeming cities of the nation. No one can read their writings and speeches without being struck by the fact that many of them believed that it was their Christian duty to right the wrongs created by the processes of industrialization. Such belief was the motive force behind the Social Gospel, a movement which swept through the Protestant churches in the 1890s and 1900s. Its goal was to align churches, frankly and aggressively, on the side of the downtrodden, the poor, and working people—in other words, to make Christianity relevant to this world, not the next. It is difficult to measure the influence of the Social Gospel, but it seared the consciences of millions of Americans, particularly in urban areas. And it triumphed in the organization in 1908 of the Federal Council of Churches of Christ in America, with its platform which condemned exploitative capitalism and proclaimed the right of workers to organize and to enjoy a decent standard of living. Observers at the Progressive party's national convention of 1912 should not have been surprised to hear the delegates sing, spontaneously and emotionally, the Christian call to arms, "Onward, Christian Solders!"

The faith which inspired the singing of "Onward, Christian Soldiers!" had significant implications for progressive reforms. Progressives used moralistic appeals to make people feel the awful weight of wrong in the world and to exhort them to accept personal responsibility for its eradication. The resultant reforms could be generous in spirit, but they could also seem intolerant to the people who were "reformed." Progressivism sometimes seemed to envision life in a small town Protestant community or an urban drawing room—a vision sharply different from that of Catholic or Jewish immigrants. Not every progressive shared the evangelical ethos, much less its intolerance, but few of the era's reforms were untouched by the spirit and techniques of Protestant revivalism.

Science also had a pervasive impact on the methods and objectives of progressivism. Many leading reformers were specialists in the new disciplines of statistics, economics, sociology, and psychology. These new social scientists set out to gather data on human behavior as it actually was and to discover the laws which governed it. Since social scientists accepted environmentalist and interventionist assumptions implicitly, they believed that knowledge of natural laws would make it possible to devise and apply solutions to improve the human condition. This faith underpinned the optimism of most progressives and predetermined the methods used by almost all reformers of the time: investigation of the facts and application of social-science knowledge to their analysis; entrusting trained experts to decide what should be done; and, finally, mandating government to execute reform.

These methods may have been rational, but they were also compatible with progressive moralism. In its formative period, American social science was heavily infused with ethical concerns. An essential purpose of statistics, economics, sociology, and psychology was to improve and uplift. Leading practitioners of these disciplines, for example, Richard T. Ely, an economist at the University of Wisconsin, were often in the vanguard of the Social Gospel. Progressives blended science and religion into a view of human behavior which was unique to their generation, which had grown up in an age of revivals and come to maturity at the birth of social science.

All of progressivism's distinctive features found expression in muckraking—the literary spearhead of early twentieth-century reform. Through the medium of such new ten-cent magazines as *McClure's, Everybody's* and *Cosmopolitan*, the muckrakers exposed every dark aspect and corner of American life. Nothing escaped the probe of writers such as Ida M. Tarbell, Lincoln Steffens, Ray Stannard Baker, and Burton J. Hendrick—not big business, politics, prostitution, race relations, or even the churches. Behind the exposes of the muckrakers lay the progressive attitude toward industrialism: it was here to stay, but many of its aspects seemed to be deplorable. These could be improved, however, if only people became aware of conditions and determined to ameliorate them. To bring about such awareness, the muckrakers appealed to their readers' consciences. Steffens' famous series, published in book form as *The Shame of the Cities* in 1904, was frankly intended to make people feel guilty for the corruption which riddled their cities. The muckrakers also used the social scientists' method of careful and painstaking gathering of data—and with devastating effects. The investigative function—which was later largely taken over by governmental agencies—proved absolutely vital to educating and arousing Americans.

All progressive crusades shared the spirit and used the techniques discussed here, but they did so to different degrees and in different ways. Some voiced a greater willingness to accept industrialism and even to extol its potential benefits; others expressed more strongly the outrage against its darker aspects. Some intervened through voluntary organizations; others relied on government to achieve changes. Each reform reflected a distinctive balance between the claims of Protestant moralism and of scientific rationalism. Progressives fought among themselves over these questions even while they set to the common task of applying their new methods and ideas to the problems of a modern society. . . .

In this analysis we have frequently pointed to the differences between the rhetoric, intentions, and results of progressive reform. The failure of reform always to fulfill the expectations of its advocates was not, of course, unique to the progressive era. Jacksonian reform, Reconstruction, and the New Deal all exhibited similar ironies and disappointments. In each case, the clash between reformers with divergent purposes, the inability to predict how given methods of reform would work in practice, and the ultimate waning of popular zeal for change all contributed to the disjuncture of rationale, purpose, and achievement. Yet the gap between these things seems more obvious in the progressive era because so many diverse movements for reform took place in a brief span of time and were accompanied by resounding rhetoric and by high expectations for the improvement of the American social and political environment. The effort to change so many things all at once, and the grandiose claims made for the moral and material betterment which would result, meant that disappointments were bound to occur.

Yet even the great number of reforms and the uncommonly high expectations for them cannot fully account for the consistent gaps which we have observed between the stated purposes, real intentions, and actual results of progressivism. Several additional factors, intrinsic to the nature of early twentieth-century reform, help to explain the ironies and contradictions.

One of these was the progressives' confident reliance on modern methods of reform. Heirs of recent advances in natural science and social science, they enthusiastically devised and applied new techniques to improve American government and society. Their methods often worked; on the other hand, progressive programs often simply did not prove capable of accomplishing what had been expected of them. This was not necessarily the reformers' fault. They hopefully used untried methods even while they lacked a science of society which was capable of solving all the great problems which they attacked. At the same time, the progressives' scientific methods made it possible to know just how far short of success their programs had sometimes fallen. The evidence of their failures thus was more visible than in any previous era of reform. To the progressives' credit, they usually published that evidence—for contemporaries and historians alike to see.

A second aspect of early twentieth-century reform which helps to account for the gaps between aims and achievements was the deep ambivalence of the progressives about industrialism and its consequences. Individual reformers were divided, and so was their movement as a whole. Compared to many Americans of the late 1800s, the progressives fundamentally accepted an industrial society and sought mainly to control and ameliorate it. Even reformers who were intellectually committed to socialist ideas often acted the part of reformers, not radicals.

Yet progressivism was infused and vitalized, as we have seen, by people truly angry with their industrial society. Few of them wanted to tear down the modern institutions of business and commerce, but their anger was real, their moralism was genuine, and their passions were essential to the reforms of their time.

The reform movement never resolved this ambivalence about industrialism. Much of its rhetoric and popular passion pointed in one direction—toward some form of social democracy—while its leaders and their programs went in another. Often the result was confusion and bitterness. Reforms frequently did not measure up to popular, antibusiness expectations, indeed, never were expected to do so by those who designed and implemented them. Even conservative, ameliorative reformers like Theodore Roosevelt often used radical rhetoric. In doing so, they misled their followers and contributed to the ironies of progressivism.

Perhaps most significant, progressives failed to achieve all their goals because, despite their efforts, they never fully came to terms with the divisions and conflicts in American society. Again and again, they acknowledged the existence of social disharmony more fully and frankly than had nineteenth-century Americans. Nearly every social and economic reform of the era was predicated on the progressive recognition that diverse cultural and occupational groups had conflicting interests, and that the responsibility for mitigating and adjusting those differences lay with the whole society, usually the government. Such recognition was one of the progressives' most significant achievements. Indeed, it stands among the most important accomplishments of liberal reform in all of American history. For, by frankly acknowledging the existence of social disharmony, the progressives committed the twentieth-century United States to recognizing—and to lessening—the inevitable conflicts of a heterogeneous industrial society.

Yet the significance of the progressives' recognition of diversity was compromised by the methods and institutions which they adopted to diminish or eliminate social and economic conflict. Expert administrative government turned out to be less neutral than the progressives believed that it would be. No scientific reform could be any more impartial than the experts who gathered the data or than the bureaucrats who implemented the programs. In practice, as we have seen, administrative government often succumbed to the domination of special interests.

It would be pointless to blame the progressives for the failure of their new methods and programs to eradicate all the conflicts of an industrial society, but it is perhaps fair to ask why the progressives adopted measures which tended to disguise and obscure economic and social conflict almost as soon as they had uncovered it. For one thing, they honestly believed in the almost unlimited potentialities of science and administration. Our late twentieth-century skepticism of these wonders should not blind us to the faith with which the progressives embraced them and imbued them with what now seem magical properties. For another, the progressives were reformers, not radicals.

It was one thing to recognize the existence of economic and social conflict, but quite another thing to admit that it was permanent. By and large, these men and women were personally and ideologically inclined to believe that the American society was, in the final analysis, harmonious, and that such conflicts as did exist could be resolved. Finally, the class and cultural backgrounds of the leading progressives often made them insensitive to lowerclass immigrant Americans and their cultures. Attempts to reduce divisions sometimes came down to imposing middle-class Protestant ways on the urban masses. In consequence, the progressives never fulfilled their hope of eliminating social conflict. Reformers of the early twentieth century saw the problem more fully than had their predecessors, but they nonetheless tended to consider conflicts resolved when, in fact, they only had been papered over. Later twentieth-century Americans have also frequently deceived themselves in this way.

Thus progressivism inevitably fell short of its rhetoric and intentions. Lest this seem an unfairly critical evaluation, it is important to recall how terribly ambitious were the stated aims and true goals of the reformers. They missed some of their marks because they sought to do so much. And, despite all their shortcomings, they accomplished an enormous part of what they set out to achieve.

Progressivism brought major innovations to almost every facet of public and private life in the United States. The political and governmental systems particularly felt the effects of reform. Indeed, the nature of political participation and the uses to which it was put went through transitions as momentous as those of any era in American history. These developments were complex, as we have seen, and it is no easy matter to sort out who was helped and who was hurt by each of them or by the entire body of reforms. At the very least, the political changes of the progressive era significantly accommodated American public life to an urban-industrial society. On balance, the polity probably emerged neither more nor less democratic than before, but it did become better suited to address, or at least recognize, the questions and problems which arose from the cities and factories of the nation. After the progressive era, just as before, wealthier elements in American society had a disproportionate share of political power, but we can hardly conclude that this was the fault of the progressives.

The personal and social life of the American people was also deeply affected by progressivism. Like the era's political changes, the economic and social reforms of the early twentieth century were enormously complicated and are difficult to summarize without doing violence to their diversity. In the broadest sense, the progressives sought to mitigate the injustice and the disorder of a society now dominated by its industries and cities. Usually, as we have observed, the quests for social justice and social control were extricably bound together in the reformers' programs, with each group of progressives having different interpretations of these dual ends. Justice sometimes took second place to control. However, before one judges the reformers too harshly for that, it is well to remember how bad urban social conditions were in the late nineteenth century and the odds against which the reformers fought. It is also well to remember that they often succeeded in mitigating the harshness of urban-industrial life.

The problems with which the progressives struggled have, by and large, continued to challenge Americans ever since. And, although the assumptions and techniques of progressivism no longer command the confidence which early twentieth-century Americans had in them, no equally comprehensive body of reforms has ever been adopted in their place. Throughout this study, we have criticized the progressives for having too much faith in their untried methods. Yet if this was a failing, it was also a source of strength, one now missing from reform in America. For the essence of progressivism lay in the hopefulness and optimism which the reformers brought to the tasks of applying science and administration to the high moral purposes in which they believed. The historical record of their aims and achievements leaves no doubt that there were many men and women in the United States in the early 1900s who were not afraid to confront the problems of a modern industrial society with vigor, imagination, and hope. They of course failed to solve all those problems, but no other generation of Americans has done conspicuously better in addressing the political, economic, and social conditions which it faced.

POSTSCRIPT

Did the Progressives Fail?

In spite of their differences, both Abrams's and Link and McCormick's interpretations make concessions to their respective critics. Link and McCormick, for example, admit that the intended reforms did not necessarily produce the desired results. Furthermore, the authors concede that many reformers were insensitive to the cultural values of the lower classes and attempted to impose middle-class Protestant ways on the urban masses. Nevertheless, Link and McCormick argue that in spite of the failure to curb the growth of big business, the progressive reforms did ameliorate the worst abuses of the new urban industrial society. Although the Progressives failed to solve all the major problems of their times, they did set the agenda that still challenges the reformers of today.

Abrams also makes a concession to his critics when he admits that "progressivism had real lasting effects for the blunting of the sharper edges of selfinterest in American life, and for the reduction of the harsher cruelties suffered by the society's underprivileged." Yet the thrust of his argument is that the progressive reformers accomplished little of value. While Abrams probably agrees with Link and McCormick that the Progressives were the first group to confront the problems of modern America, he considers their intended reforms inadequate by their very nature. Because the reformers never really challenged the inequalities brought about by the rise of the industrial state, maintains Abrams, the same problems have persisted to the present day.

Historians have generally been sympathetic to the aims and achievements of the progressive historians. Many, like Charles Beard and Frederick Jackson Turner, came from the Midwest and lived in model progressive states like Wisconsin. Their view of history was based on a conflict between groups competing for power, so it was easy for them to portray progressivism as a struggle between the people and entrenched interests.

It was not until after World War II that a more complex view of progressivism emerged. Richard Hofstadter's *Age of Reform* (Alfred A. Knopf, 1955) was exceptionally critical of the reformist view of history as well as of the reformers in general. Born of Jewish immigrant parents and raised in cities in New York, the Columbia University professor argued that progressivism was a moral crusade undertaken by WASP families in an effort to restore older Protestant and individualistic values and to regain political power and status. Both Hofstadter's "status revolution" theory of progressivism and his profile of the typical Progressive have been heavily criticized by historians. Nevertheless, he changed the dimensions of the debate and made progressivism appear to be a much more complex issue than had previously been thought.

Most of the writing on progressivism for the past 20 years has centered around the "organizational" model. Writers of this school have stressed the role of the "expert" and the ideals of scientific management as basic to an understanding of the Progressive Era. This fascination with how the city manager plan worked in Dayton or railroad regulation in Wisconsin or the public schools laws in New York City makes sense to a generation surrounded by bureaucracies on all sides. Two books that deserve careful reading are Robert Wiebe's *The Search for Order, 1877–1920* (Hill & Wang, 1967) and the wonderful collection of essays by Samuel P. Hayes, *American Political History as Social Analysis* (Knoxville, 1980), which brings together two decades' worth of articles from diverse journals that were seminal in exploring ethnocultural approaches to politics within the organizational model.

In a highly influential article written for the *American Quarterly* in spring 1970, Professor Peter G. Filene proclaimed "An Obituary for the 'Progressive Movement.'" After an extensive review of the literature, Filene concluded that since historians cannot agree on its programs, values, geographical location, members, and supporters, there was no such thing as a Progressive movement. Few historians were bold enough to write progressivism out of the pantheon of American reform movements. But Filene put the proponents of the early-twentieth-century reform movement on the defensive. Students who want to see how professional historians directly confronted Filene in their refusal to attend the funeral of the Progressive movement should read the essays by John D. Buenker, John C. Burnham, and Robert M. Crunden in *Progressivism* (Schenkman, 1977).

Three works provide an indispensable review of the literature of progressivism in the 1980s. Link and McCormick's *Progressivism* (Harlan Davidson, 1983) deserves to be read in its entirety for its comprehensive yet concise coverage. More scholarly but still readable are the essays on the new political history in McCormick's *The Party Period and Public Policy: American Politics From the Age of Jackson to the Progressive Era* (Oxford University Press, 1986). The more advanced student should consult Daniel T. Rodgers, "In Search of Progressivism," *Reviews in American History* (December 1982). While admitting that Progressives shared no common creed or values, Rodgers nevertheless feels that they were able "to articulate their discontents and their social visions" around three distinct clusters of ideas: "The first was the rhetoric of antimonopolism, the second was an emphasis on social bonds and the social nature of human beings, and the third was the language of social efficiency."

ISSUE 9

Was Prohibition a Failure?

YES: David E. Kyvig, from *Repealing National Prohibition,* 2d ed. (The University of Chicago Press, 1979, 2000)

NO: J. C. Burnham, from "New Perspectives on the Prohibition 'Experiment' of the 1920s," *Journal of Social History, Volume 2* (Fall 1968)

ISSUE SUMMARY

YES: David E. Kyvig admits that alcohol consumption declined sharply in the prohibition era but that federal actions failed to impose abstinence among an increasingly urban and heterogeneous populace that resented and resisted restraints on their individual behavior.

NO: J. C. Burnham states that the prohibition experiment was more a success than a failure and contributed to a substantial decrease in liquor consumption, reduced arrests for alcoholism, fewer alcohol-related diseases and hospitalizations, and destroyed the old-fashioned saloon that was a major target of the law's proponents.

$\mathbf{A}$mericans, including many journalists and scholars, have never been shy about attaching labels to their history, and frequently they do so to characterize particular years or decades in their distant or recent past. It is doubtful, however, that any period in our nation's history has received as many catchy appellations as has the decade of the 1920s. Described at various times as the "Jazz Age," the "Roaring Twenties," the "prosperity decade," the "age of normalcy," or simply the "New Era," these are years that obviously have captured the imagination of the American public, including the chroniclers of the nation's past.

In 1920, the Great War was over, and President Woodrow Wilson received the Nobel Peace Prize despite his failure to persuade the Senate to adopt the Covenant of the League of Nations. The "Red Scare," culminating in the Palmer raids conducted by the Justice Department, came to an embarrassingly fruitless halt, and Republican Warren Harding won a landslide victory in the campaign for the presidency, an election in which women, buoyed by the ratification of the Nineteenth Amendment, exercised their suffrage rights for the first time in national politics. In Pittsburgh, the advent of the radio age was symbolized by the broadcast of election results by KDKA, the nation's first commercial radio station. F. Scott Fitzgerald and Sinclair Lewis each published their first important novels and thereby helped to usher in the most significant American literary renaissance since the early nineteenth century.

During the next nine years, Americans witnessed a number of amazing events: the rise and fall of the Ku Klux Klan; the trial, conviction, and execution of anarchists Nicola Sacco and Bartolomeo Vanzetti on murder charges and the subsequent legislative restrictions on immigration into the United States; battles over the teaching of evolution in the schools epitomized by the rhetorical clashes between William Jennings Bryan and Clarence Darrow during the Scopes trial in Dayton, Tennessee; the Harding scandals; "talking" motion pictures; and, in 1929, the collapse of the New York Stock Exchange, symbolizing the beginning of the Great Depression and bringing a startling end to the euphoric claims of business prosperity that had dominated the decade.

The 1920s are also remembered as the "dry decade," as a consequence of the ratification of the Eighteenth Amendment and the passage by Congress of the Volstead Act that prohibited the manufacture, sale, or transportation of alcoholic beverages. The implementation of national prohibition represented a continuation of the types of reforms designed by Progressives to improve the quality of life for the American citizenry; however, the illicit manufacture and trade of alcohol and the proliferation of speakeasies, where patrons seemed to flaunt the law with impunity, raise questions about the effectiveness of such legislation. Did prohibition work, or was it a noble, but failed, experiment? The selections that follow address this matter from different perspectives.

David Kyvig points out that the Volstead Act did not specifically prohibit the use or purchase of alcoholic beverages and that liquor continued to be provided by various sources, including gangland bootleggers, to meet consumer demand. Despite efforts to enforce the law, the federal government failed to create an adequate institutional network to insure compliance. Hence, although the consumption of alcohol did drop during the decade of the 1920s, legislation failed to eliminate drinking or to produce a feeling that such a goal was even within reach.

J. C. Burnham, on the other hand, argues that enforcement of the prohibition laws was quite effective in many places. Moreover, in addition to reducing the per capita consumption of alcohol, the enactment of prohibition legislation led to several positive social consequences. For example, during the 1920s, fewer people were arrested for public drunkenness, and there were substantially fewer Americans treated for alcohol-related diseases. All in all, he concludes, prohibition was more of a success than a failure.

YES

David E. Kyvig

America Sobers Up

When the Eighteenth Amendment took effect on January 17, 1920, most observers assumed that liquor would quickly disappear from the American scene. The possibility that a constitutional mandate would be ignored simply did not occur to them. "Confidence in the law to achieve a moral revolution was unbounded," one scholar of rural America has pointed out, explaining that "this was, after all, no mere statute, it was the Constitution." The assistant commissioner of the Internal Revenue Service, the agency charged with overseeing the new federal law, predicted that it would take six years to make the nation absolutely dry but that prohibition would be generally effective from the outset. Existing state and federal law enforcement agencies were expected to be able to police the new law. Initial plans called for only a modest special enforcement program, its attention directed to large cities where the principal resistance was anticipated. Wayne Wheeler of the Anti-Saloon League confidently anticipated that national prohibition would be respected, and estimated that an annual federal appropriation of five million dollars would be ample to implement it. The popular evangelist Billy Sunday replaced his prohibition sermon with one entitled "Crooks, Corkscrews, Bootleggers, and Whiskey Politicians—They Shall Not Pass." Wartime prohibition, which only banned further manufacture of distilled spirits and strong beer (with an alcohol content exceeding 2.75 percent) had already significantly reduced consumption. Few questioned the Volstead Act's capacity to eliminate intoxicants altogether. Americans accustomed to a society in which observation and pressure from other members of a community encouraged a high degree of conformity did not foresee that there would be difficulties in obtaining compliance with the law. They did not realize that the law would be resented and resisted by sizable elements in an increasingly urban and heterogeneous society where restraints on the individual were becoming far less compelling.

Within a few months it became apparent that not every American felt obliged to stop drinking the moment constitutional prohibition began. In response to consumer demand, a variety of sources provided at first a trickle and later a growing torrent of forbidden beverages. Physicians could legally prescribe "medicinal" spirits or beer for their patients, and before prohibition was six months old, more than fifteen thousand, along with over fifty-seven thousand pharmacists, obtained licenses to dispense liquor. Grape juice or concentrates could be legitimately shipped and sold and, if the individual purchaser chose, allowed to ferment. Distributors learned to "attach "warning" labels, reporting that United States Department of Agriculture tests had determined that, for instance, if permitted to sit for sixty days the juice would turn into wine of twelve percent alcohol content. The quadrupled output and rising prices of the California grape industry during the decade showed that many people took such warnings to heart.

Other methods of obtaining alcoholic beverages were more devious. Some "near-beer," which was legally produced by manufacturing genuine beer, then removing the three to five percent alcohol in excess of the approved one-half percent, was diverted to consumers before the alcohol was removed. In other instances, following government inspection, alcohol was reinjected into near-beer, making what was often called "needle beer." Vast amounts of alcohol produced for industrial purposes were diverted, watered down, and flavored for beverage purposes. To discourage this practice, the government directed that industrial alcohol be rendered unfit to drink by the addition of denaturants. Bootleggers did not always bother to remove such poisons, which cost some unsuspecting customers their eyesight or their lives.

Theft of perhaps twenty million gallons of good preprohibition liquor from bonded warehouses in the course of the decade, as well as an undeterminable amount of home brewing and distilling, provided more palatable and dependable beverages. By 1930 illegal stills provided the main supply of liquor, generally a high quality product. The best liquor available was that smuggled in from Canada and from ships anchored on "Rum Row" in the Atlantic beyond the twelve-mile limit of United States jurisdiction. By the late 1920s, one million gallons of Canadian liquor per year, eighty percent of that nation's greatly expanded output, made its way into the United States. British shipment of liquor to islands which provisioned Rum Row increased dramatically. Exports to the Bahamas, for example, went from 944 gallons in 1918 to 386,000 gallons in 1922. The tiny French islands of St. Pierre and Miguelon off the coast of Newfoundland imported 118,600 gallons of British liquor in 1922, "quite a respectable quantity," a British official observed, "for an island population of 6,000." Bootlegging, the illicit commercial system for distributing liquor, solved most problems of bringing together supply and demand. Government appeared unable—some claimed even unwilling—to halt a rising flood of intoxicants. Therefore, many observers at time, and increasing numbers since the law's repeal, assumed that prohibition simply did not work. . . .

The Volstead Act specified how the constitutional ban on "intoxicating liquors . . . for beverage purposes" was to be enforced. What the statute did not say had perhaps the greatest importance. While the law barred manufacture, transport, sale, import, or export of intoxicants, it did not specifically make their purchase or use a crime. This allowed continued possession of intoxicants obtained prior to prohibition, provided that such beverages were only for personal use in one's own home. Not only did the failure outlaw use render prohibition harder to enforce by eliminating possession as *de facto* evidence of crime, but also it allowed the purchaser and consumer of alcoholic beverages to defend his own behavior. Although the distinction was obviously artificial, the consumer could and did insist that there was nothing illegal about his drinking, while at the same time complaining that failure of government efforts to suppress bootlegging represented a break down of law and order.

Adopting the extreme, prohibitionist view that any alcohol whatsoever was intoxicating, the Volstead Act outlawed all beverages with an alcoholic content of .5 percent or more. The .5 percent limitation followed a traditional standard used to distinguish between alcoholic and nonalcoholic beverages for purposes of taxation, but that standard was considered by many to be unrealistic in terms of the amount of alcohol needed to produce intoxication. Wartime prohibition, after all, only banned beer with an alcohol content of 2.75 percent or more. Many did not associate intoxication with beer or wine at all but rather with distilled spirits. Nevertheless, the only exception to the .5 percent standard granted by the Volstead Act, which had been drafted by the Anti-Saloon League, involved cider and fruit juices; these subjects of natural fermentation were to be illegal only if declared by a jury to be intoxicating in fact. The Volstead Act, furthermore, did permit the use of intoxicants for medicinal purposes and religious sacraments; denatured industrial alcohol was exempted as well.

The Eighteenth Amendment specified that federal and state governments would have concurrent power to enforce the ban on intoxicating beverages. Therefore the system which evolved to implement prohibition had a dual nature. Congress, anticipating general compliance with the liquor ban as well as cooperation from state and local policing agencies in dealing with those violations which did occur, created a modest enforcement program at first. Two million dollars was appropriated to administer the law for its first five months of operation, followed by $4,750,000 for the fiscal year beginning July 1, 1920. The Prohibition Bureau of the Treasury Department recruited a force of only about fifteen hundred enforcement agents. Every state except Maryland adopted its own antiliquor statute. Most state laws were modeled after the Volstead Act, though some dated from the days of state prohibition and several imposed stricter regulations or harsher penalties than did the federal statute. State and local police forces were expected to enforce these laws as part of their normal duties. Critics at the time and later who claimed that no real effort was made to enforce national prohibition because no large enforcement appropriations were forthcoming need to consider the assumptions and police practices of the day. No general national police force, only specialized customs and treasury units, existed. Furthermore, neither federal nor state officials initially felt a need for a large special force to carry out this one task. The creators of national prohibition anticipated only a modest increase in the task facing law-enforcement officials.

Most Americans obeyed the national prohibition law. Many, at least a third to two-fifths of the adult population if Gallup poll surveys in the 1930s are any indication, had not used alcohol previously and simply continued to abstain. Others ceased to drink beer, wine, or spirits when to do so became illegal. The precise degree of compliance with the law is difficult to determine because violation levels cannot be accurately measured. The best index of the extent to which the law was accepted comes from a somewhat indirect indicator.

Consumption of beer, wine, and spirits prior to and following national prohibition was accurately reflected in the payment of federal excise taxes on alcoholic beverages. The tax figures appear reliable because bootlegging lacked sufficient profitability to be widespread when liquor was legally and conveniently obtainable. The amount of drinking during prohibition can be inferred from consumption rates once alcoholic beverages were again legalized. Drinking may have increased after repeal; it almost certainly did not decline. During the period 1911 through 1915, the last years before widespread state prohibition and the Webb-Kenyon Act began to significantly inhibit the flow of legal liquor, the per capita consumption by Americans of drinking age (15 years and older) amounted to 2.56 gallons of absolute alcohol. This was actually imbibed as 2.09 gallons of distilled spirits (45 percent alcohol), 0.79 gallons of wine (18 percent alcohol), and 29.53 gallons of beer (5 percent alcohol). In 1934, the year immediately following repeal of prohibition, the per capita consumption measured 0.97 gallons of alcohol distributed as 0.64 gallons of spirits, 0.36 gallons of wine, and 13.58 gallons of beer (4.5 percent alcohol after repeal). Total alcohol consumption, by this measure, fell by more than 60 percent because of national prohibition. Granting a generous margin of error, it seems certain that the flow of liquor in the United States was at least cut in half. It is difficult to know whether the same number of drinkers each consumed less or, as seems more likely, fewer persons drank. The crucial factor for this discussion is that national prohibition caused a substantial drop in aggregate alcohol consumption. Though the figures began to rise almost immediately after repeal, not until 1970 did the annual per capita consumption of absolute alcohol reach the level of 1911–15. In other words, not only did Americans drink significantly less as a result of national prohibition, but also the effect of the law in depressing liquor usage apparently lingered for several decades after repeal.

Other evidence confirms this statistical picture of sharply reduced liquor consumption under prohibition. After the Volstead Act had been in force for a half dozen years, social worker Martha Bensley Bruere conducted a nationwide survey of drinking for the National Federation of Settlements. Her admittedly impressionistic study, based upon 193 reports from social workers across the country, focused on lower-class, urban America. Social workers, who generally favored prohibition, perhaps overrated the law's effectiveness. Nevertheless, Bruere's book provided probably the most objective picture of prohibition in practice in the mid-1920s.

The Bruere survey reported that adherence to the dry law varied from place to place. The Scandinavians of Minneapolis and St. Paul continued to drink. On the other hand, prohibition seemed effective in Sioux Falls, South Dakota. In Butte, Montana, the use of intoxicants had declined, though bootleggers actively plied their trade. Idaho, Oregon, and Washington had generally accepted prohibition, and even in the West Coast wet bastion, San Francisco, working-class drinking appeared much reduced. The Southwest from Texas to Los Angeles was reported to be quite dry. The survey cited New Orleans as America's wettest city, with bootlegging and a general disregard of the law evident everywhere. In the old South, prohibition was said to be effectively enforced for Negroes but not whites. Throughout the Midwest, with some exceptions, residents of rural areas generally observed prohibition, but city dwellers appeared to ignore it. In the great metropolises of the North and East, with their large ethnic communities—Chicago, Detroit, Cleveland, Pittsburgh, Boston, New York, and Philadelphia—the evidence was overwhelming that the law was neither respected nor observed.

Throughout the country, Bruere suggested, less drinking was taking place than before prohibition. Significantly, she reported the more prosperous upper and middle classes violated the alcoholic beverage ban far more frequently than did the working class. Illicitly obtained liquor was expensive. Yale economist Irving Fisher, himself an advocate of prohibition, claimed that in 1928 on the average a quart of beer cost 80¢ (up 600 percent from 1916), gin $5.90 (up 520 percent), and corn whiskey $3.95 (up 150 percent) while average annual income per family was about $2,600. If nothing else, the economics of prohibition substantially reduced drinking by lower-class groups. Thus prohibition succeeded to a considerable degree in restraining drinking by the very social groups with whom many advocates of the law had been concerned. The Bruere study, therefore, offered cheer to drys. Yet her report also demonstrated that acceptance of prohibition varied with ethnic background and local custom as well as economics. Community opinion appeared more influential than federal or state laws or police activity. People in many parts of the United States voluntarily obeyed the Eighteenth Amendment, but elsewhere citizens chose to ignore it. In the latter part of the decade, violations apparently increased, both in small towns and large cities. In Detroit it reportedly became impossible to get a drink "unless you walked at least ten feet and told the busy bartender what you wanted in a voice loud enough for him to hear you above the uproar."

Any evidence to the contrary notwithstanding, national prohibition rapidly acquired an image, not as a law which significantly reduced the use of alcoholic beverages, but rather as a law that was widely flouted. One Wisconsin congressmen, writing to a constituent after a year of national prohibition, asserted, "I believe that there is more bad whiskey consumed in the country today than there was good whiskey before we had prohibition and of course we have made a vast number of liars and law violators through the Volstead Act." In part this commonly held impression stemmed from the substantial amount of drinking which actually did continue. Even given a 60 percent drop in total national alcohol consumption, a considerable amount of imbibing still took place. Yet the image also derived in part from the unusually visible character of those prohibition violations which did occur.

Drinking by its very nature attracted more notice than many other forms of law-breaking. It was, in the first place, generally a social, or group, activity. Moreover, most drinking took place, Bruere and others acknowledged, in urban areas where practically any activity was more likely to witnessed. Bootleggers had to advertise their availability, albeit carefully, in order to attract customers. The fact that the upper classes were doing much of the imbibing further heightened its visibility. Several additional factors insured that many Americans would have a full, perhaps even exaggerated, awareness of the extent to which the prohibition law was being broken.

The behavior of those who sought to profit by meeting the demand for alcoholic beverages created an indelible image of rampant lawlessness. National prohibition provided a potentially very profitable opportunity for persons willing to take certain risks. "Prohibition is a business," maintained the best known and most successful bootlegger of all, Al Capone of Chicago. "All I do is supply a public demand." Obtaining a supply of a commodity, transporting it to a marketplace, and selling it for an appropriate price were commonplace commercial activities; carrying out these functions in the face of government opposition and without the protections of facilities, goods, and transactions normally provided by government made bootlegging an unusual business. Indeed bootleggers faced the problem—or the opportunity— that hijacking a competitor's shipment of liquor often presented the easiest and certainly the cheapest way of obtaining a supply of goods, and the victim of such a theft had no recourse to regular law enforcement agencies. Nor, for better or worse, could bootleggers expect government to restrain monopolistic practices, regulate prices, or otherwise monitor business practices. Consequently, participants in the prohibition-era liquor business had to develop their own techniques for dealing with competition and the pressures of the marketplace. The bootlegging wars and gangland killings, so vividly reported in the nation's press, represented, on one level, a response to a business problem. . . .

Violence was commonplace in establishing exclusive sales territories, in obtaining liquor, or in defending a supply. In Chicago, for instance, rival gangs competed intensely. Between September 1923 and October 1926, the peak period of struggle for control of the large Chicago market, an estimated 215 criminals died at the hands of rivals. In comparison, police killed 160 gangsters during the same period. Although by conventional business standards the violence level in bootlegging remained high, it declined over the course of the 1920s. Consolidation, agreement on markets, regularizing of supply and delivery all served to reduce turbulence. John Torrio and Al Capone in Chicago, Charles Solomon in Boston, Max Hoff in Philadelphia, Purple Gang in Detroit, the Mayfield Road Mob in Cleveland, and Joseph Roma in Denver imposed some order on the bootlegging business in their cities. The more than a thousand gangland murders in New York during prohibition reflect the inability of Arnold Rothstein, Lucky Luciano, Dutch Schultz, Frank Costello, or any other criminal leader to gain control and put an end to (literally) cut-throat competition in the largest market of all. . . .

Ironically, the federal government in its efforts to enforce national prohibition often contributed to the image of a heavily violated law. Six months after the Eighteenth Amendment took effect, for example, Jouett Shouse, an Assistant Secretary of the Treasury whose duties included supervising prohibition enforcement, announced that liquor smuggling had reached such (portions that it could no longer be handled by the 6,000 agents of the Customs Bureau. Shouse estimated that 35,000 men would be required to guard the coasts and borders against the flood of liquor pouring into the country. The Assistant Secretary attributed the problem to an unlimited market for smuggled whiskey and the 1,000 percent profits which could be realized from its sale.

During the 1920 presidential campaign, Republican nominee Warren G. Harding pledged to enforce the Volstead Act "as a fundamental principle of the American conscience," implying that the Wilson administration had neglected its duty. Despite his known fondness for drink, Harding attracted dry support with such statements while his opponent, the avowedly wet James A. Cox, floundered. Once inaugurated, President Harding tried to fulfill his campaign promise but met with little success. He explained to his wet Senate friend, Walter Edge of New Jersey, "Prohibition is a constitutional mandate and I hold it to be absolutely necessary to give it a fair and thorough trial." The president appointed the Anti-Saloon league's candidate, Roy A. Haynes, as commissioner of prohibition and gave the corpulent, eternally optimistic Haynes a generally free hand in selecting personnel to wage battle against bootlegging. Harding began to receive considerable mail from across the country complaining about the failure of the dry law. As reports of prohibition violations increased, Harding became more and more disturbed. Never much of a believer in prohibition himself, Harding had, nevertheless, been willing as a senator to let the country decide whether it wanted the Eighteenth Amendment, and now as president he deplored the wholesale breaking of the law. In early 1923, having gradually realized the importance of personal example, Harding gave up his own clandestine drinking. In a speech in Denver just prior to his death, Harding appealed rigorously for observance of prohibition in the interest of preventing lawlessness, corruption, and collapse of national moral fiber. "Whatever satisfaction there may be in indulgence, whatever objection there is to the so-called invasion of personal liberty," the president asserted, "neither counts when the supremacy of law and the stability of our institutions are menaced." Harding's rhetoric, although intended to encourage compliance with prohibition, furthered the image of a law breaking down.

A report by Attorney General Harry Daugherty to President Calvin Coolidge shortly after Harding's death suggested the extent to which the Volstead Act was being violated in its early years of operation. Daugherty indicated that in the first forty-one months of national prohibition, the federal government had initiated 90,330 prosecutions under the law. The number of cases had been rising: 5,636 were settled in April 1923, 541 than in the initial six months of prohibition. The number of new cases doubled between fiscal 1922 and fiscal 1923. The government obtained convictions in 80 percent of the terminated cases. These figures showed, the attorney general argued, that prohibition enforcement was becoming increasingly effective. They could just as well be seen, however, as an indication of an enormous and increasing number of violations.

The prohibition cases brought into federal court most certainly represented only a small fraction of actual offenses. They nevertheless seemed to be more than the court and prison system could handle. In 1920, 5,095 of the 34,230 cases terminated in the federal courts involved prohibition violation; during 1929, 75,298 prohibition cases alone were concluded. In 1920, federal prisons contained just over 5,000 inmates; ten years later they contained over 12,000, more than 4,000 of whom were serving time for liquor violations. The courts were so overworked that they frequently resorted to the expedient of "bargain days." Under this system, on set days large numbers of prohibition violators would plead guilty after being given prior assurance that they would not receive jail sentences or heavy fines. By 1925, pleas of guilty, without jury trials, accounted for over 90 percent of the convictions obtained in federal courts. The legal system appeared overwhelmed by national prohibition.

As president, Calvin Coolidge found prohibition enforcement to be the same headache it had been for his predecessor. Like Harding, Coolidge was constantly under pressure from Wayne Wheeler and other dry leaders to improve enforcement. He received hundreds of letters deploring the rate of Volstead Act violations and urging forceful action. Coolidge merely acknowledged receipt of letters on the subject, avoiding any substantial response. As it did with many other issues, the Coolidge administration sought to avoid the prohibition question as much as possible. Other than seeking Canadian and British cooperation in halting smuggling, and holding White House breakfasts for prestigious drys, few federal initiatives were taken while Coolidge remained in office. The picture of rampant prohibition violation stood unchallenged.

Congress, once having adopted the Volstead Act and appropriated funds for its enforcement, assumed its job was done and avoided all mention of prohibition during the law's first year of operation. Evidence of violations, however, quickly provoked dry demands that Congress strengthen the prohibition law. Whenever Congress acted, it drew attention to the difficulties of abolishing liquor. When it failed to respond, as was more frequently the case, drys charged it with indifference to law breaking. Whatever it did, Congress proved unable to significantly alter prohibition's image.

After Harding's inauguration, Congress learned that retiring Attorney General A. Mitchell Palmer had ruled that the Volstead Act placed no limit on the authority of physicians to prescribe beer and wine for medicinal purposes." Senator Frank B. Willis of Ohio and Representative Robert S. Campbell of Kansas moved quickly to correct this oversight by introducing a bill that would forbid the prescription of beer and rigidly limit physicians' authority to prescribe wine and spirits. Only one pint of liquor would be permitted to be dispensed for a patient during any ten-day period, under their plan. Well-prepared dry spokesmen completely dominated the hearings on the Willis-Campbell bill, insisting that this substantial source of intoxicants be eliminated. Physicians and pharmacists protested that beer possessed therapeutic value and that Congress had no right to restrict doctors in their practice of medicine. Nevertheless, in the summer of 1921 the bill passed the House by a vote of 250 to 93, and the Senate by 39 to 20. The Willis-Campbell Act reflected congressional determination to shut off the liquor supply, but like the Volstead Act, it did not resolve the problem of imposing abstinence on those willing to ignore the law in order to have a drink.

For years, Congress continued to wrestle with the problem of creating and staffing an effective federal enforcement organization. The Volstead Act delegated responsibility for implementing national prohibition to an agency of the Bureau of Internal Revenue in the Department of the Treasury. The act exempted enforcement agents from civil service regulations, making them political appointees. The Anti-Saloon League, through its general counsel,

Wayne B. Wheeler, relentlessly pressed Harding and Coolidge to name its candidates to positions in the enforcement agency. The prohibition unit, beset by patronage demands and inadequate salaries, attracted a low caliber of appointee and a high rate of corruption. By 1926 one out of twelve agents had been dismissed for such offenses as bribery, extortion, solicitation of money, conspiracy to violate the law, embezzlement, and submission of false reports. A senator who supported prohibition argued lamely that this record was no worse than that of the twelve apostles, but he could not disguise the enforcement unit's very tarnished reputation.

Even if the agency had been staffed with personnel of better quality, its task would have been overwhelming. It received little cooperation from the Department of Justice, with which it shared responsibility for prosecuting violators. Furthermore, the prohibition unit lacked both the manpower and the money to deal with the thousands of miles of unpatrolled coastline, the millions of lawbreaking citizens, and the uncountable hordes of liquor suppliers. The agency focused its efforts on raiding speakeasies and apprehending bootleggers, but this task alone proved beyond its capacity and discouraged a series of prohibition commissioners.

Congress steadily increased enforcement appropriations but never enough to accomplish the goal. In 1927 prohibition agents were finally placed under civil service, and in 1930 the Prohibition Bureau was at last transferred to the Justice Department. As useful as these congressional steps may have been, they came long after the enforcement effort had acquired a dismal reputation and doubts as to whether prohibition could possibly be effective had become deeply ingrained.

Early in 1929 Congress made a determined effort to compel greater adherence to national prohibition. A bill introduced by Washington senator Wesley L. Jones drastically increased penalties for violation of the liquor ban. Maximum prison terms for first offenders were raised from six months to five years, and fines were raised from $1,000 to $10,000. The Jones "Five-and-Ten" Bill, as it was called, passed by lopsided majorities in Congress and signed into law by Coolidge days before he left office, did not improve prohibition's effectiveness but strengthened its reputation as a harsh and unreasonable statute.

During the 1920s the Supreme Court did more than either the Congress or the president to define the manner in which national prohibition would be enforced and thereby to sharpen the law's image. As a Yale law professor and earlier as president, William Howard Taft had opposed a prohibition amendment because he preferred local option, disliked any changes in the Constitution, and felt national prohibition would be unenforceable. But when the Eighteenth Amendment was ratified, Taft, a constant defender the sanctity of democratically adopted law, accepted it completely and even became an advocate of temperance by law. He condemned critics of national prohibition, saying, "There isn't the slightest chance that the constitutional amendment will be repealed. You know that and I know it." As chief justice from 1921 until 1930, he sought to have the prohibition laws strictly enforced and took upon himself the writing of prohibition decisions. The opinions handed down by the Taft Court during the 1920s greatly influenced conceptions of the larger implications of the new law as well as the actual course of prohibition enforcement. . . .

While in reality national prohibition sharply reduced the consumption of alcohol in the United States, the law fell considerably short of expectations. It neither eliminated drinking nor produced a sense that such a goal was within reach. So long as the purchaser of liquor, the supposed victim of a prohibition violation, participated in the illegal act rather than complained about it, the normal law enforcement process simply did not function. As a result, policing agencies bore a much heavier burden. The various images of lawbreaking, from contacts with the local bootlegger to Hollywood films to overloaded court dockets, generated a widespread belief that violations were taking place with unacceptable frequency. Furthermore, attempts at enforcing the law created an impression that government, unable to cope with lawbreakers by using traditional policing methods, was assuming new powers in order to accomplish its task. The picture of national prohibition which emerged over the course of the 1920s disenchanted many Americans and moved some to an active effort to bring an end to the dry law.

J. C. Burnham  **NO**

New Perspectives on the Prohibition "Experiment" of the 1920's

Recently a number of historians have shown that the temperance movement that culminated in national prohibition was central to the American reform tradition. Such writers as James H. Timberlake have demonstrated in detail how the Eighteenth Amendment was an integral part of the reforms of the Progressive movement. Yet we commonly refer to the "prohibition experiment" rather than the "prohibition reform." This characterization deserves some exploration. The question can be raised, for example, why we do not refer to the "workmen's compensation law experiment."

One explanation may be that of all of the major reforms enacted into law in the Progressive period, only prohibition was decisively and deliberately repealed. The Sixteenth and Seventeenth Amendments are still on the books; the Eighteenth is not. For historians who emphasize the theme of reform, referring to prohibition as an experiment gives them the option of suggesting that its repeal involved no loss to society. To characterize the repeal of prohibition as a major reversal of social reform would seriously impair the view that most of us have of the cumulative nature of social legislation in the twentieth century.

We have been comfortable for many decades now with the idea that prohibition was a great social experiment. The image of prohibition as an experiment has even been used to draw lessons from history: to argue, for example, that certain types of laws—especially those restricting or forbidding the use of liquor and narcotics—are futile and probably pernicious. Recently, however, some new literature has appeared on prohibition, whose total effect is to demand a re-examination of our customary view.

The idea that prohibition was an experiment may not survive this renaissance of scholarship in which the reform and especially Progressive elements in the temperance movement are emphasized. But it is profitable, at least for the purposes of this article, to maintain the image of an experiment, for the perspectives available now permit a fresh evaluation of the experiment's outcome.

Specifically, the prohibition experiment, as the evidence stands today, can more easily be considered a success than a failure. While far from clear-cut, the balance of scholarly evidence has shifted the burden of proof to those who would characterize the experiment a failure. . . .

From *Journal of Social History,* 1968–1969, pp. 51–52, 55–58. Copyright © 1968 by Journal of Social History. Reproduced with permission of Journal of Social History via Copyright Clearance Center.

The American prohibition experiment grew out of the transformation that the combination of Progressive reformers and businessmen wrought in the temperance movement. Beginning in 1907 a large number of state and local governments enacted laws or adopted constitutional provisions that dried up—as far as alcoholic beverages were concerned—a substantial part of the United States. The success of the anti-liquor forces, led by the Anti-Saloon League, was so impressive that they were prepared to strike for a national prohibition constitutional amendment. This issue was decided in the 1916 Congressional elections, although the Amendment itself was not passed by Congress until December 22, 1917. A sufficient number of states ratified it by January 16, 1919, and it took effect on January 16, 1920.

In actuality, however, prohibition began well before January, 1920. In addition to the widespread local prohibition laws, federal laws greatly restricted the production and sale of alcoholic beverages, mostly, beginning in 1917, in the guise of war legislation. The manufacture of distilled spirits beverages, for example, had been forbidden for more than three months when Congress passed the Eighteenth Amendment late in 1917. The Volstead Act of 1919, passed to implement the Amendment, provided by law that wartime prohibition would remain in effect until the Amendment came into force.

The Eighteenth Amendment prohibited the manufacturing, selling, importing, or transporting of "intoxicating liquors." It was designed to kill off the liquor business in general and the saloon in particular; but at the same time the Amendment was not designed to prohibit either the possession or drinking of alcoholic beverages. At a later time the courts held even the act of buying liquor to be legal and not part of a conspiracy. Most of the local and state prohibition laws were similar in their provisions and intent. The very limited nature of the prohibition experiment must, therefore, be understood from the beginning.

At the time, a number of union leaders and social critics pointed out that the Eighteenth Amendment constituted class legislation; that is, the political strength of the drys lay among middle class Progressives who wanted, essentially, to remove the saloon from American life. The Amendment permitted those who had enough money to lay in all the liquor they pleased, but the impecunious workingman was to be deprived of his day-to-day or week-to-week liquor supply. The class aspect of prohibition later turned out to have great importance. Most of the recent revisionist writers have concentrated upon the interplay between prohibition and social role and status.

The primary difficulty that has stood in the way of properly assessing the prohibition experiment has been methods of generalization. Evidence gathered from different sections of the country varies so radically as to make weighing of evidence difficult. In addition, there has been a great deal of confusion about time: When did prohibition begin? What period of its operation should be the basis for judgment? The difficulties of time and place are particularly relevant to the fundamental question of enforcement.

As the country looked forward to prohibition after the elections of 1916, widespread public support, outside of a few urban areas, was expected to make prohibition a success both initially and later on. It was reasonable to expect that enforcement would be strict and that society both institutionally and informally would deal severely with any actions tending to revive the liquor trade. These expectations were realistic through the years of the war, when prohibition and patriotism were closely connected in the public mind. Only some years after the passage of the Volstead Act did hopes for unquestionably effective enforcement fade away. In these early years, when public opinion generally supported enforcement, the various public officials responsible for enforcement were the ones who most contributed to its breakdown. This breakdown in many areas in turn led to the evaporation of much public support in the country as a whole.

Successive Congresses refused to appropriate enough money to enforce the laws. Through its influence in Congress the Anti-Saloon League helped to perpetuate the starvation of the Prohibition Bureau and its predecessors in the name of political expediency. Huge sums spent on prohibition, the drys feared, would alienate many voters—and fearful Congressmen—more or less indifferent to prohibition. The prohibitionists therefore made the claim that prohibition was effective so that they would not have to admit the necessity of large appropriations for enforcement. A second act of irresponsibility of the Congresses was acquiescing in exempting the enforcement officers from Civil Service and so making the Prohibition Bureau part of the political spoils system. League officials who had written this provision into the Volstead Act hoped by using their political power to dictate friendly appointments, but the record shows that politics, not the League, dominated federal enforcement efforts. Not until 1927 did the Prohibition Bureau finally come under Civil Service.

The men charged with enforcement, the Presidents of the 1920's, were, until Hoover, indifferent to prohibition except as it affected politics. Wilson, although not a wet, vetoed the Volstead Act, and it was passed over his veto. Harding and Coolidge were notoriously uninterested in enforcing prohibition. When Hoover took office in 1929 he reorganized the administration of enforcement, and his effectiveness in cutting down well established channels of supply helped give final impetus to the movement for a re-evaluation of prohibition.

In some areas prosecutors and even judges were so unsympathetic that enforcement was impossible. Elsewhere local juries refused to convict in bootlegging cases. These local factors contributed greatly to the notable disparities in the effectiveness of prohibition from place to place.

By a unique concurrent enforcement provision of the Eighteenth Amendment, state and local officials were as responsible for enforcement as federal authorities. The Anti-Saloon League, because of its power in the states, expected to use existing law enforcement agencies and avoid huge federal appropriations for enforcement. Contrary to the expectations of the League, local officials were the weakest point in enforcement. Most of the states—but not all—enacted "little Volstead" acts; yet in 1927 only eighteen of the forty-eight states were appropriating money for the enforcement of such acts. Local enforcement in many Southern and Western areas was both severe and effective; in other areas local enforcement was even more unlikely than federal enforcement. For years the entire government of New Jersey openly defied the Eighteenth Amendment, and it was clear that the governor was not troubled a bit about his oath of office. Some states that had enforced their own prohibition laws before 1919 afterward made no attempt to continue enforcement.

With such extreme variations in the enforcement of prohibition over the United States, judging the over-all success of the experiment on the basis of enforcement records is hazardous. Bootlegging in New York, Chicago, and San Francisco clearly was not necessarily representative of the intervening territory, and vice versa.

An easier basis for generalizing about the effectiveness of enforcement is the impact that prohibition had on consumption of alcohol. Here the second major complication mentioned crops up: the availability of liquor varied greatly from time to time and specifically from an initial period of effectiveness in 1919–1922 to a later period of widespread violation of the law, typically 1925–1927.

In the early years of national prohibition, liquor was very difficult to obtain. In the later years when the laws were being defied by well-organized bootleggers operating through established channels, the supply increased. By the late 1920's, for example, the domestic supply of hard liquor in northern California was so great that the price fell below the point at which it was profitable to run beverages in from Canada by ship. In the last years of prohibition it became very easy—at least in some areas with large populations—to obtain relatively good liquor. Many people, relying on their memories, have generalized from this later period, after about 1925, to all of the prohibition years and have come, falsely, to the conclusion that enforcement was neither real nor practical. Overall one can say that considering the relatively slight amount of effort put into it, enforcement was surprisingly effective in many places, and particularly in the early years.

Both so-called wet and dry sources agree that the amount of liquor consumed per capita decreased substantially because of prohibition. The best figures available show that the gallons of pure alcohol ingested per person varied widely over four different periods. In the period 1911–1914, the amount was 1.69 gallons. Under the wartime restrictions, 1918–1919, the amount decreased to .97. In the early years of national prohibition, 1921–1922, there was still further decrease to .73 gallons. In the later years of prohibition, 1927–1930, the amount rose to 1.14 gallons.

These figures suggest that great care must be used in making comparisons between "before" prohibition and "after." Statistics and memories that use 1920 as the beginning of prohibition are misleading, since not only were federal laws in force before then but there was also extensive state prohibition. The peak of absolute consumption of beer, for example, was reached in the years 1911–1914, not 1916–1918, much less 1919. The real "before" was sometime around 1910.

The best independent evidence of the impact of prohibition can be found in the available figures for certain direct and measurable social effects of alcohol consumption. The decrease from about 1915 to 1920–1922 in arrests for drunkenness, in hospitalization for alcoholism, and in the incidence of other diseases, such as cirrhosis of the liver, specifically related to drinking was remarkable. The low point of these indexes came in 1918–1921, and then they climbed again until the late 1920's. Because of confusion about when prohibition began, the significance of these well known statistics has seldom been appreciated: there is clear evidence that in the early years of prohibition not only did the use of alcohol decrease but American society enjoyed some of the direct benefits promised by proponents of prohibition.

Undoubtedly the most convincing evidence of the success of prohibition is to be found in the mental hospital admission rates. There is no question of a sudden change in physicians' diagnoses, and the people who had to deal with alcohol-related mental diseases were obviously impressed by what they saw. After reviewing recent hospital admission rates for alcoholic psychoses, James V. May, one of the most eminent American psychiatrists, wrote in 1922: "With the advent of prohibition the alcoholic psychoses as far as this country is concerned have become a matter of little more than historical interest. The admission rate in the New York state hospitals for 1920 was only 1.9 percent [as compared with ten percent in 1909–1912]." For many years articles on alcoholism literally disappeared from American medical literature.

In other words, after World War I and until sometime in the early 1920's, say, 1922 or 1923, when enforcement was clearly breaking down, prohibition was generally a success. Certainly there is no basis for the conclusion that prohibition was inherently doomed to failure. The emasculation of enforcement grew out of specific factors that were not organically related to the Eighteenth Amendment.

Nor is most of this analysis either new or controversial. Indeed, most of the criticism of prohibition has centered around assertions not so much that the experiment failed but that it had two more or less unexpected consequences that clearly show it to have been undesirable. The critics claim, first, that the Eighteenth Amendment caused dangerous criminal behavior; and, second, that in spite of prohibition more people drank alcohol than before. If a candid examination fails to confirm these commonly accepted allegations, the interpretation of prohibition as a failure loses most of its validity. Such is precisely the case.

During the 1920's there was almost universal public belief that a "crime wave" existed in the United States. In spite of the literary output on the subject, dealing largely with a local situation in Chicago, there is no firm evidence of this supposed upsurge in lawlessness. Two criminologists, Edwin H. Sutherland and C. H. Gehlke, at the end of the decade reviewed the available crime statistics, and the most that they could conclude was that "there is no evidence here of a 'crime wave,' but only of a slowly rising level" These admittedly inadequate statistics emphasized large urban areas and were, it should be emphasized, *not* corrected to reflect the increase in population. Actually no statistics from this period dealing with crime are of any value whatsoever in generalizing about crime rates. Apparently what happened was that in the 1920's the long existent "underworld" first became publicized and romanticized. The crime wave, in other words, was the invention of enterprising journalists feeding on some sensational crimes and situations and catering to a public to whom the newly discovered "racketeer" was a covert folk hero.

Even though there was no crime wave, there was a connection between crime and prohibition, as Frederick Lewis Allen suggested in his alliterative coupling of "Alcohol and Al Capone." Because of the large profits involved in bootlegging and the inability of the producers and customers to obtain police protection, criminal elements organized and exploited the liquor business just as they did all other illegal activities. It would be a serious distortion even of racketeering, however, to emphasize bootlegging at the expense of the central criminal-directed activity, gambling. Since liquor-related activities were not recognized as essentially criminal in nature by substantial parts of the population, it is difficult to argue that widespread violation of the Volstead Act constituted a true increase of crime. Nevertheless, concern over growing federal "crime" statistics, that is, bootlegging cases, along with fears based on hysterical journalism, helped to bring about repeal.

We are left, then, with the question of whether national prohibition led to more drinking than before. It should first be pointed out not only that the use of 1920 as the beginning of prohibition is misleading but that much of the drinking during the 1920's was not relevant to the prohibition of the Eighteenth Amendment and Volstead Act. Private drinking was perfectly legal all of the time, and possession of liquor that had been accumulated by the foresighted before prohibition was entirely lawful. The continued production of cider and wine at home was specifically provided for also. Indeed, the demand for wine grapes was so great that many grape growers who in 1919 faced ruin made a fortune selling their grapes in the first years of the Amendment. Ironically, many an old lady who made her own wine believed that she was defying prohibition when in fact the law protected her.

We still face the problem of reconciling the statistics quoted above that show that alcohol consumption was substantially reduced, at one point to about half of the pre-prohibition consumption, with the common observation of the 1920's that as many or more people were drinking than before.

What happened, one can say with hindsight, was predictable. When liquor became unavailable except at some risk and considerable cost, it became a luxury item, that is, a symbol of affluence and, eventually, status. Where before men of good families tended not to drink and women certainly did not, during the 1920's it was precisely the sons and daughters of the "nice" people who were patronizing the bootleggers and speakeasies, neither of which for some years was very effectively available to the lower classes. This utilization of drinking as conspicuous consumption was accompanied by the so-called revolution in manners and morals that began among the rebellious intellectuals around 1912 and reached a high point of popularization in the 1920's when the adults of the business class began adopting the "lower" social standards of their children.

We can now understand why the fact was universally reported by journalists of the era that "everyone drank, including many who never did before." Drinking, and often new drinking, was common among the upper classes, especially among the types of people likely to consort with the writers of the day. The journalists and other observers did indeed report honestly that they saw "everyone" drinking. They seldom saw the lower classes and almost never knew about the previous drinking habits of the masses. The situation was summed up by an unusually well-qualified witness, Whiting Williams, testifying before the Wickersham Commission. A vice-president of a Cleveland steel company, he had for many years gone in disguise among the working people of several areas in connection with handling labor problems. He concluded:

> . . . very much of the misconception with respect to the liquor problem comes from the fact that most of the people who are writing and talking most actively about the prohibition problem are people who, in the nature of things, have never had any contact with the liquor problem in its earlier pre-prohibition form and who are, therefore, unduly impressed with the changes with respect to drinking that they see on their own level; their own level, however, representing an extremely small proportion of the population.
>
> The great mass who, I think, are enormously more involved in the whole problem, of course, in the nature of things are not articulate and are not writing in the newspapers.

The important point is that the "everyone" who was reported to be drinking did not include working-class families, i.e., the pre-ponderant part of the population. Clark Warburton, in a study initiated with the help of the Association Against the Prohibition Amendment, is explicit on this point: "The working class is consuming not more than half as much alcohol per capita as formerly." The classic study is Martha Bensley Bruère's. She surveyed social workers across the country, and the overwhelming impression (even taking account of urban immigrant areas where prohibition laws were flouted) was that working people drank very much less than before and further, as predicted, that prohibition had, on the balance, substantially improved conditions among low-income Americans.

Even in its last years the law, with all of its leaks, was still effective in cutting down drinking among the workers, which was one of the primary aims of prohibition. Here, then, is more evidence of the success of the prohibition experiment. Certainly the Anti-Saloon League did succeed in destroying the old-fashioned saloon, the explicit target of its campaign.

Taking together all of this evidence of the success of prohibition, especially in its class differential aspects, we are still left with the question of why the law was repealed.

The story of repeal is contained largely in the growth of the idea that prohibition was a failure. From the beginning, a number of contemporary observers (particularly in the largest cities) saw many violations of the law and concluded that prohibition was not working. These observers were in the minority, and for a long time most people believed that by and large prohibition was effective. Even for those who did not, the question of repeal—once appeals to the Supreme Court had been settled—simply never arose. Bartlett C. Jones has observed, "A peculiarity of the Prohibition debate was the fact that repeal, called an absolute impossibility for much of the period, became irresistibly popular in 1932 and 1933. Not even enemies of prohibition considered absolute repeal as an alternative until quite late, although they upheld through all of these years their side of the vigorous public debate about the effectiveness and desirability of the prohibition laws.

In the early days of prohibition, the predominant attitudes toward the experiment manifested in the chief magazines and newspapers of the country were either ambivalent acceptance or, more rarely, impotent hostility. In 1923–1924 a major shift in the attitudes of the mass circulation information media occurred so that acceptance was replaced by nearly universal outright criticism accompanied by a demand for modification of the Volstead Act. The criticism was based on the assumption that Volsteadism, at least, was a failure. The suggested solution was legalizing light wines and beers.

The effectiveness of the shift of "public opinion" is reflected in the vigorous counterattack launched by the dry forces who too often denied real evils and asserted that prohibition was effective and was benefitting the nation. By claiming too much, especially in the late 1920's, the drys discredited that which was really true, and the literate public apparently discounted all statements that might show that prohibition was at least a partial success, partly on the rigidly idealistic basis that if it was a partial failure, it was a total failure.

Great impetus was given to sentiment hostile to prohibition by the concern of respectable people about the "crime wave." They argued, plausibly enough given the assumptions that there was a crime wave and that prohibition was a failure, that universal disregard for the Eighteenth Amendment was damaging to general respect for law. If the most respectable elements of society, so the argument went, openly showed contempt for the Constitution, how could anyone be expected to honor a mere statute? Much of the leadership of the "anti's" soon came from the bar associations rather than the bar patrons.

Coincident with this shift in opinion came the beginning of one of the most effective publicity campaigns of modern times, led by the Association Against the Prohibition Amendment. At first largely independent of liquor money, in the last years of prohibition the AAPA used all it could command. By providing journalists with reliable information, the AAPA developed a virtual monopoly on liquor and prohibition press coverage." In the late 1920's and early 1930's it was unusual to find a story about prohibition in small local papers that did not have its origin-free of charge, of course—with the AAPA.

The AAPA had as its announced goal the modification of the Volstead Act to legalize light wines and beers. The organization also headed up campaigns to repeal the "little Volstead" acts most states had enacted. By the late 1920's the AAPA beat the Anti-Saloon League at its own game, chipping away at the state level. State after state, often by popular vote, did away with the concurrent enforcement acts. Both the wets and the drys viewed state repeals and any modification of the Volstead Act as only steps toward full repeal. Perhaps they were correct; but another possibility does need examination.

Andrew Sinclair, in the most recent and thorough examination of the question, contends that modification of the Volstead Act to legalize light wines and beers would have saved the rest of the prohibition experiment. It is difficult to differ with Sinclair's contention that complete repeal of the Eighteenth Amendment was unprovoked and undesirable.

When President Hoover appointed the Wickersham Commission, public opinion was almost unanimous in expecting that the solution to the prohibition problem would be modification. The Commission's report strengthened the expectation. Not even the Association Against the Prohibition Amendment hoped for more than that, much less repeal. But suddenly an overwhelming surge of public sentiment brought about the Twenty-First Amendment denouement.

The cause of this second sudden shift in opinion was the Great Depression that began about 1929. Jones has shown convincingly that every argument used to bring about repeal in 1932–1933 had been well known since the beginning of prohibition. The class aspect of the legislation, which had been so callously accepted in 1920, was suddenly undesirable. The main depression-related argument, that legalization of liquor manufacture would produce a badly needed additional tax revenue, was well known in the 1910's and even earlier. These rationalizations of repeal were masks for the fact that the general public, baffled by the economic catastrophe, found a convenient scapegoat: prohibition. (The drys had, after all, tried to credit prohibition for the prosperity of the 1920's.) The groundswell of public feeling was irresistible and the entire "experiment, noble in motive and far-reaching in purpose," was not modified but thrown out with Volsteadism, bathwater, baby, and all.

Because the AAPA won, its explanations of what happened were accepted at face value. One of the lasting results of prohibition, therefore, was perpetuation of the stereotypes of the wet propaganda of the 1920's and the myth that the American experiment in prohibition (usually misunderstood to have outlawed personal drinking as well as the liquor business) was a failure. Blanketed together here indiscriminately were all of the years from 1918 to 1933.

More than thirty years have passed since the repeal of the Eighteenth Amendment. Surely the AAPA has now had its full measure of victory and it is no longer necessary for historians to perpetuate a myth that grew up in another era. For decades there has been no realistic possibility of a resurgence of prohibition in its Progressive form—or probably any other form.

The concern now is not so much the destruction of myth, however; the concern is that our acceptance of the myth of the failure of prohibition has prevented us from exploring in depth social and especially sociological aspects of the prohibition experiment. Recent scholarship, by treating prohibition more as a reform than an experiment, has shown that we have been missing one of the most interesting incidents of twentieth-century history.

POSTSCRIPT

Was Prohibition a Failure?

For many historians, the 1920s marked an era of change in the United States, from international involvement and war to isolationism and peace, from the feverish reform of the Progressive era to the conservative political retrenchment of "Republican ascendancy," from the entrenched values of Victorian America to the cultural rebellion identified with the proliferation of "flivvers," "flappers," and hip flasks. In 1931, Frederick Lewis Allen focused on these changes in his popular account of the decade, *Only Yesterday*. In a chapter entitled "The Revolution of Morals and Manners," Allen established a widely accepted image of the 1920s as a period of significant social and cultural rebellion. An excellent collection of essays that explores this issue is John Braeman, Robert H. Bremner, and David Brody, eds., *Change and Continuity in Twentieth Century America: The 1920s* (Ohio State University Press, 1968).

The history of the temperance and prohibition movements in the United States is effectively presented in Andrew Sinclair, *Prohibition: The Era of Excess* (Harper & Row, 1962), Joseph R. Gusfield, *Symbolic Crusade: Status Politics and the American Temperance Movement* (University of Illinois Press, 1963), James H. Timberlake, *Prohibition and the Progressive Movement* (1963), Norman H. Clark, *Deliver Us from Evil: An Interpretation of American Prohibition* (W. W. Norton, 1976), and Thomas R. Pegram, *Battling Demon Rum: The Struggle for a Dry America, 1800–1933* (Ivan R. Dee, 1998). Mark E. Lender and James Kirby Martin provide an excellent survey that includes a chapter on the rise and fall of the prohibition amendment in *Drinking in America* (The Free Press, 1982).

There are a number of important overviews of the 1920s. Among the more useful are John D. Hicks, *Republican Ascendancy, 1921–1933* (Harper & Row, 1960), a volume in The New American Nation Series; Roderick Nash, *The Nervous Generation: American Thought, 1917–1930* (Rand McNally, 1970); and two volumes by Paul Carter, *The Twenties in America*, 2d ed. (Harlan Davidson, 1975) and *Another Part of the Twenties* (Columbia University Press, 1977). The classic sociological study by Robert and Helen Lynd, *Middletown: A Study in Contemporary American Culture* (Harcourt, Brace, 1929) explores the values of a group of "typical" Americans of the 1920s.

The economic history of the decade is discussed in George Soule, *Prosperity Decade: From War to Depression, 1917–1929* (Holt, Rinehart & Winston, 1947); Peter Fearon, *War, Prosperity, and Depression* (University of Kansas Press, 1987); and John Kenneth Galbraith, *The Great Crash, 1929*, rev. ed. (Houghton Mifflin, 1989). For a critical biography of the decade's most notable business leader, see Keith Sward, *The Legend of Henry Ford* (Rinehart, 1948).

The status of women in the decade after suffrage receives general treatment in William H. Chafe, *The Paradox of Change: American Women in the*

20th Century (Oxford University Press, 1991) and, more thoroughly, in Dorothy M. Brown, *Setting a Course: American Women in the 1920s* (Twayne, 1987). Discussions of feminism in the 1920s are competently presented in William L. O'Neill, *Everyone Was Brave: The Rise and Fall of Feminism in America* (University of Illinois Press, 1973); Susan D. Baker, *The Origins of the Equal Rights Amendment: Feminism Between the Wars* (Greenwood Press, 1981); and Nancy F. Cott, *The Grounding of Feminism* (Yale University Press, 1987). David M. Kennedy, *Birth Control in America: The Career of Margaret Sanger* (Yale University Press, 1970) examines an important issue that attracted the interest of many women's groups in the 1920s, while Jacqueline Dowd Hall, *Revolt Against Chivalry: Jessie Daniel Ames and the Women's Campaign Against Lynching* (Columbia University Press, 1979) explores the role of women in the area of race relations.

Race is also the focal point of several studies of the Harlem Renaissance. The best of these works include Nathan Irvin Huggins, *Harlem Renaissance* (Oxford University Press, 1971); David Levering Lewis, *When Harlem Was in Vogue* (Alfred A. Knopf, 1981); and Cary D. Wintz, *Black Culture and the Harlem Renaissance* (Rice University Press, 1988).

Recent scholarship on the Ku Klux Klan in the 1920s has focused on its grassroots participation in local and state politics. Klan members are viewed less as extremists and more as political pressure groups whose aims were to gain control of various state and local governmental offices. The best overview of this perspective is Shawn Lay, ed., *The Invisible Empire in the West: Toward a New Historical Appraisal of the Ku Klux Klan of the 1920s* (University of Illinois Press, 1992). For additional approaches to the KKK's activities in the "Roaring Twenties," see Charles C. Alexander, *The Ku Klux Klan in the Southwest* (University of Kentucky Press, 1965); Kenneth T. Jackson, *The Ku Klux Klan in the City, 1915-1930* (Oxford University Press, 1967); Kathleen M. Blee, *Women of the Klan: Racism and Gender in the 1920s* (University of California Press, 1991); and Nancy MacLean, *Behind the Mask of Chivalry: The Making of the Second Ku Klux Klan* (Oxford University Press, 1994).

ISSUE 10

Did the New Deal Prolong the Great Depression?

YES: Gary Dean Best, from *Pride, Prejudice, and Politics: Roosevelt Versus Recovery, 1933–1938* (Praeger, 1990)

NO: Roger Biles, from *A New Deal for the American People* (Northern Illinois University Press, 1991)

ISSUE SUMMARY

YES: Professor of history Gary Dean Best argues that Roosevelt established an antibusiness environment with the creation of the New Deal regulatory programs, which retarded the nation's economic recovery from the Great Depression until World War II.

NO: Professor of history Roger Biles contends that, in spite of its minimal reforms and non-revolutionary programs, the New Deal created a limited welfare state that implemented economic stabilizers to avert another depression.

The catastrophe triggered by the 1929 Wall Street debacle crippled the American economy, deflated the optimistic future most Americans assumed to be their birthright, and ripped apart the values by which the country's businesses, farms, and governments were run. During the next decade, the inertia of the Great Depression stifled their attempts to make ends meet.

The world depression of the 1930s began in the United States. The United States had suffered periodic economic setbacks—in 1873, 1893, 1907, and 1920—but those slumps had been limited and temporary. The omnipotence of American productivity, the ebullient American spirit, and the self-deluding thought "it can't happen here" blocked out any consideration of an economic collapse that might devastate the capitalist economy and threaten U.S. democratic government.

All aspects of American society trembled from successive jolts; there were 4 million unemployed people in 1930 and 9 million more by 1932. Those who had not lost their jobs took pay cuts or worked for scrip. There was no security for those whose savings were lost forever when banks failed or stocks declined.

Manufacturing halted, industry shut down, and farmers destroyed wheat, corn, and milk rather than sell them at a loss. Worse, there were millions of homeless Americans—refugees from the cities roaming the nation on freight trains, victims of the drought or the Dust Bowl seeking a new life farther west, and hobo children estranged from their parents.

Business and government leaders alike seemed immobilized by the economic giant that had fallen to its knees. Herbert Hoover, the incumbent president at the start of the Great Depression, attempted some relief programs. However, they were ineffective considering the magnitude of the unemployment, hunger, and distress.

As governor of New York, Franklin D. Roosevelt (who was elected president in 1932) had introduced some relief measures, such as industrial welfare and a comprehensive system of unemployment remedies, to alleviate the social and economic problems facing the citizens of the state. Yet his campaign did little to reassure his critics that he was more than a "Little Lord Fauntleroy" rich boy who wanted to be the president. In light of later developments, Roosevelt may have been the only presidential candidate to deliver more programs than he actually promised.

The first "hundred days" of the New Deal attempted to jump-start the economy with dozens of recovery and relief measures. On inauguration day, FDR told the nation "the only thing we have to fear is fear itself." A bank holiday was immediately declared. Congress passed the Emergency Banking Act, which pumped Federal Reserve notes into the major banks and stopped the wave of bank failures. Later banking acts separated commercial and investment institutions, and the Federal Deposit Insurance Corporation (FDIC) guaranteed people's savings from a loss of up to $2,500 in member banks. A number of relief agencies were set up that provided work for youth and able-bodied men on various state and local building projects. Finally the Tennessee Valley Administration (TVA) was created to provide electricity in rural areas not serviced by private power companies.

In 1935 the Supreme Court ended the First New Deal by declaring both the Agriculture Adjustment Administration and National Recovery Act unconstitutional. In response to critics on the left who felt that the New Deal was favoring the large banks, big agriculture, and big business, FDR shifted his approach in 1935. The Second New Deal created the Works Project Administration (WPA), which became the nation's largest employer in its eight years of operation. Social Security was passed, and the government guaranteed monthly stipends for the aged, the unemployed, and dependent children. Labor pressured the administration for a collective bargaining bill. The Wagner Act established a National Labor Relations Board to supervise industry-wide elections. The steel, coal, automobile and some garment industries were unionized as membership tripled from 3 million in 1933 to 9 million in 1939.

With the immediate crisis over, entrenched conservatives in Congress blocking new legislation and World War II looming, the New Deal ended by 1938. In the first selection, historian Gary Dean Best argues that with its swollen government agencies, promotion of cartels, confiscatory taxes, and dubious antitrust lawsuits, the New Deal prolonged the depression. But historian Roger Biles contends that, in spite of its minimal reform programs, the New Deal created a limited welfare state that implemented economic stabilizers to avert another depression.

YES

Gary Dean Best

Pride, Prejudice and Politics: Roosevelt Versus Recovery, 1933–1938

This book had its genesis in the fact that I have for a long time felt uncomfortable with the standard works written about Franklin Delano Roosevelt and the New Deal, and with the influence those works have exerted on others writing about and teaching U.S. history. Although I approach the subject from a very different perspective, Paul K. Conkin's preface to the second edition of *The New Deal* (1975) expressed many of my own misgivings about writings on the subject. Conkin wrote that "pervading even the most scholarly revelations was a monotonous, often almost reflexive, and in my estimation a very smug or superficial valuative perspective—approval, even glowing approval, of most enduring New Deal policies, or at least of the underlying goals that a sympathetic observer could always find behind policies and programs."

Studies of the New Deal such as Conkin described seemed to me to be examples of a genre relatively rare in U.S. historiography—that of "court histories." . . .

But, like most historians teaching courses dealing with the Roosevelt period, I was captive to the published works unless I was willing and able to devote the time to pursue extensive research in the period myself. After some years that became possible, and this book is the result.

My principal problem with Roosevelt and the New Deal was not over his specific reforms or his social programs, but with the failure of the United States to recover from the depression during the eight peacetime years that he and his policies governed the nation. I consider that failure tragic, not only for the 14.6 percent of the labor force that remained unemployed as late as 1940, and for the millions of others who subsisted on government welfare because of the prolonged depression, but also because of the image that the depression-plagued United States projected to the world at a crucial time in international affairs. In the late 1930s and early 1940s, when U.S. economic strength might have given pause to potential aggressors in the world, our economic weakness furnished encouragement to them instead.

From the standpoint, then, not only of our domestic history, but also of the tragic events and results of World War II, it has seemed to me that Roosevelt's failure to generate economic recovery during this critical period deserved more attention than historians have given it.

Most historians of the New Deal period leave the impression that the failure of the United States to recover during those eight years resulted from Roosevelt's unwillingness to embrace Keynesian spending. According to this thesis, recovery came during World War II because the war at last forced Roosevelt to spend at the level required all along for recovery. This, however, seemed to me more an advocacy of Keynes' theories by the historians involved that an explanation for the U.S. failure to recover during those years. Great Britain, for example, managed to recover by the late 1930s without recourse to deficit spending. By that time the United States was, by contrast, near the bottom of the list of industrial nations as measured in progress toward recovery, with most others having reached the predepression levels and many having exceeded them. The recovered countries represented a variety of economic systems, from state ownership to private enterprise. The common denominator in their success was not a reliance on deficit spending, but rather the stimulus they furnished to industrial enterprise.

What went wrong in the United States? Simplistic answers such as the reference to Keynesianism seemed to me only a means of avoiding a real answer to the question. A wise president, entering the White House in the midst of a crippling depression, should do everything possible to stimulate enterprise. In a free economy, economic recovery means *business* recovery. It follows, therefore, that a wise chief executive should do everything possible to create the conditions and psychology most conducive to business recovery—to encourage business to expand production, and lenders and investors to furnish the financing and capital that are required. An administration seeking economic recovery will do as little as possible that might inhibit recovery, will weigh all its actions with the necessity for economic recovery in mind, and will consult with competent business and financial leaders, as well as economists, to determine the best policies to follow. Such a president will seek to promote cooperation between the federal government and business, rather than conflict, and will seek to introduce as much consistency and stability as possible into government economic policies so that businessmen and investors can plan ahead. While obviously the destitute must be cared for, ultimately the most humane contribution a liberal government can make to the victims of a depression is the restoration of prosperity and the reemployment of the idle in genuine jobs.

In measuring the Roosevelt policies and programs during the New Deal years against such standards, I was struck by the air of unreality that hung over Washington in general and the White House in particular during this period. Business and financial leaders who questioned the wisdom of New Deal policies were disregarded and deprecated because of their "greed" and "self-interest," while economists and business academicians who persisted in calling attention to the collision between New Deal policies and simple economic realities were dismissed for their "orthodoxy." As one "orthodox" economist pointed out early in the New Deal years,

> economic realism . . . insists that policies aiming to promote recovery will, in fact, ratard recovery if and where they fail to take into account correctly of stubborn facts in the existing economic situation and of the arithmetic

of business as it must be carried out in the economic situation we are trying to revive. The antithesis of this economic realism is the vaguely hope-
ful or optimistic idealism in the field of economic policy, as such, which
feels that good intentions, enough cleverness, and the right appeal to the
emotions of the people ought to insure good results in spite of inconvenient facts.

Those "inconvenient facts" dogged the New Deal throughout these years, only
to be stubbornly resisted by a president whose pride, prejudices, and politics
would rarely permit an accommodation with them.

Most studies of the New Deal years approach the period largely from the
perspective of the New Dealers themselves. Critics and opponents of
Roosevelt's policies and programs are given scant attention in such works
except to point up the "reactionary" and "unenlightened" opposition with
which Roosevelt was forced to contend in seeking to provide Americans with
"a more abundant life." The few studies that have concentrated on critics and
opponents of the New Deal in the business community have been by unsympathetic historians who have tended to distort the opposition to fit the caricature drawn by the New Dealers, so that they offer little to explain the impact
of Roosevelt's policies in delaying recovery from the depression.

The issue of *why* businessmen and bankers were so critical of the New
Deal has been for too long swept under the rug, together with the question of
how Roosevelt and his advisers could possibly expect to produce an economic
recovery while a state of war existed between his administration and the
employers and investors who, alone, could produce such a recovery. Even a
Keynesian response to economic depression is ultimately dependent on the
positive reactions of businessmen and investors for its success, as Keynes well
knew, and those reactions were not likely to be as widespread as necessary
under such a state of warfare between government and business. Businessmen,
bankers, and investors may have been "greedy" and "self-interested." They
may have been guilty of wrong perceptions and unfounded fears. But they are
also the ones, in a free economy, upon whose decisions and actions economic
recovery must depend. To understand their opposition to the New Deal
requires an immersion in the public and private comments of critics of
Roosevelt's policies. The degree and nature of business, banking, and investor
concern about the direction and consequences of New Deal policies can be
gleaned from the hundreds of banking and business periodicals representative
of every branch of U.S. business and finance in the 1930s, and from the letters
and diaries of the New Deal's business and other critics during the decade.

Statistics are useful in understanding the history of any period, but particularly periods of economic growth or depression. Statistics for the
Roosevelt years may easily be found in *Historical Statistics of the United States*
published by the Bureau of the Census, U.S. Department of Commerce (1975).
Some of the trauma of the depression years may be inferred from the fact that

the population of the United States grew by over 17 million between 1920 and 1930, but by only about half of that (8.9 million) between 1930 and 1940.

Historical Statistics gives the figures . . . for unemployment, 1929–1940. These figures are, however, only estimates. The federal government did not monitor the number of unemployed during those years. Even so, these figures are shocking, indicating as they do that even after the war had begun in Europe, with the increased orders that it provided for U.S. mines, factories, and farms, unemployment remained at 14.6 percent.

One characteristic of the depression, to which attention was frequently called during the Roosevelt years, was the contrast between its effects on the durable goods and consumer goods industries. Between 1929 and 1933, expenditures on personal durable goods dropped by nearly 50 percent, and in 1938 they were still nearly 25 percent below the 1929 figures. Producers' durable goods suffered even more, failing by nearly two-thirds between 1929 and 1933, and remaining more than 50 percent below the 1929 figure in 1938. At the same time, expenditures on nondurable, or consumer, goods showed much less effect. Between 1929 and 1933 they fell only about 14.5 percent, and by 1938 they exceeded the 1929 level. These figures indicate that the worst effects of the depression, and resultant unemployment, were being felt in the durable goods industries. Roosevelt's policies, however, served mainly to stimulate the consumer goods industries where the depression and unemployment were far less seriously felt.

One consequence of Roosevelt's policies can be seen in the U.S. balance of trade during the New Deal years. By a variety of devices, Roosevelt drove up the prices of U.S. industrial and agricultural products, making it difficult for these goods to compete in the world market, and opening U.S. markets to cheaper foreign products. . . . With the exception of a $41 million deficit in 1888, these were the only deficits in U.S. trade for a century, from the 1870s to the 1970s.

. . . [W]hile suicides during the Roosevelt years remained about the same as during the Hoover years, the death rate by "accidental falls" increased significantly. In fact, according to *Historical Statistics,* the death rate by "accidental falls" was higher in the period 1934–1938 than at any other time between 1910 and 1970 (the years for which figures are given).

Interestingly, the number of persons arrested grew steadily during the depression years. In 1938 nearly twice as many (554,000) were arrested as in 1932 (278,000), and the number continued to increase until 1941. And, while the number of telephones declined after 1930 and did not regain the 1930 level until 1939, the number of households with radios increased steadily during the depression years. And Americans continued to travel. Even in the lowest year, 1933, 300,000 Americans visited foreign countries (down from 517,000 in 1929), while the number visiting national parks, monuments, and such, steadily increased during the depression—in 1938 nearly five times as many (16,331,000) did so as in 1929 (3,248,000).

Comparisons of the recovery of the United States with that of other nations may be found in the volumes of the League of Nations' *World Economic Survey* for the depression years. [A] table (from the volume of 1938/39) shows comparisons of unemployment rates. From this it can be seen that in 1929 the United States had the lowest unemployment rate of the countries listed; by 1932 the United States was midway on the list, with seven nations reporting higher unemployment rates and seven reporting lower unemployment. By mid-1938, however, after over five years of the New Deal, only three nations had higher unemployment rates, while twelve had lower unemployment. The United States, then, had lost ground in comparison with the other nations between 1932 and 1938.

The *World Economic Survey* for 1937/38 compared the levels of industrial production for 23 nations in 1937, expressed as a percentage of their industrial production in 1929. . . . It must be remembered that the figures for the United States reflect the level of industrial production reached just before the collapse of the economy later that year. Of the 22 other nations listed, 19 showed a higher rate of recovery in industrial production that the United States, while only 3 lagged behind. One of these, France, had followed policies similar to those of the New Deal in the United States. As the *World Economic Survey* put it, both the Roosevelt administration and the Blum government in France had "adopted far-reaching social and economic policies which combined recovery measures with measures of social reform." It added: "The consequent doubt regarding the prospects of profit and the uneasy relations between businessmen and the Government have in the opinion of many, been an important factor in delaying recovery," and the two countries had, "unlike the United Kingdom and Germany," failed to "regain the 1929 level of employment and production." The *World Economic Survey* the following year (1939) pointed out that industrial production in the United States had fallen from the 92.2 to 65 by June 1938, and hovered between 77 and 85 throughout 1939. Thus, by the end of 1938 the U.S. record was even sorrier than revealed by the [data].

Every survey of American historians consistently finds Franklin Delano Roosevelt ranked as one of this nation's greatest presidents. Certainly, exposure to even a sampling of the literature on Roosevelt and the New Deal can lead one to no other conclusion. Conventional wisdom has it that Roosevelt was an opportune choice to lead the United States through the midst of the Great Depression, that his cheerful and buoyant disposition uplifted the American spirit in the midst of despair and perhaps even forestalled a radical change in the direction of American politics toward the right or the left. Roosevelt's landslide reelection victory in 1936, and the congressional successes in 1934, are cited as evidence of the popularity of both the president and the New Deal among the American people. Polls by both Gallup and the Democratic National Committee early in the 1936 campaign, however, give a very different picture, and suggest that the electoral victories can be as accurately accounted for in terms of the vast outpourings of federal money in 1934 and 1936, and the inability or unwillingness of Landon to offer a genuine alternative to the New Deal in the latter year. To this must be added the fact that after early 1936 two of the most unpopular New Deal programs—the NRA and the AAA—had been removed as issues by the Supreme Court.

Conventional wisdom, in fact, suffers many setbacks when the Roosevelt years are examined from any other perspective than through a pro–New Deal Prism—from the banking crisis of 1933 and the first inaugural address, through the reasons for the renewed downturn in 1937, to the end of the New Deal in 1937–1938. The American present has been ill-served by the inaccurate picture that has too often been presented of this chapter in the American past by biographers and historians. Roosevelt's achievements in alleviating the hardship of the depression are deservedly well known, his responsibility for prolonging the hardship is not. His role in providing long-overdue and sorely needed social and economic legislation is in every high school American history textbook, but the costs for the United States of his eight-year-long war against business recovery are mentioned in none.

Such textbooks (and those in college, too) frequently contain a chapter on the Great Depression, followed by one on the New Deal, the implication being that somewhere early in the second of the chapters the depression was ended by Roosevelt's policies. Only careful reading reveals that despite Roosevelt's immense labors to feed the unemployed, only modest recovery from the lowest depths of the depression was attained before the outbreak of World War II. Roosevelt, readers are told, was too old-fashioned, too conservative, to embrace the massive compensatory spending and unbalanced budgets that might have produced a Keynesian recovery sooner. But World War II, the books tell us, made such spending necessary and the recovery that might have occurred earlier was at last achieved.

Generations of Americans have been brought up on this version of the New Deal years. Other presidential administrations have been reevaluated over the years, and have risen or fallen in grace as a result, but not the Roosevelt administration. The conventional wisdom concerning the Roosevelt administration remains the product of the "court historians," assessments of the New Deal period that could not have been better written by the New Dealers themselves. The facts, however, are considerably at variance with this conventional wisdom concerning the course of the depression, the reasons for the delay of recovery, and the causes of the recovery when it came, finally, during World War II.

From the uncertainty among businessmen and investors about the new president-elect that aborted a promising upturn in the fall of 1932, to the panic over the prospect of inflationary policies that was a major factor in the banking crisis that virtually paralyzed the nation's economy by the date of his inauguration, Roosevelt's entry into the White House was not an auspicious beginning toward recovery. The prejudices that were to guide the policies and programs of the New Deal for the next six years were revealed in Roosevelt's inaugural address, although the message was largely overlooked until it had become more apparent in the actions of the administration later. It was an attitude of hostility toward business and finance, of contempt for the profit motive of capitalism, and of willingness to foment class antagonism for political benefit. This was not an attitude that was conducive to business recovery, and the programs and policies that would flow from those prejudices would prove, in fact, to be destructive of the possibility of recovery.

There followed the "hundred days," when Roosevelt rammed through Congress a variety of legislation that only depressed business confidence more. The new laws were served up on attractive platters, with tempting descriptions—truth in securities, aid for the farmer, industrial self-regulation— but when the covers were removed the contents were neither attractive nor did they match the labels. By broad grants of power to the executive branch of the government, the legislation passed regulation of the U.S. economy into the hands of New Dealers whose aim was not to promote recovery but to carry out their own agendas for radical change of the economic system even at the expense of delaying recovery. Thus, truth in securities turned to paralysis of the securities markets, aid for the farmer became a war against profits by pro- cessors of agricultural goods, and industrial self-regulation became government control and labor-management strife. International economic cooperation as a device for ending the depression was abandoned for an isolationist approach, and throughout 1933 the threat of inflation added further uncertainty for businessmen and investors.

The grant of such unprecedented peacetime authority to an American president aroused concern, but these after all were only "emergency" powers, to be given up once recovery was on its way. Or were they? Gradually the evidence accumulated that the Tugwells and the Brandeisians intended to insti- tutionalize the "emergency" powers as permanent features of American eco- nomic life. By the end of 1933, opposition to the New Deal was already sizable. Business alternated between the paralysis of uncertainty and a modest "recovery" born of purchases and production inspired by fear of higher costs owing to inflation and the effects of the AAA and NRA. The implementation of the latter two agencies in the fall of 1933 brought a renewed downturn that improved only slightly during the winter and spring. A renewed legislative onslaught by the New Deal in the 1934 congress, combined with labor strife encouraged by the provisions of the NIRA, brought a new collapse of the economy in the fall of 1934, which lowered economic indices once again to near the lowest levels they had reached in the depression.

The pattern had been established. The war against business and finance was under way, and there would be neither retreat nor cessation. Roosevelt's pride and prejudices, and the perceived political advantages to be gained from the war, dictated that his administration must ever be on the offensive and never in retreat. But the administration suffered defeats, nevertheless, and embarrassment. The Supreme Court proved a formidable foe, striking down both the NRA and the AAA. Dire predictions from the administration about the implications for the economy of the loss of the NRA proved embarrassing when the economy began to show gradual improvement after its departure. But defeat did not mean retreat. Under the goading of Felix Frankfurter and his disciples, Roosevelt became even more extreme in his verbal and legislative assault against business. Their attempts to cooperate with the Roosevelt administration having been spurned, businessmen and bankers awakened to the existence of the war being waged upon them and moved into opposition.

Roosevelt gloried in their opposition and escalated the war against them in the 1936 reelection campaign.

Reelected in 1936 on a tidal wave of government spending, and against a lackluster Republican campaigner who offered no alternative to the New Deal, Roosevelt appeared at the apogee of his power and prestige. His triumph was, however, to be short-lived, despite an enhanced Democratic majority in Congress. A combination of factors was about to bring the New Deal war against business to a stalemate and eventual retreat. One of these was his ill-advised attempt to pack the Supreme Court with subservient justices, which aroused so much opposition even in his own party that he lost control of the Democrat-controlled Congress. More important, perhaps, was the growing economic crisis that the Roosevelt administration faced in 1937, largely as a result of its own past policies. The massive spending of 1936, including the payment of the veterans' bonus, had generated a speculative recovery during that year from concern about inflationary consequences. Fears of a "boom" were increased as a result of the millions of dollars in dividends, bonuses, and pay raises dispensed by businesses late in 1936 as a result of the undistributed profits tax. The pay raises, especially, were passed on in the form of higher prices, as were the social security taxes that were imposed on businesses beginning with 1937. Labor disturbances, encouraged by the Wagner Labor Act and the Roosevelt alliance with John L. Lewis' Congress of Industrial Organizations in the 1936 campaign, added further to the wage-price spiral that threatened as 1937 unfolded. Massive liquidations of low-interest government bonds, and sagging prices of the bonds, fueled concern among bankers and economists, and within the Treasury, that a "boom" would imperil the credit of the federal government and the solvency of the nation's banks whose portfolios consisted mainly of low-interest government bonds.

In considering the two principal options for cooling the "boom"—raising interest rates or cutting federal spending—the Roosevelt administration chose to move toward a balanced budget. It was a cruel dilemma that the New Dealers faced. All knew that the economy had not yet recovered from the depression, yet they were faced with the necessity to apply brakes to an economy that was becoming overheated as a consequence of their policies. Moreover, the reduction in consumer purchasing power caused by the cuts in federal spending was occurring at the same time that purchasing power was already being eroded as a result of the higher prices that worried the administration. Private industry, it should have been obvious, could not "take up the slack," since the Roosevelt administration had done nothing to prepare for the transition from government to private spending that John Maynard Keynes and others had warned them was necessary. The New Dealers had been far too busy waging war against business to allow it the opportunity to prepare for any such transition.

In fact, far from confronting the emergency of 1937 by making long-overdue attempts to cooperate with business in generating recovery, Roosevelt was busy pressing a new legislative assault against them. Denied passage of his legislative package by Congress during its regular 1937 session, Roosevelt called a special session for November despite evidence that the economy had begun a new downturn. Even the collapse of the stock market, within days after his announcement of the special session, and the growing unemployment that soon followed, did not deter Roosevelt from his determination to drive the legislative assault through it. With the nation in the grips of a full-blown economic collapse, Roosevelt offered nothing to the special session but the package of antibusiness legislation it had turned down in the regular session. Once again he was rebuffed by Congress. The nation drifted, its economic indices falling, with its president unwilling to admit the severity of the situation or unable to come to grips with what it said about the bankruptcy of the New Deal policies and programs.

By early 1938, Roosevelt was faced with problems similar to those he had faced when he first entered the White House five years earlier, but without the political capital he had possessed earlier. In 1933 the Hoover administration could be blamed for the depression. In 1938 the American people blamed the Roosevelt administration for retarding recovery. Five years of failure could not be brushed aside. Five years of warfare against business and disregard of criticism and offers of cooperation had converted supporters of 1933 into cynics or opponents by 1938. Even now, however, pride, prejudice, and politics dominated Roosevelt, making it impossible for him to extend the needed olive branch to business. The best that he could offer in 1938 was a renewal of federal spending and more of the same New Deal that had brought the nation renewed misery. In the 1938 congressional session he continued to press for passage of the antibusiness legislation that had been rejected by both sessions of 1937.

But Congress was no longer the pliant body it had been in 1933, and in the 1938 congressional elections the people's reaction was registered when the Republicans gained 81 new seats in the House and 8 in the Senate—far more than even the most optimistic Republican had predicted. If the message was lost on Roosevelt, it was obvious to some in his administration, notably his new Secretary of Commerce Harry Hopkins and his Secretary of the Treasury Henry Morgenthau. Two of the earliest business-baiters in the circle of Roosevelt advisers, they now recognized the bankruptcy of that course and the necessity for the administration to at last strive for recovery by removing the obstacles to normal and profitable business operation that the New Deal had erected. This was not what Roosevelt wanted to hear, nor was it what his Frankfurter disciples wanted him to hear. These latter knew, as Hopkins and Morgenthau had learned earlier, just which Rooseveltian buttons could be pushed to trigger his antibusiness prejudices and spite. A battle raged within the New Deal between the Frankfurter radicals and the "new conservatives," Hopkins and Morgenthau, amid growing public suspicion that the former were not interested in economic recovery.

It was not a fair battle. Hopkins and Morgenthau knew how to play the game, including use of the press, and had too many allies. They did not hesitate to talk bluntly to Roosevelt, perhaps the bluntest talk he had heard since the death of Louis McHenry Howe. Moreover, Roosevelt could afford the loss of a Corcoran and/or a Cohen, against whom there was already a great deal of congressional opposition, but a break with both Hopkins and Morgenthau would have been devastating for an administration already on the defensive.

Gradually the Frankfurter radicals moved into eclipse, along with their policies, to be replaced increasingly by recovery and preparedness advocates, including many from the business and financial world.

Conventional wisdom has it that the massive government spending of World War II finally brought a Keynesian recovery from the depression. Of more significance, in comparisons of the prewar and wartime economic policies of the Roosevelt administration, is the fact that the war against business that characterized the former was abandoned in the latter. Both the attitude and policies of the Roosevelt administration toward business during the New Deal years were reversed when the president found new, foreign enemies to engage his attention and energies. Antibusiness advisers were replaced by businessmen, pro-labor policies became pro-business policies, cooperation replaced confrontation in relations between the federal government and business, and even the increased spending of the war years "trickled down" rather than "bubbling up." Probably no American president since, perhaps, Thomas Jefferson ever so thoroughly repudiated the early policies of his administration as Roosevelt did between 1939 and 1942. This, and not the emphasis on spending alone, is the lesson that needs to be learned from Roosevelt's experience with the depression, and of the legacy of the New Deal economic policies.

The judgment of historians concerning Roosevelt's presidential stature is curiously at odds with that of contemporary observers. One wonders how scholars of the Roosevelt presidency are able so blithely to ignore the negative assessments of journalists, for example, of the stature of Raymond Clapper, Walter Lippmann, Dorothy Thompson, and Arthur Krock, to name only a few. Can their observations concerning Roosevelt's pettiness and spitefulness, their criticism of the obstacles to recovery created by his anticapitalist bias, and their genuine concern over his apparent grasp for dictatorial power be dismissed so cavalierly? Is there any other example in U.S. history of an incumbent president running for reelection against the open opposition of the two previous nominees of his own party? Will a public opinion poll ever again find 45 percent of its respondents foreseeing the likelihood of dictatorship arising from a president's policies? Will a future president ever act in such a fashion that the question will again even suggest itself to a pollster? One certainly hopes not.

Perhaps the positive assessment of Roosevelt by American historians rests upon a perceived liberalism of his administration. If so, one must wonder at their definition of liberalism. Surely a president who would pit class against class for political purposes, who was fundamentally hostile to the very basis of a free economy, who believed that his ends could justify very illiberal means, who was intolerant of criticism and critics, and who grasped for dictatorial power does not merit description as a liberal. Nor are the results of the Gallup poll mentioned above consistent with the actions of a liberal president. If the perception is based on Roosevelt's support for the less fortunate "one-third" of the nation, and his program of social legislation, then historians need to be reminded that such actions do not, in themselves, add up to liberalism, they having been used by an assortment of political realists and demagogues—of the left and the right—to gain and hold power.

There were certainly positive contributions under the New Deal, but they may not have outweighed the negative aspects of the period. The weight of the negative aspects would, moreover, have been much heavier except for the existence of a free and alert press, and for the actions of the Supreme Court and Congress in nullifying, modifying, and rejecting many of the New Deal measures. When one examines the full range of New Deal proposals and considers the implications of their passage in the original form, the outline emerges of a form of government alien to any definition of liberalism except that of the New Dealers themselves. Historians need to weigh more thoroughly and objectively the implications for the United States if Roosevelt's programs had been fully implemented. They need also to assess the costs in human misery of the delay in recovery, and of reduced U.S. influence abroad at a critical time in world affairs owing to its economic prostration. We can only speculate concerning the possible alteration of events from 1937 onward had the United States faced the world with the economic strength and military potential it might have displayed had wiser economic policies prevailed from 1933 to 1938. There is, in short, much about Roosevelt and the New Deal that historians need to reevaluate.

A New Deal for the American People

$\mathbf{A}$t the close of the Hundred Days, Franklin D. Roosevelt said, "All of the proposals and all of the legislation since the fourth day of March have not been just a collection of haphazard schemes, but rather the orderly component parts of a connected and logical whole." Yet the president later described his approach quite differently. "Take a method and try it. If it fails admit it frankly and try another. But above all, try something." The impetus for New Deal legislation came from a variety of sources, and Roosevelt relied heavily at various times on an ideologically diverse group of aides and allies. His initiatives reflected the contributions of, among others, Robert Wagner, Rexford Tugwell, Raymond Moley, George Norris, Robert LaFollette, Henry Morgenthau, Marriner Eccles, Felix Frankfurter, Henry Wallace, Harry Hopkins, and Eleanor Roosevelt. An initial emphasis on recovery for agriculture and industry gave way within two years to a broader-based program for social reform; entente with the business community yielded to populist rhetoric and a more ambiguous economic program. Roosevelt suffered the opprobrium of both the conservatives, who vilified "that man" in the White House who was leading the country down the sordid road to socialism, and the radicals, who saw the Hyde Park aristocrat as a confidence man peddling piecemeal reform to forestall capitalism's demise. Out of so many contradictory and confusing circumstances, how does one make sense of the five years of legislative reform known as the New Deal? And what has been its impact on a half century of American life?[1]

A better understanding begins with the recognition that little of the New Deal was new, including the use of federal power to effect change. Nor, for all of Roosevelt's famed willingness to experiment, did New Deal programs usually originate from vernal ideas. Governmental aid to increase farmers' income, propounded in the late nineteenth century by the Populists, surfaced in Woodrow Wilson's farm credit acts. The prolonged debates over McNary-Haugenism in the 1920s kept the issue alive, and Herbert Hoover's Agricultural Marketing Act set the stage for further federal involvement. Centralized economic planning, as embodied in the National Industrial Recovery Act, flowed directly from the experiences of Wilson's War Industries Board; not surprisingly, Roosevelt chose Hugh Johnson, a veteran of the board, to head the National Recovery Administration. Well established in England and Germany before the First World War, social insurance appeared in a handful of states—notably

Wisconsin—before the federal government became involved. Similarly, New Deal labor reform took its cues from the path-breaking work of state legislatures. Virtually alone in its originality, compensatory fiscal policy seemed revolutionary in the 1930s. Significantly, however, Roosevelt embraced deficit spending quite late after other disappointing economic policies and never to the extent Keynesian economists advised. Congress and the public supported the New Deal, in part, because of its origins in successful initiatives attempted earlier under different conditions.

Innovative or not, the New Deal clearly failed to restore economic prosperity. As late as 1938 unemployment stood at 19.1 percent and two years later at 14.6 percent. Only the Second World War, which generated massive industrial production, put the majority of the American people back to work. To be sure, partial economic recovery occurred. From a high of 13 million unemployed in 1933, the number under Roosevelt's administration fell to 11.4 million in 1934, 10.6 million in 1935, and 9 million in 1936. Farm income and manufacturing wages also rose, and as limited as these achievements may seem in retrospect, they provided sustenance for millions of people and hope for many more. Yet Roosevelt's resistance to Keynesian formulas for pump priming placed immutable barriers in the way of recovery that only war could demolish. At a time calling for drastic inflationary methods, Roosevelt introduced programs effecting the opposite result. The NRA restricted production, elevated prices, and reduced purchasing power, all of which were deflationary in effect. The Social Security Act's payroll taxes took money from consumers and out of circulation. The federal government's $4.43 billion deficit in fiscal year 1936, impressive as it seemed, was not so much greater than Hoover's $2.6 billion shortfall during his last year in office. As economist Robert Lekachman noted, "The 'great spender' was in his heart a true descendant of thrifty Dutch Calvinist forebears." It is not certain that the application of Keynesian formulas would have sufficed by the mid-1930s to restore prosperity, but the president's cautious deflationary policies clearly retarded recovery.[2]

Although New Deal economic policies came up short in the 1930s, they implanted several "stabilizers" that have been more successful in averting another such depression. The Securities and Exchange Act of 1934 established government supervision of the stock market, and the Wheeler-Rayburn Act allowed the Securities and Exchange Commission to do the same with public utilities. Severely embroiled in controversy when adopted, these measures have become mainstays of the American financial system. The Glass-Steagall Banking Act forced the separation of commercial and investment banking and broadened the powers of the Federal Reserve Board to change interest rates and limit loans for speculation. The creation of the Federal Deposit Insurance Corporation (FDIC) increased government supervision of state banks and significantly lowered the number of bank failures. Such safeguards restored confidence in the discredited banking system and established a firm economic foundation that performed well for decades thereafter.

The New Deal was also responsible for numerous other notable changes in American life. Section 7(a) of the NIRA, the Wagner Act, and the Fair Labor Standards Act transformed the relationship between workers and business and breathed life into a troubled labor movement on the verge of total extinction. In the space of a decade government laws eliminated sweatshops, severely curtailed child labor, and established enforceable standards for hours, wages and working conditions. Further, federal action eliminated the vast majority of company towns in such industries as coal mining. Although Robert Wagner and Frances Perkins dragged Roosevelt into labor's corner, the New Deal made the unions a dynamic force in American society. Moreover, as Nelson Lichtenstein has noted, "by giving so much of the working class an institutional voice, the union movement provided one of the main political bulwarks of the Roosevelt Democratic party and became part of the social bedrock in which the New Deal welfare state was anchored."[3]

Roosevelt's avowed goal of "cradle-to-grave" security for the American people proved elusive, but his administration achieved unprecedented advances in the field of social welfare. In 1938 the president told Congress: "Government has a final responsibility for the well-being of its citizenship. If private co-operative endeavor fails to provide work for willing hands and relief for the unfortunate, those suffering hardship from no fault of their own have a right to call upon the Government for aid; and a government worthy of its name must make fitting response." The New Deal's safety net included low-cost housing; old-age pensions; unemployment insurance; and aid for dependent mothers and children, the disabled, the blind, and public health services. Sometimes disappointing because of limiting eligibility requirements and low benefit levels, these social welfare programs nevertheless firmly established the principle that the government had an obligation to assist the needy. As one scholar wrote of the New Deal, "More progress was made in public welfare and relief than in the three hundred years after this country was first settled."[4]

More and more government programs, inevitably resulting in an enlarged administrative apparatus and requiring additional revenue, added up to a much greater role for the national government in American life. Coming at a time when the only Washington bureaucracy most of the people encountered with any frequency was the U.S. Postal Service, the change seemed all the more remarkable. Although many New Deal programs were temporary emergency measures, others lingered long after the return of prosperity. Suddenly, the national government was supporting farmers, monitoring the economy, operating a welfare system, subsidizing housing, adjudicating labor disputes, managing natural resources, and providing electricity to a growing number of consumers. "What Roosevelt did in a period of a little over 12 years was to change the form of government," argued journalist Richard L. Strout. "Washington had been largely run by big business, by Wall Street. He brought the government to Washington." Not surprisingly, popular attitudes toward government also changed. No longer willing to accept economic deprivation and social dislocation as the vagaries of an uncertain existence, Americans tolerated—indeed, came to expect—the national government's involvement in the problems of everyday life. No longer did "government" mean just "city hall."[5]

The operation of the national government changed as well. For one thing, Roosevelt's strong leadership expanded presidential power, contributing to what historian Arthur Schlesinger, Jr., called the "imperial presidency."

Whereas Americans had in previous years instinctively looked first to Capitol Hill, after Roosevelt the White House took center stage in Washington. At the same time, Congress and the president looked at the nation differently. Traditionally attentive only to one group (big business), policymakers in Washington began responding to other constituencies such as labor, farmers, the unemployed, the aged, and to a lesser extent, women, blacks, and other disadvantaged groups. This new "broker state" became more accessible and acted on a growing number of problems, but equity did not always result. The ablest, richest, and most experienced groups fared best during the New Deal. NRA codes favored big business, and AAA benefits aided large landholders; blacks received relief and government jobs but not to the extent their circumstances merited. The long-term result, according to historian John Braeman, has been "a balkanized political system in which private interests scramble, largely successfully, to harness governmental authority and/or draw upon the public treasury to advance their private agendas."[6]

Another legacy of the New Deal has been the Roosevelt revolution in politics. Urbanization and immigration changed the American electorate, and a new generation of voters who resided in the cities during the Great Depression opted for Franklin D. Roosevelt and his party. Before the 1930s the Democrats of the northern big-city machines and the solid South uneasily coexisted and surrendered primacy to the unified Republican party. The New Deal coalition that elected Roosevelt united behind common economic interests. Both urban northerners and rural southerners, as well as blacks, women, and ethnic immigrants, found common cause in government action to shield them from an economic system gone haywire. By the end of the decade the increasing importance of the urban North in the Democratic party had already become apparent. After the economy recovered from the disastrous depression, members of the Roosevelt coalition shared fewer compelling interests. Beginning in the 1960s, tensions mounted within the party as such issues as race, patriotism, and abortion loomed larger. Even so, the Roosevelt coalition retained enough commitment to New Deal principles to keep the Democrats the nation's majority party into the 1980s.[7]

Yet for all the alterations in politics, government, and the economy, the New Deal fell far short of a revolution. The two-party system survived intact, and neither fascism, which attracted so many followers in European states suffering from the same international depression, nor communism attracted much of a following in the United States. Vital government institutions functioned without interruption and if the balance of powers shifted, the national dremained capitalistic; free enterprise and private ownership, not socialism, emerged from the 1930s. A limited welfare state changed the meld of the public and private but left them separate. Roosevelt could be likened to the British conservative Edmund Burke, who advocated measured change to offset drastic alterations—"reform to preserve." The New Deal's great achievement was the application of just enough change to preserve the American political economy.

Indications of Roosevelt's restraint emerged from the very beginning of the New Deal. Rather than assume extraordinary executive powers as Abraham Lincoln had done in the 1861 crisis, the president called Congress into special session. Whatever changes ensued would come through normal governmental activity. Roosevelt declined to assume direct control of the economy, leaving the nation's resources in the hands of private enterprise. Resisting the blandishments of radicals calling for the nationalization of the banks, he provided the means for their rehabilitation and ignored the call for national health insurance and federal contributions to Social Security retirement benefits. The creation of such regulatory agencies as the SEC confirmed his intention to revitalize rather than remake economic institutions. Repeatedly during his presidency Roosevelt responded to congressional pressure to enact bolder reforms, as in the case of the National Labor Relations Act, the Wagner-Steagall Housing Act, and the FDIC. The administration forwarded the NIRA only after Senator Hugo Black's recovery bill mandating 30-hour workweeks seemed on the verge of passage.

As impressive as New Deal relief and social welfare programs were, they never went as far as conditions demanded or many liberals recommended. Fluctuating congressional appropriations, oscillating economic conditions, and Roosevelt's own hesitancy to do too much violence to the federal budget left Harry Hopkins, Harold Ickes, and others only partially equipped to meet the staggering need. The president justified the creation of the costly WPA in 1935 by "ending this business of relief." Unskilled workers, who constituted the greatest number of WPA employees, obtained but 60 to 80 percent of the minimal family income as determined by the government. Roosevelt and Hopkins continued to emphasize work at less than existing wage scales so that the WPA or PWA never competed with free labor, and they allowed local authorities to modify pay rates. They also continued to make the critical distinction between the "deserving" and "undeserving" poor, making sure that government aided only the former. The New Deal never challenged the values underlying this distinction, instead seeking to provide for the growing number of "deserving" poor created by the Great Depression. Government assumed an expanded role in caring for the disadvantaged, but not at variance with existing societal norms regarding social welfare.

The New Deal effected no substantial redistribution of income. The Wealth Tax Act of 1935 (the famous soak-the-rich tax) produced scant revenue and affected very few taxpayers. Tax alterations in 1936 and 1937 imposed no additional burdens on the rich; the 1938 and 1939 tax laws actually removed a few. By the end of the 1930s less than 5 percent of Americans paid income taxes, and the share of taxes taken from personal and corporate income levies fell below the amount raised in the 1920s. The great change in American taxation policy came during World War II, when the number of income tax payers grew to 74 percent of the population. In 1942 Treasury Secretary Henry Morgenthau noted that "for the first time in our history, the income tax is becoming a people's tax." This the New Deal declined to do.[8]

Finally, the increased importance of the national government exerted remarkably little influence on local institutions. The New Deal seldom dictated and almost always deferred to state and local governments—encouraging, cajoling, bargaining, and wheedling to bring parochial interests in line with national objectives. As Harry Hopkins discovered, governors and mayors angled to obtain as many federal dollars as possible for their constituents but with no strings attached. Community control and local autonomy, conditions thought to be central to American democracy, remained strong, and Roosevelt understood the need for firm ties with politicians at all levels. In his study of the New Deal's impact on federalism, James T. Patterson concludes: "For all the supposed power of the New Deal, it was unable to impose all its guidelines on the autonomous forty-eight states. . . . What could the Roosevelt administration have done to ensure a more profound and lasting impression on state policy and politics? Very little."[9]

Liberal New Dealers longed for more sweeping change and lamented their inability to goad the president into additional action. They envisioned a wholesale purge of the Democratic party and the creation of a new organization embodying fully the principles of liberalism. They could not abide Roosevelt's toleration of the political conservatives and unethical bosses who composed part of the New Deal coalition. They sought racial equality, constraints upon the southern landholding class, and federal intrusion to curb the power of urban real estate interests on behalf of the inveterate poor. Yet to do these things would be to attempt changes well beyond the desires of most Americans. People pursuing remunerative jobs and the economic security of the middle class approved of government aiding the victims of an unfortunate economic crisis but had no interest in an economic system that would limit opportunity. The fear that the New Deal would lead to such thoroughgoing change explains the seemingly irrational hatred of Roosevelt by the economic elite. But, as historian Barry Karl has noted, "it was characteristic of Roosevelt's presidency that he never went as far as his detractors feared or his followers hoped."[10]

The New Deal achieved much that was good and left much undone. Roosevelt's programs were defined by the confluence of forces that circumscribed his admittedly limited reform agenda—hostile judiciary; powerful congressional opponents, some of whom entered into alliances of convenience with New Dealers and some of whom awaited the opportunity to build on their opposition; the political impotence of much of the populace; the pugnacious independence of local and state authorities; the strength of people's attachment to traditional values and institutions; and the basic conservatism of American culture. Obeisance to local custom and the decision to avoid tampering with the fabric of American society allowed much injustice to survive while shortchanging blacks, women, small farmers, and the "unworthy" poor. Those who criticized Franklin Roosevelt for an unwillingness to challenge racial, economic, and gender inequality misunderstood either the nature of his electoral mandate or the difference between reform and revolution—or both.

If the New Deal preserved more than it changed, that is understandable in a society whose people have consistently chosen freedom over equality. Americans traditionally have eschewed expanded government, no matter how efficiently managed or honestly administered, that imposed restraints on personal success—even though such limitations redressed legitimate grievances or righted imbalances. Parity, most Americans believed, should not be purchased with the loss of liberty. But although the American dream has always entailed individual success with a minimum of state interference, the profound shock of capitalism's near demise in the 1930s undermined numerous previously unquestioned beliefs. The inability of capitalism's "invisible hand" to stabilize the market and the failure of the private sector to restore prosperity enhanced the consideration of stronger executive leadership and centralized planning. Yet with the collapse of democratic governments and their replacement by totalitarian regimes, Americans were keenly sensitive to any threats to liberty. New Deal programs, frequently path breaking in their delivery of federal resources outside normal channels, also retained a strong commitment to local government and community control while promising only temporary disruptions prior to the return of economic stability. Reconciling the necessary authority at the federal level to meet nationwide crises with the local autonomy desirable to safeguard freedom has always been one of the salient challenges to American democracy. Even after New Deal refinements, the search for the proper balance continues.

Notes

1. Otis L. Graham Jr., and Meghan Robinson Wander, eds., *Franklin D. Roosevelt, His Life and Times: An Encyclopedic View* (Boston: G. K. Hall, 1985), p. 285 (first quotation); Harvard Sitkoff, "Introduction," in Sitkoff, *Fifty Years Later*, p. 5 (second quotation).

2. Richard S. Kirkendall, "The New Deal as Watershed: The Recent Literature," *Journal of American History* 54 (March 1968), p. 847 (quotation).

3. Graham and Wander, *Franklin D. Roosevelt, His Life and Times*, p. 228 (quotation).

4. Leuchtenburg, "The Achievement of the New Deal," p. 220 (first quotation); Patterson, *America's Struggle against Poverty, 1900-1980*, p. 56 (second quotation).

5. Louchheim, *The Making of the New Deal: The Insiders Speak*, p. 15 (quotation).

6. John Braeman, "The New Deal: The Collapse of the Liberal Consensus," *Canadian Review of American Studies* 20 (Summer 1989), p. 77.

7. David Burner, *The Politics of Provincialism: The Democratic Party in Transition, 1918-1932* (New York: Alfred A. Knopf, 1968).

8. Mark Leff, *The Limits of Symbolic Reform*, p. 287 (quotation).

9. James T. Patterson, *The New Deal and the States: Federalism in Transition* (Princeton: Princeton University Press, 1969), p. 202.

10. Barry D. Karl, *The Uneasy State: The United States from 1915 to 1945* (Chicago: University of Chicago Press, 1983), p. 124.

POSTSCRIPT

Did the New Deal Prolong the Great Depression?

Both Biles and Best agree that the New Deal concentrated a tremendous amount of power in the executive branch of the government. They also acknowledge that it was World War II—not the New Deal's reform programs—that pulled the United States out of the depression. But the two historians disagree with each other in their assumptions and assessments of the New Deal.

Best argues that the New Deal was radical in its anti-business assumptions. His conservative critique is similar to Jim Powell's *FDR's Folly: How Roosevelt and His New Deal Prolonged the Great Depression* (Crown Forum, 2003). Powell has been a senior fellow since 1988 at the Cato Institute in Washington, D.C., a well-known conservative and libertarian think tank that has produced a number of policymakers who have staffed the Reagan and two Bush presidential administrations. Powell argues that the New Deal itself with its short-sighted programs increased the size and power of the federal government, which prevented the country from ending the depression more quickly. Powell's critique is based on the conservative assumptions of the well-known free-market advocates Milton Friedman and Anna Jacobson Schwartz, who argue in *A Monetary History of the United States, 1867–1960* (Princeton University Press, 1963) that the Great Depression was a government failure, brought on primarily by Federal Reserve policies that abruptly cut the money supply. This view runs counter to those of Peter Temin, *Did Monetary Forces Cause the Depression?* (Norton, 1976), Michael A. Bernstein, *The Great Depression: Delayed Recovery and Economic Change in America* (Cambridge University Press, 1987), and the readable and lively account of John Kenneth Galbraith, *The Great Crash* (Houghton Mifflin, 1955), which argue that the crash exposed various structural weaknesses in the economy that caused the depression.

Both Best's and Powell's analysis can be faulted on several grounds. For example, they underestimate the enormity of the economic crisis facing the country on the eve of Roosevelt's inauguration. Bank failures were rampant, farmers declared "farm holidays" and destroyed crops to keep up prices, and an assassin tried to kill the president-elect in Miami. As Roosevelt often quipped, "People don't eat in the long run, they eat every day." His immediate response to the crisis was the "100 days" New Deal recovery programs.

Best and Powell agree with other liberal and radical New Deal analysts that it was World War II and not the New Deal that brought us out of the Great Depression. If this is true, didn't the recovery take place because of the enormous sums of money that the government pumped into the defense industries and the armed services that reduced the unemployment rate to almost 0 percent?

Historian Roger Biles argues that the New Deal was a non-revolution compared to the economic and political changes that were taking place in communist Russia, fascist Italy, and Nazi Germany. The New Deal, in his view, was not so new. Social insurance appeared earlier in several states, notably Wisconsin. The economic planning embodied in the National Industrial Recovery Act extends back to President Wilson's World War I War Industries Board. The use of the federal government to aid farmers was begun with President Wilson's Farm Credit Act and continued during the Harding, Collidge, and Hoover administrations.

Although the recovery doesn't come about until World War II, Biles admits that the New Deal changed the relationship between the federal government and the people. The New Deal stabilized the banking industry and stock exchange. It ameliorated the relationship of workers with business with its support of the Wagner Act and the Fair Standard Labor Act. Social Security provided a safety net for the aged, the unemployed, and the disabled. In politics, urbanization and immigration cemented a new Democratic coalition in 1936 with the conservative South around common economic interests until the 1980s when racial issues and the maturing of a new suburban middle class fractured the Democratic majority.

Biles' analysis basically agrees with the British historian Anthony J. Badger who argues in *The New Deal* (Hill and Wang, 1989) that the New Deal was a "holding operation" until the Second World War created the "political economy of modern America." Both Biles and Badger argue that once the immediate crisis of 1933 subsided, opposition to the New Deal came from big business, conservative congressmen, and local governments who resisted the increasing power of the federal government. As the Office of War Information told Roosevelt, the American people's post-war aspirations were "compounded largely of 1929 values and the economics of the 1920s, levend with a handover from the makeshift controls of the war."

The most recent annotated bibliography is Robert F. Himmelberg, *The Great Depression and the New Deal* (Greenwood Press, 2001). The conservative case with full bibliographical references is contained in Powell's *FDR's Folly*. See also Robert Eden's edited *The New Deal and Its Legacy: Critique and Reappraisal* (Greenwood Press, 1989). Two important collections of recent writings are David E. Hamilton, ed., *The New Deal* (Houghton Mifflin, 1999) and Colin Gordon, ed., *Major Problems in American History 1920–1945* (Houghton Mifflin, 1999). Finally Steve Fraser and Gary Gerstle edited a series of social and economic essays, which they present in *The Rise and Fall of the New Deal Order, 1930–1980* (Princeton University Press, 1989).

Out of vogue but still worth reading are the sympathetic studies of the New Deal by William Leuchtenburg, *Franklin D. Roosevelt and the New Deal* (Harper and Row, 1963) and his interpretative essays written over 30 years in *The FDR Years: On Roosevelt and His Legacy* (Columbia University Press, 1985). See also the beautifully written but never to be completed second and third volumes of Arthur M. Schlesinger, Jr.'s *The Coming of the New Deal* (Houghton Mifflin, 1959) and *The Politics of Upheaval* (Houghton Mifflin, 1960), which advances the interpretation of the first and second New Deal, found in most American history survey textbooks.

ISSUE 11

Was It Necessary to Drop the Atomic Bomb to End World War II?

YES: Robert James Maddox, from "The Biggest Decision: Why We Had to Drop the Atomic Bomb," *American Heritage* (May/June 1995)

NO: Tsuyoshi Hasegawa, from *Racing the Enemy: Stalin, Truman and the Surrender of Japan* (The Belknap Press of Harvard University Press, 2005)

ISSUE SUMMARY

YES: Professor of American history Robert James Maddox contends that the atomic bomb became the catalyst that forced the hard-liners in the Japanese army to accept the emperor's plea to surrender, thus avoiding a costly, bloody invasion of the Japanese mainland.

NO: Professor of American history Tsuyoshi Hasegawa argues that the Soviet entrance into the war played a greater role in causing Japan to surrender than did the dropping of the atomic bombs.

$\mathbf{A}$merica's development of the atomic bomb began in 1939 when a small group of scientists led by well-known physicist Albert Einstein called President Franklin D. Roosevelt's attention to the enormous potential uses of atomic energy for military purposes. In his letter, Einstein warned Roosevelt that Nazi Germany was already experimenting in this area. The program to develop the bomb, which began very modestly in October 1939, soon expanded into the $2 billion Manhattan Project, which combined the talents and energies of scientists (many of whom were Jewish refugees from Hitler's Nazi Germany) from universities and research laboratories across the country. The Manhattan Project was the beginning of the famed military-industrial-university complex that we take for granted today.

Part of the difficulty in reconstructing the decision to drop the atomic bomb lies in the rapidity with which events moved in the spring of 1945. On May 7, 1945, Germany surrendered. Almost a month earlier the world was stunned by the death of FDR, who was succeeded by Harry Truman, a former

U.S. senator who was chosen as a compromise vice presidential candidate in 1944. The man from Missouri had never been a confidant of Roosevelt. Truman did not even learn of the existence of the Manhattan Project until 12 days after he became president, at which time Secretary of War Henry L. Stimson advised him of a "highly secret matter" that would have a "decisive" effect upon America's postwar foreign policy.

Because Truman was unsure of his options for using the bomb, he approved Stimson's suggestion that a special committee of high-level political, military, and scientific policymakers be appointed to consider the major issues. The committee recommended unanimously that "the bomb should be used against Japan as soon as possible . . . against a military target surrounded by other buildings . . . without prior warning of the nature of the weapon."

A number of scientists disagreed with this report. They recommended that the weapon be tested on a desert island before representatives of the United Nations and that an ultimatum be sent to Japan warning of the destructive power of the bomb. These young scientists suggested that the bomb be used if the Japanese rejected the warning, and only "if sanction of the United Nations (and of public opinion at home) were obtained."

A second scientific committee created by Stimson rejected both the test demonstration and warning alternatives. This panel felt that if the bomb failed to work during the demonstration, there would be political repercussions both at home and abroad. If a specific warning was given, the American military leader were afraid that POWs would be stationed in the target area.

Thus, by the middle of June 1945, the civilian leaders were unanimous that the atomic bomb should be used. During the Potsdam Conference in July, Truman learned that the bomb had been successfully tested in New Mexico. The big three—Truman, Atlee, and Stalin—issued a warning to Japan to surrender or suffer prompt and utter destruction. When the Japanese equivocated in their response, the Americans replied by dropping an atomic bomb on Hiroshima on August 6, which killed 100,000 people, and a second bomb on August 9, which leveled the city of Nagasaki. During this time the emperor pleaded with the Japanese military to end the war. On August 14 the Japanese accepted the terms of surrender with the condition that the emperor not be treated as a war criminal.

Was it necessary to drop the atomic bombs on Japan in order to end the war? In the following selections, two viewpoints are advanced. Robert James Maddox, a long-time critic of cold war revisionist history, argues that Truman believed that the use of the atomic bomb would shorten the war and save lives, particularly American ones. Maddox also asserts that the bombs at Hiroshima and Nagasaki allowed the emperor to successfully plead with army hard-liners to end the war. Professor Tsuyoshi Hasegawa casts the use of the atomic bomb in a wider setting. "Truman issued the Potsdam Proclamation," he says, "not as a warning to Japan, but to justify the use of the atomic bomb." He also challenges "the commonly held view that the atomic bomb provided the immediate and decisive knockout blow to Japan's will to fight. Instead, the Soviet entry into the war played a greater role than the atomic bombs in inducing Japan to surrender."

YES

Robert James Maddox

The Biggest Decision: Why We Had to Drop the Atomic Bomb

On the morning of August 6, 1945, the American B-29 Enola Gay dropped an atomic bomb on the Japanese city of Hiroshima. Three days later another B-29, *Bock's Car*, released one over Nagasaki. Both caused enormous casualties and physical destruction. These two cataclysmic events have preyed upon the American conscience ever since. The furor over the Smithsonian Institution's *Enola Gay* exhibit and over the mushroom-cloud postage stamp last autumn are merely the most obvious examples. Harry S. Truman and other officials claimed that the bombs caused Japan to surrender, thereby avoiding a bloody invasion. Critics have accused them of at best failing to explore alternatives, at worst of using the bombs primarily to make the Soviet Union "more manageable" rather than to defeat a Japan they knew already was on the verge of capitulation.

By any rational calculation Japan was a beaten nation by the summer of 1945. Conventional bombing had reduced many of its cities to rubble, blockade had strangled its importation of vitally needed materials, and its navy had sustained such heavy losses as to be powerless to interfere with the invasion everyone knew was coming. By late June advancing American forces had completed the conquest of Okinawa, which lay only 350 miles from the southernmost Japanese home island of Kyushu. They now stood poised for the final onslaught.

Rational calculations did not determine Japan's position. Although a peace faction within the government wished to end the war—provided certain conditions were met—militants were prepared to fight on regardless of consequences. They claimed to welcome an invasion of the home islands, promising to inflict such hideous casualties that the United States would retreat from its announced policy of unconditional surrender. The militarists held effective power over the government and were capable of defying the emperor, as they had in the past, on the ground that his civilian advisers were misleading him.

From *American Heritage*, May/June 1995, pp. 70–74, 76–77 © 1995 by Forbes, Inc. Reprinted by permission of *American Heritage* magazine, a division of Forbes, Inc.

Okinawa provided a preview of what invasion of the home islands would entail. Since April 1 the Japanese had fought with a ferocity that mocked any notion that their will to resist was eroding. They had inflicted nearly 50,000 casualties on the invaders, many resulting from the first large-scale use of kamikazes. They also had dispatched the superbattleship *Yamato* on a suicide mission to Okinawa, where, after attacking American ships offshore, it was to plunge ashore to become a huge, doomed steel fortress. *Yamato* was sunk shortly after leaving port, but its mission symbolized Japan's willingness to sacrifice everything in an apparently hopeless cause.

The Japanese could be expected to defend their sacred homeland with even greater fervor, and kamikazes flying at short range promised to be even more devastating than at Okinawa. The Japanese had more than 2,000,000 troops in the home islands, were training millions of irregulars, and for some time had been conserving aircraft that might have been used to protect Japanese cities against American bombers.

Reports from Tokyo indicated that Japan meant to fight the war to a finish. On June 8 an imperial conference adopted "The Fundamental Policy to Be Followed Henceforth in the Conduct of the War," which pledged to "prosecute the war to the bitter end in order to uphold the national polity, protect the imperial land, and accomplish the objectives for which we went to war." Truman had no reason to believe that the proclamation meant anything other than what it said.

Against this background, while fighting on Okinawa still continued, the President had his naval chief of staff, Adm. William D. Leahy, notify the Joint Chiefs of Staff (JCS) and the Secretaries of War and Navy that a meeting would be held at the White House on June 18. The night before the conference Truman wrote in his diary that "I have to decide Japanese strategy—shall we invade Japan proper or shall we bomb and blockade? That is my hardest decision to date. But I'll make it when I have all the facts."

⋅⟨❂⟩⋅

Truman met with the chiefs at three-thirty in the afternoon. Present were Army Chief of Staff Gen. George C. Marshall, Army Air Force's Gen. Ira C. Eaker (sitting in for the Army Air Force's chief of staff, Henry H. Arnold, who was on an inspection tour of installations in the Pacific), Navy Chief of Staff Adm. Ernest J. King, Leahy (also a member of the JCS), Secretary of the Navy James Forrestal, Secretary of War Henry L. Stimson, and Assistant Secretary of War John J. McCloy. Truman opened the meeting, then asked Marshall for his views. Marshall was the dominant figure on the JCS. He was Truman's most trusted military adviser, as he had been President Franklin D. Roosevelt's.

Marshall reported that the chiefs, supported by the Pacific commanders Gen. Douglas MacArthur and Adm. Chester W. Nimitz, agreed that an invasion of Kyushu "appears to be the least costly worthwhile operation following Okinawa." Lodgment in Kyushu, he said, was necessary to make blockade and bombardment more effective and to serve as a staging area for the invasion of Japan's main island of Honshu. The chiefs recommended a target date of

November 1 for the first phase, code-named Olympic, because delay would give the Japanese more time to prepare and because bad weather might postpone the invasion "and hence the end of the war" for up to six months. Marshall said that in his opinion, Olympic was "the only course to pursue." The chiefs also proposed that Operation Cornet be launched against Honshu on March 1, 1946.

***

Leahy's memorandum calling the meeting had asked for casualty projections which that invasion might be expected to produce. Marshall stated that campaigns in the Pacific had been so diverse "it is considered wrong" to make total estimates. All he would say was that casualties during the first thirty days on Kyushu should not exceed those sustained in taking Luzon in the Philippines— 31,000 men killed, wounded, or missing in action. "It is a grim fact," Marshall said, "that there is not an easy, bloodless way to victory in war." Leahy estimated a higher casualty rate similar to Okinawa, and King guessed somewhere in between.

King and Eaker, speaking for the Navy and the Army Air Forces respectively, endorsed Marshall's proposals. King said that he had become convinced that Kyushu was "the key to the success of any siege operations." He recommended that "we should do Kyushu now" and begin preparations for invading Honshu. Eaker "agreed completely" with Marshall. He said he had just received a message from Arnold also expressing "complete agreement." Air Force plans called for the use of forty groups of heavy bombers, which "could not be deployed without the use of airfields on Kyushu." Stimson and Forrestal concurred.

Truman summed up. He considered "the Kyushu plan all right from the military standpoint" and directed the chiefs to "go ahead with it." He said he "had hoped that there was a possibility of preventing an Okinawa from one end of Japan to the other," but "he was clear on the situation now" and was "quite sure" the chiefs should proceed with the plan. Just before the meeting adjourned, McCloy raised the possibility of avoiding an invasion by warning the Japanese that the United States would employ atomic weapons if there were no surrender. The ensuing discussion was inconclusive because the first test was a month away and no one could be sure the weapons would work.

In his memoirs Truman claimed that using atomic bombs prevented an invasion that would have cost 500,000 American lives. Other officials mentioned the same or even higher figures. Critics have assailed such statements as gross exaggerations designed to forestall scrutiny of Truman's real motives. They have given wide publicity to a report prepared by the Joint War Plans Committee (JWPC) for the chiefs' meeting with Truman. The committee estimated that the invasion of Kyushu, followed by that of Honshu, as the chiefs proposed, would cost approximately 40,000 dead, 150,000 wounded, and 3,500 missing in action for a total of 193,500 casualties.

That those responsible for a decision should exaggerate the consequences of alternatives is commonplace. Some who cite the JWPC report profess to see more sinister motives, insisting that such "low" casualty projections call into question the very idea that atomic bombs were used to avoid heavy losses. By discrediting that justification as a cover-up, they seek to bolster their contention that the bombs really were used to permit the employment of "atomic diplomacy" against the Soviet Union.

The notion that 193,500 anticipated casualties were too insignificant to have caused Truman to resort to atomic bombs might seem bizarre to anyone other than an academic, but let it pass. Those who have cited the JWPC report in countless op-ed pieces in newspapers and in magazine articles have created a myth by omitting key considerations: First, the report itself is studded with qualifications that casualties "are not subject to accurate estimate" and that the projection "is admittedly only an educated guess." Second, the figures never were conveyed to Truman. They were excised at high military echelons, which is why Marshall cited only estimates for the first thirty days on Kyushu. And indeed, subsequent Japanese troop buildups on Kyushu rendered the JWPC estimates totally irrelevant by the time the first atomic bomb was dropped.

✦✦✦✦

Another myth that has attained wide attention is that at least several of Truman's top military advisers later informed him that using atomic bombs against Japan would be militarily unnecessary or immoral, or both. There is no persuasive evidence that any of them did so. None of the Joint Chiefs ever made such a claim, although one inventive author has tried to make it appear that Leahy did by braiding together several unrelated passages from the admiral's memoirs. Actually, two days after Hiroshima, Truman told aides that Leahy had "said up to the last that it wouldn't go off."

Neither MacArthur nor Nimitz ever communicated to Truman any change of mind about the need for invasion or expressed reservations about using the bombs. When first informed about their imminent use only days before Hiroshima, MacArthur responded with a lecture on the future of atomic warfare and even after Hiroshima strongly recommended that the invasion go forward. Nimitz, from whose jurisdiction the atomic strikes would be launched, was notified in early 1945. "This sounds fine," he told the courier, "but this is only February. Can't we get one sooner?" Nimitz later would join Air Force generals Carl D. Spaatz, Nathan Twining, and Curtis LeMay in recommending that a third bomb be dropped on Tokyo.

Only Dwight D. Eisenhower later claimed to have remonstrated against the use of the bomb. In his *Crusade in Europe*, published in 1948, he wrote that when Secretary Stimson informed him during the Potsdam Conference of plans to use the bomb, he replied that he hoped "we would never have to use such a thing against any enemy," because he did not want the United States to be the first to use such a weapon. He added, "My views were merely personal and immediate reactions; they were not based on any analysis of the subject."

Eisenhower's recollections grew more colorful as the years went on. A later account of his meeting with Stimson had it taking place at Ike's headquarters in Frankfurt on the very day news arrived of the successful atomic test in New Mexico. "We'd had a nice evening at headquarters in Germany," he remembered. Then, after dinner, "Stimson got this cable saying that the bomb had been perfected and was ready to be dropped. The cable was in code . . . 'the lamb is born' or some damn thing like that." In this version Eisenhower claimed to have protested vehemently that "the Japanese were ready to surrender and it wasn't necessary to hit them with that awful thing." "Well," Eisenhower concluded, "the old gentleman got furious."

⤳⟨◉⟩⤶

The best that can be said about Eisenhower's memory is that it had become flawed by the passage of time. Stimson was in Potsdam and Eisenhower in Frankfurt on July 16, when word came of the successful test. Aside from a brief conversation at a flag-raising ceremony in Berlin on July 20, the only other time they met was at Ike's headquarters on July 27. By then orders already had been sent to the Pacific to use the bombs if Japan had not yet surrendered. Notes made by one of Stimson's aides indicate that there was a discussion of atomic bombs, but there is no mention of any protest on Eisenhower's part. Even if there had been, two factors must be kept in mind. Eisenhower had commanded Allied forces in Europe, and his opinion on how close Japan was to surrender would have carried no special weight. More important, Stimson left for home immediately after the meeting and could not have personally conveyed Ike's sentiments to the President, who did not return to Washington until after Hiroshima.

On July 8 the Combined Intelligence Committee submitted to the American and British Combined Chiefs of Staff a report entitled "Estimate of the Enemy Situation." The committee predicted that as Japan's position continued to deteriorate, it might "make a serious effort to use the USSR [then a neutral] as a mediator in ending the war." Tokyo also would put out "intermittent peace feelers" to "weaken the determination of the United Nations to fight to the bitter end, or to create inter-allied dissension." While the Japanese people would be willing to make large concessions to end the war, "For a surrender to be acceptable to the Japanese army, it would be necessary for the military leaders to believe that it would not entail discrediting warrior tradition and that it would permit the ultimate resurgence of a military Japan."

Small wonder that American officials remained unimpressed when Japan proceeded to do exactly what the committee predicted. On July 12 Japanese Foreign Minister Shigenori Togo instructed Ambassador Naotaki Sato in Moscow to inform the Soviets that the emperor wished to send a personal envoy, Prince Fuminaro Konoye, in an attempt "to restore peace with all possible speed." Although he realized Konoye could not reach Moscow before the Soviet leader Joseph Stalin and Foreign Minister V. M. Molotov left to attend a Big Three meeting scheduled to begin in Potsdam on the fifteenth, Togo sought to have negotiations begin as soon as they returned.

American officials had long since been able to read Japanese diplomatic traffic through a process known as the MAGIC intercepts. Army intelligence (G-2) prepared for General Marshall its interpretation of Togo's message the next day. The report listed several possible constructions, the most probable being that the Japanese "governing clique" was making a coordinated effort to "stave off defeat" through Soviet intervention and an "appeal to war weariness in the United States." The report added that Undersecretary of State Joseph C. Grew, who had spent ten years in Japan as ambassador, "agrees with these conclusions."

Some have claimed that Togo's overture to the Soviet Union, together with attempts by some minor Japanese officials in Switzerland and other neutral countries to get peace talks started through the Office of Strategic Services (OSS), constituted clear evidence that the Japanese were near surrender. Their sole prerequisite was retention of their sacred emperor, whose unique cultural/religious status within the Japanese polity they would not compromise. If only the United States had extended assurances about the emperor, according to this view, much bloodshed and the atomic bombs would have been unnecessary.

A careful reading of the MAGIC intercepts of subsequent exchanges between Togo and Sato provides no evidence that retention of the emperor was the sole obstacle to peace. What they show instead is that the Japanese Foreign Office was trying to cut a deal through the Soviet Union that would have permitted Japan to retain its political system and its prewar empire intact. Even the most lenient American official could not have countenanced such a settlement.

❧

Togo on July 17 informed Sato that "we are not asking the Russians' mediation in *anything like unconditional surrender* [emphasis added]." During the following weeks Sato pleaded with his superiors to abandon hope of Soviet intercession and to approach the United States directly to find out what peace terms would be offered. "There is... no alternative but immediate unconditional surrender," he cabled on July 31, and he bluntly informed Togo that "your way of looking at things and the actual situation in the Eastern Area may be seen to be absolutely contradictory." The Foreign Ministry ignored his pleas and continued to seek Soviet help even after Hiroshima.

"Peace feelers" by Japanese officials abroad seemed no more promising from the American point of view. Although several of the consular personnel and military attachés engaged in these activities claimed important connections at home, none produced verification. Had the Japanese government sought only an assurance about the emperor, all it had to do was grant one of these men authority to begin talks through the OSS. Its failure to do so led American officials to assume that those involved were either well-meaning individuals acting alone or that they were being orchestrated by Tokyo. Grew characterized such "peace feelers" as "familiar weapons of psychological warfare" designed to "divide the Allies."

Some American officials, such as Stimson and Grew, nonetheless wanted to signal the Japanese that they might retain the emperorship in the form of a constitutional monarchy. Such an assurance might remove the last stumbling block to surrender, if not when it was issued, then later. Only an imperial rescript would bring about an orderly surrender, they argued, without which

Japanese forces would fight to the last man regardless of what the government in Tokyo did. Besides, the emperor could serve as a stabilizing factor during the transition to peacetime.

There were many arguments against an American initiative. Some opposed retaining such an undemocratic institution on principle and because they feared it might later serve as a rallying point for future militarism. Should that happen, as one assistant Secretary of State put it, "those lives already spent will have been sacrificed in vain, and lives will be lost again in the future." Japanese hard-liners were certain to exploit an overture as evidence that losses sustained at Okinawa had weakened American resolve and to argue that continued resistance would bring further concessions. Stalin, who earlier had told an American envoy that he favored abolishing the emperorship because the ineffectual Hirohito might be succeeded by "an energetic and vigorous figure who could cause trouble," was just as certain to interpret it as a treacherous effort to end the war before the Soviets could share in the spoils.

There were domestic considerations as well. Roosevelt had announced the unconditional surrender policy in early 1943, and it since had become a slogan of the war. He also had advocated that peoples everywhere should have the right to choose their own form of government, and Truman had publicly pledged to carry out his predecessor's legacies. For him to have formally *guaranteed* continuance of the emperorship, as opposed to merely accepting it on American terms pending free elections, as he later did, would have constituted a blatant repudiation of his own promises.

Nor was that all. Regardless of the emperor's actual role in Japanese aggression, which is still debated, much wartime propaganda had encouraged Americans to regard Hirohito as no less a war criminal than Adolf Hitler or Benito Mussolini. Although Truman said on several occasions that he had no objection to retaining the emperor, he understandably refused to make the first move. The ultimatum he issued from Potsdam on July 26 did not refer specifically to the emperorship. All it said was that occupation forces would be removed after "a peaceful and responsible" government had been established according to the "freely expressed will of the Japanese people." When the Japanese rejected the ultimatum rather than at last inquire whether they might retain the emperor, Truman permitted the plans for using the bombs to go forward.

Reliance on MAGIC intercepts and the "peace feelers" to gauge how near Japan was to surrender is misleading in any case. The army, not the Foreign Office, controlled the situation. Intercepts of Japanese military communications, designated ULTRA, provided no reason to believe the army was even considering surrender. Japanese Imperial Headquarters had correctly guessed that the next operation after Okinawa would be Kyushu and was making every effort to bolster its defenses there.

General Marshall reported on July 24 that there were "approximately 500,000 troops in Kyushu" and that more were on the way. ULTRA identified new units arriving almost daily. MacArthur's G-2 reported on July 29 that "this threatening development, if not checked, may grow to a point where we attack on a ratio of one (1) to one (1) which is not the recipe for victory." By the time the first atomic bomb fell, ULTRA indicated that there were 560,000 troops in southern Kyushu (the actual figure was closer to 900,000), and projections for November 1 placed the number at 680,000. A report, for medical purposes, of July 31 estimated that total battle and non-battle casualties might run as high as 394,859 *for the Kyushu operation alone.* This figure did not include those men expected to be killed outright, for obviously they would require no medical attention. Marshall regarded Japanese defenses as so formidable that even after Hiroshima he asked MacArthur to consider alternate landing sites and began contemplating the use of atomic bombs as tactical weapons to support the invasion.

The thirty-day casualty projection of 31,000 Marshall had given Truman at the June 18 strategy meeting had become meaningless. It had been based on the assumption that the Japanese had about 350,000 defenders in Kyushu and that naval and air interdiction would preclude significant reinforcement. But the Japanese buildup since that time meant that the defenders would have nearly twice the number of troops available by "X-day" than earlier assumed. The assertion that apprehensions about casualties are insufficient to explain Truman's use of the bombs, therefore, cannot be taken seriously. On the contrary, as Winston Churchill wrote after a conversation with him at Potsdam, Truman was tormented by "the terrible responsibilities that rested upon him in regard to the unlimited effusions of American blood."

Some historians have argued that while the first bomb *might* have been required to achieve Japanese surrender, dropping the second constituted a needless barbarism. The record shows otherwise. American officials believed more than one bomb would be necessary because they assumed Japanese hard-liners would minimize the first explosion or attempt to explain it away as some sort of natural catastrophe, precisely what they did. The Japanese minister of war, for instance, at first refused even to admit that the Hiroshima bomb was atomic. A few hours after Nagasaki he told the cabinet that "the Americans appeared to have one hundred atomic bomb . . . they could drop three per day. The next target might well be Tokyo."

Even after both bombs had fallen and Russia entered the war, Japanese militants insisted on such lenient peace terms that moderates knew there was no sense even transmitting them to the United States. Hirohito had to intervene personally on two occasions during the next few days to induce hard-liners to abandon their conditions and to accept the American stipulation that the emperor's authority "shall be subject to the Supreme Commander of the Allied Powers." That the militarists would have accepted such a settlement before the bombs is farfetched, to say the least.

Some writers have argued that the cumulative effects of battlefield defeats, conventional bombing, and naval blockade already had defeated Japan. Even without extending assurances about the emperor, all the United States had to do was wait. The most frequently cited basis for this contention is the *United States Strategic Bombing Survey,* published in 1946, which stated that Japan would have surrendered by November 1 "even if the atomic bombs had not been dropped, even if Russia had not entered the war, and even if no invasion had been planned or contemplated." Recent scholarship by the historian Robert P. Newman and others has demonstrated that the survey was "cooked" by those who prepared it to arrive at such a conclusion. No matter. This or any other document based on information available only after the war ended is irrelevant with regard to what Truman could have known at the time.

⚜

What often goes unremarked is that when the bombs were dropped, fighting was still going on in the Philippines, China, and elsewhere. Every day that the war continued thousands of prisoners of war had to live and die in abysmal conditions, and there were rumors that the Japanese intended to slaughter them if the homeland was invaded. Truman was Commander in Chief of the American armed forces, and he had a duty to the men under his command not shared by those sitting in moral judgment decades later. Available evidence points to the conclusion that he acted for the reason he said he did: to end a bloody war that would have become far bloodier had invasion proved necessary. One can only imagine what would have happened if tens of thousands of American boys had died or been wounded on Japanese soil and then it had become known that Truman had chosen not to use weapons that might have ended the war months sooner.

Tsuyoshi Hasegawa

Racing the Enemy: Stalin, Truman, and the Surrender of Japan

Assessing the Roads Not Taken

The end of the Pacific War was marked by the intense drama of two races: the first between Stalin and Truman to see who could force Japan to surrender and on what terms; and the second between the peace party and the war party in Japan on the question of whether to end the war and on what conditions. To the very end, the two races were inextricably linked. But what if things had been different? Would the outcome have changed if the key players had taken alternative paths? Below I explore some counterfactual suppositions to shed light on major issues that determined the outcome of the war.

What if Truman had accepted a provision in the Potsdam ultimatum allowing the Japanese to retain a constitutional monarchy? This alternative was supported by Stimson, Grew, Forrestal, Leahy, McCloy, and possibly Marshall. Churchill also favored this provision, and it was part of Stimson's original draft of the Potsdam Proclamation. Undoubtedly, a promise to retain the monarchy would have strengthened the peace party's receptivity of the Potsdam ultimatum. It would have led to intense discussion much earlier among Japanese policymakers on whether or not to accept the Potsdam terms, and it would have considerably diminished Japan's reliance on Moscow's mediation.

Nevertheless, the inclusion of this provision would not have immediately led to Japan's surrender, since those who adhered to the mythical notion of the *kokutai* would have strenuously opposed the acceptance of the Potsdam terms, even if it meant the preservation of the monarchy. Certainly, the three war hawks in the Big Six would have objected on the grounds that the Potsdam Proclamation would spell the end of the armed forces. But peace advocates could have accused the war party of endangering the future of the imperial house by insisting on additional conditions. Thus, the inclusion of this provision would have hastened Japan's surrender, though it is doubtful that Japan would have capitulated before the atomic bomb was dropped on Hiroshima and the Soviet Union entered the war. The possibility of accepting the Potsdam terms might have been raised immediately after the atomic bombing on Hiroshima. This provision might have tipped the balance in favor of the peace party after the Soviet invasion, thus speeding up the termination of the war.

Why, then, didn't Truman accept this provision? One explanation was that he was concerned with how the public would react to a policy of appeasement. Domestic public opinion polls indicated an overwhelmingly negative sentiment against the emperor, and inevitably Archibald McLeish, Dean Acheson, and others would have raised strident voices of protest. Byrnes had warned that a compromise with the emperor would lead to the crucifixion of the president.

But would it have? Although public opinion polls were overwhelmingly against the emperor, newspaper commentaries were evenly split between those who advocated the abolition of the emperor system and those who argued that the preservation of the monarchical system could be compatible with eradication of Japanese militarism. Truman could have justified his decision on two powerful grounds. First, he could have argued that ending the war earlier would save the lives of American soldiers. Second, he could have explained that this decision was necessary to prevent Soviet expansion in Asia, though he would have had to present this argument carefully so as not to provoke a strong reaction from the Soviet Union.

Truman's refusal to include this provision was motivated not only by his concern with domestic repercussions but also by his own deep conviction that America should avenge the humiliation of Pearl Harbor. Anything short of unconditional surrender was not acceptable to Truman. The buck indeed stopped at the president. Thus, as long as Truman firmly held to his conviction, this counterfactual supposition was not a real alternative.

But the story does not end here. Another important, hidden reason motivated Truman's decision not to include this provision. Truman knew that the unconditional surrender demand without any promise to preserve a constitutional monarchy would be rejected by the Japanese. He needed Japan's refusal to justify the use of the atomic bomb. Thus so long as he was committed to using the atomic bomb, he could not include the provision promising a constitutional monarchy.

What if Truman had asked Stalin to sign the Potsdam Proclamation without a promise of constitutional monarchy?   In this case, Japanese policymakers would have realized that their last hope to terminate the war through Moscow's mediation was dashed. They would have been forced to confront squarely the issue of whether to accept the Potsdam surrender terms. The ambiguity of the emperor's position, however, still remained, and therefore the division among policymakers was inevitable, making it likely that neither the cabinet nor the Big Six would have been able to resolve the differences.

Japan's delay in giving the Allies a definite reply would surely have led to the dropping of the atomic bombs and Soviet participation in the war. Would Japan have surrendered after the first atomic bomb? The absence of a promise to preserve the monarchical system in the Potsdam terms would have prevented the peace party, including Hirohito and Kido, from acting decisively to accept surrender. Ultimately, the Soviet invasion of Manchuria would still have provided the coup de grace.

What if Truman had invited Stalin to sign the Potsdam Proclamation and included the promise to allow the Japanese to maintain a constitutional monarchy? This would have forced Japanese policymakers to confront the issue of whether to accept the Potsdam terms. Undoubtedly, the army would have insisted, if not on the continuation of the war, at least on attaching three additional conditions to the Potsdam Proclamation in order to ensure its own survival. But the promise of preserving the monarchical system might have prompted members of the peace party to intercede to end the war before the first atomic bomb, although there is no guarantee that their argument would have silenced the war party. The most crucial issue here is how the emperor would have reacted to the Potsdam terms had they contained the promise of a constitutional monarchy and been signed by Stalin in addition to Truman, Churchill, and Chiang Kai-shek. Undoubtedly, he would have been more disposed to the Potsdam terms, but the promise of a constitutional monarchy alone might not have induced the emperor to hasten to accept the ultimatum. A shock was needed. It is difficult to say if the Hiroshima bomb alone was sufficient, or whether the combination of the Hiroshima bomb and Soviet entry into the war was needed to convince the emperor to accept surrender. Either way, surrender would have come earlier than it did, thus shortening the war by several days.

Nevertheless, these counterfactual suppositions were not in the ream of possibility, since Truman and Byrnes would never have accepted them, for the reasons stated in the first counterfactual. The atomic bomb provided them with the solution to previously unsolvable dilemmas. Once the solution was found to square the circle, Truman and Byrnes never deviated from their objectives. An alternative was available, but they chose not to take it.

This counterfactual was dubious for another reason. If Stalin had been asked to join the ultimatum, he would never have agreed to promise a constitutional monarchy. Stalin's most important objective in the Pacific War was to join the conflict. The promise of a constitutional monarchy might have hastened Japan's surrender before the Soviet tanks crossed the Manchurian border—a disaster he would have avoided at all costs. This was why Stalin's own version of the joint ultimatum included the unconditional surrender demand. Had Stalin been invited to join the ultimatum that included the provision allowing Japan to retain a constitutional monarchy, he would have fought tooth and nail to scratch that provision. Ironically, both Stalin and Truman had vested interests in keeping unconditional surrender for different reasons.

What if Hiranuma had not made an amendment at the imperial conference on August 10, and the Japanese government had proposed accepting the Potsdam Proclamation "with the understanding that it did not include any demand for a change in the status of the emperor under the national law"? Hiranuma's amendment was an egregious mistake. Although the three war hawks in the Big Six attached three additional conditions to acceptance, they lacked the intellectual acumen to connect their misgivings to the fundamental core of the *kokutai* debate. Without Hiranuma's amendment the emperor would have supported the one-conditional acceptance of the Potsdam terms as formulated at the first imperial conference;

this condition was compatible, albeit narrowly, with a constitutional monarchy that Stimson, Leahy, Forrestal, and Grew would have accepted. If we believe Ballantine, Byrnes and Truman might have accepted the provision. But Hiranuma's amendment made it impossible for the American policymakers to accept this condition without compromising the fundamental objectives of the war.

On the other hand, given Truman's deep feelings against the emperor, even the original one condition—retention of the emperor's status in the national laws—or even the Foreign Ministry's original formula (the preservation of the imperial house) might have been rejected by Truman and Byrnes. Nevertheless, either formula might have been accepted by Grew, Dooman, and Ballantine, and would have strengthened the position advocated by Stimson, Leahy, Forrestal, and McCloy that Japan's first reply should be accepted.

What if the Byrnes Note had contained a clear indication that the United States would allow the Japanese to retain a constitutional monarchy with the current dynasty? The rejection of Japan's conditional acceptance of the Potsdam terms as amended by Hiranuma was not incompatible with the promise of a constitutional monarchy. The lack of this promise triggered the war party's backlash and endangered the peace parry's chances of ending the war early. Had the Byrnes Note included the guarantee of a constitutional monarchy under the current dynasty, Suzuki would not have temporarily defected to the war party, and Yonai would not have remained silent on August 12. War advocates would have opposed the Byrnes Note as incompatible with the *kokutai*. Nevertheless, a promise to preserve the monarchy would have taken the wind out of their sails, especially, given that the emperor would have more actively intervened for the acceptance of the Byrnes Note. Stalin would have opposed the Byrnes Note if it included the provision for a constitutional monarchy, but Truman was prepared to attain Japan's surrender without the Soviet Union anyway. This scenario thus might have resulted in Japan's surrender on August 12 or 13 instead of August 14.

Without the atomic bombs and without the Soviet entry into the war, would Japan have surrendered before November 1, the day Operation Olympic was scheduled to begin? The *United States Strategic Bombing Survey*, published in 1946, concluded that Japan would have surrendered before November 1 without the atomic bombs and without Soviet entry into the war. This conclusion has become the foundation on which revisionist historians have constructed their argument that the atomic bombs were not necessary for Japan's surrender. Since Barton Bernstein has persuasively demonstrated in his critique of the *Survey* that its conclusion is not supported by its own evidence, I need not dwell on this supposition. The main objective of the study's principal author, Paul Nitze, was to prove that conventional bombings, coupled with the naval blockade, would have induced Japan to surrender before November 1. But Nitze's conclusion was repeatedly contradicted by the evidence provided in the *Survey* itself. For instance, to the question, "How much longer do you think the war might have continued had the atomic bomb not been dropped?" Prince Konoe answered: "Probably it would have lasted all this year." Bernstein introduced numerous other testimonies by Toyoda, Kido, Suzuki, Hiranuma, Sakomizu, and others to contradict the *Survey*'s conclusion. As Bernstein asserts, the *Survey* is "an unreliable guide."

The Japanese leaders knew that Japan was losing the war. But defeat and surrender are not synonymous. Surrender is a political act. Without the twin shocks of the atomic bombs and Soviet entry into the war, the Japanese would never have accepted surrender in August.

Would Japan have surrendered before November 1 on the basis of Soviet entry alone, without the atomic bomb? Japanese historian Asada Sadao contends that without the atomic bombs but with Soviet entry into the war, "there was a possibility that Japan would not have surrendered before November 1." To Asada the shock value was crucial. Whereas the Japanese anticipated Soviet entry into the war, Asada argues, the atomic bombs came as a complete shock. By contrast, Bernstein states: "In view of the great impact of Soviet entry . . . in a situation of heavy conventional bombing and a strangling blockade, it does seem quite probable—indeed, far more likely than not—that Japan would have surrendered before November without the use of the A-bomb but after Soviet intervention in the war. In that sense . . . there may have been a serious 'missed opportunity' in 1945 to avoid the costly invasion of Kyushu without dropping the atomic bomb by awaiting Soviet entry."

The importance to Japan of Soviet neutrality is crucial in this context. Japan relied on Soviet neutrality both militarily and diplomatically. Diplomatically, Japan pinned its last hope on Moscow's mediation for the termination of the war. Once the Soviets entered the war, Japan was forced to make a decision on the Potsdam terms. Militarily as well, Japan's Ketsu-go strategy was predicated on Soviet neutrality; indeed, it was for this reason that the Military Affairs Bureau of the Army Ministry constantly overruled the intelligence section's warning that a Soviet invasion might be imminent. Manchuria was not written off, as Asada claims; rather, the military was confident that Japan could keep the Soviets neutral, at least for a while. When the Soviets invaded Manchuria, the military was taken by complete surprise. Despite the bravado that the war must continue, the Soviet invasion undermined the confidence of the army, punching a fatal hole in its strategic plan. The military's insistence on the continuation of war lost its rationale.

More important, however, were the political implications of the Soviet expansion in the Far East. Without Japan's surrender, it is reasonable to assume that the Soviets would have completed the occupation of Manchuria, southern Sakhalin, the entire Kurils, and possibly half of Korea by the beginning of September. Inevitably, the Soviet invasion of Hokkaido would have been raised as a pressing issue to be settled between the United States and the Soviet Union. The United States might have resisted the Soviet operation against Hokkaido, but given the Soviets' military strength, and given the enormous casualty figures the American high command had estimated for Olympic, the United States might have conceded the division of Hokkaido as Stalin had envisaged. Even if the United States succeeded in resisting Stalin's pressure, Soviet military conquests in the rest of the Far East might have led Truman to concede some degree of Soviet participation in Japan's postwar occupation. Whatever the United States might or might not have done regarding the Soviet operation in Hokkaido or the postwar occupation of Japan, Japanese leaders were well aware of the danger of allowing Soviet expansion to continue beyond Manchuria, Korea, Sakhalin, and the Kurils. It was for this reason that the Japanese policymakers came together at the last moment to surrender under the Potsdam terms, that the military's insistence on continuing the war collapsed, and that the military accepted surrender relatively easily. Japan's decision to surrender was above all a political decision, not a military one. Therefore, even without the atomic bombs, the war most likely would have ended shortly after Soviet entry into the war—before November 1.

Would Japan have surrendered before November 1 on the basis of the atomic bomb alone, without the Soviet entry into the war? The two bombs alone would most likely not have prompted the Japanese, to surrender, so long as they still had hope that Moscow would mediate peace. The Hiroshima bombing did not significantly change Japan's policy, though it did inject a sense of urgency into the peace party's initiative to end the war. Without the Soviet entry into the war, it is not likely that the Nagasaki bomb would have changed the situation. Anami's warning that the United States might have 100 atomic bombs and that the next target might be Tokyo had no discernible impact on the debate. Even after the Nagasaki bomb, Japan would most likely have still waited for Moscow's answer to the Konoe mission.

The most likely scenario would have been that while waiting for the answer from Moscow, Japan would have been shocked by the Soviet invasion in Manchuria sometime in the middle of August, and would have sued for peace on the Potsdam terms. In this case, then, we would have debated endlessly whether the two atomic bombs preceding the Soviet invasion or the Soviet entry would have had a more decisive impact on Japan's decision to surrender, although in this case, too, clearly Soviet entry would have had a more decisive impact.

Richard Frank, who argues that the atomic bombings had a greater impact on Japan's decision to surrender than Soviet involvement in the war, relies exclusively on contemporary sources and discounts postwar testimonies. He emphasizes especially the importance of Hirohito's statement at the first imperial conference, the Imperial Rescript on August 15, and Suzuki's statements made during cabinet meetings. This methodology, though admirable, does not support Frank's conclusion. Hirohito's reference to the atomic bomb at the imperial conference comes from Takeshita's diary, which must be based on hearsay. None of the participants who actually attended the imperial conference remembers the emperor's referring to the atomic bomb. The Imperial Rescript on August 15 does refer to the use of the "cruel new bomb" as one of the reasons for the termination of the war, with no mention of Soviet entry into the war. But during his meeting with the three marshals on August 14, the emperor referred to both the atomic bomb and Soviet entry into the war as the decisive reasons for ending the war. Moreover, the Imperial Rescript to the Soldiers and Officers issued on August 17 refers to Soviet entry as the major reason for ending the war and makes no reference to the atomic bomb. In contemporary records from August 6 to August 15 two sources (the Imperial Rescript on August 15 and Suzuki's statement at the August 13 cabinet meeting) refer only to the impact of the atomic bomb, three sources only to Soviet entry (Konoe on August 9, Suzuki's statement to his doctor on August 13, and the Imperial Rescript to Soldiers and Officers on August 17), and seven sources both to the atomic bomb and Soviet involvement. Contemporary evidence does not support Frank's contention.

Without Soviet participation in the war in the middle of August, the United States would have faced the question of whether to use the third bomb sometime after August 19, and then the fourth bomb in the beginning of September, most likely on Kokura and Niigata. It is hard to say how many atomic bombs it would have taken to convince Japanese policymakers to abandon their approach to Moscow. It is possible to argue, though impossible to prove, that the Japanese military would still have argued for the continuation of the war after a third or even a fourth bomb.

Could Japan have withstood the attacks of seven atomic bombs before November 1? Would Truman and Stimson have had the resolve to use seven atomic bombs in succession? What would have been the impact of these bombs on Japanese public opinion? Would the continued use of the bombs have solidified or eroded the resolve of the Japanese to fight on? Would it have hopelessly alienated the Japanese from the United States to the point that it would be difficult to impose the American occupation on Japan? Would it have encouraged the Japanese to welcome the Soviet occupation instead? These are the questions we cannot answer with certainty.

On the basis of available evidence, however, it is clear that the two atomic bombs on Hiroshima and Nagasaki alone were nor decisive in inducing Japan to surrender. Despite their destructive power, the atomic bombs were not sufficient to change the direction of Japanese diplomacy. The Soviet invasion was. Without the Soviet entry into the war, the Japanese would have continued to fight until numerous atomic bombs, a successful allied invasion of the home islands, or continued aerial bombardments, combined with a naval blockade, rendered them incapable of doing so.

Legacies

The Bomb in American Memory

After the war was over, each nation began constructing its own story about how the war ended. Americans still cling to the myth that the atomic bombs dropped on Hiroshima and Nagasaki provided the knockout punch to the Japanese government. The decision to use the bomb saved not only American soldiers but also the Japanese, according to this narrative. The myth serves to justify Truman's decision and ease the collective American conscience. To this extent, it is important to American national identity. But as this book demonstrates, this myth cannot be supported by historical facts. Evidence makes clear that there were alternatives to the use of the bomb, alternatives that the Truman administration for reasons of its own declined to pursue. And it is here, in the evidence of roads not taken, that the question of moral responsibility comes to the fore. Until his death, Truman continually came back to this question and repeatedly justified his decision, inventing a fiction that he himself later came to believe. That he spoke so often to justify his actions shows how much his decision to use the bomb haunted him.

On August 10 the Japanese government sent a letter of protest through the Swiss legation to the United States government. This letter declared the American use of the atomic bombs to be a violation of Articles 22 and 23 of the Hague Convention Respecting the Laws and Customs of War on Land, which prohibited the use of cruel weapons. It declared "in the name of the Japanese Imperial Government as well as in the name of humanity and civilization" that "the use of the atomic bombs, which surpass the indiscriminate cruelty of any other existing weapons and projectiles," was a crime against humanity, and demanded that "the further use of such inhumane weapons be immediately ceased." Needless to say, Truman did not respond to this letter. After Japan accepted the American occupation and became an important ally of the United States, the Japanese government has never raised any protest about the American use of the atomic bombs. The August 10 letter remains the only, and now forgotten, protest lodged by the Japanese government against the use of the atomic bomb.

To be sure, the Japanese government was guilty of its own atrocities in violation of the laws governing the conduct of war. The Nanking Massacre of 1937, biological experiments conducted by the infamous Unit 731, the Bataan March, and the numerous instances of cruel treatment of POWs represent only a few examples of Japanese atrocities. Nevertheless, the moral lapses of the Japanese do not excuse those of the United States and the Allies. After all, morality by definition is an absolute rather than a relative standard. The forgotten letter that the Japanese government sent to the United States government on August 10 deserves serious consideration. Justifying Hiroshima and Nagasaki by making a historically unsustainable argument that the atomic bombs ended the war is no longer tenable. Our self-image as Americans is tested by how we can come to terms with the decision to drop the bomb. Although much of what revisionist historians argue is faulty and based on tendentious use of sources, they nonetheless deserve credit for raising an important moral issue that challenges the standard American narrative of Hiroshima and Nagasaki.

The Stalinist Past

Soviet historians, and patriotic Russian historians after the collapse of the Soviet Union, justify the Soviet violation of the Neutrality Pact by arguing that it brought the Pacific War to a close, thus ending the suffering of the oppressed people of Asia and the useless sacrifices of the Japanese themselves. But this book shows that Stalin's policy was motivated by expansionist geopolitical designs. The Soviet leader pursued his imperialistic policy with Machiavellian ruthlessness, deviousness, and cunning. In the end he managed to enter the war and occupy those territories to which he felt entitled. Although he briefly flirted with the idea of invading Hokkaido, and did violate the provision of the Yalta Agreement to secure a treaty with the Chinese as the prerequisite for entry into the war, Stalin by and large respected the Yalta limit. But by occupying the southern Kurils, which had never belonged to Russia until the last days of August and the beginning of September 1945, he created an intractable territorial dispute known as "the Northern Territories question" that has prevented rapprochement between Russia and Japan to this day. The Russian government and the majority of Russians even now continue to cling to the myth that the occupation of the southern Kurils was Russia's justifiable act of repossessing its lost territory.

Stalin's decisions in the Pacific War are but one of many entries in the ledger of his brutal regime. Although his imperialism was not the worst of his crimes compared with the Great Purge and collectivization, it represented part and parcel of the Stalin regime. Certainly, his conniving against the Japanese and the blatant land-grabbing that he engaged in during the closing weeks of the war are nothing to praise. Although the crimes committed by Stalin have been exposed and the new Russia is making valiant strides by shedding itself of the remnants of the Stalinist past, the Russians, with the exception of a few courageous historians, have not squarely faced the historical fact that Stalin's policy toward Japan in the waning months of the Pacific War was an example of the leader's expansionistic foreign policy. Unless the Russians come to this realization, the process of cleansing themselves of the Stalinist past will never be completed.

The Mythology of Victimization and the Role of Hirohito

It took the Japanese a little while to realize that what happened to the Kurils during the confused period between August 15 and September 5 amounted to annexation of Japan's inherent territory, an act that violated the Atlantic Charter and the Cairo Declaration. But the humiliation the Japanese suffered in the four-week Soviet-Japanese War was not entirely a result of the Soviet occupation of the Kurils. The Soviet occupation of the Kurils represented the last of many wrongs that the Soviets perpetrated on the Japanese, beginning with the violation of the Neutrality Pact, the invasion of Manchuria, Korea, southern Sakhalin, and the deportation and imprisonment of more than 640,000 prisoners of war. The "Northern Territories question" that the Japanese have demanded be resolved in the postwar period before any rapprochement with the Soviet Union (and Russia after 1991) is a mere symbol of their deep-seated resentment of and hostility toward the Russians who betrayed Japan when it desperately needed their help in ending the war.

Together with the Soviet war against Japan, Hiroshima and Nagasaki have instilled in the Japanese a sense of victimization. What Gilbert Rozman calls the Hiroshima syndrome and the Northern Territories syndrome are an inverted form of nationalism. As such they have prevented the Japanese from coming to terms with their own culpability in causing the war in Asia. Before August 14, 1945, the Japanese leaders had ample opportunities to surrender, for instance, at the German capitulation, the fall of Okinawa, the issuance of the Potsdam Proclamation, the atomic bomb on Hiroshima, and Soviet entry into the war. Few in Japan have condemned the policymakers who delayed Japan's surrender. Had the Japanese government accepted the Potsdam Proclamation unconditionally immediately after it was issued, as Sato and Matsumoto argued, the atomic bombs would not have been used, and the war would have ended before the Soviets entered the conflict. Japanese policymakers who were in the position to make decisions—not only the militant advocates of war but also those who belonged to the peace party, including Suzuki, Togo, Kido, and Hirohito himself—must bear the responsibility for the war's destructive end more than the American president and the Soviet dictator.

In postwar Japan, Hirohito has been portrayed as the savior of the Japanese people and the nation for his "sacred decisions" to end the war. Indeed, without the emperor's personal intervention, Japan would not have surrendered. The cabinet and the Big Six were hopelessly divided, unable to make a decision. Only the emperor broke the stalemate. His determination and leadership at the two imperial conferences and his steadfast support for the termination of the war after the decisive meeting with Kido on August 9 were crucial factors leading to Japan's surrender.

This does not mean, however, that the emperor was, in Asada's words, "Japan's foremost peace advocate, increasingly articulate and urgent in expressing his wish for peace." He was, as all other Japanese leaders at that time, still pinning his hope on Moscow's mediation, rejecting the unconditional surrender demanded by the Potsdam Proclamation until the Soviet entry into the war. After the Soviets joined the fight, he finally changed his mind to accept the Potsdam terms. In Japan it has been taboo to question the motivation that led Hirohito to accept surrender. But the findings of this book call for a reexamination of his role in the ending of the Pacific War. His delay in accepting the Allied terms ensured the use of the bomb and Soviet entry into the war.

Although Hirohito's initiative after August 9 should be noted, his motivation for ending the war was not as noble as the "sacred decision" myth would have us believe. His primary concern was above all the preservation of the imperial house. He even flirted with the idea of clinging to his political role. Despite the myth that he said he did not care what happened to him personally, it is likely that he was also in fact deeply concerned about the safety of his family and his own security. At the crucial imperial conference of August 10, Hiranuma did not mince words in asking Hirohito to take responsibility for the tragedy that had befallen Japan. As Konoe, some of the emperor's own relatives, and Grew, the most ardent supporter of the Japanese monarchy, argued, Hirohito should have abdicated at the end of the war to make a clean break with the Showa period that marked anything but what "Showa" meant: enlightened peace. His continuing reign made Japan's culpability in the war ambiguous and contributed to the nation's inability to come to terms with the past.

Thus this is a story with no heroes but no real villains, either—just men. The ending of the Pacific War was in the last analysis a human drama whose dynamics were determined by the very human characteristics of those involved: ambition, fear, vanity, anger, and prejudice. With each successive decision, the number of remaining alternatives steadily diminished, constraining ever further the possibilities, until the dropping of the bomb and the destruction of the Japanese state became all but inevitable. The Pacific War could very well have ended differently had the men involved made different choices. But they did not.

So they left it for us to live with the legacies of the war. The question is, Do we have the courage to overcome them?

POSTSCRIPT

Was It Necessary to Drop the Atomic Bomb to End World War II?

The "official" history defends the use of the atomic bombs against Japan. After some early doubts by some publicists and church leaders, the hardening cold war with Russia after 1947 caused the decision makers to defend their policy. The atomic bombs were dropped for military reasons. It forced the Japanese to end the war quickly and saved both Japanese and American lives. In a much quoted article, "The Decision to Use the Atomic Bomb," *Harper's Magazine* 194 (February, 1947), former Secretary of Defense Henry L. Stimson asserted that the two invasions of Kyushu and Honshu might be expected to cost over a million casualties to American forces. While the real military estimates for the invasions were nowhere near a million, Truman's ghost writers in his *Memoirs I, Year of Decisions* (Doubleday, 1955) estimated casualties at 500,000.

The official interpretation was basically unchallenged until the 1960s when a revisionist school emerged, which blamed the Americans rather than the Russians for the cold war. In a series of articles and a published doctoral dissertation, *Atomic Diplomacy: Hiroshima and Potsdam* (Simon and Schuster, 1965, rev. ed. 1985), Gar Alperovitz argued that President Truman reversed Roosevelt's policy of cooperation with our Russian allies, rejected alternatives such as a test demonstration, blockade, or a specific warning, and dropped the bombs to make the Russians more manageable in Eastern Europe. Not all historians, even revisionists, accepted Alperovitz's use of the bomb as a trump card. Critics argued that Alperovitz had too narrow a perspective and did not see the continuity in policy between the Roosevelt and Truman administrations. Alperovitz also was selective in his use of sources and quoted from participants whose memory was faulty or self-serving. He especially relied on the diary of Secretary of War Henry L. Stimson, a 77-year-old career diplomat whom Truman respected but whose advice he rejected. Finally, Alperovitz made Truman appear to be more decisive in making decisions than he really was and that the Japanese government was united and willing to surrender if the Americans allowed the imperial dynasty to survive.

Most revisionists did not go as far as Alperovitz in arguing that the bombs were dropped primarily for political reasons. Moderate revisionists such as Barton J. Bernstein who has written at least two dozen articles on the subject accept the premise that while military objectives were important, there was a diplomatic "bonus" whereby sole possession of the bomb gave us military superiority over the Russians. This edge lasted until the fall of 1949 when the Russians successfully tested their own A-bomb.

The new orthodoxy among historians was a moderate revisionist interpretation of both military and political objectives. Such an interpretation was unheard of by the general public. When the Smithsonian tried to host a full-scale fiftieth anniversary exhibit of the events surrounding the A-bomb, a huge controversy developed. Under pressure from the Air Force Associated, the American Legion, and Congress, the original exhibit was cancelled. Only the Enola Gay, the plane that dropped the first bomb on Hiroshima, was displayed with minimal comment. For a full-scale analysis of the controversy and the development of A-bomb historiography, see Barton J. Bernstein, "Afterward: The Struggle Over History: Defining the Hiroshima Narrative," in Philip Nobile, ed., *Judgment at the Smithsonian* (Marlowe, 1995), and Michael J. Hogan, ed., *Hiroshima as History and Memory* (Cambridge University Press, 1996). See also Barton J. Bernstein, "The Atomic Bombings Reconsidered," *Foreign Affairs* (January/February 1995) where he argues that the distinction between civilian and military casualties became blurred with the saturation bombing of enemy targets in World War II.

In the plethora of books and articles published in 1995 on the fiftieth anniversary of the dropping of the atomic bomb, Professor Robert James Maddox's *Weapons for Victory: The Hiroshima Decision Fifty Years Later* (University of Missouri Press, 1995) stands out in its defense of the military reasons why Truman dropped the bomb. A long review essay by Donald Kagan on "Why America Dropped the Bomb," *Commentary* (September 1995) and "Letters from Readers" in the December 1995 issue thank Maddox and make similar points.

Maddox makes a compelling case for the military circumstances surrounding the decision to drop the atomic bomb on Japan. The Americans had suffered 50,000 casualties in the capture of the island of Okinawa in the spring of 1945. This was considered a preview of the impending invasion of Japan. Maddox points out that estimates of casualties were mere guesswork at a given time and that Army Chief of Staff George C. Marshall himself increased these numbers considerably when he realized that the Japanese were stationing hundreds of thousands of troops on their main islands.

Tsuyoshi Hasegawa has written the most recent scholarly account of why the Japanese surrendered. In *Racing the Enemy: Stalin, Truman and the Surrender of Japan,* Hasegawa has done extensive research in Russian and Japanese archives as well as American archives. He bypasses the usual debate between traditionalists and revisionists, which argues whether the bomb was dropped for military or political reasons. By engaging in multi-archival research, Hasegawa examines the varied and often conflicting political, military, and territorial objectives in ending the war of Truman, Stalin, the emperor, and the Japanese military. Hence, with the title *Racing with the Enemy,* Hasegawa lets no one off the hook. Truman never seriously considered other options to dropping the bomb because he wanted to avenge the sneak attack at Pearl Harbor. As he wrote a group of church leaders a few days after the bombings of Hiroshima and Nagasaki: "I was greatly disturbed over the unwarranted attack by the Japanese on Pearl Harbor and their murder of our prisoners of war. The only language they seem to understand is the one we have been using to bomb them. When you have to deal with a beast, you have to treat him as a beast."

Unlike most revisionists, however, Hasegawa is just as critical of the policies of the Russians and the Japanese. Stalin had his own expansionist aims. He was determined to recover the territories promised him at the Yalta Conference of February 1945 for his entrance into the Asian war once Germany was defeated. Stalin demanded and was given back all the possessions and territorial spheres of influence in Asia that Russia lost to Japan after the 1904–1905 Russo-Japanese war. After the first bomb was dropped, Stalin rushed his entry into the Asian war by a week and proceeded to take even the Northern Sakalin Islands, which was not part of the Yalta agreements. Hasegawa is also one of the few historians to seriously explore the Japanese decision-making process. He moves beyond the seminal research of *Japan's Decision to Surrender* (Stanford University Press, 1954) written over 50 years ago by his former teacher, Robert J. C. Butow, who discussed conflicts between the extreme militarists and the Japanese moderates who wanted to pursue a surrender with the condition of keeping the emperor as the nominal leader of the country. While Butow and most Japanese view the emperor as a hero who broke the deadlock between hard-liners and moderates in ending the war, Hasegawa views the emperor's intervention in the deadlock not as a "noble" decision to end the war, but as an attempt that was ultimately successful "to preserve the imperial house." Hasegawa's most controversial contention is that "the bomb provided a solution to the previously unsolvable dilemma that faced Truman: to achieve Japan's unconditional surrender before Soviet entry into the war. Truman issued the Potsdam Proclamation, not as a warning to Japan, but to justify the use of the atomic bomb. This challenges the commonly held view that the atomic bomb provided the immediate and decisive knockout blow to Japan's will to fight. Indeed, the Soviet entry into the war played a greater role than the atomic bombs in inducing Japan to surrender (p. 5). This interpretation conflicts with Richard B. Frank's *Downfall: The End of the Imperial Japanese Empires* (Random House, 1999), which argues that when the emperor announced his decision in the early morning hours to surrender, he gave three reasons: (1) the fear of a domestic upheaval; (2) inadequate defense preparations to resist the invasion; (3) the vast destructiveness of the atomic bomb and the air attacks. The emperor, says Frank, did not refer to Soviet intervention (p. 345). *Downfall* basically substantiates the arguments of Professor Maddox.

In addition to the Bernstein essay and Hogan collection, J. Samuel Walker has provided two useful essays on "The Decision to Use the Bomb: A Historiographical Update," *Diplomatic History* 14 (Winter 1990) and "Recent Literature on Truman's Atomic Bomb Decision: The Search for Middle Ground," *Diplomatic History* 29/2 (April 2005). A useful collection of primary sources is Robert H. Ferrell, ed., *Truman and the Bomb: A Documentary History* (High Plains Publishing, 1996), and Michael B. Stoff, Jonathan F. Fanton, and R. Hal Williams, eds., *The Manhattan Project: A Documentary Introduction to the Atomic Age* (Temple University Press, 1991), which contains facsimilier of original documents.

On the Internet . . .

Cold War Hot Links

This page contains links to Web pages on the Cold War that a variety of people have created. They run the entire spectrum of political thought and provide some interesting views on the Cold War and the state of national security.

http://www.stmartin.edu/~dprice/cold.war.html

Civil Rights: A Status Report

Kevin Hollaway is the author of this detailed history of black civil rights from the discovery of the New World to the present. In his own words, "It is not my intent to complain about the present state of Black America, nor to provide excuses. My intent is [to] provide excuses. My intent is [to] provide an unbiased picture of Black American history; something that is often missing from many classrooms in America."

http://www.earthlink.net/~civilrightsreport/

The History Place Presents: The Vietnam War

This page of History Place offers comprehensive timelines of U.S. involvement in the Vietnam conflict from 1945 to 1975, with quotes and analysis. You can also jump to specific events and topics, such as the Tet Offensive, the Geneva Conference, and the Pentagon Papers.

http://www.historyplace.com/unitedstates/vietnam

American Immigration Resources on the Internet

This site contains many links to American immigration resources on the Internet. It includes a site on children's immigration issues, the Immigration and Naturalization Service home page, and a forum on immigration.

http://www.immigration-usa.com/resource.html

The White House

Visit the home page of the White House for direct access to information about commonly requested federal services, the White House Briefing Room, and the presidents and vice presidents. The "Virtual Library" allows you to search White House documents, listen to speeches, and view photos. See in particular George W. Bush, "Remarks at the 2002 Graduation Exercise of the United States Military Academy," West Point, New York, June 1, 2002 (www.whitehouse.gov/news/releases/2002/06/20020601-3.html [accessed March 2005]) and *The National Security Strategy of the United States*, Washington, D.C., September 2002 (www.whitehouse.gov/nsc/nss.html [accessed March 2005]).

http://www.whitehouse.gov/

PART 3

The Cold War and Beyond

*W*orld War II ended in 1945, but the peace that everyone had hoped for never came. By 1947 a "Cold War" between the Western powers and the Russians was in full swing. In 1949, China came under communist control, the Russians developed an atomic bomb, and communist subversion of high-level officials in the State and Treasury Departments of the U.S. government was uncovered. A year later American soldiers were fighting a hot war of "containment" against communist expansion in Korea. By 1968, President Lyndon Johnson had escalated America's participation in the Vietnam War and then tried to negotiate peace, which was accomplished by President Nixon in January 1973.

From 1950 to 1974, most Americans were economically well-off. Presidents Harry S. Truman, Dwight D. Eisenhower, and John F. Kennedy managed an economy whose major problem was keeping inflation under control. From the 1950s through 1968, African Americans and women rose up and demanded that they be granted their civil, political, and economic rights as first-class citizens.

The last quarter of the twentieth century continued America's fluctuation between affluence and anxiety. Controversy surrounds whether President Ronald Reagan's policies were responsible for the demise of the Soviet Union's empire. The reputations of Presidents Nixon, Reagan, Clinton, and Bush are heavily dependent upon the future course of America's prosperity and power in the twenty-first century.

One of the problems left over from the twentieth century is still controversial with few solutions in sight. Can America remain a nation of immigrants and still regain its core culture as well as be secure from terrorism? Is a prosperous, growing economy compatible with the large number of immigrants—both legal and illegal—entering the country?

- Did Communism Threaten America's Internal Security after World War II?

- Did the *Brown* Decision Fail to Desegregate and Improve the Status of African Americans?

- Was the Americanization of the War in Vietnam Inevitable?

- Was Richard Nixon America's Last Liberal President?

- Did President Reagan Win the Cold War?

- Should America Remain a Nation of Immigrants?

- Is George W. Bush the Worst President in American History?

ISSUE 12

Did Communism Threaten America's Internal Security After World War II?

YES: John Earl Haynes and Harvey Klehr, from *Venona: Decoding Soviet Espionage in America* (Yale University Press, 1999)

NO: Richard M. Fried, from *Nightmare in Red: The McCarthy Era in Perspective* (Oxford University Press, 1990)

ISSUE SUMMARY

YES: History professors John Earl Haynes and Harvey Klehr argue that army code-breakers during World War II's "Venona Project" uncovered a disturbing number of high-ranking U.S. government officials who seriously damaged American interests by passing sensitive information to the Soviet Union.

NO: Professor of history Richard M. Fried argues that the early 1950s were a "nightmare in red" during which American citizens had their First and Fifth Amendment rights suspended when a host of national and state investigating committees searched for Communists in government agencies, Hollywood, labor unions, foundations, universities, public schools, and even public libraries.

The 1917 triumph of the Bolshevik revolution in Russia and the ensuing spread of revolution to other parts of Eastern Europe and Germany led American radicals to believe that the revolution was near. It also led to a wave of anti-Bolshevik hysteria. In the fall of 1919 two groups of radicals—one native-born, the other foreign-born—formed the Communist and Communist Labor parties. Ultimately they would merge, yet between them they contained only 25,000 to 40,000 members.

The popular "front" policy, which lasted from 1935 to 1939, was the most successful venture undertaken by American Communists. The chief aim of the American Communists became not to increase party membership but to infiltrate progressive organizations. They achieved their greatest successes in the labor movement, which badly needed union organizers. As a consequence Communists controlled several major unions, such as the West Coast long-shoremen and the electrical workers, and attained key offices in the powerful

United Autoworkers. Many American novelists, screenwriters, and actors also joined communist front organizations, such as the League of American Writers, and the Theatre Collective produced "proletarian" plays.

In the 1930s and 1940s the American Communist Party's primary success was its ability to establish a conspiratorial underground in Washington. The release of the Venona intercepts of American intelligence during World War II indicates that some 349 American citizens and residents had a covert relationship with Soviet intelligence agencies.

During the war the Federal Bureau of Investigation (FBI) and the Office of Strategic Services (OSS) conducted security clearances that permitted Communist supporters to work at high-level jobs if they met the qualifications. This changed in February 1947. In order to impress the Republicans that he wished to attack communism at home, President Harry S. Truman issued an executive order that inaugurated a comprehensive investigation of the loyalty of all government employees by the FBI and the Civil Service Commission.

Truman's loyalty program temporarily protected him from charges that he was "soft" on communism. His ability to ward off attacks against his soft containment policy against communism ran out in his second term. Alger Hiss, a high-level state department official, was convicted in 1949 of lying about his membership in the Ware Communist cell group. In September Truman announced to the American public that the Russians had successfully tested an atomic bomb. Shortly thereafter the Chinese Communists secured control over all of China when their nationalist opponents retreated to the island of Taiwan. Then on June 24, 1950, North Korea crossed the "containment" line at the 38th parallel and attacked South Korea.

The Republican response to these events was swift, critical, and partisan. Before his conviction, Hiss had been thoroughly investigated by the House Un-American Activities Committee. Had he led President Franklin D. Roosevelt and others to a sell-out of the Eastern European countries at the Yalta Conference in February 1945? Who lost China? Did liberal and leftist state department officials stationed in China give a pro-Communist slant to U.S. foreign policies in Asia?

Within this atmosphere Truman's attempt to forge a bipartisan policy to counter internal subversion of government agencies by Communists received a mortal blow when Senator Joseph A. McCarthy of Wisconsin publicly identified 205 cases of individuals who appeared to be either card-carrying members or loyal to the Communist Party.

How legitimate was the second great red scare? Did communism threaten America's internal security in the cold war era? In the following selections, John Earl Haynes and Harvey Klehr contend that a sizeable number of high-level U.S. government officials passed sensitive information to Russian intelligence, while Richard M. Fried argues that the 1950s became a "red nightmare" when state and national government agencies overreacted in their search for Communists, violating citizens' rights of free speech and a defense against self-incrimination under the First and Fifth Amendments.

261

YES

John Earl Haynes
and Harvey Klehr

Venona and the Cold War

The Venona Project began because Carter Clarke did not trust Joseph Stalin. Colonel Clarke was chief of the U.S. Army's Special Branch, part of the War Department's Military Intelligence Division, and in 1943 its officers heard vague rumors of secret German-Soviet peace negotiations. With the vivid example of the August 1939 Nazi-Soviet Pact in mind, Clarke feared that a separate peace between Moscow and Berlin would allow Nazi Germany to concentrate its formidable war machine against the United States and Great Britain. Clarke thought he had a way to find out whether such negotiations were under way.

Clarke's Special Branch supervised the Signal Intelligence Service, the Army's elite group of code-breakers and the predecessor of the National Security Agency. In February 1943 Clarke ordered the service to establish a small program to examine ciphered Soviet diplomatic cablegrams. Since the beginning of World War II in 1939, the federal government had collected copies of international cables leaving and entering the United States. If the cipher used in the Soviet cables could be broken, Clarke believed, the private exchanges between Soviet diplomats in the United States and their superiors in Moscow would show whether Stalin was seriously pursuing a separate peace.

The coded Soviet cables, however, proved to be far more difficult to read than Clarke had expected. American code-breakers discovered that the Soviet Union was using a complex two-part ciphering system involving a "one-time pad" code that in theory was unbreakable. The Venona code-breakers, however, combined acute intellectual analysis with painstaking examination of thousands of coded telegraphic cables to spot a Soviet procedural error that opened the cipher to attack. But by the time they had rendered the first messages into readable text in 1946, the war was over and Clarke's initial goal was moot. Nor did the messages show evidence of a Soviet quest for a separate peace. What they did demonstrate, however, stunned American officials. Messages thought to be between Soviet diplomats at the Soviet consulate in New York and the People's Commissariat of Foreign Affairs in Moscow turned out to be cables between professional intelligence field officers and Gen. Pavel Fitin, head of the foreign intelligence directorate of the KGB in Moscow. Espionage, not diplomacy, was the subject of these cables. One of the first cables rendered into coherent text was a 1944 message from KGB officers in

New York showing that the Soviet Union had infiltrated America's most secret enterprise, the atomic bomb project.

By 1948 the accumulating evidence from other decoded Venona cables showed that the Soviets had recruited spies in virtually every major American government agency of military or diplomatic importance. American authorities learned that since 1942 the United States had been the target of a Soviet espionage onslaught involving dozens of professional Soviet intelligence officers and hundreds of Americans, many of whom were members of the American Communist party (CPUSA). The deciphered cables of the Venona Project identify 349 citizens, immigrants, and permanent residents of the United States who had had a covert relationship with Soviet intelligence agencies. Further, American cryptanalysts in the Venona Project deciphered only a fraction of the Soviet intelligence traffic, so it was only logical to conclude that many additional agents were discussed in the thousands of unread messages. Some were identified from other sources, such as defectors' testimony and the confessions of Soviet spies.

The deciphered Venona messages also showed that a disturbing number of high-ranking U.S. government officials consciously maintained a clandestine relationship with Soviet intelligence agencies and had passed extraordinarily sensitive information to the Soviet Union that had seriously damaged American interests. Harry White—the second most powerful official in the U.S. Treasury Department, one of the most influential officials in the government, and part of the American delegation at the founding of the United Nations—had advised the KGB about how American diplomatic strategy could be frustrated. A trusted personal assistant to President Franklin Roosevelt, Lauchlin Currie, warned the KGB that the FBI had started an investigation of one of the Soviets' key American agents, Gregory Silvermaster. This warning allowed Silvermaster, who headed a highly productive espionage ring, to escape detection and continue spying. Maurice Halperin, the head of a research section of the Office of Strategic Services (OSS), then America's chief intelligence arm, turned over hundreds of pages of secret American diplomatic cables to the KGB. William Perl, a brilliant young government aeronautical scientist, provided the Soviets with the results of the highly secret tests and design experiments for American jet engines and jet aircraft. His betrayal assisted the Soviet Union in quickly overcoming the American technological lead in the development of jets. In the Korean War, U.S. military leaders expected the Air Force to dominate the skies, on the assumption that the Soviet aircraft used by North Korea and Communist China would be no match for American aircraft. They were shocked when Soviet MiG-15 jet fighters not only flew rings around U.S. propeller-driven aircraft but were conspicuously superior to the first generation of American jets as well. Only the hurried deployment of America's newest jet fighter, the F-86 Saber, allowed the United States to match the technological capabilities of the MiG-15. The Air Force prevailed, owing more to the skill of American pilots than to the design of American aircraft.

And then there were the atomic spies. From within the Manhattan Project two physicists, Klaus Fuchs and Theodore Hall, and one technician,

David Greenglass, transmitted the complex formula for extracting bombgrade uranium from ordinary uranium, the technical plans for production facilities, and the engineering principles for the "implosion" technique. The latter process made possible an atomic bomb using plutonium, a substance much easier to manufacture than bomb-grade uranium.

The betrayal of American atomic secrets to the Soviets allowed the Soviet Union to develop atomic weapons several years sooner and at a substantially lower cost than it otherwise would have. Joseph Stalin's knowledge that espionage assured the Soviet Union of quickly breaking the American atomic monopoly emboldened his diplomatic strategy in his early Cold War clashes with the United States. It is doubtful that Stalin, rarely a risk-taker, would have supplied the military wherewithal and authorized North Korea to invade South Korea in 1950 had the Soviet Union not exploded an atomic bomb in 1949. Otherwise Stalin might have feared that President Harry Truman would stanch any North Korean invasion by threatening to use atomic weapons. After all, as soon as the atomic bomb had been developed, Truman had not hesitated to use it twice to end the war with Japan. But in 1950, with Stalin in possession of the atomic bomb, Truman was deterred from using atomic weapons in Korea, even in the late summer when initially unprepared American forces were driven back into the tip of Korea and in danger of being pushed into the sea, and then again in the winter when Communist Chinese forces entered the war in massive numbers. The killing and maiming of hundreds of thousands of soldiers and civilians on both sides of the war in Korea might have been averted had the Soviets not been able to parry the American atomic threat.

Early Soviet possession of the atomic bomb had an important psychological consequence. When the Soviet Union exploded a nuclear device in 1949, ordinary Americans as well as the nation's leaders realized that a cruel despot, Joseph Stalin, had just gained the power to destroy cities at will. This perception colored the early Cold War with the hues of apocalypse. Though the Cold War never lost the potential of becoming a civilization-destroying conflict, Stalin's death in March 1953 noticeably relaxed Soviet-American tensions. With less successful espionage, the Soviet Union might not have developed the bomb until after Stalin's death, and the early Cold War might have proceeded on a far less frightening path.

Venona decryptions identified most of the Soviet spies uncovered by American counterintelligence between 1948 and the mid-1950s. The skill and perseverance of the Venona code-breakers led the U.S. Federal Bureau of Investigation (FBI) and British counterintelligence (MI5) to the atomic spy Klaus Fuchs. Venona documents unmistakably identified Julius Rosenberg as the head of a Soviet spy ring and David Greenglass, his brother-in-law, as a Soviet source at the secret atomic bomb facility at Los Alamos, New Mexico. Leads from decrypted telegrams exposed the senior British diplomat Donald Maclean as a major spy in the British embassy in Washington and precipitated his flight to the Soviet Union, along with his fellow diplomat and spy Guy Burgess. The arrest and prosecution of such spies as Judith Coplon, Robert Soblen, and Jack Soble was possible because American intelligence was able to read Soviet reports about their activities. The charges by the former Soviet spy Elizabeth Bentley that several dozen mid-level government officials, mostly secret Communists, had assisted Soviet intelligence were corroborated in Venona documents and assured American authorities of her veracity.

With the advent of the Cold War, however, the spies clearly identified in the Venona decryptions were the least of the problem. Coplon, Rosenberg, Greenglass, Fuchs, Soble, and Soblen were prosecuted, and the rest were eased out of the government or otherwise neutralized as threats to national security. But that still left a security nightmare. Of the 349 Americans the deciphered Venona cables revealed as having covert ties to Soviet intelligence agencies, less than half could be identified by their real names and nearly two hundred remained hidden behind cover names. American officials assumed that some of the latter surely were still working in sensitive positions. Had they been promoted and moved into policy-making jobs? Had Muse, the unidentified female agent in the OSS, succeeded in transferring to the State Department or the Central Intelligence Agency (CIA), the successor to the OSS? What of Source No. 19, who had been senior enough to meet privately with Churchill and Roosevelt at the Trident Conference? Was the unidentified KGB source Bibi working for one of America's foreign assistance agencies? Was Donald, the unidentified Navy captain who was a GRU (Soviet military intelligence) source, still in uniform, perhaps by this time holding the rank of admiral? And what of the two unidentified atomic spies Quantum and Pers? They had given Stalin the secrets of the uranium and plutonium bomb: were they now passing on the secrets of the even more destructive hydrogen bomb? And how about Dodger, Godmother, and Fakir? Deciphered Venona messages showed that all three had provided the KGB with information on American diplomats who specialized in Soviet matters. Fakir was himself being considered for an assignment representing the United States in Moscow. Which of the American foreign service officers who were also Soviet specialists were traitors? How could Americans successfully negotiate with the Soviet Union when the American negotiating team included someone working for the other side? Western Europe, clearly, would be the chief battleground of the Cold War. To lose there was to lose all: the task of rebuilding stable democracies in postwar Europe and forging the NATO military alliance was America's chief diplomatic challenge. Yet Venona showed that the KGB had Mole, the appropriate cover name of a Soviet source inside the Washington establishment who had passed on to Moscow high-level American diplomatic policy guidance on Europe. When American officials met to discuss sensitive matters dealing with France, Britain, Italy, or Germany, was Mole present and working to frustrate American goals? Stalin's espionage offensive had not only uncovered American secrets, it had also undermined the mutual trust that American officials had for each other.

The Truman administration had expected the end of World War II to allow the dismantling of the massive military machine created to defeat Nazi Germany and Imperial Japan. The government slashed military budgets, turned weapons factories over to civilian production, ended conscription, and returned millions of soldiers to civilian life. So, too, the wartime intelligence and security apparatus was demobilized. Anticipating only limited need for foreign intelligence and stating that he wanted no American Gestapo, President Truman abolished America's chief intelligence agency, the Office of Strategic Services. With the coming of peace, emergency wartime rules for security vetting of many government employees lapsed or were ignored.

In late 1945 and in 1946, the White House had reacted with a mixture of indifference and skepticism to FBI reports indicating significant Soviet espionage activity in the United States. Truman administration officials even whitewashed evidence pointing to the theft of American classified documents in the 1945 *Amerasia* case because they did not wish to put at risk the continuation of the wartime Soviet-American alliance and wanted to avoid the political embarrassment of a security scandal. By early 1947, however, this indifference ended. The accumulation of information from defectors such as Elizabeth Bentley and Igor Gouzenko, along with the Venona decryptions, made senior Truman administration officials realize that reports of Soviet spying constituted more than FBI paranoia. No government could operate successfully if it ignored the challenge to its integrity that Stalin's espionage offensive represented. In addition, the White House sensed that there was sufficient substance to the emerging picture of a massive Soviet espionage campaign, one assisted by American Communists, that the Truman administration was vulnerable to Republican charges of having ignored a serious threat to American security. President Truman reversed course and in March 1947 issued a sweeping executive order establishing a comprehensive security vetting program for U.S. government employees. He also created the Central Intelligence Agency, a stronger and larger version of the OSS, which he had abolished just two years earlier. In 1948 the Truman administration followed up these acts by indicting the leaders of the CPUSA under the sedition sections of the 1940 Smith Act. While the Venona Project and the decrypted messages themselves remained secret, the substance of the messages with the names of scores of Americans who had assisted Soviet espionage circulated among American military and civilian security officials. From the security officials the information went to senior executive-branch political appointees and members of Congress. They, in turn, passed it on to journalists and commentators, who conveyed the alarming news to the general public.

Americans' Understanding of Soviet and Communist Espionage

During the early Cold War, in the late 1940s and early 1950s, every few months newspaper headlines trumpeted the exposure of yet another network of Communists who had infiltrated an American laboratory, labor union, or government agency. Americans worried that a Communist fifth column, more loyal to the Soviet Union than to the United States, had moved into their institutions. By the mid-1950s, following the trials and convictions for espionage-related crimes of Alger Hiss, a senior diplomat, and Julius and Ethel Rosenberg for atomic spying, there was a widespread public consensus on three points: that Soviet espionage was serious, that American Communists assisted the Soviets, and that several senior government officials had betrayed the United States. The deciphered Venona messages provide a solid factual basis for this consensus. But the government did not release the Venona decryptions to the public, and it successfully disguised the source of its information about Soviet espionage. This decision denied the public the incontestable evidence afforded by the messages of the Soviet Union's own spies. Since the information about Soviet espionage and American Communist participation derived largely from the testimony of defectors and a mass of circumstantial evidence, the public's belief in those reports rested on faith in the integrity of government security officials. These sources are inherently more ambiguous than the hard evidence of the Venona messages, and this ambiguity had unfortunate consequences for American politics and Americans' understanding of their own history.

The decision to keep Venona secret from the public, and to restrict knowledge of it even within the government, was made essentially by senior Army officers in consultation with the FBI and the CIA. Aside from the Venona codebreakers, only a limited number of military intelligence officers, FBI agents, and CIA officials knew of the project. The CIA in fact was not made an active partner in Venona until 1952 and did not receive copies of the deciphered messages until 1953. The evidence is not entirely clear, but it appears that Army Chief of Staff Omar Bradley, mindful of the White House's tendency to leak politically sensitive information, decided to deny President Truman direct knowledge of the Venona Project. The president was informed about the substance of the Venona messages as it came to him through FBI and Justice Department memorandums on espionage investigations and CIA reports on intelligence matters. He was not told that much of this information derived from reading Soviet cable traffic. This omission is important because Truman was mistrustful of J. Edgar Hoover, the head of the FBI, and suspected that the reports of Soviet espionage were exaggerated for political purposes. Had he been aware of Venona, and known that Soviet cables confirmed the testimony of Elizabeth Bentley and Whittaker Chambers, it is unlikely that his aides would have considered undertaking a campaign to discredit Bentley and indict Chambers for perjury, or would have allowed themselves to be taken in by the disinformation being spread by the American Communist party and Alger Hiss's partisans that Chambers had at one time been committed to an insane asylum.

There were sensible reasons . . . for the decision to keep Venona a highly compartmentalized secret within the government. In retrospect, however, the negative consequences of this policy are glaring. Had Venona been made public, it is unlikely there would have been a forty-year campaign to prove that the Rosenbergs were innocent. The Venona messages clearly display Julius Rosenberg's role as the leader of a productive ring of Soviet spies. Nor would there have been any basis for doubting his involvement in atomic espionage, because the deciphered messages document his recruitment of his brother-in-law, David Greenglass, as a spy. It is also unlikely, had the messages been made public or even circulated more widely within the government than they did, that Ethel Rosenberg would have been executed. The Venona messages do not throw her guilt in doubt; indeed, they confirm that she was a participant in her husband's espionage and in the recruitment of her brother for atomic espionage. But they suggest that she was essentially an accessory to her husband's activity, having knowledge of it and assisting him but not acting as a principal. Had they been introduced at the Rosenberg trial, the Venona messages would have confirmed Ethel's guilt but also reduced the importance of her role.

Further, the Venona messages, if made public, would have made Julius Rosenberg's execution less likely. When Julius Rosenberg faced trial, only two Soviet atomic spies were known: David Greenglass, whom Rosenberg had recruited and run as a source, and Klaus Fuchs. Fuchs, however, was in England, so Greenglass was the only Soviet atomic spy in the media spotlight in the United States. Greenglass's confession left Julius Rosenberg as the target of public outrage at atomic espionage. That prosecutors would ask for and get the death penalty under those circumstances is not surprising.

In addition to Fuchs and Greenglass, however, the Venona messages identify three other Soviet sources within the Manhattan Project. The messages show that Theodore Hall, a young physicist at Los Alamos, was a far more valuable source than Greenglass, a machinist. Hall withstood FBI interrogation, and the government had no direct evidence of his crimes except the Venona messages, which because of their secrecy could not be used in court; he therefore escaped prosecution. The real identities of the sources Fogel and Quantum are not known, but the information they turned over to the Soviets suggests that Quantum was a scientist of some standing and that Fogel was either a scientist or an engineer. Both were probably more valuable sources than David Greenglass. Had Venona been made public, Greenglass would have shared the stage with three other atomic spies and not just with Fuchs, and all three would have appeared to have done more damage to American security than he. With Greenglass's role diminished, that of his recruiter, Julius Rosenberg, would have been reduced as well. Rosenberg would assuredly have been convicted, but his penalty might well have been life in prison rather than execution.

There were broader consequences, as well, of the decision to keep Venona secret. The overlapping issues of Communists in government, Soviet espionage, and the loyalty of American Communists quickly became a partisan battleground. Led by Republican senator Joseph McCarthy of Wisconsin, some conservatives and partisan Republicans launched a comprehensive attack on the loyalties of the Roosevelt and Truman administrations. Some painted the entire New Deal as a disguised Communist plot and depicted Dean Acheson, Truman's secretary of state, and George C. Marshall, the Army chief of staff under Roosevelt and secretary of state and secretary of defense under Truman, as participants, in Senator McCarthy's words, in "a conspiracy on a scale so immense as to dwarf any previous such venture in the history of man. A conspiracy of infamy so black that, when it is finally exposed, its principals shall be forever deserving of the maledictions of all honest men." There is no basis in Venona for implicating Acheson or Marshall in a Communist conspiracy, but because the deciphered Venona messages were classified and unknown to the public, demagogues such as McCarthy had the opportunity to mix together accurate information about betrayal by men such as Harry White and Alger Hiss with falsehoods about Acheson and Marshall that served partisan political goals.

A number of liberals and radicals pointed to the excesses of McCarthy's charges as justification for rejecting the allegations altogether. Anticommunism further lost credibility in the late 1960s when critics of U.S. involvement in the Vietnam War blamed it for America's ill-fated participation. By the 1980s many commentators, and perhaps most academic historians, had concluded that Soviet espionage had been minor, that few American Communists had assisted the Soviets, and that no high officials had betrayed the United States. Many history texts depicted America in the late 1940s and 1950s as a "nightmare in red" during which Americans were "sweat-drenched in fear" of a figment of their own paranoid imaginations. As for American Communists, they were widely portrayed as having no connection with espionage. One influential book asserted emphatically, "There is no documentation in the public record of a direct connection between the American Communist Party and espionage during the entire postwar period."

Consequently, Communists were depicted as innocent victims of an irrational and oppressive American government. In this sinister but widely accepted portrait of America in the 1940s and 1950s, an idealistic New Dealer (Alger Hiss) was thrown into prison on the perjured testimony of a mentally sick anti-Communist fanatic (Whittaker Chambers), innocent progressives (the Rosenbergs) were sent to the electric chair on trumped-up charges of espionage laced with anti-Semitism, and dozens of blameless civil servants had their careers ruined by the smears of a professional anti-Communist (Elizabeth Bentley). According to this version of events, one government official (Harry White) was killed by a heart attack brought on by Bentley's lies, and another (Laurence Duggan, a senior diplomat) was driven to suicide by more of Chambers's malignant falsehoods. Similarly, in many textbooks President Truman's executive order denying government employment to those who posed security risks, and other laws aimed at espionage and Communist subversion, were and still are described not as having been motivated by a real concern for American security (since the existence of any serious espionage or subversion was denied) but instead as consciously antidemocratic attacks on basic freedoms. As one commentator wrote, "The statute books groaned under several seasons of legislation designed to outlaw dissent."

Despite its central role in the history of American counterintelligence, the Venona Project remained among the most tightly held government secrets. By the time the project shut down, it had decrypted nearly three thousand messages sent between the Soviet Union and its embassies and consulates around the world. Remarkably, although rumors and a few snippets of information about the project had become public in the 1980s, the actual texts and the enormous import of the messages remained secret until 1995. The U.S. government often has been successful in keeping secrets in the short term, but over a longer period secrets, particularly newsworthy ones, have proven to be very difficult for the government to keep. It is all the more amazing, then, how little got out about the Venona Project in the fifty-three years before it was made public.

Unfortunately, the success of government secrecy in this case has seriously distorted our understanding of post-World War II history. Hundreds of books and thousands of essays on McCarthyism, the federal loyalty security program, Soviet espionage, American communism, and the early Cold War have perpetuated many myths that have given Americans a warped view of the nation's history in the 1930s, 1940s, and 1950s. The information that these messages reveal substantially revises the basis for understanding the early history of the Cold War and of America's concern with Soviet espionage and Communist subversion.

In the late 1970s the FBI began releasing material from its hitherto secret files as a consequence of the passage of the Freedom of Information Act (FOIA). Although this act opened some files to public scrutiny, it has not as yet provided access to the full range of FBI investigative records. The enormous backlog of FOIA requests has led to lengthy delays in releasing documents; it is not uncommon to wait more than five years to receive material. Capricious and zealous enforcement of regulations exempting some material from release frequently has elicited useless documents consisting of occasional phrases interspersed with long sections of redacted (blacked-out) text. And, of course, even the unexpurgated FBI files show only what the FBI learned about Soviet espionage and are only part of the story. Even given these hindrances, however, each year more files are opened, and the growing body of FBI documentation has significantly enhanced the opportunity for a reconstruction of what actually happened.

The collapse of the Union of Soviet Socialist Republics in 1991 led to the opening of Soviet archives that had never been examined by independent scholars. The historically rich documentation first made available in Moscow's archives in 1992 has resulted in an outpouring of new historical writing, as these records allow a far more complete and accurate understanding of central events of the twentieth century. But many archives in Russia are open only in part, and some are still closed. In particular, the archives of the foreign intelligence operations of Soviet military intelligence and those of the foreign intelligence arm of the KGB are not open to researchers. Given the institutional continuity between the former Soviet intelligence agencies and their current Russian successors, the opening of these archives is not anticipated anytime soon. However, Soviet intelligence agencies had cooperated with other Soviet institutions, whose newly opened archives therefore hold some intelligence-related material and provide a back door into the still-closed intelligence archives.

But the most significant source of fresh insight into Soviet espionage in the United States comes from the decoded messages produced by the Venona Project. These documents, after all, constitute a portion of the materials that are still locked up in Russian intelligence archives. Not only do the Venona files supply information in their own right, but because of their inherent reliability they also provide a touchstone for judging the credibility of other sources, such as defectors' testimony and FBI investigative files.

Stalin's Espionage Assault on the United States

Through most of the twentieth century, governments of powerful nations have conducted intelligence operations of some sort during both peace and war. None, however, used espionage as an instrument of state policy as extensively as did the Soviet Union under Joseph Stalin. In the late 1920s and 1930s, Stalin directed most of the resources of Soviet intelligence at nearby targets in Europe and Asia. America was still distant from Stalin's immediate concerns, the threat to Soviet goals posed by Nazi Germany and Imperial Japan. This perception changed, however, after the United States entered the world war in December 1941. Stalin realized that once Germany and Japan were defeated, the world would be left with only three powers able to project their influence across the globe: the Soviet Union, Great Britain, and the United States. And of these, the strongest would be the United States. With that in mind, Stalin's intelligence agencies shifted their focus toward America.

The Soviet Union, Great Britain, and the United States formed a military alliance in early 1942 to defeat Nazi Germany and its allies. The Soviet Union quickly became a major recipient of American military (Lend-Lease) aid, second only to Great Britain; it eventually received more than nine billion dollars. As part of the aid arrangements, the United States invited the Soviets to greatly expand their diplomatic staffs and to establish special offices to facilitate aid arrangements. Thousands of Soviet military officers, engineers, and technicians entered the United States to review what aid was available and choose which machinery, weapons, vehicles (nearly 400,000 American trucks went to the Soviet Union), aircraft, and other matériel would most assist the Soviet war effort. Soviet personnel had to be trained to maintain the American equipment, manuals had to be translated into Russian, shipments to the Soviet Union had to be inspected to ensure that what was ordered had been delivered, properly loaded, and dispatched on the right ships. Entire Soviet naval crews arrived for training to take over American combat and cargo ships to be handed over to the Soviet Union.

Scores of Soviet intelligence officers of the KGB (the chief Soviet foreign intelligence and security agency), the GRU (the Soviet military intelligence agency), and the Naval GRU (the Soviet naval intelligence agency) were among the Soviet personnel arriving in America. These intelligence officers pursued two missions. One, security, was only indirectly connected with the United States. The internal security arm of the KGB employed several hundred thousand full-time personnel, assisted by several million part-time informants, to ensure the political loyalty of Soviet citizens. When the Soviets sent thousands of their citizens to the United States to assist with the Lend-Lease arrangement, they sent this internal security apparatus as well. A significant portion of the Venona messages deciphered by American code-breakers reported on this task. The messages show that every Soviet cargo ship that arrived at an American port to pick up Lend-Lease supplies had in its crew at least one, often two, and sometimes three informants who reported either to the KGB or to the Naval GRU. Their task was not to spy on Americans but to watch the Soviet merchant seamen for signs of political dissidence and potential defection. Some of the messages show Soviet security officers tracking down merchant seamen who had jumped ship, kidnapping them, and spiriting them back aboard Soviet ships in disregard of American law. Similarly, other messages discuss informants, recruited or planted by the KGB in every Soviet office in the United States, whose task was to report signs of ideological deviation or potential defection among Soviet personnel.

A second mission of these Soviet intelligence officers, however, was espionage against the United States. . . . The deciphered Venona cables do more than reveal the remarkable success that the Soviet Union had in recruiting spies and gaining access to many important U.S. government agencies and laboratories dealing with secret information. They expose beyond cavil the American Communist party as an auxiliary of the intelligence agencies of the Soviet Union. While not every Soviet spy was a Communist, most were. And while not every American Communist was a spy, hundreds were. The CPUSA itself worked closely with Soviet intelligence agencies to facilitate their espionage. Party leaders were not only aware of the liaison; they actively worked to assist the relationship.

Information from the Venona decryptions underlay the policies of U.S. government officials in their approach to the issue of domestic communism. The investigations and prosecutions of American Communists undertaken by the federal government in the late 1940s and early 1950s were premised on an assumption that the CPUSA had assisted Soviet espionage. This view contributed to the Truman administration's executive order in 1947, reinforced in the early 1950s under the Eisenhower administration, that U.S. government employees be subjected to loyalty and security investigations. The understanding also lay behind the 1948 decision by Truman's attorney general to prosecute the leaders of the CPUSA under the sedition sections of the Smith Act. It was an explicit assumption behind congressional investigations of domestic communism in the late 1940s and 1950s, and it permeated public attitudes toward domestic communism.

The Soviet Union's unrestrained espionage against the United States from 1942 to 1945 was of the type that a nation directs at an enemy state. By the late 1940s the evidence provided by Venona of the massive size and intense hostility of Soviet intelligence operations caused both American counterintelligence professionals and high-level policy-makers to conclude that Stalin had already launched a covert attack on the United States. In their minds, the Soviet espionage offensive indicated that the Cold War had begun not after World War II but many years earlier.

Richard M. Fried

"Bitter Days": The Heyday of Anti-Communism

Even independent of [Joseph] McCarthy, the years 1950–1954 marked the climax of anti-communism in American life. The Korean stalemate generated both a bruising debate over containment and a sourness in national politics. Korea's sapping effect and a series of minor scandals heightened the Democratic Party's anemia. In addition, the 1950 congressional campaign, revealing McCarthyism's apparent sway over the voters and encouraging the GOP's right wing, signaled that anti-communism occupied the core of American political culture. "These," said liberal commentator Elmer Davis in January 1951, "are bitter days—full of envy, hatred, malice, and all uncharitableness."

Critics of these trends in American politics had scant power or spirit. Outside government, foes of anti-Communist excesses moved cautiously lest they be redbaited and rarely took effective countermeasures. Liberals seldom strayed from the safety of the anti-Communist consensus. Radicals met the hostility of the dominant political forces in Cold War America and fared poorly. In government, anti-communism ruled. Senate resistance to McCarthy was scattered and weak. In the House, HUAC [House Un-American Activities Committee] did much as it pleased. [President Harry S.] Truman upheld civil liberties with occasional eloquence, but he remained on the defensive, and his Justice Department often seemed locked in near-alliance with the Right in Congress. [Dwight D.] Eisenhower, when not appeasing the McCarthyites, appeared at times no more able to curb them than had Truman.

Even at his peak, McCarthy was not the sole anti-Communist paladin, though he cultivated that impression. As McCarthyism in its broader sense outlived the personal defeat of McCarthy himself, so, in its prime, it exceeded his reach. Its strength owed much to the wide acceptance, even by McCarthy's critics, of the era's anti-Communist premises. Along with McCarthy, they made the first half of the 1950s the acme of noisy anti-communism and of the ills to which it gave birth.

Soon after the 1950 campaign, skirmishing over the Communist issue renewed in earnest. In December Senator Pat McCarran joined the hunt for subversives by creating the Senate Internal Security Subcommittee (SISS). As chairman of that panel (and the parent Judiciary Committee), the crusty

From Richard M. Fried, *Nightmare in Red: The McCarthy Era in Perspective* (Oxford University Press, 1990). Copyright © 1990 by Oxford University Press, Inc. Reprinted by permission of Oxford University Press, Inc. Notes omitted.

Nevada Democrat packed it with such like-minded colleagues as Democrats James Eastland and Willis Smith and Republicans Homer Ferguson and William Jenner. While McCarthy darted about unpredictably, McCarran moved glacially but steadily to his objective, crushing opposition.

McCarran's panel spotlighted themes that McCarthy had raised giving them a more sympathetic hearing than had the Tydings Committee. In February 1951, federal agents swooped down on a barn in Lee, Massachusetts, seized the dead files of the Institute of Pacific Relations (IPR) and trucked them under guard to Washington. After sifting this haul, a SISS subcommittee opened an extended probe of the IPR, which led to a new inquest on "who lost China" and resulted in renewed loyalty and security proceedings, dismissals from the State Department and prosecution—all to McCarthy's greater, reflected glory.

The subcommittee acquired a reputation—more cultivated than deserved—for honoring due process. SISS was punctilious on some points: evidence was formally introduced (when an excerpt was read, the full text was put in the record); hearings were exhaustive (over 5,000 pages); witnesses were heard in executive session before they named names in public; their credentials and the relevance of their testimony were set forth; and some outward courtesies were extended.

The fairness was only skin-deep, however. Witnesses were badgered about obscure events from years back and about nuances of aging reports. Diplomat John Carter Vincent was even asked if he had plans to move to Sarasota, Florida. When he termed it a most "curious" question, counsel could only suggest that perhaps the Florida Chamber of Commerce had taken an interest. The subcommittee strove to ensnare witnesses in perjury. One China Hand called the sessions "generally Dostoyevskian attacks not only on a man's mind but also his memory." To have predicted Jiang's decline or Mao's rise was interpreted as both premeditating and helping to cause that outcome.

A product of the internationalist do-goodery of YMCA leaders in the 1920s, the IPR sought to promote peace and understanding in the Pacific. It had both national branches in countries interested in the Pacific and an international secretariat. Well funded by corporations and foundations in its palmier days, the IPR had more pedigree than power. McCarran's subcommittee insisted that IPR's publications pushed the Communist line on China. Louis Budenz testified that the Kremlin had assigned Owen Lattimore the job of giving the IPR journal, *Pacific Affairs*, a Party-line tilt. Budenz claimed that when he was in the Party, he received "official communications" describing Lattimore (and several China Hands) as Communists.

McCarran's panel spent a year grilling Lattimore, other IPR officials, and various China experts and diplomats as it tried to knit a fabric of conspiracy out of its evidence and presuppositions. McCarran claimed that, but for the machinations of the coterie that ran IPR, "China today would be free and a bulwark against the further advance of the Red hordes into the Far East." He charged that the IPR-USSR connection had led to infiltration of the government by persons aligned with the Soviets, of faculties by Red professors, and of textbooks by pro-Communist ideas. He called Lattimore "a conscious and articulate instrument of the Soviet conspiracy."

The hearings revealed naiveté about communism, showed that IPR principals had access to important officials during the war, and turned up levels of maneuvering that sullied IPR's reputation for scholarly detachment. Proven or accused Reds did associate with the IPR and may well have sought leverage through it. There were tendentious claims in IPR publications, as in one author's simplistic dichotomy of Mao's "democratic China" and Jiang's "feudal China." Lattimore was a more partisan editor of *Pacific Affairs* than he conceded. However, in political scientist Earl Latham's measured assessment, the hearings "show something less than subversive conspiracy in the making of foreign policy, and something more than quiet routine." Nor was it proven that IPR had much influence over policy. Perhaps the China Hands had been naive to think that a reoriented policy might prevent China's Communists from falling "by default" under Soviet control and thus might maintain American leverage. Yet those who argued that unblinking support of Jiang could have prevented China's "loss" were more naive still.

Unable to prove, in scholarly terms, its thesis of a successful pro-Communist conspiracy against China, SISS could still carry it politically. The loyalty-security program helped enforce it. New charges, however stale, motivated the State Department Loyalty-Security Board to reexamine old cases of suspected employees, even if they had been previously cleared. Moreover, nudged by the Right, Truman toughened the loyalty standard in April 1951, putting a heavier burden of proof on the accused. Thus under Hiram Bingham, a Republican conservative, the Loyalty Review Board ordered new inquiries in cases decided under the old standard. . . .

The purge of the China Hands had long-term impact. American attitudes toward China remained frozen for two decades. Battered by McCarthyite attacks, the State Department's Far Eastern Division assumed a conservative bunkerlike mentality. Selected by President John F. Kennedy to shake the division up, Assistant Secretary of State Averell Harriman found it "a disaster area filled with human wreckage." Personnel who did not bear wounds from previous battles were chosen to handle Asian problems. Vincent's successor on the China desk was an impeccably conservative diplomat whose experience lay in Europe. JFK named an ambassador to South Vietnam whose prior work had been with NATO. In the 1950s, the field of Asian studies felt the blindfold of conformity as the momentum of U.S. foreign policy carried the country toward the vortex of Vietnam.

꒰◉꒱

The IPR Investigation was but one of many inquiries during the early 1950s that delved into Communist activities. The Eighty-first Congress spawned 24 probes of communism; the Eighty-second, 34; and the Eighty-third, 51. HUAC busily sought new triumphs. In 1953, 185 of the 221 Republican Congressmen asked to serve on it. But HUAC faced the problem all monopolies meet when competitors pour into the market. Besides McCarran and McCarthy, a Senate labor subcommittee probed Red influences in labor unions, two committees combed the U.N. Secretariat for Communists, and others dipped an oar in when the occasion arose.

In part HUAC met the competition with strenuous travel. Hearings often bore titles like "Communist Activities in the Chicago Area"—or Los Angeles, Detroit, or Hawaii. The Detroit hearings got a musician fired, a college student expelled, and UAW Local 600 taken over by the national union. In 1956 two Fisher Body employees were called before a HUAC hearing in St. Louis. When angry fellow workers chalked such slogans as "Russia has no Fifth amendment" on auto bodies and staged a work stoppage, the two men were suspended. The impact of junketing congressional probers was often felt in such local fallout rather than in federal punishments (though many witnesses were cited for contempt of Congress). That indeed was the point. A witness might use the Fifth Amendment to avoid perjury charges, but appearing before a committee of Congress left him open to local sanctions.

Lawmakers fretted over communism in the labor movement. The presence of left-wing unionists in a defense plant offered a frequent pretext for congressional excursions. HUAC addressed the issue often; McCarthy, occasionally; House and Senate labor subcommittees paid close heed. The liberal anti-Communist Hubert Humphrey held an inquiry designed both to meet the problem and to protect clean unions from scattershot redbaiting. Lest unions be handled too softly, in 1952 Pat McCarran, Herman Welker, and John Marshall Butler conceived the formidably labeled "Task Force Investigating Communist Domination of Certain Labor Organizations."

Attacks on radical union leadership from both within and without the labor movement proliferated in the early 1950s. During 1952 hearings in Chicago, HUAC jousted with negotiators for the Communist-led United Electrical Workers just as they mounted a strike against International Harvester. In 1953 McCarthy's subcommittee also bedeviled UE locals in New York and Massachusetts. Such hearings often led to firings and encouraged or counterpointed raids by rival unions. They hastened the decline of the left wing of the labor movement.

The UE was beset on all sides. When the anti-communist International United Electrical Workers Union (IUE), led by James Carey, was founded, Truman Administration officials intoned blessings. The Atomic Energy Commission pressured employers like General Electric to freeze out the UE; IUE literature warned that plants represented by the UE would lose defense contracts. The CIO lavishly funded Carey's war with the UE. Three days before a 1950 election to decide control of a Pittsburgh area local, the vocal anti-Communist Judge Michael Musmanno arrived at a plant gate to campaign for the IUE. Bedecked in naval uniform, he was convoyed by a detachment of National Guardsmen, bayonets fixed and flags unfurled. Many local Catholic clergy urged their flocks to vote for the IUE on the basis of anti-communism. Carey's union won a narrow victory.

These labor wars sometimes produced odd bedfellows. Carey criticized McCarthy, but the latter's 1953 Boston hearings helped the IUE keep control of key GE plants in the area. GE management declared before the hearings that it would fire workers who admitted they were Reds; it would suspend those who declined to testify and, if they did not subsequently answer the charges, would dismiss them. Thus besieged, the UE often settled labor disputes on a take-what-it-could basis.

Where left-wing unions maintained reputations for effective bargaining, anti-communism had limited effect. The UE's tactical surrender of its youthful militancy probably eroded its rank-and-file support more than did any redbaiting. Yet the Longshoremen's Union, despite Smith Act prosecutions against its leaders in Hawaii and the effort to deport Harry Bridges, kept control of West Coast docks. (Indeed, having come to tolerate Bridges by the 1950s, business leaders had lost enthusiasm for persecuting him.) Similarly, the Mine, Mill and Smelter Workers Union held onto some strongholds despite recurrent redbaiting. Weaker leftist unions like the United Public Workers or the Fur and Leather Workers succumbed to raiding and harassment.

In an era when mainline labor was cautious, organizing initiatives often did originate with more radical unions and so fell prey to anti-Communist attack. In 1953 a CIO retail workers' union, some of whose organizers were Communists, struck stores in Port Arthur, Texas. A commission of inquiry named by Governor Allen Shivers (then seeking reelection) found "clear and present danger" of Communist sway over Texas labor. Shivers claimed he had foiled a Communist-led union's "well-laid plans to spread its tentacles all along the Gulf Coast and eventually into *your* community." Other Southern organizing drives succumbed to redbaiting too.

By the 1950s, labor's assertiveness had waned; where it persisted, it met defeat; and new organizing drives were few. Internal dissent—indeed, debate— was virtually stilled. Its momentum sapped and its membership reduced by over a third, the CIO merged with the AFL in a 1955 "shotgun wedding." Having won a place within the American consensus, labor paid a dear price to keep it.

Conservatives feared Communist influence in the nation's schools as well as in its factories. The influence of the "Reducators" and of subversive ideas that ranged, in various investigators' minds, from outright communism to "progressive education" perennially intrigued legislators at the state and national levels.

The Communists' long-running control of the New York Teachers Union alarmed the Senate Internal Security Subcommittee. Previously, the 1940–41 Rapp-Coudert inquiry had led to the dismissal of a number of New York City teachers. In 1949 the Board of Education began a new purge. From 1950 to early 1953, twenty-four teachers were fired and thirty-four resigned under investigation. By one estimate, over three hundred New York City teachers lost their jobs in the 1950s. SISS thus served to reinforce local activities with its 1952-53 hearings in New York City. The refusal by Teachers Union leaders to testify about their affiliations established grounds for their dismissal under Section 903 of the city charter.

Ultimately, the probers failed in their aim to expose Marxist-Leninist propagandizing in Gotham's classrooms. Bella Dodd, a former Communist and Teachers Union leader, claimed that Communist teachers who knew Party dogma "cannot help but slant their teaching in that direction." A Queens College professor said he knew a score of students whom the Communists had "ruined" and turned into "misfits." Yet aside from a few parents' complaints and "one case where I think we could prove it," the city's school superintendent had no evidence of indoctrination. Though Communists had obviously acquired great leverage in the Teachers Union, SISS located its best case of university subversion in a book about *China*.

HUAC quizzed educators too, but its scrutiny of the movie industry earned higher returns when it resumed its inquiry into Hollywood in 1951. By then the Hollywood Ten* were in prison, the film industry's opposition to HUAC was shattered, and the blacklist was growing. Fear washed through the movie lots. The economic distress visited on Hollywood by the growth of television further frazzled nerves. Said one witness, the renewed assault was "like taking a pot shot at a wounded animal." When subpoenaed, actress Gale Sondergaard asked the Screen Actors Guild for help, its board rebuffed her, likening her criticism of HUAC to the Communist line. The Screen Directors Guild made its members take a loyalty oath.

Yet few secrets were left to ferret out: the identity of Hollywood's Communists had long ceased to be a mystery. Early in the 1951 hearings, Congressman Francis Walter even asked why it was "material . . . to have the names of people when we already know them?" For HUAC, getting new information had become secondary to conducting ceremonies of exposure and penitence. Would the witness "name names" or not?

Of 110 witnesses subpoenaed in 1951, 58 admitted having had Party involvements. Some cogently explained why they had since disowned communism. Budd Schulberg recalled that while he was writing *What Makes Sammy Run*, the Party told him to submit an outline, confer with its literary authorities, and heed its artistic canons. *The Daily Worker* received his book favorably, but after being updated on Party aesthetics, the reviewer wrote a second piece thrashing the novel. One screenwriter recalled how the Party line on a studio painters' strike shifted perplexingly in 1945: we "could walk through the picket lines in February, and not in June."

Witnesses seeking to steer between punishment and fingering co-workers faced tearing ethical choices. Naming known Reds or those previously named might stave off harm, but this ploy was tinged with moral bankruptcy. Some soured ex-Communists did resist giving names, not wanting, in actor Larry Parks's phrase, to "crawl through the mud to be an informer." Some named each other; some said little, ducking quickly behind the Fifth Amendment. Others told all. The 155 names that writer Martin Berkeley gave set a record. Others gabbed freely. Parrying with humor the oft-asked question—would he defend America against the Soviets?—actor Will Geer, already middle-aged, cheerfully agreed to fight in his way: growing vegetables and entertaining the wounded. The idea of people his vintage shouldering arms amused him; wars "would be negotiated immediately."

In this as in all inquiries, witnesses trod a path set with snares. The courts disallowed the Hollywood Ten's use of the First Amendment to avoid testifying, so a witness's only protection was the Fifth Amendment guarantee against self-incrimination. Even this route crossed minefields. *Blau v. U.S.*

---

*[The Hollywood Ten were members of the film industry who refused to testify before Congress in 1947 about communist infiltration of the industry.—Ed.]

(1950) ruled that one might plead the Fifth legitimately to the question of Party membership. However, the 1950 case of *Rogers v. U.S.* dictated caution: one had to invoke the Fifth at the outset, not in the middle, of a line of questions inching toward incrimination. Having testified that she herself held a Party office, the court ruled, Jane Rogers had waived her Fifth Amendment privilege and could not then refuse to testify about others.

HUAC tried to quick-march Fifth-takers into pitfalls. One gambit was a logical fork: if answering would incriminate him, a witness might use the Fifth; but if innocent, he could not honestly do so. Thus, the committee held, the witness was either guilty or lying—even though the courts did not accept this presumption of guilt. However, a new odious category, the "Fifth-Amendment Communist," was born. Such witnesses, whether teachers, actors, or others, rarely hung onto their jobs.

Legal precedent also demanded care in testifying about associations. One witness pled the Fifth in response to the question of whether he was a member of the American Automobile Association. HUAC members enjoyed asking if witnesses belonged to the Ku Klux Klan, hoping to nettle them into breaking a string of refusals to answer. On their part, witnesses devised novel defenses like the so-called "diminished Fifth." A witness resorting to the "slightly diminished Fifth" would deny present CP membership but refuse to open up his past or that of others; those using the "fully diminished Fifth," on the other hand, testified about their own pasts but no one else's. (The "augmented Fifth" was like the slightly diminished Fifth, but the witness also disclaimed any sympathy for communism.)

The question of whether to testify freely or take the Fifth convulsed the higher precincts of American arts and letters. Writer Lillian Hellman, subpoenaed in 1952, took the bold step of writing HUAC's chairman that she would take the Fifth only if asked to talk about others. She realized that by answering questions about herself, she waived her privilege and was subject to a contempt citation, but better that than to "bring bad trouble" to innocent people. She simply would not cut her conscience "to fit this year's fashions." When she testified, she did invoke the Fifth but scored a coup with her eloquent letter and managed to avoid a contempt citation. In 1956 the playwright Arthur Miller also refused to discuss other people but, unlike Hellman, did not take the Fifth. (His contempt citation was later overturned.)

Art came to mirror politics. Miller had previously written *The Crucible*, whose hero welcomed death rather than implicate others in the seventeenth-century Salem witch trials. Admirers stressed the play's relevance to modern witch-hunts. In contrast, Elia Kazan, who had named names, directed the smash movie *On the Waterfront*, whose hero (Marlon Brando), implored by a fighting priest (Karl Malden) to speak out, agreed to inform against criminals in a longshoremen's union. None of these works dealt with communism, but their pertinence to current political issues was not lost. Among the arbiters of American culture, these moral choices prompted heated debate, which still reverberated in the 1980s.

The issues were not only philosophical. The sanctions were real. Noncooperative witnesses were blacklisted, their careers in Hollywood shattered.

Many drifted into other lines of work. Many became exiles, moving to Europe, Mexico, or New York. Some suffered writer's block. Some families endured steady FBI surveillance and such vexations as sharply increased life insurance premiums (for an assertedly dangerous occupation). Being blacklisted so dispirited several actors that their health was impaired, and premature death resulted. Comedian Philip Loeb, blacklisted and unemployable, his family destroyed, committed suicide in 1955.

Even though several hundred members of the entertainment industry forfeited their livelihoods after HUAC appearances, the studios, networks, producers, and the committee itself did not admit publicly that a blacklist existed. (Privately, some were candid. "Pal, you're dead," a soused producer told writer Millard Lampell. "They told me that I couldn't touch you with a barge pole.") In this shadow world, performers and writers wondered if their talents had indeed eroded. Had one's voice sharpened, one's humor dulled?

For blacklisting to work, HUAC's hammer needed an anvil. It was duly provided by other groups who willingly punished hostile or reluctant witnesses. American Legion publications spread the word about movies whose credits were fouled by subversion; Legionnaires (and other local true believers) could pressure theatre owners, if necessary, by trooping down to the Bijou to picket offending films. The mere threat of such forces soon choked off the supply of objectionable pictures at the source. Indeed, Hollywood, responding to broad hints from HUAC and to its own reading of the political climate, began making anti-Communist potboilers. These low-budget "B" pictures did poorly at the box office. They provided insurance, not profits.

Though entertainment industry moguls justified screening employees' politics by citing the threat from amateur censors, usually professional blacklisters made the system work. Blacklisting opened up business vistas on the Right. In 1950 American Business Consultants, founded by three ex-FBI agents, published *Red Channels*, a compendium listing 151 entertainers and their Communist-front links. *Counterattack*, an ABC publication started in 1947, periodically offered the same type of information. In 1953 an employee left ABC to establish Aware, Inc., which sold a similar service. Companies in show biz subscribed to these countersubversive finding aids and paid to have the names of those they might hire for a show or series checked against "the files." Aware charged five dollars to vet a name for the first time, two dollars for rechecks. It became habit for Hollywood, radio and TV networks, advertisers, and stage producers (though blacklisting had its weakest hold on Broadway) not to employ entertainers whose names cropped up in such files.

A few found ways to evade total proscription. Writers could sometimes submit work under pseudonyms. Studios asked some writers on the blacklist to doctor ailing scripts authored by others. The blacklisted writers received no screen credits and were paid a pittance, but at least they were working. Ostracized actors did not have this option. Said comedian Zero Mostel: "I am a man of a thousand faces, all of them blacklisted." A TV producer once called a talent agent to ask, "Who have you got like John Garfield?" He had Garfield himself, the agent exclaimed; but, of course, the blacklisted Garfield was taboo.

Unlike actors, blacklisted writers could also find work in television, which devoured new scripts ravenously. As in film, some used assumed names. Others worked through "fronts" (whence came the title of Woody Allen's 1976 movie). They wrote, but someone else put his name to the script (and might demand up to half of the income). Mistaken-identity plot twists worthy of a Restoration comedy resulted. One writer using a pseudonym wrote a script that he was asked, under a second pseudonym, to revise. Millard Lampell submitted a script under a phony name; the producers insisted that the script's writer appear for consultation; told that he was away and unavailable, they went for a quick fix: they asked Lampell to rewrite his own (unacknowledged) script.

The obverse of blacklisting was "clearance." Desperate actors or writers could seek absolution from a member of the anti-Communist industry. Often, not surprisingly, the person to see was one who had played a part in creating the blacklist. Roy Brewer, the chief of the International Alliance of Theatrical Stage Employees, had redbaited the leftist craft guilds, but helped rehabilitate blacklistees, as did several conservative newspaper columnists. The American Legion, which issued lists of Hollywood's undesirables, also certified innocence or repentance. A listee might get by with writing a letter to the Legion. Or he might be made to list suspect organizations he had joined and to tell why he joined, when he quit, who invited him in, and whom he had enticed. Thus the written route to clearance might also require naming names.

To regain grace, some sinners had to repent publicly, express robust patriotism in a speech or article, or confess to having been duped into supporting leftist causes. Typically, a blacklistee had to be willing to tell all to the FBI or to HUAC. Even liberal anti-Communists were "graylisted," and some had to write clearance letters. Humphrey Bogart had bought trouble by protesting the 1947 HUAC hearings against the Hollywood Ten. In his article, "I'm No Communist," he admitted he had been a "dope" in politics. Actor John Garfield, whose appearance before HUAC sent his career and life into a tailspin, was at the time of his death about to publish an article titled "I Was a Sucker for a Left Hook."

Like teachers and entertainers, charitable foundations also triggered the suspicion of congressional anti-Communists. These products of capitalism plowed back into society some of the vast wealth of their Robber Baron founders, but conservatives found their philanthropic tastes too radical. In 1952 a special House committee led by Georgia conservative Eugene Cox inquired into the policies of tax-exempt foundations. Did not "these creatures of the capitalist system," asked Cox, seek to "bring the system into disrepute" and to assume "a socialistic leaning"? . . .

How deeply did anti-communism gouge the social and political terrain of the 1950s? With dissent defined as dangerous, the range of political debate obviously was crimped. The number of times that books were labeled dangerous, thoughts were scourged as harmful, and speakers and performers were rejected as outside the pale multiplied. Anti-Communist extremism and accompanying pressures toward conformity had impact in such areas as artistic expression, the labor movement, the cause of civil rights, and the status of minorities in American life.

For some denizens of the Right, threats of Communist influence materialized almost anywhere. For instance, Illinois American Legionnaires warned that the Girl Scouts were being spoonfed subversive doctrines. Jack Lait and Lee Mortimer's yellow-journalistic *U.S.A. Confidential* warned parents against the emerging threat of rock and roll. It bred dope use, interracialism, and sex orgies. "We know that many platter-spinners are hopheads. Many others are Reds, left-wingers, or hecklers of social convention." Not every absurdity owed life to the vigilantes, however. A jittery Hollywood studio cancelled a movie based on Longfellow's "Hiawatha" for fear it would be viewed as "Communist peace propaganda."

Books and ideas remained vulnerable. It is true that the militant Indiana woman who abhorred *Robin Hood's* subversive rob-from-the-rich-and-give-to-the-poor message failed to get it banned from school libraries. Other locales were less lucky. A committee of women appointed by the school board of Sapulpa, Oklahoma, had more success. The board burned those books that it classified as dealing improperly with socialism or sex. A spokesman claimed that only five or six "volumes of no consequence" were destroyed. A librarian in Bartlesville, Oklahoma, was fired for subscribing to the *New Republic, Nation,* and *Negro Digest.* The use of UNESCO [United Nations Educational, Scientific, and Cultural Organization] materials in the Los Angeles schools became a hot issue in 1952. A new school board and superintendent were elected with a mandate to remove such books from school libraries.

Local sanctions against unpopular artists and speakers often were effective. In August 1950, a New Hampshire resort hotel banned a talk by Owen Lattimore after guests, apparently riled by protests of the Daughters of the American Revolution and others, remonstrated. Often local veterans—the American Legion and Catholic War Veterans—initiated pressures. The commander of an American Legion Post in Omaha protested a local production of a play whose author, Garson Kanin, was listed in *Red Channels.* A founder of *Red Channels* warned an American Legion anti-subversive seminar in Peoria, Illinois, that Arthur Miller's *Death of a Salesman,* soon to appear locally, was "a Communist dominated play." Jaycees and Legionnaires failed to get the theatre to cancel the play, but the boycott they mounted sharply curbed the size of the audience.

Libraries often became focal points of cultural anxieties. Not every confrontation ended like those in Los Angeles or Sapulpa, but librarians felt they were under the gun. "I just put a book that is complained about away for a while," said one public librarian. Occasionally, books were burned. "Did you ever try to burn a book?" asked another librarian. "It's *very* difficult." Onethird of a group of librarians sampled in the late 1950s reported having removed "controversial" items from their shelves. One-fifth said they habitually avoided buying such books.

Academics, too, were scared. Many college and university social scientists polled in 1955 confessed to reining in their political views and activities. Twenty-seven percent had "wondered" whether a political opinion they had expressed might affect their job security or promotion; 40 percent had worried that a student might pass on "a warped version of what you have said and lead to false ideas about your political views." Twenty-two percent had at times "refrained from expressing an opinion or participating in some activity in order not to embarrass" their institution. Nine percent had "toned down" recent writing to avoid controversy. One teacher said he never expressed his own opinion in class. "I express the recognized and acknowledged point of view." Some instructors no longer assigned *The Communist Manifesto*.

About a hundred professors actually lost jobs, but an even greater number of frightened faculty trimmed their sails against the storm. Episodes far short of dismissal could also have a chilling effect. An economist at a Southern school addressed a business group, his talk, titled "Know Your Enemy," assessed Soviet resources and strengths. He was denounced to his president as a Communist. Another professor was assailed for advocating a lower tariff on oranges. "If I'd said potatoes, I wouldn't have been accused unless I had said it in Idaho." Some teachers got in mild trouble for such acts as assigning Robert and Helen Lynds' classic sociological study, *Middletown*, in class or listing the Kinsey reports on human sexuality as recommended reading. A professor once sent students to a public library to read works by Marx because his college's library had too few copies. Librarians logged the students' names.

The precise effect of all this professed anxiety was fuzzy. Many liberals claimed that Americans had been cowed into silence, that even honest anti-Communist dissent had been stilled, and that basic freedoms of thought, expression, and association had languished. The worriers trotted out appropriate comparisons: the witch trials in Salem, the Reign of Terror in France, the Alien and Sedition Acts, Know-Nothingism, and the Palmer raids. Justice William O. Douglas warned of "The Black Silence of Fear." Prominent foreigners like Bertrand Russell and Graham Greene decried the pall of fear they observed in America. On July 4, 1951, a *Madison Capital-Times* reporter asked passersby to sign a paper containing the Bill of Rights and parts of the Declaration of Independence. Out of 112, only one would do so. President Truman cited the episode to show McCarthyism's dire effects. McCarthy retorted that Truman owed an apology to the people of Wisconsin in view of that paper's Communist-line policies. Some McCarthy allies upheld the wisdom of refusing to sign any statement promiscuously offered.

McCarthy's defenders ridiculed the more outlandish laments for vanished liberties. A New York rabbi who blamed "McCarthyism" for the current spree of college "panty raids" offered a case in point. Conservative journalist Eugene Lyons was amused by an ACLU spokesman, his tonsils flaring in close-up on television, arguing "that in America no one any longer dares open his mouth." Such talk, said Lyons, led to "hysteria over hysteria." In their apologia for McCarthy, William F. Buckley and L. Brent Bozell snickered at such silliness. They found it odd that, in a time when left-of-center ideas were supposedly being crushed, liberals seemed to monopolize symposia sponsored by the major universities, even in McCarthy's home state, and that Archibald MacLeish and Bernard De Voto, two of those who condemned the enervating climate of fear, had still managed to garner two National Book

Awards and a Pulitzer Prize. To Buckley and Bozell, the only conformity present was a proper one—a consensus that communism was evil and must be fought wholeheartedly.

But did such an argument miss the point? The successes enjoyed by prominent, secure liberals were one thing; far more numerous were the cases of those less visible and secure who lost entertainment and lecture bookings, chances to review books, teaching posts, even assembly-line jobs. The fight over the Communist menace had gone far beyond roistering debate or asserting the right of those who disagree with a set of views not to patronize them. People, a great number of whom had committed no crime, were made to suffer.

POSTSCRIPT

Did Communism Threaten America's Internal Security After World War II?

$\mathbf{T}$he "Venona Transcripts" represent only one set of sources depicting the Soviet spy apparatus in the United States. The Venona papers were not released to the public until 1995. Haynes and Klehr have also collaborated on two recent documentary collections based on the archives of the American Communist Party, which had been stored for decades in Moscow and were opened to foreign researchers in 1992. See *The Secret World of American Communism* (Yale University Press, 1995) and *The Soviet World of American Communism* (Yale University Press, 1998), both of which contain useful collections of translated Russian documents, which are virtually impossible to access. Haynes and Klehr's work also substantiates charges made by Allen Weinstein and his translator, former KGB agent Aleksandr Vassilieo, in *The Haunted Wood: Soviet Espionage in America* (Random House, 1999).

According to Fried, 24 teachers from New York City were fired and 34 resigned while under investigation between 1950 and early 1953. According to one estimate, over 300 teachers in the city lost their jobs because of their political beliefs. Similar dismissals took place in public universities and colleges across the country. Book burnings were rare, but many public libraries discarded pro-Communist books or put them in storage. In Bartlesville, Oklahoma, in 1950, librarian Ruth Brown was fired from her job after 30 years, ostensibly for circulating magazines like *The New Republic* and *The Nation*, which were deemed subversive. Actually, many agree that she was fired for supporting civil rights activism, a fact that the American Library Association left out when defending her. See Louise S. Robinson, *The Dismissal of Miss Ruth Brown: Civil Rights, Censorship, and the American Library* (University of Oklahoma Press, 2000).

Four books represent a good starting point for students: M. J. Heale, *American Anticommunism: Combating the Enemy Within, 1830–1970* (Johns Hopkins University Press, 1990) extends Americans' fears of subversion back to the Andrew Jackson years; Ellen Schrecker, *The Age of McCarthyism: A Brief History With Documents* (Bedford Books, 1994) blames both political parties for the excesses of the anti-Communist assault against radicals who were fighting against status quo race relations in the 1930s and 1940s; John Earl Haynes, *Red Scare or Red Menace? American Communism and Anticommunism in the Cold War* Era (Ivan R. Dee, 1996), which argues that anticommunism was a reasonable response to a real threat; and Richard Gid Powers, *Not Without Honor: The History of American Anticommunism* (Free Press, 1995), which portrays anticommunism as a mainstream political movement with many variations.

ISSUE 13

Did the *Brown* Decision Fail to Desegregate and Improve the Status of African Americans?

YES: Peter Irons, from *Jim Crow's Children: The Broken Promise of the Brown Decision* (Viking Press, 2002)

NO: Richard Kluger, from *Simple Justice: The History of Brown v. Board of Education and Black America's Struggle for Equality* (Alfred A. Knopf, 2004)

ISSUE SUMMARY

YES: Peter Irons argues that, despite evidence that integration improves the status of African Americans, the school integration prescribed by the *Brown* decision was never seriously tried, with the consequence that major gaps between white and black achievement persist and contribute to many of the social problems confronting African Americans today.

NO: Richard Kluger concludes that fifty years after the *Brown* decision, African Americans are better educated, better housed, and better employed than they were before 1954 in large part because the Supreme Court's ruling spawned the modern civil rights movement that culminated in the Civil Rights Act of 1964, the 1965 Voting Rights Act, and many programs of Lyndon Johnson's Great Society that were designed to improve the status of African Americans.

On May 17, 1954, the United States Supreme Court announced the results of its deliberation in the cases of *Brown v. Board of Education of Topeka et al.* In a unanimous decision engineered by new Chief Justice Earl Warren, the Court paved the way for the collapse of a legally supported racial segregation system that had dominated black-white relations in the United States. This landmark ruling also represented a victory for the National Association for the Advancement of Colored People (NAACP), the nation's leading civil rights organization.

The Court's decision created a generally celebratory atmosphere throughout the nation's African American communities, despite the fact that many blacks remained concerned about the ultimate impact the end of Jim Crow schools would have on those black educators who had derived their professional livelihoods from the separate educational systems in the South. Most, however, saw the case as a vital step in finally eliminating separate and unequal facilities throughout the country. In contrast, the *Brown* decision sent shock waves through the white South, and even as local school board representatives publicly announced that they would comply with the Court's ruling, back-channel efforts were quickly underway to block biracial schools. Unintentionally aided by the Supreme Court's refusal to establish a definite time frame by which desegregation of public schools should take place, many white southerners interpreted the Court's dictum to act "with all deliberate speed" to mean "never." Claiming that they were only protecting ancient regional mores from the intrusive arm of the federal government, these individuals followed the lead of a group of over 100 southern Congressmen who signed "The Southern Manifesto," which charged the Warren Court with abuse of power and pledged resistance to the enforcement of *Brown*. In the face of this program of "massive resistance," brief episodes of school integration, such as in Little Rock, Arkansas, in 1957, proved to be the exceptions to the rule, and by 1964 only 2 percent of the African American students in the South attended integrated schools. Not until the Supreme Court invalidated "freedom of choice" plans in the South and endorsed busing as an instrument of desegregation did the *Brown* decision have much impact. By 1972, some 37 percent of all African American students in the states of the former Confederacy were attending majority white schools; this figure peaked in 1988 at 43 percent. Busing, however, was a highly controversial remedy that generated resistance for the first time in the North, especially in Boston, which was ravaged by riots and racial violence.

Since the 1990s, the Supreme Court has seemed to turn away from the model set by the Warren Court and made it easier for school districts to avoid desegregation orders already in place. Similarly, the Court has stymied many affirmative action plans designed by universities and professional schools to diversify their student populations. In addition, some African American leaders have begun working to re-establish strong schools for their children within black neighborhoods rather than relying upon instruction at predominately white schools. As a result, "resegregation" is a term that has emerged to describe the reality of the nation's educational system in the early twenty-first century.

The selections that follow summarize the results of desegregation since 1954 and assess the legacy of *Brown* for African Americans and the nation as a whole. In the first essay, Peter Irons concludes that despite evidence that integration works, it was never seriously tried in much of the country. Consequently, a gap remains between blacks and whites. The Court's ruling in *Brown*, says Irons, remains unfulfilled.

In the second essay, Richard Kluger offers a more optimistic appraisal. In an updated version of his definitive study *Simple Justice* first published in 1976, Kluger contends that with the aid of the *Brown* decision, desegregation proceeded at a relatively rapid pace, despite southern defiance, and set the stage for key civil rights successes that continue to benefit the African American community.

Jim Crow's Children: The Broken Promise of the *Brown* Decision

Linda Brown was eight years old and in the third grade at Monroe Elementary School in Topeka, Kansas, when the case bearing her name was filed on February 28, 1951. This two-story brick building had thirteen classrooms and served black students from kindergarten through eighth grade. Directly across the street from the school was a playground area, where the older students played softball. Younger children used smaller playgrounds on the north and south ends of the building.

Today, the Monroe school has been transformed into a museum, where visitors can troop through the renovated classrooms, look at photo displays, and watch a video about the history of the *Brown* case. The weed-covered playground across from the school has been spruced up, and friendly, helpful guides from the National Park Service are ready to answer questions about the school and the historic case that challenged the segregation imposed on Linda Brown and other black children in Topeka's elementary schools. One question, however, lies beyond their ability to answer. Have things improved for Topeka's black students in the years since the Supreme Court decided in 1954 that Jim Crow schools violated the Constitution? One person with an answer to that question is Linda Brown, who still lives in Topeka and whose children and grandchildren attended integrated schools. "Sometimes I wonder if we really did the children and the nation a favor by taking this case to the Supreme Court," she told a reporter in 1994, who visited Topeka on the fortieth anniversary of the *Brown* decision. "I knew it was the right thing for my father and others to do then," she said. "But after nearly forty years, we find the court's ruling remains unfulfilled." . . .

One salient fact underscores [the] discussion of Jim Crow education over the past two centuries: there has not been a single year in American history in which at least half of the nations black children attended schools that were largely white. To be sure, pushing school integration past this "halfway" point was never the goal of the civil rights lawyers and activists who labored for so long to end the system of de jure segregation that separated black and white students in southern and order states. Their goal was simply to make sure that school assignments were no longer based solely on race. At the same time, however, many of these lawyers and activists pursued the larger, more ambitious goal of using the courts to achieve the maximum possible racial mixture of students. They urged the courts to order school boards and officials to employ a variety of means—including busing and "metropolitan" desegregation plans—that would overcome the entrenched de facto segregation of residential areas and their neighborhood schools. The failure of those efforts, after the political backlash that ended the short-lived period of "forced busing," cannot be entirely blamed on the Supreme Court and the decisions that ended judicial supervision of school districts that had achieved "unitary" status. Yet, the Court quite clearly yielded to political pressure, and reflected in its decisions the increasingly conservative mood of the American public, which has endorsed school integration in numerous public opinion polls but has balked at concrete plans to implement that policy in their own cities and neighborhoods. It is fair to conclude that school integration has failed, or—put more honestly—was never seriously tried.

The failure of integration over the past half-century, after the imposition by law during the previous century of inferior Jim Crow schools on the vast majority of black children, adds force to the statement of Justice John Marshall Harlan in 1896 that whites constituted the dominant race "in prestige, in achievements, in education, in wealth and in power." The historic and persisting gap between blacks and white—measured by any part of Harlan's yardstick—is largely the consequence of generations of Jim Crow education. This single factor lies at the root of the problems that afflict or touch virtually every member of America's urban black population of some 25 million people: higher rates of crime, domestic violence, drug and alcohol abuse, teen pregnancy, low-wage jobs, unemployment, infant mortality, lowered life expectancy, and many other indices of social pathology. Singling out one factor to explain a multitude of complex social problems may appear simplistic and reductionist. But there is no denying that the system of Jim Crow schooling has given millions of America's black residents inferior education as children, has consigned them to unskilled jobs as adults, and has made it difficult to escape the urban ghettos into which rural migrants were confined by poverty and white hostility.

There is also no denying that many blacks have overcome the legacy of Jim Crow education and have joined a growing black middle class. The numbers of black doctors, lawyers, engineers, managers, and other professionals have increased since the adoption of "affirmative action" plans by colleges, corporations, and government agencies. But, much like school integration imposed through busing, affirmative action plans imposed through racial "preferences" have produced their own political backlash; federal judges have struck down such programs at the University of Texas and other schools, and the Supreme Court has rejected minority "set-aside" plans designed to channel more public funds to minority-owned firms. Even the modest gains in black education and employment have been slowed, and in some cases reversed, as the economic boom of the 1990s has gone bust and given way to recession and retrenchment in recent years.

One measure of the damaging impact of school resegregation on black students can be found in the report issued in August 2001 of the federally funded National Assessment of Educational Progress on tests of math skills of students in the fourth, eighth, and twelfth grades. On the positive side, the NEAP report showed that the math scores of fourth- and eighth-graders had improved since 1990. Disturbingly, the scores of high school seniors, which had risen slightly during the past decade, dropped sharply between 1996 and 2000. Broken down by race, the NEAP figures show a huge performance gap between black and white students at every grade level. For example, the number of white eighth-graders who scored at the "proficient" or "advanced" levels in math grew from 19 percent in 1990 to 34 percent in 2000, while only 5 percent of blacks scored at those levels in both years. Educational experts attributed the decline in twelfth-grade scores of black students to the substandard schools which most attend. Ann Wilkens of the Educational Trust, a nonprofit organization that works to improve urban schools, stressed the impact of poor math skills on the job prospects of black students. Back in the 1950s, "people could go to work in factories with basic skills," she said. "But in the 1990s, you're seeing a growing gap between the races in the ability to participate at the high levels of society."

Studies like the NEAP report, and similar measures of academic performance on the SAT test, provide growing evidence that the increasing resegregation of American public schools is threatening to turn the "growing gap" between black and white students into a racial chasm. The failure of school integration, largely a consequence of the broken promise of the *Brown* decision, becomes an even more bitter pill to swallow in light of the clear evidence that integration works. More precisely, attending school with substantial numbers of white students improves the academic performance of black children. This reflects, of course, the advantages that majority-white schools have in terms of better-trained, more experienced, and more highly paid teachers, with access to better laboratory and library resources, a wider range of courses, particularly the Advanced Placement courses that challenge students and prepare them for college-level work, and a greater number and variety of extracurricular activities.

In his 2001 report, *Schools More Separate*, Gary Orfield of the Harvard Civil Rights Project summed up the demonstrated benefits of integrated schools for black students. Orfield cited "evidence that students from desegregated educational experiences benefit in terms of college going, employment, and living in integrated settings as adults." Black students who attend integrated high schools, and who then graduate from integrated colleges and universities, make up the majority of black professionals. Orfield and his colleague, Dean Whitla, released a study in 1999 on *Diversity and Legal Education*, which focused on elite laws schools and reported that "almost all of the black and Latino students who made it into those schools came from integrated educational backgrounds."

Integrated education has benefits that go beyond academic performance. A report by Michael Kurleander and John Yun of the Harvard Civil Rights Project in 2000 compiled surveys of students, concluding that "both white and minority students in integrated school districts tend to report by large majorities that they have learned to study and work together and that they are highly confident about their ability to work in such settings as adults. Students report that they have learned a lot about the other group's background and feel confident about the ability to discuss even controversial racial issues across racial lines." These studies illustrate the truth of Thurgood Marshall's statement, during his argument before the Supreme Court of the Little Rock school case in 1958. "Education is not the teaching of the three R's. Education is the teaching of the overall citizenship, to learn to live together with fellow citizens," Marshall told the justices.

Many people, liberals and conservatives alike, believe that the Supreme Court ended the Jim Crow system with its historic *Brown* decision in 1954. Those who profess this belief also claim that black students, now able to compete with whites on a level playing field, have only themselves to blame for doing poorly in school and failing to achieve the test scores required for admission to prestigious colleges. These advocates of "blaming the victim" fail to recognize any connection between the social and economic problems that burden the black ghetto population, and the Jim Crow educational system that has created and perpetuates the urban black underclass. After all, they argue, more than two generations of blacks have gone to schools that are no longer segregated by race, and are protected from discrimination in finding jobs and places to live by federal and state civil rights laws. Consequently, those blacks who can't find decent jobs, and who live in decaying urban ghettos, cannot blame the Jim Crow schools of past generations for their problems. Nor can they blame the Supreme Court for deciding that "resegregation" based on residential housing patterns is not something that federal judges can remedy, and for allowing the number of one-race schools to increase every year.

In my opinion, those who argue that courts have no further responsibility to remedy the damaging effects of Jim Crow schooling on America's black population are either naive or callous. To assume that two generations of "desegregation" can erase the educational harm of the preceding five or six generations is simply wrong. Studies of the continuing impact of yesterday's Jim Crow schools on today's black children are persuasive. The best compilation of these studies, *The Black-White Test Score Gap*, edited in 1998 by Christopher Jencks and Meredith Phillips, argues that grandparents "pass along their advantages and disadvantages to parents, who then pass them along to the next generation of children." Pushed back several generations, this commonsense observation has a cumulative and highly damaging effect, given the very low educational levels of blacks during the century before the *Brown* decision. Even when black families match whites in years of schooling and income, "it can take more than one generation for successful families to adopt the 'middle-class' parenting practices that seem most likely to increase children's cognitive skills." Jencks and Phillips conclude that "it could take several generations before reductions in socioeconomic inequality produce their full benefits" in higher school performance by black children.

A paradox emerges from these studies. If the past effects of Jim Crow schooling have such harmful consequences on today's black students, what benefits would they obtain from greater "reintegration" of schools? Many black leaders and educators have given up on the ideal of integration and now press for improving the quality of the one-race schools that most urban black children attend. "At this political moment, integration of the schools has been an abysmal failure," Doris Y. Wilkinson wrote in 1996. A leading black sociologist at the University of Kentucky, Wilkinson argues that the "benefits gained from obligatory school integration do not outweigh the immeasurable cultural and psychological losses." These losses include the black school as a community center and resource, the leadership training of black students in their own teams, clubs, and activities, and the close involvement of black parents in their children's education. "What has been neglected in integration history" since the *Brown* decision, Wilkinson claims, "has been a rational assessment of the emotional, motivational, learning, and community impact of abolishing the black school on poor and working-class African American children."

Another black sociologist, Leslie Innis of Florida State University, was herself a "desegregation pioneer" in the 1960s. Her study of other blacks who were among the first to attend formerly white schools shows that "the pioneers generally feel they have paid too high an emotional and psychological price for what they now perceive as too little change in the "whole system of race relations." The pioneers "do not seem to have fared any better in terms of objective social status criteria such as education, occupation, and income than their peers who went to segregated schools," writes Innis. She asserts that a "deepening dissatisfaction with the educational system has created feelings of alienation and anger" among many blacks. "These feelings have generated a call for new educational policies to be considered. Among these new policies are schools that are racially separate but equal in all important aspects—buildings, facilities, books, and personnel."

Given the growing chorus of black educators and activists who have literally given up on integration, would it not be more helpful to the millions of black children who now attend virtually all-black schools to abandon the futile efforts to achieve racial balance through busing and other means of moving children from their neighborhood schools? In place of these policies, for which there currently exists hardly any political clout, why not campaign for better-trained and better-paid teachers in urban schools, new buildings, more computers and science labs, and more rigorous standards in language and math skills? These are, in fact, the proposals to improve American schools that are currently fashionable. Other plans—giving vouchers for private school tuition to children from "failing" public schools, creating more "magnet" schools with specialized programs, expanding the Teacher Corps of highly motivated college graduates—have gained influential sponsors in Congress and state governments.

However laudable their goals, these and other "school reform" proposals have two major drawbacks. First, they do not address the serious problems of the "total environment" of the urban ghettos in which close to half of all black children live. This is the environment with high crime rates, low income, few cultural resources, and very high rates—more than 70 percent in most big cities—of female-headed households in which single mothers have little time or energy to help their children with homework, and most often are barely literate themselves. However good their schools and teachers, black children from this environment come to school with obstacles to effective learning that few white children must overcome.

The second drawback of current school reform proposals is that they rely largely on standardized testing to measure results. One consequence of " teaching to the test" is that school officials pressure teachers to rely on old-fashioned methods of rote learning, the mainstay of Jim Crow schools before the *Brown* decision. Creativity, curiosity, and critical thinking are stifled, and the pressure on teachers in largely black and Hispanic schools to raise test scores and avoid "failing" grades for their schools becomes intense. *The New York Times* reported in June 2001 that many fourth-grade teachers in the city's schools, the grade in which testing begins, are requesting transfers to other grades, to escape the "test pressure" that forces them to use a lockstep curriculum.

If the current push for school reforms that will not change the unbalanced racial composition of most schools means that integration has failed, is there any point in assigning the blame for this failure? We can point the finger at individuals and institutions: Justice Felix Frankfurter's insistence on the "all deliberate speed" formula in the second *Brown* decision; President Dwight Eisenhower's failure to speak out in support of court orders; the "war on the Constitution" waged by Governor Orval Faubus and other southern politicians; the Supreme Court's refusal to allow school buses to cross district lines in the *Milliken* case; and the Court's explicit approval of "one-race" schools in decisions that ended judicial oversight of desegregation orders. In a broader sense, however, the blame rests with the "dominant race" in America. Whites created the institution of slavery; whites fashioned the Jim Crow system that replaced slavery with segregation; whites spat on black children, threw rocks at buses, and shut down entire school districts to avoid integration; and white parents abandoned the cities when neighborhoods and schools passed the "tipping point" and became too black for comfort.

This is not an indictment of a race, merely an acknowledgment of reality. Many whites took part in the abolitionist crusade, fought and died in the Civil War to end slavery, campaigned to end the Jim Crow system, and kept their children in public schools that had become largely black. Most white Americans, in fact, profess their belief in school integration; two-thirds of those polled in 1994 agreed that integration has "improved the quality of education for blacks," and two-fifths said the same for white students. Belief in an ideal and support for its implementation, however, are not the same. Substantially more than two-thirds of whites oppose busing for "racial balance" in the schools, and most say they would move out of their present neighborhood if it became more than 20 percent black. The phenomenon of "white flight" shows that many people have put their attitudes into action.

Perhaps we should accept the reality that Jim Crow schools are here to stay, and make the best of the situation. Kenneth W. Jenkins, who headed the NAACP chapter in Yonkers, New York, was removed from that post by the national organization in 1996 for questioning the protracted litigation to integrate his city's segregated schools. "This thing is not working," he said. "I support integration, but I don't think integration is the goal. The goal is quality education." Even a dedicated NAACP lawyer, Ted Shaw, voiced his frustration at the futility of litigation to integrate urban schools. "You're beating your head up against the wall until it's bloody. At some point you have to ask, 'Should I continue to beat up against this wall?' To ask that question is not a terrible thing."

Perhaps the best person to answer Jenkins and Shaw, and others who share their frustration—white and black alike—is Thurgood Marshall, who put his whole life into struggling against the Jim Crow system. It is worth repeating here the words he wrote in 1974, dissenting in the *Milliken* case: " Desegregation is not and was never expected to be an easy task. Racial attitudes ingrained in our Nation's childhood and adolescence are not quickly thrown aside in its middle years." Marshall concluded: "In the short run, it may seem to be the easiest course to allow our great metropolitan areas to be divided up each into two cities—one white, the other black—but it is a course, I predict, our people will ultimately regret."

Richard Kluger  **NO**

Visible Man: Fifty Years After *Brown*

Exorcism is rarely a pretty spectacle. It is frequently marked by violent spasms and protracted trauma, and so it has been over the five decades since *Brown* launched the nation's effort to rid itself of the consuming demons of racism. The Supreme Court's ruling may be visualized as the cresting wave of a tidal movement resulting from the great economic earthquake of 1929. Not until then had American society seriously acknowledged that its most sacred obligation went beyond the protection of property and capital to its citizens' needs for daily subsistence. People were no longer to be viewed as an infinitely disposable market commodity. The New Deal of Franklin Roosevelt became the first national program since the end of Reconstruction in the South in 1876 to treat black Americans as recognizably human. Worldwide conflicts with fascism and communism added to he country's consciousness that its African Americans had not been precisely the beneficiaries of the social order; a system that inflicted so much pain and hardship was understood by many to be in urgent need of repair—if only the signal were given. It was in this receptive soil that Chief Justice Warren and his eight robed brethren planted the seed of *Brown v. Board of Education of Topeka, Kansas.*

At a stroke the Court had erased the most flagrant remaining insignia of slavery. No longer could the African American be relegated to the status of official pariah. No longer could whites look right through him as if he were, in the title words of Ralph Ellison's soon-to-become-classic 1952 novel, an "Invisible Man."

The mass movement spawned by *Brown* was unmistakably under way within six months of the Court's issuing its open-ended implementation decree. It began in the Deep South, in Montgomery, Alabama, when a fortythree-year-old seamstress and active NAACP member named Rosa Parks refused to surrender her seat to a white passenger and move to the back of a city bus as the local ordinances required. Within days, thanks to the leadership of Martin Luther King, Jr., Mrs. Parks's pastor, all blacks were refusing to ride Montgomery's buses in a massive display of resentment over the continuing humiliation of Jim Crow. With dignity, courage, and resolve that was capturing the nation's attention, Montgomery's African Americans made their boycott stick for more than a year. By the end of it, the Supreme Court had struck down segregation laws in public transportation just as it had in public education.

Over the next dozen years the Warren Court would hand down decision after decision that followed the path *Brown* had opened. Segregation was outlawed in public parks and recreation areas, on or at all transportation facilities (waiting rooms and lunch counters as well as the carriers themselves), in libraries and courtrooms and the facilities of all public buildings, and in hotels, restaurants, and other enterprises accommodating the public. It was declared unlawful to list on a ballot the race of a candidate for public office. Black witnesses could no longer be addressed by their first names in Southern courtrooms. Sexual relations between consenting blacks and whites were removed from the criminal decalogue, and in 1967, with scarcely a murmur of objection in the land, the high court ruled that state laws forbidding the rite most hateful to the cracker mentality—the joining of white and black in holy matrimony—were unconstitutional. Within that same dozen years the Court issued historic rulings in two other areas of critical importance to African Americans. The sweeping "one man, one vote" decisions of *Baker v. Carr* in 1962 and *Reynolds v. Sims* in 1964 mandated massive legislature reapportionment that resulted in significantly increased representation of urban areas where blacks were concentrated. In the criminal justice realm, the Court markedly improved the ability of accused criminals to defend themselves; *Miranda v. Arizona, Escobedo v. Illinois*, and *Gideon v. Wainwright* were the landmark cases.

Once ordered by the Court, desegregation proceeded at a relatively rapid pace in most categories. Streetcars and eating places and amusement parks were, after all, settings for transient commingling of the races; schools, though, were something else. There the interracial contact would last six to eight hours a day, and was from interaction with one another as much as immersion in their lesson book that schoolchildren were acculturated. So it was the schoolhouse that became the arena for the South's fiercest show of hostility to desegregation. The most rabid elements in the region pledged "massive resistance" to the command and were abetted in that resolve by the so-called Southern Manifesto issued in the spring of 1956 by 101 U.S. Senators and members of the House of Representatives, a politically potent assemblage who termed *Brown* "a clear abuse of judicial power" that had substituted the Justices' "personal, political, and social ideas for the established law of the land."

The popular and amiable President of the United States, Dwight D. Eisenhower, might reasonably have been expected to place the prestige of his august office behind the Supreme Court's monumental ruling. Yet this soldier of formidable rectitude never did so, except in the most offhand way. Declining to say whether he agreed with the *Brown* decision, Ike lamely remarked, "I think it makes no difference whether or not I endorse it. The Constitution is as the Supreme Court interprets it, and I must conform to that and do my very best to see that it is carried out in this country." It might have been carried out far sooner and less bruisingly if the President had urged the country to obey *Brown*, not just because it was a ruling of the nation's ultimate court but because it was right. For him to stand above the battle was to lend aid and comfort to the forces of resistance. "If Mr. Eisenhower had come through," recalled former Justice Tom Clark after he had retired from the bench, "it would have changed things a lot."

Thus unchallenged by the executive and legislative branches of the federal government, the South succeeded for ten years in largely evading and defying the Supreme Court's directive to end racial separation in public schools. Only a trickle of black students was allowed to enter the white schools of Old Dixie, and even then this small brave band often had to endure menacing taunts and the spittle of die-hard white supremacists. A decade after *Brown*, not even one in fifty African American pupils was attending classes with whites in the eleven states with the largest proportion of black residents. Meanwhile, the rest of the nation looked on not overly concerned, preferring to see the South's stalling tactics as a regional problem and turning a blind eye to the depth and virulence of their own uncodified racism and the *de facto* segregation in their urban ghettos.

John F. Kennedy became the first U.S. President to commit his administration, if belatedly and somewhat reluctantly, to broad action to improve the condition of black America. That burden no longer rested, as it had since *Brown* was promulgated, almost entirely upon the Supreme Court and the rest of the federal judiciary. Government protection was extended to freedom riders who risked their necks to protest the continuing disenfranchisement of Southern blacks and other inequities in the old fire-breathing bastions of Jim Crow. The Justice Department pushed the Interstate Commerce Commission to issue a blanket order ending segregation at all rail, air, and bus facilities, and its enforcement was rapid. The government initiated suits to force recalcitrant school districts to desegregate, and the pace of the process now quickened: 31 districts in 1961, 46 districts in 1962, 166 districts in 1963. All branches of the federal government were urged to step up their hiring of blacks, and federally funded contractors were similarly pushed. But because Democrat Kennedy hesitated to cross swords with the powerful Southern wing of his party, fearing that a clash would scuttle the rest of his legislative program, he delayed for more than two years before signing an executive order prohibiting discrimination in all housing that received direct federal subsidies and in the much broader sector of the home-building market financed by government-guaranteed mortgages. . . .

[F]ive months and three days before he was slain, Kennedy ended his fragile working relationship with the entrenched Southern bloc on Capitol Hill and sent Congress the most sweeping civil-rights law proposed in nearly a century. The bill bore this heading: "An act to enforce the constitutional right to vote, to confer jurisdiction upon the district courts of the United States to provide injunctive relief against discrimination in public accommodations, to authorize the Attorney General to institute suits to protect constitutional rights in public facilities and public education, to extend the Commission on Civil Rights, to prevent discrimination in federally assisted programs, to establish a Commission on Equal Employment Opportunity, and for other purposes." And to oversee this disestablishment of racism, the Justice Department would be empowered to go to court in the name of black Americans who could ill afford the time, energy, and cost of suing sovereign states and their subdivisions whose laws and policies effectively frustrated the desegregation process. . . .

During Lyndon Johnson's first months in the White-House, Malcolm X demeaned him as "a Southern cracker—that's all he is." Perhaps black leaders feared that the new President would prove the reincarnation of the last man named Johnson to occupy the White House; he, too, was a Southerner succeeding a murdered friend of the blacks. But Lyndon, born poor in the bleak west Texas hill country and never forgetting his hardscrabble origins, was not Andrew; he was, rather, a consummate practitioner of legislative deal-making, whose glad-handing could turn bone-crushing if need be. His expansive rhetoric and carrot-and-stick enticements drew together liberal and moderate lawmakers of both parties and fashioned a program that advanced the rights of African Americans far beyond what Kennedy, for all his good intentions, could probably ever have accomplished. The Senate passed the 1964 Civil Rights Act a year to the day after Kennedy sent it to Congress.

Over the next ten years, with inconstant degrees of enthusiasm, the federal-government put the 1964 rights bill to a great deal of use. And having outflanked the Dixiecrat power base in the Senate, where he had presided so ably as majority leader, Johnson kept pushing civil-rights measures through Congress during his remaining five years in the Oval Office. In 1965 the Voting Rights Act restricted "tests and devices" used to foil and intimidate would-be black voters and assigned federal registrars and observers to bolster the voter-recruitment efforts of civil-rights workers in the field. Within a decade the number of blacks on Southern voting rolls was triple the total on the day the Kennedy-Johnson administration had taken office. Before long, Congress was responding to LBJ's fervent requests by passing the Elementary and Secondary Education Act, providing unprecedented federal funds to help local school districts—and, in the process, arming Washington with a weighty financial club to enforce compliance with the desegregation orders of the federal courts. The widely welcomed education bill was part of a proliferating series of imaginative new federal programs aimed at declaring war on poverty and ignorance throughout the nation. Together—aid to schools, Model Cities, the Office of Economic Opportunity, Head Start, VISTA, the Fair Housing Act, legal services for the poor, consumer protection laws, and Medicare to tend the ailing elderly— the President labeled them stepping-stones to a Great Society, one that would benefit no sector of its people more than black Americans. . . .

Among African Americans who were to enjoy such a reward was fifty-nine-year-old Thurgood Marshall, the emblematic "Mr. Civil Rights," as the press had dubbed him. In 1967, after Marshall had served as a U.S. Circuit Court judge and the nation's Solicitor General, Johnson nominated him to the Supreme Court, the arena where he had so often appeared to advance the rights of his race. After a bloc of Southern Senators took a final turn at tormenting him by holding up his nomination for months, Marshall was confirmed as the ninety-sixth man to sit on the nation's highest tribunal—and its first African American. He would remain there for twenty-five years, and while never its brightest light and often ailing, he proved an unflinching protector of the civil rights and civil liberties of all Americans. . . .

❧❦❧

Scanning the half-century since *Brown* was handed down from the white marble temple of justice close by the nation's Capitol, what can we say with confidence about the transforming effect of the event on the national psyche and the condition of African Americans in particular?

At the least, we can say it brought to an end more than three centuries of an officially sanctioned mind-set embracing white supremacy and excusing a massive and often pitiless oppression. At long last a roster of magnanimous Justices had been moved to instruct the country that such beliefs and the resulting conduct were unconscionable and intolerable under the law. But delegitimizing the racist caste system could not magically remake the chastened former master class into overnight paragons of decency, eager to extend to their darker ex-captives full and equal access to their shared society's bounty. The lash, though, had been cast away for good. To gain their due, black Americans soon discovered, they would have to go on the march, under the banner of lawful entitlement, and not wait to be gifted with the nation's long withheld kindness. En route, they now felt licensed to vent a rage they had so long repressed for fear of swift reprisal. Their march did not proceed without its perils—or rewards.

By almost every measurable standard, African Americans as a group were significantly better off in 2004 than they had been in 1954. They were better educated and housed, more gainfully employed in more demanding jobs, more self-confident and highly regarded by their white countrymen, and had made undemable contributions to the mainstream culture. No one any longer questioned that jazz and blues were art. The black presence was ubiquitous, even where blacks were not there in person. Its impact had become detectable in nearly every aspect of Americans' daily lives: how they talk, dress, eat, play, fix their hair, sing their national anthem, even how they shake hands. Black artists were no longer a sub-category, catering only or mainly to black audiences. Black athletes dominated their fields. Every U.S. Cabinet now included one or two African Americans; the Supreme Court likewise had an all-but-obligatory black seat; the Congressional Black Caucus, at times numbering more than forty members, was a formidable voting bloc in legislative decision-making; the "Old Dominion" of Virginia had elected a black governor, and almost every major American city had at one time or another chosen a black mayor. Even in the corporate world, still a mostly white preserve, black executives were emerging, though generally in the lower echelons. The nation's biggest stock brokerage firm and the largest entertainment conglomerate chose African Americans as their CEO. . . .

For all these heartening signs of far greater black prominence and white acceptance in American daily life, there was no denying that mixed with the good news were too many remnants of an aching disparity between the races that time and good intentions had not cured.

❧❦❧

Why haven't African Americans progressed further toward equality of both opportunity and attainment? Why hasn't the nation achieved true racial integration?

One plausible explanation is that the American fondness for quick fixes and ready expedients does not compute in a realm with so many complex emotional variables. The evolution of human habits and attitudes takes time, and while the United States has not yet fully solved its most intractable social dilemma, neither has it shied away altogether. But some on both sides of the color line remain convinced that further measures to encourage interracial bonding will prove fruitless. There are many whites who believe that America has done enough to redress black grievances by substantially correcting its formerly prejudicial laws, thinking, and conduct. For those blacks willing to try earnestly to overcome their acknowledged historic disadvantages, these whites say, the way upward is open, so that African Americans should no longer be indulged as perpetual invalids, and the groans of the self-pitying among them should fall on deaf ears. In stark contrast, a substantial segment of black Americans believe—or have been persuaded—that white hatred toward them runs so deep in the American ethos that it will never yield more ground than it is forced to. And no one, they note, is forcing it. Indeed, the opposite seems to be true: instead of structured social initiatives, there have been retreats and rollbacks by mean-spirited government policymakers, so that for far too many blacks there has been little or no progress.

Such polarizing views, not without some truth to them, miss the larger picture.

The uniqueness of the African American experience cannot be fully grasped by white Americans without an understanding that for many, if not for most, blacks, their color—of whatever hue—has been and remains the indelible, shaping, and often ruling factor in their existence. Their skin cannot be shed. It is a daily reminder of the cumulative and all too frequently sorry history of their race in America. However much improved their status or however loud the proclamations by white America that racial equality is in the offing, the suspicion lingers among blacks, along with so many bitter memories, that they can never measure up and will always be seen in whites' hurtful eyes as water-bearers, tap dancers, and clowning inferiors. It is a suspicion steeped in the reality that white America has never said forthrightly that it is sorry for the enormity of the pain both physical and spiritual long inflicted on its black people—or faced up to the effort and cost truly required to undo the remnants of that atrocity.

"A society that places so much premium on 'getting ahead,'" wrote Andrew Hacker in *Two Nations*, "cannot afford to spare much compassion for those who fall behind." Hacker got it half right. It is not that America cannot do so; it *will not* do so—or, at any rate, has not yet seriously considered the matter. By the governments it has put in place and the leaders it has chosen since *Brown*, the nation has not acted in good faith—except for a short season all but forgotten now—to better educate, house, and employ those whom it had long abused. Halfhearted (or less) seemed good enough: witness the rapidity with which the "war on poverty" was shut down before it could be granted time to take hold. Why make sacrifices in the form of tax dollars, job set-asides, and "affirmative action" and thereby elevate African Americans into fully competitive rivals for society's material rewards? It made better economic sense to keep them disadvantaged in a Darwinian world where the fittest prevail.

Consider housing. Conspired against by laws, customs, crass real-estate agents, profiteering landlords, redlining bankers, merciless federal mortgage insurers, and thoughtless urban renewal planners, most black Americans who broke free from the white-supremacist South found themselves systematically penned into urban slums and their children isolated in one-race schools. When *Brown* finally ordered the gates unlocked and fair-housing laws were passed to encourage a black diaspora, few whites cheered; their property values might suffer. When busing was introduced as the only practicable method of integrating inner-city pupils, white objectors took to the hills by the legion, and soon few of them were left to integrate with. A generation later, segregation was returning to many areas. Fair-housing laws, meanwhile, were being honored far more in the breach than the practice. Yet African America persevered, a sizable black middle class emerged, and interracial communities have gradually become a spreading phenomenon. Still, no politician who reads his or her polling numbers seriously calls for a domestic Marshall Plan that could put an end to derelict black neighborhoods where so many remain mired in misery. Americans simply seem more dedicated to exploring outer space than to saving their inner cities; we lavish our wealth on outsized vehicles and state-of-the-art weaponry rather than on improving young minds or caring for the public health. The race issue has come to be regarded not as fertile ground for progressive policymakers but a burial ground for political activists of the stripe who once believed that government could lift the destitute, hound the predatory, and serve the common good. Now the liberating impulse has been largely co-opted by the political right, devoted to freeing private enterprise from allegedly incessant government meddling. The result has been an extreme maldistribution of the nation's wealth that outrages remarkably few Americans. Only an unpredictable wind shift toward altruism seems likely to power a new national consensus that identifies government as neither enemy nor savior but as a useful tool when put prudently to the task. As long as those put in charge of it profess to hate it, government cannot be the prime mover in the pursuit of justice.

If white America may be faulted for having too strictly rationed its generosity toward the black community within it, what may be ventured about the role of African America in assessing why, for all the statistical evidence of progress, the racial gulf still seems so obstinately wide?

Like its white counterpart, black America has never been a monolithic unit, its attitudes varying with history, geography, degree of assimilation, and even skin pigmentation. And with the steady expansion of the black middle class, new fissures have riddled African Americans' racial solidarity; the embittered poor are less forgiving toward their perceived oppressors than the newly prospering are. But regardless of their station in life, stagnant or evolving, the nation's blacks have understandably been haunted by twin fears: (1) Does the rest of America really accept them as equally human members of society, no longer a subspecies? (2) Has their escape from flagrant oppression taken them to the point where they can vie with confidence to achieve their individual potential? Neither is a rhetorical question.

Deep skepticism about the answer to the first question has fed the temptation among African Americans to blame many of their frustrations and disappointments on an intractable racism that some insist has scarcely abated. "Victimology is today nothing less than a keystone of cultural blackness," contends John McWhorter. The time is at hand, he argues, for blacks to address their failures and stop turning for solace to a defiantly separate—and distancing—cultural identity. Certainly there has always been a running debate within the African American community, as inside all ethnic groups, over the extent to which blacks can and should conform their conduct—their speech, dress, appearance, tastes—to white norms in order to win acceptance and advancement and yet not lose the essence of their beings. Expanded opportunities in the post-*Brown* age have intensified this concern. But to view, for example, the quest for academic excellence or entrepreneurial expertise as "acting white" and thus a denial of one's own core identity is to answer white flight with black flight. Why should a proudly practiced African American subculture be thought of as fatally diminished by flowing into the mainstream instead of being regarded as a powerful tributary that adds great life force to the national current?

Sadly, the rewards of interracial and transcultural blending have been spurned by many younger African Americans in the nation's high schools and colleges, precisely where the future is taking shape. Mingling with white classmates is often taken—whether out of long-smoldering resentment, fear of being rejected or patronized, or for some other phobic cause—as a denial of one's African American roots, while white students, detecting only a large threatening chip on their black schoolmates' shoulders and failing to perceive it as an expression of natural cultural affinities or a confession of insecurity, have often responded inhospitably, adding to the rancorous standoff. Nor have adult overseers helped matters. Administrators at many white-majority universities, in the misguided belief they were insulating their campuses against racial tension, have accomplished the opposite by setting aside blacksonly dormitories, or parts thereof, to accommodate African American students who wish to segregate themselves. But what sort of lesson has been taught by such invitations to group avoidance in settings where young people migrate to be stimulated by new ideas and to gain understanding through exposure to fresh cultural influences?

A far more telling lesson was offered on the op-ed page of *The New York Times* on the first Fourth of July of the third millennium of the Christian Era by black scholar Roger Wilkins, nephew of the longtime executive secretary of the NAACP, Roy Wilkins. Without naming her, Wilkins took issue with the in-your-face remark by acclaimed black novelist Toni Morrison that she had never in her life felt like an American. "Well, I have—all my life," wrote Wilkins, stressing that he had never felt himself less of an American because he stemmed from slaves "who in their stolen lives built so much of this country." Having begun his education before *Brown* in a segregated one-room schoolhouse in Missouri, Wilkins conceded that black living conditions in the United States remained far from satisfactory, "but the change has nevertheless been so dramatic that my belief in American possibilities remains profound." At the end he held out hope for renewed citizen action "harnessed to our founding ideas to improve American life and even to transform some American hearts."

Genuine social justice has been an oft-announced but rarely pursued ambition throughout history and probably was never achieved by any enduring society or civilization. Within the recent past the world has witnessed the collapse of Soviet-style Marxism, whose ideology enshrined an egalitarian state of selfless citizens—never mind that they were ruthlessly lorded over by a council of privileged cutthroats. The mission of defining, creating, and sustaining a truly just society on a thronged planet, manifestly unfair from its creation, is rendered almost insuperably difficult for a people like ours, a vast, clamorous, polyglot and polychromatic, beaverishly purposeful multitude, without its match on earth. Good-hearted but grasping, earnest yet impatient, easily distractable, and prone to trade its avowed humanitarian principles for triumphalism, America is a colossus of contradictions. For a certainty, justice of any type cannot materialize in such an untidy place without the binding up of its constituent elements. And that is unlikely ever to occur unless and until Americans of every variety acknowledge that what separates them is small change when counted against all they hold in common. Possessing soul is not a uniquely black or white state of grace, any more than owning a white or black skin, or a beige, olive, sallow, or ruddy one is a mark of either superiority or disgrace. A precept, let us admit in candor but with hope, that is more easily stated than lived.

POSTSCRIPT

Did the *Brown* Decision Fail to Desegregate and Improve the Status of African Americans?

The fiftieth anniversary of the Supreme Court's ruling in *Brown* has generated numerous appraisals of the decision's legacy. In Brown v. Board of Education: *Caste, Culture, and the Constitution* (University Press of Kansas, 2003), law professors Robert J. Cottrol, Raymond T. Diamond, and Leland B. Ware emphasize that beyond attacking the "separate but equal" doctrine, *Brown* offered the American people a view of the beneficial role that an activist judiciary could play in resolving some of the nation's most difficult social problems. Derrick Bell is far less sanguine about the ability of the courts to challenge white dominance in *Silent Covenants*: Brown v. Board of Education *and the Unfulfilled Hopes for Racial Reform* (Oxford University Press, 2004). Charles T. Clotfelter, in *After* Brown: *The Rise and Retreat of School Desegregation* (Princeton University Press, 2004), recognizes the incomplete nature of school desegregation but describes the interracial contact derived from the Court's ruling as having a transformative impact on intergroup relations that has benefited both African Americans and whites. Charles J. Ogletree Jr., *All Deliberate Speed: Reflections on the First Half-Century of* Brown v. Board of Education (W. W. Norton, 2004) argues that the promises of integrated public education and full racial equality were undermined by the Supreme Court's refusal to set a specific date by which segregation must end. Albert L. Samuels, *Is Separate Unequal? Black Colleges and the Challenge to Desegregation* (University Press of Kansas, 2004) examines the impact of the *Brown* decision on historically black colleges and universities (HBCUs). For an excellent summary of the *Brown* case and its legacy, see Waldo Martin, Brown v. Board of Education: *A Brief History With Documents* (Bedford/St. Martin's Press, 1998) and James T. Patterson, Brown v. Board of Education: *A Civil Rights Milestone and Its Troubled Legacy* (Oxford University Press, 2001). Both the *Journal of Southern History* (May 2004) and the *Journal of American History* (June 2004) commemorated the fiftieth anniversary of the *Brown* decision with scholarly retrospectives by distinguished historians.

Regardless of how one assesses the impact of *Brown*, many scholars, including Kluger, view the decision as the starting point for the civil rights movement. Michael Klarman's *From Jim Crow to Civil Rights: The Supreme Court and the Struggle for Racial Equality* (Oxford University Press, 2004) challenges this assessment by concluding that *de jure* segregation would have been eliminated fairly quickly even without the Court's supportive verdict in 1954. In recent years, historians of the civil rights movement have argued that the struggle for African American equality began much earlier in the twentieth century and laid the groundwork for the successes of the 1950s and 1960s. *"We Return Fighting": The Civil Rights Movement in the Jazz Age* (Northeastern University Press, 2001) focuses on the role of the NAACP in the post–World War I era. Patricia Sullivan, *Days of Hope: Race and Democracy in the New Deal Era* (University of North Carolina Press, 1996) makes a case for the 1930s and 1940s as the true watershed for civil rights activity, while Richard Dalfiume, "The 'Forgotten Years' of the Negro Revolution," *Journal of American History* (June 1968) and John Dittmer, *Local People: The Struggle for Civil Rights in Mississippi* (University of Illinois Press, 1994) make a strong case for the Second World War as the stimulus for civil rights successes in the Cold War era.

The literature on the civil rights movement is extensive. August Meier, Elliott Rudwick, and Francis L. Broderick, eds., *Black Protest Thought in the Twentieth Century* (2d. ed.; Bobbs-Merrill, 1971) presents a collection of documents that places the activities of the 1950s and 1960s in a larger framework. The reflections of many of the participants of the movement are included in Howell Raines, *My Soul Is Rested: The Story of the Civil Rights Movement in the Deep South* (G. P. Putnam, 1977). Students should also consult Aldon D. Morris, *The Origins of the Civil Rights Movement: Black Communities Organizing for Change* (Free Press, 1984). August Meier's contemporary assessment, "On the Role of Martin Luther King," *Crisis* (1965), in many ways remains the most insightful analysis of King's leadership. More detailed studies include David L. Lewis, *King: A Critical Biography* (Praeger, 1970); Stephen B. Oates, *Let the Trumpet Sound: The Life of Martin Luther King, Jr.* (Harper and Row, 1982); and David J. Garrow's Pulitzer Prize–winning *Bearing the Cross: Martin Luther King, Jr., and the Southern Christian Leadership Conference* (William Morrow, 1986). Taylor Branch's *Parting the Waters: America in the King Years, 1954-63* (Simon & Schuster, 1988), which won the Pulitzer Prize, and *Pillar of Fire: America in the King Years, 1963-1968* (Simon & Schuster, 1998) are beautifully written narratives. Finally, the texture of the civil rights movement is captured brilliantly in Henry Hampton's documentary series "Eyes on the Prize."

A critical assessment of the legacy of the civil rights movement is presented in two books by political scientist Robert C. Smith: *We Have No Leaders: African Americans in the Post–Civil Rights Era* (State University of New York Press, 1994) and *Racism in the Post–Civil Rights Era: Now You See It, Now You Don't* (State University of New York Press, 1996).

ISSUE 14

Was the Americanization of the War in Vietnam Inevitable?

YES: Brian VanDeMark, from *Into the Quagmire: Lyndon Johnson and the Escalation of the Vietnam War* (Oxford University Press, 1991)

NO: H. R. McMaster, from *Dereliction of Duty: Lyndon Johnson, Robert McNamara, the Joint Chiefs of Staff, and the Lies That Led to Vietnam* (HarperCollins, 1997)

ISSUE SUMMARY

YES: Professor of history Brian VanDeMark argues that President Lyndon Johnson failed to question the viability of increasing U.S. involvement in the Vietnam War because he was a prisoner of America's global containment policy and because he did not want his opponents to accuse him of being soft on communism or endanger support for his Great Society reforms.

NO: H. R. McMaster, an active-duty army tanker, maintains that the Vietnam disaster was not inevitable but a uniquely human failure whose responsibility was shared by President Johnson and his principal military and civilian advisers.

$\mathbf{A}$t the end of World War II, imperialism was coming to a close in Asia. Japan's defeat spelled the end of its control over China, Korea, and the countries of Southeast Asia. Attempts by the European nations to reestablish their empires were doomed. Anti-imperialist movements emerged all over Asia and Africa, often producing chaos.

The United States faced a dilemma. America was a nation conceived in revolution and was sympathetic to the struggles of Third World nations. But the United States was afraid that many of the revolutionary leaders were Communists who would place their countries under the control of the expanding empire of the Soviet Union. By the late 1940s the Truman administration decided that it was necessary to stop the spread of communism. The policy that resulted was known as containment.

Vietnam provided a test of the containment doctrine in Asia. Vietnam had been a French protectorate from 1885 until Japan took control of it during

World War II. Shortly before the war ended, the Japanese gave Vietnam its independence, but the French were determined to reestablish their influence in the area. Conflicts emerged between the French-led nationalist forces of South Vietnam and the Communist-dominated provisional government of the Democratic Republic of Vietnam (DRV), which was established in Hanoi in August 1945. Ho Chi Minh was the president of the DRV. An avowed Communist since the 1920s, Ho had also become the major nationalist figure in Vietnam. As the leader of the anti-imperialist movement against French and Japanese colonialism for over 30 years, Ho managed to tie together the communist and nationalist movements in Vietnam.

A full-scale war broke out in 1946 between the communist government of North Vietnam and the French-dominated country of South Vietnam. After the Communists defeated the French at the battle of Dien Bien Phu in May 1954, the latter decided to pull out. At the Geneva Conference that summer, Vietnam was divided at the 17th parallel, pending elections.

The United States became directly involved in Vietnam after the French withdrew. In 1955 the Republican president Dwight D. Eisenhower refused to recognize the Geneva Accord but supported the establishment of the South Vietnamese government. In 1956 South Vietnam's leader, Ngo Dinh Diem, with U.S. approval, refused to hold elections, which would have provided a unified government for Vietnam in accordance with the Geneva Agreement. The Communists in the north responded by again taking up the armed struggle. The war continued for another 19 years.

Both President Eisenhower and his successor, John F. Kennedy, were anxious to prevent South Vietnam from being taken over by the Communists, so economic assistance and military aid were provided. Kennedy's successor, Lyndon B. Johnson, changed the character of American policy in Vietnam by escalating the air war and increasing the number of ground forces from 21,000 in 1965 to a full fighting force of 550,000 at its peak in 1968.

The next president, Richard Nixon, adopted a new policy of "Vietnamization" of the war. Military aid to South Vietnam was increased to ensure the defeat of the Communists. At the same time, American troops were gradually withdrawn from Vietnam. South Vietnamese president Thieu recognized the weakness of his own position without the support of U.S. troops. He reluctantly signed the Paris Accords in January 1973 only after being told by Secretary of State Henry Kissinger that the United States would sign them alone. Once U.S. soldiers were withdrawn, Thieu's regime was doomed. In spring 1975 a full-scale war broke out, and the South Vietnamese government collapsed.

In the following selection, Brian VanDeMark argues that President Johnson failed to question the viability of increasing U.S. involvement in Vietnam because he was a prisoner of America's global containment policy and he did not want his opponents to accuse him of being soft on communism. In the second selection, H. R. McMaster argues that the Vietnam disaster was not inevitable but a uniquely human failure whose responsibility was shared by Johnson and his civilian and military advisers.

YES

Brian VanDeMark

Into the Quagmire

Vietnam divided America more deeply and painfully than any event since the Civil War. It split political leaders and ordinary people alike in profound and lasting ways. Whatever the conflicting judgments about this controversial war—and there are many—Vietnam undeniably stands as the greatest tragedy of twentieth-century U.S. foreign relations.

America's involvement in Vietnam has, as a result, attracted much critical-scrutiny, frequently addressed to the question, "Who was guilty?"—"Who led the United States into this tragedy?" A more enlightening question, it seems, is "How and why did this tragedy occur?" The study of Vietnam should be a search for explanation and understanding, rather than for scapegoats.

Focusing on one important period in this long and complicated story—the brief but critical months from November 1964 to July 1965, when America crossed the threshold from limited to large-scale war in Vietnam—helps to answer that question. For the crucial decisions of this period resulted from the interplay of longstanding ideological attitudes, diplomatic assumptions and political pressures with decisive contemporaneous events in America and Vietnam.

Victory in World War II produced a sea change in America's perception of its role in world affairs. Political leaders of both parties embraced a sweepingly new vision of the United States as the defender against the perceived threat of monolithic communist expansion everywhere in the world. This vision of American power and purpose, shaped at the start of the Cold War, grew increasingly rigid over the years. By 1964–1965, it had become an iron-bound and unshakable dogma, a received faith which policymakers unquestionably accepted—even though the circumstances which had fostered its creation had changed dramatically amid diffused authority and power among communist states and nationalist upheaval in the colonial world.

Policymakers' blind devotion to this static Cold War vision led America into misfortune in Vietnam. Lacking the critical perspective and sensibility to reappraise basic tenets of U.S. foreign policy in the light of changed events and local circumstances, policymakers failed to perceive Vietnamese realities accurately and thus to gauge American interests in the area prudently. Policymakers, as a consequence, misread an indigenous, communist-led nationalist movement as part of a larger, centrally directed challenge to world order and stability; tied American fortunes to a non-communist regime of slim popular legitimacy and effectiveness; and intervened militarily in the region far out of proportion to U.S. security requirements.

An arrogant and stubborn faith in America's power to shape the course of foreign events compounded the dangers sown by ideological rigidity. Policymakers in 1964–1965 shared a common postwar conviction that the United States not only should, but could, control political conditions in South Vietnam, as elsewhere throughout much of the world. This conviction had led Washington to intervene progressively deeper in South Vietnamese affairs over the years. And when—despite Washington's increasing exertions—Saigon's political situation declined precipitously during 1964–1965, this conviction prompted policymakers to escalate the war against Hanoi, in the belief that America could stimulate political order in South Vietnam through the application of military force against North Vietnam.

Domestic political pressures exerted an equally powerful, if less obvious, influence over the course of U.S. involvement in Vietnam. The fall of China in 1949 and the ugly McCarthyism it aroused embittered American foreign policy for a generation. By crippling President Truman's political fortunes, it taught his Democratic successors, John Kennedy and Lyndon Johnson [LBJ], a strong and sobering lesson: that another "loss" to communism in East Asia risked renewed and devastating attacks from the right. This fear of reawakened McCarthyism remained a paramount concern as policymakers pondered what course to follow as conditions in South Vietnam deteriorated rapidly in 1964–1965.

Enduring traditions of ideological rigidity, diplomatic arrogance, and political vulnerability heavily influenced the way policymakers approached decisions in Vietnam in 1964–1965. Understanding the decisions of this period fully, however, also requires close attention to contemporary developments in America and South Vietnam. These years marked a tumultuous time in both countries, which affected the course of events in subtle but significant ways.

Policymakers in 1964–1965 lived in a period of extraordinary domestic political upheaval sparked by the civil rights movement. It is difficult to overstate the impact of this upheaval on American politics in the mid-1960s. During 1964–1965, the United States—particularly the American South—experienced profound and long overdue change in the economic, political, and social rights of blacks. This change, consciously embraced by the liberal administration of Lyndon Johnson, engendered sharp political hostility among conservative southern whites and their deputies in Congress—hostility which the politically astute Johnson sensed could spill over into the realm of foreign affairs, where angry civil rights opponents could exact their revenge should LBJ stumble and "lose" a crumbling South Vietnam. This danger, reinforced by the memory of McCarthyism, stirred deep political fears in Johnson, together with an abiding aversion to failure in Vietnam.

LBJ feared defeat in South Vietnam, but he craved success and glory at home. A forceful, driving President of boundless ambition, Johnson sought to harness the political momentum created by the civil rights movement to enact a far-reaching domestic reform agenda under the rubric of the Great Society. LBJ would achieve the greatness he sought by leading America toward justice and opportunity for all its citizens, through his historic legislative program.

Johnson's domestic aspirations fundamentally conflicted with his uneasy involvement in Vietnam. An experienced and perceptive politician, LBJ knew his domestic reforms required the sustained focus and cooperation of Congress. He also knew a larger war in Vietnam jeopardized these reforms by drawing away political attention and economic resources. America's increasing military intervention in 1964–1965 cast this tension between Vietnam and the Great Society into sharp relief.

Johnson saw his predicament clearly. But he failed to resolve it for fear that acknowledging the growing extent and cost of the war would thwart his domestic reforms, while pursuing a course of withdrawal risked political ruin. LBJ, instead, chose to obscure the magnitude of his dilemma by obscuring America's deepening involvement as South Vietnam began to fail. That grave compromise of candor opened the way to Johnson's eventual downfall.

Events in South Vietnam during 1964–1965 proved equally fateful. A historically weak and divided land, South Vietnam's deeply rooted ethnic, political, and religious turmoil intensified sharply in the winter of 1964–1965. This mounting turmoil, combined with increased communist military attacks, pushed Saigon to the brink of political collapse.

South Vietnam's accelerating crisis alarmed American policymakers, driving them to deepen U.S. involvement considerably in an effort to arrest Saigon's political failure. Abandoning the concept of stability in the South *before* escalation against the North, policymakers now embraced the concept of stability *through* escalation, in the desperate hope that military action against Hanoi would prompt a stubbornly elusive political order in Saigon.

This shift triggered swift and ominous consequences scarcely anticipated by its architects. Policymakers soon confronted intense military, political, and bureaucratic pressures to widen the war. Unsettled by these largely unforeseen pressures, policymakers reacted confusedly and defensively. Rational men, they struggled to control increasingly irrational forces. But their reaction only clouded their attention to basic assumptions and ultimate costs as the war rapidly spun out of control in the spring and summer of 1965. In their desperation to make Vietnam policy work amid this rising tide of war pressures, they thus failed ever to question whether it could work—or at what ultimate price. Their failure recalls the warning of a prescient political scientist, who years before had cautioned against those policymakers with "an infinite capacity for making ends of [their] means."

The decisions of 1964–1965 bespeak a larger and deeper failure as well. Throughout this period—as, indeed, throughout the course of America's Vietnam involvement—U.S. policymakers strove principally to create a viable noncommunist regime in South Vietnam. For many years and at great effort and cost, Washington had endeavored to achieve political stability and competence in Saigon. Despite these efforts, South Vietnam's political disarray persisted and deepened, until, in 1965, America intervened with massive military force to avert its total collapse.

Few policymakers in 1964–1965 paused to mull this telling fact, to ponder its implications about Saigon's viability as a political entity. The failure to reexamine this and other fundamental premises of U.S. policy—chief among them Vietnam's importance to American national interests and Washington's ability to forge political order through military power—proved a costly and tragic lapse of statesmanship. . . .

❦

The legacy of Vietnam, like the war itself, remains a difficult and painful subject for Americans. As passions subside and time bestows greater perspective, Americans still struggle to understand Vietnam's meaning and lessons for the country. They still wonder how the United States found itself ensnared in an ambiguous, costly, and divisive war, and how it can avoid repeating such an ordeal in the future.

The experience of Lyndon Johnson and his advisers during the decisive years 1964–1965 offers much insight into those questions. For their decisions, which fundamentally transformed U.S. participation in the war, both reflected and defined much of the larger history of America's Vietnam involvement.

Their decisions may also, one hopes, yield kernels of wisdom for the future; the past, after all, can teach us lessons. But history's lessons, as Vietnam showed, are themselves dependent on each generation's knowledge and understanding of the past. So it proved for 1960s policymakers, whose ignorance and misperception of Southeast Asian history, culture, and politics pulled America progressively deeper into the war. LBJ, [Secretary of State Dean] Rusk, [Robert] McNamara, [McGeorge] Bundy, [Ambassador Maxwell] Taylor—most of their generation, in fact—mistakenly viewed Vietnam through the simplistic ideological prism of the Cold War. They perceived a deeply complex and ambiguous regional struggle as a grave challenge to world order and stability, fomented by communist China acting through its local surrogate, North Vietnam.

This perception, given their mixture of memories—the West's capitulation to Hitler at Munich, Stalin's postwar truculence, Mao's belligerent rhetoric—appears altogether understandable in retrospect. But it also proved deeply flawed and oblivious to abiding historical realities. Constrained by their memories and ideology, American policymakers neglected the subtle but enduring force of nationalism in Southeast Asia. Powerful and decisive currents—the deep and historic tension between Vietnam and China; regional friction among the Indochinese states of Vietnam, Laos, and Cambodia; and, above all, Hanoi's fanatical will to unification—went unnoticed or unweighed because they failed to fit Washington's worldview. Although it is true, as Secretary of State Rusk once said, that "one cannot escape one's experience," Rusk and his fellow policymakers seriously erred by falling uncritical prisoners of their experience.

Another shared experience plagued 1960s policymakers like a ghost: the ominous specter of McCarthyism. This frightful political memory haunted LBJ and his Democratic colleagues like a barely suppressed demon in the national psyche. Barely ten years removed from the traumatic "loss" of China and its devastating domestic repercussions, Johnson and his advisers remembered its consequences vividly and shuddered at a similar fate in Vietnam. They talked about this only privately, but then with genuine and palpable fear. Defense Secretary McNamara, in a guarded moment, confided to a newsman in the spring of 1965 that U.S. disengagement from South Vietnam threatened "a disastrous political fight that could . . . freeze American political debate and even affect political freedom."

Such fears resonated deeply in policymakers' minds. Nothing, it seemed, could be worse than the "loss" of Vietnam—not even an intensifying stalemate secured at increasing military and political risk. For a President determined to fulfill liberalism's postwar agenda, Truman's ordeal in China seemed a powerfully forbidding lesson. It hung over LBJ in Vietnam like a dark shadow he could not shake, an agony he would not repeat.

McCarthyism's long shadow into the mid-1960s underscores a persistent and troubling phenomenon of postwar American politics: the peculiar vulnerability besetting liberal Presidents thrust into the maelstrom of world politics. In America's postwar political climate—dominated by the culture of anticommunism—Democratic leaders from Truman to Kennedy to Johnson remained acutely sensitive to the domestic repercussions of foreign policy failure. This fear of rightwing reaction sharply inhibited liberals like LBJ, narrowing what they considered their range of politically acceptable options, while diminishing their willingness to disengage from untenable foreign commitments. Thus, when Johnson did confront the bitter choice between defeat in Vietnam and fighting a major, inconclusive war, he reluctantly chose the second because he could not tolerate the domestic consequences of the first. Committed to fulfilling the Great Society, fearful of resurgent McCarthyism, and afraid that disengagement meant sacrificing the former to the latter, LBJ perceived least political danger in holding on.

But if Johnson resigned never to "lose" South Vietnam, he also resigned never to sacrifice his cherished Great Society in the process. LBJ's determination, however understandable, nonetheless led him deliberately and seriously to obscure the nature and cost of America's deepening involvement in the war during 1964–1965. This decision bought Johnson the short-term political maneuverability he wanted, but at a costly long-term political price. As LBJ's credibility on the war subsequently eroded, public confidence in his leadership slowly but irretrievably evaporated. And this, more than any other factor, is what finally drove Johnson from the White House.

It also tarnished the presidency and damaged popular faith in American government for more than a decade. Trapped between deeply conflicting pressures, LBJ never shared his dilemma with the public. Johnson would not, or felt he dare not, trust his problems with the American people. LBJ's decision, however human, tragically undermined the reciprocal faith between President and public indispensable to effective governance in a democracy. Just as tragically, it fostered a pattern of presidential behavior which led his successor, Richard Nixon, to eventual ruin amid even greater popular political alienation.

Time slowly healed most of these wounds to the American political process, while reconfirming the fundamental importance of presidential credibility in a democracy. Johnson's Vietnam travail underscored the necessity of public trust and support to presidential success. Without them, as LBJ painfully discovered, Presidents are doomed to disaster.

Johnson, in retrospect, might have handled his domestic dilemma more forthrightly. An equally serious dilemma, however, remained always beyond his—or Washington's—power to mend: the root problem of political disarray in South Vietnam. The perennial absence of stable and responsive government in Saigon troubled Washington policymakers profoundly; they understood, only too well, its pivotal importance to the war effort and to the social and economic reforms essential to the country's survival. Over and over again, American officials stressed the necessity of political cooperation to their embattled South Vietnamese allies. But to no avail. As one top American in Saigon later lamented, "[Y]ou could tell them all 'you've got to get together [and stop] this haggling and fighting among yourselves,' but how do you make them do it?" he said. "How do you make them do it?"

Washington, alas, could not. As Ambassador Taylor conceded early in the war, "[You] cannot order good government. You can't get it by fiat." This stubborn but telling truth eventually came to haunt Taylor and others. South Vietnam never marshaled the political will necessary to create an effective and enduring government; it never produced leaders addressing the aspirations and thus attracting the allegiance of the South Vietnamese people. Increasing levels of U.S. troops and firepower, moreover, never offset this fundamental debility. America, as a consequence, built its massive military effort on a foundation of political quicksand.

The causes of this elemental flaw lay deeply imbedded in the social and political history of the region. Neither before nor after 1954 was South Vietnam ever really a nation in spirit. Divided by profound ethnic and religious cleavages dating back centuries and perpetuated under French colonial rule, the people of South Vietnam never developed a common political identity. Instead, political factionalism and rivalry always held sway. The result: a chronic and fatal political disorder.

Saigon's fundamental weakness bore anguished witness to the limits of U.S. power. South Vietnam's shortcomings taught a proud and mighty nation that it could not save a people in spite of themselves—that American power, in the last analysis, offered no viable substitute for indigenous political resolve. Without this basic ingredient, as Saigon's turbulent history demonstrated, Washington's most dedicated and strenuous efforts will prove extremely vulnerable, if not futile.

This is not a happy or popular lesson. But it is a wise and prudent one, attuned to the imperfect realities of an imperfect world. One of America's sagest diplomats, George Kennan, understood and articulated this lesson well when he observed: "When it comes to helping people to resist Communist pressures, . . . no assistance . . . can be effective unless the people themselves have a very high degree of determination and a willingness to help themselves. The moment they begin to place the bulk of the burden on us," Kennan warned, "the whole situation is lost." This, tragically, is precisely what befell America in South Vietnam during 1964–1965. Hereafter, as perhaps always before—*external* U.S. economic, military, and political support provided the vital elements of stability and strength in South Vietnam. Without that *external* support, as events following America's long-delayed withdrawal in 1973 showed, South Vietnam's government quickly failed.

Washington's effort to forge political order through military power spawned another tragedy as well. It ignited unexpected pressures which quickly overwhelmed U.S. policymakers, and pulled them ever deeper into the war. LBJ and his advisers began bombing North Vietnam in early 1965 in a desperate attempt to spur political resolve in South Vietnam. But their effort boomeranged wildly. Rather than stabilizing the situation, it instead unleashed forces that soon put Johnson at the mercy of circumstances, a hostage to the war's accelerating momentum. LBJ, as a result, began steering with an ever looser hand. By the summer of 1965, President Johnson found himself not the controller of events but largely controlled by them. He had lost the political leader's "continual struggle," in the words of Henry Kissinger, "to rescue an element of choice from the pressure of circumstance."

LBJ's experience speaks powerfully across the years. With each Vietnam decision, Johnson's vulnerability to military pressure and bureaucratic momentum intensified sharply. Each step generated demands for another, even bigger step—which LBJ found increasingly difficult to resist. His predicament confirmed George Ball's admonition that war is a fiercely unpredictable force, often generating its own inexorable momentum.

Johnson sensed this danger almost intuitively. He quickly grasped the dilemma and difficulties confronting him in Vietnam. But LBJ lacked the inner strength—the security and self-confidence—to overrule the counsel of his inherited advisers.

Most of those advisers, on the other hand—especially McGeorge Bundy and Robert McNamara—failed to anticipate such perils. Imbued with an overweening faith in their ability to "manage" crises and "control" escalation, Bundy and McNamara, along with Maxwell Taylor, first pushed military action against the North as a lever to force political improvement in the South. But bombing did not rectify Saigon's political problems; it only exacerbated them, while igniting turbulent military pressures that rapidly overwhelmed these advisers' confident calculations.

These advisers' preoccupation with technique, with the application of power, characterized much of America's approach to the Vietnam War. Bundy and McNamara epitomized a postwar generation confident in the exercise and efficacy of U.S. power. Despite the dark and troubled history of European intervention in Indochina, these men stubbornly refused to equate America's situation in the mid-1960s to France's earlier ordeal. To them, the United States possessed limitless ability, wisdom, and virtue; it would therefore prevail where other western powers had failed.

This arrogance born of power led policymakers to ignore manifest dangers, to persist in the face of ever darkening circumstances. Like figures in Greek tragedy, pride compelled these supremely confident men further into disaster. They succumbed to the affliction common to great powers throughout the ages—the dangerous "self-esteem engendered by power," as the political philosopher Hans Morgenthau once wrote, "which equates power and virtue, [and] in the process loses all sense of moral and political proportion."

Tradition, as well as personality, nurtured such thinking. For in many ways, America's military intervention in Vietnam represented the logical fulfillment of a policy and outlook axiomatically accepted by U.S. policymakers for nearly two decades—the doctrine of global containment. Fashioned at the outset of the Cold War, global containment extended American interests and obligations across vast new areas of the world in defense against perceived monolithic communist expansion. It remained the lodestar of America foreign policy, moreover, even as the constellation of international forces shifted dramatically amid diffused authority and power among communist states and nationalist upheaval in the post-colonial world.

Vietnam exposed the limitations and contradictions of this static doctrine in a world of flux. It also revealed the dangers and flaws of an undiscriminating, universalist policy which perceptive critics of global containment, such as the eminent journalist Walter Lippmann, had anticipated from the beginning. As Lippmann warned about global containment in 1947:

> Satellite states and puppet governments are not good material out of which to construct unassailable barriers [for American defense]. A diplomatic war conducted as this policy demands, that is to say conducted indirectly, means that we must stake our own security and the peace of the world upon satellites, puppets, clients, agents about whom we can know very little. Frequently they will act for their own reasons, and on their own judgments, presenting us with accomplished facts that we did not intend, and with crises for which we are unready. The "unassailable barriers" will present us with an unending series of insoluble dilemmas. We shall have either to disown our puppets, which would be tantamount to appeasement and defeat and loss of face, or must support them at an incalculable cost. . . .

Here lay the heart of America's Vietnam troubles. Driven by unquestioning allegiance to an ossified and extravagant doctrine, Washington officials plunged deeply into a struggle which itself dramatized the changed realities and complexities of the postwar world. Their action teaches both the importance of re-examining premises as circumstances change and the costly consequences of failing to recognize and adapt to them.

Vietnam represented a failure not just of American foreign policy but also of American statesmanship. For once drawn into the war, LBJ and his advisers quickly sensed Vietnam's immense difficulties and dangers—Saigon's congenital political problems, the war's spiraling military costs, the remote likelihood of victory—and plunged in deeper nonetheless. In their determination to preserve America's international credibility and protect their domestic political standing, they continued down an ever costlier path.

That path proved a distressing, multifaceted paradox. Fearing injury to the perception of American power, diminished faith in U.S. resolve, and a conservative political firestorm, policymakers rigidly pursued a course which ultimately injured the substance of American power by consuming exorbitant lives and resources, shook allied confidence in U.S. strategic judgment, and shattered liberalism's political unity and vigor by polarizing and paralyzing American society.

Herein lies Vietnam's most painful but pressing lesson. Statesmanship requires judgment, sensibility, and, above all, wisdom in foreign affairs—the wisdom to calculate national interests prudently and to balance commitments with effective power. It requires that most difficult task of political leaders: "to distinguish between what is desireable and what is possible, . . . between what is desireable and what is essential."

This is important in peace; it is indispensable in war. As the great tutor of statesmen, Carl von Clausewitz, wrote, "Since war is not an act of senseless passion but is controlled by its political object, the value of this object must determine the sacrifices to be made for it in *magnitude* and also in *duration.* Once the expenditure of effort exceeds the value of the political object," Clausewitz admonished, "the object must be renounced. . . ." His maxim, in hindsight, seems painfully relevant to a war which, as even America's military commander in Vietnam, General William Westmoreland, concluded, "the vital security of the United States was not and possibly could not be clearly demonstrated and understood. . . ."

LBJ and his advisers failed to heed this fundamental principle of statesmanship. They failed to weigh American costs in Vietnam against Vietnam's relative importance to American national interests and its effect on overall American power. Compelled by events in Vietnam and, especially, coercive political pressures at home, they deepened an unsound, peripheral commitment and pursued manifestly unpromising and immensely costly objectives. Their failure of statesmanship, then, proved a failure of judgment and, above all, of proportion.

H. R. McMaster

 **NO**

Dereliction of Duty

The Americanization of the Vietnam War between 1963 and 1965 was the product of an unusual interaction of personalities and circumstances. The escalation of U.S. military intervention grew out of a complicated chain of events and a complex web of decisions that slowly transformed the conflict in Vietnam into an American war.

Much of the literature on Vietnam has argued that the "Cold War mentality" put such pressure on President Johnson that the Americanization of the war was inevitable. The imperative to contain Communism was an important factor in Vietnam policy, but neither American entry into the war nor the manner in which the war was conducted was inevitable. The United States went to war in Vietnam in a manner unique in American history. Vietnam was not forced on the United States by a tidal wave of Cold War ideology. It slunk in on cat's feet.

Between November 1963 and July 1965, LBJ made the critical decisions that took the United States into war almost without realizing it. The decisions, and the way in which he made them, profoundly affected the way the United States fought in Vietnam. Although impersonal forces, such as the ideological imperative of containing Communism, the bureaucratic structure, and institutional priorities, influenced the president's Vietnam decisions, those decisions depended primarily on his character, his motivations, and his relationships with his principal advisers.

Most investigations of how the United States entered the war have devoted little attention to the crucial developments which shaped LBJ's approach to Vietnam and set conditions for a gradual intervention. The first of several "turning points" in the American escalation comprised the near-contemporaneous assassinations of Ngo Dinh Diem and John F. Kennedy. The legacy of the Kennedy administration included an expanded commitment to South Vietnam as an "experiment" in countering Communist insurgencies and a deep distrust of the military that manifested itself in the appointment of officers who would prove supportive of the administration's policies. After November 1963 the United States confronted what in many ways was a new war in South Vietnam. Having deposed the government of Ngo Dinh Diem and his brother

Nhu, and having supported actions that led to their deaths, Washington assumed responsibility for the new South Vietnamese leaders. Intensified Viet Cong activity added impetus to U.S. deliberations, leading Johnson and his advisers to conclude that the situation in South Vietnam demanded action beyond military advice and support. Next, in the spring of 1964, the Johnson administration adopted graduated pressure as its strategic concept for the Vietnam War. Rooted in Maxwell Taylor's national security strategy of flexible response, graduated pressure evolved over the next year, becoming the blueprint for the deepening American commitment to maintaining South Vietnam's independence. Then, in August 1964, in response to the Gulf of Tonkin incident, the United States crossed the threshold of direct American military action against North Vietnam.

The Gulf of Tonkin resolution gave the president carte blanche for escalating the war. During the ostensibly benign "holding period" from September 1964 to February 1965, LBJ was preoccupied with his domestic political agenda, and McNamara built consensus behind graduated pressure. In early 1965 the president raised U.S. intervention to a higher level again, deciding on February 9 to begin a systematic program of limited air strikes on targets in North Vietnam and, on February 26, to commit U.S. ground forces to the South. Last, in March 1965, he quietly gave U.S. ground forces the mission of "killing Viet Cong." That series of decisions, none in itself tantamount to a clearly discernable decision to go to war, nevertheless transformed America's commitment in Vietnam.

◦◉◦

Viewed together, those decisions might create the impression of a deliberate determination on the part of the Johnson administration to go to war. On the contrary, the president did not want to go to war in Vietnam and was not planning to do so. Indeed, as early as May 1964, LBJ seemed to realize that an American war in Vietnam would be a costly failure. He confided to McGeorge Bundy, ". . . looks like to me that we're getting into another Korea. It just worries the hell out of me. I don't see what we can ever hope to get out of this." It was, Johnson observed, "the biggest damn mess that I ever saw. . . . It's damn easy to get into a war, but . . . it's going to be harder to ever extricate yourself if you get in." Despite his recognition that the situation in Vietnam demanded that he consider alternative courses of action and make a difficult decision, LBJ sought to avoid or to postpone indefinitely an explicit choice between war and disengagement from South Vietnam. In the ensuing months, however, each decision he made moved the United States closer to war, although he seemed not to recognize that fact.

The president's fixation on short-term political goals, combined with his character and the personalities of his principal civilian and military advisers, rendered the administration incapable of dealing adequately with the complexities of the situation in Vietnam. LBJ's advisory system was structured to achieve consensus and to prevent potentially damaging leaks. Profoundly insecure and distrustful of anyone but his closest civilian advisers, the president viewed the JCS [Joint Chiefs of Staff] with suspicion. When the situation in Vietnam seemed to demand military action, Johnson did not turn to his military advisers to determine how to solve the problem. He turned instead to his civilian advisers to determine how to postpone a decision. The relationship between the president, the secretary of defense, and the Joint Chiefs led to the curious situation in which the nation went to war without the benefit of effective military advice from the organization having the statutory responsibility to be the nation's "principal military advisers."

⋞◉⋟

What Johnson feared most in 1964 was losing his chance to win the presidency in his own right. He saw Vietnam principally as a danger to that goal. After the election, he feared that an American military response to the deteriorating situation in Vietnam would jeopardize chances that his Great Society would pass through Congress. The Great Society was to be Lyndon Johnson's great domestic political legacy, and he could not tolerate the risk of its failure. McNamara would help the president first protect his electoral chances and then pass the Great Society by offering a strategy for Vietnam that appeared cheap and could be conducted with minimal public and congressional attention. McNamara's strategy of graduated pressure permitted Johnson to pursue his objective of not losing the war in Vietnam while postponing the "day of reckoning" and keeping the whole question out of public debate all the while.

McNamara was confident in his ability to satisfy the president's needs. He believed fervently that nuclear weapons and the Cold War international political environment had made traditional military experience and thinking not only irrelevant, but often dangerous for contemporary policy. Accordingly, McNamara, along with systems analysts and other civilian members of his own department and the Department of State, developed his own strategy for Vietnam. Bolstered by what he regarded as a personal triumph during the Cuban missile crisis, McNamara drew heavily on that experience and applied it to Vietnam. Based on the assumption that carefully controlled and sharply limited military actions were reversible, and therefore could be carried out at minimal risk and cost, graduated pressure allowed McNamara and Johnson to avoid confronting many of the possible consequences of military action.

⋞◉⋟

Johnson and McNamara succeeded in creating the illusion that the decisions to attack North Vietnam were alternatives to war rather than war itself. Graduated pressure defined military action as a form of communication, the object of which was to affect the enemy's calculation of interests and dissuade him from a particular activity. Because the favored means of communication (bombing fixed installations and economic targets) were not appropriate for the mobile forces of the Viet Cong, who lacked an infrastructure and whose strength in the South was political as well as military, McNamara and his colleagues pointed to the infiltration of men and supplies into South Vietnam as proof that the source and center of the enemy's power in Vietnam lay north of the seventeenth parallel, and specifically in Hanoi. Their definition of the enemy's Source of strength was derived from that strategy rather than from a critical examination of the full reality in South Vietnam—and turned out to be inaccurate.

Graduated pressure was fundamentally flawed in other ways. The strategy ignored the uncertainty of war and the unpredictable psychology of an activity that involves killing, death, and destruction. To the North Vietnamese, military action, involving as it did attacks on their forces and bombing of their territory, was not simply a means of communication. Human sacrifices in war evoke strong emotions, creating a dynamic that defies systems analysis quantification. Once the United States crossed the threshold of war against North Vietnam with covert raids and the Gulf of Tonkin "reprisals," the future course of events depended not only on decisions made in Washington but also on enemy responses and actions that were unpredictable. McNamara, however, viewed the war as another business management problem that, he assumed, would ultimately succumb to his reasoned judgment and others' rational calculations. He and his assistants thought that they could predict with great precision what amount of force applied in Vietnam would achieve the results they desired and they believed that they could control that force with great precision from halfway around the world. There were compelling contemporaneous arguments that graduated pressure would not affect Hanoi's will sufficiently to convince the North to desist from its support of the South, and that such a strategy would probably lead to an escalation of the war. Others expressed doubts about the utility of attacking North Vietnam by air to win a conflict in South Vietnam. Nevertheless, McNamara refused to consider the consequences of his recommendations and forged ahead oblivious of the human and psychological complexities of war.

Despite their recognition that graduated pressure was fundamentally flawed, the JCS were unable to articulate effectively either their objections or alternatives. Interservice rivalry was a significant impediment. Although differing perspectives were understandable given the Chiefs' long experience in their own services and their need to protect the interests of their services, the president's principal military advisers were obligated by law to render their best advice. The Chiefs' failure to do so, and their willingness to present single-service remedies to a complex military problem, prevented them from developing a comprehensive estimate of the situation or from thinking effectively about strategy.

When it became clear to the Chiefs that they were to have little influence on the policy-making process, they failed to confront the president with their objections to McNamara's approach to the war. Instead they attempted to work within that strategy in order to remove over time the limitations to further action. Unable to develop a strategic alternative to graduated pressure, the Chiefs became fixated on means by which the war could be conducted and pressed for an escalation of the war by degrees. They hoped that graduated pressure would evolve over time into a fundamentally different strategy, more in keeping with their belief in the necessity of greater force and its more resolute application. In so doing, they gave tacit approval to graduated pressure during the critical period in which the president escalated the war. They did not recommend the total force they believed would ultimately be required in Vietnam and accepted a strategy they knew would lead to a large but inadequate commitment of troops, for an extended period of time, with little hope for success.

⌘

McNamara and Lyndon Johnson were far from disappointed with the joint Chiefs' failings. Because his priorities were domestic, Johnson had little use for military advice that recommended actions inconsistent with those priorities. McNamara and his assistants in the Department of Defense, on the other hand, were arrogant. They disparaged military advice because they thought that their intelligence and analytical methods could compensate for their lack of military experience and education. Indeed military experience seemed to them a liability because military officers took too narrow a view and based their advice on antiquated notions of war. Geopolitical and technological changes of the last fifteen years, they believed, had rendered advice based on military experience irrelevant and, in fact, dangerous. McNamara's disregard for military experience and for history left him to draw principally on his staff in the Department of Defense and led him to conclude that his only real experience with the planning and direction of military force, the Cuban missile crisis, was the most relevant analogy to Vietnam.

While they slowly deepened American military involvement in Vietnam, Johnson and McNamara pushed the Chiefs further away from the decision-making process. There was no meaningful structure through which the Chiefs could voice their views—even the chairman was not a reliable conduit. NSC meetings were strictly *pro forma* affairs in which the president endeavored to build consensus for decisions already made. Johnson continued Kennedy's practice of meeting with small groups of his most trusted advisers. Indeed he made his most important decisions at the Tuesday lunch meetings in which Rusk, McGeorge Bundy, and McNamara were the only regular participants. The president and McNamara shifted responsibility for real planning away from the JCS to ad hoc committees composed principally of civilian analysts and attorneys, whose main goal was to obtain a consensus consistent with the president's pursuit of the middle ground between disengagement and war. The products of those efforts carried the undeserved credibility of proposals that had been agreed on by all departments and were therefore hard to oppose. McNamara and Johnson endeavored to get the advice they wanted by placing conditions and qualifications on questions that they asked the Chiefs. When the Chiefs' advice was not consistent with his own recommendations, McNamara, with the aid of the chairman of the Joint Chiefs of Staff, lied in meetings of the National Security Council about the Chiefs' views.

Rather than advice McNamara and Johnson extracted from the JCS acqui-escence and silent support for decisions already made. Even as they relegated the Chiefs to a peripheral position in the policy-making process, they were careful to preserve the facade of consultation to prevent the JCS from opposing the administration's policies either openly or behind the scenes. As American involvement in the war escalated, Johnson's vulnerability to disaffected senior military officers increased because he was purposely deceiving the Congress and the public about the nature of the American military effort in Vietnam. The president and the secretary of defense deliberately obscured the nature of decisions made and left undefined the limits that they envisioned on the use of force. They indicated to the Chiefs that they would take actions that they never intended to pursue. McNamara and his assistants, who considered com-munication the purpose of military action, kept the nature of their objective from the JCS, who viewed "winning" as the only viable goal in war. Finally, Johnson appealed directly to them, referring to himself as the "coach" and them as "his team." To dampen their calls for further action, Lyndon Johnson attempted to generate sympathy from the JCS for the great pressures that he was feeling from those who opposed escalation.

The ultimate test of the Chiefs' loyalty came in July 1965. The adminis-tration's lies to the American public had grown in magnitude as the American military effort in Vietnam escalated. The president's plan of deception depended on tacit approval or silence from the JCS. LBJ had misrepresented the mission of U.S. ground forces in Vietnam, distorted the views of the Chiefs to lend credibility to his decision against mobilization, grossly understated the numbers of troops General Westmoreland had requested, and lied to the Congress about the monetary cost of actions already approved and of those awaiting final decision. The Chiefs did not disappoint the president. In the days before the president made his duplicitous public announcement concern-ing Westmoreland's request, the Chiefs, with the exception of commandant of the Marine Corps Greene, withheld from congressmen their estimates of the amount of force that would be needed in Vietnam. As he had during the Gulf of Tonkin hearings, Wheeler lent his support to the president's deception of Congress. The "five silent men" on the Joint Chiefs made possible the way the United States went to war in Vietnam.

Several factors kept the Chiefs from challenging the president's subterfuges. The professional code of the military officer prohibits him or her from engag-ing in political activity. Actions that could have undermined the administra-tion's credibility and derailed its Vietnam policy could not have been undertaken lightly. The Chiefs felt loyalty to their commander in chief. The Truman-MacArthur controversy during the Korean War had warned the Chiefs about the dangers of overstepping the bounds of civilian control. Loyalty to their services also weighed against opposing the president and the secretary of defense. Harold Johnson, for example, decided against resignation because he thought he had to remain in office to protect the Army's interests as best he could. Admiral McDonald and Marine Corps Commandant Greene compromised their views on Vietnam in exchange for concessions to their respective services. Greene achieved a dramatic expansion of the Marine Corps, and McDonald ensured that the Navy retained control of Pacific Command. None of the Chiefs had sworn an oath to his service, however. They had all sworn, rather, to "support and defend the Constitution of the United States."

General Greene recalled that direct requests by congressmen for his assessment put him in a difficult situation. The president was lying, and he expected the Chiefs to lie as well or, at least, to withhold the whole truth. Although the president should not have placed the Chiefs in that position, the flag officers should not have tolerated it when he had.

Because the Constitution locates civilian control of the military in Congress as well as in the executive branch, the Chiefs could not have been justified in deceiving the peoples' representatives about Vietnam. Wheeler in particular allowed his duty to the president to overwhelm his obligations under the Constitution. As cadets are taught at the United States Military Academy, the JCS relationship with the Congress is challenging and demands that military officers possess a strong character and keen intellect. While the Chiefs must present Congress with their best advice based on their professional experience and education, they must be careful not to undermine their credibility by crossing the line between advice and advocacy of service interests.

Maxwell Taylor had a profound influence on the nature of the civil-military relationship during the escalation of American involvement in Vietnam. In contrast to Army Chief of Staff George C. Marshall, who, at the start of World War II, recognized the need for the JCS to suppress service parochialism to provide advice consistent with national interests, Taylor exacerbated service differences to help McNamara and Johnson keep the Chiefs divided and, thus, marginal to the policy process. Taylor recommended men for appointment to the JCS who were less likely than their predecessors to challenge the direction of the administration's military policy, even when they knew that that policy was fundamentally flawed. Taylor's behavior is perhaps best explained by his close personal friendship with the Kennedy family; McNamara; and, later, Johnson. In contrast again to Marshall, who thought it important to keep a professional distance from President Franklin Roosevelt, Taylor abandoned an earlier view similar to Marshall's in favor of a belief that the JCS and the president should enjoy "an intimate, easy relationship, born of friendship and mutual regard."

◦✿◦

The way in which the United States went to war in the period between November 1963 and July 1965 had, not surprisingly, a profound influence on the conduct of the war and on its outcome. Because Vietnam policy decisions were made based on domestic political expediency, and because the president was intent on forging a consensus position behind what he believed was a middle policy, the administration deliberately avoided clarifying its policy objectives and postponed discussing the level of force that the president was willing to commit to the effort. Indeed, because the president was seeking domestic political consensus, members of the administration believed that ambiguity in the objectives for fighting in Vietnam was a strength rather than a weakness. Determined to prevent dissent from the JCS, the administration concealed its development of "fall-back" objectives.

Over time the maintenance of U.S. credibility quietly supplanted the stated policy objective of a free and independent South Vietnam. The principal civilian planners had determined that to guarantee American credibility, it was not necessary to win in Vietnam. That conclusion, combined with the belief that the use of force was merely another form of diplomatic communication, directed the military effort in the South at achieving stalemate rather than victory. Those charged with planning the war believed that it would be possible to preserve American credibility even if the United States armed forces withdrew from the South, after a show of force against the North and in the South in which American forces were "bloodied." After the United States became committed to war, however, and more American soldiers, airmen, and Marines had died in the conflict, it would become impossible simply to disengage and declare America's credibility intact, a fact that should have been foreseen. The Chiefs sensed the shift in objectives, but did not challenge directly the views of civilian planners in that connection. McNamara and Johnson recognized that, once committed to war, the JCS would not agree to an objective other than imposing a solution on the enemy consistent with U.S. interests. The JCS deliberately avoided clarifying the objective as well. As a result, when the United States went to war, the JCS pursued objectives different from those of the president. When the Chiefs requested permission to apply force consistent with their conception of U.S. objectives, the president and McNamara, based on their goals and domestic political constraints, rejected JCS requests, or granted them only in part. The result was that the JCS and McNamara became fixated on the means rather than on the ends, and on the manner in which the war was conducted instead of a military strategy that could connect military actions to achievable policy goals.

Because forthright communication between top civilian and military officials in the Johnson administration was never developed, there was no reconciliation of McNamara's intention to limit the American military effort sharply and the Chiefs' assessment that the United States could not possibly win under such conditions. If they had attempted to reconcile those positions, they could not have helped but recognize the futility of the American war effort.

The Joint Chiefs of Staff became accomplices in the president's deception and focused on a tactical task, killing the enemy. General Westmoreland's "strategy" of attrition in South Vietnam, was, in essence, the absence of a strategy. The result was military activity (bombing North Vietnam and killing the enemy in South Vietnam) that did not aim to achieve a clearly defined objective. It was unclear how quantitative measures by which McNamara interpreted the success and failure of the use of military force were contributing to an end of the war. As American casualties mounted and the futility of the strategy became apparent, the American public lost faith in the effort. The Chiefs did not request the number of troops they believed necessary to impose a military solution in South Vietnam until after the Tet offensive in 1968. By that time, however, the president was besieged by opposition to the war and was unable even to consider the request. LBJ, who had gone to such great lengths to ensure a crushing defeat over Barry Goldwater in 1964, declared that he was withdrawing from the race for his party's presidential nomination.

Johnson thought that he would be able to control the U.S. involvement in Vietnam. That belief, based on the strategy of graduated pressure and McNamara's confident assurances, proved in dramatic fashion to be false. If the president was surprised by the consequences of his decisions between November 1963 and July 1965, he should not have been so. He had disregarded the advice he did not want to hear in favor of a policy based on the pursuit of his own political fortunes and his beloved domestic programs.

The war in Vietnam was not lost in the field, nor was it lost on the front pages of the *New York Times* or on the college campuses. It was lost in Washington, D.C., even before Americans assumed sole responsibility for the fighting in 1965 and before they realized the country was at war; indeed, even before the first American units were deployed. The disaster in Vietnam was not the result of impersonal forces but a uniquely human failure, the responsibility for which was shared by President Johnson and his principal military and civilian advisers. The failings were many and reinforcing: arrogance, weakness, lying in the pursuit of self-interest, and, above all, the abdication of responsibility to the American people.

POSTSCRIPT

Was the Americanization of the War in Vietnam Inevitable?

The book from which VanDeMark's selection was excerpted is a detailed study of the circumstances surrounding the decisions that President Lyndon Johnson made to increase America's presence in Vietnam via the bombing raids of North Vietnam in February 1965 and the introduction of ground troops the following July. VanDeMark agrees with McMaster that Johnson did not consult the Joint Chiefs of Staff about the wisdom of the policy of escalating the war. In fact, Johnson's decisions of "graduated pressure" were made in increments by the civilian advisers surrounding Secretary of Defense Robert McNamara. The policy, if it can be called such, was to prevent the National Liberation Front and its Viet Cong army from taking over South Vietnam. Each service branch fought its own war without coordinating with one another or with the government of South Vietnam. In VanDeMark's view, U.S. intervention was doomed to failure because South Vietnam was an artificial and very corrupt nation-state created by the French and later supported by the Americans. It was unfortunate that the nationalist revolution was tied up with the Communists led by Ho Chi Minh, who had been fighting French colonialism and Japanese imperialism since the 1920s—unlike Korea and Malaysia, which had alternative, noncommunist, nationalist movements.

Why did Johnson plunge "into the quagmire"? For one thing, Johnson remembered how previous Democratic presidents Franklin D. Roosevelt and Harry S. Truman had been charged with being soft on communism and accused of losing Eastern Europe to the Russians after the Second World War and China to the Communists in the Chinese Civil War in 1949. In addition, both presidents were charged by Senator Joseph McCarthy and others of harboring Communists in U.S. government agencies. If Johnson was tough in Vietnam, he could stop communist aggression. At the same time, he could ensure that his Great Society social programs of Medicare and job retraining, as well as the impending civil rights legislation, would be passed by Congress.

As an army officer who fought in the Persian Gulf War, McMaster offers a unique perspective on the decision-making processes used by government policymakers. McMaster spares no one in his critique of what he considers the flawed Vietnam policy of "graduated pressure." He says that McNamara, bolstered by the success of America during the Cuban Missile Crisis, believed that the traditional methods of fighting wars were obsolete. Johnson believed in McNamara's approach, and the president's own need for consensus in the decision-making process kept the Joint Chiefs of Staff out of the loop.

Unlike other military historians, who generally absolve the military from responsibility for the strategy employed during the war, McMaster argues that the Joint Chiefs of Staff were responsible for not standing up to Johnson and telling him that his military strategy was seriously flawed. McMaster's views are not as new as some reviewers of his book seem to think. Bruce Palmer, Jr., in *The Twenty-Five Year War: America's Military Role in Vietnam* (University Press of Kentucky, 1984), and Harry G. Summers, Jr., in *On Strategy: A Critical Analysis of the Vietnam War* (Presidio Press, 1982), also see a flawed strategy of war. Summers argues that Johnson should have asked Congress for a declaration of war and fought a conventional war against North Vietnam.

One scholar has claimed that over 7,000 books about the Vietnam War have been published. The starting point for the current issue is Lloyd Gardner and Ted Gittinger, eds., *Vietnam: The Early Decisions* (University of Texas Press, 1997). See also Larry Berman, *Planning a Tragedy: The Americanization of the War in Vietnam* (W. W. Norton, 1982) and *Lyndon Johnson's War* (W.W. Norton, 1989); David Halberstam, *The Best and the Brightest* (Random House, 1972); and Lloyd C. Gardner, *Pay Any Price: Lyndon Johnson and the Wars for Vietnam* (Ivan Dee, 1995). Primary sources can be found in the U.S. Department of State's two-volume *Foreign Relations of the United States, 1964–1968: Vietnam* (Government Printing Office, 1996) and in the relevant sections of one of the most useful collections of primary sources and essays, *Major Problems in the History of the Vietnam War*, 2d ed., by Robert J. McMahon (Houghton Mifflin, 2000).

The bureaucratic perspective can be found in a series of essays by George C. Herring entitled *LBJ and Vietnam: A Different Kind of War* (University of Texas Press, 1995). Herring is also the author of the widely used text *America's Longest War: The United States and Vietnam* (Alfred A. Knopf, 1986). A brilliant article often found in anthologies is by historian and former policymaker James Thompson, "How Could Vietnam Happen: An Autopsy," *The Atlantic Monthly* (April 1968). An interesting comparison of the 1954 Dien Bien Phu and 1965 U.S. escalation decisions is Fred I. Greenstein and John P. Burke, "The Dynamics of Presidential Reality Testing: Evidence From Two Vietnam Decisions," *Political Science Quarterly* (Winter 1989–1990). A nice review essay on Vietnam's impact on today's military thinking is Michael C. Desch's "Wounded Warriors and the Lessons of Vietnam," *Orbis* (Summer 1998).

ISSUE 15

Was Richard Nixon America's Last Liberal President?

YES: Joan Hoff-Wilson, from "Richard M. Nixon: The Corporate Presidency," in Fred I. Greenstein, ed., *Leadership in the Modern Presidency* (Harvard University Press, 1988)

NO: Bruce J. Schulman, from *The Seventies: The Great Shift in American Culture, Society, and Politics* (The Free Press/Simon & Schuster, 2001)

ISSUE SUMMARY

YES: According to professor of history Joan Hoff-Wilson, the Nixon presidency reorganized the executive branch and portions of the federal bureaucracy and implemented domestic reforms in civil rights, welfare, and economic planning, despite its limited foreign policy successes and the Watergate scandal.

NO: According to Professor Bruce J. Schulman, Richard Nixon was the first conservative president of the post–World War II era who undermined the Great Society legislative program of President Lyndon Baines Johnson and built a new Republican majority coalition of white, northern, blue-collar workers, and southern and sunbelt conservatives.

Richard Milhous Nixon was born in Yorba Linda in Orange County, California, on January 9, 1913. When he was nine, his family moved to Whittier, California. He attended Whittier College, where he excelled at student politics and debating. He earned a tuition-paid scholarship to Duke University Law School and graduated third out of a class of 25 in 1937. He returned to Whittier and for several years worked with the town's oldest law firm.

Nixon had hopes of joining a bigger law firm, but World War II intervened. He joined the navy as a lieutenant, junior grade, where he served in a Naval Transport Unit in the South Pacific for the duration of the war. Before his discharge from active duty, Republicans asked him to run for a seat in California's 12th congressional district in the House of Representatives. He won the primary and defeated Jerry Vorhees, a New Deal Democratic incumbent, in the general election of 1946. In that year, the Republicans gained control of Congress for the first time since 1930.

During Nixon's campaign against Vorhees, he accused Vorhees of accepting money from a communist-dominated political action committee. This tactic, known as "red-baiting," was effective in the late 1940s and early 1950s because the American public had become frightened of the communist menace. In 1950, Nixon utilized similar tactics in running for the U.S. Senate against Congresswoman Helen Gahaghan Douglas. He won easily.

Young, energetic, a vigorous campaign orator, and a senator from the second largest state in the Union with impeccable anticommunist credentials, Nixon was chosen by liberal Republicans to become General Dwight D. Eisenhower's running mate in the 1952 presidential election. In the election, Eisenhower and Nixon overwhelmed the Democrats. Nixon became the second-youngest vice president in U.S. history and actively used the office to further his political ambitions.

The 1960 presidential campaign was one of the closest in modern times. Nixon, who was considered young for high political office at that time, lost to an even younger Democratic senator from Massachusetts, John F. Kennedy. Out of 68 million votes cast, less than 113,000 votes separated the two candidates.

In 1962, Nixon was persuaded to seek the governorship of California on the premise that he needed a power boost to keep his presidential hopes alive for 1964. Apparently, Nixon was out of touch with state politics. Governor Pat Brown defeated him by 300,000 votes.

Nixon then left for New York City and became a partner with a big-time Wall Street legal firm. He continued to speak at Republican dinners, and he supported Barry Goldwater of Arizona for the presidency in March 1968. After Goldwater's decisive defeat by Lyndon B. Johnson, Nixon's political fortunes revived yet again. In March 1965, Johnson announced that he was not going to run again for the presidency. Nixon took advantage of the opening and won the Republican nomination.

During the 1968 presidential campaign, Nixon positioned himself between Democratic Vice President Hubert Humphrey, the liberal defender of the Great Society programs, and the conservative, law-and-order, third-party challenger Governor George Wallace of Alabama. Nixon stressed a more moderate brand of law and order and stated that he had a secret plan to end the war in Vietnam. He barely edged Humphrey in the popular vote, but Nixon received 301 electoral votes to 191 for Humphrey. Wallace received nearly 10 million popular votes and 46 electoral college votes.

This background brings us to Nixon's presidency. Was Nixon an effective president? In the following sections, Joan Hoff-Wilson argues that Nixon achieved a number of domestic policy successes in the areas of civil rights, welfare, and economic planning, and in the reorganization of the executive branch and some federal agencies. But Professor Bruce J. Schulman disagrees. He believes that President Nixon was the first conservative president of the post–World War II era who undermined the Great Society legislative programs of Lyndon Baines Johnson and built a new Republican majority coalition of northern white blue-collar workers and southern white conservatives and sunbelt space-age employees and its retirement communities.

YES

Joan Hoff-Wilson

Richard M. Nixon:
The Corporate Presidency

Richard Milhous Nixon became president of the United States at a critical juncture in American history. Following World War II there was a general agreement between popular and elite opinion on two things: the effectiveness of most New Deal domestic policies and the necessity of most Cold War foreign policies. During the 1960s, however, these two crucial postwar consensual constructs began to break down; and the war in Indochina, with its disruptive impact on the nation's political economy, hastened their disintegration. By 1968 the traditional bipartisan, Cold War approach to the conduct of foreign affairs had been seriously undermined. Similarly, the "bigger and better" New Deal approach to the modern welfare state had reached a point of diminishing returns, even among liberals.

In 1968, when Richard Nixon finally captured the highest office in the land, he inherited not only Lyndon Johnson's Vietnam war but also LBJ's Great Society. This transfer of power occurred at the very moment when both endeavors had lost substantial support among the public at large and, most important, among a significant number of the elite group of decision makers and leaders of opinion across the country. On previous occasions when such a breakdown had occurred within policy- and opinion-making circles—before the Civil and Spanish American Wars and in the early years of the Great Depression—domestic or foreign upheavals had followed. Beginning in the 1960s the country experienced a similar series of failed presidents reminiscent of those in the unstable 1840s and 1850s, 1890s, and 1920s.

In various ways all the presidents in these transitional periods failed as crisis managers, often because they refused to take risks. Nixon, in contrast, "[couldn't] understand people who won't take risks." His proclivity for risk taking was not emphasized by scholars, journalists, and psychologists until after he was forced to resign as president. "I am not necessarily a respecter of the status quo," Nixon told Stuart Alsop in 1958; "I am a chance taker." Although this statement was made primarily in reference to foreign affairs, Nixon's entire political career has been characterized by a series of personal and professional crises and risky political policies. It is therefore not surprising that as president he rationalized many of his major foreign and domestic

Reprinted by permission of the publisher from "Richard M. Nixon: The Corporate Presidency" by Joan Hoff-Wilson in LEADERSHIP IN THE MODERN PRESIDENCY, edited by Fred I. Greenstein, pp. 164–167, 189–198, Cambridge, Mass.: Harvard University. Notes omitted.

initiatives as crises (or at least as intolerable impasses) that could be resolved only by dramatic and sometimes drastic measures.

A breakdown in either the foreign or domestic policy consensus offers both opportunity and danger to any incumbent president. Nixon had more opportunity for risk-taking changes at home and abroad during his first administration than he would have had if elected in 1960 because of the disruptive impact of war and domestic reforms during the intervening eight years. Also, he inherited a wartime presidency, with all its temporarily enhanced extralegal powers. Although the Cold War in general has permanently increased the potential for constitutional violations by presidents, only those in the midst of a full-scale war (whether declared or undeclared) have exercised with impunity what Garry Wills has called "semi-constitutional" actions. Although Nixon was a wartime president for all but twenty months of his five and one-half years in office, he found that impunity for constitutional violations was not automatically accorded a president engaged in an undeclared, unsatisfying, and seemingly endless war. In fact, he is not usually even thought of, or referred to, as a wartime president.

Periods of war and reform have usually alternated in the United States, but in the 1960s they burgeoned simultaneously, hastening the breakdown of consensus that was so evident by the time of the 1968 election. This unusual situation transformed Nixon's largely unexamined and rather commonplace management views into more rigid and controversial ones. It also reinforced his natural predilection to bring about change through executive fiat. Thus a historical accident accounts in part for many of Nixon's unilateral administrative actions during his first term and for the events leading to his disgrace and resignation during his second.

The first few months in the Oval Office are often intoxicating, and a new president can use them in a variety of ways. But during the socioeconomic confusion and conflict of the late 1960s and early 1970s, some of the newly appointed Republican policy managers (generalists) and the frustrated holdover Democratic policy specialists (experts) in the bureaucracy unexpectedly came together and began to consider dramatic policy changes at home and abroad. Complex interactions between these very different groups produced several significant shifts in domestic and foreign affairs during the spring and summer of 1969. A radical welfare plan and dramatic foreign policy initiatives took shape.

The country had elected only one other Republican president since the onset of FDR's reform administrations thirty-six years earlier. Consequently, Nixon faced not only unprecedented opportunities for changing domestic policy as a result of the breakdown in the New Deal consensus, but also the traditional problems of presidential governance, exacerbated in this instance by bureaucratic pockets of resistance from an unusual number of holdover Democrats. Such resistance was not new, but its magnitude was particularly threatening to a distrusted (and distrustful) Republican president who did not control either house of Congress. Nixon's organizational recommendations for containing the bureaucracy disturbed his political opponents and the liberal press as much as, if not more than, their doubts about the motivation behind many of his substantive and innovative suggestions on other domestic issues such as welfare and the environment.

Because much of the press and both houses of Congress were suspicious of him, Nixon naturally viewed administrative action as one way of obtaining significant domestic reform. Moreover, some of his initial accomplishments in administratively redirecting U.S. foreign policy ultimately led him to rely more on administrative actions at home than he might have otherwise. In any case, this approach drew criticism from those who already distrusted his policies and priorities. Nixon's covert and overt expansion and prolongation of the war during this period reinforced existing suspicions about his personality and political ethics. In this sense, liberal paranoia about his domestic programs fueled Nixon's paranoia about liberal opposition to the war, and vice versa. By 1972, Nixon's success in effecting structural and substantive change in foreign policy through the exercise of unilateral executive power increasingly led him to think that he could use the same preemptive administrative approach to resolve remaining domestic problems, especially following his landslide electoral victory. . . .

Foreign Policy Scorecard

It was clearly in Nixon's psychic and political self-interest to end the war in Vietnam as soon as possible. Although he came to office committed to negotiate a quick settlement, he ended up prolonging the conflict. As a result, he could never build the domestic consensus he needed to continue the escalated air and ground war (even with dramatically reduced U.S. troop involvement) and to ensure passage of some of his domestic programs. For Nixon (and Kissinger) Vietnam became a symbol of influence in the Third World that, in turn, was but one part of their geopolitical approach to international relations. Thus the war in Southeast Asia had to be settled as soon as possible so as not to endanger other elements of Nixonian diplomatic and domestic policy.

Instead, the president allowed his secretary of state to become egocentrically involved in secret negotiations with the North Vietnamese from August 4, 1969, to January 25, 1972 (when they were made public). As a result, the terms finally reached in 1973 were only marginally better than those rejected in 1969. The advantage gained from Hanoi's agreement to allow President Nguyen Van Thieu to remain in power in return for allowing North Vietnamese troops to remain in South Vietnam can hardly offset the additional loss of twenty thousand American lives during this three-year-period—especially given the inherent weaknesses of the Saigon government by 1973. On the tenth anniversary of the peace treaty ending the war in Vietnam, Nixon admitted to me that "Kissinger believed more in the power of negotiation than I did." He also said that he "would not have temporized as long" with the negotiating process had he not been "needlessly" concerned with what the Soviets and Chinese might think if the United States pulled out of Vietnam precipitately. Because Nixon saw no way in 1969 to end the war quickly except through overt massive bombing attacks, which the public demonstrated in 1970 and 1971 it would not tolerate, there was neither peace nor honor in

Vietnam by the time that war was finally concluded on January 27, 1973; and in the interim he made matters worse by secretly bombing Cambodia.

The delayed ending to the war in Vietnam not only cast a shadow on all Nixon's other foreign policy efforts but also established secrecy, wiretapping, and capricious personal diplomacy as standard operational procedures in the conduct of foreign policy that ultimately carried over into domestic affairs. Despite often duplicitous and arbitrary actions, even Nixon's strongest critics often credit him with an unusual number of foreign policy successes.

Although fewer of his foreign policy decisions were reached in a crisis atmosphere than his domestic ones, Nixon's diplomatic legacy is weaker than he and many others have maintained. For example, the pursuit of "peace and honor" in Vietnam failed; his Middle Eastern policy because of Kissinger's shuttling ended up more show than substance; his Third World policy (outside of Vietnam and attempts to undermine the government of Allende in Chile) were nearly nonexistent; détente with the USSR soon foundered under his successors; and the Nixon Doctrine has not prevented use of U.S. troops abroad. Only rapprochement with China remains untarnished by time because it laid the foundation for recognition, even though he failed to achieve a "two China" policy in the United Nations. This summary is not meant to discredit Richard Nixon as a foreign policy expert both during and after his presidency. It is a reminder that the lasting and positive results of his diplomacy may be fading faster than some aspects of his domestic policies.

Outflanking Liberals on Domestic Reform

Presidents traditionally achieve their domestic objectives through legislation, appeals in the mass media, and administrative actions. During his first administration Nixon offered Congress extensive domestic legislation, most of which aimed at redistributing federal power away from Congress and the bureaucracy. When he encountered difficulty obtaining passage of these programs, he resorted more and more to reform by administrative fiat, especially at the beginning of his second term. All Nixonian domestic reforms were rhetorically linked under the rubric of the New Federalism. Most competed for attention with his well-known interest in foreign affairs. Most involved a degree of the boldness he thought necessary for a successful presidency. Most increased federal regulation of nondistributive public policies. Most were made possible in part because he was a wartime Republican president who took advantage of acting in the Disraeli tradition of enlightened conservatism. Most offended liberals (as well as many conservatives), especially when it came to implementing certain controversial policies with legislation. Many were also undertaken in a crisis atmosphere, which on occasion was manufactured by individual members of Nixon's staff to ensure his attention and action.

In some instances, as political scientist Paul J. Halpern has noted, Nixon's long-standing liberal opponents in Congress "never even bothered to get the facts straight" about these legislative and administrative innovations; the very people who, according to Daniel Moynihan, formed the "natural constituency" for most of Nixon's domestic policies refused to support his programs. It may well have been that many liberals simply could not believe that Nixon would ever do the right thing except for the wrong reason. Thus they seldom took the time to try to determine whether any of his efforts to make the 1970s a decade of reform were legitimate, however politically motivated. Additionally, such partisan opposition made Nixon all the more willing to reorganize the executive branch of government with or without congressional approval.

My own interviews with Nixon and his own (and others') recent attempts to rehabilitate his reputation indicate that Nixon thinks he will outlive the obloquy of Watergate because of his foreign policy initiatives—not because of his domestic policies. Ultimately, however, domestic reform and his attempts at comprehensive reorganization of the executive branch may become the standard by which the Nixon presidency is judged.

Environmental Policy

Although Nixon's aides cite his environmental legislation as one of his major domestic achievements, it was not high on his personal list of federal priorities, despite polls showing its growing importance as a national issue. White House central files released in 1986 clearly reveal that John Ehrlichman was initially instrumental in shaping the president's views on environmental matters and conveying a sense of crisis about them. Most ideas were filtered through him to Nixon. In fact Ehrlichman, whose particular expertise was in land-use policies, has been described by one forest conservation specialist as "the most effective environmentalist since Gifford Pinchot." Ehrlichman and John Whitaker put Nixon ahead of Congress on environmental issues, especially with respect to his use of the permit authority in the Refuse Act of 1899 to begin to clean up water supplies before Congress passed any "comprehensive water pollution enforcement plan."

"Just keep me out of trouble on environmental issues," Nixon reportedly told Ehrlichman. This proved impossible because Congress ignored Nixon's recommended ceilings when it finally passed (over his veto) the Federal Water Pollution Control Act amendments of 1972. Both Ehrlichman and Whitaker agreed then and later that it was "budget-busting" legislation designed to embarrass the president on a popular issue in an election year. Statistics later showed that the money appropriated could not be spent fast enough to achieve the legislation's stated goals. The actual annual expenditures in the first years after passage approximated those originally proposed by Nixon's staff.

Revamping Welfare

Throughout the 1968 presidential campaign Nixon's own views on welfare remained highly unfocused. But once in the Oval Office he set an unexpectedly fast pace on the issue. On January 15, 1969, he demanded an investigation by top aides into a newspaper allegation of corruption in New York City's Human Resources Administration. Nixon's extraordinary welfare legislation originated in a very circuitous fashion with two low-level Democratic holdovers from the Johnson administration, Worth Bateman and James Lyday.

These two bureaucrats fortuitously exercised more influence on Robert Finch, Nixon's first secretary of health, education and welfare, than they had been able to on John W. Gardner and Wilbur J. Cohn, Johnson's two appointees. Finch was primarily responsible for obtaining Nixon's approval of what eventually became known as the Family Assistance Program (FAP).

If FAP had succeeded in Congress it would have changed the emphasis of American welfare from providing services to providing income; thus it would have replaced the Aid to Families with Dependent Children (AFDC) program, whose payments varied widely from state to state. FAP called for anywhere from $1,600 (initially proposed in 1969) to $2,500 (proposed in 1971) for a family of four. States were expected to supplement this amount, and in addition all ablebodied heads of recipient families (except mothers with preschool children) would be required to "accept work or training." However, if a parent refused to accept work or training, only his or her payment would be withheld. In essence, FAP unconditionally guaranteed children an annual income and would have tripled the number of children then being aided by AFDC.

A fundamental switch from services to income payments proved to be too much for congressional liberals and conservatives alike, and they formed a strange alliance to vote it down. Ironically, FAP's final defeat in the Senate led to some very impressive examples of incremental legislation that might not have been passed had it not been for the original boldness of FAP. For example, Supplementary Security Income, approved on October 17, 1972, constituted a guaranteed annual income for the aged, blind, and disabled.

The demise of FAP also led Nixon to support uniform application of the food stamp program across the United States, better health insurance programs for low-income families, and an automatic cost-of-living adjustment for Social Security recipients to help them cope with inflation. In every budget for which his administration was responsible—that is, from fiscal 1971 through fiscal 1975—spending on all human resource programs exceeded spending for defense for the first time since World War II. A sevenfold increase in funding for social services under Nixon made him (not Johnson) the "last of the big spenders" on domestic programs.

Reluctant Civil Rights Achievements

Perhaps the domestic area in which Watergate has most dimmed or skewed our memories of the Nixon years is civil rights. We naturally tend to remember that during his presidency Nixon deliberately violated the civil rights of some of those who opposed his policies or were suspected of leaking information. Nixon has always correctly denied that he was a conservative on civil rights, and indeed his record on this issue, as on so many others, reveals as much political expediency as it does philosophical commitment. By 1968 there was strong southern support for his candidacy. Consequently, during his campaign he implied that if elected he would slow down enforcement of federal school desegregation policies.

Enforcement had already been painfully sluggish since the 1954 *Brown v. Board of Education* decision. By 1968 only 20 percent of black children in the South attended predominantly white schools, and none of this progress had occurred under Eisenhower or Kennedy. Moreover, the most dramatic improvement under Johnson's administration did not take place until 1968, because HEW deadlines for desegregating southern schools had been postponed four times since the passage of the 1964 Civil Rights Act. By the spring of 1968, however, a few lower court rulings, and finally the Supreme Court decision in *Green v. Board of Education,* no longer allowed any president the luxury of arguing that freedom-of-choice plans were adequate for rooting out racial discrimination, or that de facto segregation caused by residential patterns was not as unconstitutional as *de jure* segregation brought about by state or local laws.

Despite the real national crisis that existed over school desegregation, Nixon was not prepared to go beyond what he thought the decision in *Brown* had mandated, because he believed that de facto segregation could not be ended through busing or cutting off funds from school districts. Nine days after Nixon's inauguration, his administration had to decide whether to honor an HEW-initiated cutoff of funds to five southern school districts, originally scheduled to take place in the fall of 1968 but delayed until January 29, 1969. On that day Secretary Finch confirmed the cutoff but also announced that the school districts could claim funds retroactively if they complied with HEW guidelines within sixty days. This offer represented a change from the most recent set of HEW guidelines, developed in March 1968, which Johnson had never formally endorsed by signing.

At the heart of the debate over various HEW guidelines in the last half of the 1960s were two issues: whether the intent of the Civil Rights Act of 1964 had been simply to provide freedom of choice or actually to compel integration in schools; and whether freedom-of-choice agreements negotiated by HEW or lawsuits brought by the Department of Justice were the most effective ways of achieving desegregation. Under the Johnson administration the HEW approach, based on bringing recalcitrant school districts into compliance by cutting off federal funding, had prevailed. Nixon, on the other hand, argued in his First Inaugural that the "laws have caught up with our consciences" and insisted that it was now necessary "to give life to what is in the law." Accordingly, he changed the emphasis in the enforcement of school desegregation from HEW compliance agreements to Justice Department actions—a legal procedure that proved very controversial in 1969 and 1970, but one that is standard now.

Nixon has been justifiably criticized by civil rights advocates for employing delaying tactics in the South, and particularly for not endorsing busing to enforce school desegregation in the North after the April 20, 1971, Supreme Court decision in *Swann v. Charlotte-Mecklenburg Board of Education.* Despite the bitter battle in Congress and between Congress and the executive branch after *Swann,* the Nixon administration's statistical record on school desegregation is impressive. In 1968, 68 percent of all black children in the South and 40 percent in the nation as a whole attended all-black schools. By the end of 1972, 8 percent of southern black children attended all-black schools, and a little less than 12 percent nationwide. A comparison of budget outlays is equally revealing. President Nixon spent

$911 million on civil rights activities, including $75 million for civil rights enforcement in fiscal 1969. The Nixon administration's budget for fiscal 1973 called for $2.6 billion in total civil rights outlays, of which $602 million was earmarked for enforcement through a substantially strengthened Equal Employment Opportunity Commission. Nixon supported the civil rights goals of American Indians and women with less reluctance than he did school desegregation because these groups did not pose a major political problem for him and he had no similar legal reservations about how the law should be applied to them.

Mixing Economics and Politics

Nixon spent an inordinate amount of time on domestic and foreign economic matters. Nowhere did he appear to reverse himself more on views he had held before becoming president (or at least on views others attributed to him), and nowhere was his aprincipled pragmatism more evident. Nixon's failure to obtain more revenue through tax reform legislation in 1969, together with rising unemployment and inflation rates in 1970, precipitated an effort (in response to a perceived crisis) to balance U.S. domestic concerns through wage and price controls and international ones through devaluation of the dollar. This vehicle was the New Economic Policy, dramatically announced on August 15, 1971, at the end of a secret Camp David meeting with sixteen economic advisers. Largely as a result of Treasury Secretary Connally's influence, Nixon agreed that if foreign countries continued to demand ever-increasing amounts of gold for the U.S. dollars they held, the United States would go off the gold standard but would at the same time impose wage and price controls to curb inflation. The NEP perfectly reflected the "grand gesture" Connally thought the president should make on economic problems, and the August 15 television broadcast dramatized economic issues that most Americans, seldom anticipating longrange consequences, found boring.

When he was not trying to preempt Congress on regulatory issues, Nixon proposed deregulation based on free-market assumptions that were more traditionally in keeping with conservative Republicanism. The administration ended the draft in the name of economic freedom and recommended deregulation of the production of food crops, tariff and other barriers to international trade, and interest rates paid by various financial institutions. Except for wage and price controls and the devaluation of the dollar, none of these actions was justified in the name of crisis management. In general, however, political considerations made Nixon more liberal on domestic economic matters, confounding both his supporters and his opponents.

Nixon attributes his interest in international economics to the encouragement of John Foster Dulles and his desire as vice-president in the 1950s to create a Foreign Economic Council. Failing in this, he has said that his travels abroad in the 1950s only confirmed his belief that foreign leaders understood economics better than did American leaders, and he was determined to remedy this situation as president. Nixon faced two obstacles in this effort: Kissinger (because "international economics was not Henry's bag"), and

State Department officials who saw "economic policy as government to government," which limited their diplomatic view of the world and made themso suspicious or cynical (or both) about the private sector that they refused to promote international commerce to the degree that Nixon thought they should. "Unlike the ignoramuses I encountered among economic officers at various embassies in the 1950s and 1960s," Nixon told me, "I wanted to bring economics to the foreign service."

Because of Nixon's own interest in and knowledge of international trade, he attempted as president to rationalize the formulation of foreign economic policy. After 1962, when he was out of public office and practicing law in New York, he had specialized in international economics and multinational corporations—definitely not Henry Kissinger's areas of expertise. In part because they were not a "team" on foreign economic policy and in part because Nixon bypassed the NSC almost entirely in formulating his New Economic Policy, Nixon relied not on his national security adviser but on other free-thinking outsiders when formulating foreign economic policy.

Next to John Connally, Nixon was most impressed with the economic views of Peter G. Peterson, who, after starting out in 1971 as a White House adviser on international economic affairs, became secretary of commerce in January 1972. Although Connally and Peterson appeared to agree on such early foreign economic initiatives as the NEP and the "get tough" policy toward Third World countries that nationalized U.S. companies abroad, as secretary of commerce Peterson ultimately proved much more sophisticated and sensitive than the secretary of the treasury about the United States' changed economic role in the world. In a December 27, 1971, position paper defending Nixon's NEP, Peterson remarked that the new global situation in which the United States found itself demanded "shared leadership, shared responsibility, and shared burdens. . . . The reform of the international monetary systems," he said, must fully recognize and be solidly rooted in "the growing reality of a genuinely interdependent and increasingly competitive world economy whose goal is mutual, shared prosperity—not artificial, temporary advantage." At no point did Peterson believe, as Connally apparently did, that "the simple realignment of exchange rates" would adequately address the economic realignment problems facing the international economy.

In 1971 Nixon succeeded in establishing an entirely new cabinet-level Council on International Economic Policy (CIEP), headed by Peterson. This was not so much a reorganization of functions as it was an alternative to fill an existing void in the federal structure and to provide "clear top-level focus on international economic issues and to achieve consistency between international and domestic economic policy." For a variety of reasons—not the least of which was Kissinger's general lack of interest in, and disdain for, the unglamorous aspects of international economics—the CIEP faltered and finally failed after Nixon left office. Its demise seems to have been hastened by Kissinger's recommendation to the Congressional Commission on Organization of Foreign Policy that it be eliminated, despite the fact that others, including Peterson, testified on its behalf. The CIEP was subsequently merged with the Office of the Special Trade Representative.

≈❀≈

Even with Nixon's impressive foreign and domestic record, it cannot be said that he would have succeeded as a managerial or administrative president had Watergate not occurred. Entrenched federal bureaucracies are not easily controlled or divested of power even with the best policy-oriented management strategies. That his foreign policy management seems more successful is also no surprise: diplomatic bureaucracies are smaller, more responsive, and easier to control than their domestic counterparts. Moreover, public concern (except for Vietnam) remained minimal as usual, and individual presidential foreign policy initiatives are more likely to be remembered and to appear effective than domestic ones. Nonetheless, the real importance of Nixon's presidency may well come to rest not on Watergate or foreign policy, but on his attempts to restructure the executive branch along functional lines, to bring order to the federal bureaucracy, and to achieve lasting domestic reform. The degree to which those Nixonian administrative tactics that were legal and ethical (and most of them were) became consciously or unconsciously the model for his successors in the Oval Office will determine his final place in history.

Although Nixon's corporate presidency remains publicly discredited, much of it has been privately preserved. Perhaps this is an indication that in exceptional cases presidential effectiveness can transcend popular (and scholarly) disapproval. What Nixon lacked in charisma and honesty, he may in the long run make up for with his phoenixlike ability to survive disaster. Nixon has repeatedly said: "No politician is dead until he admits it." It is perhaps an ironic commentary on the state of the modern presidency that Richard Nixon's management style and substantive foreign and domestic achievements look better and better when compared with those of his immediate successors in the Oval Office.

"Down to the Nut-Cutting": The Nixon Presidency and American Public Life

. . . Nixon's ambitious and cunning policy agenda would poison American politics and fragment American society. His presidency, often deliberately, sometimes unintentionally, drilled a deep well of cynicism about national politics—about the possibilities for community and communication, about the capacity of government to address the nation's needs, about the dignity and necessity of public service itself. In the process, Nixon shifted the balance of power in American politics and the terms of debate in American culture. . . .

Tricky Dick

. . . Nixon's resentments persisted as well: his crude disregard for Jews, his contempt for African Americans, his hatred of the press. But most of all he hated the establishment, for its wealth and connections, its intellectual and cultural hauteur, its exclusiveness. "In this period of our history, the leaders and the educated class are decadent," President Nixon instructed his chief of staff, H. R. Haldeman. The educated become "brighter in the head, but weaker in the spine." The nation's elite, in Nixon's mind, no longer possessed any character. Nixon would prove it to them, and prove it in the most cunning of ways.

Nixon's presidency presented more than just a fascinating, and baffling, psychological profile. It even accomplished more than the unprecedented abuse of power Americans have too narrowly labeled "Watergate." His administration also posed a crucial historical problem about the evolution of contemporary American politics and public policy. Was Nixon the last of the liberals, or the first of the conservatives? Did his domestic presidency mark the last gasp of postwar liberalism—of energetic, activist government? Or did it mark the onset of a new, more cautious era—of small government, fiscal conservatism, diverting resources and initiative from the public to the private sector?

In some ways, Nixon did seem like the last interventionist liberal. He doubled the budgets for the National Endowment for the Arts (NEA) and the

National Endowment for the Humanities (NEH). He proposed a guaranteed income for all Americans, signed the nation's principal environmental protection laws, and expanded affirmative action for racial minorities. Under Nixon's watch, the regulatory state swelled; federal agencies began monitoring nearly every aspect of American life. The Nixon administration created the Occupational Health and Safety Administration and instituted the first peacetime wage and price controls in U.S. history.

Nixon even conceded that "I am now a Keynesian in economics." He embraced the idea that a humming economy was the responsibility of the federal government and that the White House should actively intervene in economic affairs, carefully calibrating the policy controls, to ensure robust growth and low unemployment. Nixon even dispensed with the gold standard, that most reassuring symbol of conservative fiscal orthodoxy.

By the middle of his first term, Nixon's seeming unwillingness to crush liberalism and disband social programs angered many committed conservatives. Patrick Buchanan, the president's in-house right-wing fire-eater, warned that conservatives felt Nixon had betrayed them. "They are the niggers of the Nixon administration," Buchanan fumed in a scathing seven-page memo.

On the other hand, the Nixon era seemed to initiate a new, more conservative era in American politics. Nixon intervened on behalf of southern school districts, supporting efforts to curtail busing and slow the pace of school desegregation. He attacked the Warren Court, replacing such liberal icons as Abe Fortas and Earl Warren with Warren Burger and William Rehnquist (and even unsuccessfully attempted to appoint two southern conservatives to the Supreme Court). He dismantled, or at least attempted to eliminate, the principal agencies of 1960s liberalism, such as the Office of Economic Opportunity (which ran Lyndon Johnson's war on poverty) and the legal services program. While he signed the popular legislation restricting air and water pollution, Nixon also established procedures for economic cost-benefit review of all environmental regulations. And he made it clear that officials should scrap or water down any pollution control that might slow the economy or antagonize business.

Nixon also pioneered what came to be called devolution—transferring authority from the federal government to state and local governments and from the public sector to the private sphere. Through a complicated series of initiatives—a combination of block grants, revenue sharing, and the like—Nixon consigned to the states policy areas that had been the responsibility of the federal government. He also took problems and programs that had been thought to require public attention and shifted them to business and the private sector. Indeed, when Nixon left office in August 1974, CBS Evening News commentator Rod MacLeish described devolution as Nixon's major achievement. "As president," MacLeish told a national television audience, "Mr. Nixon made serious policy efforts to disburse responsibility as well as money for the alleviation of our domestic problems."

By the end of his first term, Nixon had embraced small government as his campaign theme. Concluding that cutting government could become a winning strategy, Nixon declared in his second inaugural address that "government must learn to take less from people so that people can do more for themselves." Reversing John F. Kennedy's famous call for collective sacrifice, Nixon instructed, "In our own lives, let each of us ask—not just what will government do for me, but what can I do for myself?"

Faced with such a contradictory record, Nixon watchers have been tempted to split the difference. But Nixon the president did more than combine economic liberalism with social conservatism. He was no mere transitional president, a passage from one era to another that embraced elements of both, although many scholars have portrayed him as such. Others have dismissed Nixon as nothing more than opportunistic, swaying with the prevailing political winds. Primarily interested in foreign affairs, Nixon viewed domestic policy as a nuisance; he would do anything so long as it would not cost him votes.

Splitting the difference, however, mistakes not only Nixon's character, but his presidency's decisive influence on American political culture. Although Nixon was both a transitional president and an opportunist, those assessments miss his historical significance—the ways that the man (the psychological puzzle) and the policies (the historical problem) intertwined.

Not for nothing did Nixon earn the nickname Tricky Dick. Nixon was indeed the first of the conservatives. He fooled many observers, then and now, because he pursued this conservative agenda—this assault on public life—in a particularly devious sort of way. Unlike Barry Goldwater before him and Ronald Reagan after him, Nixon never took on big government directly. He rarely assailed the liberal establishment he so furiously hated and so openly resented. He did not attack liberal programs or the agencies and political networks that undergirded them. Rather, he subtly, cunningly undermined them. Nixon wanted to destroy the liberal establishment by stripping it of its bases of support and its sources of funds. . . .

Toward a Guaranteed Income?

Of all Richard Nixon's domestic policies, the most celebrated and the most controversial proposal never actually materialized: the Family Assistance Plan (FAP). In August 1969, Nixon appeared before the nation with a radical scheme, a far-reaching program the federal government had never before even contemplated—a minimum guaranteed income for every American family. Nixon proposed to abolish the existing welfare system with its labyrinthine series of benefits: AFDC (Aid to Families with Dependent Children), food stamps, housing subsidies, furniture grants. Nixon also promised to eliminate the army of social workers who ran the system and the mountains of paperwork they produced—to get rid of all that and simply replace it with direct cash grants to the poor.

"We face an urban crisis, a social crisis—and at the same time, a crisis of confidence in the capacity of government to do its job," Nixon explained when he announced the program. "Our states and cities find themselves sinking in a welfare quagmire, as case loads increase, as costs escalate, and as the welfare system stagnates enterprise and perpetuates dependency." The system, he complained, "created an incentive for fathers to desert their families," it spawned grossly unequal variations in benefits levels, it forced poor children to begin "life in an atmosphere of handout and dependency."

An ominous "welfare crisis" loomed by the time Nixon took command of the war on poverty. Between 1960 and 1975 the number of relief recipients doubled, from 7 to 14 million people. Including in-kind assistance—food stamps, Medicaid, public housing—more than 24 million Americans received means-tested benefits by the end of the Nixon years. By highlighting the problems of poverty, Lyndon Johnson's Great Society and the agencies it created had focused attention on the impoverished. Daniel Patrick Moynihan, the former Kennedy-Johnson poverty warrior who ran Nixon's Urban Affairs Council, became especially concerned with the explosion of AFDC costs in New York City. Although the economy hummed and unemployment had actually decreased, New York's welfare caseload had tripled in only five years. Moynihan and Nixon became convinced (wrongly) that New York's troubles portended the imminent collapse of the national welfare system.

Most observers, across the American political spectrum, agreed that something had to be done about welfare. On the far left, welfare radicals like the National Welfare Rights Organization (NWRO) sought to empower the poor. A group representing mostly single mothers, the NWRO encouraged poor people to apply for public assistance—to demand welfare as a right, not to accept it reluctantly and shamefully. And in fact, the vast expansion in caseloads during the 1960s stemmed not from growing numbers of people eligible for welfare but from a huge increase in the number of already eligible poor people who applied for welfare. In 1960, only about one-third of the Americans eligible for welfare actually received it; by the early 1970s, the figure had climbed to 90 percent, thanks in part to the agitation of advocates like the NWRO.

At the other end of the spectrum, free market economist Milton Friedman, a leading conservative guru, promoted his plan for a negative income tax. The grab-bag of welfare programs, Friedman asserted, served only the interests of the legislators who enacted them and the bureaucrats who administered them. Poverty resulted not from failed institutions, broken homes, or the legacy of slavery, but from a pure and simple shortage of cash. Government could cure poverty by dispensing money directly to the needy through the tax system; Americans earning less than an established minimum would receive money from the Internal Revenue Service (IRS) just as those above the threshold paid in their taxes. The negative income tax would allow poor citizens to purchase the goods and services they needed rather than the ones their congressmen and social workers insisted they should have.

Friedman was no great ally of public assistance, and he wanted to get government out of the welfare business. That sentiment appealed to Nixon. "Nixon didn't like welfare workers," his aide Martin Anderson recalled in a television documentary. A shift to cash grants would undermine the entire welfare establishment, circumventing the bureaucrats, the psychologists, and the social workers.

Nixon embraced the radical analyses of Friedman and the NWRO, rejecting the proposals for moderate, incremental welfare reform circulating on Capitol Hill and within the social service agencies. He would replace the entire AFDC system with a national minimum standard, available to the welfare poor and working poor alike. "What I am proposing," Nixon announced, "is that the Federal Government build a foundation under the income of every American family with dependent children that cannot care for itself—and wherever in America that family may live." A federal minimum would support all such families, intact or "broken," working or on welfare. The program would include work incentives (to encourage earnings, benefits would be reduced by only fifty cents for every dollar earned) and work requirements (every recipient except mothers of preschool children would have to accept employment or job training). "A guaranteed income," Nixon explained, distinguishing his plan from rival proposals, "establishes a right without any responsibilities. Family assistance recognizes a need and establishes a responsibility."

Nixon seemingly pressed for a liberal goal: one that would expand welfare and extend benefits to millions of working poor. A guaranteed income for all Americans truly aimed to unite the fractured nation, to make every citizen a member of a national community with national standards. Assistance for every family seemed to envision everyone as part of the same national family. But however extravagant the hopes of FAP supporters, Nixon's guaranteed income plan pursued an authentically conservative objective. Nixon sought to dismantle the welfare system and the agencies and programs that administered it, eliminate the social workers who ran them, and starve the liberal networks they nourished.

Certainly Nixon cared more about undercutting his liberal opposition than about putting FAP into effect. While analysts disagreed then and today about Nixon's commitment to welfare reform, he certainly made little effort to secure its passage. Despite Moynihan's urging that he spend political capital to secure congressional approval, the president remained on the sidelines, allowing his most far-reaching policy proposal to wither and die.

And expire it did. Congressional Democrats and their liberal allies denounced Nixon's guaranteed minimum as too low. Demanding a much higher income floor—roughly four times the level Nixon offered—the NWRO urged supporters to "Zap FAP." The NWRO also encouraged Americans to "Live Like a Dog" on the proposed budget, which they computed to just nineteen cents a meal per person. Mainstream liberal organizations like the National Association for the Advancement of Colored People, the American Friends Service Committee, and the Methodist church also denounced Nixon's plan. Meanwhile, conservatives opposed FAP because it would extend public assistance to millions more Americans and add billions of dollars to the federal budget.

Representative Wilbur Mills (D, Arkansas), chairman of the Ways and Means Committee, steered FAP through the House, adding sweeteners for the states that offered low benefits. But the Senate Finance Committee, largely controlled by southern and rural legislators, buried the plan. Nixon resubmitted FAP three times but never worked to secure its passage. In 1972, when Democratic presidential candidate George McGovern announced his own proposed "demogrant" of a thousand dollars for every man, woman, and child in the United States, the FAP passed into oblivion. The very idea of replacing the welfare system with cash grants became the stuff of derisive jokes.

Denounced by both left and right, FAP ended up on the ash heap of history, but it was no failure for Richard Nixon. By introducing the guaranteed income program, Nixon divided his opponents and torpedoed more generous proposals for welfare reform. His apparent boldness in meeting the welfare crisis insulated Nixon from criticism; no one could claim that he fiddled while New York and other cities burned (or at least went broke). At the same time, the president's solicitude for the working poor, antipathy to the welfare bureaucracy, and stringent work requirements appealed to blue-collar voters and appeased the Republican right wing. Even in defeat, Nixon had pulled off a remarkable tactical victory.

The Silent Majority

Nixon's indirect, underhanded strategy with regard to welfare, environmental protection, housing, and the arts represented more than a career politician's cunning or a pathological liar's need to be devious. Every one of these maneuvers advanced Nixon's larger political objective: his ambition to transform American politics by creating a new majority coalition in the United States.

Nixon had long envisioned such a realignment. His 1968 campaign had hinged on winning over two sets of voters that normally remained loyal Democrats but appeared ready to switch parties. First, Nixon targeted white southerners. By hinting he would slow the pace of desegregation, Nixon's "southern strategy" drew Dixie's yellow-dog Democrats and prosperous new migrants to the metropolitan South into the emerging Republican majority. Second, Nixon went after blue-collar northerners—white ethnics who for generations had voted their pocketbooks and supported liberal Democrats, but had recently become alarmed about the social issues—crime, drugs, loose morals, streets filled with antiwar protestors and black militants.

In 1968, white southerners seemed ripe for this strategy. Many had opposed the civil rights revolution and resented the northern liberals they felt had imposed on them an odious second Reconstruction. In 1964, many southerners had abandoned the Democrats—the "Party of the Fathers"—and cast votes for Senator Barry Goldwater, and outspoken opponent of the Civil Rights Act. Goldwater won five Deep South states.

Nixon certainly welcomed the votes of disgruntled segregationists. The campaign enlisted South Carolina senator Strom Thurmond, the former Dixiecrat leader and recent convert to the GOP, to rally white southerners. Thurmond promised that Nixon would support local control of public schools. Nixon even hired a Thurmond protégé to coordinate his campaign in the South and bombarded the region with advertisements warning against wasted votes for Alabama governor George Wallace, the hero of massive resistance running a third-party campaign for president.

Still, in 1968 Nixon carefully chose not to tread in Thurmond or Goldwater's footsteps. The campaign recognized that Wallace had locked up the Deep South. Nixon understood that overt racial appeals for the Wallace vote would alienate moderates, and even many conservatives, in the burgeoning suburbs of the metropolitan South. So Nixon largely conceded the segregationist, rural

Deep South that Goldwater had won and constructed a plurality connecting the Sunbelt with blue-collar Rustbelt neighborhoods.

In a very close race, Nixon's strategists focused on middle-class white voters in the industrializing subdivisions of the peripheral South. The population of the South's major metropolises, Nixon recognized, had doubled or even tripled in the 1950s and 1960s. New suburbs were crowded with professionals and skilled workers from outside the South and young families who had come of age after the *Brown* decision and found massive resistance self-defeating.

In September 1968, Nixon launched a campaign swing through Dixie in Charlotte, North Carolina. There, he addressed a polite, well-dressed, middle class crowd. He made his familiar stump appeal to forgotten Americans, never even mentioning race. Pressed later by an interviewer, he staked out a middle ground, affirming support for *Brown* but criticizing the Democrats and the courts for pushing too hard, too fast. Nixon cleverly laid out a moderate approach, neither championing minority rights like Hubert Humphrey nor defending segregation and states' rights like Goldwater and Wallace. He simultaneously endorsed local desegregation efforts—the nominally color-blind freedom-of-choice plans that had enrolled a few black students in formerly all-black schools across the South and Southwest—and opposed openly race-conscious remedies like busing that threatened dramatic changes in the status quo.

That strategy appealed to crucial swing voters in the 1968 election, helping the Republican standard-bearer win Virginia, the Carolinas, Florida, Tennessee, and Kentucky. Nixon's southern strategy offered more than a short-term political prize. It was premised on the fundamental demographic and political shifts that would continue throughout the Seventies and would give a new shape to American life.

A young political consultant named Kevin Phillips diagnosed this power shift in a series of position papers for the Nixon campaign and in a 1969 book, *The Emerging Republican Majority*. Phillips identified a new locus of power in national politics, a region he called the Sunbelt that connected the booming subdivisions of the metropolitan South, the sun country of Florida and southern California, and the desert Southwest. Phillips described the Sunbelt's conservative leanings and its potential as the foundation for a political realignment. The "huge postwar white middle class push to the Florida-California sun country" seemed to be forging a new political era. "The persons most drawn to the new sun culture are the pleasure-seekers, the bored, the ambitious, the space-age technicians and the retired—a super-slice of the rootless, socially mobile group known as the American middle class." The region's politics, he concluded, "is bound to cast a lengthening national shadow."

Nixon and his top advisers recognized the growing influence of the Sunbelt South in national politics. Shortly after becoming president, Nixon changed his voting residence from New York to Florida. "The time has come," he declared in 1970, "to stop kicking the South around." He detected not only the rise of the Sunbelt but the growing influence of a Sunbelt mind-set in American life generally. The South and Southwest seemed to embody a new set of cultural attitudes about race, taxation, defense, government spending, and social mores—Sunbelt attitudes that might eventually spread into the suburbs and working-class neighborhoods of the old North.

In August 1970, while vacationing in San Clemente, Pat Buchanan alerted Nixon to *The Real Majority,* a political manual for the coming decade by Richard M. Scammon and Ben J. Wattenberg. Hoping to revive their own party, these two disaffected Democrats mapped the political landscape in Nixonian terms. The voter in the center, they asserted, the key to assembling a winning coalition, was a "47 year old Catholic housewife in Dayton, Ohio whose husband is a machinist." Since the 1930s, she and her blue-collar husband had always voted Democratic. According to Scammon and Wattenberg, they had voted their pocketbooks, looking to liberal Democrats for strong unions, high wages, cheap mortgages, and college loans for their children. But now, at the end of the 1960s, they might defect to the Republicans and vote conservative on social issues. "To know that the lady in Dayton is afraid to walk the streets alone at night," Scammon and Wattenberg explained, "to know that she has a mixed view about blacks and civil rights because before moving to the suburbs she lived in a neighborhood that became all black, to know that her brother-in-law is a policeman, to know that she does not have the money to move if her new neighborhood deteriorates, to know that she is deeply distressed that her son is going to a community junior college where LSD was found on campus— to know all this is the beginning of contemporary political wisdom."

The book thrilled Nixon. If he did nothing to deny blue-collar workers their fat pay envelopes and hit hard on rioters, protesters, and drugs, he could forge a new conservative majority. "P [the president] talked about Real Majority and need to get that thinking over to all our people," Haldeman reported. "Wants to hit pornography, dope, bad kids." Nixon himself asserted that the Republicans needed to "preempt the Social Issue in order to get the Democrats on the defensive. We should aim our strategy primarily at disaffected Democrats, a blue-collar workers, and at working-class white ethnics. We should," the president concluded, "set out to capture the vote of the forty-seven-year-old Dayton housewife."

Nixon made wooing these voters—Americans he famously named the Silent Majority in a 1969 speech—the subject of concerted effort. Indeed for several years, Nixon envisioned creating a new political party—he usually called it the Independent Conservative party—to foster a wholesale realignment of American politics. This new party would unite white southerners, the Silent Majority, and traditionally Republican rural and suburban conservatives around social issues. It would ostracize the socially liberal, economically conservative eastern establishment—Wall Street and business Republicans like Nelson Rockefeller who had long dominated Republican party affairs—and attack liberal Democrats for playing so heavily to "the fashionable, but unrepresentative constituencies of the young, the poor, the racial minorities, and the students."

Nixon envisioned a new party that would appeal to the "Okie from Muskogee," the hero of Merle Haggard's 1969 country and western hit. "I'm proud to be an Okie from Muskogee," Haggard declared, "a place where even squares can have a ball." Nixon admired Haggard's anthem as the authentic voice of the Silent Majority; Haggard's Oklahoma town honored the values of millions of worried, disgruntled Americans. "We don't smoke marijuana in Muskogee," the singer explained. "We don't take our trips on LSD. We don't burn our draft cards down on Main Street. We like livin' right and bein' free." The song so impressed the president that Nixon invited Haggard to perform at the White House.

To build this new political agenda, Nixon not only inflamed the Silent Majority about social issues and appealed to the national pride of working Americans. He also took a number of concrete steps. First, he reached out to organized labor. Recognizing the social conservatism and deep-rooted patriotism of union Democrats, Nixon believed he could pry their votes away from the party of FDR. After National Guardsmen shot and killed antiwar marchers at Kent State University, 150,000 hard hats paraded for flag and country down New York's Broadway. Outraged that New York's liberal mayor had dropped the flag on city hall to half-staff in honor of the slain antiwar protesters, the construction workers denounced (and even beat up a handful of) hippies and student radicals, defended the war in Vietnam, and supported their president in the White House. Nixon deeply appreciated the construction workers' show of support, and the march reinforced his determination to incorporate labor into his New American Majority. The president offered generous loopholes for organized labor in his wage and price controls, horrifying Wall Street and business interests.

Second, Nixon named Texas governor John Connally, a former protégé of Lyndon Johnson, as his secretary of the treasury. By naming Connally to his cabinet and grooming him as his successor, Nixon hoped to entice conservative southern Democrats into his new majority. The president also understood that Connally would happily dispense with Republican economic orthodoxy and keep working people happy about their paychecks while Nixon stung the Democrats on social issues.

Nixon also valued Connally's Lone Star state charisma. Henry Kissinger thought that "there was no American public figure Nixon held in such awe. Connally's swaggering self-assurance," Kissinger reflected, "fulfilled Nixon's image of how a leader should act; he found it possible to emulate this conduct only in marginal comments on memoranda, never face to face." And Nixon never denigrated Connally behind his back, "a boon not granted to many."

In August 1971, under Connally's leadership, Nixon reversed field on economic policies. He adopted wage and price controls to cool inflation, a series of tax cuts to stimulate the economy in time for the 1972 elections, and he closed the gold window and allowed the dollar to float against other currencies, ending the Bretton Woods monetary system that had stabilized the international currency markets since World War II.

His mission accomplished, Connally returned to his native Texas in 1972 and took control of "Democrats for Nixon." The president imagined Connally as his natural successor. "By structuring it right," Haldeman recalled Nixon's ruminations in his diary, "we could develop a new majority party. Under a new name. Get control of the Congress without an election, simply by realignment, and make a truly historic change in the entire American political structure." From this coalition, with Nixon and Connally as "the strong men," Connally "clearly would emerge as the candidate for the new party in '76, and the P would strongly back him in that."

As the 1972 election approached, Nixon made little use of traditional party labels, touting his connections to Democrats like Connally and downplaying his own Republican affiliation. "Use the new American Majority," he told Haldeman, "not Republican majority." Nixon would seek the "election of Congressman and Senators who will support the P[resident], not who are Republicans."

Nixon even trumpeted his frequent escapes to La Casa Pacifica, his seaside retreat in San Clemente, California, as an assault on the establishment. Appealing to his new conservative majority, Nixon instructed his staff to tout his San Clemente home as the "Western White House." White House communications director Herb Klein informed reporters that the "San Clemente operation gives Westerners a symbolic share in the business of government. . . ." It proved that "Government is not an exclusively Eastern institution."

Nixon recognized by 1971 that the center of the American political spectrum had shifted toward the right. The archetypal Dayton housewife and her machinist husband were becoming fed up with liberals, bureaucracy, and big government. Many of them had moved to southern California, the outskirts of Houston, the suburbs of Charlotte and Atlanta. Increasingly these one-time loyal Democrats and millions of others like them believed that government programs helped only other people, not themselves. "We've had enough social programs: forced integration, education, housing," Nixon told his chief of staff as the 1972 election approached. "People don't want more on welfare. They don't want to help the working poor, and our mood has to be harder on this, not softer."

Nixon instructed his staff to adopt a tougher, more openly conservative stance. Attorney General John Mitchell launched a furious attack against black militants and student protesters in *Women's Wear Daily*. Mitchell tore into "these stupid kids" on college campuses and "the professors are just as bad if not worse. They don't know anything. Nor do these stupid bastards who are ruining our educational institutions." This country, Mitchell warned, "is going so far right you are not even going to recognize it." Nixon applauded his attorney general's hard line. "John—Good Job," he wrote. "Don't back off."

Nixon's strategy paid rich dividends in November 1972. He won reelection by a landslide over Democratic challenger George McGovern, in the process assembling the new majority of his fondest political dreams. Both organized labor and the white South went heavily for Nixon in 1972.

After winning reelection, Nixon decided to promote what he called a conservative revolution. "Now I planned to give expression to the more conservative values and beliefs of the New Majority throughout the country," Nixon recalled in his memoirs, "and use my power to put some teeth in my new American Revolution." Sounding his new conservative theme, Nixon declared in his second inaugural address, "Let us remember that America was not built by government but by people; not by welfare, but by work."

Still, the president understood that although Americans opposed expansive government in principle, in practice they demanded many specific public programs. Nixon understood, as he put it in a cabinet meeting, that "government spending is a lousy issue. People are for spending." The only way to slash popular programs was to portray cuts as "the only way to avoid inflation and higher taxes. . . . You never win," the president explained, "on the question of screwing up rich kids. You have to hit on higher taxes. You never debate the programs. By cutting the budget back, we are avoiding more taxes, and that's the line we have to use."

The budget thus became the instrument of Nixon's conservative revolution. The president set stringent targets for the fiscal year ending June 1973; to reach them, he refused to spend more than $12 billion that the Congress had already appropriated. This infuriated the Congress, which soon would debate whether these "impoundments" merited impeachment.

The impoundments were just the beginning. Having sundered the liberal policy networks and collapsed the liberal electoral coalition, Nixon next aimed to slash domestic spending. In February 1973, he proposed a shocking budget for the 1974 fiscal year, featuring deep cuts in government programs. Nixon proposed to eliminate urban renewal, impacted-area aid for school districts near military bases, hospital construction grants, soil management payments to farmers, and the Rural Electrification Administration. He slashed spending on milk for schoolchildren, mental health facilities, compensatory education for poor students. He meant to reverse the Great Society, calling for the abolition of the Office of Economic Opportunity, the vanguard of Lyndon Johnson's war on poverty.

Nixon would see neither his new American revolution nor his new majority politics through to completion. By the time he unveiled his rightward shift and his harsh budgets, the nation had become obsessed with the unfolding story of scandal in the White House. But, oddly, Nixon's personal failures—a scandal so large that he would become the first (and thus far only) president driven from office—would only aid his larger agenda. In trusting too much in government," Nixon intoned, "we have asked more of it than we can deliver." The time has come to turn away from activist government and replace it with "a new feeling of self-discipline.

In retrospect, most observers have read Nixon's declaration ironically; Watergate certainly proved that Americans had trusted too much in Nixon's government. But although the scandals brought down a Republican conservative and helped to elect the only Democratic president of the era, their principal effect was to discredit government itself. Watergate only intensified Americans' alienation from public life: their contempt for the secrecy, inefficiency, and failures of "big government.". . .

⁂

In fact, Watergate impressed many contemporary observers as a bizarre series of events presided over by a singular villain; it had been "historic but irrelevant." A year after Nixon left office, CBS News correspondent Bruce Morton concluded that "the fact is Watergate didn't change much." A decade later, many pundits echoed Morton's assessment. "Most experts," the *Los Angeles Times* reported on the tenth anniversary of Nixon's ouster, "find no evidence that the traumatic ousting of a U.S. President has caused any basic change in public attitudes about either the American system of government or the persons who occupy public positions." Sure, public confidence in government waned after Watergate, but it had been declining since the race riots and antiwar protests of the mid-1960s.

Still, Nixon's presidency, and its dramatic end, nourished a profound unease with a direction that American life had taken. And the scandal's most conspicuous and enduring effect ironically realized some of Richard Nixon's most grandiose objectives. Watergate gave a boost to conservatism and conservative Republican politicians. That effect did not immediately appear; in the first blip after Nixon's ruin, the Republicans took a bath as the Democrats won big in the 1974 midterm elections. In 1976, enough resentment persisted that Gerald Ford, Nixon's pardoner, narrowly lost the presidency to an unknown whose platform consisted of a fairly convincing promise that he would never lie to the American people.

But the general trends bolstered conservatives. The ultimate lesson of Watergate remained "you can't trust the government." The scandal reinforced a generalized antigovernment passion whose main effect worked against Democrats and liberals and for Republicans and conservatives. Even President Jimmy Carter represented a more conservative faction of the Democratic party: southern, fiscally responsible, suspicious of labor unions and government regulation.

When convicted felon and former attorney general John Mitchell left Washington, reporters mocked his earlier prediction. "In the next ten years," Mitchell had prophesied, "this country will go so far to the right you won't recognize it." Reporters shook their heads, but John Mitchell would have the last laugh.

And perhaps his chief would enjoy it. In retirement, Nixon would witness his enemies in disarray, their conception of government as the instrument of national purpose discredited, their vision of an inclusive national community debased. . . .

POSTSCRIPT

Was Richard Nixon America's Last Liberal President?

J oan Hoff-Wilson is one of the few professional historians to render a positive evaluation of President Nixon. She places him in the context of the late 1960s and early 1970s, when support for big government, New Deal, Great Society programs had dimmed, and the bipartisan, anticommunist foreign policy consensus had been shattered by the Vietnam War. She gives him high marks for vertically restructuring the executive branch of the government and for attempting a similar reorganization of the federal bureaucracy.

Unlike most defenders of Nixon, Hoff-Wilson considers Nixon's greatest achievement to be domestic. Although Nixon was a conservative, the welfare state grew during his presidency. In the area of civil rights, between 1968 and 1972, affirmative action programs were implemented, and schools with all black children in the southern states declined from 68 percent to 8 percent. Even on such Democratic staples as welfare, the environment, and economic planning, Nixon outflanked the liberals.

Hoff-Wilson has fleshed out her ideas in much greater detail in *Nixon Reconsidered* (Basic Books, 1994). British conservative cabinet minister and historian Jonathan Aitken has also written a favorable and more panoramic view of the former president entitled *Nixon: A Life* (Regnery Gateway, 1993).

Historian Stephen E. Ambrose's three-volume biography on Nixon (Simon & Schuster, 1987–1991) also substantiates Hoff-Wilson's emphasis on Nixon's domestic successes. Ambrose's evaluation is even more remarkable because he was a liberal historian who campaigned for George McGovern in 1972 and had to be talked into writing a Nixon biography by his publisher. In domestic policy, Ambrose told *The Washington Post* on November 26, 1989, Nixon "was proposing things in '73 and '74 he couldn't even make the front pages with—national health insurance for all, a greatly expanded student loan operation, and energy and environmental programs." With regard to foreign policy, both Ambrose and Aitken disagree with Hoff-Wilson; they consider Nixon's foreign policy substantial and far-sighted. In the second volume of his biography, *Nixon: The Triumph of a Politician, 1962–1972* (Simon & Schuster, 1989), Ambrose concludes that the president was "without peer in foreign relations where 'profound pragmatic' vision endowed him with the potential to become a great world statesman."

Professor Bruce Schulman disagrees with historians like Hoff-Wilson who see Nixon as the last liberal or with others who view him as a mere political opportunist. Schulman makes a strong case that Nixon pretended to support liberal measures in his first term such as increased national funding for the arts and humanities, enforcement of environmental laws, more public housing and a guaranteed annual income for poverty-ridden citizens. But as Schulman points out, many of these programs would be passed to private agencies or state and local governments through the use of block grants and revenue-sharing mechanisms. In the case of Family Assistance Program, Schulman believes Nixon expected Congress to kill the idea because it was too extreme for conservatives and didn't guarantee enough income to appease the radicals.

Schulman makes a strong case that Nixon spent the 1968 and 1972 presidential campaigns building a new conservative Republican majority. An avid reader, Nixon absorbed the ideas of Kevin Phillips, *The Emerging Republican Majority* (1969) and Richard M. Scammon and Ben J. Wattenberg's *The Real Majority* (1970). These authors suggested that the president could fashion a majority coalition of white southern Democratic conservatives, who disliked the civil rights acts; northern blue-collar workers who were more concerned about riots, increased crime, and use of illegal drugs than economic issues; and finally, migrants to the sunbelt states of Florida, Arizona, and southern California who retired or worked in space-age technological industries. Critics like veteran *The Washington Post* columnist David Broder disagree with this analysis. Because Nixon was obsessed with his reelection campaign in 1972, the president funneled all the money into his personal reelection campaign organization known as CREEP and defunded the money that the Republican National Committee could have used to support state and local candidates. The result was a 49-state electoral college victory for Nixon over his anti-war Democratic opponent George McGovern while the Democrats maintained strong majorities in the House of Representatives and the United States Senate. Had Nixon expended his political capital on state and local races, perhaps the Watergate burglary might not have happened. For Broder's comments, see the PBS 3-hour production on *Nixon: The American Experience* (1991) available on videotape or DVD.

Schulman believes that Watergate did not reinforce the belief that the system worked to curb an abuse of presidential power. Instead, it reinforced the negative attitude toward government that the American public had experienced with Lyndon Johnson's credibility gap in managing the Vietnam War. Nixon's former attorney general and campaign manager John Mitchell had it right in 1974 when he told a group of disbelieving reporters: "In the next ten years, this country will go so far to the right you won't recognize it." Reporters shook their heads but Reagan was elected for two terms in the 1980s, and in 1994, the Republicans swept the Democrats out of the House and controlled both houses of Congress for the first time since 1946.

In addition to the books mentioned, students should begin their research with Melvin Small's *The Presidency of Richard Nixon* (1999), a fair and balanced study in the University Press of Kansas' American Presidency series complete with footnotes and bibliography. David Greenberg has a fascinating study of *Nixon's Shadow: The History of an Image* (Norton, 2003), which chronicles the life and career of his images in search of the real Nixon. Jeff Hay has edited a series of secondary interpretations of *Richard Nixon* (2001) in the Greenhaven Press series on *Presidents and Their Decisions*. Interestingly, Hay neglects the domestic side, which Professor Hoff-Wilson claims were Nixon's major successes. This gap is filled by Allen J. Matusow's critical *Nixon's Economy: Booms, Busts, Dollars & Votes* (University of Kansas Press, 1998). Other biographies worth consulting include the liberal historian Herbert Parmet's panoramic *Richard Nixon and His America* (Little, Brown, 1990), the first to be based on Nixon's pre-presidential papers. Less thoroughly researched in primary sources but more insightful is *The New York Times* reporter Tom Wicker's *One of Us: Richard Nixon and the American Dream* (Random House, 1991).

In order to gain a real feel for the Nixon years, you should consult contemporary or primary accounts. Nixon himself orchestrated his own rehabilitation in *RN: The Memoirs of Richard Nixon* (Grosset & Dunlop, 1978); *The Real War* (Warner Books, 1980); *Real Peace* (Little, Brown, 1984); *No More Vietnams* (Arbor House, 1985); and *In the Arena: A Memoir of Victory, Defeat and Renewal* (Simon & Schuster, 1990). Nixon's own accounts should be compared with former national security adviser Henry Kissinger's memoirs *White House Years* (Little, Brown, 1979). *The Haldeman Diaries: Inside the Nixon White House* (Putnam, 1994), which is the subject of Kutler's review essay, is essential for any undertaking of Nixon. Haldeman's account fleshes out the daily tensions of life in the Nixon White House and adds important details to the Nixon and Kissinger accounts. Other primary accounts include Kenneth W. Thompson, ed., *The Nixon Presidency: Twenty-Two Intimate Perspectives of Richard M. Nixon, Portraits of American Presidents series,* vol. 6 (University Press of America, 1987), which contains a series of discussions with former officials of the Nixon administration conducted by the White Burkett Miller Center for the Study of Public Affairs at the University of Virginia.

Three of the best review essays on the new historiography about America's thirty seventh president are "Theodore Draper: Nixon, Haldeman, and History," *The New York Review of Books* (July 14, 1994); Sydney Blumenthal, "The Longest Campaign," *The New Yorker* (August 8, 1994); and Stanley I. Kutler, "Et tu, Bob?" *The Nation* (August 22–29, 1994), a critical review of *The Haldeman Diaries* that also contains a CD version, available on Sony Imagesoft, which contains 60 percent more of the original text than the book, as well as home movies, photos, and biographical information on the Nixon staff.

Researchers who want a first-hand glimpse of Nixon should take a trip to the National Archives and listen to some of the 4,000 hours of tape, many of which have been declassified and released earlier than the papers of other presidents because of the Watergate scandal. Stanley I. Kutler has edited some of them in *The Abuse of Power: The New Nixon Tapes* (Touchstone Books, 1998). Nixon's view can be compared with Haldeman's *Diaries* as well as *The Kissinger Transcripts* (New Press, 1998), edited by William Burr. Nixon's presidential papers, after several court suits, have also ended up in the National Archives. A sample of some of these papers can be found in Bruce Oudes, ed., *From the President: Richard Nixon's Secret Files* (Harper & Row, 1989).

ISSUE 16

Did President Reagan Win the Cold War?

YES: John Lewis Gaddis, from *The Cold War: A New History* (Penguin Press, 2005)

NO: Daniel Deudney and G. John Ikenberry, from "Who Won the Cold War," *Foreign Policy* (Summer 1992)

ISSUE SUMMARY

YES: Professor of history John Lewis Gaddis argues that President Reagan combined a policy of militancy and operational pragmatism that perplexed his hard-line advisers when he made the necessary compromises to bring about the most significant improvement in Soviet-American relations since the end of World War II.

NO: Professors of political science Daniel Deudney and G. John Ikenberry contend that the cold war ended only when Soviet president Gorbachev accepted Western liberal values and the need for global cooperation.

T he term *cold war* was first coined by the American financial whiz and presidential adviser Bernard Baruch in 1947. Cold War refers to the extended but restricted conflict that existed between the United States and the Soviet Union from the end of World War II in 1945 until 1990. Looking back, it appears that the conflicting values and goals of a democratic/capitalist United States and a communist Soviet Union reinforced this state of affairs between the two countries. Basically, the Cold War ended when the Soviet Union gave up its control over the Eastern European nations and ceased to be a unified country itself.

The Nazi invasion of Russia in June 1941 and the Japanese attack on America's Pacific outposts in December united the United States, Great Britain, and the Soviet Union against the Axis powers during World War II. Nevertheless, complications ensued during the top-level Allied discussions to coordinate war strategy. The first meeting between the big three took place in Teheran in 1943 followed by another at Yalta in February 1945. These high-level negotiations were held under the assumption that wartime harmony among Great Britain, the United States, and the Soviet Union would continue; that Stalin, Churchill, and Roosevelt would lead the postwar world as they had conducted the war; and that the details of the general policies and agreements would be resolved at a less pressing time.

But none of these premises were fulfilled. By the time the Potsdam Conference (to discuss possible action against Japan) took place in July 1945, Churchill had been defeated in a parliamentary election, Roosevelt had died, and President Harry S. Truman had been thrust, unprepared, into his place. Of the big three, only Stalin remained as a symbol of continuity. Details about the promises at Teheran and Yalta faded into the background. Power politics, nuclear weapons, and mutual fears and distrust replaced the reasonably harmonious working relationships of the three big powers during World War II.

By 1947 the Truman administration had adopted a conscious policy of containment toward the Russians. This meant maintaining the status quo in Europe through various U.S. assistance programs. The NATO alliance of 1949 completed the shift of U.S. policy away from its pre–World War II isolationist policy and toward a commitment to the defense of Western Europe.

In the 1960s the largest problem facing the two superpowers was controlling the spread of nuclear weapons. The first attempt at arms control took place in the 1950s. After Stalin died in 1953, the Eisenhower administration made an "open-skies" proposal. This was rejected by the Russians, who felt (correctly) that they were behind the Americans in the arms race. In the summer of 1962 Soviet premier Nikita Khrushchev attempted to redress the balance of power by secretly installing missiles in Cuba that could be employed to launch nuclear attacks against U.S. cities. This sparked the Cuban Missile Crisis, the high point of the Cold War, which brought both nations to the brink of nuclear war before the Russians agreed to withdraw the missiles.

During the Leonid Brezhnev–Richard Nixon years, the policy of détente (relaxation of tensions) resulted in a series of summit meetings. Most important was the SALT I agreement, which outlawed national antiballistic missile defenses and placed a five-year moratorium on the building of new strategic ballistic missiles.

Soviet-American relations took a turn for the worse when the Soviets invaded Afghanistan in December 1979. In response, President Jimmy Carter postponed presenting SALT II to the Senate and imposed an American boycott of the 1980 Olympic Games, which were held in Moscow.

Détente remained dead during President Ronald Reagan's first administration. Reagan not only promoted a military budget of $1.5 trillion over a five-year period, he also was the first president since Truman to refuse to meet the Soviet leader. Major changes, however, took place during Reagan's second administration. In the following selections, John Lewis Gaddis argues that President Reagan combined a policy of militancy and operational pragmatism to bring about significant improvements in Soviet-American relations, while Daniel Deudney and G. John Ikenberry credit Soviet President Mikhail Gorbachev with ending the cold war because he accepted Western liberal values and the need for global cooperation.

YES

John Lewis Gaddis

The Cold War: A New History

Soon to declare his own candidacy for the presidency of the United States, [Ronald] Reagan had already made it clear what *he* thought of détente: "[I]sn't that what a farmer has with his turkey—until thanksgiving day?" His rise to power, like that of Deng, Thatcher, and John Paul II, would also have been difficult to anticipate, but at least his acting skills were professionally acquired. His fame as a film star predated the Cold War, even World War II, and gave him a head start when he went into politics. It also caused his opponents—sometimes even his friends—to underestimate him, a serious mistake, for Reagan was as skillful a politician as the nation had seen for many years, and one of its sharpest grand strategists ever. His strength lay in his ability to see beyond complexity to simplicity. And what he saw was simply this: that because détente perpetuated—and had been meant to perpetuate—the Cold War, only killing détente could end the Cold War.

Reagan came to this position through faith, fear, and self-confidence. His faith was that democracy and capitalism would triumph over communism, a "temporary aberration which will one day," he predicted in 1975, "disappear from the earth because it is contrary to human nature." His fear was that before that happened human beings would disappear as the result of a nuclear war. "[W]e live in a world," he warned in 1976, "in which the great powers have aimed . . . at each other horrible missiles of destruction . . . that can in minutes arrive at each other's country and destroy virtually the civilized world we live in." It followed that neither communism nor nuclear weapons should continue to exist, and yet détente was ensuring that both did. "I don't know about you," he told a radio audience in 1977, "but I [don't] exactly tear my hair and go into a panic at the possibility of losing détente." It was that jaunty self-confidence—Reagan's ability to threaten détente without seeming threatening himself—that propelled him to a landslide victory over Carter in November, 1980, thereby bringing him to power alongside the other great contemporaries, and the other great actors, of his age.

There was one more—as it happened, another Pole—whose name few people would have known only a few months earlier. A short, squat man with a drooping mustache and jerky Charlie Chaplin–like movements, he had seen the shootings at the Gdansk shipyard in 1970, and had been sacked from his job there in 1976 for trying to organize the workers. Now, on August 14, 1980, with protests mounting once again, the shipyard director was trying to calm an angry crowd. Lech Wałęsa scrambled up on an excavator behind him, tapped him on the shoulder, and said: "Remember me?" Two weeks later—after lots of scrambling to rally his supporters from atop excavators, trucks, and the shipyard gate—Wałęsa announced the formation of the first independent and self-governing trade union ever in the Marxist-Leninist world. The pen with which he co-signed the charter for *Solidarność* (Solidarity) bore the image of John Paul II. And from Rome the pontiff let it be known, quietly but unmistakably, that he approved.

It was a moment at which several trends converged: the survival of a distinctive Polish identity despite the attempts of powerful neighbors, over several centuries, to try to smother it; the church's success in maintaining its autonomy through decades of war, revolution, and occupation; the state's incompetence in managing the post–World War II economy, which in turn discredited the ruling party's ideology. But trends hardly ever converge automatically. It takes leaders to make them do so, and here the actor-priest from Kraków and the actor-electrician from Gdansk played to each other's strengths—so much so that plans began to be made to remove them both from the stage.

The agent was Mehmet Ali Agca, a young Turk who may have plotted to kill Wałęsa on a January, 1981, visit to Rome, and who did shoot and almost kill the pope in St. Peter's Square on May 13, 1981. Agca's ties to Bulgarian intelligence quickly became clear. Soviet complicity was more difficult to establish, but it strains credulity to suggest that the Bulgarians would have undertaken an operation of this importance without Moscow's approval. The Italian state prosecutor's official report hinted strongly at this: "In some secret place, where every secret is wrapped in another secret, some political figure of great power . . . mindful of the needs of the Eastern bloc, decided that it was necessary to kill Pope Wojtyla." The pope's biographer put it more bluntly: "The simplest and most compelling answer . . . [is that] the Soviet Union was not an innocent in this business."

John Paul II recovered, attributing his survival to divine intervention. But Solidarity found its survival increasingly at risk as Kremlin leaders, alarmed that any communist government would share power with anybody, pressed the Polish authorities to suppress it. "Our friends listen, agree with our recommendations, but do practically nothing," Brezhnev fumed, "[a]nd the counterrevolution is advancing on every front." It could even take hold within the U.S.S.R. itself: what was happening in Poland was "having an, influence . . . in the western oblasts of our country," K.G.B. chief Yuri Andropov warned. "Additionally, . . . spontaneous demonstrations have flared up in parts of Georgia, [with] groups of people shooting anti-Soviet slogans . . . So we have to take strict measures here as well."

Apart from warning the Poles and cracking down on its own dissidents, however, it was not at all clear what the Soviet Union could do about the challenge Solidarity posed. Reagan's election ensured that any occupation of Poland would provoke an even harsher response than Carter's to the invasion of Afghanistan; meanwhile the Red Army was bogged down in that latter country with costs and casualties mounting and no exit strategy in sight. The Soviet economy could hardly stand the strain of supporting Eastern Europe, something it would have to do if, as seemed certain in the event of military action against Poland, the West imposed still further sanctions. Moreover, the Polish situation was not like the one in Czechoslovakia in 1968. General Anatoly Gribkov recalls warning his superiors:

> In Czechoslovakia, events developed beginning with the highest echelons of power. In Poland, on the other hand, it is the people rising up who have all stopped believing in the government of the country and the leadership of the Polish United Workers Party . . . The Polish armed forces arc battle-ready and patriotic. They will not fire on their own people.

By December, 1981, the Politburo had decided *not* to intervene: "[E]ven if Poland falls under the control of 'Solidarity,' that is the way it will be," Andropov told his colleague. "If the capitalist countries pounce on the Soviet Union, . . . that will be very burdensome for us. We must be concerned above all with our own country." The Kremlin's top ideologist, Mikhail Suslov, agreed: "If troops are introduced, that will mean a catastrophe. I think we have reached a unanimous view here on this matter, and there can be no consideration at all of introducing troops."

This was a remarkable decision in two respects. It meant, first, the end of the Brezhnev Doctrine, and hence of the Soviet Union's willingness—extending all the way back through Hungary in 1956 and East Germany in 1953—to use force to preserve its sphere of influence in Eastern Europe. But it also acknowledged that the world's most powerful Marxist-Leninist state no longer represented proletarians beyond its borders, for in Poland at least the workers themselves had rejected that ideology. Had these conclusions become known at the time, the unraveling of Soviet authority that took place in 1989 might well have occurred eight years earlier.

But they did not become known: in a rare instance of successful dramatization, the Politburo convinced the new Polish leader, General Wojciech Jaruzelski, that the U.S.S.R. was *about* to intervene. Desperate to avoid that outcome, he reluctantly imposed martial law on the morning of December 13, 1981, imprisoned the organizers of Solidarity, and abruptly ended the experiment of granting workers autonomy Within a workers' state. Ever the actor, Lech Wałęsa had his line ready for the occasion. "This is the moment of your defeat," he told the men who came to arrest him. "These are the last nails in the coffin of Communism."

⋅⟨⊙⟩⋅

On March 30, 1981, six weeks before the attempt on the pope's life, another would-be assassin shot and almost killed Reagan. The Soviet Union had nothing to do with this attack: it was the effort, rather, of a demented young man, John W. Hinckley, to impress his own movie star idol, the actress Jodie Foster.

The improbable motive behind this near-fatal act suggests the importance and vulnerability of individuals in history, for had Reagan's vice president, George H. W. Bush, succeeded him at that point, the Reagan presidency would have been a historical footnote and there probably would not have been an American challenge to the Cold War status quo. Bush, like most foreign policy experts of his generation, saw that conflict as a permanent feature of the international landscape. Reagan, like Wałęsa, Thatcher, Deng, and John Paul II, definitely did not.

He shared their belief in the power of words, in the potency of ideas, and in the uses of *drama* to shatter the constraints of conventional wisdom. He saw that the Cold War itself had become a convention: that too many minds in too many places had resigned themselves to its perpetuation. He sought to break the stalemate—which was, be believed, largely psychological—by exploiting Soviet weaknesses and asserting western strengths. His preferred weapon was public oratory.

The first example came at Notre Dame University on May 17, 1981, only a month and a half after Reagan's brush with death. The pope himself had been shot five days earlier, so this could have been an occasion for somber reflections on the precariousness of human existence. Instead, in the spirit of John Paul II's "be not afraid," a remarkably recovered president assured his audience "[t]hat the years ahead are great ones for this country, for the cause of freedom and the spread of civilization." And then he made a bold prediction, all the more striking for the casualness with which he delivered it:

> The West won't contain communism, it will transcend communism. It won't bother to . . . denounce it, it will dismiss it as some bizarre chapter in human history whose last pages are even now being written.

This was a wholly new tone after years of high-level pronouncements about the need to learn to live With the U.S.S.R. as a competitive superpower. Now Reagan was focusing on the *transitory* character of Soviet power, and on the certainty with which the West could look forward to its demise.

The president developed this theme in an even more dramatic setting on June 8, 1982. The occasion was a speech to the British Parliament, delivered at Westminster with Prime Minister Thatcher in attendance. Reagan began by talking about Poland, a country which had "contributed mightily to [European] civilization" and was continuing to do so "by being magnificently unreconciled to oppression." He then echoed Churchill's 1946 "Iron Curtain" speech by reminding his audience:

> From Stettin in the Baltic to Varna on the Black Sea, the regimes planted by totalitarianism have had more than 30 years to establish their legitimacy. But none—not one regime—has yet been able to risk free elections. Regimes planted by bayonets do not take root.

Karl Marx, Reagan acknowledged, had been right: "We are witnessing today a great revolutionary crisis, . . . where the demands of the economic order are conflicting directly with those of the political order." That crisis was happening, though, not in the capitalist West, but in the Soviet Union, a country "that runs against the tides of history by denying human freedom and human dignity," while "unable to feed its own people." Moscow's nuclear capabilities could not shield it from these facts: "Any system is inherently unstable that has no peaceful means to legitimize its leaders." It followed then, Reagan concluded—pointedly paraphrasing Leon Trotsky—that "the march of freedom and democracy . . . will leave Marxism-Leninism on the ash-heap of history."

The speech could not have been better calculated to feed the anxieties the Soviet leadership already felt. Martial law had clamped a lid on reform in Poland, but that only fueled resentment there and elsewhere in Eastern Europe. Afghanistan had become a bloody stalemate. Oil prices had plummeted, leaving the Soviet economy in shambles. And the men who ran the U.S.S.R. seemed literally to exemplify its condition: Brezhnev finally succumbed to his many ailments in November, 1982, but Andropov, who succeeded him, was already suffering from the kidney disease that would take his life a year and a half later. The contrast with the vigorous Reagan, five years younger than Brezhnev but three years older than Andropov, Was too conspicuous to miss.

Then Reagan deployed religion. "There is sin and evil in the world," he reminded the National Association of Evangelicals on March 8, 1983, in words the pope might have used, "and we're enjoined by Scripture and the Lord Jesus to oppose it with all our might." As long as communists "preach the supremacy of the state, declare its omnipotence over individual man, and predict its eventual domination of all peoples on Earth, they are the focus of evil in the modern world." Therefore:

> I urge you to speak out against those who would place the United States in a position of military and moral inferiority . . . I urge you to beware the temptation of Juride—the temptation of blithely declaring yourselves above it all and label[ing] both sides equally at fault, [of ignoring] the facts of history and the aggressive impulses of an evil empire.

Reagan chose the phrase, he later admitted, "with malice aforethought. . . . I think it worked." The "evil empire" speech completed a rhetorical offensive designed to expose what Reagan saw as the central error of détente: the idea that the Soviet Union had earned geopolitical, ideological, economic, and moral legitimacy as an equal to the United States and the other western democracies in the post–World War II international system.

The onslaught, however, was not limited to words. Reagan accelerated Carter's increase in American military spending: by 1985 the Pentagon's budget was almost twice what it had been in 1980. He did nothing to revive the SALT II treaty, proposing instead START—Strategic Arms *Reduction* Talks— which both his domestic critics and the Russians derided as an effort the kill the whole arms control process. The reaction was similar when Reagan suggested *not* deploying Pershing II and cruise missiles if the Soviet Union would dismantle *all* of its SS-20S. After Moscow contemptuously rejected this "zero-option," the installation of the new NATO missiles went ahead, despite a widespread nuclear freeze movement in the United States and vociferous anti-nuclear protests in western Europe.

But Reagan's most significant deed came on March 23, 1983, when he surprised the Kremlin, most American arms control experts, and many of his own advisers by repudiating the concept of Mutual Assured Destruction. He had never thought that it made much sense: it was like two Old West gunslingers "standing in a saloon aiming their guns to each other's head—permanently." He had been shocked to learn that there were no defenses against incoming missiles, and that in the curious logic of deterrence this was supposed to be a good thing. And so he asked, in a nationally televised speech: "What if . . . we could intercept and destroy strategic ballistic missiles before they reached our own soil or that of our allies?" It was an "emperor's new clothes" question, which no one else in a position of responsibility in Washington over the past two decades had dared to ask.

The reason was that *stability* in Soviet-American relations had come to be prized above all else. To attempt to build defenses against offensive weapons, the argument ran, could upset the delicate equilibrium upon which deterrence was supposed to depend. That made sense if one thought in static terms—if one assumed that the nuclear balance defined the Cold War and would continue to do so indefinitely. Reagan, however, thought in evolutionary terms. He saw that the Soviet Union had lost its ideological appeal, that it was losing whatever economic strength it once had, and that its survival as a superpower could no longer be taken for granted. That made stability, in his view, an outmoded, even immoral, priority. If the U.S.S.R. was crumbling, what could justify continuing to hold East Europeans hostage to the Brezhnev Doctrine—or, for that matter, continuing to hold Americans hostage to the equally odious concept of Mutual Assured Destruction? Why not hasten the disintegration?

That is what the Strategic Defense Initiative was intended to do. It challenged the argument that vulnerability could provide security. It called into question the 1972 Anti-Ballistic Missile Treaty, a center-piece of SALT I. It exploited the Soviet Union's backwardness in computer technology, a field in which the Russians knew that they could not keep up. And it undercut the peace movement by framing the entire project in terms of *lowering* the risk of nuclear war: the ultimate purpose of SDI, Reagan insisted, was not to freeze nuclear weapons, but rather to render them "impotent and obsolete."

This last theme reflected something else about Reagan that almost everybody at the time missed: he was the only nuclear abolitionist ever to have been president of the United States. He made no secret of this, but the possibility that a right-wing Republican anti-communist promilitary chief executive could also be an anti-nuclear activist defied so many stereotypes that hardly anyone noticed Reagan's repeated promises, as he had put it in the "evil empire" speech, "to keep America strong and free, while we negotiate real and verifiable reductions in the world's nuclear arsenals and one day, with God's help, their total elimination."

Reagan was deeply committed to SDI: it was not a bargaining chip to give up in future negotiations. That did not preclude, though, using it as a bluff: the United States was years, even decades, away from developing a missile defense capability, but Reagan's speech persuaded the increasingly frightened Soviet leaders that this was about to happen. They were convinced, Dobrynin recalled, "that the great technological potential of the United States had scored again and treated Reagan's statement as a real threat." Having exhausted their country by catching up in offensive missiles, the suddenly faced a new round of competition demanding skills they had no hope of mastering. And the Americans seemed not even to have broken into a sweat.

The reaction, in the Kremlin, approached panic. Andropov had concluded, while still head of the K.G.B., that the new administration in Washington might be planning a surprise attack on the Soviet Union. "Reagan is unpredictable," he warned. "You should expect anything from him." There followed a two-year intelligence alert, with agents throughout the world ordered to look for evidence that such preparations were under way. The tension became so great that when a South Korean airliner accidentally strayed into Soviet airspace over Sakhalin on September 1,1983, the military authorities in Moscow assumed the worst and ordered it shot down, killing 269 civilians, 63 of them Americans. Unwilling to admit the mistake, Andropov maintained that the incident had been a "sophisticated provocation organized by the U.S. special services."

Then something even scarier happened that attracted no public notice. The United States and its NATO allies had for years carried out fall military exercises, but the ones that took place in November—designated "Able Archer 83"—involved a higher level of leadership participation than was usual. The Soviet intelligence agencies kept a close watch on these maneuvers, and their reports caused Andropov and his top aides to conclude—briefly—that a nuclear attack was imminent. It was probably the most dangerous moment since the Cuban missile crisis, and yet no one in Washington knew of it until a well-placed spy in the K.G.B.'s London headquarters alerted British intelligence, which passed the information along to the Americans.

That definitely got Reagan's attention. Long worried about the danger of a nuclear war, the president had already initiated a series of quiet contacts with Soviet officials—mostly unreciprocated—aimed at defusing tensions. The Able Archer crisis convinced him that he had pushed the Russians far enough, that it was time for another speech. It came at the beginning of Orwell's fateful year, on January 16, 1984, but Big Brother was nowhere to be seen. Instead, in lines only he could have composed, Reagan suggested placing the Soviet-American relationship in the capably reassuring hands of Jim and Sally and Ivan and Anya. One White House staffer, puzzled by the hand-written addendum to the prepared text, exclaimed a bit too loudly: "Who wrote this shit?"

Once again, the old actor's timing was excellent. Andropov died the following month, to be succeeded by Konstantin Chemenko, an enfeebled geriatric so zombie-like as to be beyond assessing intelligence reports, alarming or not. Having failed to prevent the NATO missile deployments, Foreign Minister Gromyko soon grudgingly agreed to resume arms control negotiations. Meanwhile Reagan was running for re-election as both a hawk and a dove: in November he trounced his Democratic opponent, Walter Mondale. And when

Chemenko died in March, 1985, at the age of seventy-four, it seemed an all-too-literal validation of Reagan's predictions about "last pages" and historical "ash-heaps." Seventy-four himself at the time, the president had another line ready: "How am I supposed to get anyplace with the Russians, if they keep dying on me?"

⋅◈⋅

"We can't go on living like this," Mikhail Gorbachev recalls saying to his wife, Raisa, on the night before the Politburo appointed him, at the age of fifty-four, to succeed Chernenko as general secretary of the Communist Party of the U.S.S.R. That much was obvious not just to Gorbachev but even to the surviving elders who selected him: the Kremlin could not continue to be run as a home for the aged. Not since Stalin had so young a man reached the top of the Soviet hierarchy. Not since Lenin had there been a university-educated Soviet leader. And never had there been one so open about his country 3's shortcomings, or so candid in acknowledging the failures of Marxist-Leninist ideology.

Gorbachev had been trained as a lawyer, not an actor, but he understood the uses of personality at least as well as Reagan did. Vice President Bush, who represented the United States at Chernenko's funeral, reported back that Gorbachev "has a disarming smile, warm eyes, and an engaging way of making an unpleasant point and then bouncing back to establish real communication with his interlocutors." Secretary of State George Shultz, who was also there, described him as "totally different from any Soviet leader I've ever met." Reagan himself, on meeting Gorbachev at the November, 1985, Geneva summit, found "warmth in his face and style, not the coldness bordering on hatred I'd seen in most other senior Soviet leaders I'd met until then."

For the first time since the Cold War began the U.S.S.R. had a ruler who did not seem sinister, boorish, unresponsive, senile—or dangerous. Gorbachev was "intelligent, well-educated, dynamic, honest, with ideas and imagination," one of his closest advisers, Anatoly Chernyaev, noted in his private diary. "Myths and taboos (including ideological ones) are nothing for him. He could flatten any of them." When a Soviet citizen congratulated him early in 1987 for having replaced a regime of "stonefaced sphinxes," Gorbachev proudly published the letter.

What would replace the myths, taboos, and sphinxes, however, was less clear. Gorbachev knew that the Soviet Union could not continue on its existing path, but unlike John Paul II, Deng, Thatcher, Reagan, and Wałęsa, he did not know what the new path should be. He was at once vigorous, decisive, and adrift: he poured enormous energy into shattering the status quo without specifying how to reassemble the pieces. As a consequence, he allowed circumstances—and often the firmer views of more far-sighted contemporaries—to determine his own priorities. He resembled, in this sense, the eponymous hero of Woody Allen's movie *Zelig*, who managed to be present at all the great events of his time, but only by taking on the character, even the appearance, of the stronger personalities who surrounded him.

Gorbachev's malleability was most evident in his dealings with Reagan, who had long insisted that he could get through to a Soviet leader if he could ever meet one face-to-face. That had not been possible with Brozhnev, Andropov, or Chernenko, which made Reagan all the keener to try with Gorbachev. The new Kremlin boss came to Geneva bristling with distrust: the president, he claimed, was seeking "to use the arms race . . . to weaken the Soviet Union. . . . But we can match any challenge, though you might not think so." Reagan responded that "we would prefer to sit down and get rid of nuclear weapons, and with them, the threat of war. "SDI would make that possible: the United States would even share the technology with the Soviet Union. Reagan was being emotional, Gorbachev protested: SDI was only "one man's dream." Reagan countered by asking why "it was so horrifying to seek to develop a defense against this awful threat." The summit broke up inconclusively.

Two months later, though, Gorbachev proposed publicly that the United States and the Soviet Union commit themselves to ridding the world of nuclear weapons by the year 2000. Cynics saw this as an effort to test Reagan's sincerity, but Chernyaev detected a deeper motive. Gorbachev, he concluded, had "really decided to end the arms race no matter what. He is taking this 'risk' because, as he understands, it's no risk at all—because nobody would attack us even if we disarmed completely." Just two years earlier Andropov had thought Reagan capable of launching a surprise attack. Now Gorbachev felt confident that the United States would never do this. Reagan's position 1 ad not changed: he had always asked Soviet leaders to "trust me." After meeting Reagan, Gorbachev began to do so.

A nuclear disaster did, nevertheless, occur—not because of war but as the result of an explosion at the Chernobyl nuclear power plant on April 26, 1986. This event also changed Gorbachev. It revealed "the sicknesses of our system . . . the concealing or hushing up of accidents and other bad news, irresponsibility and carelessness, slipshod work, wholesale drunkenness." For decades, he admonished the Politburo, "scientists, specialists, and ministers have been telling us that everything was safe. . . . [Y]ou think that we will look on you as gods. But now we have ended up with a fiasco." Henceforth there would have to be *glasnost'* (publicity) and *perestroika* (restructuring) within the Soviet Union itself. "Chernobyl," Gorbachev acknowledged, "made me and my colleagues rethink a great many things."

The next Reagan-Gorbachev summit, held the following October in Reykjavik, Iceland, showed how far the rethinking had gone. Gorbachev dismissed earlier Soviet objections and accepted Reagan's "zero option," which would eliminate all intermediate-range nuclear missiles in Europe. He went on to propose a 50 percent cut in Soviet and American strategic weapons, in return for which the United States would agree to honor the Anti-Ballistic Missile Treaty for the next decade while confining SDI to laboratory testing. Not to be outdone, Reagan suggested phasing out all intercontinental ballistic missiles within that period and reiterated his offer to share SDI. Gorbachev was skeptical, leading Reagan to wonder how anyone could object to "defenses against non-existent weapons." The president then proposed a return to Reykjavik in 1996:

> He and Gorbachev would come to Iceland, and each of them would bring
> the last nuclear missile from each country with them. Then they would
> give a tremendous party for the whole world. . . . The President . . . would
> be very old by then and Gorbachev would not recognize him. The Presi-
> dent would say "Hello, Mikhail." And Gorbachev would say, "Ron, is it
> you?" And then they would destroy the last missile.

It was one of Reagan's finest performances, but Gorbachev for the
moment remained unmoved: the United States would have to give up the
right to deploy SDI. That was unacceptable to Reagan, who angrily ended
the summit.

Both men quickly recognized, though, the significance of what had
happened: to the astonishment of their aides and allies, the leaders of the
United States and the Soviet Union had found that they shared an interest,
if not in SDI technology, then at least in the principle of nuclear abolition.
The logic was Reagan's, but Gorbachev had come to accept it. Reykjavik, he
told a press conference, had not been a failure: "[I]t is a breakthrough,
which allowed us for the first time to look over the horizon."

The two men never agreed formally to abolish nuclear weapons, nor
did missile defense come anywhere close to feasibility during their years in
office. But at their third summit in Washington in December, 1987, they did
sign a treaty providing for the dismantling of all intermediate-range nuclear
missiles in Europe. *"Dovorey no provorey,"* Reagan insisted at the signing
ceremony, exhausting his knowledge of the Russian language: "Trust but
verify." You repeat that at every, meeting," Gorbachev laughed. "I like it,"
Reagan admitted. Soon Soviet and American observers were witnessing the
actual destruction of the SS-20, Pershing II, and cruise missiles that had
revived Cold War tensions only a few years before—and pocketing the pieces
as souvenirs. If by no means "impotent," certain categories of nuclear weapons had surely become "obsolete." It was Reagan, more than anyone else, who
made that happen.

Gorbachev's impressionability also showed up in economics. He had
been aware, from his travels outside the Soviet Union before assuming the
leadership, that "people there . . . were better off than in our country." It
seemed that "our aged leaders were not especially worried about our undeniably lower living standards, our unsatisfactory way of life, and our falling
behind in the field of advanced technologies." But he had no clear sense of
what to do about this. So Secretary of State Shultz, a former economics
professor at Stanford, took it upon himself to educate the new Soviet leader.

Shultz began by lecturing Gorbachev, as early as 1985, on the impossibility of a closed society being a prosperous society: "People must be free to
express themselves, move around, emigrate and travel if they want to. . . .
Otherwise they can't take advantage of the opportunities available. The Soviet
economy will have to be radically changed to adapt to the new era." "You
should take over the planning office here in Moscow," Gorbachev joked,
"because you have more ideas than they have." In a way, this is what Shultz
did. Over the next several years, he used his trips to that city to run tutorials

for Gorbachev and his advisers, even bringing pie charts to the Kremlin to illustrate his argument that as long as it retained a command economy, the Soviet Union would fall further and further behind the rest of the developed world.

Gorbachev was surprisingly receptive. He echoed some of Shultz's thinking in his 1987 book, *Perestroika:* "How can the economy advance," he asked, "if it creates preferential conditions for backward enterprises and penalizes the foremost ones?" When Reagan visited the Soviet Union in May, 1988, Gorbachev arranged for him to lecture at Moscow State University on the virtues of market capitalism. From beneath a huge bust of Lenin, the president evoked computer chips, rock stars, movies, and the "irresistible power of unarmed truth." The students gave him a standing ovation. Soon Gorbachev was repeating what he had learned to Reagan's successor, George H. W. Bush: "Whether we like it or not, we will have to deal with a united, integrated, European economy. . . . Whether we want it or not, Japan is one more center of world politics. . . . China . . . is [another] huge reality. . . . All these, I repeat, are huge events typical of a regrouping of forces in the world."

Most of this, however, was rhetoric: Gorbachev was never willing to leap directly to a market economy in the way that Deng Xiaoping had done. He reminded the Politburo late in 1988 that Franklin D. Roosevelt had saved American capitalism by "borrow[ing] socialist ideas of planning, state regulation, [and] . . . the principle of more social fairness. "The implication was that Gorbachev could save socialism by borrowing from capitalism, but just how remained uncertain. "[R]epeated incantations about 'socialist values' and 'purified ideas of October,'" Chernyaev observed several months later, "provoke an ironic response in knowing listeners. . . . [T]hey sense that there's nothing behind them." After the Soviet Union collapsed, Gorbachev acknowledged his failure. "The Achilles heel of socialism was the inability to link the socialist goal with the provision of incentives for efficient labor and the encouragement of initiative on the part of individuals. It became clear in practice that a market provides such incentives best of all."

There was, however, one lesson Reagan and his advisers tried to teach Gorbachev that he did not need to learn: it had to do with the difficulty of sustaining an unpopular, overextended, and antiquated empire. The United States had, since Carter's final year in office, provided covert and sometimes overt support to forces resisting Soviet influence in Eastern Europe, Afghanistan, Central America, and elsewhere. By 1985 there was talk in Washington of a "Reagan Doctrine": a campaign to turn the forces of nationalism against the Soviet Union by making the case that, with the Brezhnev Doctrine, it had become the last great imperialist power. Gorbachev's emergence raised the possibility of convincing a Kremlin leader himself that the "evil empire" was a lost cause, and over the next several years Reagan tried to do this. His methods included quiet persuasion, continued assistance to anti-Soviet resistance movements, and as always dramatic speeches: the most sensational one came at the Brandenburg Gate in West Berlin on June 12, 1987, when—against the advice of the State Department—the president demanded: "Mr. Gorbachev, tear down this wall!"

For once, a Reagan performance fell flat the reaction in Moscow was unexpectedly restrained. Despite this challenge to the most visible symbol of Soviet authority in Europe, planning went ahead for the Intermediate-Range Nuclear Forces Treaty and the Washington summit later that year. The reason, it is now clear, is that the Brezhnev Doctrine had died when the Politburo decided, six years earlier, against invading Poland. From that moment on Kremlin leaders depended upon *threats* to use force to maintain their control over Eastern Europe—but they knew that they could not actually use force. Gorbachev was aware of this, and had even tried to signal his Warsaw Pact allies, in 1985, that they were on their own: "I had the feeling that they were not taking it altogether seriously." So he began making the point openly.

One could always "suppress, compel, bribe, break or blast," he wrote in his book *Perestroika*, "but only for a certain period. From the point of view of long-term, big-time politics, no one will be able to subordinate others. . . . Let everyone make his own choice, and let us all respect that choice." Decisions soon followed to begin withdrawing Soviet troops from Afghanistan and to reduce support for Marxist regimes elsewhere in the "third world." Eastern Europe, though, was another matter: the prevailing view in Washington as well as in European capitals on both sides of the Cold War divide was that the U.S.S.R. would never voluntarily relinquish its sphere of influence there. "Any Soviet yielding of the area," one western analyst commented in 1987, "not only would undermine the ideological claims of Communism . . . and degrade the Soviet Union's credentials as a confident global power, but also would gravely jeopardize a basic internal Soviet consensus and erode the domestic security of the system itself."

For Gorbachev, though, any attempt to *maintain* control over unwilling peoples through the use of force would degrade the Soviet system by over-stretching its resources, discrediting its ideology, and resisting the irresistible forces of democratization that, for both moral and practical reasons, were sweeping the world. And so he barrowed a trick from Reagan by making a dramatic speech of his own: he announced to the United Nations General Assembly, on December 7, 1988, that the Soviet Union would *unilaterally* cut its ground force commitment to the Warsaw Pact by half a million men. "It is obvious," he argued, "that force and the threat of force cannot be and should not be an instrument of foreign policy. . . . Freedom of choice is . . . a universal principle, and it should know no exceptions."

The speech "left a huge impression," Gorbachev boasted to the Politburo upon his return to Moscow, and "created an entirely different background for perceptions of our policies and the Soviet Union as a whole." He was right about that. It suddenly became apparent, just as Reagan was leaving office, that the Reagan Doctrine had been pushing against an open door. But Gorbachev had also made it clear, to the peoples and the governments of Eastern Europe, that the door was now open.

Daniel Deudney and
G. John Ikenberry

Who Won the Cold War?

The end of the Cold War marks the most important historical divide in half a century. The magnitude of those developments has ushered in a wide-ranging debate over the reasons for its end—a debate that is likely to be as protracted, controversial, and politically significant as that over the Cold War's origins. The emerging debate over why the Cold War ended is of more than historical interest: At stake is the vindication and legitimation of an entire world view and foreign policy orientation.

In thinking about the Cold War's conclusion, it is vital to distinguish between the domestic origins of the crisis in Soviet communism and the external forces that influenced its timing and intensity, as well as the direction of the Soviet response. Undoubtedly, the ultimate cause of the Cold War's outcome lies in the failure of the Soviet system itself. At most, outside forces hastened and intensified the crisis. However, it was not inevitable that the Soviet Union would respond to this crisis as it did in the late 1980s—with domestic liberalization and foreign policy accommodation. After all, many Western experts expected that the USSR would respond to such a crisis with renewed repression at home and aggression abroad, as it had in the past.

At that fluid historic juncture, the complex matrix of pressures, opportunities, and attractions from the outside world influenced the direction of Soviet change, particularly in its foreign policy. The Soviets' field of vision was dominated by the West, the United States, and recent American foreign policy. Having spent more than 45 years attempting to influence the Soviet Union, Americans are now attempting to gauge the weight of their country's impact and, thus, the track record of U.S. policies.

In assessing the rest of the world's impact on Soviet change, a remarkably simplistic and self-serving conventional wisdom has emerged in the United States. This new conventional wisdom, the "Reagan victory school," holds that President Ronald Reagan's military and ideological assertiveness during the 1980s played the lead role in the collapse of Soviet communism and the "taming" of its foreign policy. In that view the Reagan administration's ideological counter-offensive and military buildup delivered the knock-out punch to a system that was internally bankrupt and on the ropes. The Reagan Right's perspective is an ideologically pointed version of the more broadly held conventional wisdom on the end of the Cold War that emphasizes the success of the "peace-through-strength" strategy manifest in four decades of Western containment. After decades of waging a

From Daniel Deudney and G. John Ikenberry, "Who Won the Cold War?" *Foreign Policy*, no. 87 (Summer 1992). Copyright © 1992 by Daniel Deudney and G. John Ikenberry. Reproduced with permission of Foreign Policy via Copyright Clearance Center.

costly "twilight struggle," the West now celebrates the triumph of its military and ideological resolve.

The Reagan victory school and the broader peace-through-strength perspectives are, however, misleading and incomplete—both in their interpretation of events in the 1980s and in their understanding of deeper forces that led to the end of the Cold War. It is important to consider the emerging conventional wisdom before it truly becomes an article of faith on Cold War history and comes to distort the thinking of policymakers in America and elsewhere.

The collapse of the Cold War caught almost everyone, particularly hardliners, by surprise. Conservatives and most analysts in the U.S. national security establishment believed that the Soviet-U.S. struggle was a permanent feature of international relations. As former National Security Council adviser Zbigniew Brzezinski put it in 1986, "the American-Soviet contest is not some temporary aberration but a historical rivalry that will long endure." And to many hardliners, Soviet victory was far more likely than Soviet collapse. Many ringing predictions now echo as embarrassments.

The Cold War's end was a baby that arrived unexpectedly, but a long line of those claiming paternity has quickly formed. A parade of former Reagan administration officials and advocates has forthrightly asserted that Reagan's hardline policies were the decisive trigger for reorienting Soviet foreign policy and for the demise of communism. As former Pentagon officials like Caspar Weinberger and Richard Perle, columnist George Will, neoconservative thinker Irving Kristol, and other proponents of the Reagan victory school have argued, a combination of military and ideological pressures gave the Soviets little choice but to abandon expansionism abroad and repression at home. In that view, the Reagan military buildup foreclosed Soviet military options while pushing the Soviet economy to the breaking point. Reagan partisans stress that his dramatic "Star Wars" initiative put the Soviets on notice that the next phase of the arms race would be waged in areas where the West held a decisive technological edge.

Reagan and his administration's military initiatives, however, played a far different and more complicated role in inducing Soviet change than the Reagan victory school asserts. For every "hardening" there was a "softening": Reagan's rhetoric of the "Evil Empire" was matched by his vigorous anti-nuclearism; the military buildup in the West was matched by the resurgence of a large popular peace movement; and the Reagan Doctrine's toughening of containment was matched by major deviations from containment in East-West economic relations. Moreover, over the longer term, the strength marshaled in containment was matched by mutual weakness in the face of nuclear weapons, and efforts to engage the USSR were as important as efforts to contain it.

The Irony of Ronald Reagan

Perhaps the greatest anomaly of the Reagan victory school is the "Great Communicator" himself. The Reagan Right ignores that his anti-nuclearism was as strong as his anticommunism. Reagan's personal convictions on nuclear weapons were profoundly at odds with the beliefs of most in his administration.

Staffed by officials who considered nuclear weapons a useful instrument of statecraft and who were openly disdainful of the moral critique of nuclear weapons articulated by the arms control community and the peace movement, the administration pursued the hardest line on nuclear policy and the Soviet Union in the postwar era. Then vice president George Bush's observation that nuclear weapons would be fired as a warning shot and Deputy Under Secretary of Defense T. K. Jones's widely quoted view that nuclear war was survivable captured the reigning ethos within the Reagan administration.

In contrast, there is abundant evidence that Reagan himself felt a deep antipathy for nuclear weapons and viewed their abolition to be a realistic and desirable goal. Reagan's call in his famous March 1983 "Star Wars" speech for a program to make nuclear weapons impotent and obsolete was viewed as cynical by many, but actually it expressed Reagan's heartfelt views, views that he came to act upon. As *Washington Post* reporter Lou Cannon's 1991 biography points out, Reagan was deeply disturbed by nuclear deterrence and attracted to abolitionist solutions. "I know I speak for people everywhere when I say our dream is to see the day when nuclear weapons will be banished from the face of the earth," Reagan said in November 1983. Whereas the Right saw antinuclearism as a threat to American military spending and the legitimacy of an important foreign policy tool, or as propaganda for domestic consumption, Reagan sincerely believed it. Reagan's anti-nuclearism was not just a personal sentiment. It surfaced at decisive junctures to affect Soviet perceptions of American policy. Sovietologist and strategic analyst Michael MccGwire has argued persuasively that Reagan's anti-nuclearism decisively influenced Soviet-U.S. relations during the early Gorbachev years.

Contrary to the conventional wisdom, the defense buildup did not produce Soviet capitulation. The initial Soviet response to the Reagan administration's buildup and belligerent rhetoric was to accelerate production of offensive weapons, both strategic and conventional. That impasse was broken not by Soviet capitulation but by an extraordinary convergence by Reagan and Mikhail Gorbachev on a vision of mutual nuclear vulnerability and disarmament. On the Soviet side, the dominance of the hardline response to the newly assertive America was thrown into question in early 1985 when Gorbachev became general secretary of the Communist party after the death of Konstantin Chernenko. Without a background in foreign affairs, Gorbachev was eager to assess American intentions directly and put his stamp on Soviet security policy. Reagan's strong antinuclear views expressed at the November 1985 Geneva summit were decisive in convincing Gorbachev that it was possible to work with the West in halting the nuclear arms race. The arms control diplomacy of the later Reagan years was successful because, as *Washington Post* journalist Don Oberdorfer has detailed in *The Turn: From the Cold War to a New Era* (1991), Secretary of State George Shultz picked up on Reagan's strong convictions and deftly side-stepped hard-line opposition to agreements. In fact, Schultz's success at linking presidential unease about nuclear weapons to Soviet overtures in the face of rightwing opposition provides a sharp contrast with John Foster Dulles's refusal to act on President Dwight Eisenhower's nuclear doubts and the opportunities presented by Nikita Khrushchev's détente overtures.

Reagan's commitment to anti-nuclearism and its potential for transforming the U.S-Soviet confrontation was more graphically demonstrated at the October 1986 Reykjavik summit when Reagan and Gorbachev came close to agreeing on a comprehensive program of global denuclearization that was far bolder than any seriously entertained by American strategists since the Baruch Plan of 1946. The sharp contrast between Reagan's and Gorbachev's shared skepticism toward nuclear weapons on the one hand, and the Washington security establishment's consensus on the other, was showcased in former secretary of defense James Schlesinger's scathing accusation that Reagan was engaged in "casual utopianism." But Reagan's anomalous anti-nuclearism provided the crucial signal to Gorbachev that bold initiatives would be reciprocated rather than exploited. Reagan's anti-nuclearism was more important than his administration's military buildup in catalyzing the end of the Cold War.

Neither anti-nuclearism nor its embrace by Reagan have received the credit they deserve for producing the Soviet-U.S. reconciliation. Reagan's accomplishment in this regard has been met with silence from all sides. Conservatives, not sharing Reagan's anti-nuclearism, have emphasized the role of traditional military strength. The popular peace movement, while holding deeply antinuclear views, was viscerally suspicious of Reagan. The establishment arms control community also found Reagan and his motives suspect, and his attack on deterrence conflicted with their desire to stabilize deterrence and establish their credentials as sober participants in security policy making. Reagan's radical anti-nuclearism should sustain his reputation as the ultimate Washington outsider.

The central role of Reagan's and Gorbachev's anti-nuclearism throws new light on the 1987 Treaty on Intermediate-range Nuclear Forces, the first genuine disarmament treaty of the nuclear era. The conventional wisdom emphasizes that this agreement was the fruit of a hard-line negotiating posture and the U.S. military buildup. Yet the superpowers' settlement on the "zero option" was not a vindication of the hard-line strategy. The zero option was originally fashioned by hardliners for propaganda purposes, and many backed off as its implementation became likely. The impasse the hard line created was transcended by the surprising Reagan-Gorbachev convergence against nuclear arms.

The Reagan victory school also overstates the overall impact of American and Western policy on the Soviet Union during the 1980s. The Reagan administration's posture was both evolving and inconsistent. Though loudly proclaiming its intention to go beyond the previous containment policies that were deemed too soft, the reality of Reagan's policies fell short. As Sovietologists Gail Lapidus and Alexander Dallin observed in a 1989 *Bulletin of the Atomic Scientists* article, the policies were "marked to the end by numerous zigzags and reversals, bureaucratic conflicts, and incoherence." Although rollback had long been a cherished goal of the Republican party's right wing, Reagan was unwilling and unable to implement it.

The hard-line tendencies of the Reagan administration were offset in two ways. First, and most important, Reagan's tough talk fueled a large peace movement in the United States and Western Europe in the 1980s, a movement that put significant political pressure upon Western governments to pursue far reaching arms control proposals. That mobilization of Western opinion created a political climate in which the rhetoric and posture of the early Reagan administration was a significant political liability. By the 1984 U.S. presidential election, the administration had embraced arms control goals that it had previously ridiculed. Reagan's own anti-nuclearism matched that rising public concern, and Reagan emerged as the spokesman for comprehensive denuclearization. Paradoxically, Reagan administration policies substantially triggered the popular revolt against the nuclear hardline, and then Reagan came to pursue the popular agenda more successfully than any other postwar president.

Second, the Reagan administration's hard-line policies were also undercut by powerful Western interests that favored East-West economic ties. In the early months of Reagan's administration, the grain embargo imposed by President Jimmy Carter after the 1979 Soviet invasion of Afghanistan was lifted in order to keep the Republican party's promises to Midwestern farmers. Likewise, in 1981 the Reagan administration did little to challenge Soviet control of Eastern Europe after Moscow pressured Warsaw to suppress the independent Polish trade union Solidarity, in part because Poland might have defaulted on multibillion dollar loans made by Western banks. Also, despite strenuous opposition by the Reagan administration, the NATO allies pushed ahead with a natural gas pipeline linking the Soviet Union with Western Europe. That a project creating substantial economic interdependence could proceed during the worst period of Soviet-U.S. relations in the 1980s demonstrates the failure of the Reagan administration to present an unambiguous hard line toward the Soviet Union. More generally, NATO allies and the vocal European peace movement moderated and buffered hardline American tendencies.

In sum, the views of the Reagan victory school are flawed because they neglect powerful crosscurrents in the West during the 1980s. The conventional wisdom simplifies a complex story and ignores those aspects of Reagan administration policy inconsistent with the hardline rationale. Moreover, the Western "face" toward the Soviet Union did not consist exclusively of Reagan administration policies, but encompassed countervailing tendencies from the Western public, other governments, and economic interest groups.

Whether Reagan is seen as the consummate hardliner or the prophet of anti-nuclearism, one should not exaggerate the influence of his administration, or of other short-term forces. Within the Washington beltway, debates about postwar military and foreign policy would suggest that Western strategy fluctuated wildly, but in fact the basic thrust of Western policy toward the USSR remained remarkably consistent. Arguments from the New Right notwithstanding, Reagan's containment strategy was not that different from those of his predecessors. Indeed, the broader peace-through-strength perspective sees the Cold War's finale as the product of a long-term policy, applied over the decades.

In any case, although containment certainly played an important role in blocking Soviet expansionism, it cannot explain either the end of the Cold War or the direction of Soviet policy responses. The West's relationship with the Soviet Union was not limited to containment, but included important elements of mutual vulnerability and engagement. The Cold War's end was not simply a result of Western strength but of mutual weakness and intentional engagement as well.

Most dramatically, the mutual vulnerability created by nuclear weapons overshadowed containment. Nuclear weapons forced the United States and the Soviet Union to eschew war and the serious threat of war as tools of diplomacy and created imperatives for the cooperative regulation of nuclear capability. Both countries tried to fashion nuclear explosives into useful instruments of policy, but they came to the realization—as the joint Soviet-American statement issued from the 1985 Geneva summit put it—that "nuclear war cannot be won and must never be fought." Both countries slowly but surely came to view nuclear weapons as a common threat that must be regulated jointly. Not just containment, but also the overwhelming and common nuclear threat brought the Soviets to the negotiating table. In the shadow of nuclear destruction, common purpose defused traditional antagonisms.

A second error of the peace-through-strength perspective is the failure to recognize that the West offered an increasingly benign face to the communist world. Traditionally, the Soviets' Marxist-Leninist doctrine held that the capitalist West was inevitably hostile and aggressive, an expectation reinforced by the aggression of capitalist, fascist Germany. Since World War II, the Soviets' principal adversaries had been democratic capitalist states. Slowly but surely Soviet doctrine acknowledged that the West's behavior did not follow Leninist expectations, but was instead increasingly pacific and cooperative. The Soviet willingness to abandon the Brezhnev Doctrine in the late 1980s in favor of the "Sinatra Doctrine"—under which any East European country could sing, "I did it my way"—suggests a radical transformation in the prevailing Soviet perception of threat from the West. In 1990, the Soviet acceptance of the de facto absorption of communist East Germany into West Germany involved the same calculation with even higher stakes. In accepting the German reunification, despite that country's past aggression, Gorbachev acted on the assumption that the Western system was fundamentally pacific. As Russian foreign minister Andrei Kozyrev noted subsequently, that Western countries are pluralistic democracies "practically rules out the pursuance of an aggressive foreign policy." Thus the Cold War ended despite the assertiveness of Western hardliners, rather than because of it.

The War of Ideas

The second front of the Cold War, according to the Reagan victory school, was ideological. Reagan spearheaded a Western ideological offensive that dealt the USSR a death blow. For the Right, driving home the image of the Evil Empire was a decisive stroke rather than a rhetorical flourish. Ideological warfare was such a key front in the Cold War because the Soviet Union was, at its core, an ideological creation. According to the Reagan Right, the supreme vulnerability of the Soviet Union to ideological assault was greatly underappreciated by Western leaders and publics. In that view, the Cold War was won by the West's uncompromising assertion of the superiority of its values and its complete denial of the moral legitimacy of the Soviet system during the 1980s. Western military strength could prevent defeat, but only ideological breakthrough could bring victory.

Underlying that interpretation is a deeply ideological philosophy of politics and history. The Reagan Right tended to view politics as a war of ideas, an orientation that generated a particularly polemical type of politics. As writer Sidney Blumenthal has pointed out, many of the leading figures in the neo-conservative movement since the 1960s came to conservatism after having begun their political careers as Marxists or socialists. That perspective sees the Soviet Union as primarily an ideological artifact, and therefore sees struggle with it in particularly ideological terms. The neoconservatives believe, like Lenin, that "ideas are more fatal than guns."

Convinced that Bolshevism was quintessentially an ideological phenomenon, activists of the New Right were contemptuous of Western efforts to accommodate Soviet needs, moderate Soviet aims, and integrate the USSR into the international system as a "normal" great power. In their view, the *realpolitik* strategy urged by George Kennan, Walter Lippmann, and Hans Morgenthau was based on a misunderstanding of the Soviet Union. It provided an incomplete roadmap for waging the Cold War, and guaranteed that it would never be won. A particular villain for the New Right was Secretary of State Henry Kissinger, whose program of détente implied, in their view, a "moral equivalence" between the West and the Soviet Union that amounted to unilateral ideological disarmament. Even more benighted were liberal attempts to engage and co-opt the Soviet Union in hopes that the two systems could ultimately reconcile. The New Right's view of politics was strikingly globalist in its assumption that the world had shrunk too much for two such different systems to survive, and that the contest was too tightly engaged for containment or Iron Curtains to work. As James Burnham, the ex-communist prophet of New Right anticommunism, insisted in the early postwar years, the smallness of our "one world" demanded a strategy of "rollback" for American survival.

The end of the Cold War indeed marked an ideological triumph for the West, but not of the sort fancied by the Reagan victory school. Ideology played a far different and more complicated role in inducing Soviet change than the Reagan school allows. As with the military sphere, the Reagan school presents an incomplete picture of Western ideological influence, ignoring the emergence of ideological common ground in stimulating Soviet change.

The ideological legitimacy of the Soviet system collapsed in the eyes of its own citizens not because of an assault by Western ex-leftists, but because of the appeal of Western affluence and permissiveness. The puritanical austerity of Bolshevism's "New Soviet Man" held far less appeal than the "bourgeois decadence" of the West. For the peoples of the USSR and Eastern Europe, it was not so much abstract liberal principles but rather the Western way of life—the material and cultural manifestations of the West's freedoms—that subverted the Soviet vision. Western popular culture—exemplified in rock and roll, television, film, and blue jeans—seduced the communist world far more effectively than ideological sermons by anticommunist activists. As journalist

William Echikson noted in his 1990 book *Lighting the Night: Revolution in Eastern Europe*, "instead of listening to the liturgy of Marx and Lenin, generations of would-be socialists tuned into the Rolling Stones and the Beatles."

If Western popular culture and permissiveness helped subvert communist legitimacy, it is a development of profound irony. Domestically, the New Right battled precisely those cultural forms that had such global appeal. V. I. Lenin's most potent ideological foils were John Lennon and Paul McCartney, not Adam Smith and Thomas Jefferson. The Right fought a two-front war against communism abroad and hedonism and consumerism at home. Had it not lost the latter struggle, the West may not have won the former.

The Reagan victory school argues that ideological assertiveness precipitated the end of the Cold War. While it is true that right-wing American intellectuals were assertive toward the Soviet Union, other Western activists and intellectuals were building links with highly placed reformist intellectuals there. The Reagan victory school narrative ignores that Gorbachev's reform program was based upon "new thinking"—a body of ideas developed by globalist thinkers cooperating across the East-West divide. The key themes of new thinking—the common threat of nuclear destruction, the need for strong international institutions, and the importance of ecological sustainability—built upon the cosmopolitanism of the Marxist tradition and officially replaced the Communist party's class-conflict doctrine during the Gorbachev period.

It is widely recognized that a major source of Gorbachev's new thinking was his close aide and speechwriter, Georgi Shakhnazarov. A former president of the Soviet political science association, Shakhnazarov worked extensively with Western globalists, particularly the New York-based group known as the World Order Models Project. Goibachev's speeches and policy statements were replete with the language and ideas of globalism. The Cold War ended not with Soviet ideological capitulation to Reagan's anticommunism but rather with a Soviet embrace of globalist themes promoted by a network of liberal internationalists. Those intellectual influences were greatest with the state elite, who had greater access to the West and from whom the reforms originated.

Regardless of how one judges the impact of the ideological struggles during the Reagan years, it is implausible to focus solely on recent developments without accounting for longer-term shifts in underlying forces, particularly the widening gap between Western and Soviet economic performance. Over the long haul, the West's ideological appeal was based on the increasingly superior performance of the Western economic system. Although contrary to the expectation of Marx and Lenin, the robustness of capitalism in the West was increasingly acknowledged by Soviet analysts. Likewise, Soviet elites were increasingly troubled by their economy's comparative decline.

The Reagan victory school argues that the renewed emphasis on free-market principles championed by Reagan and then British prime minister Margaret Thatcher led to a global move toward market deregulation and privatization that the Soviets desired to follow. By rekindling the beacon of laissez-faire capitalism, Reagan illuminated the path of economic reform, thus vanquishing communism.

That view is misleading in two respects. First, it was West European social democracy rather than America's more free-wheeling capitalism that attracted Soviet reformers. Gorbachev wanted his reforms to emulate the Swedish model. His vision was not of laissez-faire capitalism but of a social democratic welfare state. Second, the Right's triumphalism in the economic sphere is ironic. The West's robust economies owe much of their relative stability and health to two generations of Keynesian intervention and government involvement that the Right opposed at every step. As with Western popular culture, the Right opposed tendencies in the West that proved vital in the West's victory.

There is almost universal agreement that the root cause of the Cold War's abrupt end was the grave domestic failure of Soviet communism. However, the Soviet response to this crisis—accommodation and liberalization rather than aggression and repression—was significantly influenced by outside pressures and opportunities, many from the West. As historians and analysts attempt to explain how recent U.S. foreign policy helped end the Cold War, a view giving most of the credit to Reagan-era assertiveness and Western strength has become the new conventional wisdom. Both the Reagan victory school and the peace-through-strength perspective on Western containment assign a central role in ending the Cold War to Western resolve and power. The lesson for American foreign policy being drawn from those events is that military strength and ideological warfare were the West's decisive assets in fighting the Cold War.

The new conventional wisdom, in both its variants, is seriously misleading. Operating over the last decade, Ronald Reagan's personal anti-nuclearism, rather than his administration's hardline, catalyzed the accommodations to end the Cold War. His administration's effort to go beyond containment and on the offensive was muddled, counter-balanced, and unsuccessful. Operating over the long term, containment helped thwart Soviet expansionism but cannot account for the Soviet domestic failure, the end of East-West struggle, or the direction of the USSR'S reorientation. Contrary to the hard-line version, nuclear weapons were decisive in abandoning the conflict by creating common interests.

On the ideological front, the new conventional wisdom is also flawed. The conservatives' anticommunism was far less important in delegitimating the Soviet system than were that system's internal failures and the attraction of precisely the Western "permissive culture" abhorred by the Right. In addition, Gorbachev's attempts to reform communism in the late-1980s were less an ideological capitulation than a reflection of philosophical convergence on the globalist norms championed by liberal internationalists. And the West was more appealing not because of its laissez-faire purity, but because of the success of Keynesian and social welfare innovations whose use the Right resisted.

Behind the debate over who "won" the Cold War are competing images of the forces shaping recent history. Containment, strength, and confrontation—the trinity enshrined in conventional thinking on Western foreign policy's role in ending the Cold War—obscure the nature of these momentous changes. Engagement and interdependence, rather than containment, are the ruling trends of the age. Mutual vulnerability, not strength, drives security politics. Accommodation and integration, not confrontation, are the motors of change.

That such encouraging trends were established and deepened even as the Cold War raged demonstrates the considerable continuity underlying the West's support today for reform in the post-Soviet transition. Those trends also expose as one-sided and self-serving the New Right's attempt to take credit for the success of forces that, in truth, they opposed. In the end, Reagan partisans have been far more successful in claiming victory in the Cold War than they were in achieving it.

POSTSCRIPT

Did President Reagan Win the Cold War?

Now that the cold war is over, historians must assess why it ended so suddenly and unexpectedly. Did President Reagan's military buildup in the 1980s force the Russians into economic bankruptcy? Gaddis gives Reagan high marks for ending the cold war. By combining a policy of militancy and operational pragmatism, says Gaddis, Reagan brought about the most significant improvement in Soviet-American relations since the end of World War II. Deudney and Ikenberry disagree. In their view the cold war ended only when the Russians saw the need for international cooperation in order to end the arms race, prevent a nuclear holocaust, and liberalize their economy. It was Western global ideas and not the hard-line containment policy of the early Reagan administration that caused Gorbachev to abandon traditional Russian communism, according to Deudney and Ikenberry.

Gaddis has established himself as the leading diplomatic historian of the cold war period. His assessment of Reagan's relations with the Soviet Union is balanced and probably more generous than that of most contemporary analysts. It is also very useful because it so succinctly describes the unexpected shift from a hard-line policy to one of détente. Gaddis admits that not even Reagan could have foreseen the total collapse of communism and the Soviet empire. While he allows that Reagan was not a profound thinker, Gaddis credits him with the leadership skills to overcome any prior ideological biases toward the Soviet Union and to take advantage of Gorbachev's offer to end the arms race. While many of the present hard-liners could not believe that the collapse of the Soviet Union was for real, Reagan was consistent in his view that the American arms buildup in the early 1980s was for the purpose of ending the arms race. Reagan, says Gaddis, accomplished this goal.

Gaddis's view of Reagan has not changed from his earlier assessment in *The United States and the End of the Cold War: Implications, Reconsiderations, Provocations* (Oxford University Press, 1992). See the eleventh edition of *Taking Sides . . . American History,* volume two. But Gaddis builds upon the new Russian sources now available from the Cold War International History Project at the Woodrow Wilson International Center as well as the published works of Gorbachev and his aides. Turning the tables on those historians who see Reagan as an "empty vessel," an actor who read a script, Gaddis compares Gorbachev to Woody Allen's movie character Zelig, "who managed to be present at all the great events of his time, but only by taking the character, even the appearance, of the stronger personalities who surrounded him." Unlike Reagan, the Russian leader knew Russia needed a new direction but did not know what the direction for his economy and foreign policy should be. Finally, Gaddis speculates that if Reagan was assassinated in 1991, his successor George Bush might not have ended the cold war.

Deudney and Ikenberry give less credit to Reagan than to global influences in ending the cold war. In their view, Gorbachev softened his hard-line foreign policy and abandoned orthodox Marxist economic programs because he was influenced by Western European cosmopolitans who were concerned about the "common threat of nuclear destruction, the need for strong international institutions, and the importance of ecological sustainability." Deudney and Ikenberry agree that Reagan became more accommodating toward the Russians in 1983, but they maintain that the cold war's end "was not simply a result of Western strength but of mutual weakness and intentional engagement as well."

There is a considerable bibliography about both the Reagan administration and the Soviet Union in assessing their roles in ending the cold war. Three *Washington Post* reporters have provided early accounts of the Reagan years. Lou Cannon's *President Reagan: the Role of a Lifetime* (Simon & Schuster, 1991) is a remarkably objective, detailed, and interesting account by a reporter who followed Reagan's career during his California gubernatorial years. Haynes Johnson's *Sleepwalking through History: America in the Reagan Years* (W.W. Norton, 1991) is more critical than Cannon but readable. Don Oberdorfer, a former Moscow correspondent for *The Washington Post*, has revised *From Cold War to a New Era: the United States and the Soviet Union, 1983-1991* (Updated edition, Johns Hopkins University Press, 1998). Oberdorfer credits Secretary of State George P. Schultz with Reagan's turnaround from a hard-line to détente approach to foreign policy. The former Stanford economics professor and policymaker weighs in with his own perceptive assessment of the Reagan administration in *Turmoil and Triumph: My Years as Secretary of State* (Scribner's, 1993).

A number of conservatives have published books and articles arguing that American foreign policy hard-liners won the cold war. Two of the most articulate essays written early from the "Reagan victory school" point of view are Arch Puddington, "The Anti-Cold War Brigade," *Commentary* (August 1990) and Owen Harries, "The Cold War and the Intellectuals," *Commentary* (October 1991). Michael Howard reviews five books on the end of the cold war in "Winning the Peace: How Both George Kennan and Gorbachev Were Right," *Times Literary Supplement* (January 8, 1993). President Reagan's death from Alzheimer's in June, 2004, also produced an outpouring of favorable assessments of America's most popular president since Eisenhower in newspapers, magazines, and television.

In some ways President Reagan is best viewed through his own writings. His *An American Life: the Autobiography* (Simon and Schuster, 1990) contains his views but is stilted and doesn't capture his essence. More successful is *The Greatest Speeches of Ronald Reagan* (NewsMax.com, 2001) compiled by his conservative son Michael Reagan. Between his acting career and his presidency Reagan wrote a lot of speeches and newspaper and radio editorials. To prove he was not an "amiable dunce," Kiron K. Skinner, et al., edited *Reagan, In His Own Hand* (Free Press, 2001).

With the opening of some of the Russian and Eastern European country's archives, we are getting a better picture, if not a more balanced view, of the cold war. The Cold War International History Project at the Woodrow Wilson International Center for scholars has collected many of these documents and its journal, the *Cold War International History Project Bulletin*, publishes important scholarly articles utilizing its archives. Mikhail Gorbachev has weighted in the fray with his own *Memoirs* (Doubleday, 1995) and *Perestroika: New Thinking for Our Country and the World* (Harper & Row, 1987). See also his latest reflections in Gorbachev and Zdenek Mlynar, *Conversations with Gorbachev: On Perestroika, the Prague Spring, and the Crossroads of Socialism,* translated by George Schriver (Columbia University Press, 2002). Earlier, historian Michael R. Beschloss and *Time Magazine,* and later, Clinton adviser Strobe Talbot interviewed Gorbachev for *At the Highest Levels: the Inside Story of the End of the Cold War* (Little, Brown, 1993), which carries the story from 1987 through the presidency of the first George Bush.

Political scientists have weighed in the controversy. In addition to the classic Deudney and Ikenberry essay, Coral Bell analyzes the *Reagan Paradox: U.S. Foreign Policy in the 1980s* (Rutgers University Press, 1989). The Mershon Center at Ohio State University has recently run a conference at which former Russian and American participants were interviewed via round table discussions. Two of the scholars, Richard K. Hermann and Richard Ned Lebow, have edited *Ending the Cold War: Interpretations, Causation and the Study of International Relations* (Palgrave/Macmillan, 2004), which raises a number of interesting counterfactual propositions even if at times the essays become overly theoretical.

The historians also weighed in as soon as Reagan left office. Both David E. Kyvig, ed., *Reagan and the World* (Greenwood Press, 1990), and Michael J. Hogan, *The End of the Cold War: Its Meaning and Implications* (Cambridge University Press, 1992), were generally unable to forecast future events. The most insightful account because of its broader perspective is Raymond Garthoff, *Détente and Confrontation: American Soviet Relations from Nixon to Reagan* (Brookings Institution, 1994).

Two interesting perspectives on the nuclear war issue are Paul Lettow, *Ronald Reagan and His Quest to Abolish Nuclear Weapons* (Random House, 2005), which supports Gaddis and Stephen J. Zaloga, *The Kremlin's Nuclear Sword: The Rise and Fall of Russia's Strategic Nuclear Forces, 1945–2000* (Smithsonian Institution, 2002).

Reagan is best assessed through the media. After all he was an actor before he became a politician. Two good starting points are PBS's *The American Experience* series two-part biography of President Ronald Reagan (2001), and CNN's *Cold War* television documentary (1998).

ISSUE 17

Should America Remain a Nation of Immigrants?

YES: Tamar Jacoby, from "Too Many Immigrants?" *Commentary* (April 2002)

NO: Patrick J. Buchanan, from *The Death of the West: How Dying Populations and Immigrant Invasions Imperil Our Country and Civilization* (Thomas Dunne Books, 2002)

ISSUE SUMMARY

YES: Social scientist Tamar Jacoby maintains that the newest immigrants keep America's economy strong because they work harder and take jobs that native-born Americans reject.

NO: Syndicated columnist Patrick J. Buchanan argues that America is no longer a nation because immigrants from Mexico and other Third World Latin American and Asian countries have turned America into a series of fragmented multicultural ethnic enclaves that lack a common culture.

Historians of immigration tend to divide the forces that encouraged voluntary migrations from one country to another into push and pull factors. Historically, the major reason why people left their native countries was the breakdown of feudalism and the subsequent rise of a commercially oriented economy. Peasants were pushed off the feudal estates of which they had been a part for generations. In addition, religious and political persecution for dissenting groups and the lack of economic opportunities for many middle-class émigrés also contributed to the migrations from Europe to the New World.

America was attractive to settlers long before the American Revolution took place. While the United States may not have been completely devoid of feudal traditions, immigrants perceived the United States as a country with a fluid social structure where opportunities abounded for everyone. By the mid-nineteenth century, the Industrial Revolution had provided opportunities for jobs in a nation that had always experienced chronic labor shortages.

There were four major periods of migration to the United States: 1607–1830, 1830–1890, 1890–1925, and 1968 to the present. In the seventeenth and eighteenth centuries, the white settlers came primarily, though not entirely, from the British Isles. They were joined by millions of African slaves. Both groups lived in proximity to several hundred thousand Native Americans. In those years the cultural values of Americans were a combination of what history professor Gary Nash has referred to as "red, white, and black." In the 30 years before the Civil War, a second phase began when immigrants came from other countries in northern and western Europe as well as China. Two European groups dominated. Large numbers of Irish Catholics emigrated in the 1850s because of the potato famine. Religious and political factors were as instrumental as economic factors in pushing the Germans to America. Chinese immigrants were also encouraged to come during the middle and later decades of the nineteenth century in order to help build the western portion of America's first transcontinental railroad and to work in low-paying service industries like laundries and restaurants.

By 1890 a third period of immigration had begun. Attracted by the unskilled jobs provided by the Industrial Revolution and the cheap transportation costs of fast-traveling, steam-powered ocean vessels, immigrants poured in at a rate of close to 1 million a year from Italy, Greece, Russia, and other countries of southern and eastern Europe. This flood continued until the early 1920s, when fears of a foreign takeover led Congress to pass legislation restricting the number of immigrants into the United States to 150,000 per year.

For the next 40 years America was ethnically frozen. The restriction laws of the 1920s favored northern and western European groups and were biased against southern and eastern Europeans. The depression of the 1930s, World War II in the 1940s, and minimal changes in the immigration laws of the 1950s kept migrations to the United States at a minimum level.

In the 1960s the immigration laws were drastically revised. The civil rights acts of 1964 and 1965, which ended legal discrimination against African Americans, were also the impetus for immigration reform. The 1965 Immigration Act represented a turning point in U.S. history. But it had unintended consequences. In conjunction with the 1990 Immigration Act, discrimination against non-European nations was abolished and preferences were given to family-based migrants over refugees and those with special skills. Immigrants from Latin American and Asian countries have dominated the fourth wave of migration and have used the loophole in the legislation to bring into the country "immediate relatives," such as spouses, children, and parents of American citizens who are exempt from the numerical ceilings of the immigration laws.

Should the United States allow the current flow of immigrants into the country to continue? In the following selection, Tamar Jacoby asserts that the newest immigrants keep America's economy strong because they work harder and take jobs that native-born workers reject. Jacoby also maintains that the newest immigrants will assimilate into mainstream culture as earlier generations did once the immigration laws provide permanence and stability. In the second selection, Patrick J. Buchanan argues that the new immigrants from Mexico, other parts of Latin America, and Asia who have been entering America since 1968 are destroying the core culture of the United States.

YES

Tamar Jacoby

Too Many Immigrants?

Of all the issues Americans have had to rethink in the wake of September 11, few seem more baffling than immigration. As polls taken in the following weeks confirmed, the attacks dramatically heightened people's fear of foreigners—not just Muslim foreigners, all foreigners. In one survey, fully two-thirds of the respondents said they wanted to stop any immigration until the war against terror was over. In Congress, the once marginal Immigration Reform Caucus quadrupled in size virtually overnight, and a roster of sweeping new proposals came to the fore: a six-month moratorium on all visas, shutting the door to foreign students, even militarizing our borders with troops and tanks.

In the end, none of these ideas came close to getting through Congress. On the issue of security, Republicans and Democrats, law-enforcement professionals and civilians alike agreed early on that it was critical to distinguish terrorists from immigrants—and that it was possible to protect the country without isolating it.

The Bush administration and Congress soon came up with similar plans based on the idea that the best defense was to intercept unwanted visitors before they reached the U.S.—when they applied for visas in their home country, were preparing to board a plane, or were first packing a lethal cargo shipment. A bipartisan bill now making its way through Congress calls for better screening of visa applications, enhanced intelligence-sharing among federal agencies, new tamper-proof travel documents with biometric data, and better tracking of the few hundred thousand foreign students already in the U.S.

But the security debate is only one front in a broader struggle over immigration. There is no question that our present policy is defective, and immigration opponents are hoping that the attacks will precipitate an all-out fight about overhauling it. Yet even if the goal is only to secure our borders, Americans are up against some fairly intractable realities.

In the aftermath of September 11, for example, there have been calls for tracking not just foreign students but all foreigners already in the country. This is not an unreasonable idea; but it would be next to impossible to implement. Even monitoring the entry and exit of visitors, as the Immigration and Naturalization Service (INS) has been charged with doing, has turned out to be a logistical nightmare—we are talking about a *half-billion* entries and probably an equal number of exits a year. (Of the total, incidentally, by far the largest number are Canadian and Mexican daily commuters, a third are

Americans, and only a tiny percentage—fewer than a million a year—are immigrants seeking to make a new life in the U.S.) If collecting this information is difficult, analyzing and acting on it are a distant dream. As for the foreign-born population as a whole, it now stands at 28 million and growing, with illegal aliens alone estimated at between seven and eight million. It would take years just to identify them, much less find a way to track them all.

To this, the more implacable immigration opponents respond that if we cannot keep track of those already here, we should simply deport them. At the very least, others say, we should move to reduce radically the number we admit from now on, or impose a five- or ten-year moratorium. In the months since September 11, a variety of more and less extreme restrictionists have come together in a loose coalition to push forward such ideas. Although the movement has so far made little headway in Washington, it has become increasingly vocal, gaining a wide audience for its views, and has found a forceful, nationally known spokesman in the former presidential candidate and best-selling author Patrick J. Buchanan.

The coalition itself is a motley assemblage of bedfellows: liberals worried about the impact of large-scale immigration on population growth and the environment, conservatives exercised about porous borders and the shattering of America's common culture, plus a sizable contingent of outright racial demagogues. The best known organization pushing for restriction is the Federation for Immigration Reform, or FAIR, which provided much of the intellectual ammunition for the last big anti-immigration campaign, in the mid-1990's.

FAIR is still the richest and most powerful of the restrictionist groups. In the months since the attacks, a consortium it leads has spent some $300,000 on inflammatory TV ads in Western states where the 2002 mid-term elections will bring immigration issues to the fore; over pictures of the nineteen hijackers, the spots argue that the only way to keep America safe is to reduce immigration severely. But FAIR no longer dominates the debate as it once did, and newer groups are springing up around it.

On one flank are grassroots cells. Scrappier and more populist than FAIR, some consist of no more than an individual with a web page or radio show who has managed to accumulate a regional following; other local organizations have amassed enough strength to influence the politics of their states, particularly in California. On the other flank, and at the national level, FAIR is increasingly being eclipsed by younger, more media-savvy groups like the Center for Immigration Studies (CIS) in Washington and the writers associated with the website VDARE, both of which aim at swaying elite opinion in New York and Washington.

Different groups in the coalition focus on different issues, and each has its own style and way of presenting itself. One organization, Project USA, has devoted itself to putting up roadside billboards—nearly 100 so far, in a dozen states—with provocative messages like, "Tired of sitting in traffic? Every day, another 8,000 immigrants arrive. Every day!!" Those in the more respectable factions spend much energy distancing themselves from the more militant or fanatical, and even those with roughly the same mandate can seem, or sound, very different.

Consider CIS and VDARE. Created in 1985 as a fact-finding arm of FAIR, CIS is today arguably better known and more widely quoted than its parent. The group's executive director, Mark Krikorian, has made himself all but indispensable to anyone interested in immigration issues, sending out daily electronic compendiums of relevant news stories culled from the national press. His organization publishes scholarly papers on every aspect of the issue by a wide circle of respected academic researchers, many of whom would eschew any association with, say, FAIR's exclusionary politics. Along with his director of research, Steven Camarota, Krikorian is also a regular on Capitol Hill, where his restrained, informative testimony is influential with a broad array of elected officials.

VDARE, by contrast, wears its political views on its sleeve—and they are deliberately provocative. Founded a few years ago by the journalist Peter Brimelow, a senior editor at *Forbes* and the author of the best-selling *Alien Nation: Common Sense About America's Immigration Disaster* (1995), VDARE is named after Virginia Dare, "the first English child born in the New World." Kidnapped as an infant and never seen again, Virginia Dare is thought to have eventually married into a local Indian tribe, or to have been killed by it— almost equally unfortunate possibilities in the minds of VDARE's writers, who make no secret of their concern about the way America's original Anglo-Saxon stock is being transformed by immigration.

The overall strength of today's restrictionist movement is hard to gauge. But there is no question that recent developments—both September 11 and the flagging American economy—have significantly boosted its appeal. One Virginia-based organization, Numbers USA, claims that its membership grew from 5,000 to over 30,000 in the weeks after the attacks. Buchanan's *The Death of the West: How Dying Populations and Immigrant Invasions Imperil Our Country and Civilization*[1]—a deliberately confrontational jeremiad—shot to the top of Amazon.com's best-seller list within days of publication, then moved to a perch in *The New York Times* top ten. Nor does it hurt that the anti-immigrant cause boasts advocates at both ends of the political spectrum. Thus, leftists repelled by the likes of Buchanan and Brimelow could read a more congenial statement of the same case in a recent, much-discussed series in the *New York Review of Books* by the distinguished sociologist Christopher Jencks.

To be sure, immigration opponents have also had some significant setbacks. Most notably, the Republican party, which stood staunchly with them in the mid-1990's in California, is now firmly on the other side of the issue—if anything, George W. Bush has become the country's leading advocate for liberalizing immigration law. But there can be no mistaking the depth of public concern over one or another of the questions raised by the restrictionists, and in the event of more attacks or a prolonged downturn, their appeal could surely grow.

In addition to national security, immigration opponents offer arguments principally about three issues: natural resources, economics, and the likelihood that today's newcomers will be successfully absorbed into American society. On the first, restrictionists contend not only that immigrants compete with us and consume our natural resources, to the detriment of the native-born, but that their numbers will eventually overwhelm us, choking the United States to death both demographically and environmentally.

Much of Buchanan's book, for example, is devoted to a discussion of population. As he correctly notes, birth rates in Europe have dropped below replacement level, and populations there are aging. By 2050, he estimates, only 10 percent of the world's people will be of European descent, while Asia, Africa, and Latin America will grow by three to four billion people, yielding "30 to 40 new Mexicos." As the developed countries "die out," huge movements of hungry people from the underdeveloped world will swamp their territory and destroy their culture. "This is not a matter of prophecy," Buchanan asserts, "but of mathematics."

Extrapolating from similar statistics, Christopher Jencks has predicted that the U.S. population may double in size over the next half-century largely as a result of the influx of foreigners. (This is a much faster rate of growth than that foreseen by virtually any other mainstream social scientist.) Jencks imagines a hellish future in which American cities will become all but unlivable and suburban sprawl will decimate the landscape. The effect on our natural resources will be devastating, as the water supply dwindles and our output of carbon dioxide soars. (To put his arguments in perspective, Jencks finds nothing new in this pattern. Immigration has always been disastrous to our ecology, he writes: the Indians who crossed the Bering Strait 13,000 years ago depleted the continent's fauna by overhunting, and many centuries later the germs brought by Europeans laid waste to the Indians.)

Not all the arguments from scarcity are quite so apocalyptic, but all begin and end with the assumption that the size of the pie is fixed, and that continued immigration can only mean less and less for the rest of us. A similar premise underlies the restrictionists' second set of concerns—that immigrants steal jobs from native-born workers, depress Americans' wages, and make disproportionate use of welfare and other government services.

Here, groups like FAIR and CIS focus largely on the portion of the immigrant flow that is poor and ill-educated—not the Indian engineer in Silicon Valley, but the Mexican farmhand with a sixth-grade education. "Although immigrants comprise about 12 percent of America's workforce," CIS reports, "they account for 31 percent of high-school dropouts in the workforce." Not only are poverty rates among these immigrants higher than among the native-born, but, the restrictionists claim, the gap is growing. As for welfare, Krikorian points out that even in the wake of the 1996 reform that denied means-tested benefits to many immigrants, their reliance on some programs—food stamps, for example—still exceeds that of native-born Americans.

The restrictionists' favorite economist is Harvard's George Borjas, the author of a widely read 1999 book, *Heaven's Door*.[2] As it happens, Borjas did not confirm the worst fears about immigrants: they do not, for example, steal Americans' jobs, and today's newcomers are no poorer or less capable than those who came at the turn of the 20th century and ultimately did fine in

America. Still, in Borjas's estimation, compared with the native-born of their era, today's immigrants are *relatively* farther behind than, say, the southern Europeans who came a century ago, and even if they do not actually take work away from Americans, they may prompt the native-born to move to other cities and thus adversely affect the larger labor market.

As a result, Borjas contends, the presence of these newcomers works to lower wages, particularly among high-school dropouts. And because of the cost of the government services they consume—whether welfare or public schooling or hospital care—they impose a fiscal drain on a number of states where they settle. In sum, immigrants may be a boon to U.S. business and to the middle class (which benefits from lower prices for the fruit the foreigners pick and from the cheap lawn services they provide), but they are an unfair burden on ordinary working Americans, who must subsidize them with higher taxes.

Borjas's claims have hardly gone unchallenged by economists on either the Right or the Left—including Jagdish Bhagwati in a heated exchange in *The Wall Street Journal* —but he remains a much-quoted figure among restrictionists, who particularly like his appealing-sounding note of concern for the native-born black poor. Borjas's book has also greatly strengthened those who propose that existing immigration policy, which is based mainly on the principle of family unification, be changed to one like Canada's that admits people based on the skills they bring.

This brings us to the third issue that worries the anti-immigration community: the apparent failure, or refusal, of large numbers of newcomers to assimilate successfully into American society, to learn our language, adopt our mores, and embrace American values as their own. To many who harp on this theme—Buchanan, the journalist Georgie Anne Geyer, the more polemical VDARE contributors—it is, frankly, the racial makeup of today's influx that is most troublesome. "Racial groups that are different are more difficult to assimilate," Buchanan says flatly, painting a nightmarish picture of newcomers with "no desire to learn English or become citizens." Buchanan and others make much of the influence of multiculturalism and identity politics in shaping the priorities of the immigrant community; his chapter on Mexican immigrants, entitled "La Reconquista," quotes extensively from extremist Chicano activists who want, he says, to "colonize" the United States.

On this point, it should be noted, Buchanan and his followers are hardly alone, and hardly original. Any number of observers who are *favorably* disposed to continued immigration have likewise raised an alarm over the radically divisive and balkanizing effects of multiculturalism and bilingual education. Where they part company with Buchanan is over the degree of danger they perceive—and what should be done about it.[3]

About one thing the restrictionists are surely right: our immigration policy is broken. Not only is the INS one of the least efficient and most beleaguered agencies in Washington—at the moment, four million authorized immigrants are waiting, some for a decade or more, for their paperwork to be processed—but official policy, particularly with regard to Mexico, is a hypocritical sham. Even as we claim to limit the flow of migrants, and force thousands to wait their turn for visas, we look the other way as hundreds of thousands enter the country without papers—illegal but welcomed by business as a cheap, pliable labor force. Nor do we have a clear rationale for the selection we end up making from the vast pool of foreigners eager to enter the country.

But here precisely is where the restrictionists' arguments are the least helpful. Take the issue of scarcity. The restrictionists construct their dire scenarios by extrapolating from the current flow of immigrants. But as anyone who follows these matters is aware, nothing is harder to predict than who and how many will come in the future. It is, for example, as easy today as it ever was to migrate to the U.S. from Puerto Rico, and wages on the island still lag woefully behind wages here. But the net flow from Puerto Rico stopped long ago, probably because life there improved just enough to change the calculus of hope that had been prodding people to make the trip.

Sooner or later, the same thing will happen in Mexico. No one knows when, but surely one hint of things to come is that population growth is slowing in Mexico, just as it slowed earlier here and in Europe. Over the past three decades, the Mexican fertility rate has dropped from an average 6.5 children per mother to a startling 2.5.

Nor are demographic facts themselves always as straightforward in their implications as the restrictionists assume. True, population is still growing faster in the underdeveloped world than in developed countries. But is this an argument against immigration, or for it? If they are to remain strong, countries *need* population—workers, customers, taxpayers, soldiers. And our own openness to immigrants, together with our proven ability to absorb them, is one of our greatest advantages over Japan and Europe, which face a demographic crisis as their ratio of workers to retirees adversely shifts. The demographer Ben Wattenberg has countered Buchanan with a simple calculation: "If we keep admitting immigrants at our current levels, there will be almost 400 million Americans by 2050." That—and only that, one might add—"can keep us strong enough to defend and perhaps extend our views and values."

❦

The argument from economics is equally unhelpful. The most commonly heard complaint about foreign workers is that they take jobs from Americans. Not only is this assertion untrue—nobody has found real evidence to support it—but cities and states with the largest immigrant populations (New York, Los Angeles, and others) boast far faster economic growth and lower unemployment than cities and states that do not attract immigrants. In many places, the presence of immigrants seems to reduce unemployment even among native-born blacks—probably because of the way immigrants stimulate economic growth.

Economists looking for a depressive effect on native-born wages have been nearly as disappointed: dozens of studies over the past two or three decades have found at most modest and probably temporary effects. Even if Borjas is right that a native-born black worker may take home $300 less a year as a result of immigration, this is a fairly small amount of money in the overall scheme of things. More to the point, globalization would have much the same effect on wages, immigrants or no immigrants. Pressed by competition from foreign imports, American manufacturers have had to change production methods and cut costs, including labor costs. If they did not, they would have to go out of business—or move to an underdeveloped country where wages are lower. In either case, the U.S. economy would end up being hurt far more than by the presence of immigrant workers—who expand the U.S. economic pie when they buy shoes and groceries and washing machines from their American neighbors and call American plumbers into their homes.

What about the costs imposed by immigrants, especially by their use of government services? It is true that many immigrants—though far from all—are poorer than native-born Americans, and thus pay less in taxes. It is also true that one small segment of the immigrant population—refugees—tends to be heavily dependent on welfare. As a result, states with large immigrant populations often face chronic fiscal problems.

But that is at the state level, and mostly in high-welfare states like California. If we shift the lens to the federal level, and include the taxes that immigrants remit to the IRS, the calculation comes out very differently: immigrants pay in more than they take out. This is particularly true if one looks at the picture over the course of an immigrant's lifetime. Most come to the U.S. as young adults looking for work—which means they were already educated at home, relieving us of a significant cost. More important, even illegal immigrants generally keep up with payroll taxes, contributing to Social Security though they may never claim benefits. According to Stephen Moore, an economist at the Cato Institute, foreign-born workers are likely to contribute as much as $2 trillion to Social Security over the next 70 years, thus effectively keeping it afloat.

The economic debate often comes down to this sort of war of numbers, but the victories on either side are rarely conclusive. After all, even 28 million immigrants form but a small part of the $12-trillion U.S. economy, and most of the fiscal costs and benefits associated with them are relatively modest. Besides, fiscal calculations are only a small part of the larger economic picture. How do we measure the energy immigrants bring—the pluck and grit and willingness to improvise and innovate?

Not only are immigrants by and large harder-working than the native-born, they generally fill economic niches that would otherwise go wanting. The term economists use for this is "complementarity." If immigrants were exactly like American workers, they would not be particularly valuable to employers. They are needed precisely because they are different: willing or able to do jobs few American workers are willing or able to do. These jobs tend to be either at the lowest rungs of the employment ladder (busboy, chambermaid, line worker in a meatpacking plant) or at the top (nurse, engineer, information-technology worker).

It is no accident that 80 percent of American farmworkers are foreign-born, or that, if there were no immigrants, hotels and restaurants in many cities would have to close their doors. Nor is it an accident that immigrants account for a third of the scientific workforce in Silicon Valley, or that Asian entrepreneurs run a quarter of the companies there. Today's supply of willing laborers from Mexico, China, India, and elsewhere matches our demand in these various sectors, and the result is good for just about everyone—business, workers, and American consumers alike.

✦

To be sure, what is good for business, or even for American consumers, may not ultimately be good for the United States—and this is where the issue of assimilation comes in. "What is a nation?" Buchanan asks. "Is America nothing more than an economic system?" If immigrants do not come to share our values, adopt our heroes, and learn our history as their own, ultimately the nation will not hold. Immigration policy cannot be a suicide pact.

The good news is that assimilation is not going nearly as badly as the restrictionists claim. Though many immigrants start out at the bottom, most eventually join the working poor, if not the middle class. And by the time they have been here twenty years, they generally do as well as or better than the native-born, earning comparable salaries and registering *lower* poverty rates.

Nor is it true that immigrants fail or refuse to learn English. Many more than in previous eras come with a working knowledge of the language—it is hard to avoid it in the world today. Despite the charade that is bilingual education, nearly all high-school students who have been educated in this country—nine out of ten of them, according to one study—prefer English to their native tongue. And by the third generation, even among Hispanics, who are somewhat slower than other immigrants to make the linguistic shift, only 1 percent say they use "more or only Spanish" at home.

Despite the handicaps with which many arrive, the immigrant drive to succeed is as strong as ever. According to one important study of the second generation, newcomers' children work harder than their U.S. classmates, putting in an average of two hours of homework a night compared with the "normal" 30 minutes. They also aspire to higher levels of educational achievement, earn better grades, drop out less frequently—and expect only the best of their new homeland. Nearly two-thirds believe that hard work and accomplishment can triumph over prejudice, and about the same number say there is no better country than the United States. As for the lure of identity politics, one of the most thorough surveys of Hispanics, conducted in 1999 by *The Washington Post*, reported that 84 percent believe it is "important" or "very important" for immigrants "to change so that they blend into the larger society, as in the idea of the melting pot."

There is also bad news. Immigrant America is far from monolithic, and some groups do worse than others both economically and culturally. While fewer than 5 percent of Asian young people use an Asian language with their friends, nearly 45 percent of Latinos sometimes use Spanish. Close to 90 percent of Chinese parents expect their children to finish college; only 55 percent of Mexicans do. Indeed, Mexicans—who account for about a quarter of the foreign-born—lag behind on many measures, including, most worrisomely, education. The average Mexican migrant comes with less than eight years of schooling, and though the second generation is outstripping its parents, it too falls well below American norms, either for other immigrants or for the native-born.

When it comes to absorbing the American common culture, or what has been called patriotic assimilation, there is no question that today's immigrants are at a disadvantage compared with yesterday's. Many Americans themselves no longer know what it means to be American. Our schools teach, at best, a travesty of American history, distorted by political correctness and the excesses of multiculturalism. Popular culture supplies only the crudest, tinniest visions of our national heritage. Even in the wake of September 11, few leaders have tried to evoke more than a fuzzy, feel-good enthusiasm for America. No wonder many immigrants have a hard time making the leap from their culture to ours. We no longer ask it of them.

Still, even if the restrictionists are right about all this, their remedy is unworkable. Given the global economy, given the realities of politics and law enforcement in the United States, we are not going to stop—or significantly reduce—the flow of immigrant workers into the country any time soon. Businesses that rely on imported labor would not stomach it; as it is, they object vociferously whenever the INS tries to enforce the law. Nor are American citizens prepared to live with the kinds of draconian measures that would be needed to implement a significant cutback or time-out. Even in the wake of the attacks, there is little will to require that immigrants carry ID cards, let alone to erect the equivalent of a Berlin Wall along the Rio Grande. In sum, if many immigrants among us are failing to adopt our common culture, we will have to look elsewhere than to the restrictionists for a solution.

◦◦◉◦◦

What, then, is to be done? As things stand today, American immigration policy and American law are perilously out of sync with reality—the reality of the market. Consider the Mexican case, not the only telling one but the most dramatic.

People born in Mexico now account for roughly 10 percent of the U.S. workforce, and the market for their labor is a highly efficient one. Very few recent Mexican migrants are unemployed; even modest economic upturns or downturns have a perceptible impact on the number trying to enter illegally, as word quickly spreads from workers in California or Kansas back to home villages in Mexico. This precise coordination of supply and demand has been drawing roughly 300,000 Mexicans over the border each year, although, even including minors and elderly parents, the INS officially admits only half that many.

One does not have to be a free-market enthusiast to find this discrepancy absurd, and worse. Not only does it criminalize badly needed laborers and productive economic activity. It also makes an ass of the law and insidiously corrupts American values, encouraging illegal hiring and discrimination against even lawful Mexican migrants.

Neither a moratorium nor a reduction in official quotas would eliminate this thriving labor exchange—on the contrary, it would only exacerbate the mismatch. Instead, we should move in the opposite direction from what the restrictionists demand, bringing the number we admit more into line with the reality of the market. The rationale for whom we ought to let in, what we should encourage and reward, is work.

This, as it happens, is precisely the direction in which President Bush was moving before September 11. A package of reforms he floated in July, arrived at in negotiations with Mexican president Vicente Fox, would have significantly expanded the number of visas for Mexican workers. The President's impulse may have been partisan—to woo Latino voters—but he stumbled onto the basis for an immigration policy that would at once serve America's interests and reflect its values. He put the core idea plainly, and got it exactly right: "If somebody is willing to offer a job others in America aren't willing to do, we ought to welcome that person to the country."

Compared with this, any other criterion for immigration policy—family reunification, country of origin, or skill level—sinks into irrelevancy. It makes no sense at all that three-quarters of the permanent visas available today should be based on family ties, while only one-quarter are employment-related. As for the Canadian-style notion of making skill the decisive factor, admitting engineers and college professors but closing the door to farmworkers, not only does this smack of a very un-American elitism but it disregards our all too palpable economic needs at the low end of the labor market.

The problem is that there is at present virtually no legal path into the U.S. for unskilled migrant laborers; unless they have relatives here, they have no choice but to come illicitly. If we accept the President's idea that immigration policy should be based on work, we ought to enshrine it in a program that makes it possible for those who want to work, and who can find a job, to come lawfully. The program ought to be big enough to meet market needs: the number of visas available the first year should match the number of people who now sneak in against the law, and in future years it should follow the natural rise and fall of supply and demand. At the same time, the new regime ought to be accompanied by serious enforcement measures to ensure that workers use this pipeline rather than continuing to come illegally outside it.

Such a policy makes sound economic sense—and also would provide a huge boost for immigrant absorption and assimilation. By definition, the undocumented are effectively barred from assimilating. Most cannot drive legally in the U.S., or, in many states, get regular care in a hospital. Nor, in most places, can they send their children to college. An indelible caste line separates them from other Americans—no matter how long they stay, how much they contribute, or how ardently they and their children strive to assimilate. If we want newcomers to belong, we should admit them legally, and find a fair means of regularizing the status of those who are already here illicitly.

But rerouting the illegal flow into legal channels will not by itself guarantee assimilation—particularly not if, as the President and Congress have suggested, we insist that workers go home when the job is done. In keeping with the traditional

Republican approach to immigration, the President's reform package included a proposal for a guest-worker program, and before September 11, both Democrats and Republicans had endorsed the idea. If we want to encourage assimilation, however, such a system would only be counterproductive.

The cautionary model in this case is Germany, which for years admitted unskilled foreigners exclusively as temporary guest workers, holding out virtually no hope that either they or their children could become German citizens. As it happened, many of these migrants remained in Germany long after the work they were imported for had disappeared. But today, nearly 40 years later, most of them still have not assimilated, and they remain, poorly educated and widely despised, on the margins of German society. Clearly, if what we hope to encourage is the putting-down of roots, any new visa program must give participants a shot at membership in the American body politic.

But how we hand out visas is only the first step in a policy aimed at encouraging immigrant absorption. Other steps would have to include the provision of basic services like instruction in English, civics classes, naturalization programs—and also counseling in more practical matters like how to navigate the American banking system. (Many newcomers, even when they start making money, are at sea in the world of credit cards, credit histories, mortgage applications, and the like.) All these nuts-and-bolts services are as essential as the larger tasks, from overhauling the teaching of American history to eliminating counterproductive programs like bilingual education and ethnic entitlements that only breed separatism and alienation.

There can be no gainsaying the risks America runs in remaining open to new immigrants. The security perils, though real enough, are the least worrisome. Legalizing the flow of needed workers and providing them with papers will help keep track of who is here and also help prevent those who wish to do us harm from entering in the first place. The more daring, long-term gamble lies in continuing to admit millions of foreigners who may or may not make it here or find a way to fit in. This is, as Buchanan rightly states, "a decision we can never undo."

Still, it is an experiment we have tried before—repeatedly. The result has never come out exactly as predicted, and the process has always been a wrenching one. But as experiments go, it has not only succeeded on its own terms; it has made us the wonder of the world. It can do so again—but only if we stop denying reality and resolve instead to meet the challenge head-on.

Notes

1. Dunne Books, 320 pp., $25.95.
2. Reviewed by Irwin M. Stelzer in the September 1999 COMMENTARY.
3. In COMMENTARY, see, for example, Linda Chavez's "Our Hispanic Predicament" (June 1998) and "What To Do About Immigration" (March 1995), and my own "In Asian America" (July–August 2000).

 **NO**

La Reconquista

$\mathbf{A}$s the [immigrant] invasion rolls on, with California as the preferred destination, sociologist William Frey has documented an out-migration of African Americans and Anglo-Americans from the Golden State in search of cities and towns like the ones they grew up in. Other Californians are moving into gated communities. A country that cannot control its borders isn't really a country anymore, Ronald Reagan warned us some twenty years ago.

Concerns about a radical change in America's ethnic composition have been called un-American. But they are as American as Benjamin Franklin, who once asked, "Why should Pennsylvania, founded by the English, become a Colony of Aliens, who will shortly be so numerous as to Germanize us instead of our Anglifying them. . . ?" Franklin would never find out if his fears were justified. German immigration was halted during the Seven Years War. Former president Theodore Roosevelt warned, "The one absolutely certain way of bringing this nation to ruin, of preventing all possibility of its continuing to be a nation at all, would be to permit it to become a tangle of squabbling nationalities."

Immigration is a necessary subject for national debate, for it is about who we are as a people. Like the Mississippi, with its endless flow of life-giving water, immigration has enriched America throughout history. But when the Mississippi floods its banks, the devastation can be enormous. Yet, by the commands of political correctness, immigration as an issue is off the table. Only "nativists" or "xenophobes" could question a policy by which the United States takes in more people of different colors, creeds, cultures, and civilizations than all other nations of the earth combined. The river is rising to levels unseen in our history. What will become of our country if the levees do not hold?

In late 1999, this writer left Tucson and drove southeast to Douglas, the Arizona border town of eighteen thousand that had become the principal invasion corridor into the United States. In March alone, the U.S. Border Patrol had apprehended twenty-seven thousand Mexicans crossing illegally, half again as many illegal aliens crossing in one month as there are people in Douglas.

While there, I visited Theresa Murray, an eighty-two-year-old widow and a great-grandmother who lives in the Arizona desert she grew up in. Her ranch house was surrounded by a seven-foot chain-link fence that was topped with coils of razor wire. Every door and window had bars on it and was wired to an alarm. Mrs. Murray sleeps with a .32-caliber pistol on her bed table, because she has been burglarized thirty times. Her guard dogs are dead; they bled to death when someone tossed meat containing chopped glass over her fence. Theresa Murray is living out her life inside a maximum-security prison, in her own home, in her own country, because her government lacks the moral courage to do its duty and defend the borders of the United States of America.

If America is about anything, it is freedom. But as Theresa Murray says, "I've lost my freedom. I can't ever leave the house unless I have somebody watch it. We used to ride our horses clear across the border. We had Mexicans working on our property. It used to be fun to live here. Now, it's hell. It's plain old hell."

While Theresa Murray lives unfree, in hellish existence, American soldiers defend the borders of Korea, Kuwait, and Kosovo. But nothing is at risk on those borders, half a world away, to compare with what is at risk on our border with Mexico, over which pass the armies of the night as they trudge endlessly northward to the great cities of America. Invading armies go home, immigrant armies do not.

Who Killed the Reagan Coalition?

For a quarter of a century, from 1968 until 1992, the Republican party had a virtual lock on the presidency. The "New Majority," created by Richard Nixon and replicated by Ronald Reagan, gave the GOP five victories in six presidential elections. The key to victory was to append to the Republican base two Democratic blocs: Northern Catholic ethnics and Southern white Protestants. Mr. Nixon lured these voters away from the New Deal coalition with appeals to patriotism, populism, and social conservatism. Success gave the GOP decisive margins in the industrial states and a "Solid South" that had been the base camp of the Democratic party since Appomattox. This Nixon-Reagan coalition proved almost unbeatable. McGovern, Mondale, and Dukakis could carry 90 percent of the black vote, but with Republicans taking 60 percent of the white vote, which was over 90 percent of the total, the GOP inevitably came out on top.

This was the Southern Strategy. While the media called it immoral, Democrats had bedded down with segregationists for a century without similar censure. FDR and Adlai Stevenson had put segregationists on their tickets. Outside of Missouri, a border state with Southern sympathies, the only ones Adlai captured in 1956 were Dixiecrat states later carried by George Wallace.

Neither Nixon nor Reagan ever supported segregation. As vice president, Nixon was a stronger backer of civil rights than Senators John F. Kennedy or Lyndon Johnson. His role in winning passage of the Civil Rights Act of 1957 was lauded in a personal letter from Dr. Martin Luther King, who hailed Vice President Nixon's "assiduous labor and dauntless courage in seeking to make Civil Rights a reality."

For a quarter century, Democrats were unable to pick the GOP lock on the presidency, because they could not shake loose the Republican grip on the white vote. With the exception of Lyndon Johnson's landslide of 1964, no Democrat since Truman in 1948 had won the white vote. What broke the GOP lock on the presidency was the Immigration Act of 1965.

During the anti-Soviet riots in East Berlin in 1953, Bertolt Brecht, the Communist playwright, quipped, "Would it not be easier . . . for the government to dissolve the people and elect another?" In the last thirty years, America has begun to import a new electorate, as Republicans cheerfully backed an immigration policy tilted to the Third World that enlarged the Democratic base and loosened the grip that Nixon and Reagan had given them on the presidency of the United States.

In 1996, the GOP was rewarded. Six of the 7 states with the largest numbers of immigrants—California, New York, Illinois, New Jersey, Massachusetts, Florida, and Texas—went for Clinton. In 2000, 5 went for Gore, and Florida was a dead heat. Of the 15 states with the most foreign-born, Bush lost 10. But of the 10 states with the smallest shares of foreign-born—Montana, Mississippi, Wyoming, West Virginia, South Dakota, South Carolina, Alabama, Tennessee, and Arkansas—Bush swept all 10.

Among the states with the most immigrants, only Texas has been reliably Republican, but now it is going the way of California. In the 1990s, Texas took in 3.2 million new residents as the Hispanic share of Texas's population shot from 25 percent to 33 percent. Hispanics are now the major ethnic group in four of Texas's five biggest cities: Houston, Dallas, San Antonio, and El Paso. "Non-Hispanic Whites May Soon Be a Minority in Texas" said a recent headline in *The New York Times*. With the Anglo population down from 60 percent in 1990 to 53 percent, the day when whites are a minority in Texas for the first time since before the Alamo is coming soon. "Projections show that by 2005," says the *Dallas Morning News*, "fewer than half of Texans will be white."

America is going the way of California and Texas. "In 1960, the U.S. population was 88.6 percent white; in 1990, it was only 75.6 percent—a drop of 13 percentage points in thirty years. . . . [By 2020] the proportion of whites could fall as low as 61 per cent." So writes Peter Brimelow of *Forbes*. By 2050, Euro-Americans, the largest and most loyal share of the electorate the GOP has, will be a minority, due to an immigration policy that is championed by Republicans. John Stuart Mill was not altogether wrong when he branded the Tories "the Stupid Party."

America is going the way of California and Texas. "In 1960, the U.S. population was 88.6 percent white; in 1990, it was only 75.6 percent—a drop of

Hispanics are the fastest-growing segment of America's population. They were 6.4 percent of the U.S. population in 1980, 9 percent by 1990, and in 2000 over 12 percent. "The Hispanic fertility rates are quite a bit higher than the white or black population. They are at the levels of the baby boom era of the 1950s," says Jeffrey Passel, a demographer at the Urban Institute. At 35.4 million, Hispanics now equal African Americans in numbers and are becoming as Democratic in voting preferences. Mr. Bush lost the African-American vote eleven to one, but he also lost Hispanics two to one.

In 1996, when Clinton carried Latino voters seventy to twenty-one, he carried first-time Latino voters ninety-one to six. Aware that immigrants could give Democrats their own lock on the White House, Clinton's men worked relentlessly to naturalize them. In the year up to September 30, 1996, the Immigration and Naturalization Service swore in 1,045,000 immigrants as new citizens so quickly that 80,000 with criminal records—6,300 for serious crimes—slipped by. [Table 1 shows] the numbers of new citizens in each of the last five years.

Table 1

1996	1,045,000
1997	589,00
1998	463,000
1999	872,000
2000	898,315

California took a third of these new citizens. As non-Latino white registration fell by one hundred thousand in California in the 1990s, one million Latinos registered. Now 16 percent of the California electorate, Hispanics gave Gore the state with hundreds of thousands of votes to spare. "Both parties show up at swearing-in ceremonies to try to register voters," says Democratic consultant William Carrick. "There is a Democratic table and a Republican table. Ours has a lot of business. Theirs is like the Maytag repairman." With fifty-five electoral votes, California, home state of Nixon and Reagan, has now become a killing field of the GOP.

Voting on referenda in California has also broken down along ethnic lines. In 1994, Hispanics, rallying under Mexican flags, opposed Proposition 187 to end welfare to illegals. In the 1996 California Civil Rights Initiative, Hispanics voted for ethnic preferences. In 1998, Hispanics voted to keep bilingual education. Anglo-Americans voted the other way by landslides.

Ron Unz, father of the "English for the Children" referendum that ended state-funded bilingual education, believes the LA riot of 1992 may have been the Rubicon on the road to the balkanization of California.

The plumes of smoke from burning buildings and the gruesome television footage almost completely shattered the sense of security of middle-class

Southern Californians. Suddenly, the happy "multicultural California" so beloved of local boosters had been unmasked as a harsh, dangerous, Third World dystopia. . . . the large numbers of Latinos arrested (and summarily deported) for looting caused whites to cast a newly wary eye on gardeners and nannies who just weeks earlier had seemed so pleasant and reliable. If multicultural Los Angeles had exploded into sudden chaos, what security could whites expect as a minority in an increasingly nonwhite California?

᯽

Except for refugees from Communist countries like Hungary and Cuba, immigrants gravitate to the party of government. The obvious reason: Immigrants get more out of government—in free schooling for their kids, housing subsidies, health care—than they pay in. Arriving poor, most do not soon amass capital gains, estates, or incomes that can be federally taxed. Why should immigrants support a Republican party that cuts taxes they don't pay over a Democratic party that will expand the programs on which they do depend?

After Ellis Island, the Democratic party has always been the first stop for immigrants. Only after they have begun to move into the middle class do the foreign-born start converting to Republicanism. This can take two generations. By naturalizing and registering half a million or a million foreign-born a year, the Democrats are locking up future presidential elections and throwing away the key. If the GOP does not do something about mass immigration, mass immigration will do something about the GOP—turn it into a permanent minority that is home to America's newest minority, Euro-Americans.

As the ethnic character of America changes, politics change. A rising tide of immigration naturally shifts politics and power to the Left, by increasing the demands on government. The rapidly expanding share of the U.S. electorate that is of African and Hispanic ancestry has already caused the GOP to go silent on affirmative action and mute its calls for cuts in social spending. In 1996, Republicans were going to abolish the U.S. Department of Education. Now, they are enlarging it. As Hispanic immigration soars, and Hispanic voters become the swing voters in the pivotal states, their agenda will become America's agenda. It is already happening. In 2000, an AFL-CIO that had opposed mass immigration reversed itself and came out for amnesty for illegal aliens, hoping to sign up millions of illegal workers as dues-paying union members. And the Bush White House—in its policy decisions and appointments—has become acutely attentive to the Hispanic vote, often as the expense of conservative principles.

America's Quebec?

Harvard economist George Borjas, who studied the issue, found no net economic benefit from mass migration from the Third World. The added costs of schooling, health care, welfare, social security, and prisons, plus the added pressure on land, water, and power resources, exceeded the taxes that immigrants contribute. The National Bureau of Economic Research puts the cost of immigration at $80.4 billion in 1995. Economist Donald Huddle of Rice University estimates that the net annual cost of immigration will reach $108 billion by 2006. What are the benefits, then, that justify the risks we are taking of the balkanization of America?

Census 2000 revealed what many sensed. For the first time since statehood, whites in California are a minority. White flight has begun. In the 1990s, California grew by three million people, but its Anglo population actually "dropped by nearly half a million . . . surprising many demographers." Los Angeles County lost 480,000 white folks. In the exodus, the Republican bastion of Orange County lost 6 percent of its white population. "We can't pretend we're a white middle class state anymore," said William Fulton, research fellow at USC's Southern California Studies Center. State librarian Kevin Starr views the Hispanization of California as natural and inevitable:

> The Anglo hegemony was only an intermittent phase in California's arc of identity, extending from the arrival of the Spanish . . . the Hispanic nature of California has been there all along, and it was temporarily swamped between the 1880s and the 1960s, but that was an aberration. This is a reassertion of the intrinsic demographic DNA of the longer pattern, which is a part of the California-Mexican continuum.

The future is predictable: With one hundred thousand Anglos leaving California each year, with the Asian population soaring 42 percent in a single decade, with 43 percent of all Californians under eighteen Hispanic, America's largest state is on its way to becoming a predominantly Third World state.

No one knows how this will play out, but California could become another Quebec, with demands for formal recognition of its separate and unique Hispanic culture and identity—or another Ulster. As Sinn Fein demanded and got special ties to Dublin, Mexican Americans may demand a special relationship with their mother country, dual citizenship, open borders, and voting representation in Mexico's legislature. President Fox endorses these ideas. With California holding 20 percent of the electoral votes needed for the U.S. presidency, and Hispanic votes decisive in California, what presidential candidate would close the door to such demands?

"I have proudly proclaimed that the Mexican nation extends beyond the territory enclosed by its borders and that Mexican migrants are an important—a very important—part of this," said President Zedillo. His successor agrees. Candidates for president of Mexico now raise money and campaign actively in the United States. Gov. Gray Davis is exploring plans to have Cinquo de Mayo, the fifth of May, the anniversary of Juarez's 1862 victory over a French army at Puebla, made a California holiday. "In the near future," says Davis, "people will look at California and Mexico as one magnificent region." Perhaps we can call it Aztlan.

⋯◈⋯

America is no longer the biracial society of 1960 that struggled to erase divisions and close gaps in a nation 90 percent white. Today we juggle the rancorous and rival claims of a multiracial, multiethnic, and multicultural country. Vice President Gore captured the new America in his famous howler, when he translated our national slogan, "E Pluribus Unum," backward, as "Out of one, many."

Today there are 28.4 million foreign-born in the United States. Half are from Latin America and the Caribbean, a fourth from Asia. The rest are from Africa, the Middle East, and Europe. One in every five New Yorkers and Floridians is foreign-born, as is one of every four Californians. With 8.4 million foreign-born, and not one new power plant built in a decade, small wonder California faces power shortages and power outages. With endless immigration, America is going to need an endless expansion of its power sources—hydroelectric power, fossil fuels (oil, coal, gas), and nuclear power. The only alternative is blackouts, brownouts, and endless lines at the pump.

In the 1990s, immigrants and their children were responsible for 100 percent of the population growth of California, New York, New Jersey, Illinois, and Massachusetts, and over half the population growth of Florida, Texas, Michigan, and Maryland. As the United States allots most of its immigrant visas to relatives of new arrivals, it is difficult for Europeans to come, while entire villages from El Salvador are now here.

The results of the Third World bias in immigration can be seen in our social statistics. The median age of Euro-Americans is 36; for Hispanics, it is 26. The median age of all foreign-born, 33, is far below that of the older American ethnic groups, such as English, 40, and Scots-Irish, 43. These social statistics raise a question: Is the U.S. government, by deporting scarcely 1 percent of an estimated eleven million illegal aliens each year, failing in its constitutional duty to protect the rights of American citizens? Consider:

- A third of the legal immigrants who come to the United States have not finished high school. Some 22 percent do not even have a ninth-grade education, compared to less than 5 percent of our native born.
- Over 36 percent of all immigrants, and 57 percent of those from Central America, do not earn twenty thousand dollars a year. Of the immigrants who have come since 1980, 60 percent still do not earn twenty thousand dollars a year.
- Of immigrant households in the United States, 29 percent are below the poverty line, twice the 14 percent of native born.
- Immigrant use of food stamps, Supplemental Social Security, and school lunch programs runs from 50 percent to 100 percent higher than use by native born.
- Mr. Clinton's Department of Labor estimated that 50 percent of the real-wage losses sustained by low-income Americans is due to immigration.
- By 1991, foreign nationals accounted for 24 percent of all arrests in Los Angeles and 36 percent of all arrests in Miami.
- In 1980, federal and state prisons housed nine thousand criminal aliens. By 1995, this had soared to fifty-nine thousand criminal aliens, a figure that does not include aliens who became citizens or the criminals sent over by Castro in the Mariel boat lift.
- Between 1988 and 1994, the number of illegal aliens in California's prisons more than tripled from fifty-five hundred to eighteen thousand.

None of the above statistics, however, holds for emigrants from Europe. And some of the statistics, on low education, for example, do not apply to emigrants from Asia.

Nevertheless, mass emigration from poor Third World countries is "good for business," especially businesses that employ large numbers at low wages. In the spring of 2001, the Business Industry Political Action Committee, BIPAC, issued "marching orders for grass-roots mobilization." *The Wall Street Journal* said that the 400 blue-chip companies and 150 trade associations "will call for continued normalization of trade with China . . . and easing immigration restrictions to meet labor needs. . . ." But what is good for corporate America is not necessarily good for Middle America. When it comes to open borders, the corporate interest and the national interest do not coincide, they collide. Should America suffer a sustained recession, we will find out if the melting pot is still working.

But mass immigration raises more critical issues than jobs or wages, for immigration is ultimately about America herself.

What Is a Nation?

Most of the people who leave their homelands to come to America, whether from Mexico or Mauritania, are good people, decent people. They seek the same better life our ancestors sought when they came. They come to work; they obey our laws; they cherish our freedoms; they relish the opportunities the greatest nation on earth has to offer; most love America; many wish to become part of the American family. One may encounter these newcomers everywhere. But the record number of foreign-born coming from cultures with little in common with Americans raises a different question: What is a nation?

Some define a nation as one people of common ancestry, language, literature, history, heritage, heroes, traditions, customs, mores, and faith who have lived together over time on the same land under the same rulers. This is the blood-and-soil idea of a nation. Among those who pressed this definition were Secretary of State John Quincy Adams, who laid down these conditions on immigrants: "They must cast off the European skin, never to resume it. They must look forward to their posterity rather than backward to their ancestors." Theodore Roosevelt, who thundered against "hyphenated-Americanism," seemed to share Adams's view. Woodrow Wilson, speaking to newly naturalized Americans in 1915 in Philadelphia, echoed T.R.: "A man who thinks of himself as belonging to a particular national group in America has yet to become an American." This idea, of Americans as a separate and unique people, was first given expression by John Jay in *Federalist 2:*

> Providence has been pleased to give this one connected country to one united people—a people descended from the same ancestors, speaking the same language, professing the same religion, attached to the same principles of government, very similar in their manners and customs, and who, by their joint counsels, arms, and efforts, fighting side by side throughout

a long and bloody war, have nobly established their general liberty and independence.

But can anyone say today that we Americans are "one united people"? We are not descended from the same ancestors. We no longer speak the same language. We do not profess the same religion. We are no longer simply Protestant, Catholic, and Jewish, as sociologist Will Herberg described us in his *Essay in American Religious Sociology* in 1955. We are now Protestant, Catholic, Jewish, Mormon, Muslim, Hindu, Buddhist, Taoist, Shintoist, Santeria, New Age, voodoo, agnostic, atheist, humanist, Rastafarian, and Wiccan. Even the mention of Jesus' name at the Inauguration by the preachers Mr. Bush selected to give the invocations evoked fury and cries of "insensitive," "divisive," and "exclusionary." A *New Republic* editorial lashed out at these "crushing Christological thuds" from the Inaugural stand. We no longer agree on whether God exists, when life begins, and what is moral and immoral. We are not "similar in our manners and customs." We never fought "side by side throughout a long and bloody war." The Greatest Generation did, but it is passing away. If the rest of us recall a "long and bloody war," it was Vietnam, and, no, we were not side by side.

We remain "attached to the same principles of government." But common principles of government are not enough to hold us together. The South was "attached to the same principles of government" as the North. But that did not stop Southerners from fighting four years of bloody war to be free of their Northern brethren.

In his Inaugural, President Bush rejected Jay's vision: "America has never been united by blood or birth or soil. We are bound by ideals that move us beyond our background, lift us above our interests, and teach us what it means to be a citizen." In his *The Disuniting of America*, Arthur Schlesinger subscribes to the Bush idea of a nation, united by shared belief in an American Creed to be found in our history and greatest documents: the Declaration of Independence, the Constitution, and the Gettysburg Address. Writes Schlesinger:

> The American Creed envisages a nation composed of individuals making their own choices and accountable to themselves, not a nation based on inviolable ethnic communities. For our values are not matters or whim and happenstance. History has given them to us. They are anchored in our national experience, in our great national documents, in our national heroes, in our folkways, our traditions, and standards. [Our values] work for us; and, for that reason, we live and die by them.

Bush Americans no longer agree on values, history, or heroes. What one-half of America sees as a glorious past the other views as shameful and wicked. Columbus, Washington, Jefferson, Jackson, Lincoln, and Lee—all of them heroes of the old America—are all under attack. Those most American of words, equality and freedom, today hold different meanings for different Americans. As for our "great national documents," the Supreme Court decisions that interpret our Constitution have not united us; for forty years they have divided us, bitterly, over prayer in school, integration, busing, flag burning, abortion, pornography, and the Ten Commandments.

Nor is a belief in democracy sufficient to hold us together. Half of the nation did not even bother to vote in the presidential election of 2000; three out of five do not vote in off-year elections. Millions cannot name their congressman, senators, or the Supreme Court justices. They do not care.

Whether one holds to the blood-and-soil idea of a nation, or to the creedal idea, or both, neither nation is what it was in the 1940s, 1950s, or 1960s. We live in the same country, we are governed by the same leaders, but can we truly say we are still one nation and one people?

It is hard to say yes, harder to believe that over a million immigrants every year, from every country on earth, a third of them breaking in, will reforge the bonds of our disuniting nation. John Stuart Mill warned that "free institutions are next to impossible in a country made up of different nationalities. Among a people without fellow-feeling, especially if they read and speak different languages, the united public opinion necessary to the working of representative government cannot exist."

We are about to find out if Mill was right.

POSTSCRIPT

Should America Remain a Nation of Immigrants?

Buchanan argues that the new immigration since 1968 from Mexico, other parts of Latin America, and Asia is destroying the core culture of the United States. He maintains that the new immigrants are responsible for America's rising crime rate; the increase in the number of households that are below the poverty level; and the increase in the use of food stamps, Supplemental Social Security, and school lunch programs. Furthermore, maintains Buchanan, low-income Americans sustain real wage losses of 50 percent because of competition from legal and illegal immigration.

Buchanan also asserts that America is losing the cultural war. He holds that the Republican Party's white-based majority under Presidents Richard Nixon and Ronald Reagan has been undermined by an immigrant-based Democratic Party. He notes that the two biggest states—California and Texas—are beset with ethnic enclaves who do not speak English and whose political and cultural values are outside the American mainstream.

Although Buchanan expresses feelings that are felt by many Americans today, his analysis lacks historical perspective. Ever since Columbus encountered the first Native Americans, tensions between immigrants and native-born people have existed. During the four peak periods of immigration to the United States, the host group has felt overwhelmed by the newest groups entering the country. Buchanan quotes Benjamin Franklin's concern about the German immigrants' turning Pennsylvania into a "Colony of Aliens, who will shortly be so numerous as to Germanize us instead of our Anglifying them." But Buchanan does not carry his observation to its logical conclusion. German immigration into the United States did not halt during the Seven Years War, as Buchanan contends. It continued during the nineteenth and early twentieth centuries, and Germans today constitute the largest white ethnic group in the country.

Buchanan also ignores the hostility accorded his own Irish-Catholic relatives by white, Protestant Americans in the 1850s, who considered the Irish crime-ridden, lazy, drunken ignoramuses living in ethnic enclaves who were unassimilable because of their "Papist" religious ceremonies. Irish males, it was said, often did not work but lived off the wages of their wives, who worked as maids. When menial jobs were performed mostly by Irish men, they were accused of lowering the wages of other working-class Americans. One may question whether the newest immigrants are different from Buchanan's own ancestors.

Jacoby gives a spirited defense of the newest immigrants. She dismisses the argument for increased immigration restriction after the September 11 attacks on the World Trade Center and the Pentagon by distinguishing between a terrorist and an immigrant. She contends that the estimates about a future population explosion in the country might be exaggerated, especially if economic conditions improve in Third World countries when the global economy becomes more balanced.

Jacoby stresses the positive impact of the new immigrants. Many of them—particularly those from India and other Asian countries—have contributed their skills to the computer industry in the Silicon Valley and other high-tech industrial parks across America. Jacoby also argues that even if poorer immigrants overuse America's health and welfare social services, many of them contribute portions of their pay to the Social Security trust fund, including illegal immigrants who might never receive a government retirement check. Jacoby does allow that although today's immigrants may be no poorer than those who came in the third wave at the turn of the twentieth century, today's unskilled immigrants are relatively further behind than the southern and eastern Europeans who came around 1900. This is the view of sociologist George J. Borjas in *Heaven's Door: Immigration and the American Economy* (Princeton University Press, 1999).

Most experts agree that changes need to be made in the U.S. immigration laws. Some groups, such as the Federation for American Immigration Reform (FAIR), would like to see a huge cut in the 730,000 legal immigrants, 100,000 refugees, and 200,000 illegal immigrants (Borjas's numbers) who came into America each year in the 1980s and 1990s. Borjas would add a point system to a numerical quota, which would take into account age, work experience, fluency in English, educational background, work experience, and the quality of one's job. Jacoby also favors an immigration policy that gives preference to immigrants with key job-related skills over those who use the loopholes in the law to reunite the members of their families. Unlike Buchanan, Jacoby maintains that the newest immigrants will assimilate as earlier groups did but only when their legal status as citizens is fully established.

There is an enormous bibliography on the newest immigrants. A good starting point, which clearly explains the immigration laws and their impact on the development of American society, is Kenneth K. Lee, *Huddled Masses, Muddled Laws: Why Contemporary Immigration Policy Fails to Reflect Public Opinion* (Praeger, 1998). Another book that concisely summarizes both sides of the debate and contains a useful glossary of terms is Gerald Leinwand, *American Immigration: Should the Open Door Be Closed?* (Franklin Watts, 1995).

Because historians take a long-range view of immigration, they tend to weigh in on the pro side of the debate. See L. Edward Purcell, *Immigration: Social Issues in American History Series* (Oryx Press, 1995); Reed Ueda's *Postwar America: A Social History* (Bedford Books, 1995); and David M. Reimers, *Still the Golden Door: The Third World War Comes to America*, 2d ed. (Columbia University Press, 1997) and *Unwelcome Strangers: American Identity and the Turn Against Immigration* (Columbia University Press, 1998).

ISSUE 18

Is George W. Bush the Worst President in American History?

YES: Sean Wilentz, from "The Worst President in History?" *Rolling Stone* (May 4, 2006)

NO: Conrad Black, from "George W. Bush, FDR, and History," *The American Spectator* (April 2005)

ISSUE SUMMARY

YES: Bancroft prize-winning historian Sean Wilentz argues that the current president ranks with Presidents James Buchanan, Andrew Johnson, and Herbert Hoover in having divided the nation, governed erratically, and left the nation worse off than when he came into office.

NO: FDR biographer Conrad Black believes that President Bush is, with the exception of FDR, the most important president since Lincoln in accomplishing a highly successful domestic and foreign policy.

The American president is the most powerful political figure in the world. The modern presidency achieved this stature in two ways. First was the dominance of America's military power in World War II. Not only was the United States victorious in both the Atlantic and Pacific theatres, our government also developed and used, with the help of its scientific and military establishments, the first atomic weapons. The ultimate decision to drop the two atomic bombs on Japan was made by President Truman.

A second way in which the modern president transcended the early presidency was the responsibility for managing the economy assumed by the national government in the 1930s. This started incrementally with the alphabet soup agencies in charge of the New Deal programs, but the Employment Act of 1946 created the Council of Economic Advisers and charged the national government with the responsibility for maintaining economic conditions that allowed individuals to find jobs.

If a newspaper placed an ad for the job of president of the United States, the starting point would be the specifications found in the United States Constitution.

A presidential job description would include the following six roles: chief of state; chief administrator; chief legislator; chief of the party (the only one not found in the Constitution); chief diplomat; and commander-in-chief. The first role—chief of state—is ceremonial, while the other five roles are political.

The president of the United States wears two hats: ceremonial and political. As *chief of state,* the president is expected to attend special events commemorating the anniversaries of our major holidays—Christmas, Memorial Day, Independence Day, Labor Day, Thanksgiving—as well as to respond to a national emergency such as Roosevelt's address to the nation declaring war on December 8, 1941, the day after the Pearl Harbor attack; Johnson's address to Congress in 1965 exhorting the nation that "We Shall Overcome" in support of the struggle for civil rights; and Bush's address to the nation after the September 11 attacks on New York City and Washington, D.C., in 2001.

Unlike other chiefs of state in countries as diverse as England and Japan, the president of the United States is two persons in one. He is both the ceremonial and political leader. Other countries divide the roles. In England, Queen Elizabeth is the ceremonial leader and Tony Blair, the prime minister, is the political. In Japan, a similar division takes place between the emperor and the prime minister of the Japanese diet.

In the early years of our history, there was a similar division between the two roles. President George Washington was the ceremonial leader. Tall, stately, aloof, and regal, Washington, the rich plantation owner with several hundred slaves, looked more like a king than did most of the European monarchs. Washington held formal presidential dinner parties and even led his cabinet meetings in a very stiff manner. Most of the political duties of the president were carried out by his secretary of the treasury and quasi–prime minister Alexander Hamilton. But President Thomas Jefferson combined the two roles. As Professor Forrest McDonald points out in *The American Presidency* (University of Kansas Press, 1994), Jefferson "republicanized" the presidency by becoming both the ceremonial and political leader. The monarch and the prime minister were fused into the American president.

The five other roles of the president were strictly political. As *chief administrator,* George Washington presided over a cabinet of four and an office staff of a dozen. Today, President George Bush has a "West Wing" full of not only cabinet leaders, but staff positions of assistants to the assistants and aides to the assistants. Managing the executive branch of the government is as much a matter of style as of substance. On one extreme was President Carter who was involved in detailed analyses of every issue. He tried to run his office in the way he ran his small business peanut factory. On the other hand, President Reagan was primarily interested in the big picture, and left the details to his staff. Most presidents fall between the two styles. President Clinton amassed a wide-ranging amount of detail in free-wheeling discussion among his advisers, while the current president is more punctual, structured, and big-picture oriented.

A role not specified in the Constitution but one that the president automatically assumes is *chief of the party.* Originally it was expected that our government would make decisions by consensus and avoid the bickering that occurred between the rival British political parties. But squabbles over Hamilton's economic policies and Washington pro-British trade policies led to the development of the first political party system of competition. But it wasn't until the Jackson years of the 1830s that the first real party system of competition took place. By the time of the Civil War, the two current major parties—Republican versus Democrat—became the chief contenders for power. Presidents like George Washington could remain aloof and disdain congressional races. But Jackson, Van Buren, Clay, and Lincoln became the leaders of loose party organizations on the state and local levels. Today, every president automatically becomes the head of his party and is expected (especially when he's popular) to campaign and raise money for the election of his party's local, state, and congressional officials.

The president is also the *Chief Legislator*. Traditionally, it was expected that the House of Representatives would appropriate the money and attend to minimal domestic affairs such as tariff bills while the Senate would handle foreign policy and give its advice and consent on any treaties negotiated with foreign governments. Today, presidents and their staff work with the party's congressional leaders in both houses and propose key legislation. Twentieth-century Democratic presidents—Wilson, FDR, and LBJ—pushed strong national government activist programs called The New Freedom, The New Deal, and The Great Society, which led to the passage of the Federal Reserve System, minimum wage laws, collective bargaining, Social Security, Medicare, Medicaid, and the major Civil Rights Acts of 1964 and 1965.

In the twentieth century, the president of the United States spent the majority of his time in office dealing with foreign affairs. As *chief diplomat,* Woodrow Wilson led the negotiations ending World War I by the Treaty of Versailles even though he was unable to get the United States to sign the treaty and join the League of Nations. FDR negotiated numerous agreements with the Allied powers during the war and was instrumental in creating the current United Nations international organization. His successor, Harry S. Truman, was responsible for financing the regional economic alliances in Western Europe such as the Marshall Plan, and for forming the North Atlantic Treaty Organization (NATO), whose purpose was to "contain" Russian expansion during the cold war. Presidents Eisenhower, Kennedy, Johnson, Nixon, Carter, and Reagan expended an enormous amount of energy trying to diffuse an arms race between the two superpowers. Gorbachev and Reagan virtually ended the cold war, but post–cold war presidents Clinton and the two Bushes encountered other problems in Eastern Europe, Africa, and the Middle East.

The major difference between the early and modern presidency can be found in the role of *commander-in-chief*. The first president, George Washington, who traveled by stagecoach from his plantation in Washington, D.C., to be inaugurated in New York City, could hardly imagine being in charge of the decision to use nuclear weapons in war with the power to blow up the world a thousand times over. Presidents have played a dominant role in determining military strategy since the Civil War when Lincoln fired a multitude of generals until he found one—Grant—who relentlessly pursued the enemy. Presidents Wilson, FDR, Truman, and LBJ were important decision makers during the two world wars, Korea, and Vietnam. A classic case of the clash between the president and his military commander occurred during the Korean War when President Truman, with the support of the Joint Chiefs of Staff, relieved the popular General Douglas McArthur of his command of the United Nations' forces during the Korean War. It was a very unpopular decision and Truman suffered a severe drop in the public opinion polls, but the president was determined to uphold his authority as commander-in-chief.

Is it possible to use these roles to evaluate our current leader? How much time must pass before we can dispense with partisanship and attempt to view any president from a detached and objective point of view? In the first essay, Pulitzer Prize–winning historian Sean Wilentz argues that the current president ranks with Presidents James Buchanan, Andrew Johnson, and Herbert Hoover in having divided the nation, governed erratically, and left the nation worse off than when he came into office. But FDR biographer Conrad Black believes that President Bush is, with the exception of FDR, the most important president since Lincoln in accomplishing a highly successful domestic and foreign policy.

YES

Sean Wilentz

The Worst President in History?

George W. Bush's presidency appears headed for colossal historical disgrace. Barring a cataclysmic event on the order of the terrorist attacks of September 11th, after which the public might rally around the White House once again, there seems to be little the administration can do to avoid being ranked on the lowest tier of U.S. presidents. And that may be the best-case scenario. Many historians are now wondering whether Bush, in fact, will be remembered as the very worst president in all of American history.

From time to time, after hours, I kick back with my colleagues at Princeton to argue idly about which president really was the worst of them all. For years, these perennial debates have largely focused on the same handful of chief executives whom national polls of historians, from across the ideological and political spectrum, routinely cite as the bottom of the presidential barrel. Was the lousiest James Buchanan, who, confronted with Southern secession in 1860, dithered to a degree that, as his most recent biographer has said, probably amounted to disloyalty—and who handed to his successor, Abraham Lincoln, a nation already torn asunder? Was it Lincoln's successor, Andrew Johnson, who actively sided with former Confederates and undermined Reconstruction? What about the amiably incompetent Warren G. Harding, whose administration was fabulously corrupt? Or, though he has his defenders, Herbert Hoover, who tried some reforms but remained imprisoned in his own outmoded individualist ethic and collapsed under the weight of the stock-market crash of 1929 and the Depression's onset? The younger historians always put in a word for Richard M. Nixon, the only American president forced to resign from office.

Now, though, George W. Bush is in serious contention for the title of worst ever. In early 2004, an informal survey of 415 historians conducted by the nonpartisan History News Network found that eighty-one percent considered the Bush administration a "failure." Among those who called Bush a success, many gave the president high marks only for his ability to mobilize public support and get Congress to go along with what one historian called the administration's "pursuit of disastrous policies." In fact, roughly one in ten of those who called Bush a success was being facetious, rating him only as the best president since Bill Clinton—a category in which Bush is the only contestant.

The lopsided decision of historians should give everyone pause. Contrary to popular stereotypes, historians are generally a cautious bunch. We assess the past from widely divergent points of view and are deeply concerned about being viewed as fair and accurate by our colleagues. When we make historical judgments, we are acting not as voters or even pundits, but as scholars who must evaluate all the evidence, good, bad or indifferent. Separate surveys, conducted by those perceived as conservatives as well as liberals, show remarkable unanimity about who the best and worst presidents have been.

Historians do tend, as a group, to be far more liberal than the citizenry as a whole—a fact the president's admirers have seized on to dismiss the poll results as transparently biased. One pro-Bush historian said the survey revealed more about "the current crop of history professors" than about Bush or about Bush's eventual standing. But if historians were simply motivated by a strong collective liberal bias, they might be expected to call Bush the worst president since his father, or Ronald Reagan, or Nixon. Instead, more than half of those polled—and nearly three-fourths of those who gave Bush a negative rating—reached back *before* Nixon to find a president they considered as miserable as Bush. The presidents most commonly linked with Bush included Hoover, Andrew Johnson and Buchanan. Twelve percent of the historians polled—nearly as many as those who rated Bush a success—flatly called Bush the worst president in American history. And these figures were gathered before the debacles over Hurricane Katrina, Bush's role in the Valerie Plame leak affair and the deterioration of the situation in Iraq. Were the historians polled today, that figure would certainly be higher.

Even worse for the president, the general public, having once given Bush the highest approval ratings ever recorded, now appears to be coming around to the dismal view held by most historians. To be sure, the president retains a considerable base of supporters who believe in and adore him, and who reject all criticism with a mixture of disbelief and fierce contempt—about one-third of the electorate. (When the columnist Richard Reeves publicized the historians' poll last year and suggested it might have merit, he drew thousands of abusive replies that called him an idiot and that praised Bush as, in one writer's words, "a Christian who actually acts on his deeply held beliefs.") Yet the ranks of the true believers have thinned dramatically. A majority of voters in forty-three states now disapprove of Bush's handling of his job. Since the commencement of reliable polling in the 1940s, only one twice-elected president has seen his ratings fall as low as Bush's in his second term: Richard Nixon, during the months preceding his resignation in 1974. No two-term president since polling began has fallen from such a height of popularity as Bush's (in the neighborhood of ninety percent, during the patriotic upswell following the 2001 attacks) to such a low (now in the midthirties). No president, including Harry Truman (whose ratings sometimes dipped below Nixonian levels), has experienced such a virtually unrelieved decline as Bush has since his high point. Apart from sharp but temporary upticks that followed the commencement of the Iraq war and the capture of Saddam Hussein, and a recovery during the weeks just before and after his re-election, the Bush trend has been a profile in fairly steady disillusionment.

How does any president's reputation sink so low? The reasons are best understood as the reverse of those that produce presidential greatness. In almost every survey of historians dating back to the 1940s, three presidents have emerged as supreme successes: George Washington, Abraham Lincoln and Franklin D. Roosevelt. These were the men who guided the nation through what historians consider its greatest crises: the founding era after the ratification of the Constitution, the Civil War, and the Great Depression and Second World War. Presented with arduous, at times seemingly impossible circumstances, they rallied the nation, governed brilliantly and left the republic more secure than when they entered office.

Calamitous presidents, faced with enormous difficulties—Buchanan, Andrew Johnson, Hoover and now Bush—have divided the nation, governed erratically and left the nation worse off. In each case, different factors contributed to the failure: disastrous domestic policies, foreign-policy blunders and military setbacks, executive misconduct, crises of credibility and public trust. Bush, however, is one of the rarities in presidential history: He has not only stumbled badly in every one of these key areas, he has also displayed a weakness common among the greatest presidential failures—an unswerving adherence to a simplistic ideology that abjures deviation from dogma as heresy, thus preventing any pragmatic adjustment to changing realities. Repeatedly, Bush has undone himself, a failing revealed in each major area of presidential performance.

The Credibility Gap

No previous president appears to have squandered the public's trust more than Bush has. In the 1840s, President James Polk gained a reputation for deviousness over his alleged manufacturing of the war with Mexico and his supposedly covert pro-slavery views. Abraham Lincoln, then an Illinois congressman, virtually labeled Polk a liar when he called him, from the floor of the House, "a bewildered, confounded and miserably perplexed man" and denounced the war as "from beginning to end, the sheerest deception." But the swift American victory in the war, Polk's decision to stick by his pledge to serve only one term and his sudden death shortly after leaving office spared him the ignominy over slavery that befell his successors in the 1850s. With more than two years to go in Bush's second term and no swift victory in sight, Bush's reputation will probably have no such reprieve.

The problems besetting Bush are of a more modern kind than Polk's, suited to the television age—a crisis both in confidence and credibility. In 1965, Lyndon Johnson's Vietnam travails gave birth to the phrase "credibility gap," meaning the distance between a president's professions and the public's perceptions of reality. It took more than two years for Johnson's disapproval rating in the Gallup Poll to reach fifty-two percent in March 1968—a figure Bush long ago surpassed, but that was sufficient to persuade the proud LBJ not to seek re-election. Yet recently, just short of three years after Bush buoyantly declared "mission accomplished" in Iraq, his disapproval ratings have been running considerably higher than Johnson's, at about sixty percent. More than half the country now considers Bush dishonest and untrustworthy, and a decisive plurality consider him less trustworthy than his predecessor, Bill Clinton—a figure still attacked by conservative zealots as "Slick Willie."

Previous modern presidents, including Truman, Reagan and Clinton, managed to reverse plummeting ratings and regain the public's trust by shifting attention away from political and policy setbacks, and by overhauling the White House's inner circles. But Bush's publicly expressed view that he has made no major mistakes, coupled with what even the conservative commentator William F. Buckley Jr. calls his "high-flown pronouncements" about failed policies, seems to foreclose the first option. Upping the ante in the Middle East and bombing Iranian nuclear sites, a strategy reportedly favored by some in the White House, could distract the public and gain Bush immediate political capital in advance of the 2006 midterm elections—but in the long term might severely worsen the already dire situation in Iraq, especially among Shiite Muslims linked to the Iranians. And given Bush's ardent attachment to loyal aides, no matter how discredited, a major personnel shake-up is improbable, short of indictments. Replacing Andrew Card with Joshua Bolten as chief of staff—a move announced by the president in March in a tone that sounded more like defiance than contrition—represents a rededication to current policies and personnel, not a serious change. (Card, an old Bush family retainer, was widely considered more moderate than most of the men around the president and had little involvement in policy-making.) The power of Vice President Dick Cheney, meanwhile, remains uncurbed. Were Cheney to announce he is stepping down due to health problems, normally a polite pretext for a political removal, one can be reasonably certain it would be because Cheney actually did have grave health problems.

Bush at War

Until the twentieth century, American presidents managed foreign wars well—including those presidents who prosecuted unpopular wars. James Madison had no support from Federalist New England at the outset of the War of 1812, and the discontent grew amid mounting military setbacks in 1813. But Federalist political overreaching, combined with a reversal of America's military fortunes and the negotiation of a peace with Britain, made Madison something of a hero again and ushered in a brief so-called Era of Good Feelings in which his Jeffersonian Republican Party coalition ruled virtually unopposed. The Mexican War under Polk was even more unpopular, but its quick and victorious conclusion redounded to Polk's favor—much as the rapid American victory in the Spanish-American War helped William McKinley overcome anti-imperialist dissent.

The twentieth century was crueler to wartime presidents. After winning re-election in 1916 with the slogan "He Kept Us Out of War," Woodrow Wilson oversaw American entry into the First World War. Yet while the doughboys returned home triumphant, Wilson's idealistic and politically disastrous campaign for American entry into the League of Nations presaged a resurgence of the opposition Republican Party along with a redoubling of American isolationism that lasted until Pearl Harbor.

Bush has more in common with post-1945 Democratic presidents Truman and Johnson, who both became bogged down in overseas military conflicts with no end, let alone victory, in sight. But Bush has become bogged down in a singularly crippling way. On September 10th, 2001, he held among the lowest ratings of any modern president for that point in a first term. (Only Gerald Ford, his popularity reeling after his pardon of Nixon, had comparable numbers.) The attacks the following day transformed Bush's presidency, giving him an extraordinary opportunity to achieve greatness. Some of the early signs were encouraging. Bush's simple, unflinching eloquence and his quick toppling of the Taliban government in Afghanistan rallied the nation. Yet even then, Bush wasted his chance by quickly choosing partisanship over leadership.

No other president—Lincoln in the Civil War, FDR in World War II, John F. Kennedy at critical moments of the Cold War—faced with such a monumental set of military and political circumstances failed to embrace the opposing political party to help wage a truly national struggle. But Bush shut out and even demonized the Democrats. Top military advisers and even members of the president's own Cabinet who expressed any reservations or criticisms of his policies—including retired Marine Corps Gen. Anthony Zinni and former Treasury Secretary Paul O'Neill—suffered either dismissal, smear attacks from the president's supporters or investigations into their alleged breaches of national security. The wise men who counseled Bush's father, including James Baker and Brent Scowcroft, found their entreaties brusquely ignored by his son. When asked if he ever sought advice from the elder Bush, the president responded, "There is a higher Father that I appeal to."

All the while, Bush and the most powerful figures in the administration, Vice President Dick Cheney and Defense Secretary Donald Rumsfeld, were planting the seeds for the crises to come by diverting the struggle against Al Qaeda toward an all-out effort to topple their pre-existing target, Saddam Hussein. In a deliberate political decision, the administration stampeded the Congress and a traumatized citizenry into the Iraq invasion on the basis of what has now been demonstrated to be tendentious and perhaps fabricated evidence of an imminent Iraqi threat to American security, one that the White House suggested included nuclear weapons. Instead of emphasizing any political, diplomatic or humanitarian aspects of a war on Iraq—an appeal that would have sounded too "sensitive," as Cheney once sneered—the administration built a "Bush Doctrine" of unprovoked, preventive warfare, based on speculative threats and embracing principles previously abjured by every previous generation of U.S. foreign policy-makers, even at the height of the Cold War. The president did so with premises founded, in the case of Iraq, on wishful thinking. He did so while proclaiming an expansive Wilsonian rhetoric of making the world safe for democracy—yet discarding the multilateralism and systems of international law (including the Geneva Conventions) that emanated from Wilson's idealism. He did so while dismissing intelligence that an American invasion could spark a long and bloody civil war among Iraq's fierce religious and ethnic rivals, reports that have since proved true. And he did so after repeated warnings by military officials such as Gen. Eric

Shinseki that pacifying postwar Iraq would require hundreds of thousands of American troops—accurate estimates that Paul Wolfowitz and other Bush policy gurus ridiculed as "wildly off the mark."

When William F. Buckley, the man whom many credit as the founder of the modern conservative movement, writes categorically, as he did in February, that "one can't doubt that the American objective in Iraq has failed," then something terrible has happened. Even as a brash young iconoclast, Buckley always took the long view. The Bush White House seems incapable of doing so, except insofar as a tiny trusted circle around the president constantly reassures him that he is a messianic liberator and profound freedom fighter, on a par with FDR and Lincoln, and that history will vindicate his every act and utterance.

THE BIGGEST FAILURES

James *Buchanan*

Like Bush, Buchanan left the country more divided and acrimonious. As a Pennsylvania Democrat with friendly feelings for Southerners, Buchanan believed he could contain the mounting controversies over slavery by playing an even hand. Yet at crucial moments—the notorious Dred Scott decision and the bloody battles over slavery in Kansas—Buchanan tilted heavily to the South. When Lincoln's election in 1860 provoked Southern states to secede, Buchanan insisted the government lacked the power to stop them. His inaction verged on disloyalty—and handed his successor a nation already torn asunder.

Andrew *Johnson*

Johnson's efforts during Reconstruction were as disastrous as the rebuilding of Iraq. A Democrat from Tennessee who assumed the presidency after Lincoln's assassination, Johnson proved bitterly hostile to newly freed slaves. His opposition to the Civil Rights Act of 1866, which promoted civil and political rights for former slaves, prompted Congress to override a presidential veto of a major bill for the first time in history. Johnson's friendliness with ex-Confederates and defiance of Congress led to his impeachment in 1868; he escaped removal from office by a single vote after his trial in the Senate.

Herbert *Hoover*

The failure of Bush's domestic agenda is unmatched since Hoover. Running for president in 1928, Hoover declared that America had come closer to "the final triumph over poverty than ever before in the hisotry of any land." A year later, when the stock-market crash sparked the Great Depression, he oversaw loans to business and modest expansion of public works—but emphasized that caring for the unfortunate must remain primarily a local and voluntary effort. His upbeat insistence that "prosperity is just around the corner" backfired, resulting in a landslide for FDR.

Bush at Home

Bush came to office in 2001 pledging to govern as a "compassionate conservative," more moderate on domestic policy than the dominant right wing of his party. The pledge proved hollow, as Bush tacked immediately to the hard right. Previous presidents and their parties have suffered when their actions have belied their campaign promises. Lyndon Johnson is the most conspicuous recent example, having declared in his 1964 run against the hawkish Republican Barry Goldwater that "we are not about to send American boys nine or ten thousand miles away from home to do what Asian boys ought to be doing for themselves." But no president has surpassed Bush in departing so thoroughly from his original campaign persona.

The heart of Bush's domestic policy has turned out to be nothing more than a series of massively regressive tax cuts—a return, with a vengeance, to the discredited Reagan-era supply-side faith that Bush's father once ridiculed as "voodoo economics." Bush crowed in triumph in February 2004, "We cut taxes, which basically meant people had more money in their pocket." The claim is bogus for the majority of Americans, as are claims that tax cuts have led to impressive new private investment and job growth. While wiping out the solid Clinton-era federal surplus and raising federal deficits to staggering record levels, Bush's tax policies have necessitated hikes in federal fees, state and local taxes, and co-payment charges to needy veterans and families who rely on Medicaid, along with cuts in loan programs to small businesses and college students, and in a wide range of state services. The lion's share of benefits from the tax cuts has gone to the very richest Americans, while new business investment has increased at a historically sluggish rate since the peak of the last business cycle five years ago. Private-sector job growth since 2001 has been anemic compared to the Bush administration's original forecasts and is chiefly attributable not to the tax cuts but to increased federal spending, especially on defense. Real wages for middle-income Americans have been dropping since the end of 2003: Last year, on average, nominal wages grew by only 2.4 percent, a meager gain that was completely erased by an average inflation rate of 3.4 percent.

The monster deficits, caused by increased federal spending combined with the reduction of revenue resulting from the tax cuts, have also placed Bush's administration in a historic class of its own with respect to government borrowing. According to the Treasury Department, the forty-two presidents who held office between 1789 and 2000 borrowed a combined total of $1.01 trillion from foreign governments and financial institutions. But between 2001 and 2005 alone, the Bush White House borrowed $1.05 trillion, more than all of the previous presidencies *combined*. Having inherited the largest federal surplus in American history in 2001, he has turned it into the largest deficit ever—with an even higher deficit, $423 billion, forecast for fiscal year 2006. Yet Bush—sounding much like Herbert Hoover in 1930 predicting that "prosperity is just around the corner"—insists that he will cut federal deficits in half by 2009, and that the best way to guarantee this would be to make permanent his tax cuts, which helped cause the deficit in the first place!

The rest of what remains of Bush's skimpy domestic agenda is either failed or failing—a record unmatched since the presidency of Herbert Hoover. The No Child Left Behind educational-reform act has proved so unwieldy, draconian and poorly funded that several states—including Utah, one of Bush's last remaining political strongholds—have fought to opt out of it entirely. White House proposals for immigration reform and a guest-worker program have succeeded mainly in dividing pro-business Republicans (who want more low-wage immigrant workers) from paleo-conservatives fearful that hordes of Spanish-speaking newcomers will destroy American culture. The paleos' call for tougher anti-immigrant laws—a return to the punitive spirit of exclusion that led to the notorious Immigration Act of 1924 that shut the door to immigrants from Southern and Eastern Europe—has in turn deeply alienated Hispanic voters from the Republican Party, badly undermining the GOP's hopes of using them to build a permanent national electoral majority. The recent pro-immigrant demonstrations, which drew millions of marchers nationwide, indicate how costly the Republican divide may prove.

The one noncorporate constituency to which Bush has consistently deferred is the Christian right, both in his selections for the federal bench and in his implications that he bases his policies on premillennialist, prophetic Christian doctrine. Previous presidents have regularly invoked the Almighty. McKinley is supposed to have fallen to his knees, seeking divine guidance about whether to take control of the Philippines in 1898, although the story may be apocryphal. But no president before Bush has allowed the press to disclose, through a close friend, his startling belief that he was ordained by God to lead the country. The White House's sectarian positions—over stem-cell research, the teaching of pseudoscientific "intelligent design," global population control, the Terri Schiavo spectacle and more—have led some to conclude that Bush has promoted the transformation of the GOP into what former Republican strategist Kevin Phillips calls "the first religious party in U.S. history."

Bush's faith-based conception of his mission, which stands above and beyond reasoned inquiry, jibes well with his administration's pro-business dogma on global warming and other urgent environmental issues. While forcing federally funded agencies to remove from their Web sites scientific information about reproductive health and the effectiveness of condoms in combating HIV/AIDS, and while peremptorily overruling staff scientists at the Food and Drug Administration on making emergency contraception available over the counter, Bush officials have censored and suppressed research findings they don't like by the Environmental Protection Agency, the Fish and Wildlife Service and the Department of Agriculture. Far from being the conservative he said he was, Bush has blazed a radical new path as the first American president in history who is outwardly hostile to science—dedicated, as a distinguished, bipartisan panel of educators and scientists (including forty-nine Nobel laureates) has declared, to "the distortion of scientific knowledge for partisan political ends."

The Bush White House's indifference to domestic problems and science alike culminated in the catastrophic responses to Hurricane Katrina. Scientists had long warned that global warming was intensifying hurricanes, but Bush ignored them—much as he and his administration sloughed off warnings from the director of the National Hurricane Center before Katrina hit. Reorganized under the Department of Homeland Security, the once efficient Federal Emergency Management Agency turned out, under Bush, to have become a nest of cronyism and incompetence. During the months immediately after the storm, Bush traveled to New Orleans eight times to promise massive rebuilding aid from the federal government. On March 30th, however, Bush's Gulf Coast recovery coordinator admitted that it could take as long as twenty-five years for the city to recover.

Karl Rove has sometimes likened Bush to the imposing, no-nonsense President Andrew Jackson. Yet Jackson took measures to prevent those he called "the rich and powerful" from bending "the acts of government to their selfish purposes." Jackson also gained eternal renown by saving New Orleans from British invasion against terrible odds. Generations of Americans sang of Jackson's famous victory. In 1959, Johnny Horton's version of "The Battle of New Orleans" won the Grammy for best country & western performance. If anyone sings about George W. Bush and New Orleans, it will be a blues number.

Presidential Misconduct

Virtually every presidential administration dating back to George Washington's has faced charges of misconduct and threats of impeachment against the president or his civil officers. The alleged offenses have usually involved matters of personal misbehavior and corruption, notably the payoff scandals that plagued Cabinet officials who served presidents Harding and Ulysses S. Grant. But the charges have also included alleged usurpation of power by the president and serious criminal conduct that threatens constitutional government and the rule of law—most notoriously, the charges that led to the impeachments of Andrew Johnson and Bill Clinton, and to Richard Nixon's resignation.

Historians remain divided over the actual grievousness of many of these allegations and crimes. Scholars reasonably describe the graft and corruption around the Grant administration, for example, as gargantuan, including a kickback scandal that led to the resignation of Grant's secretary of war under the shadow of impeachment. Yet the scandals produced no indictments of Cabinet secretaries and only one of a White House aide, who was acquitted. By contrast, the most scandal-ridden administration in the modern era, apart from Nixon's, was Ronald Reagan's, now widely remembered through a haze of nostalgia as a paragon of virtue. A total of twenty-nine Reagan officials, including White House national security adviser Robert McFarlane and deputy chief of staff Michael Deaver, were convicted on charges stemming from the Iran-Contra affair, illegal lobbying and a looting scandal inside the Department of Housing and Urban Development. Three Cabinet officers—HUD Secretary Samuel Pierce, Attorney General Edwin Meese and Secretary of Defense Caspar Weinberger—left their posts under clouds of scandal. In contrast, not a single official in the Clinton administration was even indicted over his or her White House duties, despite repeated high-profile investigations and a successful, highly partisan impeachment drive.

The full report, of course, has yet to come on the Bush administration. Because Bush, unlike Reagan or Clinton, enjoys a fiercely partisan and loyal majority in Congress, his administration has been spared scrutiny. Yet that mighty advantage has not prevented the indictment of Vice President Dick Cheney's chief of staff, I. Lewis "Scooter" Libby, on charges stemming from an alleged major security breach in the Valerie Plame matter. (The last White House official of comparable standing to be indicted while still in office was Grant's personal secretary, in 1875.) It has not headed off the unprecedented scandal involving Larry Franklin, a high-ranking Defense Department official, who has pleaded guilty to divulging classified information to a foreign power while working at the Pentagon—a crime against national security. It has not forestalled the arrest and indictment of Bush's top federal procurement official, David Safavian, and the continuing investigations into Safavian's intrigues with the disgraced Republican lobbyist Jack Abramoff, recently sentenced to nearly six years in prison—investigations in which some prominent Republicans, including former Christian Coalition executive director Ralph Reed (and current GOP aspirant for lieutenant governor of Georgia) have already been implicated, and could well produce the largest congressional corruption scandal in American history. It has not dispelled the cloud of possible indictment that hangs over others of Bush's closest advisers.

History may ultimately hold Bush in the greatest contempt for expanding the powers of the presidency beyond the limits laid down by the U.S. Constitution. There has always been a tension over the constitutional roles of the three branches of the federal government. The Framers intended as much, as part of the system of checks and balances they expected would minimize tyranny. When Andrew Jackson took drastic measures against the nation's banking system, the Whig Senate censured him for conduct "dangerous to the liberties of the people." During the Civil War, Abraham Lincoln's emergency decisions to suspend habeas corpus while Congress was out of session in 1861 and 1862 has led some Americans, to this day, to regard him as a despot. Richard Nixon's conduct of the war in Southeast Asia and his covert domestic-surveillance programs prompted Congress to pass new statutes regulating executive power.

By contrast, the Bush administration—in seeking to restore what Cheney, a Nixon administration veteran, has called "the legitimate authority of the presidency"—threatens to overturn the Framers' healthy tension in favor of presidential absolutism. Armed with legal findings by his attorney general (and personal lawyer) Alberto Gonzales, the Bush White House has declared that the president's powers as commander in chief in wartime are limitless. No previous wartime president has come close to making so grandiose a claim. More specifically, this administration has asserted that the president is perfectly free to violate federal laws on such matters as domestic surveillance and the torture of detainees. When Congress has passed legislation to limit those assertions, Bush has resorted to issuing constitutionally dubious "signing statements," which declare, by fiat, how he will interpret and execute the law in question, even when that interpretation flagrantly violates the will of Congress. Earlier presidents, including Jackson, raised hackles by offering their own view of the Constitution in order to justify vetoing congressional acts. Bush doesn't bother with that: He signs the legislation (eliminating any risk that Congress will overturn a veto), and then governs how he pleases—using the signing statements as if they were line-item vetoes. In those instances when Bush's violations of federal law have come to light, as over domestic surveillance, the White House has devised a novel solution: Stonewall any investigation into the violations and bid a compliant Congress simply to rewrite the laws.

Bush's alarmingly aberrant take on the Constitution is ironic. One need go back in the record less than a decade to find prominent Republicans railing against far more minor presidential legal infractions as precursors to all-out totalitarianism. "I will have no part in the creation of a constitutional double-standard to benefit the president," Sen. Bill Frist declared of Bill Clinton's efforts to conceal an illicit sexual liaison. "No man is above the law, and no man is below the law—that's the principle that we all hold very dear in this country," Rep. Tom DeLay asserted. "The rule of law protects you and it protects me from the midnight fire on our roof or the 3 A.M. knock on our door," warned Rep. Henry Hyde, one of Clinton's chief accusers. In the face of Bush's more definitive dismissal of federal law, the silence from these quarters is deafening.

The president's defenders stoutly contend that war-time conditions fully justify Bush's actions. And as Lincoln showed during the Civil War, there may be times of military emergency where the executive believes it imperative to take immediate, highly irregular, even unconstitutional steps. "I felt that measures, otherwise unconstitutional, might become lawful," Lincoln wrote in 1864, "by becoming indispensable to the preservation of the Constitution, through the preservation of the nation." Bush seems to think that, since 9/11, he has been placed, by the grace of God, in the same kind of situation Lincoln faced. But Lincoln, under pressure of daily combat on American soil against fellow Americans, did not operate in secret, as Bush has. He did not claim, as Bush has, that his emergency actions were wholly regular and constitutional as well as necessary; Lincoln sought and received Congressional authorization for his suspension of habeas corpus in 1863. Nor did Lincoln act under the amorphous cover of a "war on terror"—a war against a tactic, not a specific nation or political entity, which could last as long as any president deems the tactic a threat to national security. Lincoln's exceptional measures were intended to survive only as long as the Confederacy was in rebellion. Bush's could be extended indefinitely, as the president sees fit, permanently endangering rights and liberties guaranteed by the Constitution to the citizenry.

THE GREATEST SUCCESSES

George *Washington*

Unlike Bush, whose contested election sharply divided the country, the greatest hero of the American Revolution was named the nation's first president nearly by acclamation, which gave the new national government immediate credibility. During Washington's presidency, the federal machinery sketched out by the Constitution took shape. Although criticized for his administration's pomp. Washington renounced the role of Patriot King that many Americans would have gladly given him and stepped down after his second term.

Abraham *Lincoln*

Lincoln, under pressure of daily combat on American soil, did not flout the law in secret, as Bush has. He welcomed rival voices in his own cabinet, and his unconstitutional actions were ultimately approved by Congress and intended to survive only as long as the Confederacy was in rebellion. Although he came to office as moderate Republican willing to accept slavery where it already existed, he responded to Southern secession by deftly keeping border states in the Union—and by issuing his famous. Emancipation Proclamation of 1863, turning the war for the Union into a war to free the slaves.

Franklin Delano *Roosevelt*

While Bush adheres to a simplistic ideology in the face of changing realities, Roosevelt fought the Great Depression by engaging in relentless experimentation. His sweeping new programs aided businesses and the unemployed, created jobs, and improved public housing and the nation's infrastucture, notably with the Tennessee Valley Authority. After his election to an unprecedented third term, when the Japanese attack on Pearl Harbor precipitated American entry into the Second World War, Roosevelt again altered cource, changing, as he put it, from "Dr. New Deal" to "Dr. Win the War."

Much as Bush still enjoys support from those who believe he can do no wrong, he now suffers opposition from liberals who believe he can do no right. Many of these liberals are in the awkward position of having supported Bush in the past, while offering little coherent as an alternative to Bush's policies now. Yet it is difficult to see how this will benefit Bush's reputation in history.

The president came to office calling himself "a uniter, not a divider" and promising to soften the acrimonious tone in Washington. He has had two enormous opportunities to fulfill those pledges: first, in the noisy aftermath of his controversial election in 2000, and, even more, after the attacks of September 11th, when the nation pulled behind him as it has supported no other president in living memory. Yet under both sets of historically unprecedented circumstances, Bush has chosen to act in ways that have left the country less united and more divided, less conciliatory and more acrimonious—much like James Buchanan, Andrew Johnson and Herbert Hoover before him. And, like those three predecessors, Bush has done so in the service of a rigid ideology that permits no deviation and refuses to adjust to changing realities. Buchanan failed the test of Southern secession, Johnson failed in the face of Reconstruction, and Hoover failed in the face of the Great Depression. Bush has failed to confront his own failures in both domestic and international affairs, above all in his ill-conceived responses to radical Islamic terrorism. Having confused steely resolve with what Ralph Waldo Emerson called "a foolish consistency . . . adored by little statesmen," Bush has become entangled in tragedies of his own making, compounding those visited upon the country by outside forces.

No historian can responsibly predict the future with absolute certainty. There are too many imponderables still to come in the two and a half years left in Bush's presidency to know exactly how it will look in 2009, let alone in 2059. There have been presidents—Harry Truman was one—who have left office in seeming disgrace, only to rebound in the estimates of later scholars. But so far the facts are not shaping up propitiously for George W. Bush. He still does his best to deny it. Having waved away the lessons of history in the making of his decisions, the present-minded Bush doesn't seem to be concerned about his place in history. "History. We won't know," he told the journalist Bob Woodward in 2003. "We'll all be dead."

Another president once explained that the judgments of history cannot be defied or dismissed, even by a president. "Fellow citizens, *we* cannot escape history," said Abraham Lincoln. "We of this Congress and this administration, will be remembered in spite of ourselves. No personal significance, or insignificance, can spare one or another of us. The fiery trial through which we pass, will light us down, in honor or dishonor, to the latest generation."

Conrad Black  **NO**

George W. Bush, FDR, and History

The American, and to an extent the international media, many rubbing their eyes with disbelief, are starting to contemplate the possibility that George W. Bush may be a president of great historical significance. Disparaged by opponents as an accidental president, or even the beneficiary of a stolen election, and regarded even by many of his supporters as a man of insufficient intellect for his office, the ambitions he has revealed for his second term have prompted comparisons (in the *Financial Times* and elsewhere) with Franklin D. Roosevelt, who, the President says, "fascinates" him.

These comparisons with FDR are overdone. Unlike Roosevelt, George W. Bush did not enter office with unemployment at 33 percent, a collapsed banking system and farm prices, nearly half the homes in the country threatened by foreclosure and eviction. Nor will he likely have to face any such prospect as a Nazi takeover of Europe. He is unlikely to have to lead the nation to victory in the greatest war in history, and he doesn't have to conduct his office from a wheelchair, while disguising from the public the extent of his infirmity.

Some Republican traditionalists and liberal alarmists have invoked Roosevelt by predicting that Bush will now try to undo what is left of the New Deal. There is no truth in this, unless he succumbs to second term dementia and tries to abolish the FDIC guarantee of bank deposits, and to restore Prohibition.

President Bush was obliged to focus on foreign crises in his first term, and is moving to domestic reform in his second. Roosevelt dealt with the economic emergency in his first year, structural reforms such as Social Security in his second year, cranked up his workfare programs as required for the next three years, eliminated remaining unemployment with defense production and conscription in the two years before Pearl Harbor, and concluded the New Deal with the GI Bill of Rights in 1944. Prior to World War II, there wasn't much American foreign policy.

Roosevelt did say in the 1940 election campaign that "we are going to build a country in which no one is left out," but there is no evidence that President Bush thought he was paraphrasing him when he took up the same theme. President Bush has neither the regal bearing, nor the oratorical powers, nor the protean qualities of FDR.

From *The American Spectator*, April 2005, pp. 26–30, 32–33. Copyright © 2005 by American Spectator, LLC. Reprinted by permission.

Yet, with a completely different style and timetable, George W. Bush could come closer to replicating FDR's importance as both a foreign and domestic policy president than all Roosevelt's other successors in that office.

✦

Electoral facts invite a reassessment by those who did not take the president seriously before. Bill Clinton and George W. Bush are the first successive presidents of opposing parties to win two consecutive terms in American history, and the first consecutive two-term presidents since Madison and Monroe (1809–1825). The President is only the sixteenth of 42 holders of that office to win two terms, the fifteenth to win two consecutive terms, the thirteenth to win two consecutive contested terms, and, if he serves out this term in good health, he will be only the sixth president since the emergence of the modern party and electoral system (in the Jackson era) to do so. Of his five predecessors in this category, only U. S. Grant and Franklin D. Roosevelt led parties that controlled both houses of Congress in their second terms. Grant, though he rendered immense service to the country, was a largely ineffectual president. Hence the frequent current comparisons with FDR.

Incredulous media commentators endlessly repeat that George W. Bush's poll ratings are ten points below those of Ronald Reagan and Bill Clinton when they started their second terms. (They are also 20 percent below Roosevelt's when he began his third term.) This isn't really relevant. Bush and his advisers have mastered the technique of concentrating adequate political force at strategic legislative points. In the 2004 election they brought out conservative voters by putting referenda on the emotive issue of same-sex marriage on ballots in eleven states, eliciting the margin of victory in a number of those states. Bush is adequately, though not overwhelmingly, popular, but he is overwhelmingly tactically agile.

Reagan's and Clinton's partisans did not control both houses of Congress when they were re-elected. Neither did the Republicans when Dwight D. Eisenhower and Richard Nixon won landslide reelection victories. There is more of a comparison with Lyndon Johnson when he won a crushing victory in 1964 to a full term after succeeding the assassinated John F. Kennedy. President Johnson did have an ambitious program and a friendly Congress, and great legislative aptitudes, but most of his Great Society program, apart from his immense contribution to civil rights, has been a debatable legacy.

LBJ's term swiftly became mired in Vietnam. Some Democrats and media skeptics have tried to claim that the same fate awaits President Bush, but this is nonsense. Congress has fully authorized the action in Iraq, which it did not in Vietnam, the forces committed are scarcely a quarter of those at their highest point in Vietnam, and the American casualty rates are at less than 5 percent of the Vietnam level through most of that war. Despite the impositions on the National Guard, this is still essentially a volunteer military; the enemy is not being fed by overt foreign intervention on the lines of the North Vietnamese, nor by great power suppliers, as the Soviets and Chinese stoked up the enemy in Vietnam. Where Ho Chi Minh was a widely respected figure, almost no one disputes that the world is better off without Saddam Hussein, and the Iraqi election is an unanswerable legitimization of the efforts to promote power-sharing and reasonable wealth-distribution in the Middle East.

The debate over weapons of mass destruction, like the arguments that the United States should first have tracked down Osama bin Laden or secured a permanent resolution of the Israeli-Palestinian dispute before removing Saddam, was a side-show (and pretexts for doing nothing). George W. Bush prevented the United Nations, against the wishes of its own secretary general and most of the corrupt despotisms that compose much of its membership, from becoming a toothless talking society like the League of Nations, as he promised in 2003 to the General Assembly that he would (after Saddam had ignored 17 Security Council resolutions).

More importantly, he has discovered and proclaimed the only method of reversing 13 centuries of retreat by the Arab world. Though most Arabs would not spontaneously put it this way, Arab power and influence have been in retreat since the defeat of the Moors at the Battle of Tours (or Poitiers) in 732. The Arab armies were driven out of France and slowly expelled from Europe, and almost all the Arabs were eventually colonized. To conventional modern Arab opinion, their final humiliation was the establishment of the State of Israel in what Arabs claim to be Arab land, as an apparent consolation by the Great Powers for the crimes the Jews had suffered in Europe in the 1930s and '40s. The existence of Israel has been a hairshirt for the Arabs for nearly 60 years, the ultimate, constant demonstration of their enfeeblement.

If Iraq develops some plausible institutions of power-sharing and popular consultation and wealth distribution, even stopping well short of the highest standards of electoral and social democracy in the West, it will give the Arab masses a model for government that they will eventually judge to be preferable to the tyrannies in the major Arab powers that oppress their peoples, steal and squander their money, and distract them with what should be the red herring of Israel.

There were certainly some serious intelligence shortcomings before September 11, 2001, and before the invasion of Iraq. There were also costly mistakes in the early occupation phase. But these are overshadowed by the potential benefit of a reformed Iraq.

The congratulations on the Iraqi election from the president of Egypt and the head of the Arab League; the virtual Thatcherization of the Egyptian economy and Hosni Mubarak's promise of "freer" elections, the cross-community reconciliations in Lebanon in defiance of the Syrians despite the recent assassination of the leading advocate of conciliation, the self-redemption of Qaddafi, and the emergence among the Palestinians of an authentically elected leadership that is apparently prepared to discourage terrorism and seek a two-state permanent agreement with Israel, are all, at least in part, early manifestations of the impact of the Bush policy.

This is the rationale for the nation-building effort in Iraq, and the only possible method of eliminating the danger of endless Muslim, and especially Arab Muslim, disaffection on a scale that could be a menace to the whole world. If successful, this will be as great a strategic achievement as any

American president's except for Lincoln's victory in the Civil War, Franklin Roosevelt's contribution to victory in World War II and his engagement of the United States durably in Europe and the Far East, and Harry Truman's championship of NATO and the Marshall Plan, and his resistance to communism in Korea and Greece and Turkey. It would rank with Richard Nixon's normalization of relations with China and pursuit of nuclear arms limitations with the Soviet Union; and with Ronald Reagan's ultimate bloodless victory in the Cold War. (The Louisiana Purchase was also an epochal event, but the United States would eventually have seized that territory if Napoleon had not sold it to Jefferson.) This would put the current President in far more distinguished company than his detractors could imagine with any equanimity.

⋅⟨◉⟩⋅

The President's detractors are fond of claiming that he doesn't understand all these issues. But he has sketched out his motives much more clearly than Franklin D. Roosevelt described his plans, even to intimates, for assuring the defeat of the Berlin-Tokyo Axis in the world and the isolationists at home, and the renaissance of France, Germany, Italy, and Japan as democratic allies of the Americans and British. Roosevelt has justly received the credit for that inspired policy. President Bush cannot be denied the credit and responsibility for his ambitious plan to reorient the Arab world.

He has already had an immense success in discouraging terrorism. The tepid responses of the Clinton administration to the Kobar Towers, USS *Cole*, and Nairobi and Dar es Salaam embassy bombings invited the escalation that climaxed on September 11, 2001. The Bush administration should have been better prepared than it was for the assault. But since then, despite the belligerent videos of bin Laden and others, the terrorists managed only a few incidents, serious though the attacks in Madrid and Bali, in particular, were. There have been no further attacks on the United States. The cumulative effects of the international terror campaign have not amounted to 15 percent of the human devastation of 9/11/01. At the same time, thousands of terrorists and of their more promising recruits have been killed or captured. Large numbers of them have been attracted to Iraq and eliminated there, and their methods have been thoroughly discredited. No government in the world would now openly promote or assist terrorism in the way Afghanistan, Iraq, Yemen, Syria, Iran, and some other countries had been routinely doing prior to the President's response to the World Trade Center and Pentagon outrages.

The President and his advisers recognized that much of the professed solidarity with America after the 9/11 attacks was an attempt by fundamentally irresolute governments to gain leverage on the American official response to the attacks. There was also, behind the genuine sadness of all civilized people at the murder of thousands of innocent civilians, and the general respect for the bravery of New York's firemen and for the spirit of that city generally, an unspoken consolability at the novel thought of America as a victim. The President made it clear on the evening of the attacks that the United States would not remain a victim for long, that it would make no distinction between terrorists and countries that harbored or assisted terrorists, and that other governments would be judged by their conduct, as for or against the United States.

Though these positions could have been more subtly implemented at times, especially with traditional allies, they were the right policy. Anything less would have yielded to the collegiality sought by the rest of the world: that the United States is like a great St. Bernard that will do the work and take the risks, while foreigners, especially Europeans, hold the leash and give the orders. There was an informal attempt to divide the anti-terrorist world between the wronged country which had the power to resolve the problem by imposition of its military might, and the more "moderate" allies, who substituted moral shilly-shallying and even spitefulness for the strength they did not possess (because of their own lassitude and not a lack of resources).

Modern American foreign and security policy was established by President Roosevelt in 1941 in two speeches to the Congress. In January of that year, he warned that the country "must always be wary of those who with 'sounding brass and tinkling cymbal' would preach the 'ism' of appeasement." In December, in calling for a declaration of war after the attack on Pearl Harbor, he promised that the nation would "make very certain that this form of treachery never again endangers us." Ever since, the United States has not been an appeasement power and it has possessed and deployed sufficient deterrent strength to assure that no other state overtly attacked it.

On September 11, 2001, elements that thought they had found a way around American deterrence directly attacked the American civil population for the first time in history (other than, in hindsight, the first attack on the World Trade Center in 1993). Nothing less than President Bush's immediate and continuing response was necessary for the retention of the strength of American deterrence, which administrations of both parties have maintained for 60 years. No other country remotely possesses such deterrent capacity, and no ally, no matter how genuine, could be relied upon to advocate what was necessary to uphold this cornerstone of American national security.

Franklin D. Roosevelt, behind the façade of the United Nations, sought and achieved an imbalance of power in favor of the United States. The Soviet Union managed a serious military and subversive (and even in some misguided circles, intellectual) threat for 45 years before collapsing under the weight of the competition. The imbalance of power in America's favor that Roosevelt sought now exists and cannot be disguised. Many governments and intelligent people in the world are uncomfortable with American preeminence. But instead of reviling President Bush, they shall either have to accommodate to America's position, as Tony Blair does, or develop the strength and coherence to earn a greater voice in the world, as the Chinese seem to be trying to do.

The effort of the French and Germans and Russians to stand on each others' shoulders and obstruct the United States' Iraq policy, in the name of misplaced self-righteousness, was contemptible, and Bush was right to respond to it accordingly. And now he is right to mend his fences with those countries, having made his point that America will not compromise where its own security is at stake.

If this had been George W. Bush's only major foreign policy accomplishment, it would have been an entitlement to a serious position among foreign policy presidents. Assisting the Arab world to slough its tendency to corruption, despotism, and political failure; to evolve from a source of instability in the world to a justified recovery of the pride of an ancient people with a once-distinguished history, will, if he is successful, make him an outstanding foreign policy president.

⋞◉⋟

In domestic policy, the President has defeated what had threatened to become a severe recession, introduced tax cuts as important as those of Coolidge, Kennedy-Johnson, or Reagan and launched the most comprehensive educational reform in decades. He has pledged to overhaul, partially privatize, and preemptively rescue Social Security from actuarial problems, and make medical care more accessible and efficient, partly through tort reform. If he is largely successful in achieving his domestic goals, Bush would be, next to FDR, the most important domestic policy president in the country's history (excluding Lincoln's conduct of the Civil War, which does not meet normal criteria for domestic policy).

President Truman had limited success and not a great deal of originality in domestic affairs. President Nixon had more success than his legions of frenzied enemies concede, but his record was obscured and durably diminished by the Watergate debacle, even allowing for the subsidence of cant and emotionalism he attracted over much of his career. President Reagan's domestic achievements consisted mainly of his tax cuts and simplifications, the economic boom, and his genius for inspiriting the nation after Vietnam, Watergate, and the dreariness of the Carter interregnum.

The other presidents of living memory, even so elegant a leader as John F. Kennedy, so revered a president as Dwight D. Eisenhower, the obviously very able Bill Clinton, and this president's own father, were, in domestic policy terms, more or less capable caretakers. The great achievements of the Clinton administration—apart from good fiscal order, which didn't require tax increases on the scale of those that he inflicted—such as welfare reform and the Crime Bill, were largely the work of the Republican leaders in the Congress.

Theodore Roosevelt's domestic claim to greatness consists of a bout of trust-busting, and heightened railway regulation, meat-packing, and food and drug labeling legislation, and hortatory encouragements to conservation. Woodrow Wilson's rests on the Federal Reserve Act, the Clayton Anti-Trust Act, and the establishment of the Federal Trade Commission. Andrew Jackson is remembered for promoting federal government assistance to public works and suppressing secessionism, as well as decentralizing banking (causing a severe recession that swamped his hand-chosen successor). These are all significant, and TR and Wilson and Jackson were all important presidents, but George W. Bush is well placed to surpass them in the significance of his legislation.

No one expects that President Bush will easily enact his imaginative proposals for Social Security, Medicare, tort reform, durable tax reduction and simplification, and education. The partisan antagonism in the Congress is severe. But though the Republicans have only slender majorities in both houses and their party discipline is not infallible, the President is stirring public desire for action on these issues. The President has the initiative over the dazed and listless Democrats. He will have to make some concessions, but it is a reasonable supposition that he will achieve a large part of what he seeks. Even if he does not, his historical claims will rest on his foreign policy record, his tax reductions, and his education reforms. This would still be a defensible performance that would bear comparison with most of his predecessors.

His fiscal policy remains fuzzy and his pledge of spending and deficit reductions is not entirely plausible. A $650 billion current account deficit is obviously intolerable. It is not quite as grim as it appears, because about a third of it is foreign operations of American companies selling back into the United States to the ultimate profit of American shareholders. A legitimate modernization of calculation methods would deal with this. Another third is excessive oil prices and imports. This could at least be moderated by pursuing exploration and alternate energy sources more aggressively and by selling infrastructure to more consensually governed oil-exporting countries, starting with Iraq. Most of the rest of the current account deficit is effectively dumping, especially by the Chinese. This too can be combated, as some Democrats are already demanding. But it will require subtlety and perseverance to do it without provoking serious economic and strategic friction, so addicted have China and some other countries become to their ability to export on a massive and exploitive scale to the United States. Waiting for the development of an electric automobile is not an adequate response to the trade deficit.

Bush's Treasury secretaries have not had the weight of such recent holders of that office as John Connolly, George Shultz, William Simon, James Baker, Lloyd Bentsen, and Robert Rubin. He never should have signed Sarbanes-Oxley, which mires all public companies in an almost impenetrable thicket of compliance rules (see Robert L. Bartley, "No Profit: The Craze to Reform Corporate Accounting Gets Things Exactly Backward," *TAS*, December 2003-January 2004). And in addition to taking credit in his State of the Union message for prosecuting corporate criminals, the President should also discourage the arraignment of the entire corporate executive class of the country as embezzlers by his enemies in the media and overzealous prosecutors. There are now signs that this onslaught of what at times approached corporate McCarthyism is subsiding.

⚜

The group of so-called value issues represents core beliefs certainly, but they are also rallying points to the President's natural supporters on specific issues, as with the same-sex marriage question. Where Bill Clinton confused the Republicans by stealing certain natural Republican issues, as in adding 100,000 policemen, George W. Bush presses the seven values buttons to produce irresistible support for measures only slightly related to the values invoked.

President Bush could not seriously imagine that he will get a constitutional amendment about the nature of marriage, any more than Ronald Reagan thought he would get one about abortion or school prayer. That he wishes a distinction between marriage and a homosexual union of equivalent legal standing is reasonable. The stem-cell research controversy is a harder sell. The moral issues this leads to are serious and troubling, but the scientific possibilities for longer and healthier lives may not be met by his present position. Some fine-tuning should be possible and sincere Christians should be able to accept the sort of research advocated by Ronald Reagan Jr. at last year's Democratic convention.

Complaints about Bush's excessive religiosity are hard to take seriously. Franklin D. Roosevelt referred to God so often that Molotov asked Averell Harriman how an intelligent man could be so preoccupied with religion. In his first Inaugural Address he said: "Our problems, thank God, concern only material things." All his major speeches had some reference to God in them and his address on D-Day, one of the greatest of his career, was ostensibly a prayer. Dwight Eisenhower, unlike Roosevelt, was not a particularly religious man, but he began his first Inaugural Address with a prayer. Ronald Reagan wasn't a great publicly observant religious communicant either, but he began his acceptance speech of his first presidential nomination with a minute of silence in prayer for the country. All presidents bandy God about. The tastefulness of doing so is open to legitimate discussion, but the incumbent should not be unfairly singled out.

At a strictly tactical level, when the United States' most visible foreign enemy is a group of fanatical Muslim terrorists and terrorist-sponsors, it is helpful to make the point that America is not only a center of commercialization, glitz, permissiveness, and self-indulgence. The world should know that it is also a brave country that acts on belief, including a variety of widely and strongly held religious beliefs, and that the bin Laden theory that it is soft, decadent, and cowardly is a dangerous misperception.

The United States had to overcome the political legacy of Vietnam, the Beirut bombing, and Mogadishu: that it had no staying power and could not endure the sight of body bags, no matter what the cause. Every American death in Iraq is a great sadness (that much of the media mawkishly amplifies), but each is also a sacrifice in a noble cause and a reaffirmation of American moral strength. There is little evidence that the President is pandering more than rhetorically to the religious right, in judicial appointments or otherwise. To be a traditionalist is not to be a toady to a faction.

George W. Bush does not have the heroic qualities of Andrew Jackson, drummer-boy in the Revolutionary war, victorious general, champion of the frontier and of the Common Man. He has none of the panache or urbanity of the Roosevelts, the intellect or articulation of Woodrow Wilson. He does not possess the hypnotic oratorical powers or (as far as we know) the human qualities of Ronald Reagan that enabled him, with a bullet in his chest and a collapsed lung, to stroll into the hospital operating room and say that he hoped the assembled doctors and nurses were all Republicans. I doubt that even Karl Rove, brilliant political operator though he undoubtedly is, would claim that President Bush has the prepossessing personal stature of Lincoln, Washington, or Jefferson.

If he has a precedent, it could be James Knox Polk, who was rather colorless and somewhat overshadowed by such contemporaries as Henry Clay, Daniel Webster, and John C. Calhoun. But as president, he settled relations with Britain, especially the northern border, won the Mexican war, adding Texas, California, and New Mexico to the country, reduced tariffs, and restored an independent treasury system. Polk is generally reckoned by historians to be one of the country's ten best presidents. Everything is to scale. These are much more complicated times, the United States is an unprecedentedly formidable world power, and George W., unlike Polk (who did not seek re-election), is a two-term president.

The substantial achievement of his foreign and domestic objectives would install George W. Bush as the most important president since FDR, and, except for FDR, possibly the most important president since Lincoln. What he and his advisers recognize, even if most of the media do not, is that he can be a great president by concentrating his great tactical political ability on specific ambitious goals. The general perception of him may continue to lag his objective accomplishments, for a time. This doesn't affect a president's performance or historical standing and has been the lot of many other presidents, including Truman, Eisenhower, and Nixon.

At the mid-point in his administration, George W. Bush has been a successful president. He has indisputable aptitudes for leadership, unquestionable courage and integrity, and a chance to be one of America's great leaders. All who wish America and its enduring values well, should wish him well, including millions of people in the United States and throughout the world who now profess to dislike, disparage, or fear him.

POSTSCRIPT

Is George W. Bush the Worst President in American History?

Conrad Black, a well-to-do conservative publisher, recently wrote a massive and surprisingly favorable biography of *Franklin Delano Roosevelt: Champion of Freedom* (Public Affair, 2003). In the article reprinted in this reader, he argues that President George W. Bush is "the most important president since FDR, and except for FDR, possibly the most important president since Lincoln." This is high praise for a president whose public polling ratings in the spring of 2006 are in the mid to low thirtieth percentile.

But Black takes the long view. He compares Bush's 9/11 response to the terrorist attacks on the World Trade Center's twin towers, in New York City to FDR's response to the isolationists and appeasers of Hitler and the Japanese before and after the Pearl Harbor attack on December 7, 1941. Like FDR, says Black, President Bush sought to take advantage of America's paramount position in the world by strengthening the enfeebled United Nations in his own response to the defiance by Saddam Hussein of the organizations' resolutions.

Black delivers a spirited defense of both foreign and domestic policies of the president. He defends nation-building in Iraq arguing rather nastily "that Arab power and influence have been in retreat with the exception of Israel since the defeat of the Moors at the Battle of Tours in 732." He also argues that the president's tax cut, and his attempts to overhaul Social Security, reform Medicare, and engage in a comprehensive "no child left behind" education reform will surpass the domestic achievements of all other twentieth-century presidents, with the exception of FDR.

Contrary to his critics on the left, Black downplays Bush's right-wing agenda arguing that he does not want to undo the New Deal, he appoints conservatives and not religious zealots to office and uses "values" issues to rally his supporters. Furthermore, Bush's religious views are no different from that of previous presidents, especially FDR who invoked God's name on innumerable occasions.

Professor Wilentz believes that Bush will be ranked among the lowest presidents long after he leaves office. Instead of comparing him with FDR and Lincoln as Black does, Wilentz compares Bush's failures to those of Buchanan who failed to stop the Southern secession from the union, of Andrew Johnson, who made a debacle of Reconstruction and of Hoover who was inflexible in his responses to the Great Depression. Both author compare Bush with the reticent Polk, with Black crediting him for successful expansionist acquisitions in the Southwest after the Mexican War.

Wilentz believes that President Bush has abused the power of the presidency with policies that permit the torture of detainees and the wiretapping

433

of phone calls by the National Security Agency (NSA) without obtaining a court order. He also argues that he is waging "an unlimited war" on terror and refuses to follow Lincoln's example of consulting dissenting opinions from his cabinet. Bush, he argues, never consulted with the Democratic leadership and shut down dissenting voices of military generals like retired General Andrew Zunni, General Eric Shinseki, and his own father's National Security Chief Brent Scocroft, who pointed out potential problems in rebuilding Iraq once Hussein was overthrown.

Wilentz also sees President Bush as much more radical in his religious views than Black. Not even FDR ever said, as Bush has, that he was ordained by God to lead the country. Bush's positions on stem-cell research, global population control, intelligent design as replacement for evolution, the Terri Shiavo fiasco, and his appointments to the federal bench appear to be more than a mere nod and a wink to the Christian right. For a critical view of Bush's religious views, see Peter Singer, *The President of Good and Evil: the Ethics of George W. Bush* (Dutton, 2004). But Stephen Mansfield defends *The Faith of George W. Bush* (Penguin Group, Inc., 2003).

Where Black and Wilentz differ the most is on the consequences of Bush's economic policies. Conservatives like Black see the tax cuts as a stimulus and the deficits a matter of correcting the bookkeeping methods. Wilentz believes that Bush has geared tax cuts to the richest while real wages for middle-income Americans have been dropping since the end of 2003. In short, Bush took a Clinton surplus and raised "the federal deficits to staggering record levels."

Will the indictment of Dick Cheney's Chief of Staff Lewis "Scooter" Libby for a security breach in outing a CIA agent or the intrigues of convicted lobbyist Jack Abramoff with prominent Republicans tarnish the Bush administration in the verdict of history? Will the lowest sustained polls in history for an incumbent president matter? Or is President Bush correct when he responded to reporter Bob Woodward about his historical reputation? "History," Bush said, "we won't know. We'll all be dead."

The bibliography on the American presidency is enormous. The renowned diplomatic historian Thomas A. Bailey's older *Presidential Greatness: The Image and the Man from George Washington to the Present* (Appleton-Century, 1966) discusses the political biases in the Schlesinger surveys, the importance of fortuities, temperament, personalities, as well as the roles of the presidency. Bailey also gives his summary reassessments from George Washington through Lyndon Johnson. Lewis L. Gould argues that *The Modern American Presidency* (University Press of Kansas, 2003) began in the McKinley administration whose presidential secretary George Cortelyou made the administration of the office more efficient in dealing with reporters and issues that needed immediate action. In *The American Presidency: an Intellectual History* (University Press of Kansas, 1994), conservative historian Forrest McDonald concentrates on the eighteenth- and nineteenth-century roots and establishment of the presidency before deploring its institutional decline by the late twentieth century. Liberal pundit Eric Altman also deplores the lies told during the Yalta Conference, the Cuban Missile Crisis, the Gulf of Tonkin incidents, the Iran-Contra scandal, and George W. Bush's "post-truth" presidency in *When Presidents Lie: a History of Official Deception and Its Consequences* (Viking, 2004). A more balanced approach in line with Bailey's book is Max J. Skidmore, *Presidential Performance; a Comprehensive Review* (McFarland & Co., 2004) whose introduction contains footnotes of all the major polls but questions the validity of presidential rankings. Skidmore's sketches of each president are similar to those found in other collections written by top-notch historians. Two of the best are Alan Brinkley and Davis Dyer, eds., *Readers Companion to the American Presidency* (Houghton Mifflin, 2000) and Melvin I. Urofsky, ed., *The American Presidents* (Garland Publishing Group, 2000).

The presidential ratings game began in 1948 when Arthur Schlesinger, Sr., polled 55 prominent historians for *Life Magazine*, updated in 1962 with a second poll for *The New York Times Magazine*, followed in 1996 for the same magazine by his son Arthur Schlesinger, Jr. In between, at least a half dozen other polls have been conducted by historians, political scientists, and journalists. What is interesting about these polls is the agreement that Lincoln, Washington, and FDR are America's three greatest presidents.

Conservative critics complain that the criteria are biased toward activist presidents who pursued an assertive domestic program and an internationalist foreign policy with FDR as the role model. The discrepancies in the ratings are best seen in the table below, which compares the liberal historians surveyed by Schlesinger, Jr., in 1996, with the results from the conservative Intercollegiate Studies Institute from 1997. Most controversial in the Schlesinger poll is the ranking of Carter ahead of Reagan, a conservative icon as witnessed by the endless memorial services when he died in June 1994.

Table 1

Discrepancies in Ratings

President	Schlesinger 1996	ISI 1997
Clinton	low average	failure
Reagan	low average	near great
Carter	low average	failure
Nixon	failure	below average
Johnson	high average	failure
Kennedy	high average	below average
Eisenhower	high average	near great

The presidential ratings game is rightly criticized for its liberal and conservative biases, its questionable classification schemes by some political scientists and psychologists, and the inability to locate some of the presidents in the context of their times.

The best summary of bibliography and articles from the 1999 conference at Hofstra University on the rankings of presidents in "Special Issue: the

Uses and Abuses of Presidential Ratings," *White House Studies,* Volume 3, Number 1, 2003, a journal edited by Professor Robert P. Watson of Florida Atlantic University.

An interesting sidebar but relevant to this issue is Nathan Miller's *Star-Spangled Men: America's Ten Worse Presidents* (Scribner, 1998). Miller's top-ten list, like late-night host David Letterman's, includes from the bottom to the top—Carter, Taft, Harrison, Coolidge, Grant, A. Johnson, Pierce, Buchanan, Harding, and Nixon. This list is similar to the below average and failure of the other presidential polls with the exception of John Tyler who is credited with the annexation of Texas and Millard Filmore who helped form the Compromise of 1850, which forestalled the Civil War for a decade.

Most likely, President Bush's reputation will rise and fall with the way the nation-building experiment works out in Iraq. Books that defend America's informal empire include British historian Niall Ferguson, *Colossus: the Price of America's Empire* (Penguin Press, 2004) and conservative journalist Max Boot, *The Savage Wars of Peace: Small Wars and the Rise of American Power* (Basic Books, 2002). Both have written numerous articles summarizing their views. See Niall Ferguson, "The Empire Slinks Back: Why Americans don't really have what it takes to rule the world," *The New York Times Magazine* (April 27, 2003) and Max Boot, "Guess What? We're Winning [In Iraq]" *The American Interest* (Spring 2006). *Washington Times* senior White House correspondent Bill Salmon is a defendant of the president's policies in *Fighting Back: The War on Terrorism from Inside the Bush White House* (Regnery, 2002) and *Misunderestimated: the President Battles Terrorism, John Kerry and the Bush Haters* (Regan Books, 2004). Finally, Stephen Hayes tries to make the case for links between Al Qaeda and Iraq in "Case Closed," *The Weekly Standard*, November 24, 2003, though most commentators argue against this.

The bibliography about an incumbent president is very incomplete and continuous. The earliest assessments are highly partisan pro and con and are written by political scientists, journalists, and second-tier policymakers. Important assessments from cabinet officials and high-level policymakers such as Condoleeza Rice, Colin Powell, Vice President Richard Cheney, Donald Rumsfeld, and close confidant Karl Rowe will be written shortly after President Bush leaves office. Hopefully scholars will have access to the president's official papers once a presidential library is established at a major Texas university. Three of the earliest memoirs are negative. Paul O'Neill (with *New York Times* writer for Susskind), Bush's secretary of the treasury, criticizes the president's indifference to economic policy in *The Price of Loyalty* (Simon & Schuster, 2004), a complaint more recently aired by the conservative Bruce Bartlett, *Imposter: How George W. Bush Bankrupted America and Betrayed the Regan Legacy* (Doubleday, 2006), which cost him his job as a policy analyst at a conservative think tank in Dallas. Richard Clarke, the former counterterrorism czar for both Bill Clinton and George W. Bush, argues that the current president "squandered the opportunity to eliminate Al Qaeda," which "has emerged and is growing stronger in part because of our actions and inactions," see *Against All Odds: Inside America's War on Terror* (Simon & Schuster, 2004). More favorable but still critical is David Frum, *The*

Right Man: the Surprise Presidency of George Bush (Random House, 2003), a former White House aide.

Freelance *Washington Post* writer Bob Woodward, the man who with his partner Carl Bernstein broke the Watergate scandal, now gets Washington policymakers to spill their guts. *Bush at War* (Simon & Schuster, 2002) and *Plan of Attack* (Simon & Schuster, 2004) is based upon lengthy interviews with top officials including President Bush. Primary source documents can be accessed on the Internet sources listed in the part 3 opener. Two important documents are the December 2002, "U.S. National Security: A New Era," which spells out the preemption policy and National Security Council (November, 2005), "National Strategy for Victory in Iraq."

Most of the information about current politics can be gleaned from the newspapers, magazines, radio, television, and the Internet. On the liberal side are *The Washington Post, The Los Angeles Times, The Nation, The Progressive, Mother Jones, The New Republic* (increasingly less liberal), and the articles by Sy Hersh on the Washington policymakers and John Anderson on Iraq in *The New Yorker*. Conservatives also control the *Washington Times*, the editorial pages of *The Wall Street Journal, The Weekly Standard, National Review, Commentary*, and *The* (neo-isolationist) *American Conservative*. Conservatives dominate AM talk radio led by hosts Rush Limbaugh, Sean Hannity, and former White House aide and felon G. Gordon Liddy. The liberal *Air America* station struggles with a much smaller but devoted audience. Conservatives also dominate the cable news market with Ruppert Murdoch's "fair and balanced" *Fox* network. Mainstream journalism (criticized as biased by both liberals and conservatives) include *The New York Times, Time, Newsweek, U.S. News and World Report, USA Today*, cable news networks (CNN, CNBC, MSNBC), and the three major networks ABC, NBC, and CBS (Dan Rather notwithstanding).

Bush's case for preemption as a strategy of the neoconservatives is critiqued in a number of books. The fullest and most critical account is *Washington Post* reporter James Mann, *The Rise of the Vulcans: The History of Bush's War Cabinet* (Penguin Books, 2004). John B. Judis takes on nation-building in *The Folly of Empire: What George W. Bush Could Learn from Theodore Roosevelt and Woodrow Wilson* (Oxford University Press, 2004). A good summary of Judis's argument is "Imperial America," *Foreign Policy* (July/August, 2004).

Bush's military strategy has also taken some heavy hits. James Risen, "Captives Deny Qaeda worked with Bagdad," *The New York Times* (June 9, 2003); Seymour Hersh, "Selective Intelligence," *The New Yorker* (May 12, 2003); and Michael Isikoff and Mark Hosenball's response to Stephen Hayes, "Case Decidedly Not Closed," *Newsweek Web Exclusive*, November 19, 2003. *New York Times'* military correspondent Michael R. Gordon and retired General Bernard E. Trainor have followed up their critique of *The Generals War: the Inside Story of the (first) Conflict in the Gulf* (Little, Brown, 1995) with *Cobra II: the Inside Story of the Invasion and Occupation of Iraq* (Pantheon, 2006), a detailed critique of how both sides planned and fought the war.

Fred Greenstein has edited *The George W. Bush Presidency: an Early Assessment* (Johns Hopkins University Press, 2003). Jon Kraus, et al., have also edited *Transformed by Crisis: the Presidency of George W. Bush and American*

Politics (Palgrave MacMillan, 2004). Extremely useful is Ivo H. Daulder and James M. Lindsay, *America Unbound: the Bush Revolution in Foreign Policy, Revised and Updated* (Wiley, 2005), which makes the Bush foreign policy understandable to its supporters and critics.

A wide-ranging analysis with historical analogies similar to the works of Niall Ferguson are two books by Kevin Phillips, *American Dynasty: Aristocracy, Fortune, and the Politics of Deceit in the House of Bush* (Viking, 2004) and *American Theocracy: The Peril and Politics of Radical Religion, Oil and Borrowed Money in the 21st Century* (Viking, 2006) whose titles say it all. More temperate and favorable to the president is John Lewis Gaddis's *Surprise Security and the American Experience* (Harvard University Press, 2004), which traces Bush's policies of "preemption," "unilateralism," and "isolationism" back to the policies of John Quincy Adams, Andrew Jackson, and James K. Polk. Gaddis comes in for criticism in his discussion with Paul Kennedy in *The New York Times Book Review* (July 25, 2004), page 23, and also by Andrew J. Rotter, et al., in "John Gaddis's *Surprise, Security and the American Experience: A Roundtable Critique," Passport: the Newsletter of the Society for Historians of American Foreign Relations* 36/2 (August, 2005). Gaddis modified his support for Bush's policies suggesting in "Grand Strategy in the Second Term," *Foreign Affairs* (January/February 2005), that the president should speak more softly and obtain international help in restoring security in a more dangerous world.

Contributors to This Volume

EDITORS

LARRY MADARAS is a professor of history and political science at Howard Community College in Columbia, Maryland. He received a B.A. from the College of the Holy Cross in 1959 and an M.A. and a Ph.D. from New York University in 1961 and 1964, respectively. He has also taught at Spring Hill College, the University of South Alabama, and the University of Maryland at College Park. He has been a Fulbright Fellow and has held two fellowships from the National Endowment for the Humanities. He is the author of dozens of journal articles and book reviews.

JAMES M. SoRELLE is a professor of history and former chair of the Department of History at Baylor University in Waco, Texas. He received a B.A. and M.A. from the University of Houston in 1972 and 1974, respectively, and a Ph.D. from Kent State University in 1980. In addition to introductory courses in United States and world history, he teaches upper-level sections in African American, urban, and late nineteenth- and twentieth-century U.S. history and a graduate seminar on the civil rights movement. His scholarly articles have appeared in the *Houston Review, Southwestern Historical Quarterly,* and *Black Dixie: Essays in Afro-Texan History and Culture in Houston* (Texas A&M University Press, 1992), edited by Howard Beeth and Cary D. Wintz. He also has contributed entries to *The Handbook of Texas, The Oxford Companion to Politics of the World,* and *Encyclopedia of the Confederacy.*

STAFF

Larry Loeppke	Managing Editor
Jill Peter	Senior Developmental Editor
Susan Brusch	Senior Developmental Editor
Beth Kundert	Production Manager
Jane Mohr	Project Manager
Tara McDermott	Design Coordinator
Nancy Meissner	Editorial Assistant
Julie Keck	Senior Marketing Manager
Mary Klein	Marketing Communications Specialist
Alice Link	Marketing Coordinator
Tracie Kammerude	Senior Marketing Assistant
Lori Church	Pemissions Coordinator

AUTHORS

RICHARD M. ABRAMS is a professor of history at the University of California, Berkeley, where he has been teaching since 1961. He has been a Fulbright professor in both London and Moscow and has taught and lectured in many countries throughout the world, including China, Austria, Norway, Italy, Japan, Germany, and Australia. He has published numerous articles in history, business, and law journals, and he is the editor of *The Shaping of Twentieth Century America; Interpretative Essays*, 2nd ed. (Little, Brown, 1971) and the author of *The Burdens of Progress* (Scott, Foresman, 1978).

GARY DEAN BEST is a professor of history at the University of Hawaii in Hilo, Hawaii. He is a former fellow of the American Historical Association and of the National Endowment for the Humanities, and he was a Fulbright scholar in Japan from 1974 to 1975. His publications include *The Nickel and Dime Decade: American Popular Culture During the 1930s* (Praeger, 1933).

ROGER BILES is a professor in and chair of the history department at East Carolina University in Greenville, North Carolina. He is the author of *The South and the New Deal* (University Press of Kentucky, 1994) and *Richard J. Daly: Politics, Race, and the Governing of Chicago* (Northern Illinois Press, 1994).

CONRAD BLACK is a well-known publisher and author of the recent biography of *Franklin Delano Roosevelt: Champion of Freedom* (Public Affairs Press, 2003).

PATRICK J. BUCHANAN is a syndicated columnist and a founding member of three public affairs shows, *The McLaughlin Group*, the *Capital Gang*, and the *Crossfire*. He has served as senior adviser to three American presidents, ran twice for Republican nomination for president (1992 and 1996), and was the Reform Party's presidential candidate in 2000. He is the author of *A Republic, Not an Empire: Reclaiming America's Destiny* (Regnery, 1999).

JOHN C. BURNHAM teaches the history of American science at the Ohio State University and is the author of *Lester Frank Ward in American Thought and Psychoanalysis and American Medicine*.

RON CHERNOW, a graduate of Yale and Cambridge, won the National Book Award in 1990 for his first book, *The House of Morgan*, which the Modern Library cited as one of the hundred best nonfiction books of the twentieth century. His second book, *The Warburgs*, won the Eccles Prize as the best business book of 1993. His biography of John D. Rockefeller, *Titan*, was a national best seller and a National Book Critics Circle Award finalist. Both *Time* magazine and *The New York Times* listed it among the ten best books of 1998.

ALEXANDER B. CALLOW, JR., is a lecturer emeritus in American urban history at the University of California, Santa Barbara. He is the editor of *American Urban History: An Interpretative Reader with Commentaries*, 3rd ed. (Oxford University Press, 1982).

DANIEL DEUDNEY is an assistant professor in the Department of Political Science at the Johns Hopkins University in Baltimore, Maryland. He is the author of *Pax Atomica: Planetary Geopolitics and Republicanism* (Princeton University Press, 1993).

W.E.B. DU BOIS (1868–1963) was the most important African American intellectual of the twentieth century.

RICHARD M. FRIED is a professor at the University of Illinois at Chicago and the author of *The Russians are Coming! The Russians are Coming! Pageantry and Patriotism in Cold-War America* (Oxford University Press, 1998).

JOHN LEWIS GADDIS is the Robert A. Lovett Professor of History at Yale University in New Haven, Connecticut. He has also been Distinguished Professor of History at Ohio University, where he founded the Contemporary History Institute, and he has held visiting appointments at the United States Naval War College, the University of Helsinki, Princeton University, and Oxford University. He is the author of many books, including *We Now Know: Rethinking Cold War History* (Oxford University Press, 1997).

JACQUELYN DOWD HALL is the Julia Cherry Spruill Professor and director of the Southern Oral History Program at the University of North Carolina, Chapel Hill. Her research interests include U.S. women's history, southern history, working-class history, and biography. He has won a number of awards, including a Distinguished Teaching Award for graduate teaching. She is a coauthor of *Like a Family: The Making of a Southern Cotton Mill World* (University of North Carolina Press, 1987).

OSCAR HANDLIN was the Carl M. Loeb Professor of History at Harvard University in Cambridge, Massachusetts, where he has been teaching since 1941. A Pulitzer Prize–winning historian, he has written or edited more than 100 books, including *Liberty in Expansion* (Harper & Row, 1989), which he coauthored with Lilian Handlin, and *The Distortion of America*, 2nd ed. (Transaction Publishers, 1996).

LOUIS R. HARLIN is a Distinguished Professor of History Emeritus at the University of Maryland in College Park, Maryland. His publications include *Separate and Unequal: Public School Campaigns and Racism in the Southern Seaboard States, 1901–1915* (University of North Carolina Press, 1958) and *Booker T. Washington: The Wizard of Tuskegee* (Oxford University Press, 1983), which won the 1984 Pulitzer Prize for biography, the Bancroft Prize, and the Beveridge Prize.

TSUYOSHI HASEGAWA is professor of history and director of the Center for Cold War Studies at the University of California Santa Barbara.

JOHN EARL HAYNES is a twentieth-century political historian with the Library of Congress. He is coauthor, with Harvey Klehr and K. M. Anderson, of *The Soviet World of American Communism* (Yale University Press, 1998) and, with Harvey Klehr and Fridrikh I. Firsov, of *The Secret World of American Communism* (Yale University Press, 1996).

DAVID HEALY is a professor of history at the University of Wisconsin–Milwaukee and the author of several books and articles on U.S. relations in the Caribbean, including *Gunboat Diplomacy in the Wilson Era: The U.S. Navy in Haiti, 1915–1916* (University of Wisconsin–Madison, and he is currently working on a book about the Latin American policies of James G. Blaine.

LEO HERSKOWITZ is a professor of history at Queens College, City University of New York. His publications include *Courts and Law in Early New York: Selected Essays*, coedited with Milton M. Klein (Kennikat Press, 1978).

JOAN HOFF-WILSON is a professor of history at Indiana University in Bloomington, Indiana, and coeditor of the *Journal of Women's History*. She is a specialist in twentieth-century American foreign policy and politics and in the legal status of American women. She has received numerous awards, including the Berkshire Conference of Women Historians' Article Prize and the Stuart L. Bernath Prize for the best book on American diplomacy.

G. JOHN IKENBERRY, currently a Wilson Center Fellow, is a professor of political science at the University of Pennsylvania and a nonresident senior fellow at the Brookings Institution. He is the author of *After Victory: Institutions, Strategic Restraint and the Rebuilding of Order after Major Wars* (Princeton University Press, 2000) and *American Foreign Policy: Theoretical Essays*, 3rd ed. (Addison-Wesley Longman, 1998).

PETER IRONS is a well-known civil rights lawyer and scholar. He is a professor of political science and director of the Earl Warren Bill of Rights Project at the University of California, San Diego.

TAMAR JACOBY, a senior fellow at the Manhattan Institute, writes extensively on race, ethnicity, and other subjects. Her articles and book reviews have appeared in a variety of periodicals, including *The New York Times*, the *The Wall Street Journal, The New Republic, Commentary,* and *Foreign Affairs*. Before joining the institute, she was a senior writer and justice editor for *Newsweek*. Her publications include *Someone Else's House: America's Unfinished Struggle for Integration* (Basic Books, 1998).

MATTHEW JOSEPHSON, who figured among the literary expatriots in France in the 1920s, is the author of numerous critical biographies and histories of the Gilded Age, including *Edison: A Biography* (McGraw-Hill, 1963) and *The President Makers: The Culture of Politics in an Age of Enlightenment* (Putnam, 1979).

HARVEY KLEHR is the Andrew W. Mellon Professor of Politics and History at Emory University. He is coauthor, with Kyrill M. Anderson and John Earl Haynes, of *The Soviet World of American Communism* (Yale University Press, 1998) and, with John Earl Haynes and Fridrikh I. Firsov, of *The Secret World of American Communism* (Yale University Press, 1996).

RICHARD KLUGER began a career in journalism at *The Wall Street Journal*, and was a writer for *Forbes* magazine and then the *New York Post* before becoming a literary editor of the *New York Herald Tribune*. In book publishing, he served as executive editor at Simon and Schuster and editor in chief at Atheneum. In addition to his three books of social history, he has written six novels.

ROBERT KORSTAD is an assistant professor in the Department of Public Policy Studies at Duke University, where he has been teaching since 1980. He also taught at North Carolina Central University, and he has won a number of honors and awards. His work has appeared in such journals as *Journal of American History* and *Social Science History*, and he is coauthor of *Like a Family: The Making of a Southern Cotton Mill World* (University of North Carolina Press, 1987).

DAVID E. KYVIG is a professor of history at Northern Illinois University. He was awarded the Bancroft Prize for his work *Explicit and Authentic Acts: Amending the U.S. Constitution, 1776–1995*.

WALTER LaFEBER is the Noll Professor of History at Cornell University in Ithaca, New York. He is the author of several major books concerning Central America, and his most recent publications include *America, Russia, and the Cold War*, 7th ed. (McGraw-Hill, 1992) and *The American Age: United States Foreign Policy at Home and Abroad Since 1750* (W.W. Norton, 1989, 1993).

JAMES LELOUDIS is an associate professor, the associate dean for honors, and director of the James M. Johnston Center for Undergraduate Excellence at the University of North Carolina, Chapel Hill. His chief interest is in history of the modern South, with emphases on women labor, race, and reform. He is coauthor of *Like a Family: The Making of a Southern Cotton Mill World* (University of North Carolina Press, 1987) and the author of *Schooling the New South: Pedagogy, Self, and Society in North Carolina, 1880–1920* (University of North Carolina Press, 1999).

ARTHUR S. LINK was a professor at Princeton University. He is the editor-in-chief of the Woodrow Wilson papers and the author of the definitive multi-volume biography of President Wilson.

ROBERT J. MADDOX is Professor Emeritus of history at Penn State University and is the author of two dozen books and articles on recent American history with a specialty on cold war diplomacy.

ELAINE TYLER MAY is a professor of American studies and history at the University of Minnesota in Minneapolis. She has also taught at Princeton University, and her research interests include family history and gender issues. She is the author of *Barren in the Promised Land: Childless Americans and the Pursuit of Happiness* (Basic Books, 1995).

RICHARD L. McCORMICK is president of Rutgers University in New Brunswick, New Jersey. He received his Ph.D. in history from Yale University in 1976, and he is the author of *The Party Period and Public Policy: American Politics from the Age of Jackson to the Progressive Era* (Oxford University Press, 1986).

H. R. McMASTER graduated from the U.S. Military Academy at West Point in 1984. Since then, he has held numerous command and staff positions in the military, and during the Persian Gulf War he commanded Eagle Troop 2 Armored Cavalry Regiment in combat. He is the author of *A Distant Thunder* (Harper Collins, 1997).

WILLIAM H. MCNEILL, Robert A. Millikan Distinguished Service Professor at the University of Chicago, was president of the American Historical Association in 1985. The essay in this volume is his presidential address. He has written more than twenty books of which the most important is *The Rise of the West: A History of the Human Community* (1963). He received his Ph.D. from Cornell University, after studying under Carl Becker and Edward Fox. His next literary enterprise will be a biography of Arnold J. Toynbee.

GLENDA RILEY is a professor of history at Ball State University in Muncie, Indiana. She has written numerous articles and books on women in western history, including *Women and Nature: Saving the "Wild" West* (University of Nebraska Press, 1999) and *Diaries and Letters from the Western Trails, 1852: The California Trail* (University of Nebraska Press, 1997).

BRUCE J. SCHULMAN is a professor of history and director of American Studies at Boston University. A frequent contributor to publications such as *The New York Times* and the *Los Angeles Times*, Schulman lives in Brookline, Massachusetts.

CHRISTINE STANSELL is a professor of history at Princeton University in Princeton, New Jersey. She is the author of *City of Women: Sex and Class in New York*, 1790–1860 (Random House, 1986) and *American Bohemia: Art, Politics, and Modern Love* (Henry Holt, 1996).

BRIAN VANDEMARK teaches history at the United States Naval Academy at Annapolis. He served as research assistant on Clark Clifford's autobiography, *Counsel to the President: A Memoir* (Random House, 1991) and as collaborator on former secretary of defense Robert S. McNamara's Vietnam memoir, *In Retrospect: The Tragedy and Lessons of Vietnam* (Times Books, 1995).

SEAN WILENTZ, Dayton-Stockton Professor of History and director of the Program in American Studies at Princeton University, is the author of numerous books on American history and politics. He lives in Princeton, New Jersey.

Index